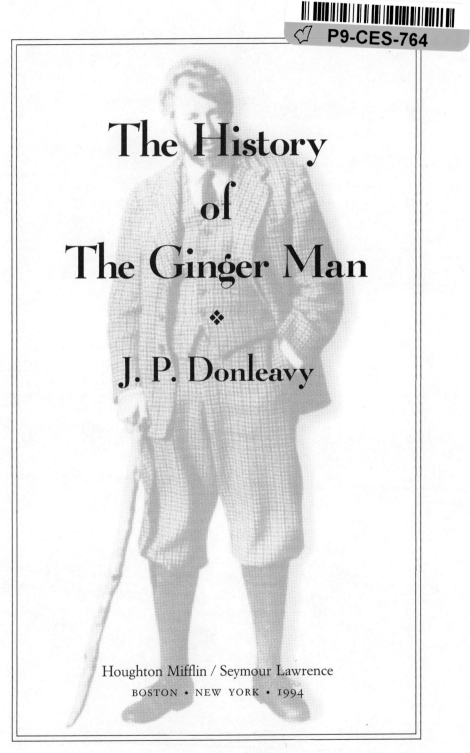

The History
of
The Ginger Man

❖

J. P. Donleavy

Houghton Mifflin / Seymour Lawrence
BOSTON • NEW YORK • 1994

For information about permission to reproduce selections
from this book, write to Permissions, Houghton Mifflin Company,
215 Park Avenue South, New York, New York 10003.

Library of Congress Cataloging-in-Publication Data

Donleavy, J. P. (James Patrick), date.
The history of The ginger man / J. P. Donleavy.
p.   cm.
ISBN 0-395-51595-5
1. Donleavy, J. P. (James Patrick), 1926–   Ginger man.
2. Donleavy, J. P. (James Patrick), 1926–   — Authorship.
3. Americans — Ireland — Dublin — History — 20th century.
4. Novelists, American — 20th century — Biography.
5. Fiction — Authorship.   I. Title.
PS3507.0686G563   1994   93-41010
823′.914 — dc20   CIP

Printed in the United States of America

RRD 10 9 8 7 6 5 4 3 2 1

Book design by Robert Overholtzer

All photographs are courtesy of J. P. Donleavy, unless otherwise
credited. The author thanks Professor Rita Donleavy and
T. J. Donleavy for permission to use photographs from the
Donleavy family archives.

Every effort has been made to locate the copyright holders of
works quoted or reproduced in this book. Any errors or omissions
are unintentional and corrections will be made in future editions if
necessary. And in this context, kind acknowledgment is made to
Neville Armstrong, Gerald Samuels & Shine, Rubinstein & Nash
& Co., Ealing Films and Kathleen Tynan, Roger Parr, Pamela
O'Malley de Crist, Jane Pratt, and Murray Sayle.

The author is grateful for permission to reprint two letters written
by John Hall Wheelock as editor on behalf of Charles Scribner's
Sons (Courtesy of Charles Scribner's Sons, an imprint of Macmillan
Publishing Company), as well as a review of *The Ginger Man*
by Peter Shaffer in *Truth,* January 1957.

Letters by Maurice Girodias are courtesy of J. P. Donleavy,
owner of The Olympia Press.

The History
of
The Ginger Man

sen' three years collecting a pile of stones that sink back into the earth. I wander the fields at night, weeping; [the first thing of our young lives are beginning to die.] The seven towers, cold constipated mornings at stool, we are men without degrees, but we have the memory of delirious fucking, handfuls of hair and the sound of the defeated at our feet, The Kosmo house is home, a barley scented womb of love. By going to America I am removing an organ from my body - to come back again is to despair and not to is to stand mumbling in the washroom of a New York Hotel There is no central theme - a step taken is never retaken - there is no possibility of return or repeat but this is, as you say, something we will never believe

These sentiments concerning my three years spent by the sea in County Wicklow, written to Gainor Stephen Crist and just prior to departing Ireland to the Isle of Man, from which I would eventually set off to the United States, recalling to him the Catacombs and two of his favorite pubs, the Kosmos House and the Seven Towers, both now demolished. I allude to the fact we would not graduate from Trinity and that one had to walk on wintry mornings two hundred yards to reach the university's outdoor latrine.

The History
of
The Ginger Man

1

IF ONE CAN NOT exactly designate, choose, or spell out the very most important moments in one's life, there being so many summits of hope and troughs of despair, it is most often those moments when one has felt the greatest relief that one can most easily recall. And it was on a mild moist morning of an Irish midland March day in the year 1978 that I received the following letter in French into my hand from one of my last remaining Paris lawyers.

63 Av. Raymond-Poincaré,
Paris, le 20 Mars 1978

Monsieur J. P. Donleavy,
Levington Park,
Mullingar,
Co. Westmeath,
Ireland.

Aff. Dte. LITTLE SOMEONE c/Garnier, Olympia Press
Ref: 137/N

Monsieur le Directeur,
I hasten to inform you that this case has now come before our Court.
I have the pleasure to tell you that your adversary's appeal has been turned down.
As soon as I obtain a copy of the Judgment I shall send it to you.
Please be assured, Monsieur Director, of my most distinguished and devoted feeling.

Jean-Martin Martinière,
Avocat au Conseil d'Etat
et a la Cour de Cassation

This communication concluded a litigation concerning *The Ginger Man* which had begun twenty-one years previously in the June of 1957 and had been variously fought in London, Paris and New York. Over the years, one did not exactly welcome the sight of legal letters, especially those coming from what seemed a remote, unfathomable, dark world of jurisprudence in Paris and further complicated by the French language. But as I spied the word *"plaisir,"* I realized that instead of having to implacably steer my legal battalions again into the battle, I could now instead indulge a moment of milder worries. And even smile, for at long last I'd put to death this interminable lawsuit, which had on many a previous waking dawn unpleasantly crept into one's consciousness.

At the end, the protagonists J. P. Donleavy, the author, the Olympia Press and Maurice Girodias, the publisher, were somewhat removed in name from the present plaintiff and defendant, respectively Garnier-Olympia Press versus The Little Someone Corporation. And I had meanwhile even become the owner of my enemy. Achieving thereby a revenge I'd nearly forgotten I'd sworn so many years before. When upon a summer morning down a little side street in the London borough of Fulham, where with a copy of the first edition of *The Ginger Man* in my hand, I smashed my fist upon its green cover format, published as it was in the pseudonymous and pornographic Traveller's Companion Series of the Olympia Press, and I declared aloud, "If it's the last thing I ever do, I will avenge this book."

And another strange irony which one could never have predicted. As I now sit looking at that same first edition published to my horror all those years ago and selling at its modest price in French francs, this selfsame copy resides now a treasure in my archives, having increased in value many a hundred times over. And in the margin of the early draft manuscript pages of this work and never published, were written the words.

Anyone
Can be a friend
So long as you don't
Get to know him
Too well

And anyone
Can be an enemy
And you get
To know him
Better
Than most

2

THE FIRST INKLINGS of the notion of the book that was to become *The Ginger Man* brewed in Ireland following American Thanksgiving Day of 1949. It was upon an afternoon of turkey, sweet potatoes, spices and Beaujolais, feasted over within a tiny house consisting of two cramped rooms, front and back on two floors, at number 1 Newtown Avenue, Blackrock, County Dublin. My host was Michael Heron and his then wife, Camilla. The latter an American dark-skinned beauty, new to Ireland and fresh from Paris, where she was a somewhat lesser chanteuse toast of the town than her friend Josephine Baker. Finding the Irish climate unbearably cold and damp, Camilla often had to remain abed to receive her guests, as she reclined stacked over with blankets and snuggled up in feather boas, while running an electric hot iron over herself to keep warm. Heron, a handsome, sensitively literate and gourmet Englishman, had shared rooms with me at 38 Trinity College, and later I married his sister, Valerie.

In these years following the end of the Second World War, the outside world's spiritually uncivilizing influences, such as cars, plumbing and neon lights, were now showing up in Ireland. A population, long without a pot to piss in, were unearthing all kinds of newfangled shiny receptacles. And the last of one's Dublin and university contemporaries were heading off to various parts of the globe. Some with chastened tails between their legs, others clutching hopeful degrees but all in search of two pennies to rub together. A few, more affluent, were grandly heading to tour exotic continents in search of further and better, if not more pleasant, particulars of life and soul. And it was upon this American Thanksgiving day I sensed that the celebratory, boisterous and resolutely careless mayhem world of Dublin which we had survived, and the benign, elegantly cloistered life within the sanc-

Michael Heron, with whom I shared rooms at Trinity College, contemplatively viewing the world and whose enlightened tastes for literature, food and wine formed a pleasantly influential background to one's university life and whose beautiful sister became my first wife.

tum of Trinity College which we had enjoyed and to which we had all originally come, were finally over.

We had been a small colony of foreign students in what was, on the surface and in language, apparently not a foreign land. But whose citizens we soon learned were deeply alien to us in other ways which we soon collectively referred to as having the "crut." This being the name applied to the inhibiting, impenetrable encasement of intellectual and sexual repression which seemed to envelop the majority of the Irish in mind and body. But to this chronic condition there had been found exceptions. And within this room, where one Americanly, thanksgivingly dined, one was reminded of the bedroom above, where the likes of the patriot, revolutionist, housepainter, poet, playwright and raconteur Brendan Behan and other Celtic amoralists had cavorted. Their lewd antics often watched stoically by two lady spinsters from the high vantage point of their window directly across the street. And at whom, during his demonstrations of freedom of the flesh, Behan would shake, insert and pull upon various appendages hoping to inspire some expression upon their implacably expressionless faces. And as no reaction would come from the spinsters, the

With me in the background, Gainor Stephen Crist with his first wife, Constance. All in our tweeds and sporting exemplary respectability, one cannot remember the extraordinary circumstances that must have existed when this photograph was taken to find the three of us in front of my rooms at number 38 Trinity College, my name just legible painted in white on the entrance behind us.

otherwise naked Behan would declare out the open top half of the window.

"Ah the blase likes of youse sedately up there are not to provoke me to remove me belt which for the sake of me own modesty I wear around me belly to hide me provocatively sensuous navel."

The Dublin trams roared past this little house from early morn till approaching midnight, and daily one would awake to the clip clop of black-plumed horses pulling hearses and carriages of mourners on their way to bury the dead at Dean's Grange Cemetery two miles farther up the road. I had on the odd occasion of missing the last tram back to my rooms at Trinity College, curled up, in the lumpy confines of a sofa in this front tiny room, once sleeping while Gainor Stephen Crist, the original occupier of this dwelling, sat across from me with a book reading the night away about Spain.

Although others who knew him well might not agree, Gainor Stephen Crist was an entirely enchanting man. He was straightly tall, elegant and precise and circumstances providing, was always supremely courteous in manner. The newlywed Crist had, with his first wife, Constance, rented for three pounds a week this small respectable

5

abode, where the local Protestant vicar, soon after their taking up residence, came to deliver his calling card one quiet Sunday afternoon. Crist, pagan sensualist though he was, was delighted at this sign of civilization from just up the street and always, provided they were not looking for money, welcomed any impromptu caller, preferring to magnify rather than oppose the condition of crut he might encounter. Even when such was usually further aggravated by the infrequent bathing of those suffering it. And as it happened upon this Sunday four o'clock teatime, setting an example, both Mr. and Mrs. Crist, there being no bath, were attempting to wash down from a bucket in the tiny kitchen. Which meant they never properly met this minister of the Church of Ireland. For, these newlyweds, at the sudden knock on their door, could only venture forth wrapped in skimpy towels to open up a crack to their narrow little hallway where, upon inquiring of the caller, Gainor's towel inadvertently fell and following the vicar's gasp, they then saw his little white card get shoved under their door.

It was upon the narrow sidewalk outside this house that I more than a few times accompanied this pleasantly saintly man Crist, with his splendidly mystical way of wasting time, to nearby public houses, where he would philosophically tackle yet another personal mishap befallen him. Such as recently sending his gray herringbone tweed suit to be dry-cleaned. Which, duly returned thoroughly washed and scrubbed, had shrunken the sleeves and trouser cuffs up to his elbows and knees. And which only suit he now had to wear to collect from the train station and carry back home a birthday present of a Great Dane puppy received from a rich American aunt. This already large animal's weak legs were not strong enough to support it and so it was borne everywhere in Crist's arms. But the canine baby beast's appetite was all devouring in these larder-bare days. Its daily diet requiring a couple of pints of milk and at least two pounds of freshly ground steak. And while Crist held starvation at bay with a sheep's head simmering on the stove, from this same aunt came a further gift, a subscription to *Fortune* magazine, well known required reading for international tycoons.

But Gainor Stephen Crist, stickler for facts though he was, and like most Americans preferring efficiency, was also, in this land where facts were avoided and efficiency shunned, tolerant and uncomplaining. In his impoverished circumstances he would peruse the pages of *Fortune* and would, with his canine birthday present grunting, good-naturedly ferry the enormous armful to the nearest pub and there with the beast collapsed at his feet he would nervously tap the bar with the edge of a half crown, ordering for himself a double Irish whiskey and a glass of draft stout plus a pint of the latter for the dog. Then with a twiddle of fingertips he would have the immediately emptied glasses refilled and announce that both he and the dog were now in the proper frame of mind to begin seriously drinking and thinking and ready to indulge another quality I found attractive in this man and which he'd already instilled in the Great Dane of being an avid listener to anything that was said.

And
Especially to some
Things
That never got
Mentioned

3

THE FADING AUTUMN of the year 1946 was a strange boom time in the world. With all its awakening hopes to provide a life dreamed of during the war. The rubble being cleared across Europe. The evil, hated enemy vanquished around the globe. And Dublin then, although rife with its slums and poverty and its shoeless children running begging through the streets, remained an unscathed oasis, unbombed and, for those who could afford, flowing with milk and honey. Bowls full of beetroot sugar to sweeten coffee in its cafes and butter to spread on its spice buns. Even more alluring was its bacon, ham, sausages, eggs and cream. Not to mention oysters, salmon, trout, prawns, saddles of lamb, and big thick steaks. Plus the limitless cascade of foamy creamy stout from its brewery to wash it all down. And these handful of ready-to-please-and-be-pleased Americans came here, each and every one of them full of great expectations. And two or three even ready to conquer the world and sporting jaunty bow ties. They frequented the pubs of Dublin which were elbow-to-elbow jammed. All day and into the evening throes of closing time as the cliche-shattering opinions flew and voices inquired.

"What are you having."

And you'd better be having something, as bartenders with sleeves rolled back handed the glasses out over the heads as the rounds of drinks were bought and the sound of mechanical corkscrews twisted their way down with a thump and pop into the necks of the bottles of stout. And it was the name of this dark brew, stout, which had confounded me when I first encountered it in James Joyce's writings. This beverage, which pumped blood through the hearts of the citizens and fueled the city and ended up flowing through pub latrines, sewers and back to the Liffey from whose headwaters it had first come. Gray parcels of it carried away out of the pub following closing time. Often to just down the street as it was from the pub Davy Byrnes. To either the top or bottom of a Georgian house, where amid the songs, stories and laughter, arguments or insults raged and fists flew in a flowering of discontent. Where nary a morally uplifting word was spoken as ladies screeched either in delight or affront, depending upon whose hand was taking a liberty. Or whose tongue was sticking in someone's ear, which was a favorite way of one lady's letting you know she was open to indecent suggestion.

At such hooleys in progress, revenge for a previous slight was widespread and disbarment common. Which at least left plenty of room for others to misbehave. Drinking may have quenched the flames of passion in some, but enough lust-incited malcontents remained to make Dublin Sodom and Gomorrah on the Liffey and then some. But this euphoric rejoicing following those first few months after the war must have been felt in other cities. And I remember having it described to me in higher tones and in a more personal manner, years later in Ireland, by a man, a multimillionaire racehorse owner, and who had come somewhat impoverished from a ravaged continental Europe to some of the still splendid streets of Oxford, and that his whole being was bursting with an exhilarating sense of freedom and such enthusiastic delight that he found himself seeking out the widest thoroughfares so that he could, arms outstretched, all the better walk along them singing to celebrate the glory of being alive. But it was in the Dublin of the time where came this greatest burst of exuberance and reveling if not rapture where it was many a time heard said at hooleys and in many a pub,

"Cheer up or I'll break your face."

And upon this dawn of world peace, these gently brash, optimistic and iconoclastic Americans arrived in Ireland to confront the wise old ways of Europe. They were to the Irish, great conquering heroes and giants from another planet. All powerful and bigger than life, striding the Dublin streets able to dominate anything they encountered. Propaganda all over Europe preached stories and printed photographs of these conquerors dispensing their chocolate and gum and patting little children on the head. But there was no doubt that these Americans possessed of their plenty were indeed a generous race, even as they were given to assume they could teach the world how to live, as indeed they finally now have done. But here and now after the war, there was no question that they were a kindly people arrived in a shrewd, calculating and war-hardened Europe.

So unself-consciously we Americans soon learned we walked in an aura of glamour to which was added the behavioral license of being at Trinity, in itself and at the time, a distinct status of some elegance in Dublin city. As for me, I complained of nothing but cold feet at night in bed and the damp chill that needed many a glass of stout to be driven from one's bones. And I was having to learn of political matters in Ireland. Having been brought up in the United States, where the creed one professed was of minor interest to others, I remember being somewhat surprised by my first encounters with university life and the whispers that one was a Catholic. And it dawns on me only now that the first Irish student friends one made were all of this religious persuasion. And my own Irish-born parents, avouching honesty, cleanliness and fair play in all one's dealings rather than religious beliefs, made me mesmerized and bedeviled by this country with its sanctimonious encrustations and the widespread penchant for evading the procreative facts of life. Albeit one soon realized that to survive in the great sea of poverty prevalent in the Dublin of the time, the oft encountered sins of lying and cheating could be seen to be required.

Ah, but then as Americans we were keeping up appearances and before the Crists had taken up residence at the address of number 1 Newtown Avenue, Blackrock, I had visited them in an abode in another more recently built suburban district, where they shared a house in two upstairs rooms rented from a respectable family in which one of the children was retarded and in which the husband appeared to have a tendency to drink. Over a short period of time Gainor's law books seemed to mysteriously and systematically disappear and it had to be finally concluded that these tomes were finding their way to a pawnbroker and were brought there by the landlord. That this would happen in holy, Catholic Ireland and in this household reeking of respectability amazed me. And it seemed unbelievably unfair to be perpetrated upon an American gentleman who, with his academic life put in jeopardy, had come these four and a half thousand miles abroad to qualify in the profession of jurisprudence and the upholding of law and justice for all. Yet Crist seemed to regard the event with a curious equanimity and understanding, which I later found could be characteristic of him when encountering the moral frailties of another.

However, it was in this house of the disappearing law books where the first of my truly Irish social engagements of an invitation to dinner took place. And that evening, stepping out to make this visit, there wasn't much evidence of the shimmering promise of life. Constance Crist, then pregnant, with an apologetic charm presented me with a mound of spinach and a boiled potato on a plate. But upon that evening in that house she was a beautifully voweled, outspoken lady, and one was fed a wonderful diatribe by my hostess, who was not exactly enamored of the Irish. And by God, when she had a mind to, did she let them have it from every moral, ethical and sanitary direction. And then with my host there occurred an animated discussion on accents and the power such wielded when emanating from the lips of those so blessed. Present also was Randall Hillis, Crist's brother-in-law, who fought as a Canadian in the war and who was at the time sharing a house out on a windswept Howth Head with George Roy Hill, later to be the famed film director. Hillis said that George Hill was attempting to perfect a British accent to perform a part in a play he was producing at Dublin's Gaiety Theatre and that Hill would be extremely envious of Crist's and my somewhat anglicized accents. As indeed both of us were even thought capable of passing as British. Proof enough that we were all much fascinated if not concerned with the pronounced class divisions in Ireland, and as Crist described it, the double-edged social sword that we as Americans wielded with our phonetics. With the further advantage that, as our quasi-British accents might slip, we had another and even better one underneath.

Now believe me when I say I may have sounded as my rearing would suggest, born in Brooklyn and raised in the Bronx, which would prompt any interested person to ask, where on earth did Crist and especially I get such accents that would be having folk get the idea we could be Englishmen. Well, curiously enough, both Crist and I had, upon each of us recalling, many an occasion and incident of having to run the risk of physically defending ourselves from fellow Americans who were unkindly crass enough to inquire,

"Hey, bud, where did you get that accent from."

And both of us certainly, especially in the U.S. Navy, had occasion to raise our fists to defend our vowels. However, even to this day, such accents can be heard in Boston as they were when I briefly lived there, and had occasion to venture into that venerable pharmacy Clough and Schackley on the corner of Beacon and Charles streets on Beacon Hill. Where elegant ladies purchased their toiletries and medical prescriptions. If such accents were not found a dime a dozen, then they were encountered at a much higher price. But both Crist and I, upon the moment of stepping ashore in Ireland, had our considerably anglicized phonetics remarked upon.

Now on another and different level of the many levels existing in Dublin, accents didn't matter a damn in this city aflood with beer and alive and aloud with festivity. Nor did they matter in the bashes, the hooleys and in the pursuit of harlotry, from the aftermath of which one awoke disorientated and bleary-eyed and often unable to speak at all. The cure generally coming following coffee in Bewley's Oriental Cafe, and when, at a decent interval after lunch, one was ready again to bash on regardless. Ah, but one did too take major steps in life between these strange parties that persisted days and sometimes weeks from one place to another all over the country. And often in the midst of such shenanigans appeared Gainor Stephen Crist especially assisting and overseeing, as he assiduously did, the moral good. "Values" and "duty" were his watchwords. "Do no evil" was his contention. And to those who did do evil, a wooling would be administered. This consisting of throwing the evildoer down on his back and, with Crist's hands dug deep in his hair, banging his head up and down on the floor while at the same time shouting the bastard's crime in his face. We became good companions because I wholeheartedly agreed with this highly effective meting out of ethical standards.

Crist, above all, was a marvelously patient man. He would quietly listen as I pontificated on my intended aspirations of conquering the universe. Or at least doing something that might get my name in the paper. And possessing that strange air of propriety of the middle westerner, Crist was always instantly ready with fatherly advice. Upon a letter plopping in the letterbox of my college rooms from Valerie in which she mentioned marriage, Crist was swift to seize me by the wrist and lead me outside the university to telegraph an immediate answer saying yes. That accomplished and as an old hand engaged in such condition, he lectured me on the codes and protocols to be observed in a contented state of matrimony. And I believed his every word. While not yet knowing that my answer agreeing to marry Valerie now frightened the life out of her.

Although growing up in America and having experienced the rough and tumble of naval life, I was still at the age of twenty only just putting my youthful years behind me and hardly ready for matrimony. But to Crist, a few years my senior, my tender youth concerned him not. He was not even to know that Valerie was tall, exquisitely formed and stunningly beautiful and had the most exquisite of British accents and that I should be very glad to marry her. She was also a speech therapist with a modestly nice income based in St. Albans in Hertfordshire and very successfully supporting herself. But I was aware that the world was a tough arena and that there was many a barefaced trauma ahead to be fought two-fisted for survival. Matrimony would also mean dislodging from one's comfortable university life, which even with Trinity's primitive plumbing, was a place of paradise. My G.I. Bill of Rights plus an allowance sent by my faithful mother gave me a considerable income to indifferently spend in this city, where my college servant, Noctor, was supporting a wife and three children on a quarter of what I might spend on an extravagant evening out and which left me constantly short of funds. And on one or two Sundays, weekend occasions actually had me broke. And such was my inextinguishable American optimism that I was left stunned and affronted to be moneyless.

For the quarterly sum of eighteen pounds, eight shillings and eleven pence, one was all found at college. Which included a sitting room, bedroom, scullery and entrance hall plus servant, gas and electricity, a daily bottle of milk and an evening meal on commons. The latter where, following a Latin prayer mouthed by a college scholar, there appeared potatoes, slabs of meat, a vegetable and a pudding, all washed down with a special brew provided by Guinness's brewery. And if one found polite people to sit next to who remembered to pass condiments and comestibles, all could be extremely pleasant. There were too, constant generous occasions of hospitality all over Dublin with very few hours ever going by without someone or something inciting some celebration. And one could drift from one to another, frequenting the innards of drawing rooms or pubs and hotels, which were a few steps in every direction all over the city. And as for country houses, one needed only someone sober enough to steer an automobile straight for a few miles or around a few dangerous corners to enter some mansion beyond some wooded copse where much eccentric goings-on would be going on and, provided you were appropriately affable, you could eat and drink to your heart's content and be merry if you could and sleep where you collapsed.

Ah, but what about literature and art. The hope to be part of which throbbed in every citizen's heart. And made the excuse for him to go on living the next day and the next with the indifferent present being made tolerable by adorning the days ahead with rosy dreams. These, for target practice, always being promptly shot down in flames by your listeners, who in a public house, need have no mind for having to please a host or hostess. And what there was of an intellectual social life, rather than being conducted in the salons of Dublin and country houses as it seemed to have been in the decades previously, was nearly entirely exercised where drink was for sale or available in one or two of the more impromptu places such as McDaid's pub or that now legendary basement redoubt, the Catacombs. Where the disgraceful could, ad lib, democratically further disgrace themselves.

There was for the citizens at large a casual carelessness about Dublin life. And with aesthetic unself-consciousness and the previously mentioned face-breaking being rampant at the time, and wine, women and song being the priority, no one knew or much cared that a so-called literary period was then hugely in the making. Comeuppance and instant amusement were all the rage, and you were as good as your last fist thrown or witticism uttered. While delving into the problem of obtaining a lifetime private income, food, not for thought but to devour, was on every mind. And if little hope of that was to be had, then a drink held in your fist was, at least for the pleasant moment, the preferred substitute. And you could rage your way toward hell taking comfort from the fact that publoads of companions were aboard on the same trip and you'd have the feeling on the way that with yourself and them with you, gone, there was no world worth talking about left.

Now, there were one or two exceptions to all this deprivation and behavior. And one of these was John Ryan, my first publisher, who presented my earliest writing, a short story, "A Party on Saturday Afternoon," in the pages of his magazine, *Envoy*. Ryan, an invariably polite, quiet and somewhat shy individual, would, when at the bar of a pub, patiently listen to anyone's stories and if prompted sufficiently could tell splendid tales of his own. He was also that rare man in Irish life who could harbor many a secret from which, I suspect, came much of the wisdom lurking in his words. Ryan, with whom I'd nearly intended to start *Envoy* but demurred when I felt it would invite the famed and ignore the unsung, was instead joined by other editors, friends of mine, and as it would seem, as always happens with good friends, the first literary effort I submitted to be published was voted down by the very man I'd introduced to join Ryan on the magazine. Ryan, however, approving the story and having heard it read aloud to his admiring, beautiful, film star sister Kathleen, and having supplied the finance to start the magazine, also supplied the final decision to publish it. And the experience serving me well and making me forever afterward a permanent outsider to literary life.

But more about the worthy Ryan. Who in Dublin was unique. As the poor mouths, the poets and the celibates roamed Dublin to cadge what they could of sustenance, Ryan was one of the few who personally had available to him both food and drink in plentisome quantity, courtesy of a mother who was as intrepid as she was charming and who ran her considerable business of the Monument Creameries. Ryan was unostentatious to the point of sometimes being a seasonably dressed vagrant. But with money to spare, and able to elect to a degree what he did with his time, he could have done as nearly all did, and spend his days racing and dining evenings at Jammets, the Red Bank or the Dolphin Hotel with jodhpured cronies. However, as much of this life as Ryan led, he always imposed upon it his abiding consciousness of the value and worth of the writers, painters and poets of the period. Nor did he ignore the nonwriting, noncomposing, nonpainting eccentrics who lurked and scurried everywhere, including Mickey Mears, the gas meter reader who rode his motorbike called Thunderbird and who always seemed to be at one's elbow ready to appreciate a bon mot.

Ryan chose too, to be interested in his native city and the relics left by so many of its literary sons, who had fled or been driven out. And no population, perhaps excepting the Viennese, has ever existed so implacably an enemy of the inspired, as did the people of Ireland. It was nearly as if to redress such wrong that Ryan had collected their books, music and pictures, and let it be known that such banned and ridiculed things were still to be seen and heard back in the creator's native land and that there remained at least one man there who kept their names alive and held them in high esteem. For Ryan was himself, as well as a publican and publisher, also a creator of painting, writing and music. And he in turn self-effacingly cherished and nourished those in the same pursuit, who, embattled, still remained in this land so hostile to their survival. It was in Ryan's uncharacteristically sumptuous Grafton Street studio where I first heard Joyce's voice reading in its strange haunting tones from *Finnegans Wake*. And where too, the then largely unknown Irish composer's compositions were played on the gramophone.

It was usually at midmorning that Ryan would appear socially, having earlier traveled in from Burton Hall, his mother's estate upon which stood her vastly splendid Georgian mansion. He'd park his car somewhere discreet in a Dublin side street and with a newspaper tucked somewhere upon his person, would stroll the distance to 37 Grafton Street, nodding recognitions as he went and watching out to avoid the worst of chancers. When confronted, he would be a ready repository for news or able to report that which was soon to become news and which was already undergoing its transition into gossip turned into a fine art. And Ryan listened to all mouths and spoke into all ears. He would never ignore, as many did, the awestruck bus conductors and sewer inspectors who edged near to be in the intellectual vicinity of the greatness of poets. Nor would turn his back on the chancers who swarmed about him exerting their charm, looking for loans or the guarantee for same in order to launch their soon-to-be-aborted money-making schemes. Thus, with Ryan invariably remaining imperturbably benign to and indulgent of all, did he become himself a dependable focus in a land where begrudgers abounded during a period of censorship and religious repression and when the philistine and pompous pedants held full sway, albeit with all kinds of shockingly prurient behavior omnipresent. And Ryan forever in Dublin's midst and privy to the deepest and darkest moments of Dublin life now seems, if less eccentric, to be yet one more of the characters to strangely lurk behind every word of *The Ginger Man*.

Who once was
A transient tourist
In that
Intimate of
Intimate cities

4

Rarely did anything happen in Dublin by plan. It was always to go out the front gates of Trinity and into the city to let come what may. Ah, but there were the odd previously designed occasions. And given this head start, the botch and bungle and faux pas had a marvelous opportunity for a field day.

As you might imagine, such a rich and handsome young man as John Ryan was, he might sooner than later, as I had already done, marry a beautiful girl. Which he did. And in so doing provided the scene for a mightily and exotically wonderful wedding day. Upon which the intrepid Gainor Stephen Crist as head usher would attend in full correctness and with due protocol, acquitting himself in the manner of the American Brahmin he was. But at that moment in Ireland he was without his proper kit for such duty and occasion. When it was suggested he rent such clothes, the suggestion was met with the steely, icy glare it deserved. And he cabled to have his morning suit and top hat expressed across the Atlantic by motor bird.

It was not till the very eve before the wedding that the postman at last knocked and Crist's sartorial social equipment, made for him by the best tailor in Dayton, Ohio, duly arrived. But his dress shirt had taken on a rather gloomy faded shade of light brown, which he insisted and then implored his long-suffering wife, Constance, who was to remain behind next day baby-sitting, to launder. Although a lady who could suddenly decide to take no nonsense from anyone and who could converse with Gainor by them both clicking their teeth in Morse code, she did duly take and soak overnight this garment in soap suds. But now in the morning the shirt had little time to dry. And the old clanking alarm clock on the mantel was ticking away the hour. Crist and Ryan and Patricia, the to-be bride, had long been delighted friends and both the latter agreed that Gainor was a master of courtliness and social procedure and it was incumbent upon Gainor to get to the church on time. And what matter a slightly sopping shirt under his tailcoat, provided the collar was presentable. And a makeshift ironing board was produced in the tiny kitchen. As the table had recently suffered irreparable damage the day before when Gainor in a rage that his morning suit had not yet arrived, had quite rightly kicked this otherwise useful piece of culinary furniture around the room.

A green door formerly on its hinges was now laid across the wobbly former frame of the kitchen table. A towel hurriedly thrown over it. The iron allowed to heat. And the rapid pressing commenced in a cloud of steam while Crist searched for his suddenly disappeared black shoes. Which had already in the last hour, along with his other pairs of shoes, been chewed beyond recognition by the Great Dane puppy gift from his aunt for whom the leather served as a canine breakfast, the poor dog not having recently got its daily ration of two pounds of steak and two pints of milk. I arrived then in the midst of all this tragedy just as Gainor was screaming,

"That goddamn dog, I'll kill. It not only is eating me out of house

Photographed in my field at Kilcoole, Patricia and John Ryan, whose lavish wedding at the time was the sensation of Dublin, and to attend which Gainor Crist had summoned his morning suit from Ohio.

and home but it is making sure I'll have no living goddamn future either."

Crist did instead find an old pair of tennis shoes. An attempt at upgrading these was quickly abandoned as efforts to remove some of the black scuffings left worse smears. But in such canvas footwear and striped trousers suspended across his shoulders by bright crimson braces, Crist now stood with desperate impatience, watching over the makeshift ironing board, where the collar of his shirt was now laid out for its final impeccable smoothing to rid of ruckles and wrinkles. But his dutiful wife suddenly had to attend to a brief call of nature. I of course stood helplessly looking on, unable to do a damn thing. But at last to Gainor's urgent insistence she returned ready to execute the final hot flattening out of his dress shirt collar. I thought I smelled the scorched smell of paint. But thought the better of alarming on the matter with time so urgently of the essence. Constance too thought she smelled burning paint. But Gainor now stood with his fists and teeth clenched hissing out the words,

"In the name of God's sacred teeth, will you iron the bloody shirt. There's no time left to worry about arson."

The iron was duly grabbed up from the surface of the green door and came down upon the shirt collar which lay there somewhat whiter than the brown it had been the evening before. But it now received from the hot electric instrument a great green oily, gaudy streak, the hues of which were more olive than emerald and more greenish blue than blue-green. And which extended collar tip to collar tip. Crist recoiling in shock backed onto a chair upon which had been placed his recently brushed silk top hat. His weight promptly reducing this silky gray elegant elevation to a squashed insignificance. As tragic as the scene had become, I could not suppress my laughter and indeed was helplessly convulsed. Crist, meanwhile, hat in his hand, brought me to task. "You think it's damn funny, don't you."

His evenly spoken words were said with such vehemence that I shamefacedly took a grip of myself and clamped my mouth tightly shut. By the reading on the mantel alarm clock, the time of the ceremony was well now nigh. Ryan himself in his own nonrented morning suit, would be already at the church and surely his about-to-be bride must soon be on her way in her Daimler chauffeured limousine. Discreetly I tried to recover my composure, as Crist, with splendid naval discipline exercised at times of crisis, picked himself up off his crushed top hat now in the shape of a saucer and giving it a few internal punches knocked it back into approximate shape. Then without a further murmur, he snatched the shirt from the green door and put it on. His tie too, which had unfortunately been tucked into one of his dress shoes, had also been chewed nearly beyond recognition. But rather than wear a piece of old rope he'd taken from a broken window sash cord, he smoothed away the tie's canine teeth puncture marks and tied it in a larger than usual Windsor knot. And at last, and if late, at least he was dressed. But I fear at the final sight I could not further control myself and doubled over with renewed laughter, I lurched helplessly out the front door.

Now, if John Ryan was always able to provide the suitable setting, Crist was always able to provide the suitable faux pas. I stood in my own morning suit and top hat just up the street in a doorway, waiting to join and apologize to Crist. Flat-footed in his sneakers, tailcoat flying, he rushed out on the street sporting this variation on a semiformal theme of deviant morning dress. No trams were passing nor were there taxis to be had. And in his desperate rush now to get to the church on time, Crist stepped directly into the very mound of merde his Great Dane puppy had that very morning laid in the gutter and concerning the insanitary nature of which Crist had already complained to me. There was something about the inevitability of this disaster which now threw me into another paroxysm and which threw Crist into a shouting frenzy,

"Goddamn this fucking country. A snake can't live here."

Of course, Crist was zoologically correct about his reptile reference, it being too cold and damp. And I now watched him raise his footwear for cleansing on the fender of the nearest parked car. And wouldn't the owner have just emerged from the apothecary shop directly across the street and from above which the two silent spinsters would view Behan's antics. Incensed at having his automobile used in this manner, he upbraided Crist and also laid hand to Crist's shoulder to delay him as he attempted to depart. A fatal error. For Crist spun around and with a straight left like a lightning bolt put your man flat on his back on the deck. And then Crist rushing out into the middle of the road, flagged down and abruptly stopped the first car going in the direction of his intended destination. And of course wouldn't it be the car carrying the bride. I stood there too dumbfounded to rush from my hiding place and also pile aboard. But how Crist smelled at this time inside the vehicle and later as head usher in the church is unrecorded. I meanwhile as it began to rain proceeded on foot and arrived at the church drenched.

Now attending at this ceremony were not a few of Europe's aristocrats and even a couple of once-crowned heads. As well as John's eccentric acquaintances there also came film star sister Kathleen's friends flown in from London, New York and Hollywood. Present too were the back-slapping higher-ups in the government, John's deceased father having been a senator. Plus every national newspaper had its photographer at the church door. And there through the massive crowds came arriving, guided now by the Garda Siochana, the bride's car. From which emerged none other than Gainor Stephen Crist, usher extraordinaire, under his crushed top hat and sporting his green-streaked collar, his chewed tie and his merde-besmirched plimsolled feet. But with the tails of his swallow coat flying as with his splendid aplomb and immaculate manners did this saintly man imperceptibly bow to the applause and then help this radiantly beautiful to-be bride to dismount from her carriage and be escorted into the blazing brightness as every flashbulb in Ireland popped. And although Crist was disguised as a vagrant, don't anybody ever dare suggest that he still didn't look every inch a fashion plate. But of course wouldn't your chap, who objected to dog shit being applied on his car and whom Crist popped one on the old schnozzola, have enough presence of mind as his head bounced off the pavement to read the conspicuously important license plate of the bride's limousine and didn't the newly wed John Ryan back from his honeymoon with the exquisite Mrs. Ryan get bombarded with writs for assault, battery and causing actual bodily harm.

But upon that happy day and at the time, finally minus the wonderfully correct diplomatic attentions of Gainor Stephen Crist, John with his new bride did contentedly sail away to his honeymoon on his yacht dressed overall and his crew saluting from the fore deck as it left Dun Laoghaire harbor, and leaving behind in Dublin, noted for its bashes and clashes, one of the most momentous bashes and clashes ever recorded or left unrecorded. For a couple of the most beautiful bisexual American ladies had arrived out of Hollywood to the wedding wearing stunning form-clinging purple dresses, their cleavage revealing their bosomy curvatures and with arses to match. These ladies would conspicuously sit on the floors of the rooms they frequented in such a manner that it was no problem to see up under their skirts, where no undergarments were worn. Such sight was to play havoc among the available men and women. And all were available. Every man's trousers out like a tent. Every woman if she hadn't already tasted the pleasures of another woman was deeply contemplating it.

But in this Sodom and Gomorrah on river Liffey, cunnilingus and horn blowing were to be the least of the sexual antics. As the cry took up that fucking was now laid on in Dublin like the hot water in the pipes of the Shelbourne Hotel. Where indeed much dress lifting and trouser dropping took place and where "Let's have a sandwich," meant a woman in between two men. However, of course Crist and I, faithful to our wives, knew better than to so engage in the carnal goings-on, I more demurring than Crist as reading bacteriology at the time and knowing the carelessness of where and into what various organs other organs were put and received, that the microbe situation could be positively catastrophic. And it wouldn't be long before disagreeably purulent exudates were manifest and haunting the psyche, there being in the Ireland of the time bacilli of a most insidious virulence.

But microorganisms apart, it was because of this innocent constellating of diverse folk of diverse inclinations that made Ryan one of the strangest characters that Dublin city has ever had in its bosom. No one understood the repression of his fellow Dubliner better, nor applauded more when it was breached. And over the years having bought the Bailey Restaurant and Bar, Ryan remained both host and acquaintance to that astonishing array and cross section of folk arriving in the Irish capital which included princes, criminals, revolutionaries, impostors and movie stars. And just as he sailed the most treacherous of these Bohemian seas, he could be a friend and comforter to both sides in libel actions, these so often erupting from the endlessly circulating gossipy letters and slanderous mouth-to-mouth reporting of the greatest series of soap operas ever to run concurrently in the history of mankind. And I suppose the Irish being a naturally playful race, such is a monument to the crut and repression perpetrated by religion on a population that frankly was in need of even more religion.

With the Irish, imagined insults are everywhere. But with a difference. Being that if you were imagining them, you could be sure they were real. And in the maelstrom of the life lived at that time, and as a diplomat in Dublin, where undiplomatic behavior was invented, Ryan had no peer. The fact that he was able to keep as lifelong friends many of those who detested even hearing another's name mentioned in the far faint distance is proof. But he was not to be, in the literal sense, pushed too far. He could and did, as Crist did when required, mete out plenty of unpoetic justice, especially when it came to aid a friend in battle. And in spite of his well-behaved retiring nature, he was one of the world's all-time best light heavyweights. And even now, these considerable years later, I can still feel the wind over my shoulder as the whoosh of his straight right fist rent the air like a thundering freight train to put manners upon some nearby vulgarian. Loutish artistic behavior could also produce a few well-deserved cuffs in and about the earlobes. Or in extreme cases, and in the manner of Crist, a wooling.

Somehow now when they ask what made that city of Dublin then so mesmerizing and bewitching, it would be that you were in a city as upon a stage, where you would appear to perform with an eager audience like your man and any man like John Ryan, ready to watch your every nuance. And of course the effort would be to make a fool of yourself and be like all the city's talented sons who one after another were driven out. But then John Ryan never played the fool and always held the fort. And then did even more in providing the ground and settings, the pub, the restaurant, the country house for those, tails up once more, who dared briefly to return, to perform yet again on Dublin's stage. And Ryan could, with his spoken words always dressed in their wonderful finery of irony, make these returnees larger than life. As if at this moment they would appear, feel and especially smell as they were back in the Dublin of that day. He would know the exact spot upon which they stood, drawn from Ryan's encyclopedic knowledge of the streets he loved and daily lived in. And here Crist, eternally delighted by this Dublin circus, played a major role amid all these walk-on parts.

Different as they were in other respects, both Crist and Ryan possessed a similar charm. Their erudition was always used to entertain but never to impress. Both savored language, rolled about on the tongue, tasted for its vintage and measuredly rationed it out to the waiting ears. Their words sounding with the same deft, intimate solemnity which they both used when, with their gently perceptible signals, they ordered drinks at a bar. Among the begrudgers, both were the least begrudging of men. And both were oft accused of lacking malice in a city so noted for such. Indeed it was unknown for either to take a friend's name in vain in a Dublin where no man's name is or was sacred. But there were differences. To the deserving, Crist would mete out justice without warning or mercy. But with Ryan, there would be a little nod of the head and his dry chuckle, which would tell you as much as any oath of condemnation shouted from the rooftops. And if Ryan did topple over into hyperbole and tell a tall tale, detouring more than a bit from credibility, you'd hear the voice of Brendan Behan announce,

"Ah but what matter. There's plenty of time later of disputing facts if a little bit of fiction has you enthralled with the truth of entertainment, said for the time being for your listening pleasure."

It was the redoubtable Brendan Behan, who first ever read manuscript pages of *The Ginger Man*. And under whose laughing vaudevillian behavior lurked much hidden haunted suffering and whose nightmarish soul blazed its brief blasphemy across Dublin, Ireland, and then the rest of the world. And who strode unkempt in his cockeyed shoes, and gave to the time an example of comportment both dreadful and profane. Which on more than one occasion was also highly insalubrious. Although he loudly proclaimed that he knew his redeemer liveth, Behan could never be thought to be a founding member of the Society for the Prevention of Sexual Desire. All and anyone were grist to his matter-of-fact cravings. He and John Ryan made wonderful opposites. Ryan on one end of the socioeconomic scale and Behan on the other, would let you share in their respective wisdom. And both who never left this capital city and were, it must be said, your true Dubliners. Of the sort who would remain attentive to your sorrows long after they are spoken. And where the graves of the departed dead are never visited because they still live alive on your lips.

And so it was that always in Dublin the ghosts abound. Sorrow and sadness pervading with its timeless profundity. It was where you could, before your own time comes, pick over dead men's bones with your own silver-plated utensils and sentimentally relive the harshest and most desperate of moments. Ryan would sometimes start the tales he told with the words "It was a bleak February in a bad year." But bleak February or bad years, there was always the nonsense spouting and the great bards thundering their daily complaint when their fancied horse lost a race. While all present and accounted for in the pub were existentially hoping there would be no delay in the buying of the next round. But there did come a bleak and silent day. When Behan finally lay in a Dublin hospital in a coma dying. And Ryan visiting looked upon that ravaged Romanesque emperor's face, and Ryan said to me, "You know, Mike, Behan despite his unkemptness and other physical frailties, always had that great luxurious head of raven black hair that would always make you want to run your fingers through it. And there lay Brendan breathing his last with that hair still luxurious and black. And it was something I'd always wanted to do and now it was a way of saying goodbye. And I reached over and just ran my fingers through Behan's hair, and his eyelids at once flickered and not that many moments later he was dead."

If the city of Dublin were ever thought to have had a king, he is and was John Ryan. Who was always one of its princes. And in the years ahead, he, who has for so many others provided memorials, is one of the very few who deserves one himself. And with the epitaph I once heard said of him. By Behan himself. Of the black luxurious hair.

Ah, you'd always
Feel kind of safe
In his presence

5

AH, BUT YOU DON'T KNOW DUBLIN. Where battles and surprises never end. And if they seemingly do, beware of enjoying victory. Friendship is on the lips but not in the heart. And just as one has completed heaping an unrelenting stream of praise upon John Ryan, I have occasion to look through some ancient files and letters. And there, by God, in handwritten black and white are statements reported to me from the Dublin of the period. These being scurrilous anecdotes and gossipy ridicule heaped upon me by the princeling John Ryan himself. And why not. It would make people listen to what you were saying. And it may be why in the Dublin of the time that most stories began with a reference to male weakness and ended with an old Gaelic refrain: "Wasn't your impotent man stark naked at the time, and in an equal state of undress was your woman feverish with desire, and alas the poor lady lingers not knowing the Gael fucks only with his fingers."

But it was not only John Ryan who was my first so-called contact with the literary world. There was briefly one other, and a Gael about whom the above refrain could never refer. I'd submitted a poem to the literary magazine called *The Bell,* for whom worked an editor called Harry Craig. Like my paintings, the poem was vaguely promising and began with the line "Soon and off the earth" and ended four or five verses later with "where the weary wind bewilders me." Craig, a man of immense charm and gentility, walked into Davy Byrnes pub and upon being introduced, mentioned that he remembered the poem and intended to publish it, and hoped that I had kept a copy because Brendan Behan, sheltering overnight in the *Bell* office, used a sheaf of manuscripts which included my poem to burn in the fireplace in order to cook his sausages for breakfast.

Now it was no revelation to me that Dublin was full of people trying

This pub became the first of the many one was to frequent, and I found myself within its precincts within an hour on my first social foray out in the city as a Trinity student. Fifty or so yards away eastward down the street at the top of a Georgian house was another venue to which carefully selected customers repaired to dine and party away the rest of the night when this pub closed.

to teach you a once-and-for-all lesson not to try to be a novelist, but they would always indulge you a bit while longer if you wanted to be a poet. However, Harry Craig was in Ireland my very first kindly admirer of one's writing. A Protestant clergyman's son and product of Trinity College, he was a gracious and compassionate man. And as he now lies peacefully dead, I'm sure he won't mind my saying just this little bit about him. He was referred to as having the looks of a Greek god. This description more likely came from and was circulated among the many homosexuals who at the time flocked to Dublin from every corner of the globe. But none of these gentlemen got a chance to get near Harry as he was besieged by women of all ages and description. And one of them, a very attractive and socially prominent English lady who favored to have love made to her while standing on her head, monopolized Harry's time. Being that Harry, of splendid physique and an outstanding athlete, was able to accomplish this while himself quaffing back a pint of stout. But for other more conservative ladies, Harry did have a handicap which hung at great length between his legs. Which observation, the English lady, who indulged her nymphomania, spread all over Dublin, with the result that Harry Craig's literary opinions were avidly listened to. And why not, for on this isle of saints and scholars, with the people so devout, this overadequacy of a monstrously big prick would be thought nobody's fault but God's.

Plus in the Dublin of the time, private parts, as much taboo as they were in public discussion, were much discoursed upon behind closed doors, where such might prove embarrassing for their owner. In any event and sad to say, the socially prominent English lady finally suffered a serious head injury in one of her sexually gymnastic sessions, leaving Harry Craig still having the looks of a Greek god and the body to go with it, a fatal attraction to the remaining women who flung themselves at him in order to cling to him for life. But nothing could stop the rumor that between his legs hung the biggest penis in Ireland, necessitating that Harry's seductions be carried out in darkness as more than one lady, seeing the instrument about to penetrate her, ran for her life. Indeed, outside any chamber wherein Harry was known to be honeymooning with a recent lady, there always gathered a curious group awaiting to see if, when Harry was having at her, there would be a scream and the lady would come fleeing out. Which once gave rise to a false alarm when Harry and a visiting Austrian countess for whose seduction he had rented a flat and had for the occasion recently painted in duck-egg blue, and wherein the overwhelming smell of paint gave them such headaches that they both came reeling out. Leaving the curiosity seekers who'd then followed them to a nearby hotel, scratching their own heads.

In Dublin I had now become a painter notorious for my nerve producing risqué female nudes with your normal pubic hair and exhibiting several still wet canvases. Such activities did get publicity, but selling only a handful of pictures at knockdown prices made me not much richer. And now, desperate to avoid a lifetime of nine-to-five employment and on the verge of marriage with Valerie, we both had gone to visit with her parents in Ilkley. Where one was now much at the mercy of their hospitality, which was, to say the least, lavish and unstinting but did not put a penny in my threadbare pocket, albeit I was still subsisting on my good mother's monthly emolument. But for all the begrudgements and treachery abounding in Dublin, there was still one man upon whom you could trust your life. And totally out of the blue Tony McInerney, by returning money I'd lent him nearly a

Being arranged before an exhibition in Dublin, my pictures are leaning outside and are hung on the wall inside my Kilcoole studio. My nerve and American brashness served me well in this endeavor, which for all my ineptitudes was serious enough to become a lifelong occupation.

year before, saved me from a fatal embarrassment of not being able to afford to buy a wedding ring. And the welcome fivers were sent with a cryptic message: "I'll bet in a million years you never thought you would ever get this."

In my utterly penurious state, the windfall at least enabled me to take Valerie to Bradford, where at the city's elite jeweler, a plain platinum ring was bought. However, the fact that I had not a pot to piss in, must have become apparent to my future mother-in-law, who

One might cringe a bit in embarrassment at my efforts to look gladly sincere on my wedding day, but never married before I was indeed delighted with my new wife, Valerie, who proved with homemade potted meat for breakfast that she could make life extremely pleasant.

conducted her mild and brief cross-examination in the privacy of their Ilkley house kitchen, to which I had been summoned and where Mrs. Heron inquired as to my prospects and assets. The then slightly vague account I gave was honest enough and, although evasive, was at least optimistically sunny. But one, as an American, feeling somewhat above all that kind of thing, took exception to this inquiry. I was in any case smitten with the beautiful and charming Valerie and had no intentions of her starving and was in fact a little bit shocked that such subject should ever be brought up. However, my prospective in-laws had envisioned that both their daughters should marry into a Yorkshire merchant's or mill owner's dynasty, whose sons had already been a long time avidly pursuing. But the Heron parents, having had enough difficulty over a previous marriage of their eldest beautiful daughter, had now more or less given up the battle to prevent marriage to someone thought not quite good enough.

The small town of Ilkley, housing textile magnates and industrialists from Bradford and Leeds, was situated in the valley of the Wharfe River and was surrounded by its moors and was originally a spa and had now become a considerably rich residential enclave to which my father-in-law had finally gravitated as he achieved affluence. With tinned food and refrigeration banned from the household because they diminished flavor, there was an extensive cold cellar brimming with beer, cheeses and such things as potted meat for breakfast and vaults of vintage wine. Riverdale, as the house was called, was a cornucopia. Over the snooker table, port and cigars followed dinner, and chocolates were available in front of the sitting room fire. But now old man Heron was confined to his rosewood and exotically etched glass–paneled and deep-carpeted bedroom. Occasionally still smoking and drinking his vintage champagne and reminding anyone who might listen of his rise from rags to riches. And I listened.

Old man Heron was not regarded with awe by his children, who would tolerate the largess but would sheepishly try to avoid his stories. Especially his son, Michael, who viewed life in more romantic terms and, groomed to take over his father's expanding business, had been sent on the grand tour during which he learned many languages as well as how to sample all of Europe's luxuries. But upon his return to Bradford, Michael could not stomach the world of textiles. Now, as old man Heron's children's lives unfolded and the prospect of grandchildren loomed, he would comment as he saw it, concerning the family's clogs-to-clogs transition in three generations, having had himself descended from a former family of some status who had lost their engineering business and grown up in a back-to-back house in a working-class district of Bradford. But the Yorkshire brand of person is a resolute and hardy one. And in the pollutants of his industrial cities, little him dismay. As might be drawn from the oft said words,

"Where there's muck, there's money."

Starting out in wool trade as a messenger boy, old man Heron vowed to make his way back up in the world. As a music lover, he taught himself to play the violin and his lunchtime leisure moments were spent each day at the free outdoor band concerts, where he stood listening at the back of the last row of seats. And with each passing year, as he continued to be promoted and had now joined a prominent textile firm, he was able to improve his comforts and pay a threepenny bit for a hard seat and then thrupence for a deck chair and finally was not only able to pay for his seat but also to buy a program. Independently, he began making up his own batch of gabardine raincoats, which he went selling at night door-to-door, and then became manager of the silk department and ultimately a director of this prestigious textile concern.

During the war the cloth trade was static and old man Heron's moment of business triumph came one day out of the blue at a board meeting. His fellow directors of the company complaining of his not appearing at his office until long after ten A.M. each day and disappearing for lunch before one P.M., when he was not to be seen again till the next morning. His habit had become to go have a slap-up pub lunch of splendid meat pie and two pints of ale, followed by a leisurely afternoon at the cinema. Upon Heron hearing the complaint, he immediately called a board meeting and for the firm's accountants to produce the firm's books. Heron then pointed out that his department was the only department that had made any profit in the past two years and that he was in fact carrying the entire firm. Under the threat of resigning, he asked for an apology from the every member of the board who in turn stood up and apologized. Upon accepting the apologies, old man Heron then rose to his own feet and announced,

"Gentlemen, I appreciate your change of heart, but I feel that such has come about under a certain duress. Therefore, I consider it appropriate to resign. And hereby resign. And a very good day and good-bye to you all."

That same afternoon, Heron emptying his desk and files, assembled his credentials and went with these to his bank manager. Whereupon that same day he had raised enough money to start his own firm, which in turn soon became more prosperous than the one he had just left and made him a substantially rich man.

These stories of old man Heron's life were told to me as he lay sick in bed in his considerable splendor, enduring his last illness. Each day, with what was persisting of my ebullient American optimism and unquenchable unconquerability, I'd play him in chess and comment upon his painting, which he'd taken up at my behest and had mastered nearly overnight. In turn he tried to teach me about the stock market and how to calculate the yield on a stock, which somehow, even as a student reading honors natural science and taught physics by E.T.S. Walton, who along with Lord Rutherford were the first men ever to split the atom, I failed to fathom. He must have only vaguely held this against me, as he later said to his wife, who remained more dubious concerning my future,

"That boy will go far."

I was relieved and pleased to hear this, as his valued opinion agreed with mine. And especially as at the time, the simple wedding that Crist had urged and highly approved of was about to come to pass. The momentum gathered from the suspicion that Valerie and I were already living together. And on a windy day with squalls of rain, the marriage ceremony was in fact pleasant enough, although my smile in the photographs seemed posed. Valerie was bought a large hat by her mother, and I wore a gray flannel suit. Michael Heron, who occasionally enjoyed proprieties, pinned roses on lapels and was best man and carried a vase of tulips to be put on the desk in the small Guiseley registry office a few miles from Ilkley, where the woman registrar read the vows and requested the fee of twelve shillings. The maids, Freda and Mary, set a wedding feast of cold chicken in lemon sauce. Bedridden as he was, old man Heron had no longer any need to climb up into the third floor of the house to try and catch Valerie and I in bed together, but did expertly open a magnum of champagne.

Luckily our honeymoon was a present and already generously paid, for following the purchase of the wedding ring, I remained abysmally broke. A hired chauffeured car took us up to the small hamlet of Kettlewell in the Dales to a tiny hotel, where, arriving in the dark, we were the only guests. The bedroom was lit by candlelight and had a large four-poster bed, and the windows overlooked a rushing stream. There was nothing to do nor anywhere to go except up on the moors, where, in my only pair of shoes, I soaked my feet. I bought myself a walking stick and attempted to make the best of the situation, and by evenings went tapping my way through the silent village after dark. Although not a soul was to be seen, this innocent air I'd suddenly adopted seemed to embarrass Valerie. But this little tribulation of the time at least distracted my attention from other worries. And to this day, I feel out of uniform without a walking stick.

My mother-in-law, with her organizational skills admired by many, had during the war become an impressive lady in the community, running an enormous catering canteen. And upon our return from our brief honeymoon, a cocktail party was thrown. The Herons' friends and relatives, most of whom were wool merchants and mill owners, arrived. Over the years, old man Heron had traditionally given, as a wedding present to the children of any of his friends who married, a set of dinner silverware. Early in the evening I'd been invited into Mr. Heron's bedroom, where, with the words "I'm not going to give you any advice," he handed me a slip of paper which turned out to be a check. For some reason, which has now become a habit of mine, I failed to look at or read what I assumed were modest numerals reflecting a gesture of goodwill from a hardened businessman. Valerie, in the privacy of the hallway, had no such daft sentimentality about the check stuffed in my pocket and asked immediately to see it. And the numerals turned out to be of a considerably large dimension.

Guests downstairs were now arriving in numbers. Being that the party was so impromptu, it was apparent that everyone in this rich community of Ilkley thought it was a shotgun marriage. Nor did Mrs. Heron dissuade them from so thinking. And none had a chance to buy a vase, dish or silver serving spoon. Instead each discreetly handed over their vellum envelopes containing these simple pieces of paper describing cash sums drawn on your better banks and which now made a substantial sheaf of envelopes in my hand. Upon Valerie calling for another accounting, it was apparent that from abject penury of only an hour or two before, one now stood possessed of modest riches. And returning to the din of the cocktail party in the deep-carpeted, rosewood-paneled front lounge of this house, I listened with animated interest to these guests and their friendly phrases, but all of whom I suspected regarded me with the deepest of deep suspicions. There having been before me a few impostors and mountebanks, some of whom in the confusion of the war were sporting double-barreled surnames and mythically alluding to their titled uncles and who attempted to wheedle their way into this mercantile prosperity, which established the social hierarchy of this town of Ilkley on Ilkley moor. However, I made no effort whatever to be anything but the reasonably nice American young man I hoped I was, born in Brooklyn and raised in the Bronx.

Ah, but even with these heaven-sent funds dropping out of the Ilkley sky, my optimism was soon to reverse upon me. From Liverpool and over the tossing Irish Sea, Valerie and I set sail again for Ireland on the mail boat. This journey so often taken amid belligerent drunken passengers, with the ship's public rooms dense with cigarette smoke, decks splattered with vomit and the boat itself rearing, rolling and pitching, which could leave you tottering and seasick for days afterward. And it was no wonder that more than occasionally a passenger, in seeking relief, would empty his pockets, neatly place the contents on the deck for identification, with a quid or two left for his heirs, and then blessing himself would leap over the ship's railings and plummet down into the dark waves. Once, having witnessed this being done, my sympathies were such for those haplessly returning to Ireland that I hesitated some seconds before alerting a member of the ship's company. Alas, I needn't have worried, this very tidy gentleman jumping was not rescued and never found.

Arriving early morning on the Dublin quays was never an event to set your heart beating with delight. There was little shelter or sustenance to be found before nine A.M. in a shut Dublin. As ladies were forbidden past six P.M. in a student's rooms, except with special permission to attend the reading room, Valerie spent the day to find us accommodation. Evening came and I went with her to Castlewood Avenue, Rathmines, a suburban area not that far from the center of the city. Going up the stairs of this modest-sized terraced house to a narrow front room, I was incredulous that people rented such tiny space to live in, where there was only a stove and a basin and one had to go outside into a communal hall to the bath and to the water closet past other doors which led to other rooms where other strangers lurked inside. Leaving no mystery as to why men build their palaces and stately homes and surround them with parklands to keep your stranger strange and as far away as possible from any proximity. And more power to such chaps.

My responsibility as a husband to support another and the thought that this is what can happen to human beings overwhelmed me. The effect on me being almost impossible to believe for someone having been through two war years of rough and a certain amount of tumble in the U.S. Navy, where one occupied barracks or crew's quarters aboard ship, and where dozens of men shared latrines and slept in open proximity. That one could be so vulnerable and that a Dublin bed-sitting-room should send me reeling back, stunned, to my rooms at Trinity took me entirely by surprise. And was probably the result of my background and the security one must have got used to growing up in what was the equivalent of a small-town suburban community in America and better known on maps as Woodlawn on the north borders of the Bronx, and where and within these handful of crisscrossing streets there had never been any serious degree of dismay in terms of living space or freedom.

Valerie left in Castlewood Avenue, as I lay back on the bed in my darkened Trinity rooms, gloomily contemplating the possible dreadful squalor that might befall me and staring at the ceilings, my heart took to pounding in such agitated manner that I thought I was having a heart attack. Struggling up from bed, I feebly dressed and hobbled down the couple of flights of stairs and faltering in front of the entrance of number 38, I looked for help in the silent empty quad of New Square. Suddenly in the dark, I spied two students exiting from their rooms and shouted for assistance. Trinity was renowned for its pranksters and mischief makers, some of whom could be extremely devilish and once in the past had even caused the death of a junior dean, and these two gentlemen of the college were quick to assume that someone was attempting a leg pull. I could, I thought, as they recognized me, even see anticipatory smiles breaking out on their faces. All of which necessitated my sounding even more plaintive in my cry for help. And especially so as I was known for being able to give a good account of myself in Dublin's frequent pub battles, when I might even issue a preliminary war whoop as I entered the fray.

Stumbling forward, I had now reached and grasped the chain encircling the flat green velvet grass of the quad. As my knees buckled, I made an extreme effort to sound my last gasp loud enough so that it could convincingly be heard. My portrayal of imminent collapse must have finally persuaded them of my plight, and the two quickened their pace to my aid.

"Thank you, thank you, I do believe I may be having a heart attack."

Now there were frowns rather than smiles on their faces as rain began to fall and they supported me under the arms out of New Square and across the cobbles of Front Square to the porter's lodge at the front gates. Dying students were not a too common occurrence as were drunken ones, but both could be treated in the same fashion, and a taxi to take me away was called. Of the two assisting gentlemen, one hailed from the north of Ireland and played college rugby and in his later professional life became a member of the British parliament. It was many years afterward when I again heard his chuckling voice just behind me as I climbed the steps of Sotheby's auction house in London's Bond Street.

"I say there, Donleavy, do you need any help."

But back upon this night and dispatched in a taxi to a Trinity College–affiliated hospital, I collected Valerie from the bed-sitter so that she could at least hear of my last wishes and the psalms to be selected sung at my obsequies. I was received staggering into the accident room, empty at the time, where the young interning doctor from Trinity's medical school and whose face I knew by sight, placed a stethoscope all over my chest. He tapped and listened and listened again. He even made me open my mouth and go "ahhha." His exhaustive examination concluded, he frowned and pronounced, "Quite frankly, there may be something wrong, but I can't find it. All I find is that you may be the best physical specimen I have ever examined. Your heart, as far as I am concerned, is in splendid condition."

Of course I had been on occasion able to run a timed practice mile in four minutes and twenty seconds. However, upon this eventful night, I still wasn't entirely convinced that I was in monumentally splendid health, but certainly I was now able to put one foot in front of the other and cautiously make my way out into the world again with the thought that my heart would hold out that little bit longer. With a bemused Valerie, I returned to the bed-sitter, and from this constricted lodgings was ready to do untold battle in the momentous struggle I envisioned was ahead that would ensure I would escape such rooms forever. Meanwhile, news of my collapse and impending death was already all over the college and a concerned solicitous get-well-soon letter was awaiting me as I arrived back at my rooms which had been sent by my tutor, the eminent Greek scholar William Bedell Stanford, whom I'm sure could have encapsulated my plight in an appropriate Hellenic homily. For he, years later upon being interviewed, contradicted nearly all opinions about me. And was quoted as saying, "I know he may have had a reputation of some obstreperous nature.

"However,
I found him
The most quietly polite
And retiring
Of young
Gentlemen"

6

Having now reared up in angered horror that the fate of a claustrophobic bed-sitting-room might ever be mine, I informed Valerie of our plight and that we must immediately garner and gather together all our assets, consisting mostly of the wedding present checks and including the modest money of hers still held in the National Provincial Bank of Ilkley, and with such funds quickly acquire land and a roof we owned over our heads. This plan did not go down well, and on this now sunny, breezy day, as we crossed Butt Bridge over the Liffey River and walked along the quay, Valerie said she wanted to keep her independence. I thought, Holy cow, what the hell is this. Am I to take all the fighting risks in life while the woman I'm married to sits on a small but reassuring amount of security.

The raging silence this produced in me over a period of the next three hours moving around Dublin was total. I was astonished at this lack of confidence in me, although one had to admit it was reasonable enough considering that only the night before I was reeling to doom as one of the world's vanquished. But as my silence continued and I let it be known her independence from now on was hers to pursue, Valerie relented and said she would throw her financial lot in with mine.

Although I could through impatience be incautious with money, I was not a squanderer or a spendthrift, having long regarded money as a daily instrument to be used rather than something to remain as security to be relied upon for the future. And one used this tool unhesitatingly if it meant providing some basic practical need to accomplish an immediate goal. And that is how I came to occupy a tiny bit of ground near Kilcoole which dotted that isolated, strange, bereft twelve-square-mile stretch of bottomland along the Wicklow coast of Ireland.

A college pal who'd also sent me the money totally unexpectedly with which I'd bought Valerie's wedding ring, had, with his inheritance, been looking at farming properties to buy, and before I went to Ilkley I accompanied him one day when he went to view a small holding near Kilcoole of just under four acres and selling for about three hundred and fifty pounds. Upon seeing the property, the friend seemed to disdain it. Certainly it was nothing resembling or anywhere near as grand as his own family farm where he had been raised. It is possible too that my pal, who could be suicidally generous, had become short of money, having already spent much entertaining friends in wining, dining and drinking, which he did with some lavishness. And on one occasion taking an entire party, including Brendan Behan, Michael Heron and Gainor Crist to Paris. The last gentleman in very typical fashion taking pleasure in introducing his host to a blind man he had in tow atop the Eiffel Tower.

At the time of his affluence, I said to my friend not to expect me to drink or contribute to his spending his legacy, which I thought ought solely to go to buy himself and his then young family somewhere to

Valerie seated outside my studio with one of her favorite cats. Never having had a tool other than a golf club or squash racket to hand before, the window above Valerie was my first ever effort to be an architect and builder.

live. However, while the money lasted, my friend in the aristocratically abandoned way of an Irish chieftain, spent on. And it was I who bought this small parcel of land not too far from the sea, where at least its couple of sheds and tumbledown cottage could become somewhere under which one's head might shelter and somewhere where one could place one's feet on soil to call one's own.

The purchase at Kilcoole was my first major transaction in life, and was in itself a financial battle. I made an offer of half the asking price and was surprised not to be turned away. Unbeknownst to me, there had been a deposit paid on a previous uncompleted sale, which would be forfeited by the original attempted purchaser when the property was finally sold. As I clung to my offer and the vendor refused to sell, the small local estate agent in the nearby town of Greystones seemed quite astonished at my refusing to even meet the vendor halfway and, as they did in Ireland, split the difference. Finally, as I stood talking to the agent over the telephone from the Grand Hotel in Greystones, in a last effort, that gentleman said with a quality of sincerity I recognized as used only when truth was being told,

"Mr. Donleavy, in splitting the difference at this stage and at this price, please believe me when I say you're getting a genuine bargain."

The estate agent's voice was so plaintive that in turn in finally agreeing to the price and purchase, I tried to sound like a normal, reasonable human being. Which clearly I no longer was and never would be again. But I had at least taken my first little step toward squiredom. By entering into a caretaker's agreement, I took immediate possession the moment the contract was signed and the check paid. And would soon acquire the wisdom that you can still stay damn poor owning your own land.

Having purchased an axe and bucket, Valerie and I attending upon my rooms at Trinity collected some college chattels and, with my disconcerted college servant, Noctor, carrying a tin trunk and a mattress and some crockery, and on this thankfully unrainy day, we exited the north side gate of Trinity where the bus to Kilcoole stopped just a few yards away. Noctor, who had been a corporal in the British Army, clicked his heels and gave a smart salute as I departed. And if I didn't at that time salute back, I do now with a little of the same sadness I felt then to know that he would no longer be available to rouse me awake in the mornings or lay out a spot of breakfast or administer in his white coat at teatime.

The bus route to Kilcoole went past Foxrock, a community of your bigger suburban homes, and on through the main streets of the sea-

The village of Kilcoole near the cottage and piece of land I'd bought in order to begin my struggle in the world of art and to which I came with my mattress from my college rooms, together with a saucepan, pail and axe, and was transported from the bus stop by the local butcher's mule and cart the mile or so to my new country abode.

side town of Bray and the smaller once fishing village of Greystones. With its large leafy gardens surrounding houses of the Burnaby Estate, Greystones was a most refined Protestant enclave on this polite bit of rocky coast. In comparison, the village of Kilcoole, four miles farther on, Valerie thought ugly and unfriendly. As we arrived, little life was evident, reminding one of a midwestern American town deserted by the populace before a gunfight. Upon inquiry at the tiny post office, the postmistress referred us to her son, who ran a small butcher shop just up the hill. Who agreed to transport our luggage and belongings in his van along the narrow, rutted dirt road which led past a cemetery where a vampire was said to be buried. Then, in an abrupt turn toward the sea and a half mile along an overgrown lane, one finally came to this isolated small holding, where, to keep surviving, I intended to put brush to canvas and occasionally typewriter keys to paper.

Although under gray skies this area could be melancholic, it also had a strange romantic beauty, which, in contemplating, made the hours just vanish away. Inland to the west, and seen starkly with each day's setting sun, rose the peaks of the greater and lesser Sugarloaf Mountains. Along the "breeches," as part of this marshy lowland bordering the Irish Sea was known, birds from all over Europe came to stop and forage. And as one cast an eye across the vast bleakness, it could shrivel the heart with loneliness. Even the buildings stood somewhat haunted, and bereft, and you'd feel abandoned and much lost as the sound of the long-beaked curlew bird's whistle would pass overhead in the evening grayness.

Out of two small rooms I soon bare-handedly made one by tearing down a partition. We spent the first few nights sleeping with the mattress on the floor. Until unhinging a door, I propped it on bricks and made a bed. With a broken edge of a knife, I cut and carved an ash sapling to use as a handle in an old rusted shovel found in a hedgerow. And dug a pool in the tiny nearby stream from which to fetch buckets of water. As I woke by dawn and had to get four miles to Greystones to catch a train to Dublin, one raged at the rain and beat the fists on the hood of the small van I'd bought which became progressively more difficult to start. And having to wait till the mailman came to help give me a push. Till finally it led to my missing more and more of my classes at Trinity. As I now seriously was faced with the idea of becoming a full-time painter and hoping somehow to make a living.

Valerie, whose habit it was to be scrupulously clean, cleaned everywhere. But for a while, itching up the legs, we thought we had fleas and perhaps we did. I'd even consulted with my zoology professor, the eminent J. Bronte Gatenby, and learned that although we could indeed be infested with Aphaniptera, we at least had not to worry about bedbugs, as it was too damp for them to survive in Ireland. However, there were other more hypochondriacal desperations to worry about. Except briefly during a school vacation, I had never worked with my hands before. And now with a slight insanity, I was throughout the day attacking hedgerows, digging a garden and risking my neck to put fallen slates back on the roof. I'd even tackled mending the rutted lane, ordering a load of gravel, which, when dumped, ended up blocking my van. And left me furiously trying to shift it into potholes. I was no longer having heart attacks but was instead now having strokes. One of which seemed to strike me like a lightning bolt and retired me to bed. The doctor summoned, reassured me my brain was not yet rupturing its blood vessels. And again I was pronounced a superfit specimen and in no time I was bouncing out of bed and spreading gravel on the lane again.

Cowering nights in front of a sparse fire, we worried about the rumors of Russian communist hordes sweeping across Europe to enslave us. And we were bound to be among the first victims, surrounded as we were by the silent fields and bogs. But I had more immediate worries and my most furious battle then was just beginning. Although still at Trinity and receiving letters of complaint from the junior dean for parking my red van outside my rooms, I had now given at the Dublin Painters Gallery on St. Stephen's Green three exhibitions. These had sold well enough to make me at least hope of making ends meet. And the exhibitions had also allowed me an early taste of fame if not fortune. My first fan letter came from the local Protestant vicar in the nearby hamlet of Delgany who extended words of encouragement and had objected to a harsh review of my pictures in the *Irish Times*. Also, Ireland's then most esteemed philosopher Arland Ussher wrote to the same newspaper to defend me. And although further kind encouraging words were to be found here and there, it was quickly dawning on me that Ireland, with its small inbred population of highly active begrudgers, was no place to expect to survive long enough to become rich and celebrated, as I innocently enough planned to do. Although I was not yet in an unmitigated hurry, there was no doubt about the realization clearly essential to my longevity, that it was to larger fields abroad that one must go.

With Valerie I expectantly set off on a trip to London, lugging my watercolors in a loose folder. On my very first call, I went to one of the best-known galleries, the Redfern in Cork Street. I was courteously invited down into the basement part of the gallery to lay my pictures out on the floor. The man, a few years older than myself, who agreed to look at my pictures, was perfectly polite and, as he leisurely contemplated some of them, actually asked me to slow down, as I was paging through my watercolors and drawings too fast. He said he regarded them as original, colorful and decorative and that I was obviously a painter of verve and talent, but that he could do nothing for me. But could do something if I were as famous as that gentleman, a novelist H. E. Bates, who was at that moment then looking at pictures in the gallery. Having my talents, albeit only relatively recently awakened as they were in the painting field, recognized and so confidently pronounced upon, and then to be told that without being famous, nothing could be done, enraged me.

Valerie, my compliant and so far patient and tolerant wife, whose heart must have mostly been sinking at my efforts to smash upward in the world, was waiting above in the gallery and was, I think, surprised at my white-faced anger. But I knew what fame was, having at least recently tasted it, albeit in the small confines of Dublin city. To me it

In my studio at Kilcoole, a commendable painting I'd done of Notre Dame, Paris, hanging on the wall. I sit at the makeshift desk and stool I'd built in order to write THE GINGER MAN, *the manuscript pages of which are by the typewriter, and where I also found lying the manuscript copy of* BORSTAL BOY, *which Behan was writing at the time he came as an uninvited guest.*

Already having discovered that authorship could find you incarcerated indoors in the same place for unconscionable lengths of time, this was my first effort to attempt to combine some pleasure with the pain of writing as I took to my newly created front lawn at Kilcoole.

simply consisted of three people, all of whom had heard of your name and were distracted enough by the knowledge to listen to what you were saying for two and sometimes even three minutes. As we left the gallery and reached the southwest corner of Cork Street and Burlington Gardens, I stopped in my tracks. Shaking my fist, I announced to the street that, goddamnit, seeing as I was contemplating it anyway, I would write a book that no one could stop and would make my name known in every nook and cranny all over the world. Quite a lot to declare on one of London's better streetcorners, where your more dignified and prosperous Londoner is wont to pass, and whose practiced indifference was supreme. And which of course could tend to leave you even angrier than you were in the first place.

We left London and took that long train and bumpy boat ride back to our small holding, where I had now seemed to have settled. And as spring approached summer in this year of 1951, I went to sit for ten stubborn days at the northern end of the sun porch I'd built on the southwest side of the cottage, and there on a makeshift stool and rickety makeshift table, I began to write *The Ginger Man*. This work long cogitating and now provoked into sooner existence by the rejection of my watercolors in what seemed that more sophisticated world out beyond Ireland but for which one now held only supreme contempt. From the reasty smell arising from next to where I now wrote, I had also ample time to contemplate the attempt I'd made at installing a drain in the concrete sun porch floor which emptied nowhere. Resolutely and stubbornly forcing word after word out of my brain, I slowly touch-typed out nearly illegible phrases from a faint typewriter ribbon. Opening words which have till now never seen the light of print and words which, certainly seem to indicate the author's rage was still simmering.

Several things mattered being alive in the agricultural, paupered, myth drugged greenery that is Ireland. These things are not love, faith or joy. These things are fire, food and booze. It is a land which best demonstrates the ingredients upon which the world fosters itself and the world fosters itself on manure. It is not a country where the stranger is killed, but where fathers, mothers, sisters, brothers and neighbours, live from day to wet day in fear of poison, the gun or the hook. Friendship is on the lips but not in the heart. Death is a visitant greeted with a shrewd glee, for another greedy mouth is dead and a fiddle plays a tune across the fairy rings and mushrooms fatten in the warm September rain.

My painting career and my cocking a snook at the art world of Dublin and whistling a fist or two in search of a begrudger's jaw had given me a certain vantage point to add to the confidence steeled by the resolve of my anger. But as one wrote farther on the page and with a hint of flourish, I appear to become a slightly more objective man of letters, carefully setting the scene and giving an indication of the bitter poverty pervading the Dublin of the day. And the words begin to come closer to those which finally appeared in *The Ginger Man*.

Today there was a rare sun of spring after a winter of dark skies, the depressant of rain and Ireland's funereal cold. Ragged white fleshed children, their faces covered in a light green phlegm, raised a din through the Georgian streets. But winter remained in the pub as it does in Ireland. O'Keefe spoke of the difficulties of being poor, the bovine shrewdness of the Irish and the need for social reform.

As I wrote further, a more formal description of the character Dangerfield, in the third dimension as it were, was given. And the first-person interior monologue of Dangerfield combined with third person, that much of *The Ginger Man* was finally written in, must have still been lying in wait to be formulated.

Kenneth O'Keefe was speaking to a tall, most respectable man, who was precise, spare and red, who wore a pair of borrowed grey flannels, an ill fitting woman's raincoat, bowler hat and had not bathed for two months. This man had attended Dartmouth College. He was drinking a bottle of Guinness having just pawned an electric fire. He was interested in the plays of Ibsen, the writings of Rousseau and Jonathan Swift and was disarmingly erudite. He had one consummate occupation which was with drink. He was married and had a year old daughter.

His name
Was
Sebastian Dangerfield

7

THE VILLAGE OF KILCOOLE was half a mile away as the crow flies and a mile's walk or drive by way of the narrow rutted lane, dusty and overgrown by summer and mud deep in winter. Walking, I occasionally stopped to visit a small church ruin and graveyard, where rumor had it that a stake had been driven through a vampire's heart buried there and over which no grass ever grew. This spookiness seemed to extend to the settlement of Kilcoole on its hill of small houses and cottages, which always seemed the last forsaken tip of civilization before one went farther south.

The clouds coming from the west more than often emptied their rain on the Wicklow Mountains leaving the sun to shine along this stretch of coast. But clement as it could be, no one seemed to stick it out in this sea-level area of land for long. It seemed at times a graveyard of dreams from which one would rage in battle to escape from this remote coast, where a brooding atmosphere seemed to forever lurk. And perhaps not surprising as there were rumors of wartime quislings, traitors and double agents from continental Europe, who, following hostilities had gravitated to this neutral country's anonymous landscape to elude the wrath of those whom they'd deceived. Such folk remained quiet outsiders, which now included me as a not so quiet pagan iconoclast.

There was still evidence of a once squirearchy in the surrounding countryside, where the several ruins of great mansions rose from their coverings of ivy. But one or two substantial houses remained still standing with a roof. One on the village's northern outskirts, surrounded in its small parkland and which housed a convent of nuns. By summer their black shapes were sometimes seen in the distance making their way to the deserted beach to swim. And haunting the landscape just to the south of my cottage, and the nearest large building, was a mansion just as gloomy as its name, Grey Fort. Although abandoned and empty many years, it still stood reasonably dry and sound. And one day I found the front door open and walked through its barren and dusty, echoing rooms. In its musty basement were strewn stacks of anti-Catholic pamphlets containing highly unfriendly words concerning the Pope, and vividly derogatory descriptions of Catholics in general. Suitably enough, it was rumored, as was nearly everything in Ireland, that Guglielmo Marconi, the inventor of a practical system of communicating intelligence without the use of connecting wires, had once occupied this house. And some truth might have attached to this, as according to the encyclopedia he had married an Irish woman.

Stories had it that the big rock jutting out from the landscape at the top of Kilcoole village marked a small common and was over the centuries a traditional meeting place of Gypsies and tinkers. And along the verges of the adjoining byways, one always saw encampments of a family or two of these traveling people crouched around their fire embers drinking tea, or by night tucked away, disappeared within their tiny canvas shells under which they slept. Their horses roamed loose down the narrow lanes grazing the "long acre," as the grass on the roadside was called. Often these piebald quadrupeds, when they panicked in the headlights of my approaching car, would then in darkness gallop before me, hoofs pounding and sparks flying. And sometimes terrifying, as trapped by my gate at the end of the long lane they would come charging back out of the blackness.

The tinkers themselves would betimes come and call to see if any tinkering could be done or a tool be indefinitely borrowed or a pony remain in a field eating one's meadow. Word soon got out and was spread about the village that nothing, not even a rusty nail, could be had out of the American. But because I had saved from drowning a tinker child fallen into a stream, word of this seemed to spread far and wide, and as I was one of the few men, if not the only man, in Ireland at the time with a beard, wherever I went for years afterward, traveling people, upon seeing me, saluted and offered me blessing as I went by.

There was a train stop on the shoreline, a full mile away along a straight road from the village. This was nothing but a bit of raised ground on this deserted stretch of sea, and one of the loneliest train stops in the world. To alight there, one had to get a message to the train driver before leaving Dublin's Harcourt Street terminus, which I had to do in my first few weeks without a car. Valerie, in meeting the train, never believed it would stop or if it did that anyone would ever get off. We then both had to wear boots in order to shortcut home across the boggy meadows, which stayed underwater through the winter. Halfway across this stretch of land between myself and the sea were my nearest neighbors, the Smiths, in their tiny cottage. And I suppose if one could have inspiration for a quiet, peaceful later life, the Smiths provided it.

A white-haired kindly, cheerful and charming retired couple in their middle eighties, they had moved out from Dublin. And now squeezed in by their large Victorian furniture lived in their three tiny rooms. And it was across their bit of meadow and past their cottage that one went to get to the sea and the station. Bowered and buried in a tangle of shrubs and trees, their tiny abode could hardly be seen. They kept chickens and had a very big gray neutered cat called Snooky, who was a good ratter. We were given eggs, and were invited for tea with homemade fruit cake. As I threw heart attacks and had strokes and was *hors de combat* at the tender age of twenty-five, and recuperating stretched out under rugs on my chaise longue brought from my rooms at Trinity, old Mr. Smith, who was eighty-six, would do odd chores for me, such as expertly installing a lock on our front cottage door. In a scrapbook, they kept photographs and newspaper cuttings they encountered of my public activities. To fetch their simple groceries, they often walked along the railway line the four miles to Greystones and back. And never uttered an unkind or discouraging word. Except to occasionally say that a loutish element were emerging across Ireland. As the turf smoke rose from their chimney and was a fainter gray against the cold winter background of the sea, I took comfort from their lonely presence.

Inland from the cottage, lived a young, friendly farming family called Farrell. They had bought the large house and farmed the land where once a British major lived who committed suicide. The Farrells grazed cattle, cows and kept a bull. And it was from them we got our daily milk. It was from old Mr. Farrell that I was given the encouragement and lessons on how to make hay. Putting it into weatherproof cocks, raked down and tied against the wind so that it would impress another farmer and fetch a good price in an auction sale. These now, my side battles in life, fought every bit as bitterly as were the struggles to write words on a page. And I could romanticize enough to imagine that I had to put the begrudgers and philistines to rout who would dare to stifle my voice. Of course one could really be so bloody-minded and determined that one wasn't that desperately concerned with these obstacle makers. But I already knew from my brief brushes with the

This distinguished-looking gentleman, with his equally distinguished and attractive wife, was my nearest neighbor at Kilcoole. As his appearance might tell, both Mr. Smith and his wife would seek instant shelter at the sound of an approaching Brendan Behan cursing his way across the fields. But one always felt one could view life with some sanguinity if one lived one's own life as they had done theirs.

literary world that they lurked and abounded in every publishing enterprise round the globe. And nothing but the unstoppable would succeed in avoiding the sabotage. Which alas was to be ceaseless.

Across the lane from the Farrells' big house, subsisted a wiry, small-statured Mr. Allen on his acre plot of land. He hailed from Leicestershire and had erected a series of adjoining shacks. Flat-roofed and tar-papered, they were neat and respectable enough, and these he rented while he industriously tilled his patch of ground. At five A.M. on summer mornings he dug up his carrots, parsnips, and cabbages, cleaned them and then with a bag strung over his bicycle would pedal twenty-five miles to Dublin to sell them in the market. Returning in the afternoon he would in short trousers pass by my studio on his sinewy, skinny legs, chewing one of his carrots, to go for a swim in the ice-cold sea. He'd been an agitator for socialism in Leicester and, having met much opposition, had come to Ireland to soothe his nerves. Although I wasn't a convert to his way of thinking I always listened patiently to his words. One day, hearing my typewriter pecking away, he inquired about what I was doing. When I told him I was writing a book he made me a present of a big, old, battered dictionary in which there was the word "papaphobia," which I was delighted to learn the meaning of as being morbid fear and dread of the Pope and Popery. With all the nearby antipapist pamphlets in the mansion Grey Fort, I thought it appropriate to promptly enter this word into the manuscript of *The Ginger Man,* where it seems solitary to exist, as I haven't seen or heard of the word since.

Back in the world of Dangerfield, I moved across a new lawn from my sun porch into an ancient stone shed, having with a sledgehammer wrought an entrance door through the back wall and installed in the south and east walls large studio windows. A smaller window faced west through which many an hour was spent watching the farmer Farrell's cattle grazing. My desk was an old door propped up by former roof joists, where I sat at my typewriter facing a few ragged reference tomes and a couple of my sculptures. Above, on the wall, was one of my earliest and quite creditable paintings of Notre Dame Cathedral in Paris. Now with my many attempted pages accumulated and drafts repeated many times, I finally had taken the bull by the horns or the bull had taken me and I proceeded nonstop into the novel. Six weeks elapsed, there was at last represented a considerable sheaf of foolscap paper, and took on the shape and weight of a manuscript with now copious notes appearing in the margin and on the backs of pages. A true sign the work had taken on a momentum.

Old man Heron had died. And at the point where the manuscript was one hundred and twenty pages long, I had gone to the Isle of Man just following his funeral. As death approached, he had decamped from Ilkley to the island, where there were no death duties. And this may have been a selfless act to preserve assets for his heirs. But it was to the island he had come on many of his wartime holidays, taking the four-hour journey alone on a Manx steamer from Liverpool, and he held this ancient small world of glens and moors emerging out of the Irish Sea, in sentimental affection. Regarding him as a fair if pragmatic man, I was left with a sense of sorrow at old man Heron's passing. But upon stepping off the bus from the airport at Douglas I was greeted by Valerie's and her brother Michael's smiling, cheerful faces. And as we repaired to Yates Wine Bar, with its cautionary signs against alcoholic overindulgence, I thought, Why not drink an ale to his memory.

In old man Heron decamping to the Isle of Man, there had to be an urgent search to find a house and for him to establish his domicile of intention. And somehow after all these years, I still remember the price of five thousand pounds, which then was considerable but in view of the house's comparatively exotic splendor, reasonable enough. Stone-built on a rock outcropping with walls three feet thick and adjoining a stream and waterfall flowing into the sea, the waves broke against the garden ramparts above which, in the island's subtropical climate, palm trees grew on the terrace.

I was not to know then that this fairly sumptuous house hovering over the sea, that old man Heron had bought before he died, was to play a significant part in the history of *The Ginger Man*. While Valerie stayed on a few more days on the Isle of Man, I returned to Kilcoole. Arriving late in the afternoon at the cottage, I found a window broken open and the sitting-room-kitchen in total disarray. Towels dirtied and clothes and food strewn everywhere. Every cooking pot blackened with soot. Nothing seemed to have been taken. Except in the small bedroom, all my shoes of which I had twenty-two pairs, were mysteriously missing.

In a panic, I went out to my studio to see if my manuscript was safe. After a few anxious moments, I finally found it lying next to and just beneath an unrecognized thumbed and ragged thick sheaf of papers. Turning the torn and stained pages, I did not have to read many words to conclude that it could not have been written by anyone else but Brendan Behan, giving as it did an account of a young Republican of heartfelt Feinian sentiments, venturing abroad with gelignite and detonators into deepest enemy territory, which happened to be Liverpool. And there, in a boardinghouse with ready-made plans to plant a bomb and prior to any such explosion, the author describing the incident was arrested, tried and sentenced and imprisoned. And these pages I read lying open next to my own manuscript pages of *The Ginger Man* were those of Behan's *Borstal Boy*.

My first ever meeting with Behan was in the Davy Byrnes pub, among a late-morning group of would-be Bohemians who were otherwise revolutionaries, horse trainers, gas meter readers, con men, ballroom dancers and professional black sheep. But all of whom had in common that they indefinitely existed upon invisible means of support. We were gathered under the most rearward of the paradisiacal murals painted by Cecil French Salkeld, whose daughter years later Behan was to marry. At the time, Behan, just released from prison for attempting to shoot a policeman, was the center of attention, which he invariably was anyway. But dressed raggedly, shirt open to his belly, and the tongues of his down-at-the-heel shoes wagging free, one would not immediately have assumed he was a man of letters. Indeed any claim by any man present of that nature would get you ridiculed to within an inch of your permanent well-being. For me, an American, the unkempt

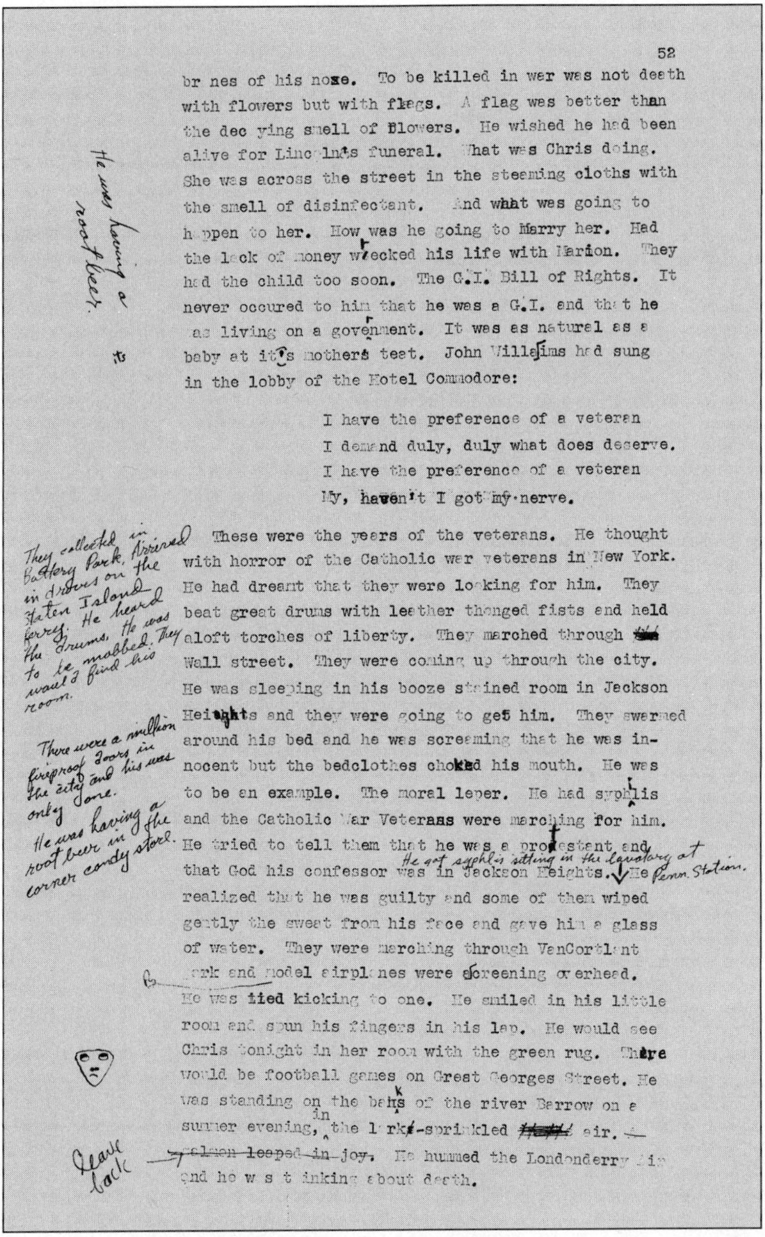

br nes of his no**x**e. To be killed in war was not death
with flowers but with fla**g**s. A flag was better than
the dec ying smell of Flowers. He wished he had been
alive for Linc ln's funeral. That was Chris doing.
She was across the street in the steaming cloths with
the smell of disinfectant. And wh**a**t was going to
h ppen to her. How was he going to Marry her. Had
the l ck of money wrecked his life with Marion. They
had the child too soon. The G.I. Bill of Rights. It
never occured to him that he was a G.I. and th t he
as living on a govenment. It was as natural as a
baby at it's mother teet. John Willa**j**ims h d sung
in the lobby of the Hotel Commodore:

> I have the preference of a veteran
> I demand duly, duly what does deserve.
> I have the preference of a veteran
> My, haven't I got my nerve.

These were the years of the veterans. He thought
with horror of the Catholic war veterans in New York.
He had dreamt that they were looking for him. They
beat great drums with leather thonged fists and held
aloft torches of liberty. They marched through the
Wall street. They were coming up through the city.
He was sleeping in his booze st ined room in Jackson
Hei**gh**ts and they were going to ge**t** him. They swarmed
around his bed and he was screaming that he was innocent but the bedclothes chok**e**d his mouth. He was
to be an example. The moral leper. He had syph**i**lis
and the Catholic War Veterans were marching for him.
He tried to tell them that he was a pro**t**estant and
that God his confessor was in Jackson Heights. He
realized that he was guilty and some of them wiped
gently the sweat from his face and gave him a glass
of water. They were marching through VanCortl nt
rk and model airpl nes were screening overhead.
He was tied kicking to one. He smiled in his little
room and sp un his fingers in his lap. He would see
Chris tonight in her room with the green rug. Th**e**re
would be football games on Grest Georges Street. He
was standing on the ba**nk**s of the river Barrow on a
summer evening, the l rk sprinkled air.
salmon leeped in joy. He hummed the Londonderry ir
and he w s t inking about death.

Handwritten margin annotations:
- He was having a root beer.
- They collected in Battery Park. Arrived in droves on the Staten Island ferry. He heard the drums. He was to be mobbed. They would find his room.
- There were a million fireproof floors in the city and his was only one. He was having a root beer in the corner candy store.
- He got syphlis sitting in the lavatory at Penn Station.
- Leave back

One of the first formal draft pages of THE GINGER MAN, *already alluding
to the censorship and bigotry then sweeping the United States. In the left
bottom of the page occurs an editorial suggestion by Brendan Behan where
he writes "leave back," referring to the phrase I was cutting, "A salmon
leaped in joy." Having at the time thought the phrase too flowery, I was
surprised later to find myself following Behan's advice, and a salmon did
leap in joy in* THE GINGER MAN.

Behan was indistinguishable from the corner boys who nightly populated the streets selling their newspapers. But in Dublin, with all equally welcomed and just as equally spurned, you had to be ready to meet anyone and be ready to drink his health and to religiously pretend that you actually listened to and admired deeply something original he had to say.

It occurred to those gathered upon this particular morning that it would be a great joke to introduce Behan and I to each other as writers. This done, Behan hearing I was an American immediately called me a narrowback. A word I had never heard before but which having the connotation of weakness was immediately taken by me as disparaging. And of course Behan was merely being academic. For at the time I did not know the word was used by the Irish immigrant who grew up in the old country to describe those of first-generation Irish born in America whose backs would not have been broadened by hard labor as were their own backs. Upon being challenged to withdraw the remark, Behan naturally repeated it. And now I was sure it was uncomplimentary. If I wasn't standing already, I stood up. And informed Behan that he could choose to have his jaw broken, his nose smashed and his head beaten off there on the spot or could elect to have it done outside in the fresh air. Behan, choosing the al fresco arrangement, followed me out through the pub's swing doors and stepping between the parked bicycles we squared off in the middle of Duke Street, which was much without automobile traffic in those days. Fists knotted at my sides like a gun cocked, I was about to make my first feinting move before unleashing a looping right to Behan's already scarred nose when Behan offered his hand to shake.

"Ah, now why should the intelligent likes of us belt each other and fight just to please the bunch of them eegits back inside the pub who wouldn't have the guts to do it themselves."

I did not yet know that Behan had just been released from prison for attempting to murder a policeman. And clearly he felt no need to demonstrate he was a dangerous man. In any event, I shook his hand but was now finding one fight becoming the same as another in Dublin. Following the first insult, there was always a great bluster and spouting of belligerent words, which were usually expected to be exchanged at length. However, coming from the highly perilous folkways society of New York, where insult could a second later be followed by a bullet or knife fatally entering your heart, one's eye watched for the first flicker of movement for such a weapon, and one did not then wait upon ceremony for it to be drawn before unleashing from the hip one's own hardest, fastest right or left cross to the jaw to produce prolonged unconsciousness in one's opponent. Having already done this several times in Dublin on the occasion of a belligerent remark, there became a distinct slowing up in the number of incidents in which unfriendly comments were made to me or about my beard. And it may have been the reason why on the occasion of the threatened battle with Behan, not one of the pub inmates bothered, as they would have done in America, to come out and watch the fight but more likely they stayed inside not wanting to abandon their drink. Thereafter, upon Behan seeing me, I would hear his shout which turned all heads up and down the elegance of Grafton Street.

"Mike Donleavy, how's your hammer hanging."

This expression used by house painters to refer to one of the tools of trade, I at the time assumed, with mild embarrassment, to refer to something hanging upon one's person elsewhere. But back upon this misty day in the cottage at Kilcoole, cleaning up, I heard whistling approaching down the lane. And it was Behan whom I confronted shuffling toward me through the wet, long grass on the lawn. And wearing, as it happened, a pair of my black patent leather dancing pumps with a bow, which, now thoroughly soaked, muddy and stretched out of shape, Behan criticized for their lack of waterproofing. Tucked under Behan's arm were my golfing shoes with rubber studs on the soles and tassels swinging loose from the laces which he referred to as being far superior footwear. Then with a total matter-of-fact unconcern, Behan explained about the twenty pairs of my pairs of shoes remaining missing.

"Now, Mike, I hate the country. And I hate the country people who live in it. A more mean and stingy miserable bunch of peasants than you'd ever want to have the displeasure of meeting in any decent reincarnation. I am only out here paying you a little friendly visit because the IRA have recently sentenced me to death in my absence, which I am happier to have done in that manner than have it be done in my presence. And in your absence I am sorry to be out here taking advantage of your hospitality, which I had to do without invitation. Now knowing, as the IRA do, my hatred of the countryside and country people, this is the last place in the world they would come looking for me. But next to hating the country and the people living in it, I hate getting my feet wet. So I borrowed your shoes I found in an old leather suitcase and brought them with me to keep me feet dry going up to the pub and wore a pair every few yards till they got wet. You'll find them flung over the fence into the field. I'm sorry if the cattle chewed a few of them. I kept these dancing yokes on my feet till last, as they wouldn't keep a flea's feet dry jumping over a bit of wet in a saucer. But now I'm ready for a swim and I would inquire if the water in the sea down there is deep enough."

Behan, although eschewing getting his feet wet, would, whenever any large body of water appeared, make for it, instantly remove his clothes and jump in. And now upon this day was intent upon a frolic in what I knew already was the bitterly cold water of the Irish Sea. Requesting my company, Behan set off for his swim with me in tow. His lack of country awareness was demonstrated halfway across a field when a horse whose nose he reached to pet nearly bit off his hand, and would have done if he hadn't tripped first into a bog hole. And then as we passed old Mr. and Mrs. Smiths' cottage, they stayed in behind their gate, polite enough at introduction, but terrified of their lives of Behan, whose opinions and irreverent language crossing the fields preceded him.

"Now, Mike, what did I tell you, these country people, frightened they are of their lives."

One did not volunteer to tell Behan that the Smiths were dyed-in-the-wool Dubliners like himself. And as I waited on the beach, ready to be summoned by a drowning man, a naked Behan plunged and disappeared into the waves. I expected him to jump out screaming from the cold, but Behan, padded in blubber like a walrus, romped the minutes away in the surf swimming and diving. That is, until spying the train approaching up from Wicklow town and on its way to Dublin. With a roar, he emerged from the waves and rushing up the beach ascended a sandy hillock near the tracks from the summit of which he wagged and waved his prick at the passing train's windows, with little regard for me, his host, being easily recognized with the only beard in Ireland. When chastened with this, Behan, as he always did, had a ready answer.

"Now, who, Mike, for the love of Jesus, would be bothered looking out and identifying you when they would be having the chance and the delight of their lives to have a brief view of a fine prick and a great pair of jangling balls just as nature made them to hang on a broth of a boy like meself."

On our return across the fields, the Smiths were nowhere to be seen, and their gate was locked and curtains drawn over their windows. Back in the cottage, Behan, with a ferocious appetite, asked for the large mixing bowl he saw and to be let attend to himself. Whereupon from the corner of my eye I watched him fill the huge piece of crockery with cornflakes, a tin of peaches, half a jar of tomato chutney, squares of cooking chocolate, pieces of bread, flour, a tin of sardines, milk, sugar, salt, spoonfuls of sugar, ketchup, baking soda, pieces of blood pudding, chopped bacon rinds and a sample of everything within reach or in sight. On top of this concoction, as if it were a blessing, he poured my only bottle of stout. Mixing the lot with a wooden spoon and with a final pouring of milk to turn the concoction further liquid, Behan then put the bowl to his lips and in several massive mouthfuls downed it. With the bowl finally empty, he smacked and wiped his lips and turned around to see me watching with openmouthed wonder.

"Ah, you know, Mike, I always like to look after my health."

Which
Would leave me
That little bit
Better than
Being
Unhealthy

8

THE NEXT THREE DAYS in Behan's company became an odyssey. Automotively I had graduated up from my unreliable small red van, which one raged over, kicked and often had to abandon in a ditch with sparks jumping across wires hanging out from behind the dashboard and then proceed on foot. As I would tramp forward cross-country in the mud, often in darkness, I swore to never own an automobile again.

But from my automotive engineers in Greystones, I was suddenly able to acquire a sedate sedan once the property of the Protestant Bishop of Meath. This dignified vehicle with its blue leather coach work started merely by pressing a small ebony button and could then accelerate to roll along at a steady forty or even fifty miles an hour. The smudged, crumpled and stained manuscript of *Borstal Boy* sticking out of his jacket side pocket, Behan seemed to revel upon his enthronement on the front seat, issuing imperatives as to where we might go from the options presented. The first selected being to pay a visit to Ernest Gebler's estate, Lake Park, an idyllic lodge nestled in its grove of pines above in the Wicklow Mountains.

From Kilcoole, we drove westward to Newtown Mount Kennedy, a village at the foot of a steep lane which rose to heights called Kilmurray. As happened on any journey with Behan, the need soon arose to visit a pub. Indeed, in open countryside, a good excuse was always required to pass one by without paying one's respects. And it had to be admitted that once inside this frequently dimmer and darker austere world, one was often relieved and glad to escape into where beer would temporarily brighten the spirit. It was where too, Behan would give his best performance as not only a brilliant mimic but in his ability to quote ad lib British laws and legal statutes, reciting chapter and verse and declaiming the more famed decisions handed down by British judges in the English courts. He could similarly quote from the Bible and even reduce to astonished tears those poor Protestants who would attempt to match skills with him and who did not possess, as he did, a photographic, encyclopedic knowledge, which even the most fanatically erudite Presbyterian in the world would envy. Behan now making his desire known to visit a pub by mimicking and declaiming as a clergyman might in giving a sermon from his pulpit.

"Verily I say to thee my dear brethren in the name of Jesus, who was unfairly tacked up crooked on the cross, that it behooves us to partake of immediate liquid refreshment or be beaten within an inch of our lives with bound copies of that God-fearing newspaper *The Catholic Herald*."

In walking and roaming the streets and his voice carrying near and far, Behan had the quality of a pied piper. And he took much pleasure in his biblical indulgence, especially as there was nothing quite as lonely and doleful as being a Protestant holding as they did their prayer meetings on a bleak Dublin evening and to which not a single passing pedestrian ever paid any attention. And Behan, at every opportunity, made references to religious convictions they espoused and sung out to Dublin's unlistening ears, his most oft repeated favorite being,

"I know that my redeemer liveth."

And these words now recited as we entered just inside the door of the pub in Newtown Mount Kennedy. Behan delivering his vowels in the most heartfelt of heartfelt manner, bending his knee in genuflection and striking it with his fist. And as he did so, an old man, clearly at the end of his life, emerged out of the shadows. It was as if he sensed Behan, who continued his religious declamation to the empty air, to be some strange oracle or faith healer who could cure the sick. And upon this early afternoon as we drank our pints of stout in the pub's semidarkness, the old man described to Behan his recent operation, which produced his presently unpleasant smell from a bag he carried under his clothing. But the infirm gentleman did not offer to buy Behan a drink, as would be regarded as normal with any Irishman joining another at any bar the world over. In Behan's eyes, to neglect to do such was heinous in the extreme, Behan turning his back to the old man, and as we left the pub he was scathing.

"The dirty, filthy, disgusting old eegit. Miserly salted away money all his life and now is afraid of dying and of leaving the money behind that's clinking in his pocket that you couldn't prize out of him with a crowbar. Wanting sympathy on the edge of the grave and wouldn't offer to buy you a drink."

Back in the car, we drove up the steep hill to the tableland a thousand or so feet higher, Behan referring to his professional calling as a house painter and that it was unhealthy work. We proceeded over the bridge crossing the Corporation of Dublin reservoir and into which Behan, for the sake, he said, of maintaining its beneficial properties, insisted we stop and he take a pee. Ceremonially describing, as he pissed, the minerals he was wholesomely adding to Dublin's water supply. But I was, and am to this day, still taken aback by Behan's vehemence concerning the sick old man. Although not that much later, I was soon to learn myself on another fateful occasion that the greatest sin any man could commit in Behan's eyes was that of not buying a drink when his turn came while a man had the money in his pocket to do so. But on this day, we had reached Roundwood. From this village it was less than two miles along a winding narrow road to Ernest Gebler's estate of Lake Park. This commodious once shooting lodge in its wooded setting stood hauntingly on the side of a hill sloping down to and overlooking the shiny black waters of Lough Dan.

Now, in any house with female staff, Behan's first act as a guest was to make familiar, first in conversation and then in activities. Although at times extremely shy himself, he would always make an overture to embrace those he regarded as his working-class brethren. If they demurred, they were then immediately disdained and gently goosed with at least one of his noticeably stubby fingers. If this produced no appropriate reaction, a long discourse would follow as Behan would assume membership of the Salvation Army and pronounce his surname in a double-barreled manner:

"I Brendan Bee-Hawn stand against the devil's evil traits. The Lord shall root out all deceitful lips and the tongue that speaketh proud things shall here and now cover you with licks and kisses."

Behan achieving a momentary complacency in his victim with his oratory would then make an outright grab. Which he did for Gebler's stoutly built cook, Bridget, who was about to marry Gebler's gardener, Micko. Bridget tolerantly and good-naturedly giggling uproariously but then screaming as an encouraged Behan attempted familiarities beyond playfulness and chased her up and down the stairs and through the halls. Meanwhile, Gebler, a reticently serious gentleman, took a poor view of his help being interfered with and was anxious that Behan either behave or be gone.

Gebler, too, had been reared in the slums of Dublin and knew Behan as a little, bare-arsed, belligerent boy swimming in the city's Grand Canal. But unlike most would-be writers in Ireland, Gebler had by dint of implacable application already become what any of them would term an international best-selling author. And was now exhibiting the fruits of what only an ambitious and dedicated writer could accomplish. His second book called *The Plymouth Adventure,* concerning the story of the *Mayflower,* was about to become a Hollywood movie, and money poured in from this best-selling work. Gebler too had recently become married to an American girl, Lea, also of Hollywood and who had been raised there, the daughter of Leatrice Joy of the Ziegfeld Follies and John Gilbert of the silent screen. This attractive lady took no such staid attitude as her husband did to Behan and was not at all alarmed by his antics. Indeed, with her stunning singing voice, she and Behan sang duets together. In fact, things, as they became musical, were going altogether well. However, although I was eagerly welcomed by Gebler, his wife maintaining I put him in a good mood, Behan in my company soon made the pair of us personae non gratae.

Behan, upon once seeing the lough below in the valley, was soon off in search of a swim. Taking with him as an entourage the entirety of the female staff of Lake Park to witness him undressing and jumping into the black ice-cold waters. And in Behan's normal naturist manner, all this seemed innocuous enough. But what became soon more conspicuous was the reinforced echoing sound of Behan's profane and obscene language which, shouted out, was now bouncing hillside to hillside from glen to glen and to the ears of Gebler's devout neighbors. As Behan, standing naked up to his arse in the ice-cold water pounded his chest in the manner of Tarzan and declaiming the more mild of his blasphemies,

"Will you give me another sup now of the almighty fruit of the juice of Joseph and the eternal spit of the horn most high."

Behan, now having well and truly worn out both our welcomes at Lake Park, huffily presented his own suggestion of another nearby destination. And so, motoring through the coconut-scented air of the golden gorse in bloom, we went on our way to the next port of call. While heading out the long Lake Park drive, Behan spoke in his sometimes shy, stammering and apologetic way.

"You know, Mike, I'd like to say a few things in respect of the bit I've now read of that writing you've got back below there in Kilcoole. I see you got me mentioned and I am proud to be there in your book, described as I am down in the Catacombs, where I often was when Dickie Wyman was the original proprietor of the place. I remember he once gave Valerie a bouquet of snowdrops with the words, Ah, my dear, I give these to you as they are scarcely suitable for me as a symbol of purity. Now in the same way I'd be paying you a compliment over your book. It's altogether a great book and one of the best pieces of writing I've ever read and the words on those pages will go around the world. And I took the liberty of making a few suggestions in the margins. Now I'll tell you one thing that you're doing that's very wise. Not a soul of them fucking jealous bastards in Dublin knows you're writing it. Not that I've come across anyway. You're a good man to keep a secret. And I remember when I came to buy the guns from your rooms in Trinity, that you never let on that the guns were stored there."

Behan was recalling a time when he and another appeared one afternoon in my rooms at 38 Trinity College, where they came to examine and negotiate over the guns, which for some time had been kept in brown paper parcels on top of my bedroom wardrobe. Behan, however, was wrong in assuming I knew such packages held firearms, and for the weeks that they remained stacked in my bedroom I had no idea of the contents. Being then far too busy with wine, women and song. And if Noctor, my servant, knew, he chose not to make mention of it. But one day following a game of tennis, I returned to number 38 having lent my key to this charming Divinity student whose packages had now long-resided in my bedroom. And there is no doubt that I was apprehensive upon seeing laid out across my sitting-room table an array of lethal submachine guns, pistols, rifles and automatic weapons alongside their appropriate boxes of ammunition. Such having been brought south on the train from Belfast to Dublin by this undergraduate friend reading Divinity. A steely-nerved son of a minor baronet, who'd been much battle-hardened in the Second World War in the African desert and landing on beachheads and fighting across Europe. And at the end of hostilities, he had collected numerous weapons and memorabilia, which, upon being demobed, he shipped home to his father's estate in the north of Ireland. Sounding out the possibilities of selling these, he discovered through Behan the interest of the IRA.

"Now, Mike, all those great guns you had there in your room. When did you know we were going to steal instead of pay for them."

Now Behan also thought I was ultrashrewd as an arms dealer because he and his accomplice, having struck a bargain with the steely-nerved baronet's son and having said they would come back in forty-eight hours with the money, planned instead to meanwhile steal the weapons. But they didn't reckon with the prescience of my steely-eyed friend, who was far ahead of them and had the weapons that very afternoon the deal was agreed, taken away to another safe place, where they were later sold to a group of Orangemen who had their money ready and by the sound of them were not averse to being up to their knees in Catholic blood and up to their knees in slaughter.

"Now, Mike, I'll say this about you, no one would ever guess you were an arms dealer and gunrunner. And clever enough at it too."

My denial of being a gunrunner only encouraged Behan to believe it was true. But it was the steely-nerved baronet's son in a series of trips from Belfast to Dublin who brought the guns to my rooms. Arriving each week and braving customs with brown paper parcels to put on top of my wardrobe. And often on the train having to sit with the muzzle end of a rifle barrel sticking up out of his shirt collar. And as the train conductor would invariably notice the gun barrel while taking my friend's ticket, he would be met with the steeliest of stares, which indicated he'd best go quickly about his business. My friend would then proceed like a wooden-legged cripple, with guns down both trouser legs, to as nonchalantly as possible stiffly stagger through the ticket barrier into Dublin. And even did this once while lugging a valise full of Lugers.

With the heathery Wicklow hills passing, Behan and I had now proceeded southward a brief distance down the road to Glendalough, where lived one of Behan's own longtime friends, Ralph Cusack. Although another case entirely from Ernest Gebler, this charmingly eccentric Anglo-Irish gentleman occupied a large Victorian mansion in its sylvan grounds, where he grew tulip bulbs for export. He was both a practicing artist and writer. As well as being of a romantic bent, Cusack exuded humanity and tolerated and perhaps even encouraged Behan's transgressions of polite behavior. However, despite his forbearing charm, Cusack could equally be of a violent nature and especially in respect of his pictures he'd painted. And should you be crassly foolish enough to venture a disparaging word concerning them, Cusack would not hesitate to perforate such canvases over your head, where they might remain as a large garland around your neck. This usually being done unsuspectingly from behind at mealtimes in the dining room just as you were finishing your pudding and before the ladies withdrew to allow the port to be passed among the gentlemen. But as violently rude and unyielding as Cusack could be to those to whom he took exception, he was overwhelmingly welcoming and kind to old friends. And on this day with actual tears in his eyes, his arms were open to embrace a wet-haired, bedraggled Behan stepping from my dignified automobile.

"Ah, my dear, dear Brendan, how good it is to see you."

"And, Ralph, I'm glad to be seen still alive and to be able to declare my patriotism in the battle to make this island into one indivisible nation. For according to Einstein's law of relativity and the bending of light, won't we one day soon, and before anybody else does, put a shamrock-branded, baptized mouse on the moon."

"Dear boy, you are the true noble savage who was preordained to inhabit the Elysian Fields and the Garden of Eden. Come now and join me for wine in our arboretum in which tranquility reigns this sunshiny day."

One felt sure these befrilled words were euphemistically spoken to soften the prospect of Behan having during his visit to be taken to task. For staying with Cusack were two maidenly and mildly lesbian English guests, Winifred and Lydia, who were notable authorities on the Pre-Raphaelite period. And these ladies had in their tweeds and stout brogues been for a long tramp on the heathery hills to sketch wildflowers and were soon to have afternoon tea on a terrace which enjoyed a splendid view down a westerly vista across Cusack's lawns while the playing of a madrigal from Cusack's ancient gramophone with its great horn came through the open French doors. And the tea had not been that long served and cups refilled and the hot scones slathered with whipped cream and dolloped with damson jam when the ladies' attentions were distracted from their auction house catalogues by a most odoriferous fume wafted to their nostrils.

"Oh dear, whatever wretched smell might that be, Winifred."

As the ladies glanced westward in the direction of the gentle breeze, there suddenly at the end of the flower-bordered prospect, and beneath a white marble plinthed statue of Aphrodite, crouched a grunting, defecating, trouserless Behan. His buttocks gleamingly exposed to the ladies. Who at once rose to their feet and shrieked. Behan, his back facing the commotion and wondering at the disturbance on the terrace, stood up and turned and, seeing the ladies, waved his considerably tumesced organ at them. Whereupon both of these gentlewomen swooned in a dead faint. Behan, not meaning to have made such a strong impression, immediately sauntered up to the terrace and, while dipping a scone in the whipped cream, dolloping on the damson jam and chewing away, was peering down upon the unconscious faces when Ralph Cusack, who had been taking me on a tour of the tulips, came running to see what the matter be.

"Ah, Ralph, wasn't I below there discreetly enough hidden by the shrubbery relieving myself to make room in my digestion for a massive bowl of food I had there earlier at Mike Donleavy's when I heard screams and found the pair of these emotionable, well-bred ladies here fallen out of their chairs."

However, upon this their day of departure, the ladies Winifred and Lydia upon their recovery told a different story to their host. Both bitterly complaining of the unsanitary and uncivilized nature of the event they'd had to witness and the disgustingly filthy penis-wagging habits of the Irish. When this news was related by Cusack to Behan in the privacy of the library, where Behan had gone to read, it met with a violent outcry, especially regarding the words describing the penis-wagging Irish. Behan raging and railing against the hypocrisy of British middle-class morals and values.

"The no-good pair of them tweedy, unctuous, fucking pharisees. Having the audacity to complain of an Irishman having an Irish crap on Irish soil. And what's more, in the fresh air and within the territorial freedom of the present republic."

Although, and usually at a discreet distance, having witnessed Behan's culpability on many an occasion, Behan now sounded so convincing in condemning the primness of the ladies that I, with an irrepressible desire to always be fair, found it difficult to take up sides in the matter. Especially knowing the purgative nature of the concoction Behan had mixed at Kilcoole, and into which one forgot to mention had also been dumped a jar of sauerkraut and one of molasses. However, the ladies had had a goodly dose of smelling salts to revive them and now having packed to travel were recovered somewhat from their ordeal and in the drawing room they were now further calmed by Cusack's administration of large snifters of brandy. And to whence Behan came with tears verging in his eyes. For he much admired Cusack and the last thing he wanted to do was to distress him. So Behan, shuffling forward with bowed head, proffered with his outstretched hand the most abject of abject apologies, to which the ladies replied,

"You beast, you worse-than-senseless thing."

Behan stunned, retreated. Back out the drawing room door and into the hall. Sad at first, he was then overtaken with smoldering fury. Sarcastically repeating again and again in his best and astonishingly authentic English pukka accent, the words, You beast, you worse-than-senseless thing. Indeed so often did he say it, it appeared he liked the sound and then began to chant it to a musical tune. But had these poor ladies Winifred and Lydia known of the revenge they were inciting by rejecting Behan's apology, they would have instead professed delight at the opportunity of witnessing his exercising his bowels on the lawn. And perhaps even put a small suitable monument there. For Behan gave them something unspeakable to take with them in their picnic basket back to London. To so commemorate and remember him by. And which upon its unsavory discovery caused both of these mildly lesbian ladies to faint again.

Right
In the
Middle of their flight
Back to
Civilization

9

DEPARTING CUSACK'S, Behan had plans unfolding and prevailed upon me to go with him up to Dublin to a hooley that night. And following a brief downing of a pint or two of stout in the Horse and Hound, located in the refined quiet precincts of the little Wicklow village of Delgany, Behan, pied piper, entertainer, sorcerer and conjurer as he was, began awakening the inhabitants to his presence. His louder declamations and singing already echoing back from the nearby hills as his tenor crooned the irreverent words to the sacredly patriotic tune of Kevin Barry.

> Would you live on women's earnings.
> Would you give up work for good.
> Would you lead a life of prostitution.
> You're goddamn right I would.

I was particularly conscious of not offending the sensibilities of these highly respectable people thereabouts, not to mention a nearby convent of cloistered nuns. Plus I was on dining terms with a most elegant gentleman, the local parish priest, Jack Hanlon, who said mass for them and heard the nuns' confessions, and whose reputation as a painter was highly esteemed. Living in the village too was the local vicar, another elegant gentleman who had written a letter in defense of me and in answer to an unpleasant critique published in the *Irish Times* concerning one of my painting exhibitions.

However, Behan's outrageous language in this genteel neck of the woods bothered me less than his interruption of an innocent people's night rest, and I told him to keep his voice down, as nearby nuns would be trying to sleep, who had taken vows of silence.

"And, Mike, not to mention vows of sublime indifference to carnal cravings. Now here's a lullaby, Mike, that would put to sleep a condemned man in his cell the night before his execution."

Behan, then, affecting an English upper-class boy's choir voice, launched into singing a cradlesong. That soon had village windows opening. Not in complaint but in silent delight and admiration. And it was astonishing how he could make such sudden transformation with his brilliant mimicry, which also embraced both the Irish rural brogue and the English cockney accent. And he would often regale me with stories of when he'd resided in the Iveagh House, an indigent men's hostel he frequented in Dublin, where, in a shilling cubicle late at night after lights-out, he would enjoy as part of his bedtime entertainment to shout out in his strongest cockney from his curtained confines.

"You bunch of no good fucking scruffulous Irish pigs, Cromwell didn't do enough to you and your filthy ways. Come on, in the name of my king and country, I'll take on the whole poltroonish fucking lot of you."

In the usual three seconds as the usually imbibed inmates were roused from sleep, and with an opportunity to wreak vengeance on what could only be an innocent singular Englishman, the dormitory floor would resound with the pounding of bare feet and shouts of, where's that limey fucker who said that. And outside Behan's cubicle, an angry inquiry would be made.

"You British cunt, come out of there and we'll see who's an Irish pig."

"Ah, bejesus, Paddy, the Blessed Virgin be my judge, it wasn't me the boyo who said that. I was saying me rosary with a decade to go of an Our Father, ten Hail Marys and a Glory Be."

Behan then letting loose another brief broadside of anti-Irishness would often bring the vigilante interrogators back. This time stretching his point of identity to absurdity, rendering another display of Irishness, throwing in a few remarks concerning the struggle to reinstate the universal use of Gaelic north and south of the border. And when the spokesman from the vigilantes inquired as to where he was from, Behan would protest with tears in his voice.

"How can you not believe me that I'm from over beyond in Roscommon and a member of the Small Farmers Union and amn't I just after getting out of me own bed into me own shoes to go looking for the fucker meself. And sure as an Irish speaker only occasionally speaking English, I wouldn't know what the word 'poltroonish' meant."

Behan would refer to these night shelters for indigent men in the same way as one might to the elegant hotels, of the Shelbourne in Dublin or Claridges in London. And in the latter city, finding himself in a similar destitute men's hostel, Rowton House in Hammersmith, Behan would, following lights-out, make similar insulting declarations concerning the English, waking the inmates from sleep in his thickest Irish brogue.

"You fucking bunch of British limey cunts, wake up the fucking lot of you. Bollocks to your fucking king. And if he's married to the fucking queen, bollocks to her too. Leave Ireland to the Irish. Up the Republic."

And as entrances to cubicles flew open and a plethora of patriotic Britishers poured out, the pounding feet would stop just outside Behan's door. And from within, Behan would let it be known, in his best Bow-bell cockney, that he was already up and ready to go looking for the Irish bastard who had insulted his king and country.

"Ah, but Jesus, Mike, let me tell you, after a close call one night, temptation would, as it always did, get the better of me. And after waiting a discreet twenty minutes or so till the indignation had subsided and inmates were nodding off to sleep again, I unleashed such a vitriolic, vicious diatribe of derision against the English that when the band of drunken limeys came roaring out again for blood, they went up and down the cubicles making each and every inhabitant speak out his allegiance to king and country, till, Jesus, didn't they come to this poor simple Kerryman with a brogue so thick you could butter both sides of a piece of bread with it at once. Jesus, I could hear his pathetic denials as they were dragging him out of his bed. But then by the sound of the limey squeals of pain, the Kerryman must have given as good as he got and broken a few jaws and noses before he himself had the living bejesus kicked out of him. And I did feel sorry for that little bit of injustice to a fellow countryman which marred my entertainment, but it was a lot better that it was him who was beset upon than me."

Myself bearded, which invariably was a target for trouble, one was always conscious, in Behan's conspicuous presence, of the possibility of a fight erupting at any moment, especially in places where Behan might be making an appearance for the first time, and especially in country districts and especially in a neighborhood where some of the residents were bound to play rugby, as was the case in the purlieu of Delgany and Greystones. And one kept a wary eye out for trouble, somehow feeling that when it came and the fists and kicks were flying, that Behan, despite his shooting at policemen and his forays with bombs to the British mainland, could easily be the first to abandon ship and leave one in the lurch. However, Behan would charmingly warn one of such an eventuality.

"Mike, when necessary for preservation of my general health and provided the safety of the nation is not at stake, I'm good at giving an excellent example of cowardly behavior."

Yet, I had known Behan, as an altercation was in its glowering, simmering stages, to break a pint glass on the edge of a pub table and snarlingly brandish the jagged edge in someone's face. Having been indoctrinated with an American brand of sportsmanship, this was not the kind of battle behavior I applauded or admired. And indeed in confronting such foul play, one was ready to administer dire consequences to the perpetrator. But now, as we safely left this Delgany pub without incident, Behan was declaiming loudly enough for the nearby nuns to hear.

"Get me Vat Sixty-nine, and I don't mean the Pope's telephone number. And while I'm drinking it, would you give the woman in the bed more anchovies. And give the nuns in the convent more cucumbers."

Before Behan launched further into his more indecently indiscreet proclamations, one seated him in one's sedate vehicle and we finally headed off toward Dublin, the late evening twilight descending upon these local wooded Wicklow hillsides. Passing through the Glen of the Downs, the automobile's windows open, Behan now in quiet reflectiveness was again talking about the manuscript of *The Ginger Man*.

"Now, Mike, you don't mind the few comments I've written in that book of yours, which I did in pencil in case you'd want to rub them out. Here and there you ridicule the Irish, and it makes me sad enough now for having to agree with you that in this petty and pathetic little country they deserve every fucking critical word you've got to utter about them. But, Jesus, despite the berating you give us, that's an awful funny book. But now, I'd only make mention of something Irish people would be sensitive about for the amount of lament and affliction it has brought, and I would only suggest it would be sort of unbecoming to point a finger at it. It would be tuberculosis I'm referring to that you describe in the book as the 'white death.' "

Behan's voice lowered as he spoke in a tone of sadness. The scent of wild garlic was blowing in through the car windows, and thick foliage of the overhanging trees made the night now doubly dark. Behan could sense that I was surprised by his remarks and he reverted to mentioning again the critical picture the manuscript gave of Ireland.

"But, Mike, the other hard things you say and the kicks you give us up the backside hole doesn't stop your book from being the great act of love I think it is for Ireland. Now some would imagine that you had in mind to write about Gainor Crist. And I'd agree he'd be a great subject and a hard man worth to figure out, but there'd be little or no resemblance I can see whatsoever. Crist was never like Dangerfield. The only similarity being that Crist is one of the few men I've ever seen managing to get credit in a pub. And if there were any more like him, it would soon bankrupt the nation. But maybe there'd be a resemblance to Crist in Dangerfield's manner, for I once overheard him at the pawn shop talking to the pawnbroker and haggling over a couple of old pieces of crockery as if he was bargaining to form a treaty between nations. And Jesus if I could fucking talk like that'd be running nations."

Behan, however, was now touching upon a part of Gainor Crist's personality which unquestionably resembled that of Dangerfield's and which had undoubtedly long intrigued if not mesmerized me. That of getting credit and raising debt all around one, and continuing to do the former as the latter bottomlessly deepened. While at the same time keeping up appearances and ignoring to economize. But then Crist seemed to gracefully accept when these appearances became frayed or were very transitory. My first ever meeting with him in the Pearl Bar in Dublin's Fleet Street took place with Crist being introduced to me in a V-necked, primrose yellow cashmere sweater borrowed from me by his brother-in-law Randall Hillis so that Crist could more fittingly present himself to get a job with a modeling agency. But even with Crist wearing my sweater, he did not hesitate to put me immediately on the defensive by rigorously cross-examining me over my chronograph watch, which was broken but which I said I was still wearing because I was able to keep a sort of time with the stopwatch mechanism, which registered one hour at one-hourly intervals. Crist would have none of this nonsense and said it was nonsense and remained totally indifferent to the possibility that at any moment one might have said, "I say there, my good fellow, by the way you're wearing my sweater."

But these were very early days in Dublin before I had myself to retreat to battle my own survival on the land. My financial circumstances, with the G.I. Bill of Rights from Uncle Sam and a flow of funds from my mother, allowed me to live with a certain profligacy. And being all found within the precincts of the college, my life during early university years had been considerably affluent. One too was without the financial responsibilities of a wife and a child and was able to repair to the monastic sanctum of Trinity and there, as the need often required, escape Dublin to recover and rest from the protracted hooleys. But with Crist having the prospect of a legacy from his reasonable rich doctor father in poor health in Ohio, there was no point in his not borrowing against this contingency to keep up appearances and maintain faith in the future. In any event, despite the jaws of debt closing and chewing around him, Crist, provided we were comfortably ensconced in a pub, never allowed to exhibit his cares or concern and seemingly remained indifferent to his own troubles, while at the same time able to console and patiently and sympathetically listen to someone else's difficulties. With a pat on the arm, he would with a fervent assurance say not to worry, that everything was going to be all right.

Behan continued to talk of writing and Dangerfield and Crist as we drove through the seaside town of Bray, a familiar and, to me, always a slightly dour place, where the likes of James Joyce's family had once briefly resided and where one often came to buy one's more serious ironmongery, such as the panes of glass to roof the conservatory under which I first sat to write *The Ginger Man.*

"But, Mike, now I'd agree to another similarity of Crist to Dangerfield in that Gainor did like a gargle and has often enough said within my hearing that a pint of plain is your only man. And that while saying that he also said he never had any intention of ever working again, as satisfied enough he would be just to go live on tinned salmon down in the Catacombs over there in Fitzwilliam Place among the damned and doomed and listen to madrigals on the gramophone and just do nothing. But for Jesus' sake, what poor innocent gramophone could ever survive for long enough to hear a madrigal in that place."

One had noticed here and there on the manuscript of *The Ginger Man,* Behan's word count tabulations, and how the logistics of authorship and producing 'literae scriptae,' as he referred to it, seemed to concern him. He mentioned that he liked to include as many songs and poems as possible in his own work, which requiring fewer written words, could, with their indentations, use up more space on the pages. Behan at the time was writing a column for the *Irish Press,* a national newspaper published in Dublin, which seemed to make him much conscious of the identity and relative rank and status that a writer might enjoy once having demonstrated this as one's vocation. Which in my case and to my surprise, he seemed to think included violence.

"Now, Mike, it's as well that I think you're a writer and that you've written a great book, as you've got an awful reputation in Dublin as being quick to take offense that no one will go near you. And that upon a dirty look you'd be hammering a man to the ground before he even had a decent chance to get a gun out of his pocket. And I'd be the last one to suggest that this on your part wasn't on many an occasion more than justified. But it would give people the impression that they couldn't utter a word of criticism in your presence. I myself now seeing you in action would think twice before I'd pass remarks to you that might incite your aggrievement. But now coming to more peaceful pursuits, I'm three years older than yourself and it would give me pause to think and make me that little bit envious that your accomplishment as a writer is every bit as advanced as my own. And I'll repeat what I said before. That book you've written contains some of the finest writing I've ever read and when it's published is going to reverberate around the world. Now I calculated you've written so far forty-five thousand words and I put the number, so as not to be conspicuous, on the top of the second page of your manuscript."

There was an apologetic sorrowful and lonely aspect to Behan's sincerity when he was attempting to let you know he was being sincere. As if he would with impunity tell lies publicly but never privately utter a falsehood. Although I was always ready to believe his words, one had due reason to be cautious of Behan's praise. I had now recently learned that my now deceased father-in-law, who had to his wife mentioned I would go far, had also later said to Valerie, who no doubt at the time was requesting the help of money,

"You as my daughter have not been raised in order to go live a peasant life raising pigs and chickens with an American tramp in an Irish hovel."

And true enough. Our primitive life, with its crisis-filled days on my small holding had progressively been closing in on one as one strove to find the doorway through which one stepped to fame and fortune while continuing to search hedgerows for scraps of wood to burn and took showers at night outside under a watering can. But uncompromising I remained. And my desperation and my ability to wildly dramatize it never seemed to get less than desperate, as I, hands blistering, wielded shovel, paintbrush and hayfork in survival. One would also unhesitatingly become one's own worst enemy kicking, or belting with a sledgehammer contraptions to pieces that refused to work. And I was frequently enough reminded of the truth, that in farming even my small patch of ground, no amount of good advice is ever taken and one learns only by committing the disaster, you were, by wiser and older minds warned against. But my deliverance and ace in the hole was now this book and what one ambitiously imagined were its earthshaking words. And even though I found Behan's remarks overly optimistic and that he should sound so presumptuously certain of himself, they were also words that in one's many bleaker and blacker moments reassured. I also sensed that Behan wanted to let me know that I was, in his eyes, doing the right thing in my now more reclusive existence, holding out in the Irish countryside.

"Now, Mike, you've done what a lot of them in Dublin talk of doing. But it remains only a dream held dearly in reserve. And the books they're writing, not a comma of them ever gets down on paper. But at least it keeps them members in good standing of the Society of Uncreative Literary Men, like Crist himself, who also wants a farm."

Anything more unlikely for this gentleman Gainor Stephen Crist I could not imagine, since I knew of Crist's interest in the concept of immaterialism and the theory he'd formulated concerning the true nature of being. His notion was based on the possibility of energy emanating from the inertia of absolute nothingness. And such energy being applied to providing a daily existence immune from labor of any kind and where as he would say, while the mind raced, eyeballs froze in stillness and stomachs rested in peace. As Crist would chip away at this monolithic philosophical structure of life lived in suspended animation as it were, I would throw in my two cents. Mostly based on the behavior of subatomic particles, and perhaps the existence of life on other planets, but wasting little time in analysis of Crist's theory, since I regarded being alive, in the better sense of the word, as the condition of one's pleasant anticipations remaining greater than one's sad regrets. And that the meaning of life only raises its question when one is sheltered, secure and sleeping and eating well.

However, one thing that I did know about Crist for certain was that he was, as a foot-washer and a sandal-wearer, different from any of us. And would, in this latter item of chaussure, following a summer day out in Dublin, return to number 1 Newtown Avenue, Blackrock, and there place his feet to leisurely cleanse in a pan of water. I as a sock-and-shoe-wearing native of New York City, and accustomed to its skyscrapers, baths, saunas and showers, and where a summer-hot pavement could sear the sole of a bare foot, would be mesmerized witnessing Crist engaging in this Christ-like and to me biblical ritual. But along with Crist's Old Testament behavior I was ready to concede there was no doubt that as exiled Americans cut off from plumbing and, often enough, hungry, a plot of land now represented a basic solution to all our problems. But even Behan had his doubts of seeing Crist in the countryside.

Sporting a bow tie and entirely clothed in his own garments and lawyer-looking shoes, a most respectably attired Gainor Crist in the first and last photograph I ever took of him in Trinity College. For he was on his way out the North Gate to the pawn shop with his electric fire in order that he might have money for a few balls of malt in the pub which he maintained would keep him as comfortably warm as any electric fire and the steam from his piss could prove it.

"Mike, you'd wonder, though, even when the hunger pangs were tolling, if old Gainor would deign lift a potato or two out of the muck or would for the boiling pot be cutting a squealing pig's throat or wringing a chicken's neck if it stopped dropping eggs."

We were now driving through the purlieu of Foxrock, an area rumored affluent. And turning right, we descended the road to Dun Laoghaire, which led on to Blackrock and Crist country, where Gainor always drew attention to the stone cross marking the pale just outside of which he lived only a step or so from his front door. And past which daily went the roaring trams and the horse-drawn hearses. In the tiny front sitting room of this house, I had on a couple of occasions slept on the small couch when the last tram had already left for Dublin and it was too far to walk back to my rooms in Trinity. And, discussions finished for the night, Crist would sit in an armchair reading by the window and be there at dawn the next morning when I woke and would find him still reading. The subject taking his intense all-night interest was Spain. And perhaps in this same way he applied himself to the study of agriculture and dreamt of having a farm.

"Mike, I suspect that somewhere back in my lineage there was, like there has been for every Irishman, some fucker tilling the land but thanks be to Jesus it's somewhere way back in my lineage."

I suspected that even Behan knew that in such idyllic country living, needy things like eggs out of hens or apples out of the trees did not come free of charge from the land. But on a barstool in Dublin and nuzzling your nose in the creamy foam of your fifth pint of stout, the imagination ignored the work of digging, dilapidations, broken tools, slates flying off in storms, automobiles not starting and, if starting, exploding, and livestock getting sick and dying. Or indeed, as I found, if everything else in one's country pursuits was going fine, a nearby farmer's cows would invariably trespass through the fence and trample one's vegetables. And if this weren't enough, there always remained, as you attempted to take a moment's leisure resting one's bones by the fireside, the growing and haunting threat of communism from behind the Iron Curtain, which, by those in the know, was rumored to soon come sweeping west out of Russia to overwhelm Europe and the rest of the world and to make everybody equal, and worse, to confiscate and collectivize every freeholder's little bit of land. Thereby snatching away from yours truly, that for which one so incessantly fought, a yet-to-be-achieved fame and fortune. And I found that Behan and I held on this subject, at least, similar sentiments.

"Mike, I wouldn't want you to breathe a word of this to anyone, especially to those IRA zealots who think they're to be the new commissars when Marxism comes, but between me and you, fuck communism. My political principles are based on the generosity of the spirit. That you taketh from those who haveth because you are the one who needeth and deserveth."

As we drove now through the leafy suburban quiet streets of Donnybrook and past the pebbled drives and walled gardens of the gable-roofed houses, not a communist nor a commissar was to be seen. And one could at least take comfort that one had become a peasant and perhaps had less to fear in submitting to Marxist doctrine and classlessness. Although I did have one advantage, in that I had a more than passing resemblance to Joseph Stalin, then in power in Russia. In any event, I was already acting in the interests of the common benefit and would on most trips to Dublin bring vegetables to distribute. And Behan told me of an incident with Tony McInerney one morning down in the Catacombs as he saw the sacks of cabbages and potatoes I had left in the big kitchen.

"Now, Mike, this doesn't show me in a great light, but I'll tell you of a time when I commented to Tony McInerney on the fact you'd brought him some dirty old sacks of vegetables and I said you were a harder man when it came to buying a drink in a pub. He was vituperative and nearly bit the head off me, saying it was more than I or anybody else had ever fucking well done to help feed his children."

We were now crossing the Grand Canal into Lower Leeson Street, a soft mist descending on Dublin and the night grown chilly and the pavements glistening and damp. It was also coming near pub closing time and I parked on the east side of a deserted St. Stephen's Green. Behan, requesting to make a quick call at a nearby public house where he might still find his erstwhile companion and poet of the people, the towering and glowering seventeen-stone Lead Pipe Daniel the Dangerous.

"Now, Mike, although he worships the Blessed Virgin and would be that bit occasionally religious, he'd nevertheless steal the shoes off a monster in a nightmare."

Although one heard bizarre stories of Lead Pipe Daniel the Dangerous's violent exploits, he was always the most benignly charming of persons in one's company. Anxious to recite his poetry and to be in every way pleasing. But it was generally agreed that when Lead Pipe Daniel and Behan were seen together in each other's company and despite their both being of a poetic and literary disposition, that these two as a pair presented a never forgotten sight that would make monsters in nightmares look like archangels and that you would not want to confront down a dark alley. Or indeed even meet in a bright and a populated place. And Behan once took my notebook and wrote in it a poem Lead Pipe Daniel had composed called "Me."

> There is a gladness in my gladness
> When I'm glad.
> There is a sadness in my sadness
> When I'm sad.
> There is a madness in my madness
> When I'm mad.
>
> But the gladness in my gladness
> And the sadness in my sadness
> And the madness in my madness
> Are fuck-all to my badness
> When I'm bad.

One recalled an elegant in mufti Dublin dinner party at which Lead Pipe Daniel was present and who always, in case anyone should doubt his financial status, allowed to have showing from his jacket breast pocket the corner of an Irish five-pound note. Also present at table, and across from Lead Pipe, sat a Trinity undergraduate who read Mental and Moral Science, a triple-barreled named gentleman who, cravated and monocled, and who, when at large in a college square, always sported an ebony silver-topped walking stick and who was now during the serving of the savory, enumerating the stimulating charms of the Anglo-Irish and in so doing referred to the Irish themselves as natives. Like a coiled spring, Lead Pipe Daniel, his long apelike arms outstretched across the table, sprang from the seat of his Chippendale dining room chair, overturning the wine glasses, and grabbed the monocled gentleman with one hand around the throat and proceeded to strangle him while punching him with his other free hand in the face.

"Don't you ever refer to the fucking Irish as fucking natives in my fucking presence, you fucking Brit."

The incident from which the monocled gentleman was saved by my nearby intervention had later prompted me to ask Behan why Lead Pipe was always so charming and lamblike in my presence and who in the case of his attack upon the monocled Trinity gent, so readily acquiesced to my restraint.

"Jesus, Mike, he's let it be known to me, that unlike the Assassin, whose looks are the only dangerous thing about him, that you are unpremeditatedly violent and he's terrified to offend you."

At this remark one did feel a bit like a gentleman to whom Behan referred as the Assassin, who, despite his name, was the most benign and harmless of men and gentle in his every way. However, he was handicapped by an insatiable curiosity and cursed with a permanent murderous expression on his face, which not only made him look as if he would kill you but was just about to do so. This impression was increased by his savagely fierce glare, which because of his uncontrollable inquisitiveness the Assassin often leveled at strange newcomers in a pub and which more than once resulted in a dangerous situation. For just after the war, and among the many ex-service personnel, there were odd members of elite parachute and commando regiments lurking about, not to mention IRA gunmen. And these folk did not welcome the Assassin's glowering attention. It was upon one such occasion that one of these former special troops was having a quiet drink when he looked up to see the Assassin glaring directly at him. And as Behan would recall,

"Ah, Mike, it shouldn't have happened to a dog. Sure the Assassin would kindly kiss the hand of anyone who came near enough to be kindly kissed. And if you weren't near enough for that, he'd declaim in your direction a love sonnet."

But this stranger, a veteran of guerilla combat having survived the war intact, upon asking who it was daring to stare at him and being told it was the Assassin, wasn't about to be now liquidated by someone in a Dublin pub. As the Assassin continued to glare and stare, the commando got up from his seat, walked over to the Assassin and, ignorant of the fact that this poor man would not hurt a flea, unleashed without preamble a right to his jaw. As the Assassin fell toward the pub floor and was being hit from every direction, it was clear he was having the living bejesus beaten out of him. Until Tony McInerney, aware that the Assassin was unable to show a friendly look upon his face, or to defend himself, leaped to his feet. McInerney, sprinting champion of Ireland, also had one of the country's fastest pairs of fists and was in principle politically opposed to your man the commando, who continued to belabor the poor Assassin. As the pub erupted in general uproar, McInerney waded in to hit your man the commando a clout that sent him ceilingward over the bar, behind which he rested stretched unconscious, a knocked-over bottle of Power's Gold Label whiskey emptying down on his head.

It was witnessing such frequent fisticuffs behavior around the Dublin pubs and myself being constantly challenged and attacked by similar folk, and having to instantly defend, that could have resulted in one's own reputation for physical tempestuousness. And now as I waited on the street for Behan and in spite of Lead Pipe Daniel's alleged fear of me, I was relieved when Behan came out alone from the pub, where he said he had investigated the lavatory from whence Daniel the Dangerous got his name, having once wrenched a length of lead pipe from the toilet wall in order to wield it upon the pub owner's head and the heads of a few of his customers at whom he wished, as Daniel the Dangerous would say, to demonstrate his aggrievement over a slight made concerning tinkers and traveling people. Behan mimicking Lead Pipe Daniel's grumbling gruff voice:

"Didn't I hit the hypocritical miserly fucker a clout on the cranium with his own fucking lead pipe I pulled out of his own fucking gent's convenience."

Behan often would recite a verse or two of a poem this dangerous man had written which referred to the Blessed Virgin but which for all the flowery, adoring words ended up being of a sacrilegious nature. And Behan could see one was not a little grateful to know this poet of the plain people of Ireland could not be found. Together on the street again, Behan and I walked along the park railings of Stephen's Green.

"Ah, Jesus, Mike, I'm glad to be back in Dublin, where there'd be maybe a familiar face and sight with every footstep you take. I'm a city rat, thankful for all the old crumbling walls, alleys, sewers and streets that I can be scurrying in and out of. And excepting yourself, who's put the countryside to good use, you can take your plots of turnips and potatoes and the mean people who till them and shove them as far as they will go up the arse of the biggest farmer you can find."

As we walked on under the leafy, thick trees of this deserted thoroughfare of Stephen's Green East, ahead in the distant shadows a solitary strange apparition approached. Which appeared to be a man bent forward pushing a wheelbarrow in which a light glowed. As we got closer, one was able to see it was in fact a man pushing a wheelbarrow in which a light glowed which gave his face a cadaverous skeletal look, like the Grim Reaper of Death. The man was wearing a pair of boots, sou'wester and trilby hat and the barrow contained a pick, shovel, pail, and as I learned later, Ireland's first Geiger counter. As we confronted to pass on the pavement, Behan endearingly greeted this gentleman as an old friend.

"Horace, how is your hammer hanging. And, does your redeemer liveth. And will he soon be opening the heavens of joy to swallow us both, Horace Bartholomew Durrow Mountmelton."

"Hello, my dear Brendan, how good it is to see you on such a fine evening as this."

"Well, Horace, to my way of observation, it looks, if you don't mind me saying, like a fucking awful evening."

"Ah, to be sure, Brendan, there appears to be a temporary indecision with the barometric pressure not knowing whether to go up or down."

"Jesus, Horace, you couldn't, with me temporarily bollixed betwixt the throes of circumstance, let me have a bob or two."

"I could indeed, Brendan, and welcome. Nothing would give me greater pleasure."

Horace, without a moment's hesitation, reached into a large inside pocket of his sou'wester and pulled out a packet of documents along with a thick sheaf of bills. Peeling off two large white English five-pound notes and bowing deeply, Horace handed them to Behan. The man's impeccable manners and the preciseness of his elegant voice made me think he was some professor of quantum theory or wave mechanics, who, like the more than a few in such rarefied pursuits knocking around Dublin with their ohm meters, had gone into permanent orbit and was now out for an airing before bedtime from one of Dublin's better mental institutions. Of course too he could have been sane enough, being that he was in the land where batteries, soda water and leprechauns were invented. In any event, Behan was now possessed of enough money which at the rate of less than a shilling for a pint, could purchase more than fifty gallons of porter or ten bottles of whiskey. Enough to keep a modest drinker like Behan drunk for a week. As this gentleman put away his roll of bank notes, he smiled and bowed and again took up the handles of his wheelbarrow and proceeded south into the shadowy mists along Stephen's Green.

"Mike, he's been my patron now for years. Buying every copyright of mine. I just tell him what I'm writing and if I've got a spare copy, give it to him or I let him see it. If not, it doesn't matter. This is just a small part advance emolument to be added on to the lot he has already given me."

As we walked beneath the drips of moisture from the park's tree branches and toward the lighted windows of the Shelbourne Hotel and to where my car was parked, Behan, as he tucked the money away in a pocket, saw the wonderment on my face.

"Sure, what's the point of being a writer if you don't get paid."

Behan indeed assiduously adhered to this principle. He was at the time being published in a column in the *Irish Press* newspaper, whose editor innocently assumed Behan would reasonably wait to be paid like other contributors at the end of the week. But found one night about midnight, while asleep in his sylvan suburban surrounds, that Behan intended to be remunerated at the end of the day his piece appeared. This editor's wife being wakened by rude shouts outside their house, and failing to inquire as to the source of the ruckus, was then assailed by small stones hitting the windowpanes, breaking one and cracking another. The editor, jumping from his bed, investigated to see Behan standing on the pebbles of the front apron of their entrance drive, his fist raised and shaking and yelling up to the window.

"Would you ever throw me down my money for my piece you published. I am without a penny in my pocket for a glass of stout. And having just walked in the rain four miles out from Dublin, my belly is screaming with the thirst that my throat is cut."

And this type of midnight alfresco remuneration could have been what influenced Behan in later years, as he would at a literary cocktail party sell a work at one end of a room and a few minutes later, crossing over, sell the same work to someone else the other side of the room. But knowing Behan and his sense of natural justice, such was no doubt perpetrated upon deserving conmen.

"Now, Mike, in fairness to myself, the one thing I do concerning a piece of writing is to keep scrupulous accounts of anyone owing me money for it."

I was to learn later that this same man, Horace Bartholomew Durrow Mountmelton, in addition to being a patron of the arts, did also have the deserved reputation of being the politest man in Ireland. And despite his present ability to be generous to Behan, he did have his times of impecuniousness. He was a longtime friend of Ernest Gebler's and would occasionally call on Gebler at his estate of Lake Park for afternoon tea. But once ended up staying, but not wanting to inconvenience Gebler, took to sleeping on a sofa in one of the smaller sitting rooms. After the days extended into some weeks of affording Mountmelton such hospitality, Gebler decided that it was time to give Horace his walking papers. Gebler, who wrote throughout the night, would only appear midafternoon, encountering Horace in his usual stiffly upright sitting position, from which Mountmelton would leap to his feet, bow and announce in his cheerful manner a long stream of complimentary banter, which never allowed Gebler to emit any harsh word of eviction. Gebler basically being a very kind man always found himself helplessly succumbing to these blandishments.

"Ah, my dear Ernie, how good it is to see you on this fine country afternoon. I trust you slept well and that your work progresses in fine fashion. The dew, I fear, has dried by now, which was sparkling on the grass this morning, as I took my constitutional following breakfast and witnessed the daffodils in their glorious profusion along your front drive. I did then go to visit your lady's garden. And here I have been keeping to give you this, a yellow, most fragrant rose, the petals of which are as soft as the dew was this morn on the grass. And I do hope you do not disapprove of my taking the liberty of plucking it. But I did so with the motive that this flower might start your day with the inspiration provided by its inestimable fragrance."

Mounting my sedate motor again, Behan and I made our way north of the Liffey quays. Where we again stopped to enter a pub, and Behan greeting and being greeted on all sides and with one of his five-pound notes ordering us bottles of stout, and he informed me that this was the pub he would frequent on impecunious days in order to drink bottles of Mountjoy Nourishing Stout, which at sixpence a bottle was a penny cheaper than a bottle of Guinness.

"You see, Mike, with the price seven pence for a bottle of Guinness, if we drink now seven bottles of Mountjoy Nourishing Stout at sixpence a bottle, you're saving a penny on each bottle and then you can go back again, south of the Liffey, with the saving and have a bottle of Guinness free of charge, as you might say. So, you see, there would be more than slums to boast of this side of the Liffey."

I had only rarely ventured to the north side of Dublin and on such occasions was either heading to the grandness of the Gresham Hotel in O'Connell Street or to catch the Aer Lingus bus to the airport from Cathal Brugha Street, or the train from Amien Street Station for Howth. And except for Behan, who sang the praises of the north side of the city, mostly all social life I had met with in Dublin was conducted in the fashionably regarded south side of the river. But where, nonetheless, one could still encounter slums the moment one stepped a few steps beyond the smart streets. And where, in solitary, walking these bereft corridors of poverty, as I often did, one would pass these broken tenements, their tattered curtained windows, the panes of glass gone and patched with cardboard. And inside on the walls see pictures of the Pope or in the dim darkness of a room, a candle glowing in front of the bleeding heart of Jesus Christ or a saint. And from Ernest Gebler's descriptions to me of Dublin slum life, one knew coughing and crying children were crowded into the Georgian rooms, sleeping one next to another on damp, torn mattresses spread across the floors, where death and disease were the daily currency of life. And Behan once while taking a pee on my Kilcoole lawn exhibited his penis as he referred to his scars of war.

"Mike, let me tell you, if you don't know already in your studies at college that there is every venereal pestilence to be had in Dublin. They would have you believe it would be coming in with the sailors on the ships, but I'm telling you the sailors would be going out with a lot worse than they had when they came in. And on such matters there'd be more in the population not knowing what the itch or burning was up their private parts that a little holy water applied wouldn't cure."

Although there was always a trace of deeper concern in his voice, it was difficult to tell if Behan was being serious when he spoke with a seemingly careless indifference concerning venereal matters. But even one's Trinity professor of bacteriology would lightheartedly open up his lectures on such as syphilis, with the caution to be skeptical of the patients who represented they had caught their infection on a toilet seat. In any event, as much as it would have been clinically enlightening, I had no desire to inspect Behan's so-called scars of war. But even with the recent advent of penicillin, I was surprised that Behan seemed nonchalant concerning the spirochete of syphilis which remained, in my eyes, an equally grievous matter as that of the tubercle of tuberculosis. But there was no doubt that the latter disease, pervasive enough in the rest of the country, was one of the scourges of Dublin's tenement slums.

"Mike, it's why you'd see in the matrimonial column of the *Evening Herald and Mail,* farmers advertising for wives, specifying that they be of stout build. It's not only as a sign they'd be strong enough to hitch them up to the plow if the horse got sick but also as being an indication that they were not wasting away with consumption and the farmer himself soon having to be sweating, digging her grave."

But Behan had no need to elaborate to me on this bane malady. As I'd learned of a young man dying and, in his last operation, had to have his testicles removed, and I had on one chill Dublin late afternoon been present down in the basement gloomy morgue of Sir Patrick Dunne's Hospital, witnessing a postmortem on a young girl where the prevalence of this disease was amply demonstrated by an almost cynical pathologist who pointed out with perfunctory indifference the many tubercular lesions on the child's internal organs. And the sadness and haunting memory of that small young life, and tiny unmourned body so alone and cold in death, and on that grim slate-gray slab, eviscerated and taken apart under the eyes of strangers, stayed with me underlying all I would ever write about Dublin.

Behan and I now drove through some dark, desolate streets into Night Town. This an area notorious back in the years for its brothels, slums and destitution, but where Behan again maintained that one found a better class of people. On the gentle slope of a hill, we stopped and I followed Behan into a tenement and up some flights of stairs into a large, high-ceilinged, smoke-filled Georgian room, crammed throbbing with voices, curses and songs. Sweating, singing faces aglow in the blaze of fire within the still elegant chimney piece. There were men, women and children of every age and Dublin description. Behan, tugging me by an elbow toward a grandmotherly old one and whispering in my ear, urging me to give her a squeeze, kiss and hug.

"These are people, Mike, who face life as they'd find it, for there is no other fucking choice they have to do otherwise. Now come here, meet this great old one. She's me own nearest and dearest, me great-grand aunt now, give her a hug. She was a whore all her life down on the quays. And now here she is enjoying herself in dignified retirement. And she loves nothing better than a good hug."

Behan, in the midst of singing a song, was, as he did in Kilcoole, filling a bowl with a concoction of food, now filling a pint glass, first with stout, then with sherry, whiskey and brandy and finally topping it off with poteen. As he finished singing the final refrain of his song, he put the pint glass to his lips and, his head thrown back, swallowed without stopping the entire pint glass of mixed beer and spirits. And as I watched the last of the liquid in the glass go down his throat, the glass suddenly dropped from his lips and, felled like a tree, he keeled over backward, to thunder his thirteen-stone weight upon the floor, shuddering the windows as screams came from the room below. The rest of the party makers seemed to regard me as Behan's keeper and bid me rid the floor of his supine unconscious presence. And were quite threatening and anxious that I remove him without delay.

"Would you ever now, you who brought him, take this drunken beast out of the midst of decent people before he does more damage."

I was not to know that most present had been that day at a wedding. And that these newlyweds had a while before our arrival and before the moment of Behan's collapse repaired to happily honeymoon in a bedroom below. Behan was limply lifted up and laid over my shoulder, and I carried him out of the room and down the stairs past the recently honeymooning newlyweds' door. Which, as we were passing, opened, and framed there, were the pair of them standing wrapped in blankets, heads covered in plaster, the entire ceiling of their room having collapsed upon them in bed. And as I descended the next flight of steps, straining under Behan's weight, with his head and arms hanging limp over my back, and the couple unleashing their bitter complaint, Behan suddenly regained consciousness and shouted back up over my shoulder to the recent bride and groom,

"Would you ever fuck off, you pair of sanctimonious eegits."

>And go
>Fuck yourselves
>Back
>In bed

10

Opening a rear door of my Austin 11.9 this night of the hooley, I dumped a comatose-again Behan in the back of this dignified automobile and drove the twenty-two miles return to Kilcoole. Parking on the lawn, I left Behan in a heap on the back seat of the car and stepped out into the fresh air of one of those rare but unforgettable bright moonlit nights of this haunting countryside. One walked across the dewy, wet meadow, hearing a curlew's mournful whistle as it flew overhead. And the distant sound of the waves gently splashing on the shore. Out on a shimmering Irish Sea, an ancient sailing ship that often plied this coast was making its way north from Wicklow Town, its pale white sail aloft in the moonlight, its starboard green lantern flickering toward the beach. Reminding one that this land could so suddenly be so tranquilly beautiful.

By morning, pounding hoofs and a sudden bellowing roar awoke me, and I jumped out of bed and looked out the window. Behan, hair dripping wet following ice-cold sea immersions, was as full as ever with life when he should have been near death from alcohol poisoning. He was in the middle of the lawn, a clump of grass in his hand and holding it out, trying to make friends with a massive bovine beast who had no similar intention. Its bulging eyes were already rolling around in its monstrous curly head, as I swept out the door of the cottage, grabbing a pitchfork kept for the purpose. The ferocious beast belonging to the neighboring farmer was now pawing the ground and sending sods of my carefully tended lawn high into the sky.

"Jesus, Mike, what's wrong at all with the ungrateful animal not wanting a bit of grass."

I shouted just in time for Behan to retreat, as the bull, with lowered horns, charged. Behan, shouting in Irish, his unlaced shoes flying off, ran across my strawberry patch and was hopelessly trying to climb the slippery bough of an ash tree. Up which a moment later he suddenly got instant assistance, the bull squarely levering him from behind, his arse mercifully between the horns and ascending skyward into the tree. Where Behan clung to the branches as the beast pawed the ground, his massive weight uprooting and nearly overturning the tree, with Behan clinging to the uppermost bough with all his might.

"Jesus, Mike, as if I needed any more reasons to hate the country-side. While you're down there, and before I fall out of the tree, would you ever tell the fucking beast in its ear in English to go away, as he doesn't understand the words 'fuck off' I'm saying to him in Gaelic."

Dodging battering and stabbing with my pitchfork, I finally maneuvered the bull amid his cows and drove the herd back through the gaping hole they'd made in the fence. And then scourging myself on brambles and blackthorns, I struggled to fill the gap with torn branches.

My days now numbered in Ireland, the event became one of my last countryside misadventures. Along with many of the frequenters of the Catacombs and of Dublin's Grafton and Harry streets, Gainor Crist had already fled or departed to England, and others of my Trinity pals had left for very foreign and distant parts. As pages now added steadily to my manuscript of *The Ginger Man,* and Valerie due to produce an heir, I had now finally decided to sell this small holding at Kilcoole, and after five years in Europe to return to America, land of the beautiful, home of the brave and oasis of the free. And there, with the book's publication, to await my justified fame and fortune and have at last those symbolic bushel baskets of dollar bills to dump on all disbelievers. But there were warning voices, such as Ernest Gebler's, to beware of the almighty world of the big, rich and prosperous over there.

A for-sale ad, cottage on four acres by the sea, was placed in the *Irish Times* newspaper. I was surprised at the sadness expressed by Farrell, my local neighboring farmer, and the Smiths, concerning my departure from this lonely, bereft stretch of coastland. There were tears in their eyes when the time came and we said we were moving away. And there they remained till one afternoon Mr. Smith gently died, and she, Mrs. Smith, died the next day following his funeral.

But then for more than a week there was no response to my ad. When suddenly walking down the long lane with his small daughter, my first possible purchaser came. A weather-beaten retired sea captain who had sailed the seven seas. He had arrived from Dublin by bus and seemed undeterred by the isolation. As he was shown around, he said that he lived on a small holding north of Dublin in an old Dublin tram which was converted to live in and which he was trying to sell. I toured the sea captain about, pointing out the defects rather than the advantages of Kilcoole, and was growing alarmed at his silence that he seemed to have no questions to raise himself and I finally asked him why. Because he said, in my years at sea I've met every kind of rogue and prince of every nationality and I'm a good judge of men and I would buy anything from you that you had to sell without question. Impressed by his good judgment, I asked him which of the world's nationalities in his opinion were the best and worst.

"The best are the Scots and the worst are Belgians. And in the last category, you might include a Rumanian or two."

As we both already knew, I didn't inquire an opinion concerning the Irish. But he soon volunteered the fact that there were too many Irish in the worst category to be able to boast of the few best. Alas, this potential purchaser and wondrous gentleman failed to sell his tram and land, and I had to place my advert again. This time an attractive and charming and most unlikely couple turned up. An RAF wing commander and his wife, a physician who had read medicine at Trinity College. And to whom my list of defects appeared pleasant challenges, as they were intending to use Kilcoole as a summer cottage. With hardly any ado, except for some negotiations over missing batteries for a radio, the sale was completed. After three years and my nearly rupture-making improvements and routine physical and nervous breakdowns, I sold Kilcoole for three times my own bitterly bargained purchase price. However, my father did come one summer to this land where he said they did not have a pot to piss in, and with a college pal, a strong swimming champion, Valentine Hinds, helping, played a large part in renovating the cottage. Putting in a concrete floor, which remained dry, and plastering the walls and sending someone for a quart or two of buttermilk each day.

As I liquidated, Ernest Gebler came down from Lake Park in his natty gent's sports car and haggled away an entire afternoon buying my chattels, from fire tongs, to milk cans, and enjoying to make bargains of most of them. However, the good thing about Gebler, who was so delighting in my discomfiture at such low prices for what I considered my priceless items, was that he would buy nearly anything offered with the only drawback being the abysmal price he'd pay. Previously, his beautiful American then wife had with her excellent taste bought two of my paintings and was even contemplating acquiring my five-seater 1935 Austin 11.9 horsepower saloon automobile, which I never tired of telling was formerly owned by the Protestant Bishop of Meath and would reach a steady sixty-five miles an hour on the straight. But Gebler, owning so many splendid vintage cars already, would not hear of buying my ecclesiastically dignified vehicle. Plus he had used these pictures of mine his lady had bought to block up holes in his estate fence to keep his neighboring farmer's sheep out. All perhaps why this exotically charming and talented woman, disenchanted with either Ireland or Gebler, who by his own smiling admission was no saint to live with, decamped back to America.

Ah, but later in the evening we repaired to the Grand Hotel, Greystones. Where white-gloved debutantes attended Friday night formal dress dances, and woe betide any gate-crashing hoi polloi who would dare breach the confines of this refined watering place on the coast of Wicklow. For there was a bevy of local rugby players within who could defend its socially comforting elegant confines. And in its light and airy dining room, which looked out over a croquet lawn to sea, Gebler and I sumptuously dined. Ernest, delighting again in the trouncing I'd taken over the dispersal of my poor belongings, now took an even greater delight in assuming a sporting attitude in insisting he pay for dinner. We quaffed wine and sipped brandy, telling and listening to each other's tales till a late hour, as we'd often done in front of a turf fire up in the forested confines of Lake Park while the rain splattered the windows and the gales blew through the pines. And Gebler spoke of his present lonely existence.

"I go to sleep at dawn. And get up late to get through another day till that day is gone, like the next day and the next. And then suddenly you stop, look back. And realize that that was becoming the life you've lived."

But Gebler was cheerful enough spending our evening in this homey family hotel, later renamed the La Touche, which had for Valerie and I become an oasis to repair to. Especially from the winter hardships of Kilcoole, when a shilling for a hot bath could replenish visions of hope, and then, over four o'clock tea in the hotel's lounge, listen to the reassuring vowels of Greystones' dowagers, among whom resided the mother of the author Samuel Beckett, literary news of whom in those days occasionally percolated from Paris to Dublin. There were also A. J. Cronin, the author, and his mother, and Father Jack Hanlon, the painter priest, and his mother. And indeed, before she bought her own house just down the road, there was my own mother, ascending and descending the stately mahogany staircase and who often stayed in this Edwardian building to be faithfully cosseted by the hotel's management and dark-uniformed staff. The wine waiter kept her wines and helped organize, with specially printed menus, the small family birthday parties she gave. And perhaps encouraged by the grandness of my mother's graciousness, there was even some effort to dance occasional attendance upon the bearded likes of me.

Gebler, even as I had now sold up, and perhaps out of his own recent isolation and loneliness, continued to press me not to leave Ireland and especially not to go to America. He was a man made wise by having to grow up teaching himself to read and write. Then self-taught as an author, he'd done exactly as he'd long plotted and planned to do, and that was to write a best-selling book. Gebler sitting and spending hundreds of hours meticulously researching in the British Museum reading room library. A seat or two away had also sat another earnest gentleman, Karl Marx, who wrote *Das Kapital.* Finally Gebler's book published in the United States swept all before it. And then Gebler would, more mournfully than cynically, pronounce upon what authors do who suddenly grow rich.

"Mike, they buy binoculars, shotguns, sports cars and fishing rods, and a big estate to use them on. And then outfitted in their new life, along with new bathrooms, wallpaper and brands of soap, they make a fatal mistake and change their women. To schemingly get toasted and roasted on glowing hot emotional coals, and subjected to a whole new set of tricks and treacheries. Which leaves that author spiritually disillusioned and minus his favorite household implements."

Although Gebler and I agreed that women were essentially the same, we also agreed that American women were a distinctive brand all on their own. And that European men were more liable than an American to take them seriously. But one felt that Gebler was once upon a time spoiled. And regretting a woman he'd left or lost. For while he wrote *The Plymouth Adventure* down a front basement room in London's Palace Gardens Terrace, and at dawn helped himself to milk to drink from neighboring porches, he had a faithful keeper and acolyte who did no man any wrong. I never met her. But about no woman have I ever heard such awed voices speak such universal praise. A Dublin girl and an accomplished actress on the Dublin stage, she seemed to be admired and loved by all. But about whom Gebler never uttered or spoke a single word. Her name was Sally Travers. Dead now. Yet one day, one knows, in her everlasting memory, will be written some amaranthine song, to be heard sung through the streets of Dublin. And one knows too that Gebler's silence only meant that, as writers do, they do more deeply conceal all that they most deeply love.

Packed in a great box I had made in Dublin, my paintings were brought to Greystones train station. From where they would go south on that lonely rail track along the shore to Cork to await passage to New York on the ocean liner *America*. My last act decamping from Ireland was to drive my trusty sedan to the Watson and Johnson Garage at Greystones, where local folklore has it, its four-wheeled ghost has been seen passing driverless on these country lanes but with Behan sedately in the passenger seat. I said good-bye to my barber, Josey, who also cut my brother T.J.'s hair who had decamped from America to take up living in our mother's house in Greystones. And Josey always could tell if Valerie was mucking about my own noncurly locks with a garden secateurs. However, when T.J. found out that Josey in his off hours tonsured the hair of the deceased, he supplied Josey with his own specially to be reserved implements delivered one day in their own embossed case.

"Now, Josey, you're only to use these on me and not on any of your departed customers to spruce them up for the grave."

I took my last ride on the train to Dublin along the precipitous cliffs overlooking the sea. And it was upon one such early journey that I composed the story "A Party on Saturday Afternoon." Arriving at Westland Row Station, I went to have a coffee and spice bun with a butter ball at Bewley's Oriental Cafe. Then exiting from the aroma of roasting coffee beans and ready to go to the airport to fly to the Isle of Man, who should I meet but Behan swaggering in his magnanimous way up Grafton Street. One first heard his loud shout, "Mike Donleavy, how's your hammer hanging," and then as he sidled up in his strangely indifferent way, he reported the very latest of latest news. That Crist, while in a restaurant in London and while dining waiting for a bus, suddenly saw the bus he had to catch unexpectedly pull up to the curb outside. Only halfway through his meal, Crist gathered up knife and fork and taking his plate of sausages, bacon and mash, popped some salt in a napkin and with a bottle of beer under his arm, rushed out the restaurant door and hopped aboard the bus, where he duly sat down and continued his meal. Behan commenting,

"Now, I'll tell you one thing, Mike, Crist may have wanted bad enough to get where he wanted to go on this bus, but whatever else we may say or think about him, one thing is a certainty that he has as a human being demonstrated his great practicality."

But later in the New World, America, I was to hear more of this story from Gainor's own lips when we would go, as I insisted we did, in order to avoid mayhem and horror, to meet and talk in Woodlawn Cemetery in New York City's upper Bronx. In Ireland, while his wife, Constance, now matriculated at Trinity, Crist had, under the dire weight of insurmountable debts and the accumulation of personal misunderstandings, which in Crist's parlance referred to bitter disputes, fled to England. But before he had done so he had taken up with an elegantly attractive fox-hunting university girl, Pamela O'Malley, from a family prominent in the southwest of Ireland, who, as a young woman of independent mind, was a rarity of the place and time, and who later became the second wife of this American man from Ohio. It was she who helped organize his life in London to be led as much as possible in a civilized manner, and saw to it that he kept appointments. And it was upon this day of taking his meal aboard the bus, that Crist had been on his way to visit his small daughter staying with relatives of his first wife. But upon arrival to see the little girl, a disagreement arose and Crist stormed off. Without a pub near at the time and another two hours to wait to catch another bus and in desperation to get away from it all, even if it was for only the briefest time, Gainor chose to go for a quiet walk in nearby Epping Forest.

"Mike, so much has gone wrong in my life that harassment and misunderstanding seems to accumulate and create about me. And the least little thing triggers off the horrors. The day I took my meal aboard the bus, I was at my wit's end and hardly knew where to turn. And I especially needed a breather and to enjoy having the considerable pleasure of seeing my very pretty and delightful little daughter. But God knows, I am bedeviled by bad luck. Within five minutes of my arrival, one of those insoluble misunderstandings erupted with my in-laws, leaving me livid and with no alternative but to abandon seeing my daughter. With time to wait until I could escape from that god-forsaken place back into the civilization of central London, I was certain to go out of my mind unless I had an unnervous break from my fast increasing heebie-jeebies, general angst, the jimjams and strain. I headed into the forest as being the nearest place where I was bound to find within nearly six thousand acres of natural woodland, and amid the hornbeam, beeches and ancient oak trees and in the sylvan and anonymous surrounds, at least a few minutes of desperately needed solace. I'd walked northward a mile and reached what must have been the center of the forest and without the sight of another human being, and began for the first time in months to feel a sense of calm. Then suddenly ahead through the shadows of trees, there was a welcoming sunlight pouring into a circular glade, an arena of tall grasses and the faded stalks of flowers through which went a path. And now within a few unbelievable seconds everything changed. I stepped out into the welcome warm rays of sunshine to walk to the other side of the glade. And as I did so, there came emerging from the opposite end of the path a solitary man. Mike, I deserve better luck. As this person approached and came near enough for one to recognize without my glasses, he was finally too near, and it was too late to politely detour rapidly from his presence and go elsewhere within this six thousand acres in which to roam. He was a man, a member of the Legion of Mary, who back in Dublin had in fact, one innocent Wednesday early afternoon come to knock on my door at 1 Newtown Avenue, Black-rock. And as it was raining and he was seeking my conversion to becoming a member of the Legion of Mary, I had asked him in. He sat on the couch and spent four hours of intense proselytization concern-ing the legion, its good works and good people, whereupon, having patiently listened without interruption I suggested we pop just a few steps away for an interlude of a little refreshment. Mike, after the second pint and exposing him to my own interest in the theory I'd formulated concerning the true nature of existence and the possibility of energy emanating from the inertia of absolute indolence, I could not extract the man from my company. He clung to me like a desperate leech, and, in the next three weeks, having been seduced by a lady whose every curvature spelled trouble and who had given him his first ever blow job, he promptly gave up the Legion of Mary, deserted his wife and children and was fired from his job. However, even more embarrassing than having set him on the road to vegetative nirvana and what I did not conceive could be his ruin, the very last thing I did before finally extricating myself from his company was to borrow his very last five shillings. Which is still owed to him. Now both of us were so stunned by this hauntingly cosmically impossible confrontation that we passed each other silently by. I did, of course, reaching the safety of the trees on the other side, turn to peek back. And just in time to see this poor sod running away for all he was worth."

And Mike
Let me tell you
It wasn't long
Before my own legs
Broke
Into a sprint

11

WORD AROUND DUBLIN already had it that following Gainor Crist's departure from his little house at 1 Newtown Avenue, Blackrock, that an occasional haunting humming could be heard of "Raggle Taggle Gypsy," one of Gainor's favorite songs. And that his ghost was seen entering O'Rourke's Pub just down the road and that the tap of the edge of a half a crown would sound on the bar to summon a pint and glass of Powers Gold Label. But Gainor was still very much alive despite his bizarre confrontation in Epping Forest. And was already toying with possible escape back to the good old U.S. of A. That place which we as Europeanized Americans assumed was always there to pick up the pieces of our lives which Europe might have sidetracked while we were at play there. That we could finally return to the New World, where hot showers would once again rain cleansing upon our heads and shoulders to rid of any old backward grime Europe had left upon our persons, and where we could exhibit our cultivated ways and step into such pursuits that befitted such dignity.

It was Gainor's strong penchant for involving in the likes of situations as the man from the Legion of Mary that gave him his mesmeric aura. He seemed to be able to find redeeming features and fascination in anyone, although he was quick to bring just retribution to those he thought evil. He was always ready and generous in offering his advice to those in deserving need, and his humane consideration and concern for even the most humble stranger knew no limits. No nervously earnest salesman or religious evangelist was ever turned away from his door. All were invited in and encouraged to present their demonstrations and, provided credit was given, whatever they were selling was bought on the spot. Especially modern contraptions like vacuum cleaners, which usually shortly later had to be repossessed. But it was never

Crist's intention not to meet his creditors in full, as he occasionally did many months later to their utter surprise. However, in celebrating such event over drinks, he would often end up having borrowed even greater sums or acquired newer and more expensive appliances.

Nevertheless, compassion for his fellow man was an almost sacred part of Crist's behavior. Few were ever left sincerely feeling that they were being duped or taken for a ride. And almost all agreed that they had pleasantly been in the company of a man they would never forget for the rest of their lives. His charm was immediate, possessed as he was of what are commonly thought of as Old World ethical codes and manners. He would jump to stand as ladies entered rooms. He would smilingly bow and click his heels upon an introduction. He would immediately, upon meeting, solicit one's opinion concerning one's health and well-being. Yet along with his splendor of deportment, Crist could be wonderfully absentminded. Which no doubt was exacerbated with the intensifying of his troubles, which had Gainor already voicing intentions that he might follow my example and return to the United States. And during my very last chat with him in Ireland, just before his own departure from Dublin to England, occurred an incident when we had assembled for Sunday afternoon tea with several others in a house Tony McInerney had temporarily rented in Howth. It was a time when he seemed to be at his most beleaguered and distracted, and Gainor and I, both locked in conversation and needing to take a pee, went up the stairs together to the water closet with Gainor being loudly reminded with shouts from behind not to pull the chain, as the lavatory needed to have the outflow of its contents gradually eased sewer-ward by the slow pouring of water from a bucket and definitely not by the rush of several simultaneous gallons plunging down from a cistern.

There was room for two in the cold confines of the water closet, where the pounding of the nearby sea could be heard coming in the window along with the drizzly mist on that day. I peed and Crist followed. And while pissing, Gainor was recounting a recent delicate matter in Dublin to which I listened avidly as it directly concerned me and a person who was rumored to insanely detest one over a liaison I had with his now wife when she was a wonderfully curvaceous single lady temporarily residing in a chamber down in the Catacombs. And it was with this bitterly aggrieved gentleman with whom Crist now had a recent and particularly unpleasant encounter at a Dublin hooley, where Gainor overheard this gentleman making offending remarks about me and my paintings.

"Mike, this most unpleasant person said your pictures were a load of shit."

Gainor, who thought me a mite more than mediocre as a painter, immediately took this gent to task for his disparagement. Whereupon the gent, a rugby player, struck out at Gainor, grazing his jaw. This was a most dreadful mistake, for in about one second the gent found himself on the floor on his back, his head bouncing on the boards as Crist, his hands locked in his hair, administered the usual wooling. Crist's philosophy of energy from indolence and his elegant slender stature gave no hint or warning of his phenomenal strength and speed. His muscles were like steel bands and his movements so swift they could hardly be seen. And the occasion for the aggrieved gent to discover this was made more ignominious as news of it spread quickly over Dublin, the man now letting it be known that he intended to gain his revenge. And this Anglo-Irish rugby player may have been one of the very few people I ever heard Gainor express a thorough dislike for or against whom he ever declared violence, and Crist said,

"Mike, he only wants to hurt me. But I want to kill him."

On the words "kill him," Crist pulled the lavatory chain. And I suppose I may have been about to express my appreciation to Gainor, for it wasn't the first time someone had undergone a wooling at Crist's hands for having uttered a disparaging word about me and my paintings. However, from below came screams and consternation as all manner of disagreeable fluid and solid matter poured down out of the ceiling into the sitting room and upon the heads of the tea-taking hapless guests. Made even sadder by the fact that this may have been one of the few ever formal occasions any of us ever had of taking tea together. Poor old Gainor, always the patrician and compassionate thoroughbred, stood nervously entwining his fingers against the yellow softness of his cashmere sweater, formerly my property, while waiting for the disturbance below to subside. While I less politely and helplessly contorted with laughter, reversed my way out of the water closet and onto the landing. Whereas Crist watched and further listened to the lamentations below, I deservedly fell backward down the stairs. At which Gainor merely frowned, gave another twiddle to his fingers and contemplatively pursed his lips.

This in my twenty-fifth year of life should have been a most solemn of solemn warnings as to what might happen to the poor likes of us in the United States. On August 1, 1951, Gainor was twenty-nine years old. And he firmly believed that, like Jesus Christ, he would be tacked up on his own cross by the age of thirty-three. Which now left a brief four years to go. And this incident of the lavatory in Howth only reminded one of another social debacle befalling Gainor, when McInerney, ever the tolerant forgiver of faux pas trespassed against him, was entertaining Crist while on a visit to Paris, which occurred shortly after Crist had met his elegant young lady Pamela, who, as Gainor could make most movie stars look pretty plain, was justifiably proud of him. And when an old friend of hers with whom she'd been to Convent School and who happened at the time also to be traveling to Paris, showed intense interest to meet Gainor, this was arranged. And I suppose on reflection this incident could vie with some which were soon to befall us in the United States.

Crist, having arrived in Paris with his little baby in tow, had holed up in a tiny, cramped back bedroom chamber on Paris's Left Bank near the corner of rue Mazarine and rue de Buci. A heat wave having descended on the city, Crist lay in his underwear vest and a pair of seersucker trousers, his baby asleep on his chest, both having taken a siesta during the hot afternoon in order to be fresh and rested to meet his girlfriend's best girlfriend. As he often did, Crist assumed his coffin state of inert suspended animation, with his eyeballs still and heartbeat at its maximum minimum. Meticulous always in his dress, he was planning to douche and change in time to present his best foot forward. However, having had a long train journey and crossing of the channel, and with the room curtains drawn, Crist fell into a deep sleep. And with his obsession with the sinking of the *Titanic,* he dreamt as he often did of a naval drill of abandoning ship and lowering life rafts over the side and just when sighting circling sharks, he woke to a sudden knocking on the door. And his baby asleep on his chest also wakened, in a state of discomfort.

"All hands on deck."

This was a summons that both Crist and I had retained from naval days. Which he now uttered as he quickly sat up and put the baby aside and felt something moistly strange on his chest, which did not immediately identify itself, being that Gainor often suffered severe olfactory impairment due to hay fever. Standing barefoot in the darkness, Gainor two-handedly, feverishly attempted to rub the matter on his chest away, suddenly realizing that the knocking on the door was the girl with whom he had the appointment. Unable to find the light switch and with no time to dress, he quickly tried to find his belt to keep his trousers up, promptly tripping into and knocking over the dressing table. Without light and without a mirror, he now distractedly with his hands felt what seemed to be something which would keep hair down and which was congealed on his chest. As he approached the door, he liberally smeared the substance back over his head with his fingers. And to another knock and with his customary élan, Gainor swept the door wide open, the hall light shining upon him and illuminating his tall figure in the doorway. Which bleary-eyed and barefoot suddenly became trouserless as such dropped around his ankles as he realized he was presenting himself smeared all over in his baby's recent excrement, which innocent feces had not the benefit of a nappy. Alas, now only wearing the upper part of his besmirched undergarment which did not reach low enough to cover his private parts, this elegant convent-bred young lady also had to face impromptu exposure to Gainor's not insubstantial genitalia.

"Oh my God."

As she uttered her words, the young lady, expecting to see this picture-book handsome swain she'd heard so much about, put her hand up to her summery flowered dress and reversed backward, as I did in Howth to tumble down the stairs. Gainor, the ever-ready gentleman, lunging forward to grab her and just managing to save her, if not from further shock at least from further fall. He did of course make other and future arrangements to meet her under more salubrious circumstances in the lobby of a much better nearby Left Bank Hôtel d'Angleterre in the rue Jacob. And she later reported that not only was he every bit as wonderful, handsome and charming as she had been led to believe but also that she had fallen deeply and hopelessly in love with him. Duly they took tea together, but no plaque seems to mark such occasion in the lobby of this hotel, where, in the eyes of this young lady beholder, the resplendent Crist redeemed himself.

However, with lavatories excepted, all now in my own life was prudent optimism. As an interim and awaiting our child's birth before embarking westward over the Atlantic Ocean, Valerie and I were to spend five months on the Isle of Man. Halfway between Ireland and England this volcanic outcropping in the Irish Sea was and remains one of the most neutral places one could ever hope to be. The Manx were not your jovial friendship-on-the-lips sort as were the Irish. Indeed, they gave one the impression of their being a withdrawn, dour, and secretly collaborating lot. But as one slowly got to know the Manx, and they, you, they proved to be a reliable and pleasantly helpful people. The island had no stigma attached to illegitimacy, gambling or wenching. Except that to this day of writing, homosexuality is banned. And birching, a punishment for the use of violence in the commission

In Ireland, O'Keefe had reasonable confidence that he
could bring about an improvement in his sexual life.
His first opportunity occured on his aunts farm in
Galway when he walked with his 17 year old cousin over
the bog to get milk from a neighbor. It was raining.
Her name was Tessie. He could tell from the tightness
in her voice that he had communicated the motives for
his presence. Having manuvered her into the driest
ditch he could find he went carefully through his rep
ertoire of seduction and was suprised when she was not
not resist his purposely obcene manuvers

*Eat this the
holding of her forearm.
flesh of her forearm.*

Spaghetti During the Depression. O'Keefe

*Dangerfield. On bed - lady shits on his chest.
Someone enters. Sebastian rises quickly rubs his
chest with his hands and sweeps his hair back.*

hyperbole
hyper Julia - the highest reverence - paid to B.U.
*hylozoism - The theory that matter has life and matter
and life are inseparable.*

The Bestial Hymn.

*Seb. sends morse code with his teeth,
On the lazy behove in God.*

A first draft manuscript page of THE GINGER MAN, which occasionally
evolved into notes, some of which produced tangents so diverse they
were not further explored.

of a crime. And let me tell you, it didn't half keep visiting vandals and ruffians minding their own peaceful business.

Over the years, the island was a traditional holiday-making place for the mill workers in the English midland cities, such as Manchester, Bradford and Leeds. With the Irish finding it a place to come to and freely commit the sin of impurity. And I heard it more than once mentioned, and perhaps a bit euphemistically, that some of the island's female population could be likened to well-plowed fields. This said of course by a "come-over," which referred to those who were not born at least five hundred years ago on the island. But what the population did to one another was different from what was accepted from a foreigner. And an ancient resentment existed over the novelist Hall Caine, who, born in Cheshire, England, and who, upon taking up permanent Manx residence, dallied with some of the island's damsels. Indeed, what else might one expect on an island isolated by mists and storm and whose male population, if not sailing the seven seas, had over the centuries past been misleading mariners to founder upon their shores for the plunder this might provide. However, the island, with its windswept lonely moors, was where one could leave open one's door at night and venture where'er one might unmolested. And those few who might be guilty of violent crimes would think twice about their next feloniousness and remember well the flogging with birch twigs they got for their last malfeasance. Proof enough that the Manx, for all their wenching and gambling, were a law-abiding, not to say highly devout, community.

But the one appropriately to see me off to the Isle of Man was none other than Valentine Horatio Coughlin. One of my erstwhile Dublin enemies whom I had fought in a mad battle of fisticuffs in the middle of Anne Street outside Davy Byrnes's pub. This following a famed altercation amid other guests in his drawing room when it got him evicted from his newly rented and decorated flat and helped break up his marriage to one of Ireland's most beautiful women. Champion whistler, champion heavyweight boxer, champion bridge player, and charming con artist when he had to be, Coughlin was the only man ever in the history of Dublin pawnshops to succeed in hocking various weights of best rump steak, which a lady assistant butcher who adored him put in his hand in unlimited, unweighed and uncharged-for quantities. Val, as he was called, was a product of a Jesuitical institution, Clongowes Wood College, one of Ireland's best schools. His words always as blunt as they were droll, he was possessed of a jaunty jollity. But Coughlin's life took a Dublin downturn when he became obsessed with revenging the catastrophic destruction of his new matrimonial abode. And it might have been more his overhearing of Gainor Crist's words spoken to the landlord who lived nearby and who rushed to inquire at the door as to what was happening to his house. And Crist, as he closed the door in his face and locked it, said,

"If you've ever heard of Iwo Jima, Bougainville, the Solomons, Normandy, and Hiroshima, you'll know that in exactly five minutes from now you won't have a house."

These words achieved fame all over Dublin, as doors splintered asunder, lamps and light fittings were demolished and full-grown people were sent crashing through windows. Coughlin's family heirlooms were broken over people's heads. Meissen figurines flew as missiles toward their targets while Crist, as ringmaster, tried to keep innocent women out of harm's way. I of course reluctantly was in the thick of it all, dishing out what justice I could to the perpetrators of evil. But the dreadful thing being that, in the melee, one of my left hooks meant for a rich gate-crashing gangster hooligan, instead of landing on his jaw, hit his dyed blond moll, who had leaped into the action to scratch out my eyes. Several of her teeth went flying out of her mouth and, like dice thrown, rattled across the floor to bounce conspicuously up against the baseboard. I of course was horrified and full of apology, but the clattering sound the teeth made bouncing across the floor seemed to incite an insane fury on all sides. Nevertheless, as the stricken lady lay unconscious on the floor, I knelt to attempt to treat her. But as I did, so her sneaky gangster husband raised a genuine Chippendale chair behind me to slam down on my head, only to find himself picked up bodily in the air by Gainor Stephen Crist, and held at a full arm's length aloft was crashed down upon Val's brand new gramophone, which unbelievably was playing a choral rendition of "Abide with Me," one of Gainor's most cherished songs. And the descent of this gent on the rotating record coincided with the last chord.

But Coughlin, dispossessed of his flat and beautiful and charming wife went searching all over Dublin to find me. I meanwhile in my Trinity rooms slept with a scalpel stuck in the side of my wardrobe, where I could grab it to stab any intruder were I to be jumped on in bed asleep. Finally Coughlin and I had it out in the middle of Duke Street when he ran into me in Davy Byrnes's pub one afternoon. The fisticuffs were brief as Coughlin, a light heavyweight, encumbered by his slower footwork, was unprepared for an unrelenting peppering of punches sent in combination from every direction. However, he was sporting enough to want to shake hands at the finish, and as a result of our fight we became firm friends. Coughlin then assuming a role of advocacy in selling my paintings and collecting the sixpences for my catalogues sold at my Dublin exhibitions. And this intrepid man, with his marvelous indifference to literature, painting and poetry and those who practiced such, was always ready for anything. As a result of searching for me all over town, he had been fired from his managerial job in a draper's shop and he now took up residence in Iveagh House, the indigent man's hostel frequented by Brendan Behan, where Coughlin was soon appointed to the position of monitor to prevent the various inmates so disposed, from pissing, shitting and vomiting all over the place.

"Mike, you've never seen such disgusting filthy behavior, with me having to contend with the likes of Brendan Behan coming in laggards drunk, roaring that his uncle wrote the national anthem and causing a near riot every night."

Coughlin often could be found, frequently alone in a nearby pub and surrounded by ancient, shawled old women cackling at his repartee as he drank red biddy, a lethally intoxicating brew which cheaply made one drunk but seemed to have no effect on Coughlin at all. Except that once following a long afternoon of drinking this concoction, he stood that evening on a streetcorner outside a restaurant where he had just consumed his favorite repast of a large mixed grill consisting of steak, blood pudding, bacon and sausages covered with fried eggs, and smoking a cigar, he suddenly disgorged the entire contents of his stomach into the gutter. But then wiping his mouth with his handkerchief he kept tucked up his shirt cuff, he re-entered the restaurant to sit down and order and devour the entirety of the meal he had just upchucked. Just, as he said, to teach his stomach a lesson.

There was a curious secrecy in these strange pubs lying to the west of Grafton Street where Coughlin's laughter could be heard thundering out through the pub walls and down these narrow side streets and alleys of Dublin's Coombe. This roaring man, who ignored fate and who loved big tits and hips on women. Who wanted children and an incentive in life and who could and did, to the delight of slum urchins, stand on the corner of Harry and Grafton streets, and by striking a match, explode his own farts in flame. And whose later London exploits and dodgy activities amassed a fortune, making him the most sought-after gentleman Scotland Yard had come across for years. And it was Valentine Horatio Coughlin who was the one last to be seen standing, waving to me as I looked out the porthole window of my motorbird as it taxied out on the runway to take off on the first leg of my ultimate trip back to the United States. And that figure who remained a staunch and faithful friend stood there till we were aloft and he had become a dot to fade out of sight.

The ancient Isle of Man, ninety or so miles northeast from Dublin, was reached in four and a half hours by "fast and luxurious turbine steamships," as these Manx vessels were described when advertised in the 1920s. Or in just thirty minutes by fast propeller plane. The island, a 227-square-mile volcanic outcropping in the Irish Sea, stretched its elongated shape twenty miles north and south and east to west, was fifteen miles wide at its broadest point. Approached by sea or air, it was often wreathed in mist to the extent that one would not know it was there. As indeed many shipwrecked wayfarers over the centuries found. And if flying by plane, one tended to try to get aboard first to sit in the less vulnerable back seats, in case there was a crash. For with any sort of gale blowing, the crosswinds would buffet and rock an aircraft to such degree that flights were often enough aborted and would overfly to Liverpool. Thus giving one an extra sense of Manx homecoming upon finding one's feet again safely on the ground.

As the month of October approached on the island, it was becoming out of season for holiday-making visitors and sparse of its summer hordes. The great long crescent promenade of Douglas, with its emptied boardinghouses, was a ghostly vision facing out over the beach and bay to the open sea. The proprietors of the hotels had departed on their own holidays and were off to such exotic places as the south of France or to take sunny cruises to distant climes. And upon this blustery day, my plane buffeted by the crosswinds finally bounced down on the runway. And a romance of a sort began with this ancient island which would endure for many years.

With what I had so far written of the manuscript The Ginger Man, and with Valerie and her mother and Madge, who looked after things in the house, I now took up residence in The Anchorage, Port-e-Vullin. And while we awaited the imminent birth of an heir, I was given a narrow bedroom in which to write in this elaborate stone house, a bastion of nearly fortified proportions, perched with its palm trees on a rugged rocky coast, its garden terraces shielding it from the sea. With whatever thoughts I must have had, I sat at a table at the window diagonally facing easterly across Ramsey Bay. From here, in the direction of Liverpool seventy-five miles away, I could stare out over the sea garden and the strand of beach. Looking up from one's desk, there was always the constant back-and-forth stream of seagulls to be seen as they traveled to and from their nests tucked into the sheer cliffs of

Maughold Head two miles farther east along this deserted coast. In immediate view was a promontory called Gro Ago, a heathery, wind-swept headland jutting into the sea with the ruins of an old mine shaft dug down through it to the shore. But for the great black-backed gulls slowly gliding by, there could be nothing lonelier to watch out upon.

By evenings, with the tide out, I walked the stony seaweed-strewn beach, or with the tide in, would climb up the slipway at the side of the house to stroll by the high road out toward Maughold Head. And no matter how inclement or chill the night winds, my battle resolve was always burning to next day swell the words of *The Ginger Man.* I learned how to light a Manx fire out of little mushrooms of newspaper. Mrs. Heron, my mother-in-law, was a stylish and handsome lady and a star hostess, and one's social life began to involve a plethora of planters, and settlers returned from Africa and the disappearing British colonies, and retired brigadiers and majors from the army. These, along with an odd rich doctor, dentist, wool or cotton merchant from the British Midlands, attended to teas and frequent cocktail parties. And one found oneself surrounded by those suspicious of my doubtful occupa-tion of painter and would-be author and, indeed, that I might be a fortune hunter waiting for my rich mother-in-law to die. Ah, but what a prize bunch of pompous, smug and disagreeably fawning bastards some of them could be. However, my untiring willingness to listen to their quite marvelously snobbish and very English bullshit and to inquire of them to spout even more of it, plus my relentless Trinity anglicized politeness, seemed to allay their suspicions of my fraudulent intent, and it made me temporarily acceptable as I passed out the pink gins and sherries and malt whiskey. In fact, I was so generous in this that it could have been that I became to be begrudgingly tolerated if not a little bit liked.

"Ah, brigadier, do, you absolutely must let me top you up. Jolly ruddy old cold gale blowing tonight, you know."

"Well, why not, pop a driblet in."

The room in which I wrote had a musty smell, which was later discovered to be caused by dry rot in the floor. Not surprising, as in the heavier seas the waves crashed against the garden rampart, trem-bling the ground and sent the sea spray up against the walls and win-dows of the house. On a clear day, it was possible from a suitably high point to see eastward to the Cumbria coastline to where were situated the villages of Egremont, St. Bees and more ominously, Seascale, an atomic power station. But life-threatening nuclear matters were only just then beginning to creep up the world panic agenda. With this medley of sights out the window, and on bright white new sheets of paper, I was now rewriting the pages that Brendan Behan had read and upon which he made his editorial marks. And to my surprise and slightly begrudging respect, I was finding that I was in fact compelled to follow each one.

Now modestly transfused by a windfall of money from the sale of the cottage at Kilcoole, my existence was accorded some of the affluence of my bachelor university days. But I was not to know that these few months passing were to be a rare period of reasonable contentment in my life. If my optimism at the time wasn't overwhelming, it certainly was enough to keep alive my expectant vision that fortune and acclaim awaited me and *The Ginger Man* in the United States.

But as a young man coming of age in America, to some considerable degree I had already tasted and experienced the conditions in which success was enjoyed. I was born in a Brooklyn hospital while my parents lived at 8 Willow Place in a period house in Brooklyn Heights. This once aristocratic area, whose residents, according to the 1939 *New York City Guide* "set the tone in manners and customs for the elite of the entire city." However, from the hospital one was then taken to live on top of one of the highest hills in the Bronx in an area called Wakefield. But from here at the age of seven, my parents, concerned that our welfare might be improved, moved a mere mile away across the valley of the Bronx River to a small community called Woodlawn. I further grew up here, called Jim by my father, Junior by my mother, sister and brother and Pat by my friends. Having been born in New York and reached the age of eighteen in the King of Cities, my teenage years were spent in a curious fairyland of privilege. Some of it attributable to Woodlawn but most of it unique to a strange room five floors up on the northeast corner of Seventh Avenue and Fifty-eighth Street. And better known as the boxing room of the New York Athletic Club. This was a curious outpost of influence not to say glamour and the memory of it helped maintain my indifference to such lack in Europe, and now at the time of my return to America, one still imagined some of this privilege left.

The title of my novel at this time of writing it on the Isle of Man was the enlarged initials of *S.D.* on a cardboard cover, to represent Sebastian Dangerfield. The many titles I'd thought of, such as *The News of Death, His Hands Refuse to Labor, The Red Sin,* seemed woefully inappropriate. And in my desperation, I was even trying one in Irish. Each morning I tapped away on my ancient steam typewriter, writing sometimes three and occasionally five pages a day as morning, afternoon and evening rolled pleasantly by, with the rest of the world elsewhere across the water, the island being altogether an idyllically isolated place to put typewriter key to paper. And that was my daily work.

My leisure each day was a brisk walk taken on the heathery headlands. In the long drawing room in front of the log fire, Earl Grey tea served every day at four and sherry at seven before dinner. The savory delicacy of potted meat was to spread on toast for breakfast. And there was always my favorite and lonely act of car drives to deserted distant beaches of the island for solitary picnics by the gray waves. Upon the sand and pebbles of a shore, where perhaps no one had been for years, a little fire was made from driftwood upon which to cook sausages, sizzle bacon and toast rolls. It was almost as if one did this in defiance of the island's utter desertedness where by winter the few pubs along lonely roads would blaze their every light outside without a single customer inside. But as darkness fell on these desolate beaches, there was a ghostly joy to sit in the warmth of the flames, the winds growing chillier and the Irish Sea washing up on the shore. And these moments were almost the last spell of complete peace and contentment I was ever to know in my life.

In the front inland side of the Anchorage garden, palm trees grew, and equally pleasant, a rushing stream and waterfall went by the side of the house splashing into the sea, where swans in their lifelong companionships came to stand and forage in the fresh water. One would see these serene great birds in the distance come sailing around the headland from farther along the coast, where they might have been lurking in nearby Ramsey town's harbor. This small port had an almost medieval air about it with its pubs along the quay, where crews of small fishing vessels drank a brew of fine ale from a local brewery in Castletown in the south of the island. With the pubs opening onto the mooring quay, one would see sailors reel out tipsy to board their vessels to sail on the high tide. Your local aristocracy confining themselves to the sedate Mitre Hotel on Main Street where sherry and pink gins were served through a hatch into its mahogany-paneled and refined sitting room. My favorite walk was along the piers to watch cargoes load and unload from the small coasters plying the port. And where one would watch navvies, whose faces had become familiar, down in the darkness of the ship's hold, sweating as they would tirelessly shovel coal.

In Ramsey by appointment, I would go up a narrow flight of stairs over a chemist's shop to sit in a strange high chair in the center of a room, where my hair was cut by my first ever female barber. A young girl who alternatively would caress and then couldn't help giggling as she managed to nip my ears as well as hair. Many of the shops could not sell you things you saw in the windows because they were there for decoration, and it would often be the only sample they had. But otherwise, the island, cut off from the world and surrounded by its high cliffs and the surf pounding upon its shores, was a magic little paradise. Its loneliness and isolation gave one an astonishing peace of mind. But even so, one day walking an empty mile-long strand, I saw a solitary man approaching from the other end of the beach. He was a gentleman called Cyril Ladyman, who, when he greeted me in the middle of this lonely foreshore, said that he had been unable to sleep the entire night before because he worried about the over-population of the world, and his voice was deeply concerned as he said,

"We will soon be sitting on each other's laps."

I made visits to the wool mills in a glen in the center of the island, where I bought bolts of Manx tweed. These I brought to Kaighen, a tailor who had a hut on the side of the road just outside a little village called Kirk Michael. Driving there, one would always admire the shadowy beauty of a canopy of trees which extended along this piece of road which went past the Palace of the Bishop of Sodor and Man. On these chillier autumn days, I'd find Kaighen busy in his small hut, a wood-burning stove keeping it snug and warm and a pair of irons always hot to put creases in the cloth. His assistant sat in a medieval manner, cross-legged up on a high bench in the corner, stitching in linings and sewing buttonholes. Kaighen, who permanently held his head cocked over to the side, was always delighted with his tailoring prospect.

"It's going to be very nice now, Mr. Donleavy, very nice. We're going to make a good job of it. It's going to fall very nicely now. A very nice job."

To avoid undue flapping about the lower leg, my instructions were to have the trouser narrow and no slit in the back of the jacket so that when out walking I avoided chill breezes from the rear. And Kaighen, not more than a year later when I had returned from the U.S. and gone to see him again, danced around with jollity and laughter, telling me that according to *Tailor and Cutter,* the journal to the trade, the very cut of my suits he'd made was exactly what was now a year later regarded as the height of London fashion. If it wasn't the case that fashion was imitating me, I simply hadn't the heart to tell Kaighen, so delighted was he far away from the big outside world in his small hut at the side of the road.

But in this interlude before setting sail for New York, all was not idyllic on the island. And I'm sure my irrepressible ego, expressed enough in the certainty about the work I was writing, was occasionally too much for my mother-in-law, Nora Heron. And more than enough for some of her stuffier guests. And one night, following a meal preceded by three sherries and accompanied by a rare claret and completed with several brandies and coffee, something snapped. I obviously had too much to drink, but also I may have had some strange premonition that *The Ginger Man* would not achieve the prediction and hoped-for great things that my boasting announced. Or that the work did not live up to the confidence I proclaimed which could sometimes be heard through the three-foot-thick walls of the Anchorage and out over the waves. But as these were battling times, one already knew, as a painter artist in Dublin, how to wage a war of survival, and I was instantly intolerable of anyone's doubt, and I also, unforgivably blunt to the skeptical, suggested to Mrs. Heron,

"Madam, the only reason you, your name or your family or anything to do with you or them, will ever be remembered by the world is because of your association with me."

These awfully unnice words, as deserving as they may have been on the occasion, were in fact said to a very nice lady, whose guest I was and who in fact had helpfully bought a few of my paintings and remained, at least on the surface, tolerant of my being a painter and of my attempt to now be a writer. For she once proudly brought her own son Michael's poetry to show her Yorkshire merchant husband. And he took one look at these accomplished lyrical efforts and loudly declared he wasn't spending money to educate his son at the best schools to waste his time writing utter drivel and rubbish like poetry.

But later in the evening of my drinking and holding an honesty night, Mrs. Heron fled to an outside social occasion, and, Valerie and I alone in the house, I suddenly rushed up the Anchorage stairs to my workroom, crashed open the door and grabbed the manuscript up from the desk. Coming out on the staircase landing, I cursed and tore at the pages, scattering them down the stairs and sinking my clawed hands into more and more of the manuscript as I ripped them out, dismembering and throwing the sheets down the stairs, followed by the manuscript itself. And as I descended the Wilton-carpeted steps, Valerie rushed to stop me, grabbing to save the pages. And being then my one and only manuscript, which I was starting to tear into tiny pieces, had it not been for this dear woman,

I might
Have scattered
The Ginger Man
Out over
The Irish Sea

12

ON A COOL, CLOUDY OCTOBER DAY, with westerly winds blowing gently across the island, we were having a picnic on Niarbyl headland from which one could look westerly across to the Mourne Mountains of Ireland. Valerie, as we lunched on the grass, suddenly said, "I think we should get back to the Anchorage as soon as possible." Guessing at what I thought was the shortest way, I drove at breakneck speed on the mostly deserted Manx roads, some of which I knew well enough, but now, in this emergency, had to chance my luck. Taking a route most famed for being part of the motorcycle tourist racecourse, known as the Mountain Road, which cut diagonally across the island and which, at least by direction, was the shortest route north back to Ramsey.

Arriving with immense relief and only in the nick of time at Port-e-Vullin, I occasionally sat and variously paced the long L-shaped drawing room downstairs, Dr. Jones having arrived the two and a quarter miles from Ramsey. And just as it was growing dark out over the seascape, and not much more than an hour following our picnic, our heir, a son, Philip, was born October 20 in what was known as the Anchorage's pink bedroom. Mrs. Heron placing news of Philip's birth in the *Times* of London, as in those socially fastidious days one was not really born until that had been done. And which immediately elicited mail order brochures on contraception.

The autumn weeks now went by watching the great yellow-headed gannets, their wings tipped with black, dive from the sky and go deep beneath the waves in a plume of spray. In westerly gales, the fishing boats would collect out in the shelter of Ramsey Bay, their lights at night gently bobbing up and down on the heavy swells. With mornings abed over breakfast of potted meat on toasted stone-ground whole-

wheat bread and Kenya coffee, one optimistically read in copies of
Country Life, with its pages of estates and country houses for sale,
always imagining one might be looking for something suitable. Philip
swaddled in thick wraps daily slept under a palm tree on the terrace
overlooking the sea. And before one sailed to the U.S.A. out of Cobh
on the good ship *America,* the only interruption of my stay on the
island was making a trip to London on what seemed to be a grand
celebratory mission, with my pockets filled with pound notes. Desmond MacNamara had made me a small replica of the blessed Oliver
Plunket's head, who in later becoming a saint, one always liked to feel
came about through Dangerfield's frequent intercessions for delivery
from crises in *The Ginger Man.* Indeed, later some seafarers in a storm
claimed that invoking Oliver Plunket's intercession, as Dangerfield
did, actually saved their lives. At any rate, it was in the contemplation
of such things that one missed the chaotic companionship of Crist and
the internecine perambulations of gossip, backbiting, and betrayal. All
solved by the dawning of love again in the lives of those others who
had escaped Dublin to see if the more civilized world of London could
improve their prospects, especially financial and where new betrayals
of their new love were ardently afoot.

"Mike. Come. London is groaning with lust."

This was an oft repeated refrain I had heard and was to hear from
Gainor. And as I headed off to Liverpool, taking the steam packet boat
slicing through the waves, with mooing cattle aboard, I imagined Crist
to be in even greater love and financial embroilments than he had been
in Dublin. Meanwhile, the steamer headed up the Mersey and docked
under the great outstretched wings of the birds on top of the Liver
building. And I boarded the train that went out from the big black
station of Lime Street and on between blackened walls and through
the bleak, gray industrial wastelands of the Midlands. Arriving in my
Manx tweeds, and with chamois gloves agrip of my luggage, I holed up
in the Hotel Russell, this great massive structure in Bedford Square not
far from Euston Station, where I had many a time arrived and departed
over the years. Often choosing to stay in the district from which
I would invariably wander southwestward into Soho, Mayfair and
beyond.

Gainor Stephen Crist and Desmond MacNamara and those folk
associated with same were on the other side of London in the area of
Earl's Court and Lexham Gardens. I taxied across and descended
down into MacNamara's dungeonlike quarters, where Gainor would
arrive by day to lie down supine on the floor and eat the cast-off bacon

rinds and other crusts thrown his way while waiting for news of his father's death in Dayton, Ohio, who, in the final days of a long illness, was now sinking rapidly. As a diagnostician, he had been a physician of some repute, known throughout the Midwest and was rumored to be a reasonably wealthy man. He was married to his third wife, his second wife being Gainor's mother. If a third wife did not leave much anticipation of considerable riches, there was nevertheless thought to be sufficient of an inheritance for Gainor to clear all his debts and have enough left to provide for some years of future comfort. And all would be better than well upon his father's demise.

During this distant deathwatch, Gainor's circumstances were at their lowest. Beset as he was on every side by seemingly unsolvable domestic matters. And with his life kept more in suspended animation than ever, he was hand-rubbingly, overwhelmingly glad to see me and drink bitter beer in the most momentous of pub crawls. Which included such shabbily exotic places as the Gargoyle and Mandrake clubs in Soho. But the first visit was to a pub known as the Bear Pit, so named because of its outside circular iron-fenced enclosure, which appeared only minus a bear within its confines. This pub was closest to where Desmond MacNamara lived, and upon whom all manner of people without a place to stay descended. MacNamara, with his strange leprechaunish image, was a lifelong vegetarian as well as one of Dublin's great sculptors, papier-mâché artists and puppeteers. He was also a worldwide center of communication, rumor and gossip, none of which was rumor or gossip but all of which was invariably true. And could give you as much of this truth as you might want or were able to digest. Always accompanied by sage remarks to guide the unwary. He remained one of the few people upon whom Behan, in the remainder of his short life, would always rely.

At the time of my visit to MacNamara's studio, his walls were variously decorated with his papier-mâché heads of friends accompanied by their sculptured winged male erected organs of regeneration. He was then in the process of making costumes for the Abbey Theatre in Dublin and had a room full of outerwear that could disguise you as a donkey, monkey, elephant or kangaroo. Suits of this last beast being the most easily fitted to our size, we set off in such on our pub crawl, courtesy of the grand arrival of none other than the bold-spirited Valentine Coughlin. And now scented with fragrances, cutting a dazzling figure, sporting his bowler hat, black kidskin gloves and rolled brolly. However, he remembered the many slights he'd received from such as the poetic intelligentsia back in Dublin, and such, if they persisted in seeking Coughlin's company, were given short shrift.

"Fuck off now, you of little faith, who wouldn't speak to me when I was cleaning the pissoirs back in the Iveagh House in Dublin and are now trying to stick your noses up my rich rear end, out of which are coming nuggets of gold."

As we drove off in his sumptuous limousine, Valentine, a kangaroo on each side of him, lounged back in the soft upholstery and roared with laughter. He was in cahoots with an equally elegant Pakistani gentleman who was never without his own gloves or his platinum-topped sword stick. Together, the latter and Coughlin had now, in a few short months, set up shell companies in Switzerland, where they pretended to export nylons free of one hundred percent duty and tax but which they in fact sent in lorry loads to be sold in southern coastal towns like Bournemouth and Brighton. And once, in emergency command of a lorry load himself, Coughlin hit a cow wandering out of a field, the lorry careering off the road to land in and become stuck in a ditch. Too late in the darkness to extricate it, Coughlin applied to and got the local constabulary to come and stand guard over it through the night while Val, one of Scotland Yard's most wanted men, retired to the nearest pub hotel to celebrate the evening away with the village locals.

It was a night of euphoria. Until one of the last pub visits came in Soho. And produced the grand finale. Where in some inebriation and following the singing of songs out of the kangaroo mouths there came some anti-British remarks. In spite of our little group being generally Anglophiles, exception was taken to cries of "No joy, no juice, you pigs no use." And these words seemingly finding us accused of being Oxford intellectuals. A momentous pub battle erupted. I got clonked on the head, remembering only that there seemed to be a staircase that descended directly into the pub and those who tried to get up it to escape the fray all came rapidly airborne back down. Attired in his kangaroo at the top of the steps stood Eddie Connell, who'd spent ten years in prison for trying to blow up the Hammersmith Bridge over the Thames. But even he was then begrudgingly pro-British, being at the time the lamplighter, who by evening lit the gas lamps on the approaches to Kensington Palace. And he was, later in life, like a few other IRA men of the time, to become a civil servant and a respected member of the British establishment.

Unconscious bodies lay over the pub floor, including, for a few moments my own. I lost my passport. And just in time before the police arrived, the little group of kangaroo-clad gentlemen were chauffeured by Coughlin to be treated in St. Mary Abbot's Hospital, where, with members of the hospital staff as an audience, much mirth ensued. I later found myself awaking somewhere in Gunterstone Road in West Kensington in the company of Crist, various ladies and several hungover IRA men. My next task being to submit myself to the American embassy for a new passport, where one underwent a lengthy interrogation by a careful young consul who viewed my bearded person with considerable suspicion and who, among other questions upon hearing I served in the U.S. Navy, asked with even greater suspicion for my naval serial number, which I said I could not remember. Whereupon I was immediately informed,

"No one ever forgets their naval serial number."

One sat now feeling being the communist spy the consul thought I was. And also now uncheerful with the prospect of having my trip canceled and my return to the U.S.A. long delayed. And then suddenly as I sat there, ready to berate this prying gentleman too ardent at his job, a number came sailing totally out of the deep blue into mind.

"Nine zero nine, five nine, zero eight."

"Ah. Yes. And let me see. Yes. Numbers in that range would just fit in with the time you enlisted in the navy."

As it turned out, I much later discovered my thoughtful IRA acquaintances had found my passport but thought it more valuable for other uses. And now following one's fresh windswept life in Ireland and the Isle of Man, London made one feel claustrophobic with its endless communities of terraced houses and streets, which lay flatly under oppressive gray skies and loomed out of its smoky mists and fogs. I even found relief in the relative openness of Kensington High Street, one of London's wider boulevards, where, following attendance at Crist's insistence at a pub called The Live and Let Live, we finally walked to this thoroughfare for lunch and spoke for hours together over our brandy and coffee. We went to sit too in the National Gallery in Trafalgar Square, where Gainor related the debacles of his recent times and love trysts in Dublin. I remembered calling to the last house he lived in up a cul-de-sac in Glenageary, where one walked in the unlocked front door. And finding it with no one home, forlornly empty and deserted. A John Ryan drawing of me still hanging on the wall in the hall. Stacks of dirty dishes all over the kitchen. Soiled clothes, books and papers strewn everywhere. A chill damp throughout the house. A feeling of loss overcoming one, sensing that the life lived up in this little cul-de-sac had come to its end. And making Ireland seem a lonely, abandoned grave of dreams.

But during my stay in London, it happened. The long, patiently awaited event. Gainor's father was dead. And at the same time this news reached him, Gainor also received by special delivery a long letter which Gainor's father wrote in his last days. This when eagerly opened meticulously recounted a litany of Gainor's indiscretions, and his improvidence, misdemeanors, misdeeds and misbehavior over the years. In the summation of which Gainor's indifference to his father's authority was singled out. And which therefore, for Gainor's own good, it had been reluctantly decided to leave Gainor nothing in his will. Gainor slowly and stoically tore the letter into the very tiniest of tiny pieces, retaining a small pile in the palm of his hand which were ceremoniously put into his mouth, chewed and swallowed, as he murmured in Spanish,

"Hasta la muerte, todo es vida."

Even this fatal and drastic news seemed not to totally discourage Gainor. In fact it seemed to be an even greater reason for him to soldier on. And I remembered that Gainor told me that three things had been traumatic in his life. Once when he had badly broken his arm, which when briefly shown to his father hurrying to an appointment, it was suggested he should go have a hot bath. Gainor later having to be brought to hospital with a serious fracture. Then as a young boy he found himself waiting frightened in a dark hospital corridor outside a private room, wherein his mother had just died. Reluctant to go in, Gainor's father made him enter and then to go and kiss his mother's cold lips as she lay dead in her hospital bed. An only child of this beautiful woman, tears came to Gainor's eyes, relating this haunting moment of his life. I learned of another trauma when walking with Crist to the west of Ireland when he stopped abruptly and asked me what was that thing on the road ahead. I went on farther to see, and returned to say it was a dead bird. Gainor then detoured off the road through the fields to circumvent the spot, and soaking his feet slogging through a bog. He then told me that when growing up in Dayton he had been sent on his birthday what he thought was a birthday present. A beautifully wrapped shoe box which had come in the mail. Unwrapping the anonymously sent gift and lifting off the cover, inside the box, and carefully swaddled in white, was a dead sparrow.

February in this fatal year of 1952 and before the disappointment not expected to come, Valerie, Philip and I got on the plane for Dublin to stay at the Shelbourne Hotel. And in those days, although beginning to dwindle in number, there were still a few of your hysterically pukka and tweedy, horsey folk about. Some so rigidly Anglo-Irish that they resembled human hawthorns strutting the lobby. Where hunt members, their vowels ringing out, would read off the fox hunting fixtures posted on the hotel lobby walls. At eleven-fifteen on this morning, I took champagne in the quiet peace of the flowered, upholstered residential lounge. An old friend of Trinity days, Jim Walsh, turned up. A six-foot four-inch gentleman of wry humor, he was an abstemious Trinity scholar, who, from the dining hall pulpit, rattled off Latin grace before evening commons, his one free meal a day. He otherwise kept himself alive counting out so many cornflakes each morning for breakfast. And curing a stammer with a splendid English accent, there was always a steely hard truth underlying the words he spoke. Then Ernest Gebler came into town in his MG sports car, and we dined under the Shelbourne's crystal chandeliers. Now, with all decisions past and committed to one's fate, and despite Gebler's warning words, America was already looming in the mind as a bright and beckoningly shiny place across the sea.

Meanwhile, Behan on his meandering travels en route through England and trying in some way to save fifteen pounds on a fare to Paris, spent a week remanded behind the grim, forbidding walls of Lewes Jail in Sussex. And upon his appearance in court, a lawyer found to represent him waxed eloquent to the judge in his defense, saying he was a model responsible citizen, successful poet, and a promising writer who contributed to Irish radio and published in Irish newspapers and was as a budding dramatist even being considered as a potential contributor to the BBC. Then, as Behan's counsel was about to launch into further and better particulars concerning his client's cultural bona fides, he was interrupted by the bench, the judge remarking,

"Yes, your model responsible citizen client served eight years in custody in 1940, three years in 1946, sentenced to death in 1945 in Ireland and commuted to twelve years penal servitude. Twice ordered out of Britain by the home secretary. Served twelve days for drunk and disorderly last month, etcetera, etcetera. I must say to you counsel that your model citizen client sounds to me a very dangerous man indeed. I order fifteen pounds fine and that he be immediately taken to the Dover boat and deported and advise that he does not return to this country."

Of course, Behan, no longer persona non grata, and proud of his Borstal and prison days, did return to England to be celebrated and feted throughout the land. But this was to be a few years on yet from the moment approaching now when I was departing from this Dublin upon whose gray granite, wet streets one had walked many a mile, detouring into battles of hate and entwining in moments of love. And one was now recalling the letters I had received from a fellow American Trinity student, who early disappeared off on the grand tour and who wrote from the deepest jungles of Africa, imploring I not return to the United States. But the die was cast by tickets and trunks. And by my family in the northern reaches of the Bronx, already awaiting their wayward, iconoclastic son, whose outspoken letters in order to be read to others had long now had to be censored. Even to the point of my father taking a scissors to excise the more defiantly dissident words.

And not
For the first
Nor last time
Would my averments
Be so treated

13

THE DRUMS WERE BEATING. America each day across the big water coming closer. That home sweet home where all was well, which was God-blessed and thought-shining in its glory to the West. Where all the good things were against the bad. Where our lives were early lived with radiant promise ahead to be fulfilled. Where one might open one's heart to what magic, what joy. Where doctors would do all to save a life by merely putting their stethoscopes over one's wallet. Where fairness and humanity could be found in unexpected places. And there was endless room to move across the valleys, mountains, deserts and plains of this massively great victorious America in whose defense our fists flew to avenge on the spot any insult to its flag or people. And yet at this time came ominous messages that one saw in letters being sent out from that land. That something was amiss. That a secretly pernicious evil had already taken hold and was beginning to pervade from coast to coast. But in remembering America from an earlier time, one did not wholly take in this certain hint of warning.

My pictures, watercolors and oils had preceded me to the boat in a big black box, traveling down that lonely, boggy coastland past the little cottage and barn where they had been painted. From the Shelbourne we went by train to Cork, changing there to proceed the few miles farther out along to the harbor and weatherbeaten town of Cobh, where we stayed the night in one of your better hotels ready to board the *America* in the morning.

Dining that evening in the hotel, and served dinner by a waiter who ceremoniously swayed back and forth as he placed our plates, Valerie sitting across from me, having just left Philip in his carrycot asleep in the bedroom, suddenly had a premonition that something was wrong and jumped up and rushed off. To find that the maid, turning down the bed and drawing the curtains, had thrown a raincoat over the carrycot completely covering it and baby Philip, who would have in a few more minutes been smothered while he slept. It was Valerie's last contact with Ireland, a place she never felt entirely at home in, and despite the general friendliness given her charm and beauty, she had to remain always conscious of the slight hostility to her Englishness. It was too to be our last association with Ireland, the Emerald Isle, as a family.

Some folk oblivious of the artistic problem of producing aesthetic balance regarded such a canine picture as obscene. Happily, not all were so dismayed, for such as my publisher Seymour Lawrence sported one of my priapic dogs on the wall of his publishing office in Boston.

By tender, we traveled out on a chill, breezy morning to the black steep sides of the *America* anchored in the bay of Cobh, the last port of call of the ill-fated *Titanic* before it sank out on the cold Atlantic. Indulging a slight inclination for privilege and at the same time exercising one's conservative nature in practical matters, we traveled cabin-class. And I was to recall that in coming to Ireland initially, one would have done so first-class, due to that strange confine, the boxing room of the New York Athletic Club, which was frequented by many a distinguished naval gentleman. For in hearing that I was off to Ireland, Commodore Harry Manning gave me a note to take down to Broadway when booking my ticket. As I did so, and never having been on a liner before, I asked the clerk what difference the commodore's note made. The eager-to-please man seemed surprised that I was unaware that, as Commodore Manning was at the time the ship's captain, I would be given the very best accommodation aboard. However, at the time there occurred a prolonged shipping strike and, following a series of false starts over a period of three days, I ended up flying to Ireland instead.

But now on my return after five years of not having paid dues to keep up my membership of the club, there was no Harry Manning to alert. And boarding this ship this windswept day, something alien and yet familiar was already dawning. In the bustle of the main deck, as passengers were directed toward their cabins, the efficient indifference of the American way of life was already evident where one's vowels and demeanor were less an advantage than one's money. One could not say this trip on the liner *America* was the most pleasant of all voyages, especially as I was now encountering the American ethic of making sure selfless service was only a thing encountered during the last hours of the voyage when attendance was danced upon one and an expectant hand would then come reaching out for a tip.

In the ensuing years I would make this ocean voyage many times, always it seemed while standing chill and windswept on the deck and always feeling the drama of seeing ahead that unforgettable sight on the last day, of those faint, thin stalks of buildings arise on the skyline, and glinting out of a gray wintry ocean. As the tugboats maneuvered the mass of this great liner into its Hudson River dock, I saw down on the quayside my mother looking up, Valerie remarking with surprise that she had no idea that my mother could appear so good-looking. Philip and Valerie were taken to my father's car while I oversaw the first of one's American problems, which could have, with just a nuance, turned into something violent and ominous. My father had sent an immensely big and strong friend from the fire department to get my luggage, and not being an accredited stevedore we came close to an altercation on the dock, especially as the man my father sent to help seemed to be the only one strong enough to shift my large crate of paintings. It was my first experience of my anglicized accent and the reasonableness one attempted to exude with such vowels, helping me to delicately navigate through the blunt rudeness of New York City. Which after Ireland and the Isle of Man suddenly seemed a place of violent chaotic mayhem, the desperate purpose of which was to make someone's next dime or dollar. And to direct such attempt toward yours truly.

My parents lived in a small, mostly white Protestant enclave called Woodlawn, described again in the *New York City Guide* of 1939 as "a middle class community on the far northern marches, where New York

The house in Woodlawn
where I lived from an early
age. Behind the three front
second-floor windows, I wrote
many pages of the manuscript
of THE GINGER MAN and
where Crist would come
with a dram of whiskey to
hand to read my notes over
my shoulder to him when
I'd become mute.

At the side of the house in
Woodlawn, my sister, Rita,
employed at the time by the
United States Steel Corporation. She was later to become
a distinguished professor in
the field of education.

City cedes to Yonkers and Mount Vernon." The area consisted of a triangular tract of hardly more than a couple of hundred acres cross-sectioned by nine streets north and south and seven streets east and west. Cut off from the rest of New York City by Van Cortlandt Park, a thousand acres to the west, which had been a former hunting ground of the Mohican Indians, Woodlawn possessed a degree of isolation, for, to the east flowed the Bronx River through its linear park, and to the south lay the sylvan acres of Woodlawn Cemetery dotted with its graves, exotic statuary, and grandiose mausoleums. This burial ground, already famed as the final resting place of some of America's robber barons as well as their socially registered descendants, was not only a splendid sanctuary for them but also for many birds and small mammals.

With its main street of Katonah Avenue, its two schools and five churches, its four or five bars and two sweetshops, where the kids congregated for their pineapple sodas, the community of Woodlawn resembled a small midwestern town and certainly would join any list of favored places to spend a childhood on the continent of North America. And typical of such places, among the first things I learned taking up residence in this white house on top of the hill on East 238th Street and where I mostly grew up, was that my father thought that instead of exhibiting and selling paintings or writing a novel, I should take the city's civil service exams and see if I could become a fireman. Later I also heard that he felt the Union Jack should be raised to fly above the house as not only my accent but my behavior was now distinctly British. But my intrepid mother was of a tolerantly different mind and had confidence in my intentions and let it be known that she would back whatever I wanted to do. With some surprise, I learned that she had kept up my membership to the New York Athletic Club all these years, just as she had my government life insurance, which one held in the navy. Her principle in all things seemed to be consistent persistence in whatever endeavor one undertook and never to waver or give up.

But I was soon to find that outside my mother and Valerie, there were to be few believers, supporters or benefactors. And as the cars endlessly traveled the highways, dawning was the quick realization that the odds were mountainously stacked against me and that my naivete had overwhelmed reality. I had already tasted fame and publication of a sort in the small art world of Dublin, but it was now eminently clear that nowhere or anywhere was there anyone waiting across this massive nation to put a laurel wreath on the head of any would-be genius full of heartfelt intentions to have his voice at least heard if not to be rich and famous. And failure could mean only two things, death or escape. For one thing was absolutely certain, that even in the unlikely event that I would be offered a job, I was not about to conform to the American mealymouthed ethic of corporate employment in any shape, manner or form. Or to tolerate, even for an instant, opposition to the work I wrote. And as I sat down now once more to again peck away at the pages, I felt that each snapping down of a typewriter key landed like a hammered nail, sealing a coffin in which was my past life of having been born and raised an American.

For having grown up in this country's culture, success always seemed to be some sudden thing that happened and all one had to do was push a certain combination of buttons that set you on your way to permanent glory. And with the right smile, the right clothes, the right friends, you just waited. But it was understood that you never made any conscious effort to succeed. That one would finally be apprised of a door through which you stepped into that place of heaven, where, as your face was lit by flashbulbs, one-hundred-dollar bills endlessly floated down on your head to pile embarrassingly up around you. And that you had to kick your claustrophobic way out of the heap.

But as an old prep school friend, Tom Gill, with whom I frequented this room, would say to me when, during the enjoyment of some exotic New York City delight, and when he felt a sobering moment or two of profundity was called for, "Pat, we live under the rich man's yoke."

But I might have been suffering even more culture shock than Valerie who at least had had the previous confrontation of having been evacuated to Canada during the Second World War where she had tasted a near version of middle-class American life. I wrote back to Europe letters to such as Crist with reports he found frightening, which described what seemed then a changing society. The once thought humane fairness of American life was undergoing an insidious corruption. Leaving the intelligent and sensitive isolated and counted fewer and fewer in number. Random violence, of gang warfare and zip guns, which was once confined to known dangerous parts of the city, was spreading. My father, watching television evenings, spoke of killing time. My brother Thomas, whom we called T.J., and who had not yet come to Ireland, I now met after many years, seemed grossly unhappy. He had taken temporarily to being a salesman of cemetery plots under the guidance of a senior, but through his lack of conviction that a preneed grave was a priority in life, he miserably failed to make a sale. And upon the one occasion that he might have done, he was ruthlessly usurped by his senior. A demonstration of our growing-up trusting backgrounds of fair play making us vulnerable to the unscrupulous. And meanwhile a man called Senator McCarthy, with accusations of communism, was seeking out and terrorizing liberals throughout the land.

In this old white house, I stationed myself upstairs in the shadowy middle bedroom, where I occupied a small desk. Following breakfast each morning I would start to write at around ten and continue until about one o'clock. Dressing then in one of my Manx tweed suits, I would take the bus, which ran along the main street of Katonah Avenue at the bottom of the hill. The bus then went past the high black railings of the Woodlawn Cemetery, a fence that took four years to paint, and when finished it was time to start again. Turning left, the bus continued along a road over which trolley tracks once ran. For nearly a mile or two in every direction with no habitation of any sort, this area was one of the loneliest and most bereft areas in the Bronx. It was along the cemetery railings that a meeting took place which involved the Lindbergh baby, one of America's most famed kidnappings. And alighting at the main gates of the cemetery, across the street was the terminus of the Lexington Avenue elevated train. Which last stop was to provide its own historically sad setting for Gainor Stephen Crist.

With no one with a beard in the entire United States except the naval Captain Sheridan in the boxing room of the New York Athletic Club, and perhaps an odd religious sect here and there, I was now constantly made aware by stares and looks of the hair on my face. My beard had become my blazing badge of defiance wherever I went, setting me immediately apart and alerting those on all sides that I was a highly suspicious character, and more than likely one of the insidious enemy spreading the creed of communism across the nation. And while this phobia besieged the United States, mercifully for my paranoia, I did deeply believe that, although at times critical, there was nothing I had ever done or would ever do that would make me disloyal to the nation.

One had already many times, on the occasion of being asked why I was growing that beard, answered that I was doing nothing but that everybody else was shaving his off. One day I even ventured forth down into the city in a red shirt and tie, albeit muted by a tweed waistcoat and jacket. Although it was wonderful for one's privacy, nothing anywhere could have set me more apart than my whiskers and made most of whom I met or encountered eager to disappear as soon as they could from one's presence. A chap even walking face-first into a closed glass door. And I suppose, all such folk in the final analysis, would be one's potential enemy ready to betray one at the merest clank and tinkle of a hammer and sickle. However, I did not seem to give way to any delusions of persecution, and there did occur one single exception to all this surrounding hostility. At exactly five minutes to three, one breezy cool day, I was taking a left turn rounding the northeast corner of Fifty-second Street and Madison Avenue. When, on this otherwise empty street and coming in the opposite direction around the same corner, I was confronted by a cheerful, smiling gentleman who dressed in a great bundle of tweed, uttering loud and clear these words, as if they were a cry of victory,

"Ah, *magnifique barbu.*"

To hear the words "bearded man" sung out with such joy by this obviously Gallic gentleman, and as if his soul had been saved, lifted my spirits no end. We both waved back at each other full of smiles. Brief as it was, it was a relief from having to employ an implacably fearless look backed by a pair of ready fists wherever I might go. Alas this was the only single time in my entire stay of twelve months in the United States when I was met with any sign of unrestrained heartfelt enthusiasm. But considerable exception to this air of hostility occurred in that aforementioned strange outpost, the boxing room of the New York Athletic Club, a venue tucked away in a southwest corner of that twenty-story version of an Italian Renaissance palace overlooking Central Park. Founded over a hundred years ago and dedicated by its originators to the pursuit of manly sports, the club was a princely redoubt for those seeking comfortable escape from the spiritually corrosive shoving and pushing of America's largest city and the hustle and bustle of its swarming masses seeking fortune, as I was, in this municipal bourse. Along with its country clubhouse, this urban, gray stone edifice housed all manner of equipment and chambers to accommodate not only an endless number of athletic activities from rowing, shooting and yachting, to squash, handball and fencing but also numerous means of restorative cures for body and mind. Based on the theory to treat the body well and the mind will take care of itself.

In the city clubhouse, one thing all sports and their venues had in common was that, except to be invited to matches or to the special cocktail lounge to drink or to the dining room to dine, women were banned. And the sweaty, noisy irreverent confines of the boxing room was the most banned place of all. Several sports were small clubs within themselves, and the boxing room was certainly one of the clubbiest, attracting as it did the more extreme of the dissident eccentric who comfortably circulated around New York on their private incomes. Among these were another assorted folk, maritime and naval types who commanded vessels at sea and who were the stalwart everyday regulars. But also could be found one or two like oneself, still looking for a private income. However, all had in common a readiness to pop a punch on anybody's nose who gave them any unwanted lip of which there could be found plenty around every streetcorner in New York. And especially encountered by these eccentric, who by their nonconformist appearance, behavior and opinions and blatantly possessed of the self-esteem of the warrior, provoked it. Of course all this sportsmanly behavior in the use of fisticuffs was before drugs, handguns, and knives, when bullets and stab wounds came into vogue.

It was my fellow classmate Thomas M. Gill at Fordham Preparatory School who had first invited me to the New York Athletic Club because he said I seemed to manage well in the prep's boxing ring and gave the impression of fearing no one. I certainly had my fears, but there was no doubt that along with a willingness to fight anyone, I also must have demonstrated rebel and dissident signs at the prep because I was finally expelled. In any event, Gill at least thought I would be an interesting specimen to see flailing about with other eccentrics in the athletic club's boxing ring. In the school's intramural contests, I had a first-round knockout or two and was now being pressed above my lightweight division by the coach to take on even bigger and better opponents. Gill, himself a light heavyweight, was no slouch in the ring, and of those he hadn't pounded to the canvas in short order, he sent flying through the ropes. And it wasn't long before the two of us were putting on boxing exhibitions of murderous intent, which had folk at the athletic club gathered to witness flying bicuspids as the blood and gore spattered the ring.

Gill and I, as well as slamming resounding punches into each other's faces and ribs, also had our intellectual contests. These especially provoked by Gill's blunt, matter-of-fact way of putting things, which were opposed to my usually erroneous romantic exaggerations, and some of our discussions were just as brutal as our battles conducted within the crimson ropes. But there were moderating arbiters in the persons of two gentlemen, both former boxing champions and highly respected referees, who, overseeing the boxing room, saw to fair play. Both were also advisers and scholars in the world of boxing. One Frank Fulham and the other Arthur Donovan, the latter being at the time world-famed as the doyen of referees and referee of the Joe Louis fights. And especially a most-famed fight of all, when Louis, previously knocked out by Schmeling, knocked out Schmeling in their return match. With the room's two boxing rings, collection of punching bags, skipping ropes and weight-lifting apparatus and the mementoes of fighters and even framed letters from a president or two, there was no question that the boxing room was a revered sanctum dedicated to the manly art of self-defense, where those of gentler dispositions feared to tread. And where Arthur Donovan and Frank Fulham always attempted to keep the maim and gore to a minimum.

Ah, but there were exceptions to the gentlemanly peacekeeping, and no hindrance was put in the way of formulating any well-deserved war between members who detested the thought of each other. And such battles were viewed silently out of the corner of each eye. But mostly the boxing room was a center of information about the boxing world, the source of which was found historically represented around the walls and in the encyclopedic knowledge both Donovan and Fulham had of the fight game. Donovan once telling me about a boxer no one at the time had ever heard of but, according to Donovan and those who'd seen him fight, was one of the most devastating ever seen in the ring. Donovan, whose eyes would light up talking about this mystery pugilist who the public were only beginning to know of, said that because of the destructive force of this fighter's victories, no manager with any kind of decent boxer with any prospects would give this man a fight because no fighter once battered to the canvas by him was ever the same afterward. And I asked the name of the fighter. Donovan answered with a whisper and chuckled as if I were being let into a well-kept conspiracy.

"His name, Pat, is Sugar Ray Robinson."

Of course this prizefighter was well heard of years later as a world champion in more than one weight division and is thought of as one of the ring's greatest ever middleweights. However, lucky for most inmates of the boxing room, the repartee and sardonic burlesque were as blisteringly wielded as were the flying fists, which latter mercifully were encased in sixteen-ounce sparring gloves. But when the likes of Frank Fulham was asked to spar a friendly round or two with a gent called Steve Brody, a socialite sportsman around town and of formidable heavyweight size and an equally brilliant boxer, some of the most devastating fights I've ever seen in the ring took place. Thunderous punches landing, with beads of sweat sprinkling the air and mouth-pieces flying. Total awed silence would reign in the boxing room as the inmates waited for one or the other of these gentlemen to lay stretched unconscious on the canvas. Frank Fulham always ending up having landed the most lethal punches.

As no money was used in the club and members signed chits, I became somewhat of an imposition on Tom Gill's generosity and it was decided that for the modest fee it entailed I should become a junior member. And except for an occasional guest that Tom might invite we seemed to be the only two young persons abroad in the vastness of this club amid these older clubmen. After a day's workout, which now consisted of a round or two in the ring, a game of squash and sometimes even a wrestling match followed by our usual retirement to the palatial tiled baths to bake in the hot room, steam in the steam room, a pummel in the power shower, swim in the pool and an occasional massage, Tom and I would repair to the club's taproom on the second floor. In this mock English setting of oak floors and beamed ceilings and a fox hunting scene rushing past across the back of the bar, there came at around five o'clock each day two white-coated and -hatted chefs who would assemble themselves at one end of the taproom, sharpening knives behind a long refectory table upon which sat a baron of roast beef and a massive ham. At one's proffering a dish, great slabs were cut and deposited on the slices of rye, pumpernickel or other breads and then upon one's desiring it, sauce or gravy would be added. This extravagant repast rendered with the compliments of the club. And often just Tom Gill and myself alone in enjoying it. There were as well selections of cheeses, crackers, butters and other hors d'oeuvres. With our appetites, Tom and I frequently came back for seconds and thirds with which to down beer from a club member's brewery. This member was also a habitué of the boxing room, who by winter looked like some abominable snowman coming up Central Park South enveloped from ears to ankles in a voluminous raccoon skin coat. He must have known how much of his brewery's beer we drank. For at the sight of Tom and I, he would stop in the middle of the Fifty-ninth Street pavement, do a little delighted jig and then demonstrate his power handshake, at which Tom and I would dutifully grimace in pain.

But my life was not free of traumas. Although possibly I exhibited other devious traits to the Jesuit tradition, the reason for my expulsion from Fordham Preparatory School was given as being a bad influence on the student body occasioned by my efforts to start my own personal fraternity of which I would be the supreme brother master. I also, of course, may have been absent without leave and sentenced to jug by

Having been expelled from Fordham Prep for being a bad influence upon the student body, myself now in the U.S. Navy, standing sockless in front of a college hall at Manhattan College. The preparatory school just behind to the left where I attended not unhappily for my last year of high school.

the prefect of discipline, a Father Shea, a meticulously stern discipli-narian who remains unforgotten by anyone who ever attended this prep school during his reign. His clipped words ordering one to write ten thousand words on why my tie should not be loose at the neck. "Jug" was the word used to designate punishment and consisted of walking in a prescribed circle in the gym or out of doors on clement days until told to stop. But my infractions deserved the most serious punishment of all, expulsion. My father exploding his Irish brogue and angrily pounding the desk of the principal with his massive fist when it was suggested that my innocent younger brother be removed as well. A young Jesuit English instructor, however, for whom I had written a theme or two he had admired, stood up for me and was equally incensed and said to the principal that I would be one of the few pupils whose presence in the school would be of some significance one day. And there was also a Mr. Songster, another young Jesuit, who, from an aristocratic family in Germany, sported a silver-knobbed ebony walk-ing stick, and who, although he did not back or defend me upon my expulsion, said he would very much miss the frequent nuisance I made of myself.

But one other to stick up for me was Tom Gill's mother, who shoutingly called the principal a bastard over the phone. However, I did have my first European indoctrination at Fordham Prep. The son of the French consul in New York sat in front of me, and when I would incite him to respond to some of my more inflammatory observations concerning his existence on earth, he would turn and resoundingly declare in French that I should lick his ass. This change of usage from the American verb "to kiss" usually associated with this act, made one realize that Europe allowed a more exotic descriptive expression, if not behavior, in dealing with unwanted attention. Alas, my French was not good enough to follow his other lengthier ripostes in that language, but I would let him have blasts back in my most fluently abusive Italian, which seemed to enrage him more than my American English. But this young Frenchman was delighted to hear that I was being kicked out of this school. Nor was it lost upon me that the principal of this educational institution, as he summarily dismissed me, would take the trouble to greet on the front steps the arrival of a pupil, a young star on Broadway, who was chauffeured there in a limousine. But had it occurred to me at the time, which it didn't, imbued as I must have been with the American ethic of equality, I could have assumed that my parents' Irish birth and our family's modest aspirations were such as to make me socially undesirable in the eyes of socially climbing folk. My father still possessed of innocence enough to intercede with an admirer of his, a Madam de Barbac, along with an old-time resident dowager of Woodlawn, to have my sister, a first-generation American, made a member of Daughters of the American Revolution.

Following my expulsion from Fordham Prep, I entered one's idea of paradise, a coeducational high school north of New York City in Westchester County called Roosevelt. This modest mock Elizabethan red brick edifice, with its small campus, was then located in open countryside and seemed after an all-boys' school, almost as if one were entering a true American life of sweaters, sweat socks and saddle shoes. And last but not least now provided a constant association with young ladies instead of the infrequent opportunity occasioned by the chaperoned tea dances at Fordham Prep. And it was here I met my first quasi-serious girlfriend one evening during a train ride south between the affluent communities of Scarsdale and Bronxville. A year older and her father dead and her mother working as a nurse, I encountered a less palmy side of American life, where they lived in a small apartment on the slightly wrong side of the tracks. However, her quiet elegance and considerable beauty and her awareness of how the world worked

Dear Mr,

First week of school I was a sincere gentelmen, the semester proceeded and I think I was a gentelmen in a cruyde sort of way with a few outbreaks here and there. I made a few moves in class and helped to make others but at this time I thought I was a good boy. I laughed a little to loud, somtemes, and others I didn't. Mabey I might have tolked a little to much but this is my nature and I think I am gifted with a good line of speech or gab. I also like to kid around in class, and so made a couple of minor mistakes but dont we all? I made a few conspicuous noises in class at the wrong time but I guess this was done to satisfy my nature. Now these wrong doings were mostly mixed together, I mean they weren't done at differint times in the season because I dont belive in keeping up with the styles in such things as these. So therefore my conduct was deplorable only after the first week then inexcusible after a few more weeks and I reached my hight about a week ago and I'm now on the short road to the bottom of the hill. But to be bold— I'd say that I'm only a fifteen year old boy that doesn't no any better and quite a stupid one at that— so people tell me.

Sincerly yours,
James P.P Danbury

P.S. I hope this letter is in order. it is 211½ words

This Dear Mr. letter was written as a punishment to a Mr. McKinney, a Jesuit novitiate instructor at Fordham Preparatory School. My tendency was to have a lot to say, if not to inspire rebellion then to incite minor disruptions and especially to protest oppression. Mr. McKinney was tolerant enough not to insist upon worse than the present letter as my chastisement. Indeed he even fought for my not being expelled, pleading to the principal at the time that my presence at the prep might be the only reason the school would ever have to boast of anyone in future years. As indeed one does now boast of Mr. McKinney.

landed her with invitations from the Ivy League colleges and as far afield as Annapolis. I found myself mildly envying her too because she kept Coca-Cola in her refrigerator, a drink regarded as being without nourishment by my mother. During nights we spent clutched together on a couch in the small sitting room, she would say, "Don't move, don't speak," as her senile grandfather, who had once prosperously built many of the houses in Bronxville, would wander in in his pajamas, and as he loomed over us in the moonlight, he would raise an arm and point a finger and intone, "I'm going right up over there now."

Her life, once privileged and rich, was now one of parsimony, and I occasionally accompanied her to her babysitting jobs, where she would listen patiently and even appreciatively to my poems. But she once made an embittered outburst at my indifference and unawareness to the sorrow, impoverishment and tragedy of American life. And it was a pity I never realized what a gem this American girl was, who, with her lucid brown eyes, abundance of brown hair, her smooth skin, her soft lips and calm voice, was so far beyond me in sophistication. But my insensibility and ignorance of the grimmer aspects of American life was due to the small-town, pleasant community of Woodlawn, and in some part to the New York Athletic Club, from which I was not expelled, and which remained a part of one's daily existence. Its great haunted rooms, always sparsely populated, and Tom and I, after trying to beat each other in chess or to a pulp in the ring, would each day following steam baths and ablutions come sit in the taproom overlooking the park and the bustle of theater customers collecting across the street at the Yiddish Arts Theater. Discussing the verities of life, we would watch the traffic lights change from red to green and green to red and people crossing Seventh Avenue as they made their way along Central Park South. Occasionally, a fire apparatus would speed out of Fifty-eighth Street, clanging and hooting around the corner. Women not being allowed in the taproom, upon more gala occasions Tom and I took ladies, one of whom was my Bronxville girlfriend, to the club to dine in what must have been and no doubt still is one of the most beautiful dining rooms with a cityscape view in America. The cheapest thing on the club menu was sautéed potatoes at fifteen cents a portion, often ordered by me in having to be conscious of a big club bill at the end of the month.

But much entertainment came free of charge through Tom Gill's father, an influential lawyer who would frequently have an invitation or free tickets somewhere for Tom and myself to amuse ourselves.

Separated from Tom's mother, his father seemed to live a bachelor's life out of a shadowy apartment just behind the club in an ornate building known as Alwyn Court, a city landmark whose facing was covered by an intricate terra-cotta French renaissance stone tapestry, and which was lonely viewed by me many times from the club's library and boxing room windows. Although I never knew precisely what Tom's father did, he seemed to manage one or two of New York's notable nightclubs and ran some of America's famed bands, which started out their careers from what was known as Glen Island Casino, a nightspot on the Westchester shore of Long Island Sound and just across a stretch of water from the club's country clubhouse. However, he did every day seem to play cards or at least visit in the massive great darkness of the card room up on the ninth floor, where one imagined that under the inverted bowls of light beamed down on the tables, large sums of money were won and lost. And every once in a while, as the chimes of the grandfather clock sounded, one would see a player get up from his seat and, puffing his cigar, cross the soft deep carpets to the corner of the vast lounge overlooking Central Park, where a ticker tape machine spewed out its long strip of paper quoting the most recent price of stocks and shares on Wall Street. A scene which prompted a remark from Tom Gill one day.

"Pat, for some people it's all play and no work."

And my first confrontations with the deeper mysteries of New York came, when Tom's father, as Tom was unavailable at the club one day, invited me to drive to Glen Island in a bulletproof limousine with a gentleman in a dark suit and a black Stetson hat, who was saluted by traffic policeman as we drove by. When we reached the casino, and as the band there rehearsed, a young lady singer came to sit on this gentleman's knee, and he put a large sparkling diamond ring on her finger. Somehow, this simple act, although alien to me, seemed to demonstrate the power of power in America. And I was learning of the artless workings of money in this great unpredictable bourse of New York, as later that day we drove down to the Lower East Side of the city, where Tom's father went on behalf of an elderly widowed client to collect rents in some tenement buildings for which he emerged with great stacks of bank notes. He once spoke of a man to whom he'd given valuable tax advice, which consisted merely of a change of accounting dates but which saved the man many hundreds of thousands of dollars. However, the man resented paying a considerably large fee of tens of thousands of dollars for such simple but valuable counsel. And one last impressionable ethic Tom's father left upon me was he refused to do business with anyone drinking or who had been drinking.

But throughout my goings and comings downtown at the New York Athletic Club, there was another most unforgettable character who was the reason why so many frequented this curious precinct known as the boxing room. Sometime past three o'clock, the door was propped open each day, which allowed the faint smell of steam and newly pressed clothes to permeate, as the boxing room door was across the corridor from the club's tailor and dry cleaning service. And pulling the door further open, one would see inside Frank Fulham, his feet in boxing shoes propped up on a desk, and wearing an old tattered robe. And it was Fulham these five years later following my departure to attend university in Europe who sat there just as I'd left him and who was now one of the few who instantly said friendly words to me in these United States.

"Jesus, if it ain't Pat Donleavy. It is, isn't it."

"It is."

"Where have you been all these recent years out of our lives. You know every once in a while people would come in here asking for you. Where's that guy gone with the fastest fists in the business. All the admirals, captains and commodores, the undertakers, the judges, the politicians and congressmen. You and Tom Gill used to put on some of the toughest fights around here."

Nothing perhaps in my stay now in America gave me greater encouragement than the cheerful welcome I received that day from Frank Fulham. Who when away from his duties as boxing instructor operated a "we knock 'em dead" exterminating service, which he was always quick to let us know dealt with bedbugs, rats and that indomitable ancient beast, the cockroach, and was not of the human kind. But such were the myriad connections effected through the boxing room that one was sure that somehow through its network that even the agency to get someone rubbed out could be found. For which, let me tell you, there was no shortage of suitable candidates.

Upon this exuberant day of seeing Frank Fulham, I went through my first workout since my years in Dublin, where all my punches thrown were in pubs and on the street. And here in the good old boxing room of the New York Athletic Club, such blows and swings were now exercised under the guise of the gentlemanly art of self-defense. But even so, within a few minutes, some collegiate boxing champ invited me into the ring for what was purported to be a friendly sparring match but was to clearly beat the absolute bloody bejesus out of me. And suddenly one felt highly inconsiderate blows raining upon one from all sides. Until I let loose a right under the man's heart which landed like a ton of cement and quickly corrected his sporting manners. And bent double, the collegiate champ gasped, "Nice shot."

Fulham enjoying the event, and it was obvious that habitués of this room still did not hesitate to knock the hell out of each other when they got into the ring. And I was now fully reminded that when any member casually invited one to spar a round or two, he was, you could be sure, planning to murder you. Meanwhile, Fulham was anxious to know what I was up to, having returned from Europe.

"Hey, Pat, tell me what are you doing."

"I've been painting pictures."

"You mean art. Like Leonardo da Vinci."

"Yes."

"Hey, that's good. You try to sell them."

"Yes."

"Hey, that's even better."

A few days later, in returning to the boxing room, and as I would, visiting it early in the afternoon before the hard-hitting habitués arrived, Frank Fulham, as usual in his old boxing gear and with his feet propped up on his desk and in his old ragged dressing gown, called me over to where he always sat by the telephone. He took up three cards and handed them to me, each with a note written on the back.

"Here you are, Pat, these are three introductions. I've talked to each of these guys, and they'd like to meet you. I said Picasso and Matisse better watch out. You just go around the corner there to Fifty-seventh Street and introduce yourself."

The three cards were to the three of the most prestigious modern art galleries on this famed boulevard. I was quite pleasantly astonished at Fulham's unhesitating help he offered and at the same time wondered how I was to break the different news that I was now writing a novel and had to find a publisher. It became apparent in the goings and comings of the boxing room that Fulham, although always ready to be amused, was also a very practical gentleman, and in addition to his exterminating service he seemed to have access to many influential pies. But knocking insectile vermin dead was his first love, and business was brisk.

"Pat, I ain't a professor of bugology for nothing. We got over fifty species of these cockroaches that will eat anything and survive our ruthless methods. The building owners, with a building so infested that nobody can live in it anymore, think they can get rid of them when they knock the place down and build a new building. But the cockroaches don't die, they just go swarming into the next building or go across the street at night and wait. Then when the new building's built and ready for occupation, and when everyone's asleep, the king of cockroaches says let's go, and they next morning are all there back again. The whole city is nothing but a breeding ground for the biggest, best-fed healthiest rats, termites, fleas, bedbugs and cockroaches in the world, plus other pests down the sewers they haven't got names for yet. That's why we got our new motto, 'We knock 'em dead for longer than just a while.' "

Out of the increasing bleakness of my return to America, and as spring approached and the pavements of New York promised to soon fry eggs, I was finding my funds inexorably dwindling despite my family's free accommodation, so I could not have been more delighted with Frank Fulham's helpful gesture. And finally when I worked up the nerve to tell him that I was presently engaged in writing a novel instead of trying to paint and sell pictures, I also avowed that I would still most certainly go and make use of his calling cards.

"Is that right, a novel, Pat. Like a book that keeps you turning over the pages in deep suspense."

"Yes, I hope so."

Hardly more was said. But toward the end of the same week, I found myself confronted by a gentleman who'd been led down from the fencing room to the other end of the fourth-floor corridor, and who in his athletic gear was shown into the boxing room to meet me. His name was Charles Rolo, who was on the board as a judge of the Book-of-the-Month Club, the well-known bonanza for authors and publishers. One most politely bowed and shook hands with Mr. Rolo, who in turn let me know that he'd heard from Frank Fulham of the brilliant novel I'd written which Frank informed him would have people standing on their chairs cheering and be a certain bestseller, Frank Fulham of course not having read a single word of the book. However, the friendly Mr. Rolo did caution that it was a long way up to this position but he'd be more than glad on Frank's recommendation to see the work and if promising recommend it to a publisher. It was such gesture as that made by Frank Fulham that gave me glimmers of hope against all the odds that I instinctively felt were accumulating and against which my own confidence was more and more desperately exerting itself. And I was even vaguely toying with taking up professional prizefighting, with Fulham as usual providing his ready course of action.

"No problem, Pat. Take your weight down to middleweight, that means no butter and no sugar. And we'll get you just the right kind of warm-up fights to take you right up to the championship."

There were others who took their steps to glory from the help that seemed available through the good offices of Frank Fulham and percolated through from many sources in the boxing room. Favors and influence could be traded amid the brewers of beer, makers of whiskey, owners of cotton and silk mills, male heads of modeling agencies and the odd tabloid newspaper publishers. There were also champions from nearly every sport, who also liked to be able to use their fists when necessary. One, such as Lawrence Tierney, a champion runner with an unpredictably serious temper which he indulged in the boxing ring and later in Hollywood when he authentically played the role on screen of the famed gangster John Dillinger. There was such as my own namesake, Brian Donlevy, the actor who portrayed many a tough-guy role in Hollywood. But if you weren't planning to set out to the West Coast for movie fame and fortune, there was Commodore Bayliss, always available, who headed the coast guard and could cruise you around New York Harbor, and even a prominent undertaker or two if you needed such service. I even felt that had I mentioned to Frank Fulham that I was intending to qualify as a mortician that he would have had in short order an arrangement ready for me to apprentice at an embalming table in one of your better New York funeral parlors, one or two of the proprietors of which, under Fulham's tutelage, liked to be handy with their fists. It not being totally unknown, according to one undertaker, for a corpse with rigor mortis settling in, to stiff-arm the embalmer one in the eye.

Although a club employee, Fulham, with his charm and influence, was more like this vast club's honorary deputy president, and he could sometimes be found in the lobby making introductions. But of the many good fights that could be witnessed in the boxing room, nearly all the best involved Fulham. And were generally fought with those few he was not exactly enamored of and who in turn did not disguise the fact that they would dearly love to knock Fulham out if not exactly kill him. However, such folk ended up coming out between the ropes from their encounter, faces and ears well reddened. But not all such protagonists were Adonis-like ex-football stars and all-around skilled athletes and famed for swan-diving at least once a year from the highest point on the Brooklyn Bridge. There was another with whom Fulham engaged in loathing contention, but this was limited to nonviolent exchanges of sarcastic words. The battle would commence whenever the bow-tied Ivy Leaguer Horace Bigelow would appear at the boxing room door. Bigelow, club librarian and the official chess instructor, ran the chess room on the ninth floor and would, as a brilliant player, have simultaneous games with seven or eight club members and beat most in less than a dozen moves. But in exchanging unparliamentary language with Fulham, Bigelow, with all his erudition, was no match. One would listen avidly to the parry and thrust of the cant and argot, not to mention an occasional Fulham obscenity.

And there was
Never any question
That this was
An athletic club
Which included words
As well as muscles
For exercise

14

ODD URGENT MESSAGES were now arriving from Gainor Stephen Crist, heralding his escape from Europe and his intention to come settle in Spanish Harlem. I was already homesick for Ireland and the Isle of Man, and, although I did not know how things were in Spanish Harlem, I wrote back warnings that dollar bills were not like autumn leaves falling off the trees. And that there was little evidence of this being the land of milk and honey and that if he arrived he would be strictly on his own. But in the old white house atop the hill, I had now settled down to a routine of sorts which daily came ablaze with my determination to write on with *The Ginger Man*. With a certain degree of silence I kept counsel with myself, taking orange juice, sausages, All-Bran, coffee and whole-wheat toast and grape jelly for breakfast. My religious application to my typewriter every morning, if nothing else, seemed to impress the household. A childhood friend up the street, Gerald McKernan, came to see me, with whom I had while growing up indulged in many a back yard adventure, invading the neighbors' privacy with creative vandalism. But there were not that many words between us before my nonconformity became grievously obvious and it became clear that I "wasn't the same Paddy Donleavy" he used to know and was instead shaking a fist in the face of the status quo. However, my childhood friend, who was handsome, charming and a brilliant athlete, was now equally so as a hearty handshaking executive. But back in our early Woodlawn days, he had no peer in imitating a back yard midnight cat fight to the extent of having every shoe in a person's bedroom flung out the window at him, nor as an outstanding middle distance runner could he ever be caught had a neighbor given chase for the more disruptive misdeeds we committed.

However, not all were as deeply suspicious of me. In the opposite direction, another couple of houses away, lived another handsome and charming childhood pal, Richard Gallagher, who'd had, more than the rest of us, to fend for himself, his father dying and leaving a family of seven children to be raised by a valiant mother. With a quiet, respectable dignity, they resided in their small house set back nearly out of sight from the street. Of a strangely humane and fair-minded intelligence, Gallagher, in spite of economy of means, paid fastidious attention to his clothes. Always presenting himself with a certain stylish elegance in immaculate shirtings and splendid sports jackets. His gray flannel trousers were always sharply creased, and his argyle socks and gleaming loafers dazzled the eye. All helping to give Woodlawn a modest reputation for the best-dressed young men. The only harsh words I ever heard him speak were once when he was considerably sick with flu and holed up in his tiny bedroom and I came visiting him one afternoon with another friend, who brought him a dirty book to read. He was appreciative of the dirty book, but when I handed him a Catholic pamphlet on how to have a happy death, he angrily opened its pages and said,

"So this is the kind of thing you bring somebody who is sick. It shows you who your friends really are."

I suppose that my sense of humor, based as it was on the last resort, was more easily indulged while I was able to spend my time off playing tennis or golf and could remain a carefree believer in one's ultimate millionaireship. Whereas Gallagher, in his young life, was pressed much closer to the realities of survival. One Christmas Eve, having worked overtime in the bowels of a post office downtown, sorting packages till three A.M. and not paid yet, he found when it was time to go home that he had no subway or bus fare. With only a few left at the sorting office and too proud to approach anyone to borrow from, he set out to walk penniless through the falling snow northward along the famed boulevard of Broadway. Gallagher trudged the more than twelve miles up across Manhattan Island, through Harlem and the Bronx, to reach Woodlawn at dawn. A feat no less dangerous or arduous than the last dozen miles to the North Pole.

Unlike me, Gallagher seemed to have no glamorous illusions about America or the life it might present. He had, as I also temporarily had, till fired, a newspaper route delivering the *Bronx Home News*. This daily family newspaper made it its policy to instill in its delivery boys an entrepreneurial sense of taking of one's first steps that a Bronx boy might take toward tycoonery or being president of the United States. To give one the sense of being in business for oneself, you bought your own newspapers from the publisher and were also presented with free samples to give away in order to find new customers and expand. Gallagher, neat, prompt and businesslike, had his route running like clockwork. Whereas mine, once prosperous under its former proprietor, was quickly diminishing in profit and customers, due to late or missed deliveries, or my flung folded papers flying misjudged into the wrong doorways. Or, as my aim became that of a marksman, knocking over objets d'art as I sailed my missile through a window opened a crack. As complaints began to pour in, the superintendent of routes, a Mr. Baumgartner, was incensed enough to raise his voice and say,

"Confound you, Donleavy, must I always have to find fault with you. You're giving the *Bronx Home News* a bad name."

Plus my aggrieved, irate tax-paying pillars of the community who subscribed to the paper shook their fists at me from their front porches. And admittedly, I would shake a fist back. But what seemed most to add to their further fury was, when I wasn't paid on time or at all, I would write my own editorial in large block letters across the top of the front page:

HOW DOES IT FEEL TO CHEAT A CHILD

But as Gallagher, hearing I was back from Europe, came this day to visit me, he did in finding me changed not particularly find fault as well. He listened sympathetically as I spoke about how things had been in Ireland and what my plans were in the United States. He had himself, after serving in the Second World War in the marine corps, joined the New York police force. He was to become lieutenant, head of the Riverfront Squad and later of homicide in Midtown Manhattan. Over the years he provided a needed escort off the big liners and through waterfront obstacles for a friend or two. Then, confronting the aftermath of hundreds of murders, Gallagher was to become, as he has occasionally described himself, a book actor. Which in Gallagher's case made him one of New York's most written about and imitated characters. And whose humanity, compassion and understanding saved many from needless anguish. A lifelong friend, Gallagher was to be, aside from Frank Fulham, one of the very few to accept me without reservations on my return to America. And years later as he sat over his whiskey at my fireside in Ireland, I asked him, a man about whom everyone had a good opinion, did he ever want one of his children to become a policeman like himself. And when he said no, I asked him why.

"Because, J.P., it gives you a bad opinion of people."

But as I ventured on my daily walk through the city down on the island of Manhattan, I did meet one other former childhood friend. After my eight o'clock breakfast routine, I touch-typed about four foolscap pages on the new typewriter I had bought myself on my last trip to London. Then, dressing in jacket, collar and tie, I descended the steep hill to wait for the bus which ran along Katonah Avenue. This short thoroughfare was mostly made up of shops and houses with a bakery, library, a grocery, two bars and two candy stores, plus a public secondary school and a few vacant lots. The bus took one to the terminus of the elevated train and passed on the way the fire station, where on lonely summer evenings I would, as a child, be given a nickel or dime by my father when I had walked the few blocks there to bring him sandwiches as he sat on his fire watch just inside the firehouse doors, tabulating the bells ringing in from around New York. My father, unmindful that I was a midnight scourge of the neighborhood, invariably treated me as a dutiful son, often patting me on the head and calling me by his own pet name, announcing to anyone interested to listen,

"Jim's a good boy."

But as odd familiar Woodlawn citizens climbed aboard or were seen on the road as one passed, there was on this bus journey always one or two emotional shocks rearing up ghostly out of the past. The first girl ever to declare her love for me stepped aboard and sat just in front across the aisle, where I was able to see her face. When we were nearly thirteen years old and blushing with her shyness, she handed me a printed-out note at class in school which she signed.

I Love You
Charlotte Gray

Quiet and reserved, she was, despite her hauntingly simple name, of some exotic middle European stock. Now a mature woman, slender and tall, she was, with her pale silken skin and exquisite face, stunningly beautiful. I then heard, when I inquired, that she had married into one of a clannish group of families of her own ethnic origin. She was a girl whose young loveliness I had never forgotten. And endured a terrible regret that I had been too shy to say I loved her as well.

While riding the elevated train I could look down into the monument mason's yards, which supplied Woodlawn Cemetery with gravestones. And then passing along by Mosholu Golf Course and above the crowded streets of the Bronx, one would pass the anonymous apartment house windows and see into all the chocolate-colored boardinghouse rooms into which failure could sentence you. If it didn't do even worse and leave you a vagrant on the street. But once deep into the city, I would more optimistically walk, mile after mile, wandering in any random direction. Astonished and stopping and staring at what I never imagined could be thought to be a beautiful city. The mysterious source of wealth of its anonymous inhabitants stacked on top of one another along Park and Fifth avenues. The utter variety of grandiose architecture, which could vie with that of Europe and which other pedestrians seemed not to notice or care about. Each intent upon getting to appointments and, if not having one, pretending they had, as I did, so as not to be arrested as I loitered. Until when the time approached three-thirty o'clock and I would move lonely in the direction of the New York Athletic Club.

But one balmily sunny day, as I was heading east and about to cross Madison Avenue on Fifty-seventh Street, I saw an unmistakable flaming red head of hair approaching, periscoped above the crowd. I stopped and waited as the figure neared and confronted me. It was none other than another childhood friend, John Duffy, with whom, in the neighborhood of Woodlawn I had shared many a momentous emotional growing-up pain. And I was not too sure that I did not see at first in his eyes a tendency for some means of escape. But always a polite and gentle gentleman unless provoked, he was on the occasion, if surprised, perfectly glad to see me. And I was now to find in him a kindred spirit and a companion with whom to stroll the New York streets and who had an encyclopedic knowledge of and love of this city.

As we spoke cautiously upon our first meeting, I should have realized that Duffy would be as different now as he was then growing up. For shortly after my arrival back from Europe, I had found myself wandering across McLean Avenue north beyond Woodlawn into Yonkers, where I had my newspaper round. As the evening was darkening, I passed by the house to which the remainder of Duffy's large family, originally of thirteen children, had moved away from Woodlawn and saw Jack, as he was called, seated under the leaves of potted palms inside the sun porch poring over a desk. With the then communist exposing mood of America and the witch-hunting across the nation, even intellectual exercise was by many assumed a sign of the liberal-minded and was un-American and unpatriotic. And with myself already stared at and regarded as suspicious by all and sundry everywhere I went, I was surprised Duffy was letting himself be seen by passersby in the street. But as I was now able to learn from the horse's mouth, this childhood friend of mine was as good a citizen as any and was writing music, having taken up the vocation of composer.

Duffy and I had been in many a growing-up scrape together, once purloining sherry and other spirits from his family's wine cellar and drinking away the night in the woods. When one of our number keeled over, he was revived by the remaining gathering pissing on him, which always led to a miraculous if violent recovery of consciousness. Then in a friendly shoving match one day outside the local sweetshop, Stellings, I, not totally accidentally, sent Duffy through a large plate glass window. No one was injured, but, as the proprietress and her sister were dignified Swiss ladies who made wonderful pineapple and strawberry sodas, it caused a scandal of sorts and considerable expensive damage for which our parent guardians had to pay. In another escapade, we aided and abetted another mutual pal to squander his prep school tuition entrusted to him by his impecunious mother. Traveling downtown to conduct an extravagant drinking spree around Times Square and repeatedly consuming a cocktail called Tom Collins. While our poor mutual pal spent days hiding out in the huge attics and cellars of his house avoiding the wrath of his mother.

My bad influence on others may have stemmed from my academic status, which had always been precarious. Having been left back and demoted once in grade school, I had always sat in dread as the dumb boy in the class. With only one other boy thought dumber and who was called Dirty Harold, was accused and reproached and blamed for everything. The whole class turning to look at him as he sat in the back in his ill-fitting and unpressed clothes, and the class, in answer to any misdemeanor, pointing fingers and accusing him in unison. Then one day, a mile away from Woodlawn, in the wasteland of Yonkers, I happened to be passing by his house, a rambling, disordered clapboard structure conspicuous in a large lot and surrounded by what seemed to be discarded and broken bits of machinery. And there was Dirty Harold standing there on a bald patch of his lawn and obviously waiting for me to be disagreeable. But I was anxious to know the purpose of one convoluted contraption, which looked useless in the extreme. But Dirty Harold launched into a most marvelously useless explanation, which then continued as to the value of each piece of rusting scrap metal and abandoned junk. When he was finished telling me of this treasure trove surrounding his house, it so impressed me that I realized I was listening to one of the most intelligent people in the class. And that seated rearward and assessed dumb like him, I must also be a victim of my repressed intelligence. And at least Dirty Harold later became a scrap metal merchant millionaire.

Ah, but wait. In those days, Christmas did come once. And our class was delegated to perform Dickens's "A Christmas Carol," as our school play. Chosen to play Scrooge, a tall, temperamental introspective boy, Regan, who combed his hair straight back and who parted it in the middle, suddenly at rehearsals finding the role unsympathetic, became stubborn, sulky and difficult and finally was sick and absent. I had had a fight once on the streetcorner near school with this boy, which I won when I bloodied his nose, and following which he became an intellectual friend. And now on this occasion of his indisposition, I was chosen to play his role. It was as if I had been ripped from my contented obscurity as a backward pupil and the struggle to memorize and repeat lines was immense and my fluffing of them appalling. My legs were still too short to let my feet touch the floor from the seat upon which I sat on stage. Happily, I was enamored of a pretty girl, Joan Skillen, who stood next to my chair. But as I was a replacement on short notice, I seemed to endear myself to the audience as I trembled in terror, trying to remember my lines and the sympathetic applause brought the house down at the final curtain. Although I was to occasionally hanker over the lore of the theatrical world, it was to be my first and last performance on stage. And the only time I was ever able to distinguish myself in an educational institution.

But being so outlawed academically then must have marked me and made one deliberately dissident. And following my expulsion from Fordham Prep, my bad influence on others must have included Duffy. For when my family separated me from the coeducational influence of Roosevelt High School, and when it was known that I was then to attend Manhattan Preparatory School, Duffy, already a student there, was promptly removed and sent off to a different school by his family. However, I still had recourse to Duffy, and now for other and mostly unfriendly reasons. Both of us had for a time been enamored of the same marvelously attractive girl, Carol, my very closest childhood friend Alan Kuntze's younger sister, whom I'd taken to the cinema and invited to Fordham Prep tea dances. But not only was I incensed over this trespass. For Duffy one day, a year or two later, by the drinking fountain in the park suddenly produced treasured photographs of my Roosevelt High School girlfriend, which he proceeded to slowly tear up in front of me before I realized what he was doing. Having myself been often threatened by Mafia children, I now in true Mafia tradition threatened to kill Duffy. And perhaps no wonder efforts were made to keep the two of us apart.

But Duffy was no stranger to other menaces and misfortunes and, like Richard Gallagher, must have also grown up through his young years without the illusions I must have had over these mightily wonderful United States. And seemed to have retained all through my years in Europe. Of the grandeur and promise it still offered. And of how one planned in daydreams to perfect one's leisure in the glow of its glamour. But there were tragic reminders of a more solemn world. Duffy's older brother called Tag, so named because of his skill in playing a peculiar Bronx game of ring-a-levio, had his head severed from his body by a passing car while retrieving a ball from a street manhole. On my way to and from school, I saw the blood left on the grass where Tag's body lay on the sloping lawn outside the big brick house on the corner overlooking where the accident had happened. And now on my return to the United States, from Duffy emerged a different view of America. That of a society maliciously wielding its prejudices and exploiting its poor and downtrodden and dispossessed. And Duffy was to be a singular friend who would always upon greeting use that word "friend."

"Hello, friend. How are you doing."

Jack Phonecious Duffy, as he was called growing up, was tall and sturdily built. He was called Phonecious as a nickname because of his extraordinarily striking face, and with his astonishingly handsome classical profile, we imagined we could find a resemblance engraved only upon some bronze from a remote period of antiquity. His waving orange-crimson locks frequently had totally strange women stopping and offering themselves to him on the street. And once, as I casually went strolling with Duffy through the neighborhood, and seeing a house alight within and hearing the sound of music, Duffy mounted the porch, knocked on the door and politely inquired in his gently quiet, unassuming and hesitant voice,

"Excuse me please for my intrusion, but I just happened to be passing and I just wondered if there was a party going on here."

Such was Duffy's elegance and charm that when the first shock of his inquiry had worn off, the door was opened and Duffy would duly be invited in. And even when he turned and waved his arm to his waiting cohorts, I and another lurking in the shadows across the street to come and join him, Duffy soothed any apprehension of his soon-to-be host.

"Oh, I hope you don't mind, they are just some of my friends."

Duffy had been as a teenager a formidable boxer, football player and a musical prodigy as well as a fashion plate. Wearing collarless jackets of outrageous pink and yellow tints, and even zoot suits with their drape shape and which required the wearer to stand astride on either a streetcorner or in front of the local sweetshop with the palm of his hand encircling upon a perpendicular plane as he polished air. And often joining Duffy was a quick-witted and acerbic raconteur, Red Walsh, who all the many years later was to become a publisher's representative and deliver a copy of the Paris-published *Ginger Man* to its first contracting American publisher. And Duffy was to compose the music for the first stage production of *The Ginger Man* in the United States, which in its turn provided a tiny atom in the matrix of American history, as its premiere took place on the eve of President John Kennedy's assassination.

Woodlawn, because of its geographical intimacy as a community and location isolated on the edge of America's then largest city, was a small forcing ground in many a teenage pursuit. Producing a handful of young musical prodigies who won amateur talent contests on the radio, either singing, playing drums or stroking the viola. As it had with Richard Gallagher, others too innovated young men's fashions. A local figure called Stevie Bennett, who, along with Alan Kuntze, pursued their various forms of rakish conservative dress. Alan Kuntze, upon spotting a pair of Norwegian leather bedroom slippers in a man's fashion magazine, decided to wear them for ordinary street wear. And having won a swimming scholarship to Trinity School downtown was soon shuffling about, spreading the awareness of this footwear everywhere until loafers came into being. My own taste in clothing was nonexistent until I was indoctrinated into what the fashionable young Woodlawn man should sport, exchanging jackets with Alan and his brother Donald, both of whom had considerable collections. But one choice I'd made from my own inventory and originally belonging to my sister, and which was a total rainbow of bright hues, met at once a stern admonition from the prefect of discipline of Fordham Prep.

"Do not. Ever. Wear that again to this school."

Alan, as well as being meticulous in dress and being older by a couple of years, was a mentor in almost all matters governing social behavior, sport and girls. Which in the last case included descriptions as to how to stimulate the pleasure-sensitive areas of the female anatomy. Or how, on introduction, to execute a firm handshake or impart a reassuring squeeze to a girlfriend's limb. He was the first to pick intellectual holes in my obtusely bigoted arguments and to suggest books, such as James T. Farrell's, to read. He was also a pal of a sophisticated Bill Pain, who'd wax emotionally impressed by films he'd seen and books he'd read, once keeping us spellbound under a summer tree in the street, describing a great film he'd just seen called *Citizen Kane.* Alan also insisted on social decorum, even when it involved one's sister. Pursuing his perfections in everything, he could be charming just as he could suddenly be blunt and hard. And then with immense charm be immediately contrite. He was a marvelous athlete, winning trophies for speed skating on ice, and by evening one would find him meticulously sharpening his racing skates. He held high school free-style swimming records and would take morning doses of glucose for breakfast and would let his fingernails grow long to get a better pull from his strokes in the water. He could also, on his way to school, waiting each morning for the bus across from the cemetery, infract his fitness by unathletically puffing on a cigarette. Which allowed me to tell my first joke I'd ever heard from a country cousin visiting Harold Farrell, who lived nearby and who, when asked if he smoked, would reply,

"Ain't never got that hot."

Among the proper Protestants in Woodlawn for whom four Protestant churches catered, there were a handful of rich Italian families along with five Irish families, all with many children and all of whom lived in big brick houses discreetly behind their lace curtains and for whom one Catholic church provided worship. Of the Irish there were the Dordans, the Deacys, the Duffys, the O'Connells and Horgans. It was from the twin brothers of the last family, who were slightly older and who, both having asthma, were sent periodically to the clear air of Denver, Colorado, that I learned to throw a lariat and could catch, as they could, someone running away by the ankle. They would return east with ore samples of gold and silver and all the practiced skills of cowboys. The Horgans held annual venison parties and kept horses in their garage on 236th Street which sometimes galloped past toward Van Cortlandt Park, where they would ride the bridle paths through the woods. They also owned a Kerry blue dog, and I had a Chesapeake Bay retriever puppy, which, when I ventured down their way, would, encouraged by the twins, be attacked and chased and bitten. But when Chess, my dog, got some months bigger, and I brought him back down the street and the Horgans' Kerry blue sailed at him, my dog stood his ground and bit the hell out of him and chased him back into his yard. And such victory was sweet.

Adjoining the community of Woodlawn were what we referred to as the first, second and third woods, inhabited by owls, hawks, chipmunks, possum, muskrat, snapping turtle, black snakes, fox and occasional deer. Indian arrowheads were still to be found in people's back gardens. And hunting wildlife was part of growing up. Alan Kuntze knew all there was to know of the lore and way of life of the American Indian. How to shimmy as Indian children did to the top of a birch tree and, holding to its top, throw oneself off to gracefully descend to the ground again. How to hunt with bow and arrow, follow trails and skin animals. Alan, with a slingshot fashioned from the fork of a dogwood branch, was as accurate as he was with a rifle, and we often ate roasted squirrel around an evening campfire. He kept pet crows and owls and had a trapping line in the swamp of the third woods, catching muskrat for their pelts, which he cured each winter and sold to the Hudson Bay Company. We also unwittingly became America's first conservationists, blocking the trenches dug for the schemes to drain the swamp in the first woods. But across which now roars the traffic of the Major Deegan Expressway.

In childhood, these growing-up years before the Second World War, we played marbles under the maple trees, and street hockey on roller skates. There were annual community parades with floats and bands and community picnics in the park, with everyone invited to enter games and contests and to win prizes. Ceremonies were conducted at a

As skilled as an American Indian, whose way of life he emulated, Alan Kuntze in Van Cortlandt Park at his trapping line, a caught muskrat in hand. Handsome and charming and a couple of years older, he was my adviser in matters of wardrobe, morals and manners.
Equally skilled as a champion swimmer and ice skater, he was also beloved by many a young woman who wept at his graveside when he was killed in an automobile accident while still a U.S. Air Force pilot in the last days of the Second World War.

famed Indian battle site, where was erected a First World War memorial, with its bronze list of names of the war dead surmounted by an eagle, and nearby was displayed a cannon. There were playing fields for baseball and football games. We had weenie roasts and made model airplanes and balsa wood gliders aerodynamically efficient enough that they would sail away out of sight in the sky. The older folk gathered summers to play horseshoes and shuffleboard and sat to swap tales on the benches as the lightning bugs flew by. My only deprivation was not ever to attend at a barn dance or to ever be taken to New York's annual rodeo. But for these omissions in one's life, there did not seem to be a trauma too great to overcome.

Ah, but before I became a tolerated friend of the Horgan twins, and when no more than about six years old, I got my first rejection of the many I was soon to get again now that I was fully grown up and returned to my native land, America. Where with the months passing and without being published and acknowledged for the work I was writing, I was beginning to feel more and more uninvited. But in recalling this youthful incident befalling me, it possibly explained a painful shyness which provided a background to my growing reclusiveness. One afternoon, my mother hearing of a children's birthday party being held at the Horgans, insisted I go. Dressed in a lavender summer suit with a big white collar, I sauntered down the road. I knocked at the back kitchen screen door, through which I could hear the festivities. And I was told by a voice within to go home, that I hadn't been invited. I returned, devastated, back up the street. But my undaunted mother took me by the hand and brought me back. I was allowed in and given something to eat and drink in the kitchen but did not venture further into what seemed the shady large grandness of the house. My mother had, as she could with a few direct but diplomatic words, shamed these shunners. Just as she did one day in one of my earliest street fights, when in fisticuffs with another boy his mother grabbed me and held my arms behind my back so that her son could hit me without hindrance. And my mother, who happened to be near, came and said to the woman,

You know,
You're going to have
To do that
For the rest of that
Boy's life

15

I<small>T WAS MANY THE TIME NOW</small> that having returned to America in this year of 1952 from such a different world and life in Europe that I recalled my childhood friend Alan Kuntze. Who I was sure would have been another sympathetic ear into which one could speak. But whose life, before I left for Ireland, was to send the first shadow of death across mine. And like all life that occurs anywhere, it can and does, with little warning, end.

It was while I was still in the navy, following the end of the war, and had hitchhiked on a military aircraft with other naval personnel from Norfolk, Virginia, and heading to New York somewhere, flying above the Maryland-Delaware peninsula, that smoke seeped out from the holes in the floor of the aircraft. All of us heading on leave and a fighter pilot passenger bemoaning the fact that, having survived six months of overseas combat, he was now to go down in the flames which were already licking up through the floor holes. I thought at least I would save all poetry I'd written and which I had with me in my ditty bag, pushing it near the hatchway to give it a kick out in the sky as the plane exploded. The pilot navigator and others were pressing fire extinguishers to the floor of the aircraft as the pilot dived down below out of the clouds. At best it seemed we could only now, if the plane didn't conflagrate first, crash-land somewhere in open country. But miraculously, there appeared below a B-52 emergency landing strip. The pilot descending in a crosswind and conducting a brilliant landing, only knocking off the top of a tree. I trudged through woods and swamps to find a road and hitchhiked by land the rest of the way to Newark, New Jersey, where I completed the journey home by train.

Having so escaped death, I was feeling much like celebrating life and, knowing Alan was expected home, I rang the Kuntze residence, where they had moved farther down into the Bronx. I was told over the telephone by Donald, Alan's older brother, that Alan, who had the evening before been celebrating his imminent discharge, had been killed in a car accident. This golden boy of so much promise. His lifelong love of being a woodsman, hunter and the follower of American Indian lore, and who planned to study to be a forester, now had his young life ended. Stricken and never wanting to forget this closest of all my friends and in the memory of his bus stop cigarette, which even then he called a coffin nail as he smoked it with such amusing ceremony, I swore to never smoke again. And I suppose if there were a heaven and if he did, in spite of his young sins, go there, he'd at least now know I had a benefit for which I now have him to thank.

But just as death had taken a once dependable friend, nothing now was dependable in the world that one remembered as America. The predominantly middle-class WASP nature of Woodlawn was being imperceptibly eroded. Of its four Protestant churches, other religious folk would soon take over one of them and arrive there in buses to worship. The more Irish of the Catholic Irish were seeping in. The mostly pleasant years of one's growing up were now ominously shrouded as more baneful human tragedies were revealed. And these now, rather than being accounts read in the city's newspapers, were told by word of mouth which gave them a just-around-the-corner reality where in fact they were all happening.

My mother, a lady of impeccable discretion and a purveyor of only the best view of any matter or person, invariably upheld and defended the reputations and respectability of all. Even that of the town drunk to whom one might listen at the last stop of the bus. She would patiently explain that he had troubles on his mind. Her belief being that some people had misfortune thrust upon them through no fault of their own. Nor did she feel there was any need to unnecessarily worry anyone, even when it involved the most mountainously consequential of disasters. An example of which occurred one evening, when my sister Rita, before retiring for the night, phoned my mother while she was taking her hot toddy and reading the next day's newspaper. Between them, they passed pleasantries of plans and weather and then said good night. It was not until the next morning that my sister Rita saw emblazoned over the full front page of New York's biggest circulation newspaper, in a now nationally famed photograph, that one of my mother's houses, where we had once lived and which she still owned, had burned down. Rita, this next day telephoning in a panic,

Rita and my always philan-
thropic mother at Royal Oak,
Michigan, where they went
to visit an unusual church.
My mother, who had much
traveled the United States,
had a special interest in
ecclesiastical architecture.

My father, myself and
younger brother, Thomas,
whose expression is of a
slightly more pessimistic view
than mine, as we stand on a
hillside of Van Cortlandt Park
in our corduroy knickerbockers.

listened as my mother explained that she had of course seen the picture the night before but thought not to mention it, as she had enjoyed her own night's sleep and why should anyone else lose hers over something that could not be rectified.

But my mother's faith in the basic goodness of people must have been often sorely tried. Having the undeserved reputation of being the richest woman in the Bronx, with folk even walking in front of her house, hoping they would slip and break a bone or two if not their ass, she was promptly sued over the fire by all and sundry and even by those trying to put it out. But it was an example of her coolness under such onslaught that only once was I ever to see her crack, albeit for only a few seconds, and over another tragedy that was to populate the coming months. But she and I continued to cross swords over calling a spade a spade and if someone did a dirty deal or took the stalks off the mushrooms in the supermarket before they were weighed, that's what they did. And that not only was it unnice but that it was deliberately dishonest. If I did not go to church or marry or worship in the Catholic faith, no God, if He were such and in His right mind, was going to think less of me than He did of those who were hypocritically devout. I challenged her that it was secretly whispered that some of the richer families and pillars of the community in Woodlawn had got that way by other than fair and honest means. And that there were bigoted tax payers in league who saw to it that ethnic undesirables did not penetrate the neighborhood.

However, as the first murders had now occurred in this tiny community, it was getting harder for my mother to keep up the appearances of neighborly respectability. A man had been shot dead by a gunman when he was held up and robbed of his wallet on his front lawn. The more profound, if not terrifying, nature of this violation being that it was this man's own front lawn and that it was in Woodlawn. But there were others in the family to whom I did not have to repeat my cavil on American life. I now sensed a disguised desperation in the daily existence of my father and my younger brother, Thomas. That whatever dreams were once dreamt in this great wide land of opportunity were now no longer dreams but nightmares. My father, sitting resigned by evening watching television, regarded it as killing time. He no longer wrote his homespun poetry or recited it, as he could do, from memory. My talented brother, who could be entertainingly, whimsically witty, now having given up his attempts to sell cemetery sites, had found a job working as a security checker in a large dress clothing chain, flying from city to city to descend without warning to take inventory of stock while worried store managers and their employees either immediately left for Mexico or chewed on their fingernails or indeed, as one did, hung themselves. And now Duffy, on our walks, told of an older, exotically beautiful married sister to whom he was a confidant and who disclosed to him her unhappy marriage and the utter broken desolateness of her life. And Duffy in sorrow and despair listening to her sympathetically, until her tragic death. These stories underlining our own despair and told as we would wander as we did down a steep hill to the bridge crossing the valley of the Bronx River and New York Central train tracks the roar from which one could hear in the silence of summer nights.

Duffy's sensibilities, tempered by the tragedies that touched his life, gave some solace to me. That I was not alone against the mealymouthed and righteous. On our many meetings, we randomly walked mile after mile throughout New York City, talking and talking. I would accompany him, buying vegetables and fish on Tenth Avenue. He was always ready to stop and loiter and look in the windows of pawnshops and funeral parlors or stroll unafraid along the streets of Hell's Kitchen. In politer places, we attended music receptions and concerts, where one or two other kindred spirits lurked. He was one of the first to whom I'd occasionally recite a line or two of one of my little poems out of *The Ginger Man,* some of which he later set to music. And Duffy, fighting his own battle for recognition and against injustice and exploitive indifference to the downtrodden and impoverished in this land, had already posted notices to that good effect on the parish bulletin board in the vestibule of the local St. Barnabas Catholic Church, where we had both been to grade school. Although I remained aloof from attempting corrective measures on those deserving, Duffy never hesitated to raise his fist in the face of any narrow-minded bigot whose prejudices were expressed in his hearing. Which in America at that time or indeed at any time since, would give you big biceps in a hurry.

By evening, finishing my workout at the New York Athletic Club, I would occasionally visit Duffy, who at that time was living in Thompson Street in Greenwich Village, farther downtown. This area, known as Little Italy, where the Pope in Rome was referred to as the Big Ginney or Mountain Wop. Although its residents were unfriendly to strangers, one took comfort from the streets' European flavor. Through a cramped dark hallway and up a creaking staircase, Duffy's must have been one of the smallest, most windowless, cold-water flats in New York. Which he occupied with a comely ballet dancing girl from Sarah Lawrence College who later became his first wife. A cat swung would bounce off all four walls, and his one window opened into an air shaft across which one could reach to take something off his neighbor's kitchen table. Only that, as Duffy said, being the kind of neighbors they were, if you tried this to borrow a little salt, they would chop your arm off, cook it and try to sell it back to you as sausage.

But the spaghetti we ate and wine we drank and words we spoke within these sunless confines made it an oasis. And Jack had lost none of his robust readiness to take a justified stand against objections voiced to his brilliant playing of the clarinet and his occasional notes rendered on the French horn. Upon such protests, he would open his door and roar a warning through the building's narrow hallways that discourtesy to Debussy would be instantly avenged. In this I admit to helping him one night, as a devout lover of Debussy, to instill a little long-term terror into one or two of the more unpleasant bullying and deserving neighbors that any more lip out of them would find a couple of pineapples rolling past their door. One did find it disheartening that as fair and as good as some Americans could still be, there seemed to be so few of them. Whereas with those to whom manners had to be taught in these United States, their number seemed legion.

Meanwhile, in the news, the Collier Brothers turned up. Two gentlemen who occupied their large town house on the West Side of Manhattan but who never threw anything away. They were finally found dead, hidden within their massive, labyrinthine, catacombed building. Each room crammed to the ceiling with their furnishings and newspapers and collected junk. The only access throughout the house were tunnels through which the brothers had to crawl to get from room to room. And one found it some relief to hear of these other nonconforming eccentrics who had been living in this nation. Then fast on the heels of the Collier Brothers came another highly publicized event affecting my life in America. And just as one had nearly had enough of the hostility one met on streets and on buses and on trains. All abruptly changed and did so overnight as a spectacular headline appeared in the newspapers.

WILLIE THE ACTOR SUTTON ARRESTED.

This gentleman was the number-one most-wanted criminal in America. And called the actor because he often assumed roles disguised as a telegraph messenger or similar to gain admittance to rob banks in which endeavor he had a reputation for never having used violence. When captured, he was adept at escaping from wherever he was imprisoned and while on the run or hiding out he had also earned the near admiration of the public for his Robin Hood good works and generosity to the poor and needy. And here there was more evidence of yet another American of staunch principles and humanity from whose existence one took a little comfort as well as felt a little sadness at his capture, which the newspapers and television now dramatized. It being revealed that the arrest took place as a result of the observance of a young man who worked in his father's tailoring establishment and who had, as is the custom in American post offices, a poster affixed in his father's shop portraying America's most-wanted criminals, the number one of whom balefully stared out at him throughout the day. Along with these photographs, a substantial reward was offered for information leading to capture.

Then on the subway train one afternoon, this young man was casually reviewing the faces seated across the aisle, when suddenly he saw among them this face he'd seen a thousand times tacked up to the back of a door in his father's tailoring shop. And he at once recognized Willie "the Actor" Sutton. When Willie left the train, the young man followed and trailed him to where he lived and alerted the police. These latter in force descended upon the area to make Willie's arrest. Sutton was found to be living as usual in his quiet, dignified manner, and dispensing help to his neighbors and even paying tuition for one of their children so he could attend college. As the human interest stories multiplied and were reported across the United States, there were probably few people in New York who did not sympathize a little with Willie Sutton. The young informant was seen on television and interviewed to tell his story. It seemed for a moment as if criminality had been put to rout by civic-minded citizens and that such good deeds would receive their well-deserved substantial reward. But such was not to be. For another day later, the young man was found in his doorway shot to death.

Upon the day following this killing, I continued my usual routine of walking to the bus, which I took to the train. On the way to school, we used to play devils and angels, skipping over these blue flagstones upon some of which a cross was marked and which reminded of a more carefree time of one's Woodlawn life. And now taking the train downtown, I had got used to adopting my deadly profound Mafia expression of letting people know not to stare too long or more than once at me. As this was the terminus I usually went aboard the last car and into a nearly empty train. But upon this day as the journey began and as we passed each station, I noticed that the cars in front were filling up and the one in which I traveled was left empty. Except that as we reached our first major express stop, the doors opened and a crowd of people,

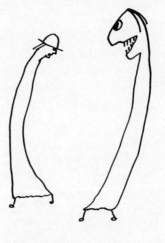

'Are you subversive?'

My drawing reflecting the mood of the time of McCarthyism in the early fifties in the United States.

pushed by those behind, came in filling the train. As we were now underground with nothing to see passing outside, I looked up and surveyed these newly assembled faces. I noticed immediately that as my eyes met theirs, there was no attempt to stare back. Quite the contrary, they seemed to nervously turn away and push farther toward the doors. Then at the next stop the entire train car emptied, with no one's gaze dwelling that extra microsecond on me to let me know I was undesirable. And what a nice relief.

Ah, but now I noticed that none of those leaving were crossing the platform to get onto other trains or were departing the station through its exit stiles, but all were instead going ahead and entering other cars of the same train. It suddenly dawning on me that it was my beard making me look suspicious and like a wanted criminal in disguise and with no one wanting to be thought identifying and unmasking me. And so it was thanks to Willie "the Actor" Sutton and his avengers, whoever they were, who had now made the city my pleasant private preserve, and the conspicuousness of my beard was not to unduly trouble me again in America.

And with only
The very briefest of glances
Required to send
Any hostile bastard scurrying
Toward quick obscurity

16

On this western side of the Atlantic, the drums were beating steadily now. If the beautiful, the brave and the wonderful were anywhere in abundance, they could not be found. All I encountered were teetering on the abyss of despondency, waiting for something even more awful to happen than a broken ass or hip, which would sentence them to an avalanche of doctor bills, which could simply wash you away. Letters more revealing of his intending departure to the New World were arriving from Gainor Stephen Crist. Mine in reply were, he found, dispiriting in the extreme. Not surprising for I penned in large printed capitals,

"IF YOU COME HERE BE PREPARED FOR THE UTMOST
IN DESPAIR."

Crist, now living in London, had been employed by the Festival of Britain as a clerk going through great ledgers and had been living in a room overlooking two tracks of a short stretch of London's underground system at Earl's Court, where the trains ran from five-thirty A.M. in the morning till one A.M. at night and, as Crist said, briefly surfaced for air as they passed beneath his window. Then, typically of Crist's life, he found a new enjoyable job traveling all over England canvassing people as to what they read, what soap they used and if they owned a TV set. But he wound up on the seafront at Blackpool, in contrary circumstances, surrounded by his first wife and second wife-to-be and his little daughter, Jane. Returning to London, he escaped to an address, Mount Ararat in Richmond, Surrey, through which area ran a road called Paradise. As I quickly looked in my encyclopedia, I found Ararat celebrated in legend as the mountain on which Noah's

Ark came to rest as the waters of the Deluge subsided. Crist, of course, was soon going to fervently wish he had stayed there. He was already alarmed by my reactions to America, asking that I did not further frighten him too much with tales of horror about the New World just before he was ready to emigrate, sailing June 12 on the *Georgic* for New York, which he later changed to booking on the S.S. *Ryndam*, June 15, 1952.

But some unexpected changes had come into one's life. A pleasant lady called Jane Pratt, who through the Zurich Jungian grapevine had heard of Valerie's presence in New York, and shortly later, hearing we were free to move, she asked Valerie if she might help her in the summer temporarily care for her grandchildren while her daughter was having another child. As the Pratts lived up in the deeper reaches of the Connecticut countryside, it was an invitation readily accepted. Meanwhile, Duffy and I attending at occasional musical gatherings, did find another friend or two. Traveling one evening to Bronxville, an isolatedly strange bit of carefully zoned suburbia forming an enclave of your more luxurious houses located just some miles north of Wood-lawn. Through this area ran Ponfield Road, over which I had so many times walked carrying home my Roosevelt High School girlfriend's books. The recital we attended was held in the large château of a Bronxville industrialist, whose son had musical aspirations, until casually meeting a girl who welcomed his amorous intentions and said she had taken precautions that she wouldn't get pregnant and, promptly in the little time it took to do so, got pregnant and demanded marriage. But here, at least this young vulnerable man was still host at this gathering, where Duffy and I met a confidently acerbic and witty lady, who was a voluptuary in all things and a marvelously brilliant blues and opera singer and actress called Tally Brown.

Tally, who lived in a sprawlingly strange windswept apartment on Riverside Drive, overlooking the Hudson River and nearly under the New York side of the George Washington Bridge, was to ease one's life considerably. A lady of solidly ample proportions, she was a wonderful cook, and Duffy and I would come to her apartment to lavishly dine and enjoy her splendid, forthright intelligence. The wine flowed, and tasting her garlic bread and spaghetti sauces and her mustard made from a grandmother's recipe made one swoon with delight. Concerning the making of the latter, Tally promised to leave me instructions in her will. It was the first time too I had come across hashish. Tally retreating to a small sitting room, where in the shadows she and her closer friends collected in a little circle, smoked as the breezes outside swept by up and down this Hudson valley. Duffy and I, both conscious of our good health, stood by politely refusing a puff but remaining appreciative of their suddenly increased good humor. However, even in this pleasant redoubt, the coinage of American life was making itself further known as more and more news came of men in nightmares and the women with whom they associated in torments much worse. And on top of it all, no one wanted to wash dishes or scrub floors anymore.

But now appearing out of the blue into my less than tranquil life, a voice from the past, and recently from Boston, came visiting to Wood-lawn. A. K. Donoghue, who had already nearly four years previous, courtesy of the American consul, sailed off from Ireland, tail between his legs, on a merchant ship, tossing, as he said, like a peanut shell on the Atlantic waves, to return via the West Indies to the U.S.A. A Harvard graduate, Donoghue first arrived at Trinity College to delve into further and better particulars of Greek and Latin. But due to the bureaucratically delayed arrival of subsistence checks on the G.I. Bill of Rights, he was in short order plunged into debt and hungry impoverishment. A condition which befell nearly all American ex-servicemen

Arthur Kenneth Donoghue sporting his graduate's gown in front of my rooms, New Square, Trinity College. A classicist, Donoghue regarded Trinity as academically superior to Harvard and would allude more often to having attended the former than the latter institution of learning.

at Trinity at the time. Who, as one of Europe's coldest winters descended, were hard put to survive the chill. And with the lack of opportunity for temporary employment, these rich and powerful world conquerors, despite the awesomeness of the United States molding their backgrounds, were turned into overnight beggars. A role the Irish simply didn't believe, so that at least the likes of an elegantly educated penniless Crist, George Roy Hill, and Ray Guild, a handsome Harvard football star, were given financial credit. And just as the impoverished poet and intellectual was tolerated and often encouraged to drink and scrounge in his day-to-day survival, so too were these former warriors, which only helped descend them into even deeper debt.

But it was a distinctly chirpier and well-heeled Donoghue arriving to stay in Woodlawn. And he was the next, following Behan, to read the manuscript of *The Ginger Man*. Donoghue, a mocker of pretensions, had always imagined that like him I grew up with a dozen pairs of hands grabbing at a bowl of boiled spuds, and while shamrocks were sprouting from my ears, Bridget would be bringing a pail of milk warm from the cow across the emerald fields of the Bronx. Nothing would dissuade him from thinking that I had, like himself, been dominated by a Boston Brahmin society keeping the Irish in their servile place. For the couple of welcome days he stayed, Valerie, he and I chewed over old times in the old sod. It being a relief to hear again the iconoclast's voice braying who'd imported blunt honesty into Ireland with the recommendation that Irishmen perform cunnilingus upon their long-suffering wives and girlfriends to ease the burdensome life of Irish womenfolk. Donoghue, whose convictions in carnal matters were supremely heartfelt and exhaustively philosophically researched, had of course in the days of uttering such tenets, yet to achieve all his goals in such matters.

However, in those days back in Ireland when conversation was just about the only entertainment indulged in and in some cases to be had, Donoghue's company was usually eagerly awaited by most of those whom Donoghue, upon meeting, did not rub the wrong way. Announcing as he would entering a room the state of his hunger both for food and a sex life. He was one of the few people to whom Brendan Behan would ever defer. Donoghue in return stating that he could not stand the sight nor the sound of Behan. Asked what he was having at Dublin's bars, it was Donoghue who, when it was someone else's round, was the first ever to order a sandwich instead of an alcoholic drink. He found himself as a result getting neither. But his principled, matter-of-fact approach to life defied rejections. And many beautiful women, who often caused his most grievous attacks of anxiety, found him unforgettably endearing.

Although he would obey some of the social rules if it opened the doors to solving some of his long-sought satisfactions, Donoghue could always be relied upon to quickly revert to his old bluntly rude ways when finding nothing was to be gained. And one could understand his reluctance to be otherwise from just one event of awareness which was to involve the health of the whole world. It was Donoghue who forthwith in that snowbound winter of 1947 must have been among the first to throw away his cigarettes when he had read in a British medical journal that cigarette smoking was a contributing cause to lung cancer. Donoghue, at the time armed with this knowledge and having taken the Irish mail boat en route to London and while waiting in a railway carriage in the Welsh train station of Holyhead, beneficially announced this news to the first smoker he met and who had, sitting across from him, just lit up a cigarette. The gentleman so informed promptly jumped up out of his seat, rushed at Donoghue, put his two hands around his neck and tried to choke him to death. Donoghue, stronger than he looked, fended him off and, standing up at the train window to attract attention and seek help, waved to the first passing guard on the train platform, who, taking one look at Donoghue, shouted back up at him,

"Shut up and sit down, you fucking ignorant Irish ape."

In the ensuing thirty or more years it took before the public was made conscious that smoking was lethal to your health, Donoghue, on the premise that his own health and longevity came first, rarely ever again breathed such word of warning to those he encountered puffing at large. And now, while visiting in Woodlawn, Donoghue, having seen my watercolors and paintings and read the existing manuscript of *The Ginger Man,* let it be known that he was moderately impressed. He had been one of my earlier disbelievers at Trinity, where, when tramping into my rooms and helping himself to food, he would stand munching away while surveying a story stuck in my typewriter and when asked to pronounce as to its quality would announce,

"It stinks."

Until one day I inserted a translated text from Horace. And when I again asked Donoghue's opinion, I heard the same refrain. It was a more cautious gentleman now who in his recent years had returned to America to become a textbook salesman representing a prestigious Boston publisher. Having studied and practiced phonetics, he had also perfected an English accent. While selling his school textbooks, he found it helped to hire a chauffeured limousine to take him to schools, where he would indulge the nun teachers in shopping trips. He took up horseback riding and became an accomplished equestrian, visiting stables and riding wherever he went. And doing so on the premise that being booted and elevated on the height of a horse, one exerted a ruling authority on those unbooted and unhorsed. His outward behavior, at least to the unpracticed eye, becoming nothing less than aristocratic in an otherwise unappreciative United States. When later he became employed at the Russian Center at Harvard, trying to eavesdrop on the matters going on behind the Iron Curtain, and when asked what had been discovered, he said,

"From all the information we get, the only two things we have found out so far is that it's gray and drab. And the only thing I've learned listening on the earphones is that I shouldn't have been doing it, as it has ruined my hearing."

The visit of a spiritually unchanged Donoghue, at least for the moment, gave some hope and a morsel of encouragement against the censorship, paranoia, and fear of the witch-hunters howling for blood across America against the original, the rebel, the bearded, the long-haired and the nonconforming. We had now agreed with Jane Pratt to come for six weeks of the summer to Connecticut, having met her and her husband and visited their secluded paradise. However, as one was learning in an America that never stopped moving or changing, the unpredictable was ready and waiting to happen around every corner. Donoghue, heading back to Boston and halfway there, the bus went on fire. As the passengers escaped and the bus burned, Donoghue sitting on the roadside was next to a lady who had lugged with her off the bus her heavy suitcase. Donoghue asked her why she had risked her life and being burnt alive just to save her old battered baggage. She simply answered that in her suitcase were all the belongings she owned in this world and if they got left behind and burned then she didn't want to live.

But worse was to face Donoghue at the end of his journey to Boston, where arriving down Lakeview Avenue in Cambridge and up a flight of stairs a letter now awaited him from Mount Ararat and from the one and only Gainor Stephen Crist. Donoghue, sitting in his mother's kitchen, read the dreaded words announcing that Crist was about to set sail from Southampton, England, for the New World and that with his passage paid and sufficient money for on board ship, he was requesting material aid in the way of a loan of twenty-five dollars to assist him upon his penniless arrival and also asking if Donoghue could also suggest some way to find a cheap room. Donoghue, who had already spent eons of time in Crist's company, as sometimes days vanished away and having already lent Crist money, which had never been repaid, the threat of Crist's descent disrupting his regulated life utterly terrified him out of his wits. Especially as Crist was one of the very few immune to Donoghue's ability to put people on the defensive. For as brutally blunt and honest as Donoghue could be with his opinions, and one who had long perfected a talent unequaled in seeking out people's weak points, Donoghue was now himself the embattled put in total and abject fear.

Of course, it was me who sent Crist Donoghue's address and suggested Crist write to Donoghue. This done perhaps not so innocently, liking as I did to keep friends in touch with each other, and to then learn from one of them how the other might be faring, and also as it was in this case to keep one's distance from Crist and avoid the calamitous events which could so easily lead to being killed in his company. And I had already written less than gently to Mount Ararat not to place hope in my aid or largess.

Dear Gainor,

It's like this. Unfortunately I will not be in New York when you expect to arrive and will be leaving about June 1st for about six weeks. Then I move to Boston. If you had me with you while looking for a job or getting a place to live people would slam doors in your face due to the fact that I have hair growing on my jaw and they would think I was a Communist Party Member. The best I can do for you if you come will be to sit in some park or better still, cemetery, and talk about Ireland or England and soothe you. There are many places for rent. You can get a room for eight dollars a week, I see them advertised in the paper. Also there are thousands of jobs but not too much salary unless you become a salesman. Spanish Harlem would be a good place to live although it's a little dangerous. As far as I know, George Roy Hill lives here. Get in touch with him, he may be able to arrange things for you. As far as I am concerned I am a little more than a bit pessimistic. *Sebastian Dangerfield* if it gets published at all will not make money, that's a certainty. The publishing game here is also a little rough. There will be no sky-pie as expected. Any money I make will be on painting. There is a saying, "It's hard but it's fair." Economically this place is much tougher than over there and I don't see how a man of your sensibilities and sensitivity will make money in this clime. If you are coming here for escape you will have to do so again. However, strangely enough your accent will be of help and may, suitably employed in the proper setting, make you money. Get in touch with the Travelers Aid bureau when you arrive, they will assist you in finding a place to live. A very pukka organization run by betrothed debutante socialites who will welcome meeting you and who may need and savor a salubrious root and ball injection. Sorry to be, if I am, so disheartening.

Guts

Although in my present circumstances, I was acutely aware that I could not afford to entertain the unpredictable Crist, whose affairs could always be trusted to be in one woeful mess, I was not to then know that Donoghue's attacks of anxiety concerning this otherwise charming man could be catastrophic. Especially as he read and reread Crist's so reasonably put words of a monetary emolument to be sent care of the American Express office, New York City. Donoghue, possessed of an insatiable childlike curiosity and naivete which allowed his imagination to conjure up awful images, now sat for days immobile with dread as he imagined a starving Crist hitchhiking from New York to Boston, and with his birdlike gait hurrying along Brattle Street in Cambridge, would turn down Lakeview Avenue, mount the porch, open the screen door and climb the stairs to beard him in his lair. And here he was, Arthur Kenneth Donoghue, an upwardly mobile American with his phonetics taped and assuming and fostering an image of the fox-hunting Anglo-Irish squire, now forced to shrink back into his chambers in Cambridge, Massachusetts. And wanting to neither see nor hear anything further whatever from the handsome, socially correct and charmingly polite man from Ohio.

The astonishing thing was that Crist was always the first to understand someone's dread and fear of him. And in such dilemma he responded with compassionate sympathy, which often made matters even more terrifying, as it meant the victim having to cling to Gainor's company. But that Donoghue could be so petrified perhaps was attributable to the young use of his imagination in thinking he was living in Ireland while early growing up in Boston. In any event, this same imagination was responsible for Donoghue becoming an astonishing scholar whose brain was able to store a good bit of the world's knowledge without of course ensuring that his opinions expressed from such erudition were always correct. But he had mastered seven languages and was an authority on human frailty, anatomy, the history of medicine, the circulation of the blood, pathology, and last but not least, knew how to light a match on the sole of his shoe. Crist loved his company, thoroughly enjoying Donoghue's display of supposed aristocratic behavior and manners and taking further delight in the slipups revealing the same old rude, crude Donoghue he knew of old who would not wait to be asked to help himself at table, but would, in a thoroughly American way, grab wine and food from under his host or hostess's nose.

European elegance unquestionably affected all of us Americans now back in our native land. Although it helped make friends and to some degree influenced people to resent you, there were no outstanding prizes for its use. But Donoghue could turn his accent on and off and did so to many a person's amazement and shock. He also took on pupils, especially Koreans, Chinese and Japanese, who although mastering English were made incomprehensible by their accents. Donoghue would socially sequester them for three months under his tutelage and then reintroduce them proudly at a party to stun their old friends with their impeccable, mellifluous Oxford accents. Donoghue at the same time would question the origin of my own vowels, many of which had come with me to Europe from the Bronx. And at least from the reactions of my classmates at Fordham Prep, public speaking seemed to be for me one of the few academic endeavors at which I wasn't abysmally inept.

But now, as the S.S. *Ryndam* plowed at a steady twenty knots toward New York City across the Atlantic with Gainor Stephen Crist on board, I found that both Donoghue and myself were attempting to compose letters to await his arrival, and largely conveying the message that he was on his own and not to depend upon help from either of us. For in addition to one's Connecticut plans, one was planning then of moving to Boston, where Donoghue told of an immensely cheap place to live in the West End, with its narrow streets and European ghetto atmosphere, where with many deserted and abandoned apartments, rents were as little and in some cases less than twenty dollars a month. And now one was about to enter another and entirely different realm amid the sylvan stretches of rural Connecticut.

But before Crist's arrival, and Valerie, Philip and my departure north to an isolated cabin on a forested hillside above the banks of the Housatonic River, there already had been the beginning of one literary encouragement, which came indirectly via a unique establishment run by the U.S. Navy called the Naval Academy Preparatory School. This scholastic institution was intended for those with an appointment to the Naval Academy who over an academic year could prepare for their entrance examination to the Naval Academy proper at Annapolis.

During the month of April, I had read James Jones's novel *From Here to Eternity* and saw a reference to the name John Hall Wheelock, who had backed the book's publication and whose name I thought the same as an instructor in English in whose class I was a pupil at this naval school. I wrote to John Hall Wheelock at Scribner's, inquiring if he were my former instructor at the Naval Academy Prep whose criticism I had found to be both helpful and kind. Toward the end of April, I received a reply that although he was not the same Wheelock from my naval days and had never taught nor indeed even been to Maryland, he suggested I send the manuscript to Scribner's anyway. And so for the first time in the nearly fifty occasions it was done, *The Ginger Man* was sent to a publisher.

However, it was in the classroom confines of this strange school overlooking the banks of the Susquehanna River in Maryland that my first serious awareness of being a writer came. The buildings and grounds were originally those of the Tome School for Boys, founded by a rich merchant gentleman of this name, who was concerned over the lack of local opportunity for the formal education of young people of modest means. Set on a sylvan height above the small hamlet of Port Deposit, where the school's founder had lived, one could see south across the Susquehanna River the rolling hills of Maryland. Now in the hands of the navy and known as officer country, the campus had a rural splendor with its gray Georgian-style buildings arranged around a grass quadrangle upon which faced the largest of these edifices, the school proper. A mansion across the green space, once the headmaster's residence, was now occupied by the commander of the naval training base, from which latter the school was separated by a golf course. There was access down a steep set of steps to the tiny town of Port Deposit. With its main street running closely parallel to the Susquehanna River and its handful of ancient frame buildings with their porches up a few steps, it was as if this tiny settlement was lost in time with no one knowing of its existence outside of the people who lived there. And in the precious few brief moments I found to just walk its one long street, I longed to, but never succeeded in, having a pineapple soda in its small-town drugstore.

In what turned out to be the last year of the war, it was as if the Naval Academy Preparatory School was a prelude to civilian life. Except that as students we resided in two large barracks on the edge of the golf course, which we were strictly forbidden to cut across to school under pain of serious disciplinary action. Instead we marched in platoons the half mile to and from classes, three and sometimes four round trips a day. Tunes booming and blaring out from the prep's own band and with "Marching through Georgia" played at least once a day. This melody heard loud and clear by the Southerners whom one suspects were making angry fists on behalf of the Confederacy as they marched. Students were comprised of those who had won appointments to the Naval Academy by exam from the fleet and civilian life and the remainder by political influence, which presented an astonishing mixture of superintelligence combined with political power and an unbelievable array of guile. With chewing gum strictly forbidden, school regulations incorporated such slogans as "Shoulder your share of the job. Do not be a slacker." However, in microseconds, the brains put together in this curious academy would invent ways of defeating all and any unwanted naval interference in our lives. The warning word "Dumbo" formulated to be whispered whenever one should be on guard at the approach of authority. And thus, with its strange collection of pupils and faculty, this school must have been and may remain one of the most curious educational institutions of all time.

There seemed to be a preponderance of Southerners in the prep, especially from the states of Mississippi and Louisiana and all with resoundingly Anglo-Saxon names. And a more romantically sentimental lot, you could never hope to meet, as they recalled in their wistful manner their idyllic existences back in the shade of their magnolia trees. Reminiscing about their high school and college proms, one could smell the perfume and sense the presence of crinoline and lace of their lady loves, with whom they yearned to be back with again. Of course, I lapped it up, even the stories of their college fraternity pranks over which they nostalgically enthused. There were some too who spent hours recalling similar hours in the blissful care and company of their black nannies and who would remind Northerners of General Sherman's troops burning house to house throughout the South and destroying Atlanta. And any slight made by any resident above the Mason-Dixon line concerning the good name of the Confederacy would provoke a challenge, with a Southerner jumping up in front of the class and, fists raised, inviting any goddamn Yankee to get up and fight. Amazingly, one or two did and quickly made the Second World War seem a very minor matter very far away.

Of course the only proper future for a southern gentleman to contemplate was the whoop whoop whoop whistling of his escort destroyers sounding fore and aft and to port and starboard, as he, an admiral on the bridge of his command battleship, sailed his fleet into combat.

But there was, like me, another less sentimental contingent from the Middle Atlantic states, with ethnically ghetto names. One a naturalist vegetarian whose Bohemian parents admonished him to never brush his teeth. And he would, without encouragement, show you his perfect yellow-brown tusks in what he professed to be a genuinely healthy smile. Along with this pleasantly eccentric chap, with his natural dentition, there were geniuses in nearly every academic category who could embarrassingly upstage the most erudite of professors from the navy at large who had been recruited to teach. With the wizards in action from the back seats of the class making such instructors' life a nightmare. Answers were shouted out to complicated algebraic equations, which the instructor lengthily wrote out on the blackboard and which were expected to take at least twenty minutes to solve, and just as the last numeral of the problem appeared, a mastermind from a back row of the class would have figured it out. With one young, exasperated officer-teacher, his patience exhausted, finally threatening,

"The next answer yelled out in this class will get the perpetrator put on a summary charge."

But what this innocent young officer instructor did not realize was that such an attempt at discipline could, through the school's political appointees, provoke the power of the United States Congress against him. In any event, for those like myself who did not want to have to bother solving questions, exams were a farce. Wizards in another class would select the correct multiple-choice answer and these would be semaphored beforehand up the stairwells and along the corridors. Or if a more serious situation demanded, report cards would be altered or even rifled from the faculty room in the dead of the night by a commando force delegated to raid across the golf course. Cheating got so cavalier that it became more a case of getting something deliberately wrong so as to allay suspicion of knowing the answers beforehand. Although nothing was new to me in this naval behavior, one had sympathy for those many who already observed the Annapolis honor system and were serious intending naval careerists who would not cheat and took more than a poor view of these old salts from the fleet who did. And one was admiring of such gentlemen who would, like their fathers and grandfathers before them, make splendid, upright, permanent naval persons. As for my own principles, the one I most strongly clung to was my objection to forfeiting my life as an ordinary seaman swabbing decks. But did not mind being killed in the service of my country as an admiral.

There were too, others skilled in the exotic. And one subtle and benign northern gentleman from an old naval family who was able to identify by smell all the available ladies' scents, enabling him to pick up limitless numbers of willing girls on trains, planes and buses upon his asking if the name he mentioned was the perfume she was wearing. But there were too those still deadly serious about the navy to whom ladies and their perfumes mattered not a damn. Above me on a two-tier bunk in the barracks slept the son of one of the navy's highest ranking admirals, who justifiably complained of the resounding bouts of laughter and the noise made in my conversations after lights-out with my nostalgically reminiscing southern friends. Further, my friend in the upper bunk let it be known that he was distracted from studying by the nautically indifferent likes of me whose constant subject of conversation was wine, women and atheism. Then following an outburst clearly provoked by my naval irreverence, and another day later following his complaint, an army of engineers, the Seabees, descended upon the barracks, and disemboweling the place in its entirety, separated bunks and converted half the place for study. Then from another student quarter, there came a complaint over the food these privileged prepsters had to eat and which was served to the large adjoining naval base. A day or two later, buses with half of Congress aboard arrived upon the training station, depositing senators and congressmen who each took a place standing between every two pupils in the long chow line and sat to dine with the Naval Academy prepsters sampling the food. Forthwith upgraded.

The school was run by a young commander with long sea duty who had been given this post as a reward for outstanding service. Early on in his administration, he called the school on parade one Wednesday to give a pep talk only to find it being greeted with student catcalls. Unable to pick out perpetrators from the mass of black sailor uniforms, and in a rightful fury and in the interests of immediate discipline, the school's weekend liberty was canceled. Dismissing the assembly, the school now confined to base and with Saturday three days away and as the political appointees alerted their congressmen and senators, there came within the hour telephone calls and cables from Washington followed by telegrams from the governors of most states in the Union. And before long the weekend liberty was reinstated, by what one must assume was a congressional decree. One imagined that this naval commander, a no-nonsense naval officer for whom this must have been an embittering experience of frustration, was justifiably ready to strangle one of these lowly ranked landlocked students who had direct access to power in Washington. And he, once having one of these recalcitrant types waiting outside his office, at least managed to trip over his chair and with an appropriate apology made to the influential student ending up on the floor on his arse.

Meanwhile, I enjoyed listening as the Southerners reminisced about their fraternities and the grand southern balls they had attended on such magical college evenings. Walking in the spice-scented air with their dates, who, for that night at least, they loved and who loved them, as the band music drifted across the campus lawns, the crickets chirping and the phosphorescent lightning bugs flying by, blinking green. I would be shown photographs they always carried of their black nannies and of whom they spoke with awed love and affection. But when I applied to a black southern college on behalf of one of the most southern of these southern gentlemen and the application arrived and he opened it with anticipation, which then turning to astonishment, fast changed into a boiling rage. As he, still in his underwear, rose, red-faced, fuming from the edge of his bunk and waving the application over his head, tramped barefoot up and down the barracks aisle shouting,

"I'll kill the fucker who did this, I'll kill him."

For weeks afterward, this aggrieved southern gent continued to roam the barracks looking to discover and throttle with his bare hands the perpetrator. And even as I reveal this these many years later, I do hope it does not incite him to come in search of me now. However, I managed at least to get him off his angry feet when I offered to assist him in training for the arrival of the Annapolis football coach and assistants who were on their way up to conduct tryouts to see if there were any football talent at the prep who could then be persuaded to make a special effort to pass their exams and come to play on the Naval Academy team. And plus, should they be outstanding players, their entrance to the academy, as we all believed, would be a foregone conclusion. My southern friend, in knowing that I was much inclined to general athletics and was possessed with a prowess at a few sports, readily agreed when I offered to put him through his paces. And so, much to my immediate relief, I was at last presented with an opportunity to divert this Southerner's sworn quest to discover and kill me.

On the evening before the tryouts, I began my friend's training, putting him through my suggested concentrated regimen and playing upon his desperation not so much to be an admiral but a football star.

By one ruse or another I was able to get him to do the first one hundred deep knee bends, push-ups and sit-ups. Then I absolutely insisted he repeat them in order to at least knock off fifteen pounds of the soft weight I said he was carrying and which flab was bound to slow down his speed. Then there were the neck exercises, the jaw, the fingers, the toes. And only when I mentioned the ears did I get a look of skepticism. Quickly explaining that it would help him get the signals correct from the quarterback in a huddle. My handiwork done, which continued till lights-out at taps, showed its results next morning when my southern friend lay inert in a long silence. Especially to my exhortation to rise and shine and hit the deck for a quick limbering-up session. His voice finally coming groaning out between his tired lips.

"You fucker, Donleavy, can't you see I can't move a muscle or get out of this bunk, never mind to stand up."

Indeed, my southern friend lay that way moaning for some days afterward and had to be supported to and from the latrine by two of his fraternity brothers. But instead of giving me dirty, unappreciative looks to my sympathetic apologies for perhaps having overworked him a little too much, he responded in the true nature of a gentlemanly Southerner, heaping all blame upon himself. There were other charming variations of these Southerners. One very pleasantly sensitive from the state of Louisiana who was a talented musician. Eschewing the philistines, he would invite me as his most appreciative one-man audience to repair to the school auditorium, which housed an organ of some splendor on which this gentleman would play Sibelius's *Finlandia* and follow with Mahler and Schubert. One day peeking in the door, we were joined by an athletic, good-looking Jewish gentleman, who, from a different rather than the wrong side of the tracks of an eastern seaboard city, was, along with appreciating music, a brilliant mimic and an antidote to all these southern gentlemen.

"Holy Jesus Christ, I don't believe it, two cultured guys in this school."

Izzy, as he was called, said he always kept his eye on the main chance in life. Which in his case turned out to be strange women in threesomes, there being a man shortage caused by the war. Returning from his weekend liberty with his Adonis good looks glowing, he would collect about him a circle of listeners whose faces he would watch change expression as he would relate his adventures, mostly of meeting up with female naval personnel in Baltimore. With three of whom he repaired to a hotel. As the shock increased on the faces around him, Izzy, the class genius at logarithms, would describe breaking the bed with the first two ladies while the third temporarily absented herself in the bathroom. Izzy, a former boatswain mate from the amphibious corps, waiting as the southern gentlemen's faces flushed red at what was considered a grossly irreverent attitude toward women, then warming to his subject and to the mostly shocked ears of his listeners, further recounted in naval parlance and in graphic detail.

"There I was, naked as the day I was born a baby in Newark, New Jersey. Now in my heroic, patriotic war effort to continue to make up for the man shortage, I fucked the first two ladies silly while the third had gone to the bathroom for a crap. And not wanting to be remiss in my patriotic duty, I knew I had to screw the third. So I left the two first ladies to each other back on the broken bed, who were raging lesbians anyway. I drunkenly crawled across the bedroom floor, crashing headfirst into the bathroom door before realizing it was closed. In the rug's dust, I went down sneezing. But patriotism again overcoming me, I came up breathing and proceeded on all fours again across the tiles of the lavatory. And nothing dismayed me, navigating toward this remaining naked objective sitting on the toilet seat. Between the port and starboard parted white thighs, I saw something dark looming ahead. I called for full engines astern. I knew I had to make soundings in order to ascertain the depth of the channel I was about to enter. I signaled slow ahead. Then I felt a hand on the back of my cranium pull me closer. It was like the great gates of the Panama Canal opening. Into the void before my eyes, I shouted "Ahoy there." I waited. Listening for the echo to come back. Then. And at long last the fading echo came back. Ahoy there. I signaled full ahead to the engine room. Then with my nose breaking a bow wave and eating my way forward hungry for this deliciousness, I had lunch, dinner and breakfast combined."

Izzy roared laughter at the gathering of shocked faces, but these weekly liberty stories he told were soon features of Sunday evening entertainment. Each story more bizarre than the last. Izzy waiting in the middle, an assemblage formed at one end of the barracks. A wicked smile creasing his face as the Southerners feigned indifference but made sure they remained within hearing distance. And one afternoon, Izzy came cornering me near my bunk. A most serious and concerned look upon his rugged face.

"Hey, Donleavy, don't think I don't know more about you than you think. We're both out of the amphibious corps and saving our lives. And I want to tell you something. You know how I like outraging these southern prima donnas. But I see you. You're always just listening. You don't smile, you don't laugh. Maybe you smile just a little. But you don't object to my filthy, disgusting descriptions. You just listen. And you know what."

Just like
The English teacher
Says
You're going to be
A writer

17

I<small>T WAS TRUE</small>, as Izzy said, that out of the amphibious corps our lives were saved. One had been assigned as a radar man to one of the amphibious landing ships medium, which had been converted to a rocket ship. Such vessels were stationed off a beach, having for three hours the firepower of a battleship, and were, with their hundred tons of rockets, chosen as a priority target to be blown out of the water by kamikaze suicide pilots during the amphibious landings. And the English teacher to whom Izzy alluded was one of the few exceptions to all the Naval Academy Prep's insubordination on the part of some of its students, and the man whose name accidentally led to my first submission as the novelist author of *The Ginger Man,* when on May 1, 1952, I first sent the manuscript to Charles Scribner's Sons, established in their Edwardian building on Fifth Avenue. And just prior to my leaving for Connecticut came the first ever publisher's reaction.

CHARLES SCRIBNER'S SONS
PUBLISHERS
597 FIFTH AVENUE, NEW YORK 17, N.Y.

Mr. James P. Donleavy,   June 5th, 1952
233 East 238th Street,
New York City.

Dear Mr. Donleavy,

We have now completed our reading of the manuscript of your *S.D.,* and I am writing you at once to give you very briefly our impressions, for whatever they may be worth.

Well, first of all, as I am sure you yourself must know, you have an extremely vigorous and fresh writing talent, with a gift for characterization which is, I suppose, the novelist's prime requisite. Secondly, this novel of yours *S.D.* (we realize that there are still a hundred pages to come), presents the reader with a concentration upon certain aspects of life, unrelieved by contrast. Such a book, for all its talent, would not be publishable. In the case of a novel such as *From Here to Eternity,* for instance, the frank depiction of certain episodes and the very heavy use of four letter words, etc., is incidental to the course of a story which does not dwell solely on these aspects.

But it's difficult to put these things into words in a letter. I note that you would like to come in and pick up the manuscript. If you will let me know in advance when you plan to come in for it, I should like to have the pleasure of meeting you, and perhaps at that time I could more adequately express our sense of your talent and the difficulties involved.

Yours sincerely,
John Hall Wheelock

I phoned to say I would collect the manuscript and on this warm sunny June day and, as I had a habit of doing approaching any new address, I reconnoitered down Fifth Avenue past the gleamingly inviting shop fronts located along part of this famed boulevard, which forms the spine from which radiates this city's geographical center of wealth. If books have splendor stacked and displayed in their shiny colorful covers, there was such in the storefront windows of Scribner's. At an entrance adjoining the bookshop, I entered an office door and, ascending a few floors in an antique elevator, I duly arrived at the Scribner's offices. Led by a receptionist to a little fenced enclosure, I soon sat with this polite, wryly smiling and kindly man, John Hall Wheelock. Who now told me that four at Scribner's had read the manuscript, and it was the opinion of three of them that *S.D.* was one of the best manuscripts ever to come to Scribner's and that the fourth person was of the opinion it was the best manuscript she had ever read. However, in Wheelock's sympathetic smile I was warned not to expect a contract to be proffered. Wheelock going on to apologetically say that because of the editorial changes in their publishing hierarchy and the climate of publishing at the time and especially in the light of the difficulties which arose from the publication of *From Here to Eternity,* he did not see how they could publish the manuscript as it stood.

Somehow one knew in these words that one's vision of a future as an author was slipping from one's grasp. Even as I persisted to say to Wheelock that in yet reworking through the manuscript that the novel might possibly undergo much change in amendments and rewriting.

We agreed that I would stay in touch. But that day, as I left Scribner's and walked back up Fifth Avenue with the manuscript under my arm and having now encountered such a glowing opinion from what could only be regarded as one of America's most revered publishing houses, famed for editors such as Maxwell Perkins and Wheelock himself, and not to have been offered an advance and contract, I was made to realize that there was little chance of finding a more liberal publisher and that instead of cataclysmic glory, *The Ginger Man*'s future in America was to be bleak.

Perhaps not so strangely, John Hall Wheelock bore an uncanny resemblance in both looks and behavior to the Wheelock I had encountered at the Naval Academy Prep. And whose English class provided its wonderful hour of pleasure with this marvelously entertaining gentleman, a chief petty officer, opening up the day's proceedings by telling his latest received risqué jokes, which, despite their banal simplicity, always reflected a verity of life. His suggestions of subjects to write upon were always original, and one responded to them. And from these assignments, he chose a selection to have read aloud by his visiting friends at gatherings at his house. Aware that I was ghostwriting several other students' themes, he never brought me to book or complained. Instead he seemed to be amused and encouraging, several times suggesting I let him show copies of my class essays to publishers with whom he had been associated in civilian life. And I had the temerity to think, as Izzy did, that he was in fact referring to me when he said that there was someone writing in the class that they would hear of one day.

However, in already presuming I was a writer, I was shy to put myself forth as one. Branded and called Shakespeare in navy boot training camp, I had been the acknowledged company poet, which mostly involved writing requested love letters to fellow seamen's girlfriends, to whom, with cynicism reeking between the lines, I would unleash salvos of marvelously sentimental endearments, which brought forth equally fervent replies. However, my similar attempts at flowery embellishment on behalf of my fellow Naval Academy prepsters often embarrassingly resulted in highly disgruntled customers, who would, chagrined, present me with a loved one's unnice response, telling them in more flowery words than mine, to fuck off and to go shove their crap up some other gullible girl's ass. Even I myself, getting such a reply from a sophisticated young lady, Joy Calverton Corbett, with whom I had attended the Ford Theater in Baltimore and who later wrote from Antioch College that if I wanted to continue my ridiculous letter writing to her, I would be getting back the same ridiculous replies.

But while there was a growing dissension to my letter writing, when instructor Chief Petty Officer Wheelock alluded to overtones of James Joyce in my ghostwritten efforts, I was alacrity itself in repairing to the Tome School library. This always singularly empty place was where I often foraged alone and on this occasion went to find out about this man Joyce, who might be imitating me. When after a long search, I finally found mention of him, it was with a certain sense of mystical awe that I read that his obscene work was banned and that he had been a dissolute undergraduate, who, frequenting houses of ill repute, consorted with medical students and led a drunken existence, carousing through the streets of the ancient capital city of Dublin. With it being three thousand miles away across the Atlantic and the country of origin of both my mother and father, news of this alleged dissolute writer aroused my first interest in Ireland. Plus the awareness that someone somewhere was producing literature banned as obscene.

But all was but a miracle in my getting an appointment to Annapolis and arriving at the Naval Academy Prep in the first place. My naval career being full of recalcitrant behavior of an almost insane and suicidal kind, ruled by my nearly hysterical refusal to do anything I considered menial, and an assault upon one's dignity. In such resolve I was helped by being a mile runner and my ability to cover any training obstacle course in pronto time. At boot camp, I had won extra leave by winning races over these prescribed hurdles and hazards. Not that difficult, as no one else was looking to overly strain himself. However, there were bases offering twenty-five-dollar war bonds as prizes, and on these I would try to break the obstacle course record. In any event, when arriving at an amphibious base located on a barren sand flat at the mouth of the Chesapeake Bay at Little Creek, Virginia, my escapes from receiving unit working details recruited for the day became legendary. Effected as they were following morning muster in front of thousands of men. Rather than have some sadist cook relish overseeing me wash pots and pans and then exercise a further authority to inspect them to see if they were clean, I would, still, even after another daredevil one or two had abandoned the idea, bolt out of the massed group of sailors while a presiding officer from a raised podium screamed over an address system in a voice I can hear even now ringing in my ears,

"Get that man. Get that man. Get him."

Of course, not ever having washed a pot or pan before, I had no idea what such cleanliness that cooks insisted upon meant. So even when extra shore patrol were put waiting for this man to burst forth from the assembled sea of navy blue, and were stationed on the long road fronting the dozens of Quonset huts which ran parallel to the base obstacle course, I still made a run for it. And the rousing cheer, which went up from three thousand or so naval personnel, did nothing to calm the anger of the lieutenant in charge. It was nearly becoming a matter now not to disappoint all those anticipating as the seconds would tick away and the suspense would mount. But as the days went by and I went uncaught, I was not to know that further shore patrol had now finally been put lurking with their truncheons at the ready and patrolling the sandy alleyways between these moundlike, corrugated, circular-roofed iron barracks. And upon the day I discovered that this further additional naval enforcement had been posted everywhere, it was too late. As a crescendo of voices rung out, "Go, go, go," I really went, for now actual hands were reaching out and one could feel the breeze of wielded truncheons as I dodged, ducking and weaving, in every direction. Literally now, running for my life. But luckily, just as the trap was closing, and, in the fraction of a second it took to do so, I finally got unseen into a Quonset hut. With doors at either end, I ran through taking off my tunic and skivvy shirt to emerge out the opposite door and to plunge both under the tap of a washing facility between the huts. And to be seen scrubbing away just as a dozen shore patrol came running from every direction. I even found a piece of old soap to add authenticity to this desperate moment. One of the posse even stopping to ask me did I see a guy running by.

"Nope, can't say I did."

It was my last attempt at outrageous escape. Leading to my final adoption of more subtle means involving much less stress and considerably less energy. As a result of my appointment to the Naval Academy and the belief that this indicated above-average intelligence, I was summoned on the base to meet one or two of the powers that be. In the amphibious corps, where lieutenants were captains of substantial-sized landing ships, even the lowest-ranked of petty officers and naval ratings wielded considerable authority. And in one signal case, there existed a first-class yeoman who simply seemed to wield influence over and above everybody, and run the entire base. This gentleman was the marvelously erudite Roger Parr. Who, with the looks of a matinee idol and possessed of many civilian academic degrees and an authority

Attired in civilian elegance, first-class yeoman and later a chief petty officer in the U.S. Navy, Roger Parr, while humanely dealing in matters of welfare, also established an oasis of culture at the naval amphibious base at Little Creek, Virginia, during the Second World War.

on Shakespeare, was also a humorous humane man. With generous sympathy, he helped many through tragedy and difficulty. And in my case, as a deserving intellectual, I was, instead of being chased by the base's entire shore patrol, able now to devise a phone call each day to the receiving unit to be called out to attend this or that facility, which enabled me to instead retire for the day to the library. Parr was also responsible for my achieving a major practical advantage in pursuing a writing career. One day seeing me peck away one-fingered over the typewriter, he insisted that I become a proper touch-typist and assured me I would never regret the time spent drilling in the initial tedium of five-finger exercises.

Parr and his cohorts were a welcome blessing from the anonymous mass of sailors who frequented the nearby city of Norfolk, surrounded as it was by military installations and one of the world's largest naval bases. On a night out on liberty, even the toughest of old salts would be seen next morning lying in their bunks wreathed in bandages. One debonair gent for whom the ladies easily fell in his bell-bottomed tailor-mades had even boasted of a date he'd made with a girl he'd met in the city's library but then found that evening when he called on the lady at her address with a bouquet of flowers, he was number seven waiting in the queue on a hall staircase. Amused by his own presumption and happily undismayed, he said that when his turn came he presented the roses, which earned him an extra kiss on the cheek for which the lady made no extra charge. And indeed agreed to let him take her out to dinner when she had finished with the last of her customers.

But from this and other stories, one was mighty glad to be able to repair to the clublike atmosphere of this base welfare office and talk away the evenings, run as it was like a Paris cafe, coffee brewing and cake at the ready. In turn I did one of the powers that be a favor and sat the high school exams for a man who never graduated and wanted to qualify to go to morticians' school when he left the navy. Embarrassingly, this gentleman, a first-class boatswain mate and a most impressive disciplinarian in his manner of commanding men, was also the petty officer who directly oversaw the very section of the receiving unit from which one had been so conspicuously bolting each day. He also had a glaring clue to my identity with my name on a nearby sign in gold letters for having broken the record and won a war bond on the obstacle course. If he recognized me, and I had a suspicion that he did, he never gave any indication. On the contrary, he spent hours describing his dream mortuary to me. Ah, but when I duly, fraudulently sat his high school exams for him, this inspired gentleman who had such wonderful plans for dealing with the dead, just barely passed.

Although I had now resorted to more subtle means to avoid menial tasks in the navy, I had previously in my reckless disregard for authority actually once been caught. Which resulted in my being briefly criminalized and imprisoned for having gone absent without leave. And had it not been for an anonymous man behind a desk who had, without my knowing it at the time, done me an immense favor, my return to academia and my brush with literary matters at the Naval Academy Prep would never have happened. Having completed radar training school in a beachside hotel in Fort Lauderdale, Florida, and endured a hurricane, which involved me in what could have been a lethal fight with a giant bully over a bunk to sleep in, I had now more peacefully been sent with a crew to the city of Miami to a receiving unit in a hotel converted to naval use to await being shipped out. As the first few days passed, I was able to leave and play golf on one of the marvelous local golf courses. Then, as an announcement was made that the transfer of the crew was imminent, we were confined to barracks, and guards posted at the hotel front door no longer allowed personnel to exit. I had long got used to this hurry-up-and-wait treatment in the navy as a quite frequent convenience adapted as an option while the navy carried out other more urgent plans, needlessly confining personnel to barracks until it suited them. This always struck me as being highly inconsiderate behavior on the part of the navy. And gauging that there were at least three days left before we would be shipped out, and too precious not to indulge in good golfing excursions, I decided to make a break for it.

The day, as they usually were in Florida, was balmy, sunny and warm. To avoid detection by the guard at the front entrance, as there was no longer free exit out the hotel front door, I repaired to the back of the hotel and a high balcony from which, holding by my fingertips, I was able to at least eliminate six feet from the fifteen or so feet to the ground. I dropped and escaped the barracks out through a back alley to a parallel street. From there in a taxi, I was off to play golf on a course where it was given free of charge to servicemen. Shooting my eighteen holes, I took a further leisured few hours dining and wining in the members' clubhouse. Returning that night to the hotel sun-kissed and alcohol-refreshed from one of Miami Beach's most beautiful golf courses, I discovered I had been wrong. This single one time, the navy for once absolutely meant what it said. The naval shore patrol were there already waiting to arrest me.

However, although more than a little worried I was assured by my captors that I wouldn't be shot immediately, and as we raced through the nighttime Miami streets in an open jeep, I found my nighttime tour full of fascination. In the brig, pleasantly located on an inland waterway near the sea, I was locked in a communal cell with what seemed to be an unrepentant group of murderers, rapists and thieves. On my prison dungarees was printed back and front of my shirt and on both thighs a big P for prisoner. My fellow criminals seemed to be charming conversationalists, philosophizing about life's untrustful vagaries and of the main things to pursue in avoiding them. One murderer, pacing back and forth reading the Bible and occasionally providing a quote. Because the prison dining room also catered to officers, served on the other side of a partition, I sampled the best food I'd ever had in the navy. Then put alone in a single cell, I was after four days suddenly given a ticket and my records and released. Instructed to take a train on which I was booked north to Washington, D.C., and from there on to an amphibious base called Solomons, I was told that I had better get there.

Although full of foreboding with the realization that my whole future in the navy was now doomed by my felony, boarding the train that evening out of Miami I entered a carpeted sanctum of mahogany elegance. I was to later learn that my crew four days previously had been shipped north, slumped in broken seats, sitting the night away in a rattling old sooty cattle car. Here in my private berth the Pullman porter had pillows puffed up and my blanket folded back on the clean sheets stretched smooth. With a decanter of chill water within hand's reach, his smiling black face inquired as to one's comfort. I said I was fine. But as I was removing toothbrush and toothpaste from my ditty bag, a naval officer with scrambled egg on his cap visor of a full commander arrived. He couldn't help but notice from the two tiny lines around my tunic cuffs that I was next to the lowest ranking sailor in the navy. When he found himself having to climb into the upper bunk above mine, his only observation of my inconvenient presence was a comment said to me with a certain amused resentment.

"Who do you know."

I was tempted to slip the commander the truth that I was a prisoner in transit. But I promptly thought better of it. Instead, by the time we reached Washington, I was by all the demeanor at my command, pretending to be, if not a nephew of President Roosevelt, at least a cousin of the secretary of the navy and on urgent top-secret naval business. Such imagined privilege must have gone to my head because I even chose on my arrival to commandeer a taxi and avail of a whole morning's leisure viewing the generously wide and beautiful boulevards of Washington, D.C. And as I was on my way to be sentenced at summary court martial, to no doubt serve further time in the brig, I thought at least I might enjoy a last few moments of freedom out in civilian life. For, back in Miami, as we paraded as prisoners out of doors under armed guard and within sight of civilians, I had already learned what it felt like to be a marked criminal. And it sure wasn't nice.

On my arrival back at this vast train station to catch a naval bus to Solomons and with the doom of my situation now descending, it would have been of immense reassurance, had I any way of knowing then that one day many years hence I would have a limousine pulled up next to the train in this same station and would be chauffeured out with the voice of John Lehman, Jr., the then actual secretary of the navy, inquiring over the car's sound system if I were comfortable and had a good trip. But now this day I traveled by uncomfortable bus to this naval base located about fifty miles southeast on an isolated toe of land sticking out into the Chesapeake Bay. With some trepidation, on arrival I handed my orders across the counter at the base's reception office to a naval yeoman. Who, in turning through the pages of my record book, looked at me quizzically. And then looked back at my papers as I assumed to look back with as much bravery as seemed appropriate while waiting for him to summon the shore patrol to put me under arrest. Finally he said,

"Hey, this is really none of my business, but you traveled all this way up here with these further orders for trial and disciplinary action just like this in your hand."

"Yes."

As I persisted to look back uncomprehendingly at him, he realized that I simply did not know what he was talking about or what I could have done if I had known. I had traveled the night along the coast of Florida, a thousand miles north, traversing these sea-level lands over the Okefenokee Swamp, through Jacksonville, Savannah and Richmond. A bell clanging as the train slowed to cross the street crossings through these sleeping villages and towns, and one peeked out to read the name of the lonely, empty passing stations. Carrying all this way with me a small slip of paper upon which was typed a naval directive toward the sentencing and doom of yours truly, seaman second-class, serially numbered 909 59 08. For a few further foolish seconds as I waited, the yeoman behind the counter suddenly tore a page out of my orders and simply said,

"You don't want this little sheet of paper in here. You just go and join your unit."

I now realized that what any old salt would have done in carrying his own records had now been done. I thanked this man I had never met before and have never seen since. And I now thank him again. For without a clean discipline record, I could never have succeeded in getting a fleet appointment to the Naval Academy. Which in itself had nearly been a lost battle. For when I heard it announced at the amphibious naval base at Little Creek, Virginia, that one could sit exams to get such an appointment, I submitted my academic school record in order to do so. But on this fairly abysmal report being reviewed, I was turned down by the officer in charge as not having a ghost of a chance. And as I stood before his desk in a gloomy Quonset hut on a sunny Virginia day, it may have been the first time in my life that I ever persisted in an effort to be let do something and especially in this case anything as unappealing as being allowed to sit an exam.

The officer, wanting to go out to play golf, finally standing and reaching for his cap, said with the utmost weariness,

"OK, sailor, if you want to take the exam that badly, I'm not going to stop you."

The mental and physical exams were spread over four days, finally ending with an interview in front of a board of officers. At this latter, one was advised to present oneself as one of the underprivileged who, through the democratic process afforded by the navy, was now given a chance to pursue the hope one always held dear of being a career naval officer. I may have even alluded to growing up in an old shack on the edge of a polluted canal where I first dreamt of a seafaring life. And also possibly described being the son of Irish immigrant parents, who although honest and hardworking didn't have a clue as to wielding influence in opening doors to the higher attainments available in American life. I could not discern any moisture in any officer's eyes, but there was no doubt that at the time I was desperate enough to absolutely believe what I was saying. And, if nothing else, I was at least free for four days of my ordeal in escaping working parties. But out of this base called Little Creek and from the ten thousand men there, only one man ended up getting an appointment. And that was me. And appropriate enough, as my old prep school pal Tom Gill was already at the Naval Academy, and considering the many times we'd both fought admirals around the ring at the New York Athletic Club, it was time now to become one of them.

But then again, it was the existence of this curious American characteristic of dispensing fairness to an underdog that one seemed to look for and expect to find on my return from Europe. And also the trait of humanity in giving somebody a break whose desperation in requesting it or needing it should have instead alerted caution in the giver to whom it might even cause serious risk. It was a pleasant practical quality one continued to recall when an officious European would go to all lengths to make life difficult and which made me have to regard Americans as being the fairest of all nationalities. Knowing that among them there were those principled with genuine compassion. Which, if it weren't the case, one would not now be writing these words.

But this day I had retired to my unit at the amphibious naval base at Solomons, which, despite my good samaritan friend who saved me from the brig, had a reputation for a certain lawless toughness. Between the constant stream of profanity, as it was generally in the navy, it was rare to hear a word of English spoken which conveyed any meaning and one was warned that these sea duty–hardened amphibious personnel were skilled at all the ruses the navy offered. I found myself the next day at morning muster standing beside a man who, as we turned right to salute, was now in front of me, as the band played the national anthem and the flag was raised. As he held his arm up, his sleeve slipped down, revealing watches worn from his wrist to elbow. Assuming that he must be either a collector, watch repairer or eager to have the correct time, I asked him what he was doing with so many watches. He said that some of his friends in the navy were careless and just not looking, so he stole them. When I showed shocked surprise at this open admission he smilingly turned to say,

"When you find a friend who is good and true, fuck him before he fucks you."

After the flag was raised and when he saw the band marching away, he said, "I think I'll see if I can join. They sound good and I'll make them sound even better." He then announced that he was a clarinetist and had played in some of America's famed bands, traveling all over the country meeting and screwing girls. At evening muster, he was tossing his philosophy back at me over his shoulder. As he said, "Man the main thing in life is that so far it costs nothing to masturbate, but you better start pulling, for they may be charging for it soon." Returning to barracks, he said, "Hey, I trust you." He invited me to see more stolen loot in his locker. Then, handing me a letter to read, he said, "See this, this is a reply from my girlfriend. Those are her lipstick kisses all over this whole letter I sent her on this sheet of paper."

Dear Sophie,
    I have rubbed my big prick all over this letter for you to kiss.
                                                     Charlie

As I held the letter up I saw Sophie's reply scrawled across the bottom.

Dear Charlie,
    I have kissed this letter all over with my lipstick. Please come and fuck me soon.
                                                     Sophie

Charlie was missing at muster next day, and I thought someone must have finally caught him stealing and turned him in. But as the band went marching by, there he was, puffing his cheeks blowing into his clarinet. And I realized I'd been in the company of another would-be poet. Who, as well as being one of the best letter writers in the navy, had, upon our parting, slipped me a further poetic piece of advice.

When you find
A girl
Who is good and true
Fuck her
Before she even faster
Fucks you

18

AND NOW in the warmth of a New York June, six years had passed since my days in the navy, and, following a totally different life in Europe, a whole new and different world of America was being revealed. Valerie, Philip and I were being ferried by the Pratts' chauffeur northward from the Bronx through Westchester's richer suburban enclaves and sixty or so miles into Connecticut. Leaving the massively spread coastal conurbation to pass through the green, cloistered peace of these small rural New England towns and villages.

Growing up, I had visited numerous times in the miles of this spacious hinterland and spent a couple of summers in this part of the world when milk was fetched from cows down the road and it was an event to hear of a motorcar passing by. We rented a mansion behind three great pine trees at Paynes Corner on Route 22, where it met Middle Patent Road. Atop the Revolutionary period house was a cupola full of hornets. From the kitchen ran a servants' staircase up to the narrow hallways and bedrooms. Beneath my corner bedroom window, where I pasted together model airplanes on the floor, snakes sunned below on the grass. Ghost stories were told by night on the big porch when visitors would come. We went to swim in a large lake in the middle of the woods behind the mansion with giant bullfrogs and big black snakes along its shore. And with our dog Chess and brother T.J., we would walk the uninhabited and seldom-traveled Middle Patent dirt road and would pass a lily pond, where a girl who lived on the nearby horse farm would, unperturbed, sun herself bare-assed on a float among the reeds.

Now one was traveling much further afield from New York City, which always seemed to exist in one's young imagination as an uninhabited wilderness reaching all the way to the North Pole. Crossing the

Housatonic River and turning into a large spread of forest, one passed odd fields with woodchuck mounds. Then coming off the blacktop road and entering upon a winding dirt track, we drove nearly a mile through a thick plantation of pines, finally arriving at a cabin in a little clearing enfolded by an impenetrable wilderness in every direction. The cabin consisted of one large living room, a bedroom, bathroom and kitchen. Two bunks on either side of a massive stone fireplace. On a wall hung a telephone operated by eccentric signals, which finally got you through to whom you wanted to speak. Disconcertingly massive spiders seemed to occasionally crawl across the bedroom ceiling. And one piece of furnishing standing in a corner was an enormous radio which, with much patient fiddling, could tune in to Europe.

Valerie went with Philip each day during the afternoons to mind Mrs. Pratt's grandchildren while she, Jane, a gracious and retiring lady, took a nap. Following a marvelously simple driving test in New Milford, I got a license to drive an eight-cylinder gray Chevrolet coupe car put at our disposal. Compared to the feeble horsepower of my European cars of the time, which even to start, I often had to crank by hand and push, this wondrous machine caused me no end of delight. When one drove out through the plantation of pines, to deliver or go fetch Valerie, it was like being on the bridge of a great battleship. Under its vast bonnet, a massively powerful engine could effortlessly move this vehicle off in third gear and propel it nearly silently along the dirt tracks and quickly accelerate it to speed on the blacktop roads. Occasionally at six P.M., one had a predinnertime cocktail with the Pratts. With George, or Gid, as he was known, turning out to be a strange, introspective bird, indeed. Who, as he sat in his sitting room in his khaki shirt and trousers, had mulled over statements of mine, which perhaps had been said a week or more previously and which he said had set his mind to thinking.

Gid Pratt too had set my mind to thinking as to who this man was or could be, who seemed not in the least to be worried about my beard nor my nonconformity, nor the communist scare raging across America. One heard he was widely known throughout these parts of Connecticut as a benevolent employer and generous benefactor, who was also accused of being liberal. But clearly he was unafraid to indulge the luxury of having his own opinions. Aware that our cabin had been newly provided with bedding and mattresses and that an amount of other furnishings had been just acquired for our comfort and finding that his supply of other and recent model Chevrolet cars was extensive, and as one would pass his brand-new combine harvesters in the fields, one could not help but become accumulatively conscious of Pratt's wherewithal. Especially after one's years in Ireland. Driving once with him to the local town of New Milford and as we passed land where I noticed cedar trees growing, I asked about them and was told he'd planted them as an amenity of beauty on what must have been many hundreds of additional acres of his estate, which I began to realize must have amounted to some thousands of acres. And one day I said to Valerie that despite the Pratts' simple, unostentatious and very private way of life, and with their positively pleasant way of presenting the existence of a chauffeur disguised as the man who got the post and the newspapers and the butler as the man who helped fix the vegetables, that the Pratts could be nothing but very rich.

Although I was at first unaware and not to say indifferent, there seemed to be a growing friction between myself and Gid Pratt. But hardly necessary to look far to find out why. As she was herself, I was also somewhat unaware of Valerie's quietly spectacular beauty, which, with her shy charm, became an irresistible attraction for anyone coming into contact with her. And that she should be in the company of, and worse, married to an impecunious and unpublished writer who could, if provoked, let you know unequivocally that not only was the work he was writing going to be published but that it would blast its way through a resisting literary world for whom the author held nothing but the deepest disregard. In America's then mood of oppressive suspicion, such words were hard even for a liberal to stomach. But I could be incited to say something resembling them to whomever I met whose sour resentment and indifference to my resolve was obvious. And meanwhile poor and unknown as I was, I remained unconcerned as to the contrast of my condition with that of having a beautiful young wife who had already quite happily endured three previous years in peasant circumstances at Kilcoole, where some folk seeing such a lady as Valerie performing the menial task of carrying a pail of water down a mucky lane dared to think I was a reprobate. But dared not at the time to call me one.

However, Pratt, if shy and retiring, was of a more candid kind. His days seemed to be spent overseeing his farm and sometimes helping his men in his fields, and he did, by his tendency to reclusiveness, intrigue me. A keen photographer, he took pictures of Valerie and Philip playing on the lawn. But signally none of me. Although I was not especially keen to be noticed or photographed, I probably would have reacted quite civilly to an invitation. Pratt said that in earlier days he did socialize somewhat and would occasionally hold a barn dance in a

Valerie in the long grass of one of our fields at Kilcoole prior to becoming a mother and our going to America.

George Pratt's photograph of Valerie with Philip on the Pratts' lawn in Connecticut.

complex of buildings which formed his rather elegant farmyard. The impression one got of the then invited were as an assortment of folk who might be referred to as socially registered Bohemians and whose interests Pratt thought might be as intellectually introspective as were his own. But he said he soon formed a less than flattering opinion of such folk and ended up preferring to avoid their company. One of course had no idea of whom he spoke, but one assumed they were your more upper-crusted of arty-crafty poets, painters and philosophers who hailed more from Park Avenue than Greenwich Village. But who perhaps might also easily fit the description of being a not too transparent bunch of rabid materialists. Rather than folk like Pratt, who had more philosophical intent and seemed to isolate himself in his own company and farm work. But had he held another barn dance, they were something I had always dreamt of being at and I would have desperately wanted to have been invited.

Although Pratt was one of the first genuinely liberal voices I was to encounter on this my return to my native land, he made me realize that despite his antipathy expressed about so-called society and the socially registered, that Pratt himself before his hair-shirt withdrawal to his rural life, and disposing of his former house with gold taps, which had been acquired by the Russians for an embassy, was himself precisely from this socially registered stratum of American life. But it was completely without warning that our evening cocktail hour was soon to be with sparks flying. My somewhat uncommunicativeness and rigid regimen of sobriety coupled with my country gentleman Trinity College anglicized accent finally seemed to have got to Pratt, who chose one moment in a prolonged pause in our conversation to announce,

"You know what I think you are. I think you're a stuffed shirt."

In the summer silence of the sylvan thousands of acres surrounding us and my face having gone several shades paler than ashen, and my fists knotted white, this statement produced in me an astonished shock of such momentousness that one could hear your proverbial flea fart out somewhere on the edge of the universe. Pratt, one was nearly sure, having no idea he was making his remark to someone who could erupt across the room in instant violence. And had done so on many a previous occasion found pointedly insulting. However, as there seemed to be much early American delicate furniture about which I admired and as an end was soon coming to our sojourn in Connecticut and for diplomacy's sake, I was prepared to use words in reply to words. But which further words could be taken as a warning. And such words meaning, say that, or anything like it again, and I'll break your ass.

"What makes you think you can say that to me."

As I rose and discontinued my presence at the cocktail hour, Pratt, at the realization that I was leaving, did murmur a few further words of polemic. For one thing was for certain. That if America was designed to make you conform, and to knock the shit out of your self-esteem, I was having none of it. And especially not from someone I thought liberal and tolerant and should know better. But I had no option but to add Pratt's personal opinion to the growingly alien world of America, and although fissures were already showing and no doubt big fractures were on the way, there was no chance of my acquiescing to the mealymouthed, who were everywhere behind their corporate shiny desks, ready to suppress, squash and snuff out any original voice who wasn't saying what they thought should be said in order that they could keep their job till retirement.

However, both the Pratts were as kindly and well meaning as they were well bred. And the matter of this falling out was over ensuing days diplomatically negotiated between Valerie and Jane Pratt, and enough words of apology were said to at least make passing confrontation not too embarrassing. Following such reconciliation as there was, Pratt came one evening to the cabin in the woods for dinner and for something as prosaic and un–stuffed shirtish as sauerkraut and frankfurters. He seemed on his most immaculate behavior to the extent that one almost preferred his previous rudeness. However, he did inquire if the cabin was populated by a variety of enormous spider, and I said I had seen an occasional one cross the bedroom ceiling. To which Pratt, a touch apologetically, said he wondered when we were going to notice them. And one could not hold any grudge against this man. He was at least one American who had listened to and thought about what I had to say. And in saying such, I could be overbearing in tooting one's own horn. In any event, Pratt was an example of the best sort of American that America can produce. And the fact that he may have been possessed of more than a modicum of the wherewithal to which most Americans aspire had not deprived him of introspective cerebration.

In the cabin in the woods, I had already written the words of *The Ginger Man,* describing Dangerfield's first day at Trinity, which was as my own, when upon that cool October first morn in that optimistic year 1946, after the war, I stepped out of the green upholstered tram, and there was the university through my apprehensive eyes. And one could, secluded in this wilderness, and while hearing the snakes glide over the previous year's dead leaves carpeting the rough ground and the muted roar of the Housatonic River below through the impenetrable forest of trees, relive walking past those college squares of flat green velvet. And as one would occasionally hear the plaintive whistles of the New York, New Haven and Hartford railway train passing just across the valley and on its way to New Milford through Brookfield and Still River, one sensed upon the ether, and muffled distant drums beating that Gainor Stephen Crist had arrived and was abroad somewhere in America. And I wondered more than a moment or two if that intrepid traveler who, with his rapid birdlike walk and nervously twiddling his thumbs, might finally be making his way through the forest lane to appear at this cabin door, his hand held out in welcome relief to grasp mine, which would be trembling in apprehension. But instead the iconoclast and dream breaker A. K. Donoghue came to be picked up from New Milford station. And in his friendly, accommodating way, to help make us feel at home, he immediately assessed our situation and informed us that we were working as servants. This made us feel swell. And when Donoghue was briefly put on display at the Pratt cocktail hour, he lost no time in capitalizing on any embarrassment that could be sniffed out of the occasion. His *pièce de résistance* presented when he conspicuously lit a match on the sole of his shoe to light Pratt's cigarette.

Summer at its height and with the approaching end to our time in Connecticut coming near, one made plans through Donoghue to move to Boston and take over a cheap apartment in the West End, which lay at the foot of Beacon Hill and extended to the Charles River. A couple, who much resembled their names, called Melvin and Deedi, who had lived there and were selling up and moving to better things. Meanwhile I was endeavoring to see as much as I could of these environs of Connecticut and the town of New Milford, which was not without its glamour and where one could occasionally come across a famed Broadway and Hollywood movie actor going into a shop with the same meaningful determination on his face with which he played his roles. And as always seemed the case in America, I could never find enough time nor the opportunity to wander and loiter along these wonderful small-town streets and see the clapboard houses rearing up from their clean, neat lawns to stand in silent peace beneath their big shady trees.

One declined an invitation to go cruise around Nova Scotia with Pratt on a more than modest-sized yacht he sheepishly revealed owning. But one was delighted to attend a farewell picnic planned by the Pratts for us, as the sojourn in Connecticut was drawing to a close. Surrounded by stony outcroppings the *fête champêtre* was held in a glade on a distant part of the Pratt estate amid a forbidding wilderness which was out on a promontory of land into a lake. And all was a marvel of delight. On a large charcoal grate, succulently tender filet mignon were grilled. Packed in ice were the best of beers and wines. Salads, fruits and cheeses in plenty. And to whet appetites were your usual canapés, bearing the better brands of caviar, ready to set sail into the mouth. From guests assembled in a great circle came music and singing. A nearby voice commented on the beautiful firelight sight of Philip playing on the lap of his mother. And no longer being the stuffed shirt I had been, Pratt in the company of an overly ingratiating lady, chose to leave what he said was the stuffy other side of the fire, to come across and sit next to me. Saying, as he departed the lady's proximity, that he was seeking the company of a kindred spirit.

Night descending now and departing the picnic, Pratt and I were both loading up the back seat of one of his new Chevrolet cars. With the interior stuffed to capacity, as it was attempted to close the door, the contents were already spilling out. And with the door bursting open again and again, Pratt began slamming it harder and harder. Finally exasperated and with a foot trying to shove back in the carload, he then attempted to kick the door shut, a big dent appearing in the shiny new steel. As I saw Pratt's indifference to this foot imprint in the car's door and then as the stacked, stuffed contents fell out all over again, and he imprinted yet another large dent, I burst out laughing, a mischievous smile then appearing on Pratt's face. Incited by my amusement and Pratt now laughing heartily himself, more kicks were rained and even deeper dents were wrought in the car doors to get them closed. Pratt, at long last relenting and acquiescing in the admission that he had more than a modicum of the world's riches and that a few deep dents in this new car merely meant he would, if he liked, just choose another out of his garage. And if that in turn was kicked out of shape he had yet another to replace it. Holding my stomach with laughter, this scene and realization leaving me unable to stand up even with the fear that I'd be bitten in the arse by a snake as I fell and rolled in the deep grass.

But car door kicks were nothing compared to what happened when the two of us finally got in the car to motor away. Pratt pressing the accelerator to the floor and with tires smoking, the car sped, propelled forward like a tank through the ever-thickening brush to plow into the surrounding growth of saplings and trees. Careering over the former and crashing into the latter. Pratt much amused as I ducked and shielded myself. Both of us now convulsed with laughter as we went bumping over the stony outcroppings. The exhaust was ripped off, the bumpers dented and twisted, fenders torn, and sundry other metal automotive fixtures disappeared as gouges rent the front, sides and bottom of the vehicle. Until at last we finally reached the safety of the dirt road which had peacefully got us to the glade in the first place. With so many citizens washing, cleaning, polishing and pampering their cars across these United States, it was a relief to have enjoyed this charming but expensively indulgent incident. And I regretted not having been more friendly with this man who was, at least to some small degree, a kindred spirit.

But I was never left far from the growing awareness, reflected by my reaction to Pratt and the knowledge that books by Mark Twain were being censored and removed from educational institutions because the work contained subversive matter, that *The Ginger Man* and all that this novel stood for would upon publication be excoriated by such as the American Legion and the Catholic Church. Not to mention all those red-blooded and upstanding in the American corporate body who sided with McCarthyism. Such coupled with the vulgarity and obscenity of their money seemed all-powerful and the influence they wielded, overwhelming. Courageous voices were alone and shunned. And a paranoia had silenced many the American citizen who had once stood up and said "I'm going to break your ass, you mealymouthed sons of bitches."

Of such dire matters, I was now glad that I had warned Crist in my letters and even suggested that if he did come westward, he bring with him the books of Franz Kafka and read them in America. But along with such advice, I did try to be helpful in other but rather dismal ways. Aware now that one was in for the long haul and that there was no pie in the sky, I noted to Crist that as he and I had in common being sailors and that tight quarters would present no problem, I repeated to him that rooms were available for eight dollars a week and that the newspaper was filled with them. But I would always try to end on a positive note, pointing out that the cemeteries still seemed peaceful enough places where we could meet and talk. And I did think that George Roy Hill, whose name was in the phone book, could be a godsend to Gainor. Hill was then directing plays in New York and seemed at least by his address in the East Sixties to have set up more than respectably in a decent part of town.

However, with the prospect of now leaving Connecticut and one's isolation out in the woods, I realized that I had at least enjoyed a sense of escape. Even from my surrounding family in Woodlawn, aware as I was, that through no fault of their own, they had been sentenced to the American way of life, which had to be abided by for survival's sake. But too, one was growing increasingly certain that even if *The Ginger Man* was to find a publisher, that upon its being published that one's passport might be revoked by the State Department and that I'd be trapped in America and that with the little money one had left, be forever doomed to stay there. With such imaginings, I was already trying to figure a way to get out and opening the atlas to look at places in Ireland to return to, my eye settling on Mizen Head, a southwest promontory on a peninsula, where the small village of Skull was located. Somehow one envisioned this a wild and deserted rugged clime, where one could do as I did at Kilcoole, cherish and put my hands down into Irish soil again and feel its loam fall through my fingers. These thoughts now, albeit belatedly, were surely heeding voices which had already warned me. Voices which were older and wiser, such as that of Ernest Gebler. Which made me acknowledge now that coming to America had been the biggest mistake of my life.

During one of the last sultry days in Connecticut, and as I lay reading on a bunk in a modicum of shady coolness by the side of the tall boulder-built fireplace, the trees were turning up the under white of their leaves through the thick forest as a storm came sweeping over the Housatonic valley. Lightning striking out of the heavens and the thunder cracking so loud it trembled the ground as it rained a deluge. I had come to the last page of a biography I was reading of Herman Melville. His was a voice, which like Edgar Allan Poe's and Stephen Foster's, had always awakened for me the sad, forlorn story which seemed to overhang so many of America's most illustrious writers, poets and composers. These three as they seemed to be, unsung, abandoned and forgotten in the last years and days of their lives. But I found it comforting that Melville had paid a passing visit with Nathaniel Hawthorne, who was the American consul in the city of Liverpool. And to be reminded of the Isle of Man only sixty or seventy miles across the water. The thought somehow haunting me out in these wilds of Connecticut as more lightning lit the room and flashed on the words I read. That Melville's latter years of life were so quiet that even his own generation thought him long dead. Then as I came to the last paragraphs of this biography, I learned that upon a gloomy, rainy day, Melville was laid to rest in the Bronx in Woodlawn Cemetery. His grave being but a stone's throw from where I had cut grass during a school vacation one summer while holding the only full-time employment I have ever had. I took some comfort that this voice which had dwelled long in obscurity but which had awakened itself again in American literature had occupied a body whose bones had lain so near where I grew up.

And when one finally left Connecticut, the unexpectedly strange thing happened that one sometimes ideally conjures up as a redress for one's self-esteem, having been slighted as it were that one evening with Gid Pratt. Sometime after we had moved to Boston, Valerie again saw Jane Pratt in New York and was told that both she and Gid were one evening at a dinner downtown in Manhattan at which the guests included none other than John Hall Wheelock. This gentleman must have confirmed to the Pratts that he had actually read my work and that I was a genuine writer of at least some modest ability. And Mrs. Pratt relating this story to Valerie, ended it saying,

It was
You know
Nice
To hear it
From somebody else

19

IN THE MIDDLE OF JULY one moved to Boston's West End, where I had already made a reconnoitering trip and now awaited Valerie and Philip's arrival. I had slowly and pleasantly strolled through the worn wonderment of this city, so much more like the Europe I had left. Pacing over its red-brick pavements, which lay through the elegant solitude of its areas of Back Bay and Beacon Hill, the latter with its gleamingly polished windows that balefully told the passerby that we be Brahmin who live within these houses of Louisburg Square. Wandering as I would, I would also proceed through the dingy darknesses of North Station, where the trains headed toward Maine and Montreal. And where one would see derelict men shuffling by in their broken shoes and begrimed white socks.

The West End housed cramped apartments in small buildings, many of which were unoccupied and empty. Beacon Hill rose to the south along with the structures which made up the complex of Massachusetts General Hospital. Westward, with its crisscrossing sailboats and rowing sculls, was the basin of the Charles River. The West End was full of many ethnic varieties. And catering to the close-knit life of these small confines were grocery stores, butcher shops, funeral parlors, family bakeries and bars. The bustling activity in its slum streets was as close as one could get to that of a European city. And always pervading the air in the summer heat was a sour-sweet smell of life's refuse and rubbish.

One took up residence behind a curtained storefront which once sold vegetables, its entrance up a step from the street. The apartment consisted of a kitchen and tiny bedroom and a cramped water closet. The kitchen, also serving as a sitting room, housed a makeshift shower and an old gas stove. The rent was eighteen dollars a month. I sung as best as I optimistically could the praises to Valerie that at the bottom of Spring Street in the park adjoining the Charles River Basin was a swimming pool. And to this latter, admission was one penny. A coin now being counted carefully. And one of which, during these hot summer days, I soon put in the turnstile to sample this recreational facility.

My study was established with a stool and dictionary in the shady coolness of the storefront. I sat at my typewriter placed on an old counter, my nostrils never without the reasty, fermenting smell of wine coming up through the floorboards, which was once made leavening in the cellar below. Melvin and Deedi, the previous occupiers, had made efforts to cheer the kitchen walls with red paint, but even this helped little to dispel the gloom as the windows opening on a narrow courtyard allowed the sun to shine for only the briefest of moments into the kitchen and then only when it was at its summer apogee. And in this womblike interior, darkness mostly reigned.

Toward the end of July, among the first letters to get shoved under the front door and to lie waiting in the shadows on the dusty, grimy floor in Spring Street was one from Gainor Stephen Crist. He had traversed the Atlantic and was now in New York living at 178 Fifth Avenue across from the Flatiron building near Twenty-third Street. He announced he was working nine to five, five days a week, at American Express, 65 Broadway. Although this company assured Gainor of a future, he said he found it very dull, his summing-up words being, "On this August 1st, 1952, I am thirty years old and homesick for all the British Isles, excluding Wales. I should like to see you when you come out of hiding and hope your situation has improved and you are less depressed."

Letters from Gainor, writing from Europe, no longer said he wanted to go live in Spanish Harlem. And I sensed he had already thought better of the idea. In any event, he was forever a one to seek and mostly find habitation on the right side of the tracks but always avoiding anything too prosaic in his residences. And now in the New World, chased by debt from the Old, it was clear that at least he had once again somehow landed on his feet. His penchant for befriending those he casually met, especially womenfolk, resulting as it often did in his being saved, not to mention being comforted and cosseted. The first hint of the latter coming in his next letter when he referred to his weekend visits in the country. Once heading out to the rurality of New Jersey in the company of a girl he met on the big ship. Her father was an abstract artist, and her mother, according to Crist, was a blunt, forthright progressive liberal who thought Gainor had strong fascist leanings because of his contention that in a so-called democracy too many disinterested people got out to vote.

Gainor's next described visit being to Sag Harbor on the end of Long Island, where another lady, a Mrs. Spenser, to whom he referred as his friend and benefactor, had a cottage. Crist finding this small once fishing village a revelation, having no idea, as he said, that such magnificent places existed. And where he was talked to, as he described, by seemingly successful artists, although rather drunken ones. Here he ate like a pig and without a driving license drove his benefactors' and hostesses' car around the countryside. I knew vividly of where he spoke. For several of my growing-up summers had been spent in a house amid the potato fields not far from the village of Bridgehampton. I played each afternoon in the sand dunes and watched the surf breaking along the miles of deserted beach. At the age of five, I had learned to swim in Sagaponack Pond. And our evening excursions for ice creams took us to Sag Harbor across the island. And it was strange now to hear Gainor refer to one's childhood haunts.

I was to hear more of Crist's first few days on the July-hot New York pavements. With little or no carfare and searching for a job and with massive holes in the soles of his shoes, Crist had to pad these with folded wads of newspaper to prevent the bottom of his feet from being scorched. He did too straight off follow my advice to ring George Roy Hill. Getting no reply, he proceeded to see if he might, by calling at Hill's address in the East Sixties, find Hill home. Hill, like Crist, rich or poor, always lived with an aura of elegance, which Gainor found, finally reaching this town house of some grandeur. Mounting the brownstone steps, he pressed the bell. And waited and waited. All was silence within. But Crist, knowing well that George would, unlike many others, be overjoyed to see him, rang again and waited further. With still no answer, he finally bent down and peered in through the letter hole. And what he saw was the very last that he would ever see again of a dear and close friend, George Roy Hill. For George had, just the day previously, boarded an aircraft to fly first-class from Idlewild Airport westward. And leaving there behind him, waiting in the hall, a large steamer trunk, packed ready to be shipped by train. And emblazoned with a prophetic address.

> George Roy Hill
> Pan Arts
> Hollywood
> California

Gainor, crestfallen and overhot in his gentlemanly attire of tweed jacket and gray flannels, and without bus or subway fare, lonely proceeded on his threadbare footwear to tramp the long way back to 178 Fifth Avenue. Years later saying he knew what it was like to walk the last mile to execution in the electric chair.

Meanwhile, August had come to Boston. In leisure moments away from my typewriter, I had taken to stepping out to sit in my khaki wear on my front stoop, which enabled me to watch a group of kids spinning their tops and especially a little black boy who could, by lying in the gutter, get his top to go spinning up the side of his nose. And one day, as I was watching this amateur circus specialist performing in the street, directly across on an opposite stoop, I heard a voice utter to me.

"Hey, do you know what you are. You're a bum."

There was no doubt in my mind as to what was going to happen to this significantly repulsive creature, so confidently perched on his stoop issuing insults. But for a moment, and judging by the similar use of words, I thought perhaps Gid Pratt might have visited the district to keep tabs on me and to keep me in my place. And my reaction was similar to the one that I'd had in Connecticut. Less ashen-faced, perhaps, but twice as angry and beaming back such burning violence smoldering in my eyes that this bugger across this narrow street assumed by my utter stillness that I was ready to rise as they did in Westerns and, with my hands lowered to my six-shooters, would at his first muscle moving fill him full of lead. But having no guns, I fully intended to get up and slowly cross the street, where, should I find him still sitting or standing, I would with both legs deeply flexed and from the level of one's kneecaps, launch a single blow, which, sailing slightly upward, would connect with his throat and drive him aloft into the darkness of the open hall doorway just behind him. But as my eyes continued in silence to bore into his and signal this very definite intention, this guy in his off-white socks and no longer disagreeably sneering, was distinctly and increasingly getting nervous. Until he finally said,

"Hey, what's a matter, you going to kill me."

As I slowly rose from my sitting position and took the first step toward him, there was no doubt that the guy did not intend to wait around to see if his question might be answered in the negative. He started to get up, at first pretending nonchalance. But as I reached midstreet, his movements hurried up more than somewhat and he was now standing on the sidewalk. I continued to slowly advance, as he with quickening steps proceeded toward the nearby streetcorner. Taking a look backward over his shoulder and seeing me follow him, he broke into a run. As he turned the corner, with one last look behind, he crashed into a vegetable display of watermelons, sending them over the sidewalk, and then squashing the pink exposed flesh of one underfoot, tripped and knocked over a full trash can. The big-bellied proprietor, who made it a habit to always cheat me two cents in my change, came running out, screaming, and continued the chase for me. And luckily for this bugger on the stoop, I never saw him back there again. For there was no question whatever that not only did I totally and absolutely intend to kill him but to do it by slow punishment, leaving his jaw and teeth intact, but delivering continuous left and right hooking blows to his midsection in order not to injure my knuckles.

However, with the gleaming golden dome of the State House presiding over Boston, there was a quality of peaceful pedestrian certitude in this city. And I roamed these streets free for the most part of belligerent stares or growled insult. On our budget of fifteen dollars a week, we lived on eggplant and lamb's kidneys fried in olive oil. With liver considered offal, it was, along with kidneys, merely twenty cents a pound, and with grapes at ten cents, living was somewhat sumptuous. My daily extravagance being the five cents spent on a copy of the *New York Times* bought at a drugstore just past the gray, forbidding edifice of the Charles Street Jail. I would, in the cool of midmorning, stroll each day, passing the back of Massachusetts General Hospital, this reminding one of one's mortality. For above the large black morgue doors were the windows of the pathology lab, where one could see steeping in formaldehyde the specimens of brains, liver, lungs and kidneys in their glass jars.

Walking the length of Charles Street, which bisects the environs of Beacon Hill, one would reach the sylvan acres of the Public Garden. Here I would find a bench to read my newspaper. Which helped me in other ways, as when I had lost sleep at night, either through shoes banging the floor above or the Italian woman's last screams at night at her husband, or after midnight when the prostitute was coming and going noisily past one's window with her clients. I would on such occasions next day desperately need a nap. So following reading a few lines, I would then put the newspaper up over my face and, with the swan boats paddling back and forth on the lake nearby, be lulled to sleep. It said a lot for these better-bred Bostonians, who did not take it amiss seeing me vagrantly reclining, albeit under that day's edition of a respectable newspaper. And I was not to know then that the many years hence, my publisher Seymour Lawrence, who was to publish the first unexpurgated hardcover edition of *The Ginger Man,* would have his elegant paneled office, where from his window on Beacon Street he looked out on these very selfsame trees and benches where I snoozed in order to write this book.

Spring Street was not without its cultural surprises. One day in late afternoon at teatime, the top of the kitchen window open into the tiny courtyard through which the occupants of the building came and went, I heard the sad music of the ancient Gaelic song "She Moved through the Fair," and followed then by the melody "The Lark in the Clear Air." This latter a ballad often played for me on the piano by John Ryan in the palatial peace of the music room of Burton Hall, the sumptuous mansion where he lived and where the song had been composed one afternoon by the composer, following a walk he had taken out along the leafy lanes surrounding Burton Hall's parklands, and where he heard the larks singing as they rose high in the sky from the fields. For some moments, in my dark redoubt I thought I was beginning to hear things and that America had finally got the best of me. But the music, I was to learn, came from a secluded confine called Elm Court, only a door or two away. And I had noticed that just up Spring Street, there was an entrance to a quiet little cloister between the buildings where a tree grew, and I was told by Donoghue that it was a Harvard outpost, where the odd oddball professor came to hole up away from Harvard at a cheap rent down this tiny, cozy cul-de-sac, where Elm Court was a peaceful exception to the noisy life of this ghetto. And where some eccentric aficionado of things Irish and beautiful must now have lived.

Having put the fear of God into a local or two who dared give me more than one dirty look, and through the neighborhood hullabaloo raised by the fat grocer over his squashed and bruised watermelons, I was able to take up my peaceful, usual late-afternoon reverie sitting on my stoop. It was an ever-changing carnival to watch the traffic of life go by and listen to the eruption of fights and arguments coming out of open windows up and down the street. And each day, there would at least once and sometimes twice come by an elderly man pushing a wheelcart. In rabbinical clothes under his black homburg hat, this gentleman collected discarded clothes, junk and other sundry paraphernalia. While commandeering his load to the safety of the confines of his apartment just behind mine, he would, looking suspiciously to either side of him, speak to no one. Then one day, having deposited his daily junk collection, he emerged from the courtyard alleyway entrance to stop in front of me where I sat.

"Hey, what do you do here. In there, I hear tap, tap, tap."

To my silence, he looked suspiciously around him and up and down the street and then continued his interrogation with a conspirational smile.

"Hey, is it legal. Hey, you a bookie. I don't tell anybody. Hey, I hear you talk. The way you speak. You are an aristocrat. What do you do, you come live around here with all these bums and no-good people. Who is the woman, is she your wife. She is more beautiful than a beautiful queen. Hey, you a Jew. Hey, you can tell me. I won't tell nobody. What do you do. Tap, tap, tap, I hear all day. You are a yid. Hey, you can tell me. Hey, you shake your head no. Hey, I know. You are. You are a yid. Such a beautiful yid like you I have never seen before. Believe me, I don't tell nobody. My son. He is a big-time lawyer. Busy, busy all the time. He lives in nice big house. Nice big lawn all around him. He try to make me move. Come live with him. I say no. Hey, don't worry, I don't tell anyone you are a yid. You can tell me you are a yid. See, I pinch you on the cheek. I know. I can tell. I can feel such a fine yid. Good-bye. I pray. I go to the synagogue now."

Crisis struck. Philip, having lost a soft piece of cloth he used to caress against his cheek, got an inguinal hernia from crying. Having to be operated upon, we now became customers of the nearby Massachusetts General Hospital. And as the cliff-hanging days went by, even the cost of the thermometer to take his temperature was a worry. However, Philip's medical care was excellent and all was finally well. But the more I wrote, the more despairing I was becoming over *The Ginger Man*. Somehow sensing in Wheelock's pleasant replies from New York to my letters that there was little hope ever to be found at Scribner's. And the whole ethic of America seeming more and more averse to me and my song. And I was also to discover the kind of attention given to America's departed great writers. Before moving to Boston, the first thing I did returning from Connecticut to New York was to visit Melville's grave. Proceeding to Woodlawn Cemetery's main office at the northeast corner of the cemetery where I had worked. Inside these somber rooms, I asked for directions, imagining that I would be immediately told just to follow a way taken by hundreds of others to this revered shrine. But the helpful lady had to go to a card index file and take some time to look up the name. Finally finding the reference, she gave me a cemetery map upon which she marked the way to the plot. And I realized that not a single solitary person must have ever bothered over the recent years to come visit this burial site, where one of America's most illustrious writers had been laid to rest and where there was a quill pen carved in relief on the stone and a poem of remembrance written for a departed son.

Writing is a singularly lonely task. And, as no one wants to let you alone to do this, the writer must buy his time and his place to sit and unless he loves noise and interruption and if he can ever afford the extravagant price, the most difficult thing for him to find is surrounding silence. All these conditions added together can sometimes, especially in a city, demand a vast price. Luckily I had in the peace of Kilcoole and the Isle of Man already assimilated some of the disciplines of writing and, like a mariner at the tiller of a ship in a storm, I could keep the bow of page progress facing into the waves to plunge continually on. But sometimes in Boston in my struggle to write, the interruptive noises would be so great that I would, midmorn, sooner than usual, go out and walk. Taking the route up Spring Street which terminated into a cross street. Here I would be early reminded to get back to my makeshift desk of a shelf and typewriter. For in front of me was a small building housing the local funeral director and his parlor, with its small sedate reception room behind its ground-floor curtained windows. But above, on the next floor, as one approached from a short distance, could always be seen peeking over the top of his open window the busy, bald, sweating pate of the undertaker as he bent over a corpse. And this reminder of imminent death would soon send me back to the typewriter in the hope of avoiding it.

Having now developed a routine, I was more and more determined it shouldn't be broken. But working the cooler mornings till just past noon, noise now was a matter to be desperately contended with. In the shabby storefront room, it was harder to hear the building inhabitants' raised voices, especially that of the Italian lady on the floor above, who would, starting at dawn and continuing like a ceaseless Gatling gun, nag and berate in both Italian and English all day long and into the night. Her husband and son resigned and submissive under the barrage. The son, a well-meaning and always trying to be helpful local delivery boy, who would bring home his accumulated dime tips and in proffering the amount and being told that he shouldn't spend a nickel to buy himself ice cream, he would sometimes wearily answer her stream of fulminations in plaintive and begging tones not to get so upset. But all one still heard from the husband were his two shoes dropping nightly with a thump on the floor above.

With Philip too now crying, and as there were no nights off for the prostitute who lived three floors higher up in the building and who through the night continued to pass back and forth outside in the alley courtyard with her customers, it was a nightmare. For a few of her disgruntled patrons already noisily drunk would now get obstreperous. And along with an explosion of screaming voices in the courtyard, there would come shoving and pushing matches. At this three A.M. I announced out from behind my darkened kitchen window that I would come out and kill the next son of a bitch who made a sound. This was a mistake. The prostitute abandoned the customer shoving her around the courtyard and made it over to my window to call me a Jew Shylock who was running a numbers racket on the horses and that I should be arrested. It was now, following this diatribe, a quarter past three A.M., and it seemed a long way away from the past elegances of one's life. But whatever I did, and it was, I fear, violent and horrendous and noisy as well, you could, without any shadow of doubt forever afterward at night in that courtyard, hear the proverbial flea fart.

Meanwhile I was learning by letter reporting on the Dublin grapevine that Gainor had left in his wake in Europe much domestic turmoil. His two marvelously beautiful and captivating little daughters were now without their father. And his astonishing rapport with Constance, his first wife, to the degree of their being able to communicate by a clicking of the teeth transmitting Morse code, had now been replaced by seemingly irreconcilable differences, this forbearing spouse having long lost her sympathy for his erratic behavior. However, Gainor had now the caring and exclusive attention of Pamela, who then began doing all any woman could to ease the problems of Crist's life. But it did not take long before such efforts were upset by the accumulated previous chaos Gainor had fomented, not to mention the new pitfalls coming down the pike. These latter invariably descending as the aftermath of previous debacle. Which then resulted in Crist having to have more than a drink or two to calm his nerves in order, as he said, to mend his fences, or be able to reflect upon how to avoid having to fix them. However, I may have been the only man on earth to know that he meant no harm to those close to him, and indeed I was myself more than once brought to tears by his heartfelt concern. And I have never found anyone before or since in my life, more compassionate, more consoling or more benignant to those he loved who were in pain. And to me, Gainor from New York communicated.

"I shall be grateful to hear how Sebastian Dangerfield is faring. I wish you all success with it. It is already, I think, a success but I was speaking more prosaically and referring to the mundane financial aspect."

A. K. Donoghue, who found the Spring Street flat for us and who lived in Cambridge, across the Charles River in the eastern environs of Harvard, was a frequent visitor and continued to read the manuscript. He suggested having one of his closest childhood Boston friends, an instructor in English at Harvard, also read the manuscript. The consensus being that I should submit the work to Little Brown and Company, whose office was just up the hill from Charles Street and overlooking the Common. The unlikelihood of a Boston publisher taking on the book still did not overcome the usual fantasies besieging one of one's massive half-yearly royalties arriving by check in an embossed vellum envelope at one's Louisburg Square residence, the private messenger respectfully saluting as one's secretary acknowledged receipt.

I now dressed in khaki shirt and chino trousers à la Gid Pratt, and not in the white-shirted manner sported by Harvard undergraduates as was decreed I should emulate by Donoghue so as to avoid being taken for a manual worker. The manuscript, which had now become a quite thick and heavy document on foolscap paper, was duly left off at Little Brown and Company, in the entrance hall of this old Boston former town house. This publisher's sedate address was situated on a corner, the one side of which was a narrow brick paved street further ascending Beacon Hill. It was also near one of Boston's most socially exclusive clubs, the Somerset, to which Donoghue referred as a place into which no Boston Irish would ever be admitted unless as servants. Being Irish and knowing a bit about this race, having lived in their country, I was glad enough to hear all this colorful news, but also having been raised in New York City I had no idea this nationality had been singled out for such rejection. Which I must confess, I did not at the time think was the most inappropriate policy in the world. In any event, this would be the second time one had deposited this manuscript in its brown paper wrapping at a publisher's reception desk to await a verdict.

I had now become quite familiar with the West End's narrow ghetto streets. And the one or two of which had literary overtones, being named as they were after authors, two of which were the essayist Emerson and the poet Whittier. But it was Blossom Street upon which I would most often walk and which would take me past the sweating, balding pate of the undertaker at work. And it was as if the same contrast and signal difference existed between the funeral parlor's front office and the embalmer above that was evident in the elegance of the front part of the Massachusetts General Hospital, where limousines often arrived to deposit their hospital patients at its imposing entrance and which contrasted with the hospital's black morgue back doors, out of which exited the funeral director's van loaded with the deceased. A scene I would often pause to watch, however, my consciousness of life and death now needing no reminders.

But there was no route away from Spring Street which was not to lead me to melancholy contemplation or to startling revelations of one sort or another. And coming out one day to the busy main thoroughfare of Cambridge Street, there unexpectedly, under front garden trees and behind an iron fence reminiscent of Dublin, was a library. I joined, and occasionally within its architectural elegance and under its rather splendid dome, I would go to randomly read anything at all that struck my interest among the newspapers and magazines. Then upon one hot afternoon, looking through the recently returned books, I came upon a volume written about America's sixty families, who, by virtue of their vast wealth, could be thought to own the United States. And as I was then subsisting on my few paltry dollars a week, I thumbed through this book's pages, recognizing some of these fabled names, and taking solace that at least there were a handful of folk about somewhere in this land who did not have to overly worry where next month's rent was coming from. Then suddenly, I came across a name described among others as one few Americans had ever heard of, but was capable of being able to buy and sell Indian maharajas. And as I eagerly read further, there it was, a name I knew. None other than my old friendly adversary and former host in Connecticut, Gid Pratt. And although I had already said it to Valerie that the Pratts could be nothing else but very rich,

It was
You know
Nice
To hear it
From somebody else

20

O N AUGUST 12, 1952, at 12:52 P.M., a Western Union Cablegram
from New York City was received in Boston and was duly delivered
early afternoon to 51A Poplar Street. Pasted to the top of the telegram
was a legend:

FOR DISTINCTIVE, SOCIALLY CORRECT
MODERN CORRESPONDENCE, INVITATIONS, ANNOUNCEMENTS,
REGRETS, GREETINGS, CONGRATULATIONS,
USE TELEGRAMS.

In the upper right-hand corner, there was even the symbol VLT,
which stood for "International Victory Letter," and Crist's message
very aptly seemed to fit Western Union's style.

DONLEAVY
51A POPLAR STREET

ARRIVING TONIGHT WITH GUILD LITTLE GELD NO
GUILE MUCH GUILT

GAINOR

I was finally to lay eyes upon the living and breathing Gainor Stephen Crist in the New World. Ray Guild, mentioned in the cable, was
a Bostonian of exotic lineage, who had grown up a close friend of
Donoghue's in the area of Cambridge. Guild, one of the most affable
and good-natured of men, when hearing of Donoghue's plan to go to
study at Trinity College, Dublin, immediately jumped on the boat with
him just as Donoghue was about to leave. Ray, an outstanding scholar
and star athlete at Harvard, was a member of the black community of

Boston and one of the first ever of your dusky variety of complexion to play on Harvard's football team. With American Indian blood in his veins and Ray's father a prominent lawyer and a pillar of the black community, Ray, good-looking and debonair and a master diplomat, was now representing one of America's prominent beer firms, spreading its name, fame and goodwill in such places as New York City's Brooklyn, and places beyond, and occasionally buying complimentary rounds for a bar's customers. And he could not meet a more ideal or congenial companion to do this with than the accommodatingly agreeable Gainor Stephen Crist, whose thirst could be trusted to be never without need of quenching.

It was through Ray Guild and Donoghue that much of our early socializing was done during our first weeks in Boston. And it was mostly among black folk who heaped hospitality upon us. Which seemed appropriate enough. For upon my return to America, I had long got used to, during my years at Trinity, associating a black face with a well-mannered and pleasant aristocracy who were a privileged lot indeed. Many having already been to Britain's best public schools and were, as the sons of the very rich and politically powerful chieftains and tribal kings in Africa, usually accompanied by a retinue of servants and marvelously solicitous and obedient womenfolk. And feasts given by such gentlemen were welcome occasions during the cold and dreary winter days of Dublin. Upon my first arrival back in America, I found myself favoring to seek out black faces among the whites to ask of directions or other matters of information one found necessary in the city. However, at first surprised by the lack of reciprocation, or much elegant semblance to my former mates at Trinity, I did not long persist.

For a dollar and seventeen cents, I nearly furnished our Boston kitchen, purchasing twenty glasses for three cents each, together with ten plates and a platter. As one or two other former Trinity people arrived at the shop front redoubt of 51A Poplar Street, it became for a brief moment a meeting place, as had my rooms at college. Besides Ray Guild and Donoghue, there was Douglas Wilson, who lived just over the river in Cambridge and who had been a frequent visitor to Kilcoole. One does not know if he were trepidatious, as he showed up down this shadowy ghetto street and he exhibited no signs of it, issuing us with our first invitation to the countryside, where his family had houses at Grafton, Vermont. There to witness over a weekend New England's spectacular turning of the leaves. And also to witness a crisis with Philip, who, when one's back was turned, managed to crawl and open a kitchen cupboard and get at some rat poison, which he was induced to vomit out copiously as a precaution but seemed to sample without harm.

Away from our narrow little street in Boston's West End, aswarm with its Italians, Poles, Jews, Czechs, Slavs and Russians, one had now at the Guilds' and Wilsons' houses at least got a glimpse of the family life which Americans aspire to. And upon Gainor's weekend arrival with Ray in Boston, he was at his cheerful best and seemed to be going great guns. Although it was never known to me for Gainor to suffer from melancholy, he would have his distracted and down moments, but even during these his priority would always be to cheer one up. His thank-you note came back to say that he had enjoyed a thoroughly wonderful weekend and had, after an arduous road journey, arrived safely back in New York to there drink beer with Ray from two to four A.M. And as always in his communications was his added encouraging word.

"Mike, I'm genuinely most impressed with SD and really feel that its publication is inevitable. Be patient, however, and don't be discouraged by preliminary disappointments should they occur."

It so far seemed that with a brand-new fresh start in the capital city of the New World that Gainor had not yet too much complicated his affairs. And was in his respectable job with American Express doing fine and hoping to do better. But in all these assumptions, I was wrong, wrong, wrong. I was to learn not that much later that new, bigger and more ominous complications had already accumulated in his life. Facts slowly emerging that someone somewhere had begun to chase him, necessitating his taking up residence out in the semisuburban wastes of Long Island, where he claimed he had also moved, having left American Express, for closer access in his new job, that of playing host on behalf of an airline to receive very important people from abroad. And forsooth, no one anywhere could do such job better. As compliments poured in to the airline's executives from such dignitaries of every description from every corner of the globe, upon whom Gainor had danced his attendance. His being the first voice who might greet them to escort them from the plane or to see them off on their departure. Even the United States State Department were dumbfounded by the paeans of praise. Ah, but the entertainment and refreshment expenses incurred by this brilliant host, Gainor Stephen Crist, were astronomical. With the bar bills crippling the airline, the otherwise appreciative executives decided that in spite of the enthusiastic VIP praise for Crist, that this host had to go.

Gainor, now with an income abruptly less, was looking for the cheapest rent possible. And wouldn't you know he would find along with it the worst kind of landlady. An Austrian from Vienna. Who older but still attractive was charmed by Crist's good looks and exquisite manners and, unable to speak or read much English, made inviting eyes at him. But when this was not reciprocated by Gainor's slight standoffishness and unexplained absences, she became increasingly suspicious of his activities and was soon steaming open his letters and attempting to read his mail. She employed such skill in this that Gainor was kept unaware of her activity. This disagreeable invasion of his privacy could at least be thought tolerable when letters were delayed only a day or two, but as the landlady had to have them translated this could extend the delay. Warming to her pastime, and the landlady finding some of the letters more bizarre than just tasty gossip, she began lending them to a friend to read, who soon began to send them on to a further friend of similar ethnicity, and she in turn invited in guests to hear the incredible contents. This latter sequence of events causing an entire month to go by, preventing Gainor getting some very urgent mail. It did not take long before minor misunderstandings in Crist's life became momentous ones and began to multiply to an incredible extent. Especially as the landlady was now attempting to blackmail Crist into seducing her.

However, in now changing his address to a new landlady, Crist, forever an ear of sympathy, quickly found himself in even deeper trouble in Flatbush, an area known as a desirable residential neighborhood. Married to a policeman, this new and reasonably attractive landlady made Crist generous maple syrup and pancake breakfasts and confided in him that she was forced to commit, to her horror, unpalatable sexual practices. These consisting of being made to stand with her hands cuffed behind her back and positioned in front of mirrors, where her husband, holding his service revolver to her head, buggered her at gunpoint. Finding Crist an attractive and compassionate listener, it did not help Gainor's peace of mind to further learn from the landlady that her husband had already murdered two people, one of whom had made a pass at her. Which promptly made Gainor conspicuously attend the Flatbush Reformed Protestant Church and to make it known that he was a member of a midwestern religious sect specializing in celibacy. But although Crist, who had read law at Trinity and taken his dinners at Lincoln's Inn in the Inns of Court in London, regarded the landlady's revelations as grave and heinous matters, and were perhaps deserving of his making a citizen's arrest, he thought, at least for the time being, that because of his own quickening problems, he might give such apprehending a miss, especially as he related to me over the telephone.

"My dear Mike, one does not mind donating one's deepest sympathies to a victim of such unwanted carnal practice by a grievously violent husband, but one does draw the line when one is handed this gentleman's spare service revolver and is then invited to fulfill his amorous role naked and candlelit in front of mirrors while he is away the weekend playing golf with his submachine gun–toting Mafia cronies in Florida."

Ah, but you'd wonder as to what were the kind of goings-on in the letters purloined and delayed delivery by the first landlady. These were for the most part brilliantly colorful accounts of carnal relations going on back in the old country which Desmond MacNamara described as achieving a grandeur of mischievous behavior that would make the old Marquis de Sade himself gasp in shock. And were further added to by a few candidly unrestrained missives written by yours truly to what turned out to be my first ever, albeit unofficial, American reading public. But it was in the comparative distant safety of Boston and over a beer or two in the West End that Gainor now revealed the stories of his first days in New York, the ensuing correspondence over which must have kept the landlady and her cohorts enthralled. It seemed that Gainor had not been overlong in stepping off the S.S. *Ryndam* when he lost his glasses with nearly the last thing he read being George Hill's Hollywood address on George's steamer trunk. And although Gainor could still read print held very close up to his eyes, he could not decipher words at a distance, this often necessitating him to question the nearby public as to what certain signs read. In this his recent life in the New World, directions on public transport were becoming vital if he were not to be deposited in oblivion. Being as he now had to head as cheaply and as quickly as possible from one distant part of the city to another on New York's unfamiliar and complicated subway system, which was capable of confusing even an Einstein. But not a thief or assailant you might hope to bring to justice.

It was on a sultry, humid late-afternoon subway station platform near the Brooklyn Bridge that Crist was attempting to head to Canarsie, an area of dispiriting flatlands smoked over by the perpetual reek of fires to which Crist was innocently going, alas at my lighthearted behest, in search of ultracheap accommodation and to free himself of the scourge of landladies. I told Crist that it once had bordering its coastline on Jamaica Bay an amusement park called Golden City. This had been a once forlorn beach resort where Crist thought he might find anonymous and isolated refuge, which he felt he desperately needed. And now waiting for the train, Crist, as he squinted about him, asked a man standing nearby on the platform if the trains stopping on that side of the station went uptown or downtown. Gainor attempting to sound as matter-of-fact as possible, as it had already, on enough occasions, become the case in America that his aristocratically British accent, combined with his politeness and elegance of behavior, was mistaken for effeminacy. Notwithstanding this impression, and Crist getting no answer, he repeated his question. And as he was in the habit of doing in order, as he said, to make people understand what the fuck he was saying, did so using an even more clipped tone.

"Excuse me, but I would appreciate very much if you could possibly tell me if this train goes uptown or downtown."

"What's a matter, bud, can't you read."

"As a matter of fact, without my glasses, I can't. So I would appreciate your telling me if this train goes uptown or downtown."

Assuming a distinctly sour expression, the man, ignoring Crist's question, belligerently grunted. And it must be said here and now that Gainor so abhorred rudeness of any kind and especially when shown to a woman that it could anger him to instant violence. His abhorrence of those discourteous also including those who lacked compassionate humanity for their fellow man. But Crist, in spite of provocation, always remained every inch of his six feet a consummate diplomat and in addressing anyone would invariably couch his statements in the most polite manner possible, often accompanied by a slight bow and delicate clicking of the heels. He himself would never hesitate to even abandon his own urgent journey in order to conduct by the elbow another fellow pedestrian to his or her sought destination. However, so far as your man on the station platform was concerned, he was having none of it, clearly assuming that Gainor was a raging homosexualist attempting to make his unpleasant acquaintance. With the rumble of an approaching train heard, and with no one else to turn to, Gainor again, urgently, one more hopeful time repeated his question just as the train's lights came into view and were approaching in the tunnel.

"Please, does this train go uptown or downtown."

Of course there was yet another deep-grained socially correct aspect to Crist's deportment, insofar as he was the most democratic of men, and no man, no matter how mentally deficient, emotionally disturbed, sexually deviant, or lowly of station in life, would not get his most kind and undivided attention. Gainor too had recently witnessed the exquisite panoply of a king's funeral back in London, and was already much homesick for the good manners he'd been long accustomed to in reciprocal British behavior. That when such a question of direction to somewhere might be raised to a brolly-toting, bowler-hatted resident of London, this would be fluently and courteously forthcoming. And if it were a lady inquiring for help of such gentleman, he would, while giving her assistance, remove his hat, bow and again tip his hat before leaving her presence.

Ah, but we were here. In the New World. Upon this island bought for beads from the Manhattan Indians, where the skyscrapers now reared and the sun blindingly reflected hot rays into these canyons. It was a humid and sultry New York day, where fumes choked the lungs, the noise of traffic assaulted the ears and on all sides machines threatened limbs and everything harried the eye. And down in this subway, where black blobs of chewing gum made unsightly spots everywhere, a large careful rat was running along between the train tracks away from the pounding, deafening noise of the approaching train. And staring malevolently back at Crist, the man, with a snarl, suddenly replied.

"This train doesn't go anywhere near to where you ought to be going, bud."

It was patently clear that this disagreeable chap was possessed of little perspicaciousness and was unmindful of the sinewy strength of the man to whom he addressed this regrettably unhelpful remark. It was with a speed that was blinding and a force that was like a bolt of lightning that Crist's fist exploded up out of nowhere and landed with such bone-shattering concussion on your man's jaw that the sound, according to a deposition given later in court by the change maker in the station kiosk, could be heard above the noise of the approaching train. His feet separated from the platform, your man, once vertical, was now horizontally sent ten feet farther away. His body in free-fall having reached the edge of the platform now tumbled over down into the tracks. Already flashing through Crist's mind was the daily lethal phenomenon of the scorched and carbonized penises encountered by pathologists in New York City morgues, and which Crist had already witnessed befalling drunks late at night, who, in pissing from subway platforms, discovered too late that when the stream of urine hit the third rail alongside the tracks it suddenly turned into an arc of electricity, and as a bolt of this shot up in its thousands of volts, electrocuted your pissing man on the spot.

"Mike, I do for God's sake deserve better luck than to have twice now been an unwilling beholder of some poor idiot with a bladderful killing himself. Everywhere there are signs forbidding spitting, but none suggesting not to urinate. And even as God forbids, I must get myself a license and a car to drive above ground as soon as possible."

This was yet another heartfelt plea from Gainor, for as a frequently late-night traveler, the New York subway system was playing an ever-increasing major role in his life. And one could sympathize. The existence of all the mysterious and distant destinations, the local trains, the expresses, the shuttles, free transfers and the separateness of one line from another all led to finding this form of rapid transit being harrowing in the extreme. Despite Gainor's ultra-yeoman-efficiency acquired in the navy, of checking and double-checking, the existence of the Myrtle Avenue line, the Canarsie, the Fulton Street, the Rockaway, not to mention the Concourse, the Jerome Avenue and White Plains lines and trains marked GG, DD, AA, BB, EF, any of which could land you up at a godforsaken last stop in Brooklyn, the Bronx or Queens. And all contributed to a nightmare of confusion for the unwary newcomer, as well as being a risk to life itself. Crist, in a telephone aside, saying,

"Pray, Mike, that I do, if it can be avoided, forever in the future stay off the Seventh Avenue–Dyre Avenue line, upon which due to witnessing a most awful event, I took a recent mistaken ride to the last stop, which was dire in the extreme. And having been on the Lexington Avenue line, how I managed to get on this line in the first place I shall never understand. The only explanation I can fathom is that I perhaps went into a catatonic state."

It was Gainor's second time witnessing this dreadful phenomenon of the carbonized penis. And upon this occasion he was in fact to a degree involved. He had left a New York pub past midnight in the area of City Hall and was on his way to a somewhat literary and liberally congenial gathering just one subway stop away. The station was called Brooklyn Bridge. Which bridge, as folklore had it, was oft sold to the unwary immigrant fresh in off Ellis Island, who might be found standing admiring its massive engineering and who, upon being offered it at a cheap price by a local con man and buying it, thought he could charge traffic admittance and who then, upon stopping his first customer to exact payment, promptly got the shit kicked out of him. Gainor was in fact amusing himself with this very thought as he came down into the dungeonlike darkness and urinic smells of the subway and, having popped his nickel in the slot to push through past the wooden arm of the turnstile, he was now putting his cuff-tucked, perfumed handkerchief up to his nose when he spotted down the end of an otherwise empty platform a gentleman undoing his fly and about to relieve himself into the tracks. Horrified at what might be about to happen, Gainor, always the good samaritan, shouted.

"Stop!"

But, as usual, wouldn't your hombre assume that Gainor was a righteous, interfering citizen about to insist upon proper public behavior. And your man was now cascading his piss down into the tracks while, busy, two-handedly maneuvering his prick, directing the stream. And at the same time he shouted back at Crist words of highly idiomatic English.

"Mind your own fucking business, buddy."

As the flaming bolt shot up the arc of urine from the tracks, these words spoken were to be this lamentable chap's last on earth. Pervading the subway air with the appalling smell of burnt flesh, the electric current had carbonized your man's penis, killing him on the spot.

"Mike, the horror was unforgettable, and here I was upon another fatal occasion back down again in the subway, hovering over a man I'd just knocked over into the selfsame tracks."

On this new occasion of horror, Crist, as he stood there the good citizen, shouted for help as he saw there were two witnesses at the other end of the platform. But they were already moving in what they deemed was the safest and fastest direction in which to vamoose as far away and as soon as possible. In fact, they had in the first place, as it turned out, already unflatteringly moved to where they were upon seeing Gainor arrive on the platform where he paced back and forth with his birdlike nervousness and would suddenly stop, bend over and with a slight paroxysm, twiddle his thumbs and fingers in a manner characteristic of the mentally unstable and who might have just stepped out for a random breath of subway air from their institutional confinement. Plus the man on the other side of the turnstile in the change booth was already keeping a wary eye out for this individual whose bodily movements appeared to give an indication of more eccentric behavior to come. And in these citizens' appraisals, they were not to be disappointed. For with Gainor now standing clasping his hands in an ecclesiastical manner, having knocked your man into the tracks, the crisis was in full swing. The victim's body stretched unconscious or already dead down in the tracks, where it had landed on top of the rat attempting to scurry out of the way. And Gainor, the while waiting, horrified, for the inevitable smell of scorched flesh and the man's last agonizing scream as he was electrocuted.

But miracle of miracles, all parts of the man's unconscious body missed being in contact with the third rail. Which, had even the tip of his finger touched, would, just like the pricks of the chaps pissing, have been carbonized and killed him instantly. However, with the thundering noise of wheels upon steel approaching, the train was already trembling the platform. Its lights seen and its destination clearly visible to all who could read. And if it made any difference to death after life, it did now present a new and much more gruesome way of the man's dying and being dead. Plus in Crist's ensuing trial for manslaughter, there would be a bigger funeral bill and damages assessed accordingly. For your man's head with his gray trilby hat still amazingly on, was lying across one of the shiny tracks. So if not to be carbonized, he was soon to be decapitated. And with the train's wheels passing over the rest of him, he would be ground up like mincemeat, leaving a trail of his thigh and pelvic bones peeking whitely up out of the gore and scattered all over, up and down the tracks. And the poor, honest, responsible, gentleman citizen, Gainor, having witnessed a similar mangled body in London's underground, and ever the good samaritan, and ever a stickler for fair play and good manners at all costs, stood his ground. Instead of like any hard-bitten New Yorker, who would have been four steps at a time up the stairs, and long gone out of the station and disappeared around several streetcorners. And Crist was shouting as loud as he could.

"Stop the train! Stop the train!"

The power cut, the man in the change booth was already out his door and vaulting over the turnstile. The train's brakes squealing and screaming, the terrified driver now could be seen, horror on his face as his train wheels bore closer and closer to crush the skull and decapitate the unconscious body lying in the tracks before him. The station attendant next to Gainor as Gainor continued to wave his arms and shout.

"For God's sake, stop the train!"

"Bud, the trains are stopped everywhere all over New York."

The two men now holding their breath as the train, with only inches left to go before running over the prostrate figure, finally came creeping to a halt. The cars emptying, a crowd collecting. The sound of police sirens on the street above. The station cordoned off. Paramedics, firemen and police pouring down the station entrance along the platform. Someone had already reported a person mangled in the subway. However, this man Gainor had socked was regaining consciousness and, fished up from the tracks, was leaving a dead rat beneath him. He was in fact, without a bone broken or indeed a scratch and with only his jaw slightly out of place, whisked off by stretcher and taken by ambulance to the hospital for observation. While Gainor Stephen Crist, ever the man trying to be reasonable with unreasonable people, was gently arrested. In the patrol car, the police, hearing Gainor's foreign and English accent, asked where he was from. And of all things and of all places, this man from Dayton, Ohio, nervously and sentimentally explained he was from Ireland.

"Hey, do they speak like that there."

"Some do. Some don't. I do."

"Hey, you don't say."

Later a couple of friendly executives of the American Express Company, having already highly valued Gainor's presence in their company, arranged for his release. It was not to be long now before the lawyer's letters arrived, seeking damages. And when the odd opportunity of telephone communication presented and Gainor reported this desperate event to me, he was already showing signs that his brief honeymoon with America was well and truly over.

> Mike pray God
> That something soon happens
> To deliver me out of this city
> Before it kills me
> Or worse
> I kill somebody

*Another one of my haunted men of the time
in whose hunched, pessimistic look one tried to
combine a lawyerly and ecclesiastic demeanor.*

21

WHEN RELATING this subway event to me, Gainor urged me to swear not ever to breathe, report, or repeat a word of it, so that no news of it would ever get back to Dublin or London, where the slanderers and gossipmongers would not only make a meal of it but exaggerate the incident out of all proportion and then would, by smoke signal, tom-tom, telegraph, overnight letter, and Morse code, disseminate it to every corner of the globe, including his ladylove, Pamela, who was already deeply apprehensive concerning his presence in the United States. And except for the Austrian landlady and her cohorts, no word of this event ever did get breathed till now.

As time passed, other matters were slowly divulged concerning the subway incident. Although the man did not ultimately press charges, Crist, when temporarily arrested, found himself subject to overnight incarceration and put in a daily lineup of others taken prisoner, who, for the benefit of detectives in order that they might better familiarize and acquaint themselves with the mannerisms and appearance of desperadoes, had paraded before them at police headquarters a selection of these to be cross-examined by loudspeaker and scrutinized under floodlights.

"My dear Mike, you have no idea as to the soul-searing degree such a ritual demoralizes one. I was under suspicion of being a subway marauder who was terrorizing stations by pushing people under trains and, because of my accent, even being suspected of being an international jewel thief and fortune hunter after the assets of money-rich widows. In which latter case, I must admit an increasingly desperate interest. But in my present state of dishabille, not to mention lack of ready cash, I can't see how I can finance to afford to suitably attire myself as a paramour and frequent the better hotels and cocktail bars in search of victims, indeed if such could ever be found in such dubious places."

But that was not to be the last, by a long chalk, of Gainor's battle of survival in New York's rapid transit system. It was in fact only the beginning of his being chased, harried and badgered. For now, Gainor, on the way to court to dispute damages attendant upon the first assault, popped yet another rude bugger right on the old schnozzola and now, among other dire matters, further faced another barrage of legal summonses, subpoenas and writs. But he of course at least had his European legal training at his fingertips, plus his achieved skills acquired in Dublin as to how to avoid and elude payment of bills, or those seeking damages, redress, indemnification, compensation, or restitution, not to mention atonement for the bestowing of grievous distress. However, a stroke of luck. It transpired that the wife of your first man whose jaw Gainor had contused was looking for him for so much unpaid back alimony that your man in court was turning to look over his shoulder to see if she might any second show up, which seemed to help make your man more readily agree to a nonastronomical settlement. The judge, in turn, short of calling Crist's adversary a sour son of a bitch who richly deserved to be belted on the old kisser, complimented Gainor on his forthright honesty and gentlemanly behavior, which he said he rarely if ever encountered on the bench.

Ah, but one signal precaution Gainor took with each new threatened lawsuit, prosecution or proceeding, was a quick change of address. So that, as he said, he might sleep more relaxedly, knowing his door was not to be broken through during the night and disagreeable people like process servers jump him as he slept. But all now seemed antipathetic. Even his attempts to commandeer the use of America's modern artifacts met with disaster. One always recalling Gainor's brilliance and joy back in the old country with the arrival one day of the miracle of a modern vacuum cleaner upon which he still owed payments but with which he caught flies, and his delight as he developed an uncanny skill in this regard, imitating George Roy Hill, who was a naval fighter pilot during the Second World War. But now chairs broke underneath where he sat. Wake-up devices and coffee makers either jumped off his various bedside tables or outright exploded. Lamps short-circuited and went on fire. And all as if to remind and assist to drive him out of the United States. Where he had so earnestly come to make money to pay off his debts in Europe and now where overnight he was being sued for more than everything he ever had. Especially by the man he popped on the old schnozzola on the way to court. Whose action for damages included the cost of extensive plastic surgery to restructure his nasal angle and return his physiognomy to its original appearance from having had his nose flattened across his face. And in telephone communication with me, I was to hear Gainor's plaintive but never defeated voice.

"Mike, this has plunged me into even greater debt and there is no need to remind you to keep further mum. But I must solve the daily problems of my existence. Before I even extricate myself out of one difficulty, I find myself in another. My life is becoming a legal mishmash of mittimus, mandamus, caveat, habere facias possessionem, habeas corpus ad testificandum. The discourtesy in this city is not innocent or accidental, it's wanton and deliberate. Chimpanzees have better manners. Why must people be insufferably rude and then, as one remonstrates, have their jaws or noses get in the way of my fist. I really do think that I deserve better luck than has befallen me. Pray tell, your advice to me to stay in Europe was all true. In fact, I read it for the second time just as I was stepping aboard the S.S. *Ryndam*, thinking it was a stray five-pound note I'd overlooked in my pocket and eagerly fetched it out with delight. But rather than its being the price of a bottle of champagne I intended to celebrate with on the eve of my voyage to America, it was instead your last letter to me before I left Europe. And alas contained information and advice I should have heeded. I have now reread it many times and have it taped to my mirror, where it is further reread while I shave in the morning."

My dear Gainor,

Big news I hereby urgently give to you. There is no good life here. They're all polishing their possessions. Everything is fake. Even the unhappiness isn't real. Sex is a disease. The populace who aren't beaten and disillusioned are instead insipid with the philosophy of self-improvement which is nothing more than a narcissistic self-devotion made further appalling by their thinking they're so wonderful because they're so selfish. It is extremely sad, and terribly bitter. Where no man has the opportunity to feel any love. Where the whole country is strangling with the tentacles of religion and the obscenity of money. This is a country of cancerous hearts and bodies and leaves one sitting in pain. The only good thing about it is they are getting what they deserve. And everyone at many dollars an hour is attending a witch doctor. All the wonderful things in me are locked up. But I'll beat them yet. If this letter doesn't stop you coming here, then I wish you bon voyage.

Yours sincerely and fondly,
Guts.

Guts was a name Gainor had for sometime come to use in addressing me. And one immodestly assumed it was a form of flattery in recognition of my continued fighting spirit in the face of overwhelming odds to which he had often been a witness back in the old sod when many a time he stood by holding hats and coats and taking bets on me to demolish the opposition as one was forced to wade into a bevy of bullies. But here in the good old U.S.A. it should have been Gainor who more appropriately might have been called Guts. Intrepidly upholding gentlemanly principles in the face of intolerable provocation. But there was no doubt that it was with a certain and rapidly increasing degree of awful resignation that this kindly, compassionate man, recently arrived in the New World in order to save his life in the Old, was already realizing that he would soon be compelled to return to the Old World again in order to save his life in the New.

"Mike, but for God's merciful blizzards, the cars on the highway never stop. The ethnic bigotry burgeons. Who in heaven's sweet sense ever dumped all these people together in such a caldron of discontent. They say happiness is everywhere. And I say back to them, have you looked at the faces."

Yet America was a place of cornucopia abundance where the shelves of stores were forever full. Where soap copiously lathered and hot water flowed through the pipes and showers sprayed cleansingly upon backs coast to coast across the United States. And where toilet paper could be had which was soft and pliant and did not sandpaper away, as it could in Europe, one's adrectal area of evacuance. But where nearly none would open up heart, mind or soul to speak of anything resembling the truth of this nightmare. But where, too, there still existed a nobleness such as that possessed by John Duffy, Tally Brown, Richard Gallagher and my own brother, T.J. The last, whose job of previously unsuccessfully selling graves was now counting dresses. And it could have meant that had he not quit his previous work, he would have had a potential customer in his new profession. For as T.J. flew into one far western town one evening to do an inventory next day, he found in the morning the store manager in the stock room hanging in a self-made noose by the neck. T.J. said the man had a terrible, terrible look on his face, and T.J. on the spot returned to the airport, flew back east and never again counted another dress.

And yet too, none of those friendly with me were ever to say nay, stop, abandon, don't go on, as I seemed still able to continue to do, in spite of Gainor's chaos and my own increasingly tenuous holding out in my tiny outpost in the narrow confines of Poplar Street, where I still wrote on in *The Ginger Man*. And where, pushed in under the door, a letter came. I was now summoned to collect my rejected manuscript back from Little Brown. And upon this humidly warm summer day, I went past the morgue doors of the Massachusetts General Hospital and the high gray stone walls of the Charles Street Jail to head along Charles Street and turn left up the hill on Beacon to enter the offices of these publishers. Instead of the manuscript awaiting me, I was asked by the receptionist to wait a few moments and was then directed up a flight of stairs and into a sedately pleasant office. There behind a desk was a man in his white shirtsleeves who stood up to greet me in my now usual clothes adapted à la Gid Pratt. This man shook my hand in that dreadful, limp manner that reassures that he might not be able to strangle you, but that he might dearly like to do so. He soon sat down with a look of concern overcoming his face along with outraged disapproval.

"This manuscript of yours. Were we to publish it here in Boston, we would be tarred and feathered."

I already suspected that nowhere, and unlikely that ever again on the North American continent, was I to receive any reception for this work resembling that already given by Scribner's. Being the well-mannered European, I politely listened and was evasive as to who I was or where I lived. It was clear from this gentleman's depth of feeling that it did not allow for him to be thought a mealymouthed poseur. But there was an air in his manner that said, How dare you write such a book and how dare you bring it here. And he must have read the work, for, with noticeable apprehension, this gentleman in his neat, clean white shirt behind the elegance of his mahogany desk in this graciously comfortable office, suddenly, rearing forward in his seat, raised his arm and pointed to the corner of the room behind me where the bulk of the manuscript of *The Ginger Man* sat on the floor at the very farthest point from this man's desk and, raising his voice in an angered accusing tone.

"There's libelous obscenity in that manuscript."

But even now, I remained undismayed as the voices were raised against this work, realizing it was nothing but the sincerest form of flattery. As he watched me rise from my chair and go pick up the manuscript, I had the feeling the gentleman behind the desk half expected me to stay and argue the point. And there was ever so the slightest sense of mystification over his face that he had taken this trouble and time to send on his pathetic way a scribbler, not yet an author whose work he clearly detested. I now wonder if back all those years there remains at such publishers any record of this submission of *The Ginger Man* under the initials of Sebastian Dangerfield and of the author's visit. For amazingly, this selfsame publisher, Little Brown and Company, was to cause me considerable difficulty much later on in my writing career. But if no record exists, there was no question but that here in this fine Boston town house, I was to find an enemy who would emerge more than once over the ensuing years.

Following this further dispiriting event concerning *The Ginger Man,* I found myself walking one early afternoon with Donoghue. We had just progressed past the back morgue doors of the Massachusetts General Hospital, and were emerging from Blossom Street into the sunnier clime along the Charles River embankment. I voiced one's gloom over the book and that I was now coming to the conclusion that the obstacles to its publication were insurmountable and that it would be a wise decision to not continue and finish it, but to throw in the towel. Donoghue, who was at the moment just passing a fire alarm box on the corner, stopped in his tracks and, his whole body slumping, he reached out and held on to the red fire stanchion. And I for a moment wondered if he were going to pull the lever for the fire brigade. But he was merely clinging for support to stop himself from falling to the ground as he gasped out his alarmed words.

"You can't do that. You can't stop. You've got to go on."

It was an amazing moment. And that someone could feel so strongly about someone else's work was a surprise, more so perhaps because of those so recently vociferous in wanting to reject it. Donoghue, however, was so crestfallen as we headed off to have a coffee in Charles Street that by the time we got there, and so as not to squelch the little that remained of cheerful optimism and to not depress the enjoyment of coffee and slice of blueberry pie for which he was paying, I reassured Donoghue that I would go on. But it was becoming increasingly difficult, with the suspicion intensifying that I was not to find a publisher in these United States. And with few small pleasures and less and less to look forward to, my confidence had already started to wane.

Melvin and Deedi, previous occupiers of the apartment, suddenly descended to remove their two beds. And one was left to sleep on a mattress on the floor where bedbugs now invaded. These unpleasant creatures seemed to come in under the apartment's permanently closed back door, which was just across a narrow hall from where lived my Jewish friend, who now passing as I sat on my stoop, tipped his homburg hat, bowed and called me Mr. Yid. Then on the advice of Donoghue's close friends the Moynahans, one managed to get a cheap bed from the St. Vincent de Paul Society, which remains the only instance of the Catholic Church in any way contributing to the writing of *The Ginger Man.*

Although much abated, there was still an occasional fight between the prostitute and her customers in the courtyard. But at least in the teeming ghetto of Boston's West End, with its smelly garbage-strewn streets, there was less conformity than was required in the rest of this lemminglike nation. However, both Valerie and I were now feeling a serious and growing yearning to be back in Europe, and to be there on nearly any terms. But there was a smidgen of encouragement left. In response to mine, a pleasant letter from Wheelock came. Although I could not see how I could change the character of the work, I still held out vague hopes that this highly thought of editor of whom Crist had heard and Scribner's might acquiesce to the difficulties first expressed concerning obscenity. In our meeting in New York, there had been mention of a thousand-dollar advance, which kept vague hope of survival in America alive. But that dream became more and more remote as I found as I wrote on that there was little or nothing in the work I could change. If anything I was becoming conscious that it was presenting even more of the problems Scribner's did not want. Especially in the matter of frank depiction of events too delicious to part with. And which in turn seemed to give rise to more outrageous matters in the telling of the tale of Dangerfield. Thus digging a deeper and deeper hole out of which no expurgation could now retrieve me.

As cheap as it was to live in the West End of Boston, our infinitesimal money, with no income, was running out. Such food items as a twenty-seven-ounce tall can of Friend pork and beans were luxuries beyond our purse, as were two for forty-nine cents. Or a ten-ounce can of Gorton's ready-to-fry codfish cakes at twenty-one cents. Or Bang-O popcorn at sixteen cents or fancy solid white tuna at twenty-nine cents. One did, at thirty-five cents for a pound package, make a magnanimous exception to purchasing Ritz crackers, which, coated with peanut butter, was one of Crist's favorite staples, and continued to buy half a pound of kidneys now reduced to fifteen cents. Valerie investigated working again as a speech therapist, but with the prevarication of the possibilities and referrals in distant different directions, that soon became an unenthusiastic route to pursue. Return to New York City was looming. And Gainor now in his communications constantly alerted one to the fact that these United States were not for us.

"Mike, why is it impossible for me to be able to pursue my daily life without strife. God knows I've tried to abide by the rules, maybe not all, nor to the letter but at least made every effort to uphold chivalry in a land boasting of freedom. But more a freedom for fucking other people up. There seems to be no escape for yours truly. And I am sadly left, an unhappy dangling puppet of the fates. Pray God that someone soon pulls for me more sympathetic strings."

Having both been five or more years away, we did expect too much of America, and for it to resemble the ethic we had known growing up there, that hard work and fair play was rewarded if not necessarily accorded the poor. And leisure, privilege and money would, as one's background ordained, be heaped upon those cultured and astute. Neither Gainor nor I really expected to confront a country ruled by corporate mores and riddled by fear and suspicion. But at least a few times it did achieve one's best anticipations, often enjoyed for little or no money. Although ten cents was a large investment in carfare, I occasionally visited Cambridge, climbing up to the station near the county jail to take the train over Longfellow Bridge and across the Charles River Basin, where along its shore were held summer orchestral concerts and where oarsmen on the ripples of the water rowed and pretty sailboats wafted back and forth in the Boston breeze. Then one came to the strange abruptness of this underground last stop at academia and Harvard Square. Where up the steps and across the street was the Harvard Coop. Donoghue had already walked me along by the elegant houses of Brattle Street and brought me to sit in Widener Library to hear poetry and music. I even ventured with him to a pub hangout of Harvard students. Where Donoghue explained that one had to beware concerning intellectual discussions held in such leisure environs, as sometimes these could be interrupted by intruding Boston Irish vulgarists, who, overhearing such conversations, would interject uncongenial disagreement and then on the premise that might makes right would threaten a fist to break the Harvard student's jaw.

I did feel it was all the more reason why I should be attired as I still was, in my khaki shirt and chino trousers and looking like a ditch-digger. Albeit one sporting the overtones of a British accent. However, Donoghue finally seemed to stomach his embarrassment of my being so dressed, and I met some of his oldest friends, native Bostonians of very Irish backgrounds and Harvard folk who were possessed of sophisticated charm indeed. One being Dr. Edward O'Rourke, the then commissioner of health in Cambridge. O'Rourke, a medical doctor with an astonishing range of interests, was of a marvelous, understanding air, diplomatic, tolerant, chuckling and assenting to all free thought. He would snatch minutes during his busy lunch hour to rush

Donoghue and I about while shooting a pleasantly cultural breeze with us. And generously, if only briefly, providing redeeming moments among the many accumulating depressing ones.

Among other of Donoghue's earliest childhood friends were Julian, and his wife, Lizzie, Moynahan. With Valerie and Philip, we visited them, in what seemed to us, from Boston's West End, their commodious Cambridge apartment. Dining on delicious heaps of spaghetti, we downed nourishingly rich and highly intoxicating Chianti wine. Julian, having been at Harvard, and Lizzie at Radcliffe, this young couple both knew of the hard lot of the Irish and the privilege the best educated of this race could achieve. With their intellectual assurance and possessed of an astonishing handsomeness, they were natural patricians free of the mealymouthedness and suspicions rife across the continent. They were eagerly able to listen to my own iconoclastic talk. And were thinkers of the kind that both Crist and I had imagined would still be found in American life. One took some comfort from the fact that these of Donoghue's friends now had read the manuscript of *The Ginger Man.* And were not dismayed.

Funds had now just about run out, and our ghetto sojourn in Boston was to be short-lived. When we left for New York, Donoghue took over living at 51A Poplar Street. The weather cooling, we were back again in the old white house atop the hill at East 238th Street. It was decided that the way to get out of the United States had to be piecemeal. Valerie made plans to depart for Europe and the Isle of Man with Philip. I returned the 558-page manuscript of *The Ginger Man* to Scribner's. I was now with minuscule money left, depending on handouts from my always dependable mother but beginning to see that in hanging on through a last-ditch stand and trying to see if I could find a publisher, one could bite the dust sooner than soon. But I would persist to wait till I could wait no longer. The attraction of the Isle of Man was that we felt we had there an ace in the hole. Old man Heron's will had provided for money that had been left to Mrs. Heron in such a way that a modest sum could be paid out to the four children at her discretion. Before we left for America, Valerie's mother had volunteered that the money so left would be at our disposal should we want or need to return to Europe.

Upon the sad nineteenth day of November, Valerie departed for Prestwick Airport in Scotland and from there to the Isle of Man. I was alone in America. And with Valerie gone and as I awaited a reaction from Scribner's, the days passing made one feel more and more barren and beaten. In the distant downstairs of the house and in the middle of the night, I could hear T.J. playing his "Knobbly Wood Concerto" on one of his three pianos and, as he sometimes astonishingly did, playing all three at once. Although not yet acute, the strain was beginning to tell and tensions were growing. For safety and solace, I now went to visit Woodlawn Cemetery. To muse among the tombstones under the huge trees along its winding lanes. I was frequently in touch with Gainor, who had most of my photographs I'd taken in Ireland and a carbon copy of the manuscript *S.D.,* which he said he often dipped into to read. One so far spoke pleasantly to him on the phone, always making sure one stayed at least fifty miles away. As benign, reasonable and pleasant as he could be, one knew of the risks he ran in this violent city and felt him as an awful threat. But I could hear a plaintive note in his voice as he would so politely say, "Mike, I completely understand your not meeting me. But because I feel you would be most interested to see the airport in action, I urge you to take an afternoon to do so."

Gainor had removed to yet another address, Clyde Street in Forest Hills, which was near the area's tennis stadium. Significantly, the street ran closely parallel to Dartmouth Street, after the name of the college in New Hampshire where Gainor had first attended university. I now agreed to go see him out at the airport at work. I took the Lexington Avenue train downtown, which was elevated half the way. And as it arrived underground, a benign-looking lady of early middle age got on at 125th Street and sat across from me. I was transfixed by her calm and contented countenance. And thought, my God, there at least goes one face that does not carry that cast of unhappiness writ deep and sour as it is on every other visage one sees. At her feet, there was a bag and an address airline tag on it, which, as she glanced away a moment, I could read. And it said British Overseas Airways, with the lady's destination writ just beneath. Totnes, Devon, England. And I remembered Gainor's words.

"Have you looked at the faces."

And here I was on my way actually going to see him and surely risking life and limb. Queens Boulevard, on which we rode in the long black airport limousine, was like some great highway to an oblivion one felt awaited both Gainor and I in the United States. Passing cemeteries in which the white upturned teeth of the tombs seemed ready to devour us. Then rearing up at the side of the road, a massive palace erected by the Elks. And as one stared ahead down this boulevard, doom seemed part of the landscape. Recently one had walked through the New York streets and heard the booming blast and throb of an ocean liner's whistle as it sounded its intention to back out into the Hudson River and sail for Europe. As the echo reverberated through the gray canyons of buildings, it clutched at one's heart.

Arriving at Idlewild, I finally found Gainor inundated by passengers. I approached an airport employee to convey the message to him that I had got there. And as he looked up and out over the milling crowd to acknowledge me, he smiled assent as he saw that I lurked, half-hidden behind a steel pillar. The airport had been for days jammed with swarming passengers and their hordes of friends seeing them off. I had already read a couple of strange accounts in the newspaper of those who, intending to fly to San Juan, Puerto Rico, had instead boarded flights which ended them up bitterly protesting in such places as Nome, Alaska, Hong Kong and Singapore. It was thought that with their speaking Spanish and their poor English, mistakes of destination were being made. Gainor, with a command of this language, seemed to be coping, as I, with hardly room to move from my redoubt behind the pillar, watched him at his station dealing with irate folk in the wrong line, overbooked seats, and excess baggage. Gainor, having previously over the telephone told me,

"Mike, you have no idea how uncooperatively violent and exasperatingly unpleasant some of these people can be. The temptation to send some of them to Spitzbergen is immense."

If not involved with his own affairs, Gainor was possibly one of the most super efficient of people, his administrative capacity in dealing with another's business, invariably swift, accurate and polite. But one immediately saw that some of these present passengers were of a totally dissimilar behavior. Impatient, pushing, noisy, demanding and screaming and all insisting on making complaint. Fights breaking out in the long lines. Gainor, trying to keep some semblance of order, remonstrated with a snarling man demanding to be first in the queue because his plane was about to leave. When Gainor said there was still adequate time, the man suddenly went berserk, drawing a flick knife, and rushed Gainor to stab him. The six-inch-long blade ending up embedded deep in the check-in desk. But Gainor seemed to keep his cool. In a lightning flash, he had your man grabbed by the wrists and immobilized. But not but a minute later and before the summoned airport police arrived, one saw this formerly bitterly vociferous and murderous complainant minus his weapon and smugly satisfied, rushing on his way to join his ready-to-leave flight to San Juan, Puerto Rico.

And I should have known and guessed when reading the newspaper reports as to whom was behind this selected handful of misdirected passengers. For Gainor had just sent this impatient Spanish-speaking fucker off on a two-stop flight to Helsinki, Finland.

However, throughout this astonishing melee and during the nearly two hours I stood at my station by the pillar, I noticed Gainor every twenty minutes or so would have a replacement and leave his post to disappear into the gents' convenience a short distance away. It was now getting late afternoon and, having seen enough, one was weary of the sight and noise, not to mention the continued risk one ran to one's life, and I decided to go home. Also needing to pee and now with the opportunity to alert Gainor to my leaving, I headed over to and entered the men's latrine. The pissoir was at the end of a longish narrow hall. But among the few pissing passengers, no Gainor was to be seen either urinating, or, in surveying the cubicles, could any black-trousered and shoed feet like his be observed taking a crap. I now thought that in my having witnessed him so many times entering this place that I was now beginning to suffer self-deception and was seeing things. I had already been experiencing acute hypochondria to the extent of almost hoping I would break a leg for relief. But even so, I now examined every inch of the latrine. The small window apertures were barred and were far too high for a man to reach. Again, as discretion would permit, and short of kneeling to peer under the door of each of the cubicles, I did, where there were no feet showing, open wide each door to see if Gainor might be there behind and standing on the seat for the sake of privacy in case someone he'd recently socked in the subway was looking for him. And still no Gainor.

I took my pee. And now slightly dazed, with depression closing in and my desperation increasing to get the fuck as far away as possible from the roaring motorbirds and from these once mud flats upon which the airport had been built, I gave up. Plus I was in fear of arrest as a soliciting homosexualist already getting dirty looks as well as an occasional inviting one, and I now proceeded out the entrance hall. But just as I was about to push through to emerge into the airport melee again, I noticed a narrow-shaped door in the wall. Waiting till the hall emptied, I reached and turned the brass knob and pulled it open. There inside the small space and cramped between the brooms and mops, his two feet stuck in pails, and with hardly an inch in which to move a muscle, was the one and only Gainor Stephen Crist, his head tilted back under a wicker-basketed gallon bottle of Chianti and his lips locked around the open end. Now suddenly turning in alarm from under his bottle to look at me, the wine was meanwhile pouring out, splashing over his hair, face, jacket, shirt, trousers and shoes.

"Good God, Mike, it's you."

And
Good God
Gainor
It's you

22

"MIKE, FOR GOD'S SAKE don't go now. Just wait another hour till I come off duty."

With a wine-soaked Gainor pleading in his reasonable way, I did reluctantly finally succumb to his blandishments to travel back with him to his apartment. Knowing already by the odd references made by him to his two flat mates, to whom he referred as Mutt and Jeff, that there was a certain degree of misunderstanding and disgruntlement between him and them. I was still remembering the poor sod in his shiny brown suit and bright orange tie, whom Gainor had sent on the wrong plane and who, instead of arriving in San Juan, Puerto Rico, after flying 1400 miles, was to end up 4000 or so miles away in the arctic clime of Helsinki, Finland. And of the other Puerto Ricans he might have also sent to even more distant foreign parts. But now in borrowed ill-fitting clothes and covered by a voluminous raincoat reaching down to his ankles, for he wore no trousers at all, we traveled back by airport limousine along through these quasisuburban and commercial wastelands to be dropped off from where it was a brief walk to Gainor's apartment.

And I should have guessed if not known. Adjoining the building's entrance, there was a cocktail bar to which ready access could be made from within Gainor's front hall. Although the stairwell was ill-smelling of dental, medicinal and cooking fumes, the apartment up another four floors was reasonably pleasant. With a modest-sized kitchen and a bathroom on one side of a hallway, there were three adjoining bedrooms on the other. The third of which was Gainor's. And which had originally been a dining room connected to the sitting room through French doors. There was indeed nearly a hint of luxury about the adequately furnished and reasonably spacious place. All except for Gainor's own bedroom, which at first he would not let me see. Then as I reminded him of having acquiesced to travel back with him instead of doing the wiser and preferred thing of returning to Woodlawn, I politely as I could insisted.

"Mike, do please believe me when I say I can't let you see in there."

"Gainor, you must. And more for the reason that you won't."

"Please, Mike, some other time."

Gainor's response contained more than a hint of chaos and disorder. And as I could just faintly make out odd shapes through the curtained French door, I was of course more eager than ever to see within his sanctum. But I no longer persisted when I could sense that he might feel it an invasion of his needed personal privacy. When he excused himself to get out of his borrowed clothes, I idly perused a subscription copy of a magazine devoted to men's fashions belonging to the persons with whom Gainor shared the apartment and to whom he now referred as being overly fastidious and positively covetous concerning their every belonging. But then my moment came. A scream of anguish erupted from Gainor's bedroom. The lights went out. And still able to see by the illumination in from the street and believing Gainor had injured himself, I rushed to push open the door. There was the smell of burning rubber.

"Mike, I've just nearly been electrocuted."

The lights of the apartment had short-circuited and Gainor had now lit candles, which were stuck in the tops of empty wine bottles. In his long underwear, he stood, holding aloft a lamp as does the Statue of Liberty, the cord of which had hugely fused. In the room, there was a double bed which dipped deeply in the center and seemed broken in the middle. Erected across it was an American Indian wigwam, the top of its support poles attached to the bedposts and reaching the ceiling. It was from within this indoor shelter that Gainor had removed the lamp. On his dressing table, along with bits of food, stale breads, bacon rinds and cheese, was another wicker gallon bottle of Chianti, a Trinity College tie knotted around its neck. Nearby stood a serenely elegant photograph of Pamela and one of his two beautiful little daughters. And out here, where Queens Boulevard seemed to have deposited Gainor in this folorn oblivion, I felt the crushing heartache that was in this scene of loneliness and isolation. Except for the sobering, cold fear of what might yet befall us, tears did well up but did not drop from my eyes.

"Mike, do please forgive me for the appalling state my bedroom is in. But I do wish that the feeble electrical appliances in this country would bloody well work without their risking killing one, which this damn lamp has now nearly done twice. I use it to be able to read in my wigwam I erected, which, made of strong deer hide, not only helps keep me warm but gives me a sense of protection while I sit in there with *S.D.,* attired comfortably in my long underwear. It also helps shield me from the noise down in the street. And these hex signs painted on the panels keep away evil spirits. See. This flap opens and I keep your manuscript and pictures quite safely in there. Indeed, without those two things to sustain me, I think I might have totally given up. I also, while squatting Indian-fashion, eat my frugal meals within. And indeed partake of sips of Chianti. Also while squatting Indian-fashion."

"Gainor, I must go. Just tell me where I catch the subway."

"Mike, stay with me, please, just a little while longer. Just give me a moment to shower, shave and dress. And then we'll both travel across to Manhattan Island together and visit Lea. You know how much you admire her singing. Meanwhile, here, have this nice little bit of cheese and let me fill you a glass of this, one of my favored wines. That's one good thing, you know, America has plenty of *la vino.* Esperanto for wine. And it is called the same in Czech and Serbo-Croat. Oh yes, I know my Esperanto these days. Indeed wine is called *'vins'* in Lettish and *'vynas'* in Lithuanian."

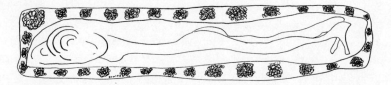

Reclining woman in a decorated sarcophagus and prone in a manner in which she might be deemed comfortable should she not again arise.

Lea was one of the more beautiful products of the fabled world of Hollywood, and was as well the former wife of Ernest Gebler, from whom she had decamped to America. Leaving behind nestled within its often mist-cloaked forest of pines, the somber rural splendor of Lake Park, and a Gebler who, following her departure and riven in pain, then sat the months away in silent reclusiveness, relieved only by a bickering household staff and my own occasional presence when we would over whiskey talk the night away. Myself predicting again to him the hopeful. That along with women, even hearts, lungs, kidneys and maybe even brains could be replaced.

And Lea was now residing in an elegant town house in the west of Greenwich Village. This alluringly attractive woman had veritably stunned the male population of Ireland with her lively presence. Her open optimism inspired poets, painters and even turned lifelong vegetarians into meat eaters overnight. Possessed of a marvelous singing voice, she would lull her admirers into contented reverie. But Gainor and I had always remained aloof from her considerable charms, reminding each other, or at least Crist reminding me, that American women were of a cast and intention that would never suit us who had got so accustomed to Europeans. But Lea instead made for both of us a charming and enthusiastic acquaintance who could do no wrong. Plus she did what was most important for me, was to buy two of my paintings which Gebler promptly expropriated and used to fence out the neighboring farmer's sheep. And I was such a good painter, no wonder she left him.

Having had to acquaint himself with the maze of the subway for his court appearances, Crist was now an expert. Without a hitch or a schnozzola to smash, we found ourselves traveling by the Fourteenth Street Canarsie Line to land safely in Manhattan. Surfacing at Fourteenth Street and proceeding on foot. And while wandering these few blocks south, we were drawn up in our tracks. When from high-up barred windows, graphically obscene shouts came screaming down at us. Gainor staying me by the arm. And as he often did now, speaking a few words in Spanish. Stopped on the street, we looked up and saw the shadowy shapes of women clutching the bars at an open window.

"Hey, you cocksuckers down there, come up and fuck us. There are too many lesbians in here."

"Guts, listen. At last, the unexpurgated voices of America speak."

Unknowingly, Gainor and I had passed the House of Detention for Women. But we had now arrived at West Eleventh Street and were climbing the brownstone steps to this town house. There was already a hint of Yuletide spirit in the air. From late Christmas shopping, Lea piled out of a taxi with armfuls of presents. She made cheering greetings as she rushed through the house. A maid in the kitchen was making drinks. But we found that even Lea was missing Europe. As she provided Gainor with his favorite whiskey, Powers Three Swallow Gold Label, I heard the pair of them listing cities and places which they referred to as finding a port in a storm. Lea, a generous hostess, there was much clinking of fresh ice in glasses and more Irish whiskey to wash down the delicious cream cheese canapés. But one could sense that her husband-to-be, John Fountain, although in a remote way pleasant, now glumly sitting in a chair and with his leather-bound Yale yearbooks neatly placed on his shelves, was not anxious to have this pair of visitors, as Gainor and I were, overlong on his doorstep. Indeed, one even sympathized with him and was equally anxious to be gone. But at least there were the moments enjoyed of the camaraderie that one felt still existed with Lea from all our previous rain-soaked and wild windswept country life in Ireland.

Following more drinks and more canapés and a song or two, Gainor and I took our leave to call upon another lady, appropriately called April. For she was, with every bit of her tall, willowy, blond beauty, a harbinger of spring. She said she had to put on her evening livery and would shortly join us. Repairing to a bar a short walk away on the borders of the Hudson River and within the moaning sound of the West Side elevated highway, we were briefly left to ourselves again. And in the bar atmosphere, once one had started, it was hard now to stop quaffing back the beer and Gainor his whiskey. Plus there was no one better than Gainor Stephen Crist inside a pub to make one feel enjoyably at home. His silent way of engaging anyone, and then as they spoke he would speak. Obeying a religious ritual of behavior and possessed of a solemn confidence, Gainor's every nuance was like an actor on a stage. The way he stood or reached for his drink or took out his cigarettes or lit one. His eyes assimilating everything. His aura introducing an unspoken camaraderie to make even the most dull bar the most salubrious in the world. At his approach, bartenders could be nearly seen assuming a physiological readiness to give the attention that this man's demeanor casually demanded. And such bartender would be the recipient of an immediate reward with Gainor's words.

"Will you have one yourself."

And always Gainor and I would refer back to the pub which was like no pub anywhere and made us never to forget that one night spent in Kells, County Meath, when on our way hitchhiking and walking to the west of Ireland, we met up with the man who was the only man there and who said he'd been on Forty-second Street and Broadway and he'd seen the lights. But who came back again to Ireland and drank away his farm, selling the fields one by one. Coming to the conclusion that with a scythe out in the meadow and the sweat coursing down your cheeks, what was the use cutting thistles when they would grow again and even more of them the next year. And sure you'd go to the hedge and look down the road. Then raising his pint of stout, he'd say,

"And I came back to this."

And that night back then, I could not drag Gainor away, as he had, as he almost invariably did in bars, established an unspoken camaraderie with this man who killed his horse riding it to exhaustion by moonlight across the countryside. And as it was with this man, so it was with Gainor. That anyone near enough by to overhear his mesmerizing comments reflecting the state of being, would, alive that moment in that bar, in that place and on that continent, know that there was nothing else to know beyond what he already knew. It was Gainor's entrance to such environs that made everyone there sense his presence and wait for him to speak, which he did then with just the very slightest hint of conspiracy. And such things that he said were always said with reassurance of comfort and encouragement in his voice.

"Mike, better days are coming."

In the same way, he ordered drinks, and then, while these were forthcoming, would reach for his cigarettes, carefully selecting one, then perusing it for further perfection, would, packing the tobacco with a tap on the back of his hand, place it in his mouth to flare it alight with a wooden match. And then, just as drinks were laid to rest in front of him on the bar, he would, as he did this night, remark to me.

"Mike, don't worry, everything is going to be all right."

And it was blissfully for a while as April swept in. Smilingly gleeful to see us and we to see her. Who had such blunt words to give anyone for advice. If you dipped your wick, expect to pay for the oil. And if your prick didn't give you any fun, have it cut off. But with April's arrival, there were words from a pair of lesbians a few feet away down the bar. And one had an immediate sense that everything, as Gainor said it would be, was quickly not going to be all right. In what could be if it chose to be a very tough bar indeed. April being the center of attraction and attention. And the battle of words and that of the fists to come started slowly enough. And instead of stevedores, meat butchers or truck drivers giving us annoyance, it was two mannish females. Who did seem to have a couple of male friends at a nearby table and both of whom were looking upon their accosting us with amusement. I knew that my beard invariably invited trouble, but the unexpurgated words of the stunning April now overheard down the bar, did even more so.

"Hey, guys, don't mind me, just go give those two bull dykes a cock between their legs to chew on with their meat grinders."

It always amazed me how it could be assumed that Gainor and I were such pushovers. Many was the battle one had in and out of the boxing ring, and one was not half bad as a wrestler. But Gainor as an adversary was something else again. Arms of crushing steel strength and fists which were administered with whiplash lightning, he was a formidable opponent. It was also a long mystery to me why it was that I was always the one to be first faced into battle to get killed while Crist chose to stand approvingly by at the sidelines, taking bets on my winning. He did say once that he liked the way I employed perfect economy in the use of my energy and also that he liked to hear my voice raised in battle cry, enunciating what I was going to do to my antagonist as I waded in, shouting, "Off to the beach fighting amphibians, we sail at break of day. And I'm going to break your ass in fifty or more pieces."

"Hey you, what did you say."

And now this was one of the lesbians speaking. Poor Gainor had had a long day of it. And for the first time in Crist's bar history, I did not immediately hear him answer this riposte to April's remark and invite a long philosophical explanatory discussion. Instead, he continued with describing to April and I some of the more amusing of his long-suffering domestic difficulties out in the bereft climes of Queens Boulevard. But the ignored lesbians, who had been making eyes at April, now said something more provocative.

"Hey, we asked you a question. Who the fuck do you think you are."

These abusively dreadful words were an indication of how weak and defenseless we looked in this rougher part of town. And certainly having in tow one of its most spectacular inhabitants, making us an even more conspicuous target. One was beginning to feel that it was time to be gone quicker than soon. Remembering that to be near big rivers in a city was always a threat to a sailor's good health. And in our present situation, with the unexpurgatedly outspoken and willowy curvaceous April, who could hammer you senseless with her few words, things could be heading for an unholy and because of their gender, one-sided war with two formidable amazonian lesbians. Again one waited, mostly wondering who might explain who we thought we were, but knowing that our silence was rapidly accruing courage to our potential adversaries and to the now two smirking gents at their ringside table. The dykes, clearly bored in an otherwise empty bar, couldn't believe their luck at the appearance of April, who, having removed her coat, and dressed in a satiny black sweater and skirt, revealed a stunning figure, which elicited the lesbians' observation.

"Hey, honey, we won't chew on pricks, we'll chew on those beautiful tits of yours."

Whoopsie doodle dandy. The night was turning out swell. Here in the environs of New York's meat market and the faint smell of dead fish. April, a former model, was married to a burgeoning businessman who was often away. She said she liked to call a spade a spade, and if the husband kept making lots of money, she wouldn't, except for either Crist or me, leave him. But there is no doubt that Crist and I this night were both thinking of leaving. For the lesbians, obviously a pair of weight lifters, looked very tough indeed. And my God, after all these months of our American sojourn enduring misunderstandings, rejections and hostilities, instead of now being presented with a wonderful opportunity to make someone deserving atone for all the indignities and suffering heaped upon us, here we were with one of New York's most beautiful women having to end up trying to protect womenkind by fighting women.

"Hey you, the tall good-looking guy, did you hear what I said we're going to do to your girlfriend."

Albeit threatening, this was a little more polite, and Crist in his gentlemanly manner immediately deferred to me as being the one referred to. But April for the first time was showing a distinct sign of nervousness, and as it would then happen her accent would always slip into a deep hillbilly southern drawl.

"I ain't going to let any ole pussykissing dyke chew on my tits and that's for sure."

However, it was at this point that I was sure Gainor, who would have made one of England's great barristers, would now respond. For he turned slowly in the direction of the lesbians. But as the seconds ticked away, he merely regarded them in silence. To which the lesbian responded in a voice even less belligerent.

"Hey, when I talk to someone and ask them a question, I expect to be answered. Especially when someone sounds like they're English."

But there was no question but Crist by far fitted the description of the tall good-looking guy. And his accent was certainly somewhat more English than mine. And it was amazing that in a land where accents were not supposed to matter, they mattered very much indeed. But I thought in the case of Gainor's arrival in America that there had been enough disagreeableness and enough folk had already been knocked unconscious into the tracks and enough others, one of whom was at that very moment far out flying over a wintry Atlantic Ocean and, probably hysterical, was flying on toward the good city of Helsinki, having to be restrained in a straitjacket. My tendency now was to swallow what was left in our drinks on the bar and if not to go to

April's pretty apartment for a nightcap, then to go quietly home and even more quietly stay there. That is if these overtly questioning folk would let us. Which by the sudden attitude now being taken by their associates at the table was seeming more and more unlikely. As they were just entering the one-sided conversation.

"Hey buddy, didn't you hear what the lady said to you."

The considerably beefy lesbians attired in unpleasantly green clothes had now sidled up closer. April in the circumstances seemed fearless enough, and I wondered if springing from her tall willowyness she packed a wallop. I knew that she had once chased another hillbilly up a mountain and whacked him with an axe when he thought he was going to rape her. She said she laughed herself silly and sick as she saw him with his pants down and his bare ass skidaddling for its life. But now out of the corner of one's eye, one saw that the bartender, who while telling the lesbians politely to mind their own business, was also reaching for something beneath the bar. And one could only wait to see whether it was a truncheon, knife or gun. But the lesbians in turn told the bartender to mind his own fucking business and, reaching out, one of them took Gainor by the arm to pull and turn him around to look at her. Gainor of course behaved unresistingly to the extent of there not being a physical contretemps. But as he attempted to gently retrieve his arm away, he did speak. In his most precise legalistic manner.

"I think perhaps, madam, you may have had too much to drink, and I'd prefer if you let go of my arm."

"Hey buddy, you leave her alone."

These latter words came from one of the guys at the ringside table, who was already up out of his chair and making for Gainor, who was further pulling away from the lesbian's grasp. The guy, shoving Gainor hard against the bar, never realizing for a second that a blistering fist was already on its way to catch him smack on the jaw and to send him flying backward, crashing into the table and chair he'd just left. As all hell broke loose, a citizen previously lurking in the dark had selected and was playing on the jukebox the Christmas carol "Silent Night." As I stood in front of April, to whom the fatter lesbian had already made an indecent suggestion, the other lesbian waded in to attack Gainor, who had knocked their friend at the table into the middle of next week but did it with such lightning efficiency and speed that the lesbian was unaware of it. Ah, but the other guy at the table who was aware was quickly wasting no time to be quickly elsewhere. But poor Gainor, even as provoked as he was, was refusing to defend himself, except to hold the lesbians at arm's length as they tried to knee and kick him in the balls.

"Get the fucker in the nuts, get him in his fucking nuts."

My own thumbs and knuckles had already been contused enough in Dublin fights, and now one needed elbow room to land immobilizing blows to the softer parts of folks' anatomies. And for the sake of Gainor's gentlemanly life and the preservation of his nuts, I realized I had to do the ungentlemanly thing and let go a few light shots into the first lesbian's belly, for the second one had already tried to grab April's tits, and April kicked out, then grabbed her coat and ran for the door, saying upon her departure,

"This little ole soul is going to get the living fuck right out of here and bring her little ole alive tits with her."

The lesbian meanwhile, clearly a jujitsu artist, trying to get me in a headlock and throw me on my back. But this plan I instantly reversed and instead, grabbing her elbow, threw her on her back. But she knew her Greco-Roman wrestling and clung on, getting me in a scissors as I sat out on the floor and got her in a grapevine, producing squeals of agony and breaking her hold. But boy, was she tough. As she got up, I was tempted to hit her a couple of hooks in the haggis. But meanwhile, the first guy Gainor had hit had slowly got back on his feet and had a bottle in hand. Plus the bartender, who obviously also had the hots for April, whose spectacular beauty was the cause of it all, and who had long since departed, was now clearly not on our side, and it was turning out to be five against two.

"Kill the English fuckers."

With this announcement, one was keeping a wary eye out for knives and bullets. But happily, the bartender was only armed with a blackjack. I couldn't believe my eyes when Gainor, in a flash picked up and downed his whiskey off the bar and in the next flash contused the second gentleman from the table with an uppercut which lifted him off the floor and nearly sent him to the ceiling. And just at that moment, I luckily ducked. The bartender, coming up behind me and wielding his blackjack, had just missed my head to land on the side of my neck and shoulder, nearly paralyzing my arm. He could see that there was murder in my eyes at his dastardly sneakiness and did, as the rest of the opposition had now done, run. To escape, they entered and slammed and locked a glass door behind them. Through which went flying my fist. And now we were running.

"Good God, Mike, are you all right."

"No."

My arm pouring blood, Gainor and I were someway down a cross street when the sound of police sirens came. We were making our way back to April's to seek some shelter and first aid. But like Gainor's own rage in his subway confrontations, another had been boiling over in me. Gainor now trying to make for calm. To hold our horses. That I would be published. That recognition of *The Ginger Man* would come. Indeed that I might even achieve more. But to be patient. Then we rang April's bell. She was such a great believer in cutting men's pricks off instead of their balls. Because she said most guys were nothing but pricks anyway. And I thought tonight we needed more of such sensible advice. But getting no answer and some justifiably rude bastard telling us she was away and objecting to the noise we made, and with Crist trying to restrain me, I again punched my hand through a pane of glass in a door. I was roaring revenge at mealymouthed America. And for the first and only time ever of my being in his company, Gainor, who signed his letters "Your affectionate friend," fled for his life. I actually laughed, and one was convulsed as I saw him disappear down the middle of Jane Street. But now bleeding badly from my torn wrist, I stopped a taxi and asked to be brought to the nearest hospital. This happened to be St. Vincent's, only a short distance away. And wherein only some months later, Dylan Thomas, the Welsh poet, died. Apologizing as I struggled to get my hand into my coat pocket for money to pay the taxi driver, he turned around, and I heard him say,

"Buddy, I don't take money for an emergency."

Again one was reminded of the humanity lurking in American life. And of the mean calculation one encountered in Europe. Remembering the similar taxi ride in my early Dublin years when, having my false heart attack, the driver leisurely taking me the longest way to the hospital and finally getting there, was mostly worried that in running up the fare I might die before he might get paid. But now around midnight, I found myself in the emergency ward of this charitable place, surrounded by nuns. Along with reciting all my most abstruse bacteriological knowledge, I was also giving an extemporaneous lecture on the nonexistence of God. And of how my own present plight proved that He couldn't exist. And if He did, I could easily beat Him in chess.

Because of the deepness of the cut, I was given a tetanus shot while an angelically beautiful nun took wry pleasure in administering a deep jab of penicillin in my arse. Now guided by my angelic nun, and with a doctor summoned, I was then brought to a small operating room to lie on my back. Refusing anesthetic, seventeen stitches were, according to my angelic and now more sympathetic nun, beautifully sewn into my ripped arm, as would, she said, befit a great work of art. And when my nun asked how I could stand the pain, I said that I had learned how to do it from the historical example set by the American Indian. Then this angelic nun, who seemed to be personally looking after me and who, listening to my random raves and my announcement that I was going to surely die, put her delicate soft hand on my brow and said, "Oh, after all I've been hearing you say, Mr. Donleavy, you're surely not ready yet to meet your maker. And he surely won't let you die."

But having been sewn up and having lost much blood, I did moments later nearly meet my maker. Again on my feet and my angelic nun escorting me ahead of her to depart the hospital, I suddenly stopped in my tracks and keeled over backward in a dead faint. Landing at the nun's feet, my head banging the floor with a crack like a thunderclap. I woke up again supine on a hospital couch, being examined to see if I had fractured my skull. With Angelica, as I now called her, saying it sounded like I had. But at dawn fully examined again, I was still in one piece with the most comprehensive and expert medical attention I have ever known in my life. However, Angelica asking that they be allowed to keep me for further observation and that she'd already arranged a bed for me in the hospital. But I said I had to go.

"Oh, Mr. Donleavy, I'm sorry you're leaving. You know we don't get many patients like you here. And if we did, I'm not too sure this might go on being a hospital."

Slowly now arising, holding onto Angelica to take my first steps, I was guided to the street. And after much pleading was allowed to kiss Angelica good-bye on the cheek. I took the nearest subway, the Seventh Avenue–Broadway line, which would bring me back again into the uttermost, northernmost Bronx. But which would deposit me two miles away from Woodlawn. It was snowing as I trudged by the boathouse of Van Cortlandt Lake, where growing up we would get our hot chocolate to drink as we ice-skated in winter. And then I trudged up across by the old winding road through the Van Cortlandt woods. With my girlfriend Ann Henry, I had often walked to school this long way. In the biting winter winds and meeting at an early eight o'clock in the morning. It was with her that my earliest philosophy was often discussed. And she thinking my reasoning pretty poor, it more often made her laugh. But into whose patiently listening ears, and tolerant of my mispronunciations and appalling grammar, I would tell my poems.

No route to school could be lonelier as we met this way each day

Ann Henry in New York's Washington Square Park. Such lady whose gurgling laughter and warm charm set one's anticipations and expectations high, but her allurements were only very rarely encountered again in other women one met later in life.

and made our way walking nearly an hour, I to Manhattan Prep and she to travel another mile and a half all the way to the banks of the Hudson to the college of Mount St. Vincent, for she was in college and I was still in high school. But in this dawn after this night and the premonitions it now brought, all the world seemed such a bowl of tears. In the squawking bluejay silence of these woods, where I hunted and played and walked and talked and held hands with the girls I loved. Each step I now took in the deepening snow, my confidence slowly draining away. And so began my gradual demise into despair from which I was never again to recover in America. Gainor's words echoing in one's mind.

> Mike there is
> For us pure of heart
> No end of
> Malice
> No end of
> Scorn

23

I HAD PREVIOUSLY WRITTEN to Valerie that from what I could gather of the publishing world, it was booming, and the sale of cheap reprints was skyrocketing. I was beginning to imagine *S.D.* selling seven thousand copies and the royalties that one might make amounting to four hundred pounds yearly. Enough in Ireland to survive on. But now with no book to write nor pictures to paint, the wait to hear no word from Scribner's and energy sapped, my decline into full-blown despair was accelerating. Gainor still advising me:

"Mike, according to John Preston, one of their authors, you're getting the recognition and respect of one of America's best editors, who has almost complete power at Scribner's. You must continue to be patient."

But with nothing left to fight, as each afternoon wore on, the greater the gloom became. I was already thinking I was wrong to resubmit the book to Scribner's and was now wishing they had rejected it outright when it had first been submitted. I again recalled my first visit there seeing Wheelock, and he had a sheaf of authors' royalty checks handed him and these were waving in front of me. And then, just as I was slowly feeling some physical recovery from my drunken night with Gainor, through the letter slot of the front door of the sun porch, the fatal news came.

CHARLES SCRIBNER'S SONS
PUBLISHERS
597 FIFTH AVENUE, NEW YORK 17, N.Y.

Mr. J. P. Donleavy,   December 18, 1952
233 East 238th Street, New York City.

Dear Mr. Donleavy,
    At last we have had a chance, two of us, to read in its entirety this

somewhat revised version of your novel, *S.D.,* and I am writing you about it now.

S.D. came up for discussion at our editorial conference yesterday, and I'm sorry to report that, in spite of our admiration for your writing talent, we are not in a position to make you an offer. As you know, I had thought there was just a chance that, with some revision, we could do the novel — in any case, you had not at the time turned in the whole thing. The difficulties which I feared might be strongly felt by our present editorial set-up still remain in the manuscript.

I am sorry to be writing a letter that can be so little inspiriting and, particularly in the case of a manuscript that reveals so much imaginative vitality and writing skill.

Will you let me know what you wish us to do about the manuscript, which we hold here pending your instructions?

With kindest regards,
Yours sincerely,
John Hall Wheelock

When I read Gainor the letter, he said not to get panicky. But the consciousness of this rejection and my present vulnerability were overwhelming. I recalled a thunderstorm in Connecticut in the middle of the night and in a lightning flash saw a fox in the woods barking in hopeless defiance up at the sky. And too, there was a vision of dying and death. I remembered a time growing up. That of one snowy Sunday morning just as the winter light was dawning and I was collecting my stack of newspapers that I was to deliver from where they were dropped and where they were now covered in snow. I reached down with my hand and seemed to grip on something soft and round, and it was a dead man's arm. Something made me look up, and I saw a window open from where he had jumped and curtains blowing out in the breeze. It was a man who owned a candy store who'd sickened with cancer and left his warm bed for the cold street. Somehow I knew the letter was fatal. And I was agonizing now to be away back in Ireland and digging my bare hands into its loam again.

But I wrote back to Wheelock, hoping to keep some door open. That there could be some reconsideration based on revisions I still intended to undertake but also that I would come and collect back the manuscript. And Gainor telephoned me back from Queens.

"Mike, I'm sincerely sorry to hear this news about the book. You mustn't be discouraged. I still firmly believe that somewhere somehow you will find a publisher. But perhaps not here. And I must confess that my own feeling for this place is transcending into deep hatred. Mike, there comes from time to time in one's life sworn situations where the resolve to do something becomes so great that all other matters pale into insignificance. Well, the sworn resolve I have committed to is to get out of here before anything else befalls me. Today is Sibelius's birthday. He is eighty-seven. And it should be some small encouragement to us who are of a less advanced age. Except I guess one might also point to all the years we have theoretically yet got left in which to thoroughly get fucked up. Especially when one considers one's past indoctrinations undergone in this land. Mike, are you there."

"Yes, I'm still here but only just."

"Well, I wonder if you remember that in school growing up as I did in Ohio that one stood at the side of one's desk every morning and saluted the stars and stripes and recited something called the Pledge of Allegiance. Which, if I may remind, states, 'I pledge allegiance to my flag of the United States of America and to the republic for which it stands, one nation, under God, indivisible, with liberty and justice for all.' This was written by a man called Francis Bellamy, who, among other things, let it now please be said, worked for an advertising company. Mike, it's those words 'liberty' and 'justice,' in which we believed and which have left us bedeviled since. Meanwhile, I trust and hope your wounds are healing. One could never have predicted that night that something actually awful was about to happen. By the way, April says to send you her love and not to forget to wear your steel jockstrap next time you go out. She did as an aside also suggest that she thought we were both badly in need of long, lingering blow jobs. Although she did not suggest that she would oblige, she did say that from her experience it was just amazing how it calmed guys down. And I shall tell you more of what she said on this subject later. She is of course just the sort of girl we need to have to stick by us when we are in trouble."

In the old white house atop the hill in Woodlawn, I was now in for the long haul and hoping to make it as short as possible. Toying with the idea of getting an agent. And suffering the slow, uncertain wait to garner enough money together to get out. A blotch of red from a penicillin reaction at last subsiding on my arm, I darned my socks and washed my underwear and went on my first outing. To a place I earnestly recommended Gainor visit for respite. The Bronx Zoo, a rare open space that existed in this part of the Bronx and through which the Bronx River flowed. People still staring at me as I traveled by the bus. Along with the spacious Botanical Gardens, the zoo was part of the many green acres that lay to the east of the Fordham University campus and the prep from which I'd been expelled. There was also Fordham Hospital, where I had been brought as a boy with a broken collarbone, and where too, unbelievably, Gainor was to shortly end up from yet another incident in the subway. But meanwhile, here I was purposely attempting to hold on to what was left of my fighting spirit, just as I sensed Gainor was trying to hold on to what was left of his sanity. Crossing to the zoo entrance, a voice accosted me.

"Hey buddy, what a roué you'd be back at the asylum."

As I looked at this smiling man with his lopsided face saying these words, I realized he was intending to be friendly and implying I'd be a big hit with his mental institution female inmates and was uttering just about the last amicable words I'd hear from a stranger in America. Then inside the zoo, while watching the happier faces of the orang-utans, tumbling and wrestling together, and while contemplating this seemingly calm animal for hints of how it achieved its composure, a man noticing my beard walked up to me.

"Hey, excuse me, are you a yid. Look how these animals are going crazy locked up like this. I'm from Russia. I am sixty-seven. I stopped work last year and now with nothing to do, I am waiting to die. I have a roommate. He is eighty-seven. He stole five sets of underwear from me. You think at his age he'd know how to behave. But he is nothing but a no-good bastard. I worked as a cutter in a tailor's. My children are like the communists. They say I want, gimme, gimme, gimme. But they don't come to see me. I get rid of this old bastard who steals my underwear and I die of loneliness."

One was glad, even for a moment, to listen to a foreign complaining voice, but not all matters unpleasant to hear were erupting in America. Valerie's letters back from the Isle of Man soon contained information that the money voluntarily promised her by Mrs. Heron on her return and left under her father's will was not now to be forthcoming. And not only that, she was also being made to pay for the electricity she used in the house. A steely hardness, along with my growing angst and reclusiveness, was settling over one. I was also beginning to regret having sold the cottage at Kilcoole and disposing of all one's pathetically insignificant treasures in life, like battered pails, old boots and bent spoons. And that little former isolated patch of tiny land by the Irish Sea and its cottage with no water, electricity or plumbing was now beginning to seem like paradise. In spite of the odd time when a somewhat semipink Bohemian poet might pay a visit. To report that reds would take over soon. Coming like a massive horde on horseback and slashing down the rich, like a combine harvester in a grain field. And on those lonely, isolated, windswept nights, this was terrifying talk when one thought next morning these red-garmented folk from Russia would be sweeping in on the beach only two fields away, and clanking us in chains would ship us off to the slave labor camp.

Against all the now accumulating odds and massive indifference, I thought there had to be a tiny spark remaining left with which to fight. For if one break, which was not my neck, did not soon come my way, I knew I'd be finished. One realized how desperate it must have been for Pamela, Gainor's faithful girlfriend, who wrote now to me asking of Gainor, for he was neglecting to write and to tell her about two pawnbrokers she was supposed to contact on his behalf in London. Of her own news, she said that all the former residents of Dublin and who were now residents of London were all still looking for the perfect job and were as a result becoming very whipped and tacked-up men. Meanwhile, a letter came back from Wheelock suggesting that when I came to pick up the manuscript that we could have a little talk, and that then he could explain the feeling at Scribner's better than he could in a letter. But I already nearly knew what would be said. It was lucky now that other encouraging words such as Gainor's had been given me. For it was clear that *The Ginger Man*'s lifelike obscenity could not find vent in this land. And as T.J. had said when he read the manuscript,

"If that book is ever published, there's going to be a lot of lampcords under the closet doors."

It seemed one had left only an awkward conceit which could protect and save one from nothing. I was still able to trade sorrows with and talk to Jack Duffy. He'd married and moved to a newer and more commodious apartment. And there was still Tally Brown, who, from her own redoubt under the George Washington Bridge on the Hudson, spoke encouraging words. And to where Gainor and I had so contentedly gone to be entertained. With meals ever more sumptuous and which ended with splendid cheeses and vintage ports. When she heard all my bad news and that I in some desperation and with one foot already sinking in the pit of doom, was planning to book on a liner soon to depart for Europe, she cried out at me over the phone.

"Mike this country needs people like you. You can't go. Fight. Get back into life. Don't let yourself slip into the pit of doom."

More snow fell. Hungry bluejay birds were raucously crying out. The sound of scraping, digging shovels and of cars getting stuck as their engines whined and raced to escape from the drifts. The drums were now pounding with a long, steady beat. I had at last got a new passport and all my attentions were toward getting out. With more snow sweeping the streets, I went by subway downtown. I walked down Fifth Avenue in my black tweed, a thornproof silverburn made by my tailor Kaighen on the Isle of Man. Arriving at Scribner's for the last time, I was conducted into a room referred to as the library as Wheelock sat me down to speak of his position.

"I do feel guilty about not publishing *S.D.* as it is and a bit like a cowardly editor. But if cuts were to be made to the manuscript, which would be required if we were to publish it, I feel it would ruin the book. I don't feel anything should be changed in the work. I could press on here against opposition and press for publication, but a lot would have to come out of the novel which I feel is intrinsic to it. But you may use my name as a recommendation. There's an agent, Diarmuid Russell, A.E.'s son, who reads everything he handles and whose office is just down Fifth Avenue. By the way, I met your friends the Pratts, and they spoke warmly of you and your very delightful wife and baby."

I dropped the book off at the agent farther down Fifth Avenue, as suggested by Wheelock, Russell himself not being there. Douglas Wilson had come to New York down from Boston for a wedding. I went to the N.Y.A.C., where I was to meet him and Gainor. We sat in the vast lounge on the ninth floor where in three lonely chairs by the window looking out and down on the snowy whiteness of Central Park, Wilson talked about his grand tour he'd made of Africa and India and reported that A. K. Donoghue was acting on the stage at the Poets' Theatre in Brattle Street and creating a sensation. Shut away from people for so long, I was enjoying company and invited Gainor back to Woodlawn. Although his image of sainthood was still largely intact, it was becoming clear that some emergency was always required to be overtaking him in his life. Several times in the middle of the night, I could hear his bare feet pass my bedroom door and go downstairs to get some Scotch whiskey, of which there was an endless supply, my father having been sent a case or two at Christmas. Next day we walked together entirely around the four hundred acres of Woodlawn Cemetery.

"Mike, I must tell you sincerely that I am thoroughly enjoying my brief sojourn here with you and the marvels of this cemetery. Also the entertaining company of your brother, T.J., who seems to have some very incisive ideas."

Of course, some of T.J.'s incisive ideas were not all flattering to Gainor, who, after he left, said Gainor was a murderer at heart without absolutely any feeling of any sort, but someone everyone thought very, very nice. One could not help but recognize some truth in T.J.'s words. But said in the context of the present chaos of Gainor's life, they were a mite unfair. However, as much as I didn't want to feel it did, even I found that everything to do with Gainor seemed to go haywire. His company was usually cheering, but now combined with my own dejection it was anathema. And which had in just one day already caused me enough angst to last a lifetime. The tension too that had long been mounting as to Scribner's decision and the long absence of a reply, which now having come, could hardly seem worse. Crist still had the borrowed carbon of the manuscript and all my photographs I had taken in the old sod, which he said served as some consolation in his tribulations and wanted not to part with them yet for they acted as a life preserver out and lost upon the great ocean of anonymity that was Queens. And he quoted me words I wrote, which he said he often whispered to himself.

"Who seeks me, beseeches my presence. Knows where I am. In my own brokenhearted sorrow. Dying alone. No one seeks me, beseeches my presence, knows where I am. Dying alone."

I told Gainor that Pamela did. She sought him and beseeched his presence. And that Mutt and Jeff were after him too, seeking him for his share of the rent. But at least for the moment out in the more isolated northern wilds of the Bronx, no one did, as far as I know, know where he was. Although Gainor seemed able to summon up resolves stronger than mine, his life seemed far more scattered, and his purposes more undecided. He had even said he thought he'd had a touch of the D.T.'s. I had already told him to get on the first boat and get back to London and stay there. Yet, using the phonetic Gaelic of my surname, he was always able to come back with a contrasting reply, as if I could find some solace in hearing of his own troubles that were anything but bliss.

"Dinnlay, to look at life through eyes distrusting is to fear. Hast thou forgotten the splendor of our days on the Emerald Isle when the west was awake. Ah, but I know what must trouble you. It's not that one expects to be loved and admired in this land, but one does not expect either to be kicked or shunned. But Mike, I thought from your forewarning letters that you were forearmed."

"Yes, Gainor, but forewarning and forearming still does not stop one from being finally beaten."

"Ah, Dinnlay, we have been badly wrong but not now for us to falter nor despond. That upon our sinking ship we shall go down like men, unsquealing and unwhimpering. Dignified on the deck. The ladies and children safely away in the lifeboats. Our dinner jackets agleam in the moonlight, raising our voices in God-worshipful song. Even as the chill water rises upon us to stifle our sound. We shall stand thus saluting at attention till the last. And be thereby the best of men."

"Gainor, your words are well taken. And I am looking at life through distrusting eyes. And as a result I am goddamn well full of fear. And I also fear I will do a hell of a lot of bloody complaining as the ship sinks."

To Gainor's efforts to provide heartening and would-be reassurance from chivalrous behavior, all my ripostes now were of a contrary and discontented nature. And it was upon the very next day following this conversation when I had repaired with darkness descending at four o'clock, to my room to write my usual long letter to Valerie and to further sit counting my pennies at my desk, my back to these three windows facing the street and over which the shades were pulled down. Making sure no one could draw a bead on me and make a hole in my head while I held together by all spiritual means what was left of my more than somewhat shattered dreams. When there came another phone call from Gainor, his voice calling out my name as if he imagined I could not hear him.

"Mike, Mike, are you there."

"Yes, Gainor, I am."

"Mike, I just a few minutes ago out here in godforsaken Queens have again short-circuited the bloody lights over which Mutt and Jeff are screaming. And I'm now waiting for the police to arrive."

"Good God, what for."

"A naked and completely berserk girl is hysterical down on the next landing. And I may need someone to go bail for me. You'll never believe this, neither will a judge or the police. I was in the bathroom having a shower and at the same time trying to shave, and trying to do two things at once I slipped in the goddamn bathtub. In reaching up to stop my fall I first tore the bloody shower head off its mooring in the wall and then a light fixture which short-circuited the lights. Just more things I'm going to have to pay someone a ransom to fix. I don't know what madness made me risk nearly electrocuting myself, but I was late for my shift at the airport. And I haven't much time to tell you this, but that is only the beginning. The shower head coming off in my grasp, the only thing left to cling to was the shower curtain and rail. And I ripped the whole bloody thing down in my fall."

Lounging back in a sofa chair in the downstairs sitting room in my dressing gown, I was now having to hold the phone away from my ear and my hand over the mouthpiece so that Gainor could not hear my convulsed laughter. His voice remaining alarmed and deadly serious as he went on to relate matters which were clearly portending legal if not criminal consequences.

"Honestly, Mike, I thought, here I am prostrated with a bruised ass in the bath and why not put in the plug, fill it up, keep my head under water and mercifully end it all. But no. Like the fool I am, I struggled up. And I hadn't yet been able to turn the water off, which was shooting out over the bath, onto the floor. Then having found at last a dry match and by a miracle a candle, I lit the bloody thing and was carrying it till of course it suddenly went out. And long enough for me to get attired and entangled in the fucking shower curtain. But then in relighting the candle and coming out into the hall, how was I to know that Mutt's girlfriend, whom I had never met and who as I've just discovered was stopping overnight on her way back to Cleveland, had been asleep in his room waiting for him to come back from his shift at the airport. Mike, you couldn't get out here, could you. It's desperate."

"Good God, Gainor, I've just undressed and am just about to take a bath. Why don't you just go gently and well wrapped up in your shower curtain and invite Mutt's girlfriend for a cocktail downstairs in the bar. It's the Yuletide season, and if she's in a blanket people will merely think you're in fancy dress."

"Mike, this is not fucking funny. With my subway track record, my story won't be believed. The whole thing is utterly too absurd. That's why I'm wasting precious moments telling you all this. It could be thought I tore this girl's clothes off. But in reality, she was in a bloody state of undress and obviously coming to use the bathroom and not knowing anyone else was in the apartment thought I was some sort of naked rapist intruder, then panicked and ran stark raving nude out into this building's hallway landing to ring every goddamn neighbor's bell for help. Who bloody well could help nobody, suffering as they all do from an acute pathological and chronic paranoia. Then in stupidly trying to calm the naked girl, I got a blanket to cover her and proceeded out into the hallway. Where, under the light and dressed in a yellow polka-dot shower curtain, of course the first neighbor in her curlers to look out her crack in the door also thought I was a rapist and slammed it shut. How could anyone think otherwise at such a scene. But, Mike, I haven't told you the most embarrassing and incriminating thing yet. I got an erection. How this could be psychologically possible under the circumstances, I'll never know. I just couldn't believe what was happening to me. It was as if in a twisted gentlemanly fashion, I didn't want to make a liar out of the girl. The terrified creature wouldn't let me approach her with the blanket and instead ran down the stairs to the next floor below. The wretched girl is still as far as I know shivering there on the landing. Where obviously no one is going to open their door. Mike, are you still there."

"Yes, Gainor, I am."

"After what's happened, I have to let you know all this in case I am arrested and arraigned and will need someone to make me at least seem I might be civilized and to bail me out."

"Gainor, show them your passport, you're a veteran of the U.S. Navy and served your country. And have never been accused of rape before. On the contrary, you've been besieged by women from the moment you set foot in high school."

"Mike, please don't try to be funny. Can you come out here. I've no time to tell you more. Because that's not all that's bloody well happened. But it's all I've got time to tell you now. Only a half-gibbering wreck can go on surviving here. The secret is to lose most of one's sanity and just keep enough left to know when people are shortchanging you. I could be bloody well arrested and locked up for several years. I know it's a lot to ask, but, Guts, can you get here."

As Gainor spoke and some of the humor wore off, I was, rather than heading out to Queens, thinking of getting down pronto to the transatlantic piers on the Hudson and running up the first gangplank I could find available on any ocean liner that I could afford to get on. But there was also no doubt that Gainor was curing me of my own comparatively feeble concerns, as he always could in reciting yet another drama befalling him. And which often had me holding the phone near to my ear and my hand over the speaker as I was convulsed in some mirth. However, I considered expedient practicality as being of the highest priority now. And showing his passport and declaring his naval serial number as a veteran of foreign war was not the worst start provided he got dressed and divested of his shower curtain. And I realized that even if I were able to solve my way on the subway system, that my showing up in Queens with a beard would only compound problems further. And one placed one's hope in knowing what a charming diplomat Gainor could be.

"Gainor, please listen to me. Just put on your clothes, a shirt and your Trinity tie, and at least you will stand some chance of convincing the girl and police of your innocence. If you get arrested, then ring me back."

"But the whole damn point, Mike, is that I may not be able to ring you back."

"OK. If I don't hear from you in an hour, I'll come out there and look out for where they've got you locked up and that should be the nearest police station to your address. But I will most likely end up saying I don't know you from Adam."

"Mike, I don't blame you, I really don't. But Mike, by the good intercession to blessed Oliver Plunket, if I get out of this, I'll take you up to Woodstock, where we can both be assured of some peace and quiet and take a brief rest."

Gainor hung up, and I waited by the phone. And after twenty minutes of reading further in Thomas O'Crohan's tale "Twenty Years a Growing," his story of life and living on the Great Blasket Island of western Ireland, I went and had my own bath. And there immersed in the water, dreaming up cartoons of fish, who were mostly eating each other, that I was now drawing for amusement, and distraction. And with which I was also hoping to make money. But in assuming the worst now as another hour passed, one's worry drove one to ring Gainor back. And I immediately took encouragement as I sensed his voice full of relief.

"Mike, for the moment I have to speak quietly so as not to be overheard. She's not preferring charges."

"Thank heavens."

"No, Mike, thank the blessed Oliver Plunket. But my God, what an unbelievable nightmare. The police arrived, about two hundred of them. Summoned by about a dozen bloody different people. It was thought the Martians had landed and Orson Welles himself was leading his legions out of his spaceship to take possession of Queens. The road cordoned off, searchlights illuminating the whole building. She, meaning Mutt's girlfriend, who has, by the way, the most incredibly fantastic figure, rang all the bells down to the ground floor. Mike, the damages I'm going to be sued for here are going to be overwhelming. And the sooner I quietly decamp with my wigwam from this address the better. Water from the shower I had neglected to turn off as I was being accused of being a rapist on the rampage, poured down into the apartment below and in turn down into the apartment below that. And to put it mildly, this apartment is now a mess of every possible bloody description. Then when the police arrived and saw my wigwam, they immediately assumed I was a total nut case, which of course I am now. But together with the neighbors jabbering their accusations and having previously complained to the landlord that this apartment had been turned into an abode of ill repute, being a mere rapist seemed a mild enough accusation. But, Mike, I did as you advised, however, and I know what I am about to tell you may seem a bit farfetched. But the girl, whose eyes I suddenly met, as there I stood surrounded by police and handcuffed ready to be taken away and hopelessly making a last-ditch effort at explaining what happened, changed her expression completely. Now, this is the astonishing thing. Her eyes had exactly the same instant expression they had of a certain sudden appeasement when she was out in the hall and glanced down and saw my erection. I don't know what she was thinking, but there was an almost inviting backward glance as she fled down the stairs to ring more bells on the lower landing. And now, giving me the exact same look again, she suddenly and unbelievably announced it was all an unfortunate misunderstanding and mistake. I was unhandcuffed. The police left. All two hundred of them. And one last jocular chap saying as he closed the door, 'Have a good day.' "

"But you did intercede to blessed Oliver Plunket."

"Yes I did. But, Mike, honest to God, I am absolutely convinced that had I not got an erection, which obviously her unbelievably attractive figure must have involuntarily provoked, I do believe I'd be sitting in a jail cell right at this bloody moment. The only trouble now being that all of this could appear in the papers because reporters and photographers were all over the place. Plus we've just sat the last hour in the sitting room facing each other, and I must confess to having had more than a drink out her bottle of her duty-free gin. She's presently gone to the bar downstairs to buy more."

"Gainor, you're mumbling a little, I can't quite hear you."

"That's because I'm seeing if my teeth are still intact. Trying to brush them in the ensuing darkness of the bathroom, I bloody well used instead of toothpaste an athlete's foot preparation. What in God's name they put in that stuff I don't know, but now I feel my teeth any second are going to drop out. But that's entirely minor. I believe as a result of my involuntary erection, I have become the object of this girl's very immediate attention if not lifelong affection. She now clearly wants me to fuck her. Such a state of affairs not making matters any easier to deal with Mutt, a most unpleasantly conscientious type who already seems resentful enough about me. Pray God, I can avoid any such additionally complicating emotional strife. Turns out she knew someone with whom I went to high school in Dayton, Ohio. That's all I can tell you now. Except that as a result of all this, I've been replaced on my shift and have missed a day's work. Which bloody hell is not going to improve my financial affairs any. I need rest. I need to escape from it all. Before I float away, borne by life's strange sadnesses. And please, Mike, I beg of you, please, please don't mention a word of this to anyone and especially not to certain people in London and Dublin who behave as central news agencies in such matters. I know you forget nothing, but for God's sake do forget this incident. But I know, as one who lives on in utter ignominy, that, Mike, you'll be writing all this down, if not for your own amusement, then for posterity's sake. Well, if you are, write this down too.

> "I can take
> Slander here
> I can take
> Slander there
> But I can't take
> Slander everywhere"

24

THE DAYS now having drifted toward Christmas and the New Year, I was now walking a mile or two to even save a dime and had by miraculous means accumulated $115 with a further $50 to go to pay for my fare overseas. Finally, my ever dependable mother giving me the remainder. *The New Yorker* magazine rejecting a first few drawings now asked to see more of my fish cartoons. Earlier having booked passage in middle January and in my desperation to secure some last-ditch foothold of achievement in the U.S., I delayed my departure and booked instead on the Cunard liner *Franconia,* sailing out of New York on February 13. But again, when more cartoons were sent, a letter came back saying they had similar ideas in the works, and their indifference made me send no more.

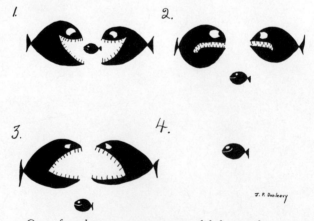

*One of my later cartoons, marine life having become
a ready symbol, for in aid of their own survival they often
swallowed one another whole.*

Gainor too I knew was contemplating his exit. But from his position ever growing more complicated with Mutt and Jeff holding onto his mail till his rent was paid, and his continued consistent reportage to me over the telephone of his dealings with money and its being wired here and there and everywhere, there seemed to be only more chaos compounded by yet more chaos in his life. Which since his rape scene in Queens and the ensuing dunning for damages and his previous indebtedness from his subway assaults and his day-to-day survival getting more and more precarious, one could not see how he could afford a ticket to get out. Nor did it seem he could get free travel by air as he might have been entitled to, and one guessed his employers must have discovered who it was who was sending folk to Helsinki. He was now spending more and more time in touch with me and indeed was planning to come stay as a guest with me in Woodlawn.

Ernest Gebler from Ireland sent me a copy of the *Irish Times* with a picture of a bullock running amok in Dublin's main thoroughfare, O'Connell Street. And this newspaper seemed also full of meanness and the overtones of the Catholic church's repression. But even this I found a brief and lovely relief from America and the gadget-crazy desires of its populace. More and more of them, always looking for any label to boast of and searching for anything to shine, anything to represent their continued whiteness of skin, cleanliness of body, sameness of mind and their camaraderie cemented by their heartfelt bigotry. My sister's husband, Jack, moving house, was already concerned that the new neighbors might see their old refrigerator, and although I had sympathy for this honest and hardworking man, this widespread American attitude made one want to dent their bloody cars and appliances and spread horseshit and cow dung everywhere across the nation.

I went to see the agent Diarmuid Russell, suggested by Wheelock. The meeting was short and not so sweet. He thought I could write but that *S.D.* was an unlikely book for publishers and that John Hall Wheelock had probably not read the book at all. Which I knew he had since he was able in our talks to vividly describe details of scenes and seemed especially taken by the stout bottles that were secreted in a pile of turf. It made me realize that this well-meaning and quite kindly agent actually didn't believe I'd even spoken to Wheelock. And with the manuscript of *S.D.* again under my arm, I walked out of an office on Fifth Avenue for the second time. And brought the manuscript to Random House on Madison Avenue. Writing back to Valerie to say that everywhere it was said that editors couldn't find authors who wrote with feeling and that there was no interesting literature to publish, and here I was putting it in front of them and their cozy little minds seize up. But then a copy of a letter I'd written to someone describing a visit to Lea and of her lavish optimism in the Fountain household and sent to Ernest Gebler immediately elicited Gebler's response that I was indeed a writer and that my manuscript should be sent to his agent, Mavis MacIntosh.

Meanwhile, as Valerie wrote back tolerantly to my continued depressing news of rejections, with my letters containing nothing but proclaimed hope and renewed resolves, her letters contained no good news either. I was now even getting reluctant to return to the Isle of Man. Full of anger as I was at Valerie's treatment by her mother, who, hearing the book was rejected by a publisher, now said that she was not allowing Valerie her money in order that I could exercise my libido. I soon let it be known that I never had any intention of ever seeking money from her or anyone else. Nor was I to be used as an excuse for someone being denied that to which they were more than morally entitled. Always having held that a moral matter was as binding as one legal and therefore legal. It seemed now a battle on both sides of the Atlantic, with it being no longer clear as to where or even if there was somewhere a promised land.

It was now every bit a certainty that with the roots of our strength withering, Gainor and I were as on a raft, isolated and adrift on an endless ocean. The sharks' fins circling. America had beaten us both. But still I felt I had, albeit three thousand miles away, Valerie's courage, faith and wisdom to in many ways depend upon. And that they were there to escape to. However, as I wrote in my letters of land and of a cottage again somewhere, even she was losing hope in any future. And as the days passed of further fruitless waiting, the lifeline between us was being relentlessly stretched and torn. I was now down to simply having to say, have faith in me. Still unable to believe that there wasn't at least one other person somewhere in America with enough or some integrity, or even the desire to grow rich by publishing S.D.

A full moon was rising and glistening white across the landscape on these December nights. Then a day came pouring rain and washed the snow away. Duffy invited me downtown for a meal, and his quiet voice and his smile would come as he bid welcome as he always would with his two reassuring words.

"Hello, friend."

And he was one of the few people I was now feeling safe with. For I was finding Gainor a more and more nightmarish ordeal. And as I tried to pound sense into him, even referring to him in letters to Valerie as a lazy, irresponsible bastard who was now planning to leave his job sending folk to Helsinki and to go on the dole. Then one would sheepishly regret such words, as I'd find he was sending money back to support his children in Europe. But with Duffy, all was a respite as we had spaghetti and Chianti. His now wife Judy had left Sarah Lawrence College to be a housewife. They had moved from their tight tiny apartment in Thompson Street to a much larger, airier, brighter place nearby at number 50 Grand Street, where they installed a concert grand piano. And I remembered that when they found a big chair and table on the street in front of their old apartment and took it in as furniture, that it made me feel that it was at least one pleasant and contradictory certainty about America that people would throw away useful and even luxurious items as garbage and refuse, which vicarious generosity one would never encounter in Europe. Although Jack and Judy did wince over my vehemence on matters American, I did try to provoke a little laughter and avoid a lot of lies. I read them the end of *The Ginger Man* just as Gainor arrived, took a glass of wine, sat down, listened and applauded. He was impossible to beat when showing his discrimination, commendation and wholehearted appreciation. But survival now was another matter and just like fighting air. And daily forbearing the time to pass. While in fold-up postal air letters, and hardly missing a day, I wrote paeans of love to Valerie.

But now closer to home, tragedy struck. Early morning, a policeman called at the door on East 238th Street to inform that T.J., having been stabbed in an affray, was in a critical condition, clinging to life downtown in Bellevue Hospital. The story unfolded that with his car remaining parked at Tenth Street, he'd left his girlfriend, with whom he'd had a fight, and then at three in the morning near Brooklyn Bridge had got into an altercation with two ethnics of the moment as T.J. referred to them, one with a knife and the other with a gun. T.J., an outstanding athlete, not only as a speed ice skater but also in track and field and as a discus thrower had, when confronted with the two armed assailants, knocked the gunman to the ground and while grappling with the assailant with the knife and lifting him up over his head to throw him at the other man reaching for a gun, was stabbed three times in the back. With both attackers briefly on the ground, T.J. ran, and running had just enough time to get far enough away not to be an easy target for the bullets whistling by. Realizing immediately as he sprinted that he was losing blood fast and might not get far, he was lucky to be able to hail a passing taxi and be brought to the hospital.

Sister Rita, my mother, myself, at the side of our Dodge car replaced by my father with a new one every two years. Again Thomas standing in front of his mother with his somber demeanor.

Following in my footsteps as he too left Fordham Prep and followed me to Manhattan Prep to be taught by brothers of de la Salle, a French order, my brother, Thomas, in front of St. John the Baptist de la Salle, whom he maintained was the only decent man in the academic movement who understood him. T.J. much cheered up in his Manhattan Prep school days, which he said were idyllic, but he decided to be deliberately photographed wearing, as he described, "the sneer of the year of 1947."

266

Misery and apprehension within one, I approached this famed New York City landmark of Bellevue and one of the oldest hospitals on the North American continent. Its great anonymous reception halls patrolled by armed security police was lined with brown benches and a motley bewildered-looking assortment of waiting patients. Having to ask directions to find the way to T.J.'s emergency ward, my English accent seemed to elicit immediate, helpful attention. Walking past medical orderlies emerging from myriad other wards, wheeling bodies under their white sheets and on the way to the morgue. Reclining back with tubes from bottles stuck into his arm, T.J. seemed alert enough. His forthright and intelligent sense of observation not deserting him on what had to be thought was his deathbed. The doctor saying that although it seemed he had not suffered any clinical shock, it was now touch and go over the next twelve hours. Back in Woodlawn, I for the first time in my life heard my mother break into sobs, but then heard her say that she would rather see T.J. dead than married to his present girlfriend. One realized that despite the battering one's confidence had already undergone that one now could not let oneself crack any further and had to undertake an even greater steely resolve to battle on and cling ever harder to the wall of the abyss and prevent falling while awaiting the strength to take the slow, clutching climb back up and out. A tension now gathering in my throat. And my tendency to speak growing less and less.

As Bellevue Hospital became a daily visit, and T.J. at last seemed to be mending from his additional wounds done by a stiletto, a thin, round blade which had punctured him in face and legs as well as lungs, one could still not chase the morbid gloom out of one's brain. So sapped by everything on every side. Lonely, without lust, without joy. Each day purposefully taking the bus to the terminus of the Lexington–Jerome Avenue line. And in the roaring noise of the train riding downtown. And before plunging underground, staring at the passing windows at all these lives stacked up in their living boxes. Arriving at Twenty-eighth Street, jammed with cars and people. All seeming wretched as one walked in the direction of sunrise to reach this vast complex of buildings located bordering the East River and occupying a dozen city blocks along First Avenue. The grim barred windows of its huge, gloomy, psychiatric building, lurking full of brooding death and violence. Which gave the name Bellevue its latency of haunting fear. Its vast corridors leading to its massive wards. The beds full of cancer patients, accident and murder victims. T.J. said that as he thought he might live instead of dying that now lying there just watching and hearing them die on all sides had shattered his last illusions.

But then for all its grimness, this was also one of the great hospitals of the world. Where, if you had any chance of living at all, they could keep you alive. It was also, as T.J. said, the kidneys and bowels of New York. Excreting out its demented and dead. Keeping full its massive, somber morgue. From which were taken daily the boxes of amputated limbs and the unclaimed deceased to the back of the hospital and a barge T.J. could see awaiting in the East River. A derrick lifting the wooden-cased corpses and lowering them into the barge's hull. To be towed on the East River up past Sutton Place of the rich and farther through Hell Gate and past the prison windows of the apprehended on Riker's Island and thence to Potter's Field on yet another island called Hart. Nothing in New York could make a greater impression than the fate awaiting the failed. As these, the tens of thousands of bodies, passed through this vast morgue of this great hospital, half of whom, unable to pay for death, are never claimed. And then who go to final rest on this small piece of land standing in view of the shore of Orchard Beach, a massive man-made crescent of sand teeming by summer with swarms of New Yorkers who come to swim and sun and occasionally drown. Growing up, I would go for the day to visit childhood friends like Alan Kuntze and Gerry McKernan, who worked there as lifeguards. Saving the living from death. Pulling those crying for help back to shore. Kneeling over their bodies to resuscitate them. The skin of these drowned turning blue and lips white when they failed.

Returning each day as I would to Woodlawn from the hospital, one would remain in a pall. Despite walking along Fifth Avenue for some cheer, and feeling a guilty response to the Christmas organ music, and the white-bearded Santa Claus ringing a bell. Then to brave the evening hours away eating at my desk in the front room, hunched over a tray of turnips, broccoli, mashed potatoes, and chicken. Could it ever leave one in any doubt about withdrawing and living forever away from this world. And go instead back to where one was surrounded by nothing but bogs, moorlands and open fields. Able to walk amid the purple heather, the cornflowers, the golden gorse, thistles and nettles. And these flora coming alive, I now found in such books as Patrick Kavanagh's *Tarry Flynn* and *The Green Fool*. Reminders, and I needed them, that a writer's life and work was worthy to the world. And that there was at least some solace in having written the first sprawling draft of *The Ginger Man*.

It turned out that Gainor's friend John Preston published by Scribner's whom he occasionally visited in Greenwich Village, when told of his publisher's reaction to *S.D.*, said I was being treated with great consideration, which he said was rare for an unknown writer and certainly meant that one day someone somewhere would publish such a manuscript. I remembered too Wheelock's words that there was hardly anything he could criticize about it as a novel. But with the thump, thump, thump pounding of daily reality, what might be in the future did leave me now with none. It seemed that only letters I wrote to Valerie allowed one to at least briefly escape out of one's own painful little world of angst. Gainor saying on the phone, "Mike, in Europe it was merely petty pilfering out of one's emotional reserves, but here in this nightmare it is wholesale rape and demolition."

Gainor also felt that Lea, who, like us decamped from Ireland and who invited us both back again and again to her house and continued to show us boundless hospitality, was a lady who in fact hated us both, if not for one particular reason then maybe for a million. And Gainor said that he was already depressed enough without being further depressed by her. It could have been that Lea had achieved respectable survival, whereas Gainor and myself, for all our struggles, were samples of the very opposite. Lea had, however, attempted to chivy along Ernie's agent Mavis MacIntosh over *S.D.*, so that as much as I might suspect Gainor's words of being true, I for the time being had to withhold judgment. But then Gainor's predicaments were now so many. And his friends in America perhaps growing fewer. Especially in matters where he had incurred indebtedness, when Gainor was likely now to resent any move or action to recover same.

"Mike, it seems that for whatever one has been accused of having done, one must then naturally expect to be disliked, hated or sued. But lawyers, Mike, they seem to come in their legions out of the woodwork. Indeed, I think this whole bloody country and its citizens have set sail out upon one vast uncontrollable sea of litigation. Upon which I would hope one day soon to have my own monetary little craft to cruise about upon the topmost waves. But, Mike, above all, beyond all, we must ourselves keep possessed of the admirable, the seraphic, and trust to fondness and charity, no matter what destiny doth deliver us in woe."

Days going by now, one's animation suspended, and able to stand less and less the brunt of misfortune. Taking one's temperature by morning and evening. And knowing numerous symptoms from medical studies, I was then choosing a matching disease that might be in the slow process of killing me. I was kept meanwhile alive by tuna fish, mushroom soup, lettuce and home-preserved peaches. My mother said if my sister, Rita, had gold she should wear it to be seen by the world. But I also sensed that despite my nonaccomplishment in the American tradition of success, that my uncompromising words and more my behavior was making itself felt on the whole of this family. Although I despaired the telephone, which seemed to ring insistently with the most purposeless interruptions to destroy one's mornings, there were still these wonderful long calls from Gainor for which I am sure he still owes the bill. He would enunciate in his precise manner his opinions and comments, which could be enjoyed and savored at a safe distance.

"Mike, forgive me if I should bore you with this. But I am still bedeviled by the event of my involuntary erection in front of Mutt's girlfriend in the chill hallway, where my member sprang to its full limits of rigidity in about the three or less seconds flat. And as it did so, it actually quivered. It positively seemed as if it were provoked by something primeval and had its own mind in the matter. Mike, can you from your broad knowledge obtained in the study of zoology possibly give me an explanation of this. I know that dinosaurs had a plexus of nerves situated at the latter end of the spine which served as a secondary brain to operate the back half of their body."

"Gainor, you are quite correct about dinosaurs, but I must in your case, based on what you have told me of the incident and the girl's physical features, assume that you were overtaken by purely hysterical, unpremeditated lust, which may have been aided and abetted by you and Mutt's girlfriend having both been to high school in Ohio."

Gainor seemed amazingly to turn my explanations over in his head, thanked me and hung up the phone. But now came a week of silence from him. And I was to later learn that he was away again visiting pals he'd made of a decidedly Bohemian couple, Justin, a painter, and Sally, his attractive heiress, who lived at Woodstock, upper New York State. A town of a thousand in the Catskill Mountains, where Gainor urged me now to come with him to sample the peace and calm that could be found in the rural surroundings but where he said a rainstorm unleashed a cloudburst, which washed out the roads. But I found myself now tending to decline invitations which took me into strange company. I preferred, with my own hopes growing fainter, to reclusively stay afloat midocean with one's tiny life preserver. It being harder and harder to awaken and come alive to rise up in the battle once more. The tentacles of despair locked around one. Sitting there in the old white house atop the hill. Deep in trouble. Staring at my fingernails. Hart Island on one's mind. And the unsung who died friendless and unmourned in this city. Their flesh and bone abandoned to be taken to be buried with the other unknown and forgotten. Under a cross bearing an inscription over their anonymous graves, "He calleth his children by name." And April had said, "J.P., what does it matter what happens to you when you die." And I wrote out in tiny capitals on a piece of paper I gave her.

IT MATTERS ALL THE DAYS YOU LIVE.

My mother, from her continued remarks about T.J.'s girlfriend, seemed to have no thought for the years T.J. had got yet to live and that it was his life. His very life. Which indeed I thought she might now see end. Although one started one's withdrawal and was even becoming fearful of stirring out, I went daily to visit T.J. in the great anonymous bowels of Bellevue. I still had left my life-giving letters of love I wrote to Valerie in Europe. And I somehow garnered enough strength to brace myself and to face everything. For now I felt that the whole family could go. One had heard the expression "big casino." And I in some way began to connect this term with catastrophic disease, that when it came to one or another member of a family it could wipe the entire family out, striking almost as a lethal pestilence sowing its seed of death. I could not believe that doctors, with the largest incomes of any professional sector in American life, were against any form of socialized medicine, which could protect from such ruinous calamity. I was more concerned now than ever that my passage was finally booked. And that at least and at last I was able to focus on that final day one could get out.

Although he seemed to have amazing powers of recovery, each day of T.J.'s survival came with relief. But there was no doubt that T.J., whatever else besieged him, had heart. The doctor admitting that they had not expected him to survive. His good physical condition and his will to live keeping him alive. Moved to another ward now, T.J. had spoken to a young man who was of an Irish background and had been to good Catholic schools. One day he noticed he had a sore on his side which got progressively bigger and grew into a hole, and he had to be removed to the hospital. His mother came each day visiting as the hole got even larger and he was slowly dying. And T.J. announced that he suspected the mother was killing the boy and now the boy was dead. As were other occupants of the ward each day when someone new appeared in their bed, and they were taken away, white sheets drawn back over their faces.

I made now every effort to get T.J. home. Out and away from the atmosphere of despair, sorrow and death. That what there might be of hope and recovery was better found back in his room, where the winter branches of a cherry tree could be seen out the window. But I could also sense that life in America was for T.J., as it was for Gainor and I, becoming impossible. I was hardly even keen to get calls from Lea, who had previously been asking Gainor and I to breakfast, which when we were unable to accept was now converted to lunch. She seemed exhilarated but told Gainor she was living out of her top emotional drawer.

"Mike, I told her so were we all. Except in our case, we had no drawers left."

I showed up first at Lea's. Ringing the doorbell and at the delay of an answer, I had looked in the window to see if anyone was home. A large fire roaring in the front living room where John Fountain was sitting alone and seemed to look vacantly out into space. Now answering the door, he welcomed me in and offering whiskey to drink, he explained Lea was still out shopping. Minutes later Gainor arrived freezing without an overcoat and in sandals and white socks. And then all of us ensconced by the fire, suddenly Fountain asked Gainor of his life and then of both our marriages and then he smiled, a killed smile, and said,

"You don't know what happiness is till you're married and then it's too late."

When Lea arrived out of a taxi and overflowing with packages, the neighbors on either side were invited in and champagne flowed. And all three men were jolted out of their doldrums. There was no doubt that if this beautiful and vivacious lady had shortcomings, she had many fewer than most. And even Ernest Gebler, left back in Ireland without her, had written me that she was innocent of any grave intent and a woman he had, and still did, deeply love.

But going to and from Bellevue Hospital day after day, I was randomly wandering and making visits elsewhere in the city. Seeing tall April, the golden girl of the rapierlike words and tumbling blond hair, who said she wanted and would get a steel priapus for Christmas to give the girl downstairs to use instead of her Great Dane. She was, in spite of her betrayal and leaving us in the lurch with the lesbians, becoming Gainor's and my mentor and mascot, and joining us on a visit to see Tally Brown. She came all bundled up as if ready to go skiing. And as arctic winds blew snow down the Hudson, and along by the barren high cliffs of the Palisades, it was nearly what we had to end up doing, only snowshoes would have proven better than skis. But inside Tally's, we were safe from the descending blizzard. Incense burned as we sumptuously dined by candlelight off pasta, filet mignon, creamed spinach, garlic bread, and exquisite Burgundy. These two ladies contrasting so much in shape and size, traded equally wise words of wisdom and kindly for dessert offered us both blow jobs to which suggestion Gainor rose to announce,

"Although I only speak for myself, I am ready, my dear ladies, in acknowledgment of your great compassion, kindness and charity to have my brains blown out if it makes, as you suggest it does, for any modicum of contentment and indeed serves as a dessert which clearly shall have no peer."

In this acoustically resounding chamber, April vocalized a song of her own called "My Jangles No Longer Jingle for Yingle Yule." Then Tally, whose unparalleled bel canto voice could tear at one's heartstrings and ranged through opera, the blues, jazz and to Stephen Foster, sang from Fauré's requiem and arias from *La Traviata*. And then came the Hungarian lament "Gloomy Sunday," which Gainor often played upon comb and paper and hummed back in the old sod. Tally's graceful fingers gently touching across the keys of her great black concert grand piano, as this haunting music and its words pervaded the sprawling drawing room and her exquisite voice rung from the words their deathful sadness. Tears welled in Gainor's eyes, and a couple of globules of moisture fell down even my own cheeks. And it almost seemed in these transcending moments that we could be back in Balscaddoon House on Howth Head in Ireland with the stormy seas pounding the cliff side.

It was as if a sacredly if brief wonderful redemption had been given us this night in Washington Heights which could preserve us through all the clobberings and defeats that had been or might yet come. And stave off for indefinite time that last and fatally depressing ignominy that Gainor and I awaited to befall us. But as I began to retreat into a shell of silence to fight my last round, this was to be nearly the very last of social occasions in America. A blizzard had fallen during the night, leaving the city silent, traffic stopped and stranded all over New York. And good ole April was the only one ready for the weather. Holed up as we were next day till early afternoon with Tally's pancakes, sausages, maple syrup, homemade raspberry jam, and coffee. With no shortage at all of further compassion, kindness and charity interspersed by laughter and croissants. Plus a tot of brandy for the road to aid us, hiking away, climbing the hill to the subway in the deep snow, when Gainor said,

"If there's any voice anywhere in this world as magnificently beautiful as Tally Brown's, I've never heard it."

With him Gainor had been carrying a book, *Berkeley's Immaterialism* by Arthur Aston Luce, M.A., Litt. D., D.D., a senior fellow and vice provost of Trinity College, Dublin, as was Berkeley himself in 1707. When asked by April about the book, Gainor waxed lyrical.

"Ah, it concerns Bishop Berkeley. A remarkable man of salty satire and teasing wit. Who selflessly devoted himself to the economic and spiritual betterment of Ireland. Recommended tar water as a general medicine. He was a believer in natural logicality and meditative philosophy. Espoused purity of sentiment and good will toward mankind. Espoused insight into principle. Theorized on the perception of space. His dictum, April, was *Esse is percipi.* To be is to be perceived."

"Well, Gainor, this ole hillbilly gal can't perceive a goddamn thing you're talking about, but I'm listening."

"April, you see. Here in my hand. A snowball. The existence of immediate objects of sensation consists of their being perceived. The whole corporeal world only exists as a set of objects of consciousness. It's all in the mind and its internal sensations."

"Well, Gainor, you sure could have fooled me. But too many of those kind of internal sensations could make you a nut case for Bellevue. And my little ole external sensation right now is to get us some goddamn transport downtown out of these snowdrifts, before somebody comes along and thinks we're looking for a fight. Hey, but you know if you two guys do go skidaddling out of here back to Europe, I think I'm really going to miss you and could die."

As we stood atop this hill down to the Hudson, these were prophetic words of April's spoken in reference to Bellevue and someone coming along looking for a fight. The winds were now swirling over the drifts of snow as a plow made its way through the streets. The area populated by apartment houses, and once reasonably respectable, was not now thought entirely safe. Her own husband away, April was concerned at Gainor's and my survival in this roughest and toughest of cities.

"Hey, J.P., you and Gainor are my dearest, closest, mostest soulmates, but you should get wised up. Like in this town where we were the other night. You see a fight about to happen, hey, gee, you just get right the hell out of there soon. And as I said before, I just didn't want to get my little ole ass all busted up by them big ole ornery bull dykes.

Not anyway while I'm still hard struggling to support a nonsupporting husband until I can get permanently rid of him and sell half my ass on a monthly lease to the highest bidder. You guys forget I was in the military and had big dirty ole dykes trying to jump and rape me all the time. Except that I was a first lieutenant, they would have been trying to stick their tongues anywhere they could get them into little ole me."

I was loathe to disclose to April Gainor's own frequent and often justifiably violent behavior caused by his quickness to anger but also provoked by his being dreadfully, eye-poppingly rude. Which was just about to happen as we approached the 175th Street station of the subway, to take April and Gainor downtown. Gainor was inquiring on my behalf for the train to take me uptown to the nether wilds of Broadway and 242d Street on the western edge of Van Cortlandt Park and had walked up to a line of people waiting for a bus. With his first question for directions receiving no answer, Gainor demanded one. And still there was silence.

"Look here, you people, can't anyone of you tell me where the goddamn nearest subway stop is of the 7th Avenue–Broadway line. One of you must know. Or is that too much for your brains to fathom. What the hell's the matter with you all. Are you all dumb. Do you understand English."

It was not for the first time in our friendship that I was tempted to tell Gainor he was on his own. That both of us having grown up in this country, he knew as much as I did about handling oneself in a strange street. And although indoctrinated with the principle of fair play and a fair fight, we were both ready for the situation to any second get unfair. Nevertheless, we were raised at a time when the world seemed to be getting bigger and better. Faster and faster. With more leisure, less work. Cleverer machines making for less to do for more of men. And nothing you dismay. Except as Gainor was finding out in Queens, that when you reached to use anything, everything, as he said, became fucked out of kilter. But with all this evolution and change, one might have also thought the place had to be getting a little more courteous too. But not so. Just as one would now awkwardly and rapidly find. While this cold day's bright sun shone blindingly on the snow. And as a man swaggered forward out of the line who looked tough enough to be acting as spokesman for the group waiting for the bus. And one was to hear again those old-fashioned provocative words said to Gainor, this once-upon-a-time paragon of diplomatic behavior, who had perhaps been one of the most courteous men who ever lived.

"Hey, bud, are you looking for a fight."

"No. As a matter of fact, I'm looking merely for directions, which surely any halfway civilized person would, considering the snow, reply to, even to the extent of informing that they do not know the answer."

For all these measuredly statesmanlike words spoken by Gainor, one could nevertheless sense rising in him a blazing anger. And with us all wanting to go home to our would-be firesides, April was pulling on Gainor's left arm as I was tugging on his right to move him backward away. April whispering in his ear,

"Hey, Gainor, come on, honeybunch, let's get the hell out of here."

"I'm not going till this rude individual apologizes."

The gauntlet dropped, the rude individual to whom Gainor referred took an astride, intimidating stance, cocking back his head, belligerence written all over his face and menace in his sneer. All the very appropriate behavior necessary to turn Gainor Stephen Crist, the erudite follower of Bishop Berkeley, into a killer.

"Well, bud, it so happens I'm not apologizing. What are you going to do about it."

Both April and I knew what Crist could do about it. And April, an admitted lover of peace, and I, who still with the pink fresh scars of my last affray to remind me, wanted, as much as April, to get the hell away out of there in one big hurry. And not to delay with splashing blood, ears bitten off and chewed, and the usual bicuspids flying everywhere. Plus police cars and ambulances in pronto abundant attendance. One was actually toying with the idea of running. When just at that moment, April suddenly stepped forward to take up a position between Gainor and his antagonist. And right smack in front and only a hairsbreadth away from the so-called rude individual, who continued to be rude.

"Hey, lady, you get the hell out of my way before you get hurt."

"And you, buster, member of pipsqueaks anonymous, had better get the fuck back in that line. Before first you get your ears pinned back, second your jaw broken, third your dumb nose flattened across your face and fourth get socked fifty miles into next Tuesday. Because after that we're going to pick you up by the ears and shake your balls off."

Now then. As the words were loud enough, a woman nearby taking a bottle of milk in from her windowsill stopped midmotion to watch. And I was immediately sure that nowhere in the annals of potential confrontational violence had one ever come across such an astonishingly long agonizing pause. And April stood. And she stands. On her honor. And on her long, tapering legs. As she always did. Even when she abandoned us to the dykes. Her stunningly blue beautiful and brave eyes staring steadily into this shocked man's face. Boring holes in his head as the seconds ticked away. Kids pulling a sleigh along the sidewalk. Another snowplow passing in the street. And your man taking a backward step. And then looking behind him, took two steps. Then three. And turning. Just as April bid him do. To join his place back again in line. And I'd remembered April once reminiscing and talking about back up there in the mountain gulch where she was born, saying her mother had her in April, when they were expecting her in May. And April said, "You see, guys, they got it all wrong, because I was born already. So eager was I.

> "To get out there
> And
> Start winning"

25

It was clear that Gainor was never going to compromise with rudeness in these United States, and although it was sad it was with enormous relief that I watched Gainor disappear with April down the snow-covered steps into the subway beneath the ground of Washington Heights. Glad I was not to have to use energy in anger and to further smash the bones in my fists hammering them on the endless supply of belligerent faces whom Gainor referred to as the ill-bred by the ill-bred.

I went on my own way to Broadway and 168th Street to take a train back to Woodlawn and to trudge the couple of miles with freezing ears and frozen feet through the woods. Remembering that along by this isolated terrain of the golf course and in similar deep snow and when not much more than seven years old, I was once lost when left behind by bigger boys who would not wait for me to catch them up. And a great black, gleaming limousine came along the road, and stopped. When I said I was crying because I was lost, I was ushered into the company of a lady sitting in the back who spoke to her chauffeur through a small speaker held in her hand. I'll never know now who this lady was who took the trouble to pick up a small vagrant to take to the nearest police station farther downtown in the area of Kingsbridge. Where I was finally rescued by my parents. But the incident must have given me a preference for large chauffeured limousines since. And for kindly ladies.

Back in the old white house, struggling against an ever present depression, I now undertook again my noncompromising and battling and rigid routine. Standing firm on my every besieged principle. But an influence was being wrought. T.J. now home was still kept to bed. In a back bedroom which we shared growing up with a high window through which one could see the sky. His life at a crossroads. He said he had been goaded day after day by a girlfriend about marriage. And about her family and all they stood for and wanted. And told then about how all the other girls had rings, had married and had cars and refrigerators. But meanwhile the same girlfriend would make him spend every penny he had ever earned taking her out to dinner. While she kept her aura of her money saved, her car got and how many other guys were desperate to marry her.

But at least T.J. had escaped from corporate America, and had, following selling cemetery plots and counting dresses, taken a job with the Bridgeport Box Lunch Company, where he was happier working long arduous hours brewing huge caldrons of coffee and making box lunches than he was finding bodies hanging in the back rooms of department stores. Remarkable for his dedication and his prodigious work, he had made a most favorable impression on his boss, who very much wanted him back and was even sending him get-well wishes and presents. But as I brought him food and let fresh air into his room every morning, I realized that T.J. desperately needed something, other than making box lunches, to occupy his time. And one afternoon I brought to his bedside a canvas, paints and brushes. Next morning he presented me with a still life of fruit on a table, complete with shadows and highlights and a work any academician studying a lifetime in Florence would have been proud of producing and exhibiting at a major exhibition. When I was somewhat incredulous, T.J. assured me.

"It's easy. An orange is round and it's colored orange. A grapefruit, you flatten a little at the top and a little at the bottom and color it yellow. An apple, you make it look as if it's ripe with a little bit of green here and a little bit of red there. The light from the window shines in so here and there, so you place a spot or two of this flake white to make it bright."

T.J. did not seem to be surprised that he was painting with the lifetime skill of a master craftsman, or was, straight from the off, executing works of art. And was now so prodigious in the production of these that I suggested he also make pottery to help use up more of his overwhelming energy. I brought him clay. Converting an old gramophone turntable into a potter's wheel, he in no time had turned the basement cellar into an Aladdin's cave of pots equally original and exquisite to his paintings. He was like a man possessed. Explaining that he worked day and night because for the first time in his life he had something satisfying to do. And even exhausted and hung over, Gainor, catching his breath on a brief visit, was stunned.

Tears streaming down his cheeks, as he sat in T.J.'s music room, listening to T.J.'s "Nobblywood Concerto," played by T.J. at an average rate of thirty-five notes a second, and which could and did disembowel one with its utter sadness. Then even sadder, T.J. played his "Nobblywood Dirge," which he then dedicated to Gainor and renamed the G.S.C. Memorial Concerto. Gainor, upon parting thanking me and saying,

"Mike, as a great lover of music, I have now in America heard some of the best there is to hear in the world. From John Duffy, Tally Brown and now T.J."

Jack O'Hare, my sister Rita's then husband, also seemed suddenly influenced by the changes affecting the household. Returning in the evenings from his studies or work to talk and listen as the family would convene between kitchen and dining room. Arguments sometimes flared and then died or got renewed again. But one night, Jack O'Hare said,

"You know I've been thinking. About us in this country. Do you know what we are. We're just a bunch of lying bastards. I don't think we've told the truth once in our lives."

Coming from this man who during the war was a major in the marine corps and whose life had been nothing but dedicated hard work and adhering to the ethic of the American way and who, while working as a policeman, was also qualifying as a lawyer, it was a victory. Especially as right at that time the United States Congress was going all out against obscene literature. Even so, I was making declarations in my letters back to Valerie that there was no question, none whatsoever, and not one chance in a million, that *S.D.* would not be published. And would finally one day quell and squash all the mealymouthed, sanctimonious and hypocritical who sneakily and not so sneakily were abroad in America. However, it was becoming more and more evident that first, someone somewhere was going to have to stand up with a public courage and declare that the undeceitful were about to rise and exist in this land.

But hardly a week had gone by back in Woodlawn before another call came across the wires to the Bronx from Queens, where Gainor too, beset by nightmares and working without sleep and then unable to sleep, seemed to be attempting more steps to retreat from the world. He rang from his redoubt on what was suddenly this cold winterish evening, the thermometer plummeting with little flurries of snow again falling on the deep drifts already piled high along the highways and streets. And where the snow had been removed, it left black gleaming ice. All was silent outside. Comfortable lights glowing within the houses. The telephone sounded off just as I was attempting to internally warm and cheer myself, having a glass of hot chocolate before bedtime.

"Mike, thank God you're there. I've got to find somewhere to hide out until I can finally get out of this country. Mike, I have, I really have had enough."

"What on earth's happened now, Gainor."

"Mike, I was put in a straitjacket, and have spent the night in a padded cell. Pray God and special intercession with blessed Oliver Plunket will save me from any more. And that I am delivered from this place ere long and that my nerves already badly shattered each day at the airport stay steady enough to sustain me long enough so that I can lug my old creaking bones up the gangway and onto a preferably British ship sailing the bloody hell out of here."

"Good God, are you all right."

"Mike, I feel like I'm under some kind of homosexual blackmail in this building. What is wrong with me that I should attract these unwanted overtures of every conceivable kind ending me up fined fifty dollars and it was only with the help of the airline I was released. Mike, I was in my wigwam over my bed looking again at your pictures of the old sod, which I may say every time I do so, renders me utterly homesick. And also reading S.D., Mike. I know you've been depressed by all your recent rejections, but you mustn't ever give up. However, in my state of deep nostalgia created by Sebastian Dangerfield and your photographs and wanting badly to be left alone by every person in this city, I thought I would just slip downstairs to the bar for a reflective tumbler or two of Irish whiskey, which the bartender now keeps for me. As you know, I'm forever grateful that the ground floor of this building provides drinking accommodation into which, thank God, there is blessedly easy access. Now following all these recent days of chaos and having worked many dreadful extra hours in long stints at the airport, trying to pay off my mounting debts, and dodging the usual knives and fists which put my life constantly in jeopardy, today I was traced there by some insufferable individual dunning me for a bill I owe who actually stood in the check-in line for half an hour and then slammed the bill instead of a ticket down in front of me."

"You hit him."

"Mike, I wish I had. But as I was relieving someone at his desk, I merely said he was looking for my twin brother who also worked at the airport but this was his day off. Luckily everyone began to hiss and tell him to get out of the line. However, then back in my wigwam and my Chianti bottle having run dry, I was so looking forward to some brief relaxation and a little drink. In any event, as I was already attired in my long underwear while in my wigwam, and being that the bar's subdued lighting would keep one out of sight and harm's way, as it were, I simply pulled on a tall pair of woolen socks up over my long johns, slipped into my shoes and put on my father's overcoat. Then, after descending to the quite populated bar, and just as I was beginning to relax following my first drink and having thought I had successfully extricated myself from a one-sided unpleasant discussion with a divorcée who was telling me that she'd just taken her husband to the cleaners for every penny he was worth and that what a happy country this is, to which I uttered my standard reply, 'Have you looked at the faces including your own, madam, in the mirror?' I then started to look for my cigarettes. Mike, I shouldn't have made the latter remark to this bitch. She suddenly hauled off and landed a resounding slap on my jaw. I actually saw Saturn and Mars and a few other of the more long-distanced stars. God knows I've always interposed chivalry at such times as when women have exasperatingly pushed me to breaking point. But this country is, with the exception of Tally and April, turning women into veritable monsters. Of course I was instantly put into considerable bad humor and unable to strike back, I was now even more desperately looking for my cigarettes, which I did not seem able to find. Now fully exasperated and angrily still digging around trying to locate my packet of Chesterfields and forgetting that I was no longer wearing my airline uniform, I took off my overcoat and then as the whole bar went suddenly quiet, I stood there in just enough light to see by, in my long underwear, white from neck to knees and green then to my ankles. Mike, you might think that's funny."

"Gainor, I'm sorry, it's a very quiet and uneventful evening up here in Woodlawn, and one is prone to being easily amused."

"Well, I haven't yet told you, and I blame and owe it to April's advice. I was wearing a jockstrap over the underwear. Only this bloody one was mistakenly washed with a red shirt back in Ireland and has stayed that color. Mike, believe me when I tell you that in all my life I have never seen anything like the expressions that were to be seen on these people's countenances. At least on those who were in a position to see and then tell everyone else, and who then got an even bigger shock thinking my privates had undergone some kind of bloody recent transvestite transplant operation which went woefully wrong and my privates were as a result bandaged up and the blood soaked through. Thank God the bartender, with whom I maintain a financial arrangement, knows me well. Jesus, Mike, I can hear you, this isn't a laughing matter."

"Gainor, that was just a little feeble croak of mirth surfacing, as it were, out of our overwhelming sea of woe. But you haven't mentioned a word about homosexuality."

"Don't worry, I'm coming to that, but with "Jingle Bells, Jingle Bells" unsuitably playing on the jukebox, the whole scene was garish in the extreme. Especially when, while I'm being seen desperately feeling myself up, I'm still trying to find a cigarette to get some nicotine quickly into my system, which, along with a large tumbler of whiskey, I hoped could temporarily paralyze my perceptions. Of course, the long tall socks I was attired in were in fact a bright, tasseled variety one wears with a kilt. If anyone in this world looked like a complete lunatic out of the institution, I did. And of course, Mike, what do you imagine could be the bloody most inconvenient next thing that happened."

"Your father's black, incredibly luxurious satin-lined overcoat disappeared."

"Yes, you're absolutely right. Mike, it could not have been taken by mistake. Some bloody bastard deliberately vanished with it, together with my apartment keys. That leaves me even a little more banjaxed, plus having to wait until Mutt or Jeff got back to the apartment to let me in. Temporarily I got loaned someone else's coat draped over me, a ladies', as it happened, with a pretty fur collar. However, with now every bloody face in the place watching me, and really thinking I was a transvestite, and as I was beginning to feel like one, I then drank too bloody much too fast than was good for me. Now, Mike, considering what had already happened, you'd think that by the law of averages I could at least expect some good thing to befall me. But I seem to have no bloody damn luck at all."

"Gainor, it's not luck you need, but unmitigatedly large sums of money, and that goes for both of us."

"Mike, that also goes without saying. But I was of course inebriated enough to chance trying to go back up to the apartment, and hoping to avoid being seen rushing up the four flights in my red jockstrap and long underwear. Which, were I seen and considering previous events, also would incite more bloody mayhem, with everybody phoning each other in the building that I was about to go on another rape rampage. But wouldn't you know that I was hardly up to the first bloody landing when the first scream emitted. Then I had to proceed all the way back up the remaining three flights and the public hallway with nearly every bloody door opening with each previous scream alerting newer and louder additional outcries. My desperate concern now to disappear out of sight before the usual police and fire squads arrived. But then getting at last to the apartment door and of course without keys and finding Mutt not there, I had to cower in my red jockstrap and long underwear. As you know, I am of a mind and firm belief that every man have unto himself his own predilections and be free to pursue pleasures of any sort that he may be inclined to find. But now, this little fat, bald, pot-bellied bugger from across the hall appears and is asking me, would I like to join him in his apartment for a homosexual romp. Mike, are you still there. Are you still listening."

"Yes, Gainor, I am. I'm even making notes."

"Well, firmly and legibly note, will you, that I declined. But in persisting, he said, 'Why not, you're in your underwear and you've got nothing better to do, plus why are you wearing a red jockstrap if you're not queer.' Mike, I simply could not fathom his reasoning for such an assumption. But for all I know in this bloody city perhaps red jock-straps are indeed worn by queers. In any event, stranded there as I was in the hall, one struggled to be diplomatically polite. But the audacity of some people is spellbinding and imposes limits on one's self control. As he wouldn't budge from the hallway, and trying to be facetiously helpful, I suggested to him that he go back into his own nice warm apartment, stick his prick in the sucking end of the vacuum cleaner, and that I'd at least try not to short-circuit the lights in the building while he was enjoying himself. Mike, he took this very well meaning suggestion of mine very badly. Said I insulted him and stalked off slamming doors. But not before informing me he knows the landlord, who is queer and who will evict me. I'm sure his remark about the landlord is not true, but if it were I'd breathe a sigh of relief to be sent packing as soon as and as far away as possible. But a squad car did arrive. And still in my underwear, the more I tried to explain in the hall what had happened in the bar downstairs the more the police thought I was a criminal lunatic. Instead of being simply arrested and charged with drunk and disorderly behavior, I was put in a straitjacket."

"Gainor, I am sorry to hear of your troubles. Why don't you go spend a day at the Bronx Zoo."

"Mike, please don't try to be funny."

"I'm not. I mean it. You'll find it an altogether charmingly calming place. Of bears, monkeys and zebras."

"Mike, I've presently got plenty of bears, monkeys and zebras in my nightmares and don't presently need real ones."

I could no longer conceive of Gainor actually being able to escape. It began to seem that wherever he went and whatever he did now in America brought detriment. I had heard from some source but had never questioned Gainor or had it authenticated that he was in some way related through family to the Amish Mennonites, a sect who held to freedom of conscience and opposed slavery and warfare. If such were the case, it would have accounted for Gainor being an inveterate foot washer. But not for him to unaccountably blunder into constant strife. The Amish too were renowned for their quiet industry and routine hard work. A characteristic that Gainor did in fact have. And it was exactly how, upon such precepts, that I was now trying to hold onto my own sanity in and keep as busy as I could my life, which was now without a core around which one's existence could center. I had to make it back to the land of Ireland or to the Isle of Man, where one could tramp the heathery moors again and civilized take tea and scones in some hostelry or drink beer before a fire in a pub. But it was as if I were fighting a losing battle in trying to remain quietly methodical in my angst-ridden and hypochondriacal state, with an occasionally rapidly beating heart. Making all efforts to keep moving, in order to be distracted and exercised. Forcing myself out in the cold under the sky and sun. Taking food that I thought would be good for me. All-Bran, scrambled eggs, sausages, brown toast and coffee for breakfast. And even cod-liver oil.

Meanwhile, T.J., who lay in bed, went on painting his masterpieces. With their exquisite grading of shadows and highlights. And I was dumbfounded as he started about his tenth picture, maintaining it was easy, like water off a duck's back, which indeed at the moment he was presently painting. On such bird each drop of moisture sparkling like a gem. While he was meticulously anointing his canvases, T.J. would talk. Telling of an old Woodlawnite and school acquaintance who'd gone further afield to another town to make his way and fortune. And who would every so often return to be seen rich and successful, slowly cruising through the Woodlawn streets in the back of a chauffeured limousine. Giving a royal wave to any nosy parker who might be watching, or anyone who might recognize him, which was nearly everyone, to whom he then patronizingly smiled and tipped his cap. But then someone from Woodlawn had accidentally come across him employed working in this distant small upstate town sweeping up in a grocery store. And the chauffeured limousine was seen no more. And

T.J. said that when he heard of this unmasking he was overcome with grief that he would not see this man passing again to whom he gave an admiring smile and a thumbs-up sign.

An editor had now read the manuscript of *S.D.* at Random House publishers, and reported on a Friday to agents that it was too long in parts and that the story slowed up, but the agents remained optimistic over a weekend when they expected to hear a final decision on Monday. For five straight days now, I had no word from Gainor, used as I was to my long, nearly daily talks with him over the telephone, which always included our plans for departure being rehearsed. As I knew he was hoping soon to get away to the quite rural peace of upstate Woodstock for a brief stay and for some light relief, I thought he must be there. But not having an address or phone number, it was impossible for me to discover. I rang his number out on the wastes of Queens, expecting to hear he'd again been arrested in his long underwear and red jockstrap and was in jail on Riker's Island in the East River. But instead got an immediate angry answer from what I presumed was one of his flatmates.

"He's not here, and I don't know where he is."

In trying his number at the airport, I had to wait, as long, fruitless inquiries were made, to be then told that he was unavailable and that no one knew when he would be back. Finally my worry mounted as to his whereabouts and although relieved not to be in his company, I was now concerned for his welfare. Then, early morning, just after finishing my ablutions following breakfast, and as I was about to sit at my desk to take my temperature, feel my pulse and try to abate the waves of angst by reassuring myself that all my readings were normal, the telephone rang and found me rushing downstairs to the sitting room.

"Good God, Gainor, where have you been. I've been trying to reach you."

"Mike, as usual you're not going to believe this. I've been these past several days in the Bronx. And in Fordham Hospital, right next to where you went to school."

I listened dumbfoundedly attentive to Gainor. My attendance at Fordham Preparatory School for three years and odd truancy days had made me much familiar with this curious area of the Bronx, where Edgar Allan Poe had lived in a little white cottage I often passed by. And Fordham Hospital was where my father had been treated when he was injured in a fire as a fireman and where as a child I had been taken when breaking a collarbone falling out of bed when I was but five years old. Brought to the hospital's accident ward, I saw a trolley wheeled by on which lay another little boy, gently moaning and accompanied by tearful parents, his smallness covered in a blood-spattered sheet and his clothes in a little pile at his feet. He had been hit by a car while playing in the street. And somehow I heard as I waited to be treated that this little boy who passed by was now dead. Leaving me forever afterward with a haunting fear and disrelish of hospitals. And these thoughts flashing through my mind as I listened further to Gainor and yet another mishappenstance in his life.

"Mike, I took your advice. And went to see the spitting cobras at the zoo. Having gone there after having been besieged by Mutt's bloody girlfriend, who indeed wants to see my prick quiver again. But that's another story I won't go into now, save to say that some women in this land are trained up by their mothers to be the killers of joy in men. And the cobras do indeed splash their white poison on the glass of their cage. And I was having such a nice day all by myself viewing scenes from nature. Strolling and reading on a sheltered bench in the sunshine, where the temperature was fifty-five degrees. Everything you said about the zoo is true. I saw two monkeys fucking, over which, unlike us poor mortals, they don't appear to waste much time, nor seem to sit around worrying much about the consequences. Then leaving the zoo and going nearby to further stroll and look at the fine building where you went to prep school and admiring its Old World architecture, and I then did in a very satisfied mood of mind have a couple of beers at a local bar before returning to the subway. I was of course carrying with me to read Luce's trusty volume *Berkeley's Immaterialism* and indeed was engrossed in it on the subway platform while waiting for the train. And, Mike, I absolutely know you're going to think I'm careless and at fault and to some degree admittedly I am, but I walked right the bloody hell off the platform and fell into the tracks. Yes, I know you're going to say why the bloody hell didn't I watch where I was going."

"Gainor, yes, that's exactly what I was going to say."

"Well, I'll tell you why. Because at that precise time, and on Berkeley's principle that 'to be is to be perceived,' I got a flash insight of how the universe came into being. And totally envisioning it all just as I was falling. But when my head hit the tracks, it knocked the perception completely out of my consciousness. I tell you, I have come to my wit's end and have now gone so far beyond that I'm practically in nirvana. But where I have really been for the last four days is in Fordham Hospital. And having had to be kept there under observation."

"Good God, you haven't cracked up."

"Morally and physically, yes, but I don't think quite mentally yet. A dim shred of reality still hovers somewhere to which I tenuously and desperately cling. However, I have certainly been left having for nearly four days to talk my way out of being permanently incarcerated in a mental institution. And trying to convince doctors that I'm sane, exactly as all true lunatics apparently attempt to do. And as you persist in doing so, they then start regarding one as being troublesome if not malicious and possibly criminally insane. But even more terrible, Mike, is the desperate, anguished feeling in knowing that whatever you say or do is going to even more convince them that one is a mental case. Having hauled me up out of the tracks and just missing the third rail and with a train as usual on its way into the station which luckily stopped but ten feet away, I was shaky and bruised and cut myself, and although admittedly unconscious for a few moments I was intact and otherwise perfectly all right. But I then overheard them saying that, having been on the platform reading as I was Luce's splendid volume on *Berkeley's Immaterialism,* I was an obvious psychiatric case trying to commit suicide. And heard that dreaded name Bellevue mentioned. All just as April predicted. Mike, if it hadn't been for someone saying I needed immediate medical attention I might now be in a padded cell."

"Gainor, you've got to, you must, whatever else you do, stay out of the subway. It's nearly an exact replica of your previous debacle only this time you were the victim."

"Mike, it's the only way I can afford to travel. I just simply walked a mite off course into the subway tracks. And Mike, considering what has happened to me so far in this country, would that the wheels of that train had only accorded me such mercy and proceeded those extra ten feet and ended my days."

Except for his collapse in the bath under the shower curtain rail, I had never before heard Gainor express a view dismal enough to suggest that he would contemplate an end to his life. But he was only to reveal now more of what had happened out in Queens the evening of the long underwear. When it transpired that the potbellied, bald homosexual, whom Gainor had told to shove his prick in the business end of a vacuum cleaner, then called the police to inform them that Gainor was a raving lunatic, threatening violence and loose on the landing, which produced a whole team of police paramedics charging up the stairs to put Gainor Stephen Crist in a straitjacket.

"Mike, I'm sure I don't have to tell you that there is no worse feeling than to have about a dozen hands grabbing you from every side as they pin you down to encase one in that most disagreeable restraint. Mike, I never ever again anywhere want to undergo that again. But having lost my temper on that occasion, I was at Fordham Hospital able to convince them that not only was I sane but that I was supersane in wanting to get the hell out of there. But there was of course a hairline fracture discovered in my skull. With the outcome of it all to be just one more sizable bill presented to me. And obviously to see if I could pay my bill, they were checking my credentials and phoned my employers. Of course some bloody no-do-gooder there told of my having sent passengers to Helsinki who wanted to go to San Juan, Puerto Rico. Then in phoning my address and getting an earful from Mutt and Jeff of red jockstrap, wigwam, long underwear and attempted rape, they were again contemplating sending me to Bellevue. I nearly went berserk but fortunately didn't. I announced in the simplest, calmest, quietest, clearest, sanest manner possible, that were I to be manhandled or put in a bloody goddamn straitjacket or that they do any similar such thing to me that the entire hospital would be bankrupted by the most stupendous ensuing litigation for damages ever mounted or devised by the hungriest bunch of contingency lawyers ever assembled on the North American continent. Miraculously, that little spiel of mine seemed to quiet everyone down. And I was given a private room and made happier than I think I have been at any other time in America, enjoying a few welcome hours of peace and calm under treatment there. Played chess and beating everyone and outwitting them in every other intellectual endeavor, I became, I believe, an object of affection for various nurses and doctors who took to paying me friendly visits. I had the undivided attention of the most charming and wonderful nurse too. Who's made me a present of quite an unusually good bottle of brandy, which I'm presently sampling. She's even rung me to see if I'm all right. Mike, I did truly enjoy strolling through the Fordham campus, whose rather impressive college buildings seemed a quite marvelous place. I passed a tiny little building in which they measure earthquakes. They even seemed to have an infirmary, which I presume was available to you when you were there as a student and were injured or had a tummyache. But I do truly think they did themselves a woeful disservice to expel you. But ah, Dinnlay, in the words of Jesus Christ, one simply murmurs under one's breath, father forgive them, for they know not what they fucking well do. And, Dinnlay, with time to contemplate in the hospital, I was thinking of S.D. I know you have described the literary world as a bunch of small-minded, self-congratulatory, timid little shits, who, aware of their own insignificance, lurk waiting ready to reject and dismiss the meritoriously original. Of course, you are entirely correct and quite rightly will keep your life forever clear of them. And by the way, Mike, you must solemnly promise to never, never reveal ever to anyone till at least twenty-five years after my death about my being restrained in a strait-jacket."

Having received anguished letters from Pamela asking me to urge Gainor to write, I did as she requested but did not disclose to her any of Gainor's reasons for not doing so. And now small interruptions of silence were coming as Gainor went on talking, and I thought I could hear the movement of brandy in its bottle. And as I clung to the phone listening and attempting to hold onto my own sanity, Gainor's voice took on a strange incantation. I had nervous thoughts that perhaps he had finally cracked and would indeed be finally, by straitjacket, hauled off to Bellevue. But there was now no one anywhere with whom I could better maintain comradeship and seek what solace I could from being in an identical predicament and probably about to suffer an identical fate. And I listened raptly as his voice droned on.

"But you know, Dinnlay, one day, and as certain as the drums now beat for us in retreat and we await to sail, even these deceivers of genius will have to come out from under their cowardly cover. To acknowledge you, if not to sing your praises. Believe and trust me in that prediction. Let it sustain you through these next days if dismal they might be. Be loyal to your royal blood. Be certain that soon the betrayers will be betrayed. And not that too far away in the future. Even as you continue to humble yourself. Your name will be spoken of in praise and in awe. Again believe me. Again trust me. Have faith that this shall be so, Dinnlay."

"Gainor, for God's sake, don't drink any more of that brandy."

"Ah indeed, Dinnlay, I can't. What do you think about that. Because I've just drunk it all. Down to the last drop. And am about to decamp to downstairs for a midmorning nightcap. And in the full covering of my airport uniform, I might add. But before I go, let me say this. Let us not let the present make us forsake the future. We both must patiently abide till relief shall come from all this disappointment and chagrin. Which shall happen as the good ship *Franconia* pulls out to midstream from its dock. To float down upon that great river, the Hudson. Passing on our left Cortlandt Street. Rector Street. And Bowling Green. Oh yes. I know the names. Then, Dinnlay, as we go out across New York Bay, past the Statue of Liberty, we shall, as former naval persons, be standing to attention on deck. Watching the tall spires of this city shrink behind us. At long last escaped as I shall be from Queens Boulevard. My highway to doom. And you relieved of your temporarily dashed hopes. And then, out there. Upon the Atlantic waves. Finally we will feel the swells of the sea under us. Heading home. Back to where both our hearts eternally lay. Where both our loved ones dwell. Where shall befall us no more ignominy. No more pain. Nor breaches of courtesy. And there shall we find. A little contentment. And where we might hear if we listen, a strange sound. From the wise owl. And ask.

> "Who doth it be
> Now
> Who hoots
> Out of a sorrow
> Cold and old
>
> "It doth
> Be me
> Who hoots"

26

As GAINOR, I and T.J. sat at the white porcelain table having breakfast in the warmly snug kitchen in Woodlawn, from Europe news came of the Irish Sea being swept by some of the worst storms in memory. Lives already lost on one of the ferries crossing from Scotland to Northern Ireland. On the Isle of Man, the Anchorage was being battered by the mountainous waves and the spray which was blowing over the house, but, with its three-foot-thick walls and high garden bastion overlooking the beach, was holding out. And Gainor hearing these tidings intoned, "May there be God's mercy on a wild, wild sea."

Sustaining one these early days of February was the knowledge that the good ship *Franconia* was already plowing the North Atlantic deeps on its way to New York to rescue one. And even perhaps Gainor. Who I knew was leaving no stone unturned under which he might find a way of getting out or, in failing that, being able to hide. But meanwhile for me came more bad news. Tumbling as it seemed routinely down the pike. And always one unable to get out of its way. The book having been read twice at Random House was finally declined. The agents, who had plans to show the novel to Farrar, Straus and Young and Harcourt Brace and were hoping to get an editor to work with, no longer seemed to want to pursue further finding a publisher. Saying they found the work very exciting and were certain of its ultimate publication but felt there was too much in the work to which publishers would take exception. Mention was made of references to the Catholic church and to scenes thought too explicit.

With not that many days left to sail, I retrieved the novel. Publishers I'd heard were swamped with stacks of manuscripts day after day. And I knew there was no way *The Ginger Man* without an agent could be plucked up out of the scramble. The manuscript went packed into my bag. At the same time, a letter arrived from Ernest Gebler, who was in London for the premiere of *The Plymouth Adventure,* the star-studded Hollywood rendition of his account of the Mayflower, which he'd originally entitled "The Dream of Poor Men." He had written in answer to one of my fiercely depressing accounts of life as I was finding it in America and the grim prospects I was experiencing for *S.D.* And sounding euphoric, Gebler wrote back saying that he had felt exactly like that in New York and also, in prophetic words, mentioned that he had an idea about French publishers who published in English in Paris. But meanwhile not to let myself be undermined by rejections and to come back and, with prices cheap, buy a farm in Ireland.

I found that although my mother could carp and criticize, she always acquiesced and came across in all the important things, relenting at my insistence and saying that she would go along with anything I wanted to do. And she had now given me enough money to return to Europe and even the promise of help there, should I need it or of help to get a farm should we ever contemplate return to the United States. I made now my last visits to the club. Taking a ride on the mechanical horse in the gym and working out on bags in the boxing room. I took my leave of Arthur Donovan and Frank Fulham. Who, hearing I was going, expressed the appropriate sadness and immediately launched into their clearly fictitious plans they pretended they had made for my ring future.

"Hey, gee, champ, we got all lined up for you a few pretty good fights at middleweight, where you could pulverize these guys. Like you and Tommy Gill used to do to each other. No kidding. You could go right up to the top of the rankings overnight."

And of course I hadn't been kidding when I thought more than once that I might actually have to get up in the ring somewhere and with a mouthpiece preserving my teeth, hope that I could batter a few opponents to the deck for my butter and bread. Plus it might have done me a lot of other good with a means of letting off steam. Especially as one had very quickly found everything wrong in this country. And life corroded by the poison of suspicion seeping deep across the nation. The falsely accused, sent down to doom. Betrayed and their lives ruined. But now at the end of my sojourn, I was also alternately finding Gainor one moment an ally, and the next, intolerably exasperating. And was beginning to wonder why I forgave him all his unforgivable transgressions. And especially through the now rapidly accumulating discomfiture he provided by the constantly occurring mayhem in his life. But then I could never forget that in the midst of all his own tribulations, he would still end up giving me encouragement. And how this could continue throughout his own ordeals and bedevilments was becoming increasingly astonishing to me. But I never thought the day could ever come when I would find Gainor comforting, which I did for the few days he had arrived in Woodlawn for some respite before making his way to Woodstock for further rest and recuperation. Now in a state of hysterical silence, with my voice gone, Gainor spoke to me and I listened and then in large, clearly legible letters, I printed out my replies to him on scraps of paper to make them look like posters.

"Mike, can you tell me why it is that wives, mistresses and children can't all live together in happy harmony and avoid this awful emotional not to mention financial fragmentation that comes by having to support several roofs to exist under. Have you any comment to make."

YES, TO BE CAUGHT ON THE HORNS OF A DILEMMA IS BAD
ENOUGH BUT TO THEN HAVE ONE OF THE HORNS A MILE UP
YOUR REAR END IS A HELL OF A SIGHT WORSE. AND THAT'S
WHY YOU HAD BETTER NOT ALL TRY TO LIVE TOGETHER

One occasionally had to remind oneself that Gainor was in fact one of the trusted efficient supervisors of passenger traffic for Pan American airways and that his associates appreciated his endless willingness to accomplish for them all sorts of favors and relieve them at their harrowing duty at their check-in desks. But I did not take too seriously Gainor's seemingly vague plans to decamp. Nor did I know that he was in touch with Pamela for money to do so. But I did know that his stepmother back in Ohio had sent him fifty dollars with the firm understanding that he would get no more. And there was no way now that I could see him climbing the gangway to a transatlantic liner or, as was now the case, that of the S.S. *Franconia* and escaping back either to England or the old sod, as the ship was scheduled to call at both Cork and Liverpool. On his desk in Woodlawn, as we exchanged thoughts, Gainor's given me verbally and mine written on scraps of paper, I chanced upon what appeared to be printed notes and asked Gainor what they were. As he picked up the sheet, he smiled as he said he had drawn up what he felt might constitute a general preamble to letters he was writing back to Europe.

"Mike, do you want to hear my averments, and perhaps record them in your diary that I see that you are keeping."

YES

" 'To whom it may concern: Please be advised of these, the facts of my life, which I now freely and happily disclose. America has been wonderful to me. I like and enjoy my work very much at the airport. It has made me very fit and limber, as I have got to keep constantly on my toes, dodging knives, punches, and sometimes bullets, which are directed at me at my check-in counter. But in rebuttal of such, I have innovated for Pan American Airways a delightful lottery of foreign destinations to which unruly passengers might surprisingly find themselves directed at no extra cost. These are called mystery rides. When not busy at work, I do a great deal of reading of the great philosophers. Then having put my mind at rest, agreeing with their conclusions, I manage to get ten hours sleep at night. I go to the opera frequently. And attend equally at the ballet. I wash my own socks and have my shirts laundered by a Chinaman who sends his daughter to Vassar and his son to Yale. I despise drink and smoking and those awful people who do. I particularly avoid pubs, and other places of serious sin. I have most happily now repaid with interest all my debts in Europe and straightened out all of my other highly fucked-up affairs. And here in the land of the free and home of the brave, I have opened up accounts with several reputably bankrupt-proof banks and have retained a broker to acquire for me some of the better stocks and shares. My surplus funds, I send to be looked after by a sedate bank in Basel, which is of course located in Switzerland. However, on the debit side, I must admit that the food and people in this country here have absolutely no taste or flavor. I haven't yet found a tailor to my liking but am still on the lookout. Nevertheless, in other gustatory and sensual matters, I am particularly delighted to disclose that one can find exotic ladies here with diamond-tipped nipples and with their vaginas lined with a new ripless, stretch-resistant tissue. I have been particularly charmed and delighted by the college-skilled ladies who give what are referred to here in America as mind-blowing blow jobs. One merely has to make a blowing motion with one's lips to have one of these former cheerleading girls reach and unbutton the necessary buttons and fish it out of one's trousers and go to work. It's proved very convenient and relieving of angst that does make one's balls shiver a lot less and prevents them sounding like castanets clacking in an empty cathedral. One must add that the apples and grapes are also very good. And the maple syrup. It's all really a matter of choice.' Do you like that, Mike. Do you approve. Is that a fair and honest assessment. I see, along with considerable amusement, slight concern on your face. You think I've cracked up. Not true. Everything is going to be all right."

YES I LIKE IT VERY MUCH
ALTHOUGH I DO
NOT AGREE THAT
EVERYTHING
IS GOING TO
BE ALL RIGHT

The old white clapboard house in Woodlawn had now become an outpost as one was gathering possessions together and packing. And making last contact with those whom I would leave behind in America. Although I thought there was a fraction of a hope that Gainor might indeed escape with me, when I then thought of the horrors chasing him I was sure he would be trapped and left in circumstances of long incarceration. And as I stood there looking at him, a weary but understanding smile broke across Gainor's face. For one thing was certain, he was delighted and relieved to find himself once more safely ensconced in Woodlawn. But his appearance reminded me of early mornings back at my rooms at Trinity when Gainor would turn up in his gown, clutching a few papers, and having spent the night drinking in the cattle markets and was now on his way to go sit his law exams. His hands trembling, the veins standing out in his wrists, his eyes reddened in an ashened face, he looked as if he had not eaten solid food or slept for days.

Knowledge spreading that I was leaving, odd parting messages came through from such as Donoghue, perhaps more American than any of us and coping in his own eccentric way better. But who called from Boston to say he was seeking analysis as to why he was getting blow jobs but could not get laid. And now in residence in Spring Street, he said that after I left, the old Jewish man with his long gray beard who lived behind still had his rich son coming to see him who continued to throw out and put in garbage cans all the old man's junk he collected at four A.M. when he would tour the local streets with his little handcart. The son trying to clean the place up. But that as soon as the son and wife left again, the old man would go out to the garbage pails, empty them and bring back in all his junk again. When he would stop Donoghue, he would say that all were bums except for the man with the beard, who was a gentleman and who used to live there with the beautiful wife and baby.

News came too from Douglas Wilson in Boston, whose life seemed also better regulated, saying among other things that even in angst there was to be found enlightenment. And he said he was simplifying his own future by studying law. He also reported the whereabouts of a mutual friend and college chum whose serenely black face one was always glad to see in Ireland and who had now returned home to Africa where he was presiding over his father's vast estate in the southern Sudan and was at the following address.

Sayid Ishak Mohammed Khalia Sherif,
Director, Zuleit Pumping Scheme,
Kosti

Ishak, a talented painter and poet, describing himself on the pumping scheme as not being wholly incompetent, aided as he was by expert and expensive advisers. I was learning too from various sources that other American folk with whom one had been acquainted at Trinity College and who had tried return to America as the solution to their lives had already, thoroughly dispirited, quietly departed without fanfare. Away from this land of the American dream. Where one wondered if it were wives who wanted most to escape. Feeling themselves betrayed by so-called unsuccessful husbands. And themselves turning into evil-humored shrews who used their energies, guile and scathing, carping sarcasm to usher and hurry their spouses onto death. And to the payout on their life insurance policy. Although my own mother kept her own counsel, I sensed my own father was in his own nightmare, ready to be expendable and, despite his animating poetry and horticulture, was beginning his final demise. But never, it appeared did he give up a devotional admiration of my mother.

With the single exception of April, I no longer spoke to anyone. But not using my voice anymore did not seem to make me any faster writing messages on pieces of paper and scribbling out advice, mostly to Gainor, whose life, at least at the moment, was suspended in hibernation. But as one sensed his plans getting more chaotic, I felt I had to be quicker with my admonitions, exhortations and warnings. And communication with him was improved, becoming almost as fast as talking, when Gainor would come and stand behind me as I sat at my typewriter and typed my replies to him, which he read over my shoulder. Some of my answers being brief indeed.

"Mike, might you be able to see your way clear to lending me just ten dollars till tomorrow afternoon, when I shall repay you at three o'clock when a draft of money arrives for me at American Express."

NO

I did in fact advance a small bit of traveling money to Gainor, which in turn he did repay as promised. And the sum assisted him to go with T.J. to attend a small gathering convened by Tally at her apartment. As I no longer wanted to see anyone, I remained, holding the fort in Woodlawn, with T.J. and Gainor vividly reporting back. There had been slight friction evident among the guests. Lea was there with John Fountain, who the whole time looked up at the ceiling or into books. But musically at least, it was according to Gainor a much enjoyed evening. To awed and stunned listeners, T.J., normally shy at such events, stepped forward and played from his repertoire his "Bronx Rhapsody in Pink." Lea's marvelous singing voice was again joined with Tally's when the two sang in duet pieces from Bizet's *Carmen*. Gainor said he was spellbound listening to a recording played of one of John Duffy's early symphonies, in which the sadness of the violas, Gainor said, could rip out your soul. As Tally's marvelous food and drink were served, Lea was talking about and wanting to go to the Canary Islands. Recommending Tenerife to Gainor as the perfect place for him to find peace. And prophetic these words would become. As none of us could ever guess then, that a place so far away was indeed to be the place of all places to play the final hours in Gainor's life. But nothing was seen of April. Who rang me this very same night to plaintively say,

"Gee, J.P., don't shut up on me will you. Shut up on the others but not me. I couldn't stand that, especially with the rest of the things that are happening in this burg. Come on. You're a good guy. Don't go. Fight it out. Battle. Beat the little turds. Don't leave me alone with all the shits."

I told April that agents, my last hope, had now declined to further handle the work. That the paranoia spread everywhere, and even among the most liberal-minded, was such that made even the mildest of words in *S.D.* actually feared.

"Hey, gee, J.P., I guess you got to go. And then you're not going to hear any more of my bedtime stories. You know, maybe the only thing after all worth having is a good marriage. And a guy like you who loves his wife. Which gives life a center, a purpose. And maybe into which you can put with hard work some faith and trust. All those things together and maybe you got something to wake up to in the morning. Hey, gee, listen to me, old cynical lips, saying these things. When my ole grandma hit my ole grandpa a good ole contusion with a board on the head to wake him up and do a little work plucking peaches from the peach tree, she killed him. 'Cause maybe that's what she wanted to do in the first place. But other than just a couple of extra shekels to jingle, what else is there supposed to be around that's supposed to be better than two people in love. But then you know, J.P., what is a guy to a girl but a prick. And you put your name on it with a wedding. And no wedding, what is a guy but a prick. And you end up, as your tits begin to sag down to your knees, looking over your shoulder, wondering where your lifetime private income is going to come from. And so with that little rendition of ole hillbilly wisdom from high up the gulch, my ole dear J.P., I wait for you to come back. And in the by and by, I bid you fond voyage over the steep ocean waves."

Along with April's predictive and weatherwise words echoing in one's mind, one also thought one could sometimes hear coming up the Hudson valley and into the northern reaches of the Bronx, the great throbbing blasts of an ocean liner's horn announcing its putting to sea. And then one morning, I did hear such a sound coming on the chill wind blowing across the snowy, cold Van Cortlandt woods. I took it as foreordainment of my certain departure. And it shortened the days now passing, as I attempted to conquer my malaise by making morning explosive bursts from my bed and trying to fight off the gloom that would slowly, inevitably settle upon me during the day. Meanwhile keeping silent in my own silence. No longer the presumptuous, positive iconoclast I had been in Dublin. Assuming my certainty over my future as a writer and painter. I had been wrong. No one was waiting in America to acclaim a work I had believed would be acclaimed. Instead the nation seemed an enemy. In my letters, I now apologized to Valerie for taking her away from the civilization of England and for introducing her to the gossipy backbiting morass of drink and dismally dissolute life to be found in Dublin. I expressed regret for then having further dragged her through the disappointments and crushed hopes that were to be mine in America. And which till I got aboard the boat, I was still not certain I had survived.

My mother away at my sister, Rita's, and my father at the firehouse, Gainor, T.J. and I kept counsel with one another over the few days in Woodlawn. Gainor giving more than the mere impression of having to hide out, as we went through the names of all those who, having given help in the past, might again do so. He represented that he still had his job and income. But he was in fact without any money at all. Having upon repayment of his loan from me to reborrow a dollar. In his room he maintained he would sleep the night soundly. But then I would find him throughout the day, coming into my room and then lying on the old four-poster bed, taking naps. His head propped up on pillows, and his injured leg from his fall into the subway tracks stretched out resting. On the bedside table, he kept a pan of water, lemon juice squeezed into it. From which he would anoint his brow and then cover his eyes with the cloth. I would, as the downstairs clock could be heard to strike three, serve tea and bring Gainor a cup and plate of crackers. At the sound of the tolling chimes, Gainor slowly blessed himself in the manner of a Catholic. On a note I wrote,

AS AN

AGNOSTIC

WOULD-BE PROTESTANT, WHY DO YOU

BLESS YOURSELF

"Mike, as I lie here in the marvelous, soothing comfort of your hospitality, back in Ireland on the north Liffey Quays at exactly this time it is eight in the evening. Night has fallen. It's cold and misting. The mail boat is casting off. Embarking across the fretful Irish Sea to Liverpool. I make this observance of blessing myself in memory of such voyage and of all those who upon this very night may be about to take it. As I have done so many heartfelt times in the past. Standing as a third-class passenger, on that stern deck. Watching the gray granite quays pass as we floated away down the dark waters of the Liffey. Attempting, as I would invariably be, to vanish from Dublin. And gone in the wan hope that I would, having done so, find better times. Then, my affairs straightened out and jingling a few coins in my pocket, be able to return. But alas such latter dream never attained."

With no one other than myself and T.J. knowing where he was and with apparently many people looking for him, Gainor continued to totally relax in the sense of safety he felt in Woodlawn. Other than to disappear in the utter wilds of the west, it was in many ways as close as one could get in America to being cut off. And especially in a house where one could hold out with a basement fruit cellar stocked full with a variety of home-bottled vegetables, including carrots, corn, tomatoes, peas, sauerkraut and string beans. And fruit such as apples, peaches, plums and pears. Also there were potatoes from my father's gardens, and whole-wheat bread and homemade butter from the country. Not to mention the still unemptied crates of whiskey which arrived at Christmas. And it was crystal clear that whatever heinous thing had befallen him, that Gainor had not lost his appetite nor his palate to enjoy alcoholic beverage.

"Mike, believe me when I say that even as I appear to be somewhat in a recuperative state and supine much of the day, that I am in fact experiencing enormous contentment in being here."

Although the menu was haphazard enough at dinner in the kitchen and sometimes held in the dining room, Gainor would, in the most quietly elegant but deliberate way, devour whatever appeared in front of him. T.J. and I would watch, astonished, as two massive helpings of beans with two large potatoes immersed in melted butter and accompanied by endless pieces of bread, would be polished off, to be then followed by two thick plate-sized hamburgers, each crowned with melted cheese and fried egg on top. But one watched him eat with immense relief, Gainor having lost weight, and making one concerned for his health. And his gusto in eating, and the white of his eyeballs brightening again, became one of the few positively encouraging things that I could see happening in his life. Or indeed in America.

Sobriety being now one of my absolute priorities, I was surprised that I did not seem to mind when Gainor quaffed back his evening whiskeys. But rather than inebriating him, it seemed to bring an incisive quickness to his speech and brilliant strategy into the long chess games that were waged late into the night. I was even enjoying washing dishes and got in a dispute with Gainor as to how this was properly done and in what sequence were cutlery and dishes to be cleansed. From my mother's advice, I opted for cutlery first, for she had also taught me how to break bread in smaller pieces before buttering it, and I thought, although she had for sometime had a cook who did so, she must also know about washing up after meals.

Gainor said he was going to write a book. Something I was the first to realize would be marvelously fascinating, if his adventures were anything to go by. But I felt, knowing how much discipline was required and how much dedication it demanded, that in both cases it would be more than Gainor had at his disposal. I wondered too, aware of his readiness to socialize with all, and especially random, strangers, if he could muster the sometimes grim resolve to suffer long bouts of isolation. I also now began to notice some of T.J.'s observations. That there were qualities of the spoiled child in Gainor, of expecting to get what he wanted. And becoming petulant in not obtaining it. Also noticeable now in his behavior was an element of ruthlessness. That it was a time to abandon ship, and every man for himself. For there seemed to be a growing indifference to the many of those who made a sacrifice of some sort to help him. However, I did take his conduct as being more a reaction to the doom-laden desperation to get out that we were both suffering. And to be away from the atmosphere of informers, accusers and denunciators who were alleging, insinuating and bearing false witness across the land. But none of whom pointed a finger at Gainor whose recently accumulated adversaries were of a different aggrievement and variety, and who were now added to those who had chased him to America in the first place. And it would have had to be concluded, as it was by an American embassy official who had once, in Dublin, when Gainor was anonymously accused of being a communist spy, examined an inch-thick file on Gainor, and who said as he closed it, "Mr. Crist, there is no doubt that you have committed numerous indiscretions and incited numerous claims against you, but there is nothing here in this file to indicate that you have at any time ever been disloyal to the United States."

The weather briefly not too cold these few days in Woodlawn, Gainor and I again went for enormously calming walks in the cemetery and sat on the benches along Van Cortlandt Park East. Gainor seemed now not to be drinking much. And certainly watching him eat was in itself an entertainment and altogether optimistic event. T.J. saying it was like witnessing the fueling of the boilers of a great ship and that one could nearly sense the massive drive shafts turning and sending gargantuan neurological energy up into Gainor's brain. And this in turn he certainly used later in the evening in our struggles over the chessboard. It was evident too now why an alcohol-free mind was of such importance. For Gainor took his chess playing very seriously. But had yet to win a game from me. I in turn would write my gamesmanship comments on my usual scrap of paper and slip them in front of him as he would after long, agonizing deliberation finally make a move.

AH YOU HAVE BLUNDERED
YET AGAIN AND YOU
ARE SOON FINIS KAPUT

It was now three months since I had finished the manuscript of *S.D.,* or at least what one could term the first final draft. And there was nothing to monitor one's days or help in weathering bouts of angst. Except to force myself out to walk. And by evening it occasionally distracted to watch boxing bouts on television. Gainor and I continuing to carry on our longer communications, me by typewriter and printed capitals and he by his verbal response while twiddling his thumbs. And sometimes he would inquire after my health.

"Mike, how are you feeling."

FOR THE FIRST TIME IN WEEKS I HAVE BEEN ABLE TO
SIT, LOOK DOWN AND NOTICE THE WEAVE OF THE CLOTH
IN MY TROUSERS AND THE SHAPE OF MY ANKLE IN
MY SOCK AND SHOE. BUT SINCE VALERIE LEFT, MY
LIFE HAS BEEN JUST ONE LONG JOYLESS BLANK. HAVE TO GET
BACK TO WRITING AGAIN. SOME PROJECT THAT WILL
TAKE MY MIND OFF MYSELF. IN AN ENTIRE YEAR
IN AMERICA ONE HAS ONLY FELT GLADNESS ABOUT
FOUR TIMES FOR PERHAPS TEN MINUTES ON EACH OCCASION.
THERE IS NO LONGER THAT PALMY PROSPECT OF FAME AND
FORTUNE THROUGH *S.D.* ALTHOUGH DEEP WITHIN ME, I STILL
BELIEVE THERE IS. THE FAME DOESN'T INTEREST ME.
NOR THE FORTUNE. BUT PROTECTION DOES. AND THE
LATTER COMES MOSTLY IN A FINANCIAL GUISE.
FOR THE FIRST TIME IN MY LIFE, I NEED A
LITTLE DREAMBOATING.

"Mike, it's all dreamboating anyway, no matter whether the dreams
come true or not."

WHEN ARE THEY GOING TO STOP POLISHING
THEIR CARS

"Never."

WHEN ARE THEY GOING TO STOP MAKING GODS
OF THEIR CHILDREN AND THEN TELLING
THEM PATRONIZING LIES

"Never."

I LEAVE HERE A BEATEN MAN. BUT VICTORIOUS BECAUSE
I WILL HAVE GOTTEN OUT. IT WOULD BE IRONIC IF
THE TWO OF US RETURN ON THE SAME BOAT

"Dinnlay, in our time here, many of the pieces of the puzzles of our
lives have fallen into place. Our futures have been ordained. We shall
for better or worse henceforth conduct our lives upon the other side of
the Atlantic. We shall live there as we can. We shall die there and be
buried there. And you may take it as an article of faith that I shall be
aboard the good ship *Franconia* when it sails."

303

Gainor was leaving that night for Queens to attempt to get his mail from Mutt and Jeff and in the morning to head for Woodstock. And behind he left with my mother his calling card. Amazingly expected by this lady who through any fuss or tribulation always observed elegant decorum. And who was as impressed by Gainor as he was by her. She had of course before her marriage spent her life in the suites of great hotels and in the luxury of private railway carriages. She had earned and learned a diplomatically courteous behavior on top of the wisdom that she had brought to the United States as a simple country girl. And it was never lifelong forgotten by any of my friends who had ever met her and were inspired by the attention she gave them. But now the time had come of leave-taking. T.J. about to drive Gainor to the train and who now stood in my room as I put on my coat to accompany him. And with the sadness of departure he was at his most charmingly benign.

"Mike, in Dublin's Grange Gorman, where such as Sean O'Sullivan, Ireland's greatest portrait painter, went to escape the scourges of drink, he said Trinity College men not only get preferential treatment but that they also piss in Wedgwood pots, upon which is emblazoned the college's heraldic insignia and which are then taken to be emptied, poured on the tulips in the garden which then bloom in Trinity's colors. And, Mike, I feel you have afforded me a similar privilege to be with you here this too little time in Woodlawn, and let me tell you, I have immensely enjoyed the solace and respite it's given me. And meeting your mother and father, both of whom I found most charming. And talking and listening to your brother, T.J., and his music and indeed seeing his extraordinary pots and paintings. All has helped renew my faith in mankind. I only wish my chess play was more deserving of your expertise. However, I am now feeling fully fit to go for a few days to round off my continued rest in Woodstock. Mike, you'd like it up there very much, and I do hope as soon as I appraise things that you will come up and join me."

IN WHAT
SURELY IS BOUND
TO BE
CHAOS

My reply was not meant cynically. For Gainor's words were not the flowery words that they might seem. They were words spoken in the most heartfelt and warm manner with tears obscuring the slightly haunted look in his eyes. And as he was deposited at the lonely elevated terminus of the last stop of the Lexington–Jerome Avenue line, he stood there a desolate, bereft figure, clutching in his cold hand the same paper bag with which he had arrived. Above us, the chill winter winds were blowing under the steel girders and snow beginning to fall. On one side fading into the darkness were the stretches of Van Cortlandt Park woods. And on the other side were the night-haunted mausoleums and graves of the cemetery. I had given Gainor a sweater to wear under just a jacket and scarf. His blue Aran Islander's cap on his head. And for footwear, he was in white socks and sandals. He had recently in a subway station and in his usual manner, lost his temper over a vending machine which failed to produce, and as he kicked it to pieces it also did the same to his shoes.

A premonition was overcoming me that this was to be the last time I would ever see Gainor. As if he were being set free to be abandoned amid wintry ocean in an open boat. Snow forecast for the whole night and the next day. And T.J., having made Gainor a sandwich to take with him, knew what was in the paper bag. Refusing at first to tell me but then admitting that within the brown crumpled folds and crusts of bread along with a few bits of stale cheese was also a long, curled-up piece of rope. And it told me more than anything else ever could of Gainor's solemn desperation. And I knew that if he did not get up that gangway and out. That the rope he had was long enough.

To
End his life
By

27

THE FUTURE had finally seemed to come. With only a matter of ten days left now till three P.M. on the Wednesday that the *Franconia* was due to sail. Prematurely packed and ready and with less and less to do, I was wondering each hour if I could survive and hang on. With all shades pulled tight closed on my front three bedroom windows, I hoped to avoid aimed bullets and the accident of stray ones. I had little desire to go to Woodstock and Gainor in giving me an invitation merely made me feel that I would risk putting myself into even greater jeopardy. I had not met any of his considerably literary and artistic friends and had no reason to think that they would be anything other than kind and friendly as had been their messages to me sent via Gainor.

Gainor, when leaving at the train terminus, said his Aran Islander's hat, flowing pink scarf, white socks and sandals, in making him look stranger than ever, plus a slightly manic demeanor he had recently adopted, had the sidewalks clearing in front of him and people moving away to distance themselves on public transport, and he was enjoying his newfound elbow room. He seemed now to be seriously hiding out from creditors. One knew that he was about to abandon his address at Queens Boulevard and could go to stay with a girlfriend who worked at the airport. A convenience he chose to avail of, since his one problem he did not have in America was attracting women, who would do anything for him. But one remained skeptical over his joining the *Franconia* despite his saying Pamela was sending him his boat fare and it was on the way. But he did seem doubly concerned now that word might leak out in any direction that he was decamping.

"Mike, even in your silence, mum's the word."

I had put my last things in my big steamer trunk and it was already awaiting in the sun porch of the old white house atop East 238th Street to be taken down to the pier. Not only the hours, but one was now counting away the very minutes as they went by. Mornings the worst for feeling an overwhelming sickening tension. And having been told about the length of rope in Gainor's bag, my anxiety was increased as to what new news I might now hear of him. I did force myself out for a walk and to return library books. Which was one of the things I was blaming Gainor for not bothering to do. My reading matter now was the *History of Ireland* and the *Reptiles of the World,* along with casual references into Boswell's Johnson. Gainor in Woodlawn had been reading Sean O'Casey's autobiography, which I now noticed was missing. As I went on my stroll, kids were sleigh-riding on the steep hill, as I once had done. And dangerously zooming out where traffic passed at the very foot of the incline. Where on the main street of Katonah Avenue, I met Mrs. Kuntze. And as I was about to leave Woodlawn for good, it seemed as if it were preordained. For this pleasant, attractive woman of outspokenness and character was the mother of Alan, Donald and of my first girlfriend, Carol, all of whom had been part of my most impressionable years growing up in America.

The Kuntze family, Donald, Carol and Alan, in front of where they lived in Woodlawn. Alan, my closest childhood friend, and Carol, my first serious girlfriend. Donald, later a distinguished physician in the field of obstetrics, was a brilliant boxer and later a collegiate wrestling champion. And with Alan and I belting away at each other with gloves, Donald taught me my first rudiments of boxing as well as Greco-Roman grappling.

And for this nice lady, I briefly broke my silence and croaked out a few words.

Returning now to the house, I was surprised to find myself missing Gainor's presence. It had all seemed strangely like a leisurely weekend in a country mansion, albeit small and located in the suburban Bronx. But when one read the Sunday newspaper and we all sat around thumbing through sections of the massively thick *New York Times,* Gainor and T.J. talked and I listened. Gainor still taking an interest in anything and everything. Especially paying rapt attention to the macabre stories told by T.J. about when he was a cemetery salesman. Gainor's recalling being informed by his stepmother concerning the expensive burial of his father, whose coffin was encased in atom bomb–proof grave liner, the price of which at the time could have salvaged Gainor's future. But T.J. cheering Gainor with an account of his making an on-site pitch one hot summer's day to a prospective customer in the cemetery about mausoleum burial above ground and the pre-need contentment this provided. And just as T.J. felt he had closed the deal and was about to produce a contract for signature, there came from just behind, and but a stone's throw away, an unholy explosion. A recent mausoleum blew up along with the recently interred contents of a coffin, a gas concentration having become explosive in the heat caused by the day's hot rays of the sun, and this previous customer, who had already availed of his pre-need contentment, was sent sky high.

I did take some comfort, however, from the fact that Gainor said that if it were the last thing he ever did in life, it was to board the good ship *Franconia* and sail on the thirteenth. And that aboard such ship we could continue our chess games, in which Gainor said his concentration could be better directed than it could while he was under his present duress ashore. If I had any fond thoughts left for America, they were still of Boston. And I almost thought I could have survived there. Where the people at least on the surface seemed easier and so much more relaxed about life. The struggling slum of the West End, and just daily survival chasing away worry about the distant future. In which Ireland was now again a prospect. A newspaper clipping arrived from Ernest Gebler with Irish country properties for sale. T.J. told me that I must be as hard as nails not to have cracked under the strain. And that my silence was a psycho block and that I would not talk again until I was on my way.

With tumbling gray-black, bleak thunderclouds, the forecast of snow struck in the form of a storm at noon the day following Gainor's night departure back to Queens. Bringing, as blizzards did, a growing silence to the city as the drifts got deeper. And not having heard further again from Gainor, I assumed all had gone well and that he had got away soon enough to the promised quiet restfulness of Woodstock.

Meanwhile, four days went by during which I further packed and, using some of my carpentry skills acquired in Kilcoole, completed making a box for my paints and brushes. I was informed too, that the time of departure of the *Franconia* had been delayed. From three P.M. to three-thirty P.M. And although sailing was still some many days away, it did add another full half hour, during which I was going to have to remain in the United States. I took the news on the chin. And decided thirty minutes was not a grievous amount of time to further wait, provided no sniper was across the Hudson River drawing a bead with telescopic sights on one from the Palisades as one stood on the *Franconia* deck. Upstairs at my desk in my dressing gown and socks, I was having pork chops and sauerkraut and listening to Boccherini's Cello Concerto in G Major on station WQXR. When there came a knock and T.J. peeked his head in the door.

"Mike, Gainor is on the phone and he doesn't sound too good. Should I tell him you're not available. But he seems pretty desperate to speak to you."

I nodded my head in assent that I would go downstairs to the telephone. The word "desperate" coming from a diplomatically sensitive T.J. in reference to Gainor most certainly did not sound good. And I knew it meant that something suitably catastrophic had happened. Anticipating the worst, I took my knife and fork, napkin and plate, with me. And as I went by the upstairs landing windows, I looked down into the garden lawn at the side of the house. The snow was more than a foot and a half deep, and it had begun to fall again. Juggling utensils, I nearly had a catastrophe myself down the stairs, a pork chop slipping off my plate. However, it tasted just as good as I picked it up and followed T.J. along the small hall and into the sitting room, where the telephone was in a corner by the fireplace. Talking to Crist here had always been like sitting in an electric chair, never knowing when the current would end one's life in shock. And my heart now I could feel was beating more rapidly as I picked up the receiver into which T.J. spoke first.

"Gainor, I am now putting Mike on the phone to you."

"Mike. I am most sorry to trouble you. But trust me when I tell you that, my God, this has been an unbelievable nightmare. And I do apologize for interrupting you in the middle of your dinner. But I have only now been able to get my hands on a telephone that works, as the snow had the lines down, and hope you can hear in all this static. Now if I don't escape from up here alive, I at least want you to record for posterity my very last days. As Scott did in his diary in the Antarctic when he and his companions perished following their journey to the pole, which in fact this entire trip of mine has resembled and may yet end in similar grief. Also, you will see why it would not be sensible for me to further recommend for you to come up here. I am at this moment slipping down a large dram of bourbon to soothe my nerves. It has simply been the most terrifying ordeal to which I have ever yet been subjected. Do please grunt, Mike, when you've heard enough and don't want to hear anymore. But I'll be as brief as I can be. But first, Mike, let me ask, Have you ever as a little boy been taken into a chamber of horrors at a fun fair. Grunt two for yes and three for no."

"Ugh. Ugh."

"Well, then, you'll know exactly what I am about to tell you was like. And grunt four if you feel any sympathy for me during the telling. My problems started on Wednesday evening when I first began to attempt to hitchhike up here in a howling blizzard. Starting at seven P.M. from the George Washington Bridge to where I had taken the subway and where April had at the same station memorably intervened and saved me from having a fight. Now, Mike, some of this story is going to sound like the same old refrain. But considering how they are not able to reproduce themselves, there would seem to be an aston-ishing population of homosexuals in this land. However, suffice to say that because of my outfit and especially my white socks and sandals and worn in the snowstorm raging at the time, my first lift was with a homosexual who assumed I was like-minded and amenable if not as desperate as he was to go with him somewhere and have the evening together and do what such gentlemen do with or to each other."

"Ugh. Ugh. Ugh. Ugh."

"Mike, I know you're not speaking, but please, for God's sake don't laugh, this was one of the most unfunny moments of my life. I was caught in the most appalling bloody damn dilemma, having in mind your remark of being on the horns of same and having one of the horns far up one's hole, which was clearly the intent of this individual with whom I had the unfortunate luck to get a lift. But with not a sign of any refuge for miles except the very occasional light of a lamppost, I was not keen to have to return out into the blizzard, the snow having caught in my sandals had already melted and so my feet were wet and of course would freeze to ice once back out in the subzero air again.

Equally, I wanted, of course, to get as much mileage as I could on the way to Woodstock, as he was going as far as New Paltz, more than half the way. But he took my reluctance to get out of the car as an invitation to fish his tumesced cock out and to ask me to go down on him. When I refused his request, he began pulling it himself."

"Ugh. Ugh. Ugh. Ugh."

"Mike, he was already beginning to drive erratically enough and given that the roads were hard-packed with snow and more falling, the entire situation was clearly becoming dangerously suicidal. Especially when this homophile was undergoing some sort of frisson prior to having an orgasm and we'd veered off the road, just missing one telegraph pole by a hairsbreadth. Mike, please, for God's sake, this was not in the least funny. We were going through a small village at the time, and he mounted somebody's bloody front lawn, knocked over a flag pole, and then, just missing a tree, mowed down the entirety of this poor unfortunate's hedge fronting of the whole of his house, and although it was obscured by snow, he then ripped off the fender of the poor bastard's parked car as he came back again out on the road. And it's simply too embarrassing to repeat what this madman was saying while all this was happening. But he did utter the word 'whoopee' several times. How we weren't killed, I'll never know."

"Ugh. Ugh. Ugh. Ugh."

"Mike, can you imagine I got out of that rolling death trap with this imbecile shouting after me that I didn't know how to have any fun. Well, he was damn right. For again, I found myself stranded on the bloody side of the road, the snow swirling down under an isolated lamppost I was standing beneath. Mike, I was only wearing the clothes you saw me in when I left Woodlawn and naturally my outfit did not encourage people to stop. But for fully fifteen minutes, with not another car coming, I was beginning to freeze to death. And then finally when one did and I stepped out to wave it down, it picked up speed and nearly ran over me in order to pass me as quickly as possible. Mike, you simply won't believe my next bloody bit of ill luck when finally a car did stop and I was offered a lift. In the most magnificent Hispano-Suiza. And into which I was most relievedly delighted to get. But the sniff of an overpowering perfume should have warned me the moment I got in the car. But certainly it temporarily felt like being rescued from being a member of a chain gang with both my feet now weighted down, solidly encased in ice. And my God, we hadn't gone more than a few hundred yards further down the road when I knew what I most feared was about to go wrong and happen. We were talking about this marvelous vehicle when he suddenly interjected to say that my profile was like that of a Greek god and my accent like that of Orson Welles."

"Ugh. Ugh. Ugh. Ugh."

"Mike, the first chance and money I get, I am going to have my face disfigured and my accent made as un-English as possible. It was bloody nearly an exact replica of my last ride. Only this time your man was reaching over and trying to open my fly as well. Mike, is that you grunting or is that more laughter. I tell you not a single moment of this journey was funny. Mike, are you still there, please grunt if you want me to hang up. But please don't laugh if you want to hear more."

"Ugh. Ugh."

"Mike, I thought there must be some bloody upper New York State convention of homosexuals, whom for some inexplicably obtuse reason I seem to attract like a magnet. Anyway, rather than risk another four or five lifts with different homosexual propositions, I stayed in the car and let this guy continue masturbating until we finally reached Woodstock. He in fact was quite well mannered, handed me his engraved calling card and merely suggested that I should feel free to keep in touch. But, Mike, having at long last reached Woodstock half-frozen and psychologically worn out, it was only then that my real troubles started."

"Ugh. Ugh. Ugh. Ugh."

"Mike, I've recently read that the gray matter of the hippocampus in the brain, if it could be somehow paralyzed, could completely wipe out the memory. Or indeed, I understand that with the whole bloody brain sufficiently cooled down, one could also avoid remembering one's previous life by being in a sort of cryonic suspension, which in one then being reanimated and reversing clinical death, can make a new start in life. And I tell you, it is dearly what I should like to do. For having arrived in Woodstock, I was to find that my would-be host, Justin, was in my hostess Sally's house, having, so to speak, commandeered it dead drunk, and that she, Sally, his once-upon-a-time lady love, had escaped a mile away, seeking safety in another house. The difficulty being that the house to which Sally had retreated, belonging to a friend, and this friend temporarily putting us both up, was expecting a house full of people the next night, so both Sally and I had to vacate, and Sally wanted Justin out of her house, and immediately. Thus, in the middle of the night, I was delegated to accomplish this. But at least my feet had thawed and I was in dry socks and woodsman's boots. When I reached Sally's house, where Justin was, he had it totally barricaded. Mike, this is about two in the morning after an already harrowing day, and I had to break in and then get Justin out of his drunken sleep. For fully ten minutes, he was repeating lines from *Macbeth* and thought I was somebody else who was a character in another of Shakespeare's plays. But after a tumbler of whiskey mixed with grapefruit juice he collected his wits and listened to Sally's various ultimata. It did not help matters of course that the last time I was in Woodstock he tripped over Sally and I wrapped around each other on the bathroom floor, albeit in a totally spiritual and nonsexual manner, when he came to use it. But he was sufficiently drunk of course and in such a stupor that holding our breaths and awaiting his wrath, he completely ignored us and as he sat on the crapper we continued our spiritually renewing antics practically between his legs."

"Ugh. Ugh. Ugh. Ugh."

"Now I left about three to wade through the drifts to a bar to call Sally to say that Justin refused to budge out of her house but that I was on my way back to her having in the bar met a lesbian who offered me a lift. Mike, just to digress and say there are so many bloody people in the world and I'm not in my short life going to get to know them all but what I should most dearly like to know now is how the fuck do I avoid now forever the few utterly impossible people I have unfortunately got to know without becoming a mute hermit in a monastery. Anyway, the cold night was bright and moonlit and full of stars and the snow stopped falling. Mike, I should have been forewarned of my bad luck with lesbians. Not to mention all manner of homosexual persons. But this particularly attractive lady was charm itself and kindly offered to drive me back to where Sally was staying and where I could at least get a bed for the night and have a desperately needed sleep. By the way, not once did the howling blizzard let up throughout my entire hitchhike up here. Mike, are you still there. Do grunt twice if you've heard enough. And three if you haven't. Because now we are coming to the utterly catastrophic part."

"Ugh. Ugh. Ugh."

"Straight off, the lesbian, who by the way was called Gertie, having told me she knew the roads, took the wrong turning and got us lost and miles away in the wrong direction. In an effort to turn the car around we got stuck and stalled in a snowdrift. My God. I thought that that was it. That it was in fact to actually be like Scott in the Antarctic. And Gertie and I were to become in the course of the rest of the night, pillars of ice. I took over the wheel of the car to try to get us out and only got us deeper in. But then and only by an utter miracle, a lorry came along with snow chains on the tires and was able to pull us back out on the road again. I retained the wheel after the lorry left and I also thought I better knew the way back to Sally's, although frankly, we could have been in Timbuktu. But with the night clear, I was, by the vestiges remembered of my celestial navigation, able to guess the way. I drove up the road and found space to turn around and headed back to the village. A car approached. And as it got closer and I instinctively went to the left side of the road, I thought what is this bloody idiot doing over on the wrong side. Of course at such an ungodly hour of the morning, I thought, this son of a bitch is obviously drunk and out of his mind. I kept cursing, 'Get out of the way, you stupid bastard,' while at the same time Gertie the lesbian couldn't be aware of what was happening to tell me that it was me who was on the wrong side of the road."

"Why?"

"Mike, you've spoken."

"Ugh. Ugh."

"And, Mike, I know why you want to know why the lesbian couldn't hear."

"Ugh. Ugh."

"Because, Mike, and God help me, despite her being a lesbian, she had my fly open and was in the process of attempting to be heterosexually otherwise engaged. But any pleasure that emanated from that fact, however, was to be forthwith terminated. Mike, we smashed head-on in a collision. Gertie was concussed, her head hitting the bottom of the dashboard. And I know this is an awfully selfish thing to admit, but my God, I was lucky not to have had her incisors guillotine my private part. She also injured her knees, God only knows how. I injured both my knees as well, and on top of my previous injuries can now barely walk at all. One of my knees is as big as a football. Thank God no one in the other car was hurt, but both cars were more than somewhat cracked up. Of course, standing out in the bloody moonlight, I was in fact about to attempt to put on a feeble act of being indignant but suddenly the chill air made me look down to see that my fly was still open and my prick hanging mournfully out. I was arrested of course for dangerous driving but luckily not for indecent exposure. The state troopers taking me before a justice of the peace, and I stood my trial down in his cellar at four A.M. The justice attired in his pajamas. While his Pekingese dog tied to the bannister of the cellar stairs was growling at me the whole time. I was fined thirty dollars for reckless driving and ten dollars for possessing no license. These were the minimum fines he could impose. Since I hadn't the money with me to meet the fines, I was taken to the Kingston jail, thence to hospital for examination of my injuries and antitetanus shots. I had been in jail eight hours when Sally came to fish me out. Mike, that's just another forty dollars I shall have to do without. This banjaxes me a bit more. I will of course be sued by the insurance company of the man whose car I struck. The police have my New York address from which I am going to finish vacating and then hide out until I can, with blessed Oliver Plunket interceding, escape the bloody hell out of here before I end up in an asylum for the insane. Justin, my male friend, has been hauled away in a psycho coma. Gertie is still under observation in the hospital. And I am living in dread that they will come for me. There is an atmosphere of real horror up here and I cannot recommend you to come to experience any of it during your last few days in the United States. Because, Mike, that wasn't all that happened. With Justin gone and nothing in the house to eat, Sally and I got drunk and went to bed together to keep warm."

"Ugh. Ugh. Ugh. Ugh."

"When we woke up, I struggled out of bed and hobbled down to the sitting room, where I found a bottle of bourbon miraculously full. Mike, Sally's house is most attractive, with this one very large, restful room with a ceiling, which goes up two floors high. Putting a blanket over my knees, I sat in a chair and put the whiskey bottle on the table beside me. I thought, My God almighty, this is about to be the first few peaceful minutes I am about to have in God knows how many hours or days. Or I even suppose, months. Then Sally dressed, came down and I told her the good news of the full bottle of whiskey. Sally, who has been most wondrously kind to me in every way, said she would go to the kitchen to see if she could find me some soda water, which I much wanted, not least because it had been invented in Ireland. Under the blanket I had placed a pillow across my two injured knees so that they could come to no further harm. Mike, right at this moment that I am speaking, I am here in Sally's house utterly alone, which will be explained when I tell you what happened. Now, as I've mentioned, this is a rather very large and attractive room built in the manner of a studio. The sort of place that you and I perhaps could find our way to comfortably living in were we sentenced to remain indefinitely in the United States, which God forbid. It has in fact a most impressive collection of modern art on the walls, which I fear only produces in me a very jumpy feeling which may not have been intended by the artists. Well, I thought to myself sitting there, I've got this far in life and through sexual molestations, a recent bloody blizzard and car crash and am still alive. And the afternoon is pleasantly fading. As only American afternoons on the northeastern seaboard can. The sun sinking a red, red blazing ball beyond the horizon of the nearby mountain. It's what I most pleasantly remember about Dartmouth when I was briefly at college there and we would build a massive snowman in the quad. And I'm contemplating being able to have a drink of what by its name purports to be a splendid sour mash southern bourbon, called, of all marvelous things, Rebel Yell. My hand resting gently around the base of the bottle, from which I had taken the cork. I heard a blue jay squawking in the snow. Mike, right at that moment, I thought, and it may make you also think that, my God, I am and we are, indelibly Americans and always shall be no matter where we shall ever go or be. Nothing ever to erase that indefinable feeling deeply bred in both of us and making us what we are."

"Ugh. Ugh. Ugh. Ugh."

"When thinking this, I must have also been unconsciously thinking that nothing further could happen to me for at least the next five minutes. And was just wondering how to explain to Sally how a condition had come about that she'd noticed in the bedroom while I was undressing to shower. Mike, it could only have been another miracle which saved me from total amputation. Sally saw and drew my horrified attention to the circle of red teeth marks around my prick. Dinnlay, you see the embarrassments were not yet over. But at least Sally, like April, I must count among the trusted good friends I still have left in America. And she does always have about her an endearing air of optimism. Somewhat attributable, I'm sure, to a modest but steady private income from a trust created by a great grandfather who had a share in a gold mine and also later discovered oil. Ah, but I digress, Mike. Sally, in her tartan tweed skirt, was crossing the floor to the kitchen in pursuit of my soda water. And I was admiring her legs. She has in fact, as many American girls do, quite stunningly attractive legs. Mike, the following happened just exactly as I am going to exactly tell you. And now that some of the static has disappeared from this line. Sally, upon this somber if sunshiny afternoon, got just a little more than halfway across this floor. When, without preamble, without a sound or any warning whatsoever, she disappeared utterly and completely from my sight. Gone. No longer there. Vanished from where she had been just a split second before and not more than thirty or so feet away across the floor. The room now empty save but for myself.

You can grunt now if you like, and if you've heard enough I'll hang up."

"Ugh. Ugh. Ugh."

"Does that mean in the parlance of three grunts for no and two for yes to continue, Mike."

"Ugh. Ugh."

"Well, I sat there. Hardly able to even be aghast. Not wanting even to know of such things as psychic phenomena. I gripped the bourbon bottle tightly by its base. Just in bloody case that too disappeared. I then lifted it up and put the open end of the bottle to my lips. Making a sound resembling glug, glug, glug, I found myself drinking as one would do water when one had been stranded a week in the desert. Glug, glug, glug, it continued to go. Down the hatch. Till, a third consumed, I came back to my senses. Or went out of my senses completely. All was silent. All was calm. I don't know now how long I sat there. It could have been two minutes, an hour, or two hours. Or a whole day. All I know was that I was getting some blessed relief from Rebel Yell. And was any second feeling a tendency to get up myself and yell all over the bloody place. Mike, I wish you could speak. But I know and trust you are still listening. I admit that I lack a certain discretion. But, my God, I seem to have no luck whatsoever. I did finally hobble up, totally terrified. Carried the whiskey bottle with me. Inch by inch I made my way across the floor. To where Sally had disappeared. And she had. She was down twenty feet below in the cellar. Luckily part of her descended on a stack of old burlap bags. Otherwise she would have broken her neck. She had been knocked unconscious with her head hitting the trap door, which had been under a rug and opened and through which she fell, plunging down to where she lay groaning until I fetched help. Now, Mike, with Justin gone and me in the sole company of this charming heiress, I am not for a second suggesting that anyone deliberately tried to murder anyone or that it was anything other than an accident. After much maneuvering, tugging and lifting, I finally carried Sally back to bed. Neither one of us now hardly being able to walk. Nor did we want to speak. In fact, we both got back under the covers and wept in each other's arms. Or rather, if truth were to be known, she was consoling me and I was weeping. But Sally's pain continued to be such that the doctor was called and he insisted on Sally's immediate hospitalization. Which turned out to require an ambulance. Mike, to stand there and see that vehicle pull away, which it barely did twenty minutes ago, made me feel just about the loneliest human being in the world. Mike, I know you're still there even though you're not saying ugh or ugh, ugh, or ugh, ugh, ugh, or ugh, ugh, ugh, ugh. I should have listened while still the other safe side of the water to all your cautions, warnings, exhortations and caveats. But if I can crawl, just crawl. If I can see, just see. If I can speak, just speak. And not even speak. I am going to get out of here. On a bus. Or train. Or bloody mule if needs be. And be back in New York. Where I shall hide out until it is time to traverse along that pier. And up that gangplank. And onto that ship. Mike, I have been utterly faithful in mind if not in body to the women who love me. But honest to God, to delay death, one does need a good, honest, unpremeditated and uncompromising fuck for distraction now and again. And, Dinnlay, even as the final curtain does come and our thought waves escape from gravity to go to dwell erstwhile and far away out upon some dim star, dead for eons out in the stellar graveyard, let it be known by those remaining back in the earthly ferment that we fought well and valiantly against the cowardly mealymouthed, hoping always not to get our asses permanently busted. And as our souls have come to rest on the nebular scrap heap. Rusting to infinity with all the other souls. Shrinking and cooling for the rest of time. I shall recall those marvelous last words April said to you.

> "Hey J.P. maybe you'd like
> To know
> That at night seals sing
> They come up out of the water
> With their big sad eyes
> With good news
> In the sweet by and by"

28

Wᴴᴵᴸᴇ ᴅᴇᴇᴘᴸʏ ᴍɪɴᴅɪɴɢ my own destiny in my own despairs, I took some encouragement from Gainor's uncanny ability, always quite unbelievably remarkable, that no matter what befell him he always seemed able to rebound from doom. And then in his quietly matter-of-fact way be able to state plausible explanations for his problems. But by the timbre of his voice, his travail now was, I knew, a dire situation. The knee swollen up like a football had become infected, making it difficult to walk. He went to the doctor who shot him full of penicillin and who cleaned the leg up a bit but left him financially destitute. And I was only to hear from him briefly once again before leaving. Informing me that he'd made a last return to Queens Boulevard, arriving late at night to try to get his mail and vacate with his few remaining possessions. And as T.J. handed me the phone at approaching eleven ᴘ.ᴍ. I felt a degree of "acerphobia," a word which Gainor used occasionally to refer to a fear of situations.

"Mike, I am speaking to you from down in the pub located at what will soon be my former apartment house, where I am hoping that my good friend the bartender here doesn't suddenly ask me to settle my bar bill. Which of course I shall do once safely across the other side of the water. I am now going to hide out, God knows where, but inform T.J. that I very much appreciate his offering to accommodate me. I can't talk to you at length now, and apologize for calling so late. But I had to wait till Mutt and Jeff were both on night duty at the airport, and safely out of the building before I could vacate my remaining possessions and also to avoid the bloody homosexualist across the hall who I feared might be lying in wait ready to call the police to put me in a straitjacket again. Mike, never should I have got behind the wheel of a car, having as an American trained myself in Ireland and England to instinctively go to the left side of the road, and I should have realized I would continue to do just that. I won't bore you now with what has just happened out here in Queens, suffice to say Mutt's girlfriend suddenly turned up just as I was dismantling my wigwam. Judging by her behavior in suddenly confronting me, this girl's a total sex maniac. Being chased hobbling around the bloody apartment in my present infirmity has just about finished me. She has clearly never forgotten my prick quivering, which, Mike, I still don't think you've adequately explained to me other than its making randy women upon sight of it insatiably unable to control themselves. And even following one's stupendous efforts to do everything possible to try to satisfy them, which seems only to incite them to wanting more. But I won't digress into zoological phenomenon. This call is principally to tell you that I am now gone from this address and to request you once again not to breathe a word to anyone about what happened in Woodstock. I fear most that the insurance people over my most recent car crash, hearing that I might be fleeing, will be after me and could of course be even waiting for me at the boat. Or worse, if news gets reported back to Europe, they could be waiting ten days hence at Liverpool for me to step off the boat. I will be in touch as usual, when least you expect. I am leaving here as soon as I down this triple shot of Power's Gold Label. Mike, I now place my trust for deliverance in the blessed Oliver Plunket."

From my present vantage point in Woodlawn and as I placed the phone back on its hook, I saw no possibility of Gainor being able to make that ship or any ship. Although Valerie was comparatively isolated on the Isle of Man, I did caution her to keep quiet concerning the considerable amount I reported about Gainor and his movements, which now consisted of visions of Crist in his red jockstrap, his dismantled wigwam over his head and making his way down his apartment house stairs as he was pursued by Mutt's naked girlfriend. I was also trying to rack my brains to remember if I'd ever witnessed Gainor actually driving a car. But realized from his background that this would have been sine qua non in growing up in America as Gainor had done in considerable affluence. And the usual brightly colored brand-new convertible would have been sitting in front of his house for his sixteenth birthday. And it would have been merely just another simple artifact expected to be part of the life of any decently rich kid in this cornucopia land, as it was for more than a few of my own contemporaries. Yet to Gainor, when speaking on his last evening to stay in Woodlawn, pleasures could be ultrasimple.

"Mike, although justifiably sad that you are unable to converse, I am truly most solemnly happy here. Just like this."

He had come up to my bedroom, having just been watching TV downstairs with T.J., and he had gone to sit in a green rocking chair, a blanket across his knees and fiddling and twiddling his fingers and thumbs, as he gently rocked back and forth. He spoke and I typed back my answers to him. But then he would become still and silent at the brutal bluntness of these replies. However, moments later he would slowly shake his head up and down in affirmation. And as Gainor further sat on in the green chair wrapped in a blanket, his mood suddenly changed as he spoke about his two little daughters and about trying to get his first wife, Constance, who was in Ireland at the time to come with them to London. Things not being good between them, he was always fearful that he might be stopped by immigration upon his arrival in England, as his original right to be there stemmed from his marriage to a British national.

"Mike, one tries and tries so hard to keep everyone happy, even to the extent of trying to comfort those in their remorse for having betrayed one. And, Mike, who am I to argue over these, your forthright if pitiless replies. Ah, but here is arrived, I must say, a gesture to warm the cockles of the heart."

T.J. had brought Gainor a tumbler of whiskey, and Gainor smiling, shaking his head yes as he took the glass and looked and sniffed into the tea-tinted liquid as he put it to his lips to take a delicate sip. Then raising his glass in a toast, he optimistically announced that he was looking forward to having his first drink at the bar aboard the boat. It was always at moments such as this over a drink and most often contemplating a future drink somewhere, that Gainor was at his magically most pleasant. As if such occasions were a preamble to the time certain to come when all his problems would be solved. In the intensity of such moments, he would place aside his whiskey, and leaning forward would indulge then a further finger-twiddling paroxysm. As he did on this very last occasion I was to see him on American soil.

"Mike, my dear Dinnlay. As I sit here in this sacred comfort, the cold winds aswirl outside, I tell you of a song. 'The Water of Tyne.' Which as I weathered the worst of my circumstances, I sometimes heard sung by girls' voices somewhere out on the distant edge of my mind. It is a sad song. Of a girl whose love is the other side of a river that flows from the ancient wilds of Northumberland and out to the sea. She is crying out for a boatman to come to row her across to him. For she is sighing and dying. Mike, my dear Dinnlay. It is as we are.

And we two wait. To be ferried back over that big and cold sea. To our loved ones. And having borne more than a root and a toot of ignominy up the rear end, let me say to you that I shall be deeply glad to go. But despite a bust here and there upon the old bones, I assure you that better days are coming. Count on it."

Of course I did not count on it. But this same day all now was haunted by having had walked for three or four miles through Van Cortlandt woods, showing Gainor the sites of my childhood. Of where we flew gliders we made, and where we hunted by gun, slingshot and bow and arrow. Where my friend Alan Kuntze trapped muskrat. I brought Gainor to secret sites where campfires had been built and potatoes and squirrel legs roasted. We strolled past the community dump, which was then encroaching on the wetlands we had tried to prevent being drained. Amid the tall cattails, big black snakes and snapping turtles lived and the red-winged blackbirds flew. We then ended up sitting on a curved enclosure of benches which half encircled one of the strangest memorials in America. And the site where the bones of the seventeen braves of Chief Ninham were buried, attesting to where the Stockbridge Indians had fought on the side of colonists and gave their lives.

"Mike, I am truly fascinated to see where you grew up in comparatively wild and open spaces and in one of the largest cities in the world."

Since Valerie left, it had been the rare day spent like that with Gainor that kept me resolute to hold on and continue to hope. And as we sat in that front room that evening, one of the last sounds now that one heard in America was a Celtic lament, which suddenly came at this strangely appropriate moment on the radio station WQXR that one had constantly listened to growing up.

"Dinnlay, they play those sad, strange strains of music, knowing that we're going."

But now following his return from Woodstock, and except for his brief call from Queens, Gainor vanished. There had been fog for three days. A letter had arrived for Gainor from Pamela, full of her sound advice, and another letter asking me to prevail upon him to write. But I was already packed up and ready to leave. Having thought that after waiting and waiting the precise moment would never come. My big steamer trunk already delivered to the ship. And now on a cold misty but thawing morn, the lonely day of departure had dawned. Snow turned to a gray slush in the streets. The last music I listened to on station WQXR was Offenbach. At one-thirty P.M., with just a bag and my typewriter, I was driven by my father and mother down to the boat. T.J., left behind, still furiously painting and turning out his pottery. If I were in any way sentimental in departure, I was also remembering words I printed out for Gainor to read on my pieces of paper I handed him.

I AM

WAITING LIKE YOU TO FLEE. TO BE GONE WITHOUT PAINFUL
PROLONGED GOOD-BYES AND BE NO LONGER HERE ON
ANYBODY'S
MIND. I AM STILL A HUMAN BEING BUT ONLY JUST
IN THE UNMITIGATED, UNRELENTING VULGARITY AND ALL THE
LIES
HOW COULD THE BEAUTY OF LOVE EVER EXIST
OR IF IT DID, EVER PERSIST HERE
THIS COUNTRY NEEDS ITS PHONY FACE SMASHED
AND A REAL ONE PUT IN ITS PLACE
AND EVEN IF I WERE ABLE TO SURVIVE HERE
I COULD NOT BEAR TO
DIE HERE

A hurricane having penetrated north from Florida, it was looking as if the trip to Liverpool on the *Franconia* could take longer than ten days. Being early to the boat, I asked my parents not to wait to see me off. My spirits, if they were not picking slightly up, were at least not any longer sinking. I had even allowed myself to toy with the thought that before leaving I would submit *The Ginger Man* to another publisher. But then realized that only some force from without and far away from the United States could ever change matters for *The Ginger Man*. My mind already casting itself back to Europe, I had come to hate America but swore that I would survive the damage it had done.

What I had left of a future was now the other side of the Atlantic, where storms were still raging over the Irish Sea. On the Isle of Man, the wind had been blowing so strong that when Valerie took little Philip out for his walks he was blown over.

From an almost deserted pier, I climbed the gangway to come on board the Cunard line's R.M.S. *Franconia*. In my silence I managed with notes to find my way to the four-berth cabin shared with two others and "squared my things away," as they said in the navy. Looking everywhere, there was no sign of Gainor on the ship, and one did not want to start slipping strange scribbles to the purser as to having seen any sign of a man in white socks and sandals toting a paper bag with a length of rope in it. I was returned now up on the deck and looking down on the pier. Not long to go. Blue peter hoisted on the main mast. Fore and aft, they were lifting away lines from their moorings. The great rope hawsers splashing in the water. The steam winches rumbling and whirring, reeling the lines back up on deck. Either side of the gangplank, sailors were standing by, waiting ready to take it up. Undoing ropes and knots. A bell ringing and a voice over the Tannoy had already sounded throughout the ship.

"All those not sailing must now go ashore, please."

I had, I really had made it. This was it. I could see the first and second mates at their stations and the captain on the wing of his bridge. Along with the rejection, the nightmare of America, the angst, melancholia and hypochondria, were at last, thank God, all over. If I died now, it would be at least peacefully. Or indeed, I could live and begin a life again. Even in these last few seconds of leaving, I was still desperately anxious to go. And staring down at the now emptied pier, I thought of Gainor. Hunted and haunted. Somewhere desperately left in this city. Where he'd been so often caught in the spiderweb of the subway. A vagabond alone on the North American continent and so very far away from a Dublin and London he in many ways loved. The solution now to his suffering, the rope in his brown paper bag. For all the worry and even anger he had caused through all the wasted time of the past few weeks, one simply didn't have it within one to put upon him blame. Only to wish him all blessings. And desperately hope for him that he would one day escape.

A white-coated waiter came out a door on deck and went in another toting a tray. It left a familiar warming smell on the cold air. Beef tea was being served in the ship's lounge. Blue peter lowered from the main mast. From high up on the ship's funnel, steam shot in the air as two blasts came of the ship's horn. I was back in dignity, holding myself askance. I stood by the ship's rails, not far from the gangplank. Always the imaginary admiral watching this last act of setting sail. Above the clattering noise, my ears could still hear ashore the sound of police sirens. Dockers now pushing and tugging to remove the gangway. The twenty-thousand-ton vessel making its first stirring in the dock. Next stop would be February 15 at Halifax, Nova Scotia. And from there, straight across the North Atlantic to Cork and Liverpool. Then suddenly, as the last rope of the gangway was cast aside, instead of joyous relief, tears welled in my eyes. A desperate inexplicable sorrow overtaking me. That I was leaving people, some of whom, like my father, I would never see again. And that poor old Gainor, who had endured through his own insufferable fault so bloody much, had not made it.

From portside, I was about to turn my attentions to the starboard to watch the tugboats at work, when on the pier there seemed to be a slight commotion. A voice shouting. A thump, thump, like feet running. The voice sounded like one I had previously known well and heard crying out in exasperation. And one had nearly expected to have such a daylight nightmare. That I would now take back with me to Europe. To forever afterward hear familiar words spoken to me by a ghost of a man I had never seen before. But was suddenly seeing now on the pier, as there and then came into sight from around the corner of the customs hut a hobbling figure struggling to make haste over the wooden planks. Moving forward almost as if one leg had to wait till the other crippled one had caught up. Scarf wound round his neck and tucked in under the lapels of his orangy brown tweed jacket. His blue Aran Islander's cap on his head. Lugging in one hand a heavy suitcase and in the other a brown paper bag. And this man who was shouting out, was none other than the one and only intrepid and resolute Gainor Stephen Crist.

"Wait for me."

The gangway was pulled back into place and held as Gainor climbed aboard. I watched as his suitcase was taken from him by a sailor. Gainor wincing, holding the rail as he stepped onto the ship's deck. His breath heaving, his head nodding up and down. And without seeing me, he disappeared aboard as the tugs hooted and the *Franconia* blasted two blasts and the echoes came back over the Hudson from the Palisades. I went back to the stern. The vessel, pushed out into the current by tugs, was slowly turned and, bow facing east, the *Franconia*, its engines throbbing, was now under way down the North River. The tall buildings of Manhattan were gray and silver under the overcast sky and veiled by a strange red-tinted mist. And a hand came to rest on my shoulder. Standing there silently behind me and smiling was Gainor. His paper bag and suitcase parked with the purser, and with a Pan American Airways pouch underarm he had returned out on deck. And one might have known, he had a cabin for four all to himself.

"Ah, Dinnlay, you did think, didn't you, that I would not make it. To sail back with you into those times of yore. And back to the nighttime sweet-scented smoke descending upon the city of Dublin.

Softness of rain falling softly. The glow of turf fires, the only warmth. The sound of music on wirelesses, the only comfort. The evening-steamed windows of the crowded trams rattling past Trinity. We return to the smell of sheep's head stew. The dark wine of the people going glug glug down the slaked throats in all the pubs. Rasp of meaningless voices becoming more meaningless as they become drunker and finally make sense. Those too, of the stone-cold hearts. The unkind, the ungenerous. The narrow minds becoming narrower. Who will go to join the others like them in the granite sepulcher of Dublin's defeated souls. The evening's loneliness as one hastens from pub to pub and the turf smoke presses down from the old gray sky. And we seek out the catacombs to raise a defiance against death. Where bad nights can always be relied upon to bring worse mornings. And yet, Dinnlay, that selfsame city we love. The noise of earth-colored beasts through the night in the cattle markets. The lash of blackbriar on their rumps. A brute voice driving them through the darkness and into the morning light of the harbor's quays, where the boat awaits to take them to slaughter in England to become British roast beef. It is how we will always remember Dublin. And where'er we go, to it shall we always want to return. Living as it does within us. Incubus of eternal sorrow. Across which the purple winds of melancholy blow. Dinnlay, we go back now to embrace all its grimness, all its default and all its failure. And we willingly do so with wide-open and all-embracing arms."

WHERE ALSO THE FIRST PRIORITY WILL BE
FOR US TO GET INTO A BAR
WHERE AS SOON AS POSSIBLE WITH DRINK WE CAN
BLOT OUT THE PAST AND DREAM AND TALK OF
A HOPEFUL FUTURE
WHILE AT THE SAME TIME WE TRY TO BORROW
AS MUCH MONEY AS POSSIBLE
FROM ANYONE WHO HAS ANY
WHICH IS USUALLY NOBODY
IN THE CITY WHOSE FLAWS
SO SPLENDIDLY PROVE
ITS PERFECTIONS

"Ah, Dinnlay, you may no longer speak with your mouth, but you have not lost your eloquence and astutely accurate observation by your pen."

AND I AM, I FEAR, ALSO LIKE THOSE IN DUBLIN
WHERE THE WANDERING POET PLEADS
CELEBRATE ME NOW BEFORE I'M
DEAD
CELEBRATE ME NOW WHILE I'M POOR AND
UNREAD
CELEBRATE ME NOW WITH A DRINK
A MEAL AND A LIFETIME ANNUITY. PLEASE DON'T LET ME DIE
BEFORE I'M RICH AND FAMOUS
AND BECOME A VACUITY

"But, Dinnlay, you say pessimistically harsh words about where we would wish to return to."

JUST AS THE IRISH CAN BE
BRILLIANT FLATTERERS
THEY CAN ALSO DISCLOSE
RUTHLESSLY TOLD
VERSIONS OF THE TRUTH

On the fantail stern we stood, the *Franconia* in the current gathering speed. Beneath us, the water eight fathoms deep. Watching the island of Manhattan silently receding in the gray mist. As if all life had ceased there. Across the sky, the sun cast a dim, blood red cold light. Passing to our starboard, Hoboken. Where there was a school which taught you how to build ships. On portside passed the fireboat station. And across town, beyond, in those streets was where April lived and St. Vincent's Hospital and the wondrous nun. Gainor, as well as knowing the depth of water flowing beneath the hull, also seemed to know the details of all we passed port and starboard. Just as he had known throughout the war, the most secret and guarded telephone number of the bunker beneath London's Mall, from which Winston Churchill conducted the Battle of Britain. And to which number Gainor phoned to make assignations with his first wife, Constance, who had refused to disclose same to him.

"And, Mike, we both know that Pier Ninety-two was the best place to be stationed during the war. Unlike being at sea aboard ship, it was marvelous for liberty. Merely a walk of a few blocks to Forty-second Street and Broadway for girls and beer. Of course while briefly there, I frequented the better hotels, which others, less particular, ignored."

As Battery Park went by, I knew that there stood a monument on

327

which were listed all the names carved in marble of the dead in the war. And it seemed as if to acknowledge this, that both Gainor and I were involuntarily, silently standing at attention. And could it be, that all these braver dead, had they not died, could have made this place we left, less ruled by the bigoted, bullying, treacherous and their demagoguery. For it seemed that the silence we left behind was that of a city which had stopped chasing us. To drive us out and away. For we were gone.

It was as if one could hear signal bells ring up on the bridge. Faster now as the knots increased and the sea foamed up astern. Through the narrows. In nine fathoms. A ferry crossing our wake on its way to Staten Island. The clutch of tall buildings of Manhattan sinking and fading now out of sight. The wind blowing harder. Seagulls crying. Passing to port was Coney Island, Brighton Beach and Rockaway. We were at last at sea. Out upon the Atlantic deeps. Making our way through the heaving ocean swells.

Mike, my dear Dinnlay,
There it goes
And we shall without hoot,
Without holler,
Commemorate this moment
For the rest of our lives

29

Even with his bad knees, Gainor was able to dance a departing jig on the deck. He had spent most of the three days prior to leaving riding from last stop to last stop and sleeping at night on the subway. Taking trains variously traveling back and forth from the Bronx to Coney Island more than twenty miles and fifty stops away. I had feared he'd never raise enough money for his ticket, but his loving and ever dependable Pamela provided once again. And of course he had nearly missed catching the *Franconia* by having fallen asleep and wakened in the environs of Canarsie. Then, near hysterical, he found himself back in Manhattan with a bare twenty minutes left to sailing.

"Mike, I had not even a last few dollars to spend on a taxi. But I can tell you, no one in the Olympics has ever covered running distances faster. All pain vanished from my knees as I skipped, hopped and tripped my way the last few blocks to the pier. The subway, which was my nemesis upon my arrival in this land, has alas also been upon my departure, my savior."

When we had been passing the mouth of the East River, entering New York Bay, one could nearly see from the *Franconia* the house at 8 Willow Place in Brooklyn Heights where my parents had first set up to live a married life and where one was conceived. My father later, when we had moved from Brooklyn to Wakefield in the Bronx and thence to Woodlawn, was, as he tended dahlias in the garden, always bemused watching me go by in the sunshine with a tennis racket or golf clubs over a shoulder, when in the old country in the misty mist I would have been toting a shovel, pitchfork or a scythe.

The certainty of my going and leaving America confirmed one inevitable thing, that my birth and having been reared there did not make me eternally American. And it might even be thought that I had been

My parents' wedding picture.

born in the wrong country. Brought up by parents to whom it was still the promised land but who themselves must have spent many a secret moment remembering and wanting to return to where they were first reared and grew up. My mother's eyes always filled with uncharacteristic tears whenever she alluded to suddenly being snatched away from her Galway home as a young girl to be brought to America and there to become thoroughly part of this mix of races, but where she always kept her Irish Catholic faith throughout her life. America physically fading now as we left its shores. But still remembering the more wished-to-be-forgotten unforgettable moments there. Where, like Gainor's homosexualist motorist, I had also indulged my own vehicle escapades, as when at the age of sixteen, having just got a license, my father let me drive one of his new Dodge cars as I did one night, having a beer too many. And found myself racing along a sharply curving lane, which sent me up through and across a suburban dweller's front lawn and over his flower garden of bright red and yellow tulips, mowing them down under my headlights. And Gainor had an explanation of such phenomenon.

"Mike, we were raising defiance against the claustrophobic status quo. And you can be absolutely certain of one thing, that such suburban people, over whose lawns such motorcars tend to go to maraud with crazy insanity at night, fly the stars and stripes on their front lawns by day. And it's as well such bloody righteous, patriotically smug citizens are occasionally reminded of their vulnerability."

This latter remark could have been thought extremely uncharacteristic talk from Gainor, who on the surface at least had always verbally extolled and upheld the honor and trust that dignified family values, especially those epitomized by photographic portraiture of mom, pop and offspring exhibiting Brahmin respectability, with such representation perched upon the shiny top of the grand piano. And it was only by dint of necessity and circumstance that a major degree of Bohemianism had insinuated itself into his life. Such now exemplified by his brown paper bag, sandals, Aran Islander's cap and his trusty rope, which might be required when things got bad enough to end it all. However, aboard the *Franconia* he immediately adopted one of my suits, a silk shirt and Trinity cravat for shipboard wear. Returning him to his previous diplomatic splendor, which he had sported when receiving and taking leave of the important persons on behalf of Pan American Airways. Indeed, on our second day at sea, with his back to me, I hardly recognized him in the ship's lounge already in the company of a group of girls who happened to be the *Franconia*'s most attractive passengers. And presto. Upon Gainor seeing me, I was no longer left to be the lonely, reclusive and silent North Atlantic traveler that I usually was. Gainor, heels clicking and bowing, instantly introduced me to whatever female shipboard fun, beauty and intelligence was available.

GAINOR HOW
PLEASE TELL ME
HOW
DO YOU DO IT

"Ah, Dinnlay, aside from allowing myself to enter my second childhood, and my having an honest and open demeanor about me, I abide by a simple motto. Bad persons vamoose, good persons come hither."

YOU DON'T SAY

"Yes I do verily say, Dinnlay. And those who may be of a doubtful category I encourage to stick around to see if they might at least prove briefly amusing, as indeed most often they do."

The ship on its way to Halifax was not very full and indeed at times seemed relatively deserted. But nowhere in the annals of human enthusiasm or among those crossing eastbound on the North Atlantic could ever be found recorded anything to exceed the amount of whole-hearted animation that was shown by Gainor Stephen Crist upon this voyage. His name being the first to appear as a participant in every contest being advertised aboard the good ship *Franconia*. Nor did any passenger ever engaged in so many activities at the same time exhibit a so utterly unfussed and unfazed demeanor or move about as Gainor did with such verve and elegance. Almost overnight his knee joints, becoming more flexibly nimble by the minute, returned to nearly normal size.

GOOD GOD
GAINOR YOU'RE UP
AND DOWN THIS
SHIP'S LADDERS LIKE A
GYMNAST

"Ah, to be sure, Dinnlay, to be sure. One must avail of quickness to fulfill so many commitments. And indeed luckily so, as I have met the most delightfully appealing young lady who is returning to Europe, just like us and who was badly disillusioned with the United States. And we discuss and talk about it in my cabin."

I assumed from Gainor's pleased expression that he too had to keep his backbone flexibly nimble for his frequent bowing and possible other activities, for one now began to encounter a smilingly gladsome young lady who seemed very little disillusioned as she was to be seen coming and going from his cabin door. Even on this second day under way, Gainor, up bright and early, was the first to hand in his slip to the guessing game, having estimated within four eggs how many had been eaten in the previous twenty-four hours. He had already won his first two matches with all comers in Ping-Pong. He also waged furious war at quoits, his eye even without his glasses devastatingly accurate. And when I lent him for the coming events a pair of black, diplomatically correct shoes to sport by day and diplomatically appropriate dancing pumps to wear by evening, his smiles were a mile wider, and his bows a fathom deeper.

"I am most grateful to you, my dear Mike, for this loan of shoes and shall refrain, I promise you, from teaching lessons to any future vending machines by kicking them to pieces."

My failure to speak and being attired in my beaver-collared, camel's hair greatcoat as I paced the deck with silver-knobbed walking stick and accompanied by a solicitous Crist, reading messages I handed him, gave rise to the stories now abounding about the ship that I was formerly of a middle European family dynasty who had ruled a province which was now a Russian satellite state and that Gainor, my chief of protocol and personal secretary, was shielding me from unwanted attention and that we were traveling incognito and tourist class to avoid being conspicuous. And of course more than a few women aboard were going out of their minds as to how to meet Gainor and if meeting him how to continue to stay close. And one was even able to witness the unprecedented phenomenon of first-class passengers longingly and enviously looking over the barrier into tourist class and to find some excuse to breach the division. Even to peeking through a boat deck porthole into the tourist-class smoke room, and then upon seeing Gainor there, to gate-crash into his company. And which did not seem to please Gainor much.

"My dear sovereign Dinnlay, you've heard the expression 'to go slumming.' I dare say we are witnessing an unseemly example of such aboard this ship. Of people who think it might be greener in our cheaper pasture. Ah, but one does tend to want now to live and let live. Indeed, happy-go-lucky is how one might describe one's present mood. And I have been occasionally happy and I have equally more than occasionally been unlucky. But here and now aboard this vessel, and for the first time I can ever recall, I am both happy and lucky at the same time."

But as Gainor was embarking upon his life of bliss, my life in the meantime aboard ship became one of a total shambles and partial nightmare. I was already feeling that bit queasy but in the shared cabin with a deep-sea diver traveling between assignments and a young kid being banished by his parents to a more disciplined life in Europe, one had one's first night's sleep shattered. The fifteen-year-old boy getting drunk and returning to the cabin, where, in the middle of the night from his top bunk across the aisle, he chose to kneel and in the darkness pee into the center of the stateroom. Both the smell and sound of splashing woke one up. And the light switched on, I left it to the deep-sea diver, a petty officer in the Royal Navy, to take remedial action. As in my case, short of hitting him, I would have only been able to hand the kid a note stating,

STOP

333

But the kid did not stop. The deep-sea diver, a most understanding gentleman, having mildly remonstrated, found himself undergoing a drenching. And pronto, the master of arms aboard the *Franconia* was summoned. Who on behalf of the Cunard line, with its long tradition of cosseting and calming passengers, very diplomatically attempted to reason with this unruly young gent. But the kid had obviously reserved even further urine for this very moment, and he unleashed a new stream of piss upon his newly arrived adversaries. This did strain the master of arms's practiced cordiality, and the kid, still in his underwear, was full of fight as the master of arms and two assistants struggled to drag him down from his bunk and away out of the cabin to be restrained and calmed elsewhere aboard.

"Don't you touch me, you bastards."

A water jug and glass smashed against the bulkhead, leaving blood from cut feet on the stateroom rug. The battle and shouts proceeding out into and along the companionway. The boy, as he struggled and screamed, was also pounding cabin doors with his feet as he was dragged by. Several passengers having already donned their life belts were in their pajamas and bundled up in coats were peeking out their doors ready to go to their muster stations to board a lifeboat and abandon ship. Only to then encounter in the companionway the ship's company attempting to subdue a now totally naked passenger, whose legs were flailing as he was pulled along shouting at the top of his lungs.

"Let go of me, you fucking limey cunts."

It seemed now as if our roles were entirely reversed, as I sought to join Gainor for peace and quiet in his cabin for what Gainor called a Chianti cocktail. But with the unruly passenger held elsewhere, I was now imposed upon to vacate the shared cabin to the deep-sea diver for two hours every afternoon so that he might do, as he intimated, some deep-sea fucking with an accommodating lady passenger he had met, whom he described as having dark and mysterious sexual wants. Meanwhile, as we approached Halifax, and the Florida storm hurried north after us, the sea swells were becoming bigger, with the roll and pitch of the ship increasing. With more than a passenger or two absenting themselves from the dining room. Where the already friendly waiter did not mind putting such missing passenger's appetizer, entree or dessert in front of Mr. Crist, to whom he would bowingly and smilingly announce as he deposited same on the table,

"*Bon appétit,* my good sir."

And Crist in turn, with alacrity, would polish off everything placed before him. But with his shipboard activities, Gainor, along with having to replenish his strength weakened in America, was now burning up immense energy. Much of which was expended in our chess games in the ship's lounge which were attracting considerable attention in our first two days at sea, being that we were eminently conspicuous in our play. I would unsportingly, graphically demonstrate with waving hands and arms over the board as to what I was about to do to Gainor's uncastled or unprotected king. And as my pincer movement of bishops and knights would close the trap for checkmate, I would draw my hand across my throat or simulate a man who had just been hanged. The fact that it was known that I did not speak seemed to add to the drama of these gestures. At such awful moments, Gainor, in plotting his next defensive move, would jump up from his seat, rush out onto the open deck and furiously pace back and forth, inhaling deeply to renew the air in his lungs. And then, grim-lipped and resolute, he would return to the board. To be slaughtered. Such moments being the only time aboard the *Franconia* that Gainor was to be seen with even the merest flicker of discontent on his face.

With the sky overcast and snow flurries blowing along the decks, we had now passed Cape Sable at 65 degrees longitude and 43 degrees latitude on the southern tip of Nova Scotia and were, with Chedabucto Head abeam, soon entering the peaceful waters of the Halifax harbor and docking at Pier 21. It was some welcome relief for me to be able to come ashore, as the Atlantic swells had now become so mountainous that there was a rumor that we might have to delay sailing and remain in port, a prospect neither Gainor nor I had reason to complain about. Meanwhile, getting our passports stamped with leave to go ashore, Gainor seemed, as we disembarked, to be beside himself with delight. Indulging his usual paroxysm of twiddling his fingers, hunching forward his head and shoulders and emitting pleased grunts as we walked out into the cold, snowbound Sunday-deserted streets of what seemed this Old World town. The sun suddenly coming out to shine as we strolled through Grafton, Barrington, and Argyle streets, redolent of the Europe we'd left. Climbing Citadel Hill along Bedford Row and up George Street we came to a church overlooking a square. And Gainor beckoned me.

"Dinnlay, follow me. We go to enter within this door."

A brochure Gainor had with him described this building we were about to enter as the Westminster Abbey of the New World. I of course, temporarily relieved of the desperation to find a future for the manuscript of *The Ginger Man*, was now reaching the point where I might start talking again. And I croaked out a few words, saying I would wait outside while he reconnoitered within the church. At the sound of my voice, Gainor immediately put his finger up to his lips for silence. And as I asked why, a cloud of concern came over Gainor's face.

"Dinnlay, on this nice stroll we are having on terra firma, I have just spotted two other travelers off the *Franconia* who might notice you speaking and therefore I am imploring you continue to keep further silent. It is not that I do not like hearing your voice again. Far from it. You have in fact a most perfect speaking voice when you speak. But, you see, the fact of the matter is I have already informed everyone aboard ship that you would not speak again until our tiny principality, the identity of which had to remain secret, was liberated from Soviet domination. It so happens too that the dear young lady, who so willingly visits my cabin and who has already bought me a few drinks plus shaving cream and my favorite toothpaste and who is about to give me some very much future-needed financial assistance, believes implicitly in the incredible tales I have, in my trance of unbridled euphoria, already divulged. The size of your castle. The nature of your labyrinthine wine cellars. Your stable of performing horses. The lot. I should now hate to think that she might suddenly feel duped and taken advantage of to find out that you are not the reigning monarch and prince we claim you to be, nor have you a vestige of horseflesh to your name, nor anciently stacked bottles of Château d'Yquem waiting to be drunk by thirsty lips. Nor that I, which I suppose is equally important, am your loyal secretary of state and chief of protocol who also has the keys to your wine cellars. Therefore, please, for both our sakes, mum must be the word."

GOOD GOD GAINOR
TO HELL
WITH MY
HORSEFLESH AND WINE
CELLARS
IT IS LITTLE ENOUGH
I ASK
BUT TO BE ABLE TO
SPEAK AGAIN

"Dinnlay, be patient. You must. At least for this very temporary time being remain silent. For both our happy contented sakes. All shall be divulged in good time. And then you may shout your head off. But meanwhile, you must admit the trip has been entirely agreeable and comfortable so far. Only nine days now, or ten, depending on the weather, to go. And we may look forward to its continuing idyllic as it has been for these first two days."

BLOODY HELL, IT MAY BE THAT WAY

FOR YOU

BUT I'VE ALREADY HAD TO ENDURE

ONE NIGHT OF

NIGHTMARE

AND I'M NOW

VERGING

ON BEING SEASICK

"Ah, Dinnlay, I am indeed sorry to hear of such disagreeableness befalling you. But do please continue your silence. You will thank me years hence when you are able to take out all these scribbles of yours you make and practically reconstruct your very life, hour by hour out of what is memorably happening to us now. Come, be of good cheer, follow me in here to look about in this nice temple of prayer from which we hear such nice singing. Come, we must go in. And please, I beg of you keep shut up."

GAINOR

BELIEVE ME WHEN I HEREBY STATE

THAT THIS WILL BE AMONG

THE VERY LAST

OF FAVORS

I SHALL DO FOR YOU

The church was a warm and welcome revelation, quite full of worshippers. There was room at the rear in the last few pews. Crist entering one and I the pew just behind him. I could suddenly see that this Amish, agnostic, atheistic, Protestant Christian, or whatever he was, was visibly touched and immediately behaving as if he were a lifelong member of this congregation. His voice in one of those vaguely familiar songs could be heard raised among the voices of the church members. Words sung to proclaim belief and trust in Jesus. And that this man so sadly crucified those many centuries ago was the true light and guide in life. Then as a voice from the altar pulpit spoke, I

337

could see Gainor's shoulders straighten and his head bow forward in genuflection as he listened to what must have been the most appropriate words he ever could have heard.

"O almighty God, we yield Thee praise and thanksgiving for our deliverance from the evils of those great and apparent dangers wherewith we were recently compassed. We acknowledge it Thy goodness that we were not delivered over as a prey unto them. And beseeching Thee still to continue such Thy mercies toward us, that all the world may know that Thou art our savior Who hath redeemed our souls from the jaws of death."

The organ music trumpeted out once more, and Gainor, along with these other dedicatedly devout, was heard singing again. Not always in tune, nor indeed using, from what I could hear, the same words. But he did manage to get through a couple of songs when a collection basket appeared which was being passed approaching down the aisle. I knew that Gainor must be short of money but did not know that he simply at the moment had not a red cent. He now plaintively half turned around to me to discreetly display his empty palm to indicate that he needed a coin for the tray. I shook my head in mild and what I thought would be amusing refusal in order to demonstrate that I was not your usual contributor to church funds, and also to show that I had limits in being taken advantage of, especially when told to shut up and wait to be given permission to speak again. Then Gainor, withdrawing his hand, proffered it a moment later, his palm outstretched again to show me the only thing in his possession and which he was now holding in reserve to contribute to the collection. This was a shirt button, white in color. But there was on his face no laughter that nearly came to mine. And I was suddenly stunned by the seriousness with which he now confronted this situation of having to drop a shirt button into the collection basket. For tears were falling down Gainor's cheeks.

The clink of coin was now getting closer with the basket only two pews away. And I was stricken. That I should have been so carelessly unfeeling as not to recognize another's heartfelt sanctity. And although it was deeply against my principles to contribute to the support of the religious, other than in matters of architecture and music, I reached into my pocket and as I took from Gainor the shirt button I gave him in exchange an American nickel. At which Gainor ever so slightly frowned. And then additionally I gave him a dime. In turn as the collection basket passed my way I was surprised to find myself taking a whole quarter to pop into this woven wicker receptacle. For somehow, although still on the North American continent, and in this marvelous church and among these wonderfully devout upright Protestant people, the music of their voices filling our ears, we clearly were both of us, overwhelmed with this unexpected opportunity to express thanksgiving for our escape. Being lofted as it were by magic carpet away into the nether reaches of where one's future lay far beyond the pitfalls of the past. And where our spirits were melded in hope once more.

As the service came to an end and as these thoughts were passing through one's mind, the organ trumpeted and the chorus of voices swelled in a last song as if to extoll a God to whom one day the whole world might pray. When just then, a beam of light came like a bolt in one of the windows. A halo glowing and blazing in yellow gold. And the cone of this eloquent illumination shone alone and only upon Gainor. And something without doubt was proclaimed. That as I stood there. It was finally explained. That I truly was.

In
The presence
Of a saint
To whom one could pray
To solve
The impossible
And beg deliverance
From evil

30

Outside returning down the hill, leaving this church where one had this apparition of Gainor's sainthood, I must have wanted to reassure myself that Gainor was only human after all and as he walked in front of me a few yards away, I dug my hands into the snow and made a snowball. Then, shouting a warning, I unleashed it and hit him on the shoulder. And there in the street began a brief snowball fight which I distinctly lost. Gainor, an outstanding baseball pitcher, promptly managed to land a snowball exploding smack in my face. Which although it did not knock me on my back, did leave me dizzily dismayed and my eyes glowing red.

"My dear Mike, I am most awfully sorry. I actually did think you would duck."

AH, BUT I LEARNED A LESSON
NEVER UNDERESTIMATE YOUR ADVERSARY
NOT EVEN IN A SNOWBALL FIGHT

As great swells from the storm rolled into Halifax harbor, the good ship *Franconia* delayed to set sail and it was marvelously pleasant to continue to enjoy an unyielding deck underfoot. In Gainor's utter transformation and in just a little more than two days, it was now almost as if he had taken over command of the vessel. And in his smiling, bowing manner, without portfolio, he did the job of any good purser, as he, quite light-footed, made his speedy way about. The older ladies as well as the young being given his courteous attentions. He had already twice won the ship's general knowledge test, getting the answers to all twenty-one questions correct, and as far as I could ascertain had organized credit with one of the barmen in the small topside smoke room. I was meanwhile holding my tongue but frequently threatened that I was going to break my silence, and then his finger would immediately go to his lips, and he'd whisper.

"Dinnlay, trust me. And one day you will thank me."

CHRIST, CRIST, YOU ARE SOMETIMES A
BASTARD
YOU'RE ALREADY POLISHING OFF EVERYTHING
FROM THE FIRST-CLASS MENU, INCLUDING
THE WOMEN
AND YOU CONTINUE TO INSIST
I SHUT UP
SO THAT I AM
UNABLE TO EQUALLY ACQUAINT MYSELF WITH
THE OPPOSITE SEX

"Dinnlay, I assure you all the ladies are already in awe of you, and everyone already loves you aboard this ship. Courteous, flattering whispers follow you where'er you go. It's all for the best. Besides, you are a most happily married man to one of the world's most beautiful and charming women. You will and shall want for nothing. You have a little baba whose looks are so attractive, it makes people stop in the street in order to vent their admiration. You go to join your little family in splendor on an island whose parliament is the world's most ancient and where they flog evildoing ruffians with the birch and no foreign harm comes to the inhabitants. You, must for the sake of all these things, Dinnlay, continue to keep your mouth shut and continue to assist in my not disillusioning the ladies."

THANKS A BLOODY BUNCH

Gainor sometimes, when noticing that I had become more frustratedly disgruntled than usual, would reach to take the sheet of paper upon which I wrote, which was in this case Cunard's blue engraved stationery of a gray-colored variety, a supply of which I took from the ship's library. And upon this occasion, he wrote his own note in large capitals to hand back to me.

DON'T MENTION IT
AND BE NO LONGER REPUDIATORY AND GLOOMY
AND DO LET ME GET YOU ANOTHER
SHERRY BEFORE DINNER

Gainor, not only with credit aboard ship, now seemed also in funds. And it were as if the ship's company could not do enough for him. Jealousy of course rearing its ugly head at nearby dining tables as Gainor might be served a whopping plate of grilled mignon of tenderloin attended by a side dish of boned breast of guinea hen with ham Lucullus. But throughout, it had to be said he did always distribute tiny portions to the nearby deserving. However, there was nearly a mutiny when he was seen to lean over and shovel up cornets of smoked salmon and beluga caviar, with people recognizing that bubbles were arise in his continuously replenished glass of white wine. Even I began to think that it was entirely possible that with his new seemingly improved financial status Gainor was in fact paying a supplement for first-class cuisine. Indeed this seemed confirmed by our accommodating waiter, who now being goaded by jealous passengers was outdoing himself.

"Sir, allow me to put to the side here for you, some *harengs frais grillé* with *sauce moutarde*."

Of course, at that, the lady at the next table, of some elegance herself and a widow of an ambassador, complained. Whereupon the waiter courteously served her with the same dish while explaining in whispers that Gainor, as well as being my chief of protocol, was an already-paid-for first-class passenger. And that I, as well as my being royalty from a damn good principality, was one of Cunard's largest shareholders. And next, a little card was presented to both Crist and I, inviting us to her commodious cabin for drinks. And my God, she too became instantly and irrevocably another infatuée of Gainor's. And, as he described, was picking up his scent and always on his trail where'er he went on the ship.

As the fourth day dawned aboard the *Franconia,* we had set sail and, Chedabucto Head abeam, entered out upon the white-capped Atlantic Ocean. Riding the northern edge of the Gulf Stream across the grand banks, the snow was falling out of deeply overcast sky and the wind was howling in the rigging. The western Atlantic basin passing beneath the hull, we were not that far out to sea when the stern of the vessel was ascending and descending in the water like an elevator, and the ship's screws occasionally fanning the wind and the bow pointing to the sky. The storm had veered unpredictably and had now caught up with us just south of Cape Race, Newfoundland, where we hit the Labrador current from the Arctic. In the brilliantly navigated *Franconia,* the rolling massive seas ahead neatly split apart by the sharp black prow, the foredeck becoming awash. It was an ocean splendor to witness as the spray of the sea descended upon those who had their sea legs.

And indeed rough it was. The ship no picnic for those of queasy stomach. Folk becoming fast sparse, disappearing to their bunks and beds below, it did not take many hours to transform the ship into a ghostly emptiness. At each seating for meals, fewer and fewer attending. Even members of the crew were vanishing. And as I struggled to stay at our humble table, my appetite now had well nigh disappeared. But Gainor, totally unperturbed, was eating anything and everything our waiter continued with kindly indulgence to provide from the first-class menu. Not that it was that much different from tourist and certainly no more nourishing. At one sitting, I had listed Gainor's smashing back a bottle of wine, devouring noodles Alfredo, sinking his incisors into roast duckling and then licking his chops, following wiping plates clean of portions of fresh pork brawn, *oeufs tartare* and split veal kidneys smothered in parsley butter. My final demise starting in the middle of this lunch, just as the last of the split veal kidneys were disappearing into Gainor's mouth, when the ship gave a sudden lurch as it slammed into a massive wave.

"Are you all right, Dinnlay. You suddenly seemed to have turned a pale version of green."

I'M OK,
BUT YOU, I FEAR,
MAY HAVE TO EAT
MY SPLIT VEAL KIDNEYS

"I shall indeed, of course, Dinnlay, see to it that no leftover embarrassment is to be seen remaining on your plate. But you must, you know, try to eat."

The very hardiest people who were left now began to desert their tables. But with one's sense of loyalty as a former naval person with Crist, I thought I would try to hang on. Remembering my first ever having been seasick en route up Chesapeake Bay aboard a U.S. Navy minesweeper when having a wonderful lunch of ham baked with pineapple, all of which I had to deposit overboard. And all of which made me not particularly favor ham and pineapple ever since. The dining room now looking quite bereft, I made an effort to at least pick at my food while Gainor had no troubles of any description, golfing down into his hole in one cup, the French asparagus spears *mousseline,* followed by peaches *flambées* in kirschwasser. But as usual, he was extremely solicitous of my discomfort.

"But too, Dinnlay, we must not let vanity get the better of us. Or let a sense of ceremony intervene. Do take your leave if you feel like yawking. If you should like to make for the open deck, the lee is on starboard at the moment."

DON'T WORRY
I WON'T YAWK HERE
I'LL GIVE MYSELF TIME TO GET THERE

I clung on till breakfast next day with just Gainor and five others left in the dining room. Gainor's advice to eat well did help settle the stomach. However, following boiled eggs and a plate of bacon, I had at this point nearly to give up. But still desperately clung on to make it to lunch, only to have to finally rush from the table just as the appetizer Helford oysters with Creole relish was served. Leaving in solemn, solitary occupation, with both plates in front of him, in a now almost completely empty dining room, Gainor Stephen Crist.

GAINOR, SORRY
TO HAVE TO DESERT YOU

"Ah, Dinnlay, you fought the battle long and well. But always remember, such discomfort is in a good cause, for we are at last on our way to Ireland. A great fine land for both sorrow and love. And where we shall be able to find festive comfort through the night in the pubs and then be able to cure our hangovers in the early morning drinking houses of Dublin."

With the captain's splendid navigation, everything on shipboard soon returned to normal when calmer seas were reached. And after a day's convalescence, I reappeared. Then under the duress that I continue to keep my mouth shut and my pen busy writing notes, I was introduced to a marvelously attractive and pleasant girl by Gainor by the reassuring name of Joyce. Who patiently read my scribbled woes. And even read the manuscript of *S.D.* And was full of every encouragement. Always marvelous what an admiringly handsome, sympathetic girl can do for one's spirits. My journey now when Gainor was otherwise occupied was so much less lonely. And as Gainor's fame spread along with my own invented fame, a few eccentric first-class passengers were now even more aggressively slumming in order to see and meet him. They were not disappointed. Splitting their sides as he performed his mimed antics as a surgeon in an operating theater botching an operation.

Meanwhile, during dinner, I was summoned to the radio shack, and, as the purser's assistant whispered in my ear, everyone in the dining room assumed that a coup had taken place in my principality and that I was about to instruct my loyal generals to execute the previous puppet government. At least this was the kind of story that Gainor always had ready to unleash on those nosy enough to want to know, and only God knows what he said as I nervously and speedily left the table. And I did break my vow to Gainor not to speak aboard ship when I tried to hear through the static the voice on the other end.

"Hello. Hello."

"Hey, J.P. It's me, April. I've been trying to get you for five days. You two guys just upped and beat it on the very night I was giving you both the best going-away party ever seen in this town in my swell new stupendous penthouse apartment high up over everything, where I'm enjoying its Florentine palace splendor like it was in the movies, lit with lights, festooned with flowers, heaped with wonderful food, bottles of all the best beers, whiskeys, bourbons and champagnes. Not to mention a bottle even of Rebel Yell for Gainor. And the whole night turned into a funeral. I had to get the hell out of that place where the girl downstairs was driving me out of my mind with what I knew she was doing with her Great Dane. Hey, J.P., turn around and come back, will you. Hey, can you hear me. Come back."

Before I could speak the static drowned out April's voice, and, the ship's radio officer losing contact, I couldn't hear her again. I stood there in the chill strangeness of dials and pinpoints of light and sound of other signals coming over the airways. The radio officer quietly solicitous, assuming from the solemnity of my face that I had received bad news. When I told Gainor, he just sat staring and remained as silent as I was. It was perhaps the only really sad moment we were to know crossing the Atlantic.

With the ship tranquil again, Gainor rushed to take part in each of the events listed in the daily program. Hurrying along the windy decks or to be met on a companionway staircase, he was always on the move.

To play anything or take part in whist or bridge or bingo. And, unbelievably, considering past injury to his knees, he employed his astonishing reflexes to beat everyone at table tennis. And I found him staring with satisfaction at his name posted as winner outside the purser's office. But with a dud partner, he came in only second at shuffleboard, and when this result was appended outside the purser's office he was more than a little miffed. But in such a sophisticated man, I simply could not believe at what I was witnessing. His wholehearted embracing of tourist-orientated shipboard life and his endless readiness to engage in every single activity. Always the first to enter the quiz competition and return his answers to the purser's office. Always the first to his seat for the recorded concert. He even presented himself as Abraham Lincoln in the fancy dress parade. His energy astonishing. His enthusiasm knowing no bounds. Daring even to suggest, instead of Abraham Lincoln, he present himself at the fancy dress parade as a madam of a bordello. But thank God, his young ladies gown proved many sizes too small.

GAINOR IT'S RUSH

RUSH RUSH

ABOARD THIS SHIP

"And why not, Dinnlay, and why not."

And Gainor, by his indefatigable example, did buck me up. And I tried to join him for morning beef tea and music at teatime. Plus the film shown at four P.M. and the cocktail hour at six. Although it was clear that Gainor was not caring a damn as to what was going on in the outside world, he would, reception conditions permitting, go to listen to the news broadcast at six-thirty P.M. He even exerted some friendly persuasion upon the kid in my cabin when, somewhat chastened, the kid was returned to shipboard life and warned not to piss again from his bunk in the middle of the night. Gainor seemed a friend and confidant to all and despite his daily appointment-filled life, there he was at nine-fifteen P.M., front row at the recorded orchestral selections and with his now silver flask of brandy given him by the ambassador's widow, who said he so reminded her of her late husband in the way he was sympathetic in manner, ministerial in mien and charming in all company. That she wanted him to have something which belonged to the man she'd married and loved. In short, just as he must have done as an acting host for Pan American Airways, Crist enchanted this ship and brought to nearly all aboard solace and comfort. His only regret being that clocks were retarded one hour at midnight, making the enjoyment of his day that bit shorter for activities. Some of which he admitted might involve the odd frisson occasioned in the time spent in the privacy of his stateroom. Where we were sitting one evening having a predinner glass of the remains of the gallon bottle of Chianti, and Gainor suddenly became a mite serious.

"As we are now midway between two continents, Dinnlay, and as I clearly see the increase in thickness of the number of sheets upon which you make your little shipboard notes, I'm sure, as it would be impossible for you not to, you must occasionally be including mention of me. So I would like to make it known that at least while I live and breathe that you promise you will never disclose what has taken place aboard this ship concerning my more personal activities."

WHY

"Because, quite simply, your often acutely observant and detailed observations might be misunderstood."

AND WHAT WOULD HAPPEN
IF I DID DISCLOSE
AND IT WERE
MISUNDERSTOOD

"Something awful usually takes place."

SORRY
TO HEAR THAT
I TAKE IT THAT
LADIES ENAMORED OF YOU
WHO CATCH YOU WITH YOUR TROUSERS DOWN
WITH ANOTHER WOMAN
GIVE YOU WHAT FOR

"Ah, Dinnlay, you have caught exactly the substance of the matter. Again, quite simply, I would as a result be savaged."

GOOD GOD

"Fingernails used as claws gouging deep ruts down my face."

BUT
DEAR ME
COULDN'T YOU RUN
FOR IT

"Not when this most oft times takes place in closed and deliberately locked rooms from which there is no escape."

HEAVENS
HOW THEN DO YOU
POSSIBLY PROTECT YOURSELF, SINCE
YOU ARE THE
QUINTESSENTIAL GENTLEMAN
AND IT IS FOR YOU
ABSOLUTELY ANATHEMA
TO EVER RAISE YOUR FIST TO WOMEN
TO WIELD THEM
EVEN A WELL-DESERVED
CLOUT
UPON THE OLD GOB

"I get under the bed."

AH WHAT A GOOD IDEA

"No, Dinnlay, it's not."

WHY

"Because under there I am then pursued by the hard poking end of a broom handle. Which is thrust deeply into any part of my anatomy that can be reached. Which means all of me."

HOLY CHRIST I SUGGEST THEN
YOU HAD BETTER KEEP YOUR
FLY CLOSED
AND I ABSOLUTELY PROMISE
NEVER WHILE YOU LIVE AND BREATHE
TO MENTION
A WORD OF YOUR
CEASELESS WIDESPREAD PHILANDERING

348

"Dinnlay, put this in your notes that I am desperate to get very old at which time it is rumored one's gonads rust up, dry up and sometimes even drop off. But meanwhile, I do everything I can to keep the buttons from popping and zip from unzipping my fly. But nature being what it is, one is prodded on to prod others which one trusts will be of the opposite sex. Nature, by the way, seems to have its own methods untaught by mankind, and, if you'll forgive the expression, it can rather fuck one up. Except for the war, Dinnlay, my father was sending me to Eton, a very English school on the river Thames where my father said the stiff collars and top hats they wear would do me a world of good. You see, Dinnlay, your mother suggested Trinity to you in Ireland, where we had the good fortune to meet. Our pretensions come from our parents' dreams for us. And then when we don't live up to our parents' dreams, we do things to make them shatter even more irrevocably. Ah, but as we soon approach Ireland again, give me your sheet of paper upon which I will write an old Orange song."

WE'RE UP TO OUR KNEES
IN CATHOLIC BLOOD
AND UP TO OUR KNEES
IN SLAUGHTER
AND IF WE HAD THE POPE
RIGHT HERE, WE'D
DROWN HIM IN
CHIANTI PORTER

Gainor raised his glass in a toast. Although I had never heard him utter a word against religion, the Catholic and Protestant war in Ireland had been one of Gainor's most consuming fascinations. And when visiting his in-laws of his first wife's in the north of Ireland, he would, when he heard of such, go anywhere to see an Orangeman's parade and listen to the fierce beating of the big Lambeg drums. Gainor seemed to especially delight in these four-foot-in-diameter instruments of percussion, the symbol of the Orangemen, which were beaten with two long canelike sticks and with such frenzy as to bloody the wrists and hands of the beater and which represented the ferocity of hatred between the two anciently belligerent tribes. And it was, he said, a battle to the death of the truthful against the dishonest, of the dirty against the clean, of the cowardly treacherous against the bravely honorable. But when asked to say which band was which, he smiled and pronounced,

"Ah, my dear Dinnlay, answering that would imply that I had taken up sides, which would be very much against my principles in such matters. However, what is not against my principles is to drink another toast in Chianti to the Pope. To the Pope, Dinnlay."

TO THE POPE

"And, Dinnlay, I trust, despite your brief indisposition caused by the heavier seas we encountered, that you are enjoying this trip as much as I am."

Gainor still presiding at his place at table and who was now shining in radiant splendor in another suit of mine, was still without the vestige of a single ounce of fat upon him. And was as ever, smashing back at a sitting, sauerkraut juice, clam chowder, fried smelts, noodles Bolognaises, braised beef à la mode, onions au jus, mashed potatoes, a portion of lamb's liver smothered in onions with an on-the-side dish of rolled ox tongue, spiced ham and galantine of chicken. He was clearly the blue-ribbon winner and the all-time champion eater of crossing the Atlantic. The easily amused waiter still dancing delighted and almost hysterical attendance upon him. And once following a substantial number of main courses and Crist wiping the plates clean of pineapple crush pie and an assortment of Wensleydale, Cheddar and Cheshire cheese, washed down by glasses of rich red wine at one shilling a glass, which I was glad to buy him, the waiter on returning to the galley door, suddenly doubled up with laughter at the stupendous, unceasing appetite of this man and dropped an entire tray of dishes. And then slipping on some butter grease, fell on his own arse. Whereupon the next waiter emerging from the kitchen tripped over him and dumped his own entire tray of chocolate custard puddings down on his head.

"Mike, despite our waiter having just broken about fifty dishes and undergone a sudden ethnic color change to his face, I regard him as one of the very best in his long suffering profession and intend to dispatch a list of commendations concerning him to Cunard's managing director as soon as we return to London."

GAINOR, THAT MIGHT BE ILL ADVISED
AS YOU MIGHT THEN BE PRESENTED WITH
AN ADDITIONAL BILL, JUDGING BY THE
AMOUNT OF FIRST-CLASS CUISINE
YOU HAVE CONSUMED

The storm left far behind, the submariner was now taking three- instead of two-hour sessions in the cabin with his lady and was polishing off two bottles of wine. While Gainor gave as explanation of his appetite that he burned inordinate amounts of energy trying to avoid being demolished by me at chess. However, he in turn had demolished all at draughts and dominoes and while waiting for new challengers, he now sat alone for periods in the ship's lounge by day and then would by evening station himself high up in the boat deck smoke room bar located behind the funnel amidships. And there I would come to find him as we merrily and now smoothly sailed on with a much appreciated lack of the ship's pitching and rolling. And Gainor on this night was quaffing a predinner sherry, as one imagined he might one day do in his London club when qualified as a barrister and taken silk in the interests of British justice. And the bartender at this bar this night, polishing glasses, nodded assent as Gainor indicated in sign language for replenishment, waving a pair of eyeglasses borrowed from his lady admirer to read the *Ocean Times,* daily delivered under one's cabin door. And on this occasion, as I entered, Gainor, upon seeing me, closed a book and immediately rose from his seat to click his heels and bow.

"Ah, your royal highness, how good it is to see you so refreshed from taking, as I trust you just did, the air on deck. Do please sit here and join me. As you see, I am, courtesy the kindness of the ambassador's widow with her husband's eyeglasses, able to read again. Being without my own specs was cause for the worst of my last hours in New York on the subway. Not being able to read signs, I daren't get off the line I was on. Ah, and I see you notice what I am reading. Got it out of the ship's library. Potted biographies of great Americans."

I THOUGHT YOU'D HAD ENOUGH
OF THAT PLACE

"And so I have had, Dinnlay. But I am also concerned that there must have been deeper reasons why we have fled from that land where all things seem dramatically possible. And indeed one knows now in one's bones that neither of us shall ever return there to live. Ah, Dinnlay, I know I have squelched your freedom of utterance. But understand I did so for what I know you will finally appreciate was for a better purpose. And perhaps it has caused you to have had to listen to me more than you'd like to. But let me now say this. America, as we grew up, Dinnlay, gave us our dreams and aspirations. And has now handed them back to us shattered. We were born in that land to the promise supreme. That life would give us whatever one wished. To have whatever one wanted. And to be whatever one wanted to be. And perhaps one goal above all was dangled in front of us and was undoubtedly the worst of all. It was that we could become president and commander in chief of that massive burgeoning nation. And follow in the footsteps made for us by Abraham Lincoln and George Washington. The latter, whose early forebears were described as gentlemen. And the former born in a backwoods cabin. Just like April was up her family gulch. Abraham helping his father clear fields and plant pumpkin seeds and take care of crops. He saw, as I did as a young boy, his mother die. And then be buried in the forest. Whereas I kissed my own mother's cold lips good-bye in her hospital bed. And watched her coffin lowered into her grave in a cemetery. And they had to hold me back because I said she was going to be lonely. And then my father would not let his second wife have any children because she might not pay enough attention to me."

I MAKE NO COMMENT

"Dinnlay, it was the same Washington under whose bridge so named where I stood hitchhiking and who in the story so told, admitted to his father that he'd chopped down the cherry tree, saying, 'Father, I cannot tell a lie, I hacked the defenseless, bloody thing down with my own highly sharpened axe.' Dinnlay, at the time of our young innocence we believed all those things. Trusted them. And always relied upon getting what we would ask Santa Claus to bring us for Christmas. Wrapped as it would be in all the colors of the rainbow. Otherwise, we would throw a foot-stamping tantrum. And in spite of all this, and do forgive me if I put it this way, but I think we duly got our faces shoved in the shit. And that we end up now preferring a more sophisticated stack of same to anoint our visage with."

AND WHICH KEEPS
OUR
OLFACTORY NERVES
IN TRIM

"And, Dinnlay, even this far out at sea, one can not shake off the nightmare of America and its strange moments to be remembered. Especially if you recall that afternoon when I lay contentedly on April's sofa just before Christmas waiting for her to return from shopping and I with all my myriad of troubles lay back on a divan in front of April's windows. *Pictures at an Exhibition* playing on the gramophone. A wood fire sparkling and crackling in the grate. A full and as yet unopened bottle of Power's Gold Label Irish whiskey nestled and resting in the crook of one's arm. And I was even reaching to dip a Ritz cracker in a bowl of whipped cheese and sour cream and chives. When I heard a loud deep bark out the window and rose up higher to see. The girl in the basement apartment beneath was returning from walking her dog. She was quite remarkably stunning as she stood a few moments and whispered in the dog's ear before descending the steps. And, Mike, I absolutely saw the dog smile. And would not believe I had until April said that she could no longer stand the noises coming up through the floor. Or indeed the happy look on the girl's face. As T.J., your brother, said, Dinnlay, There's enough in this nation to give everybody the life they want to lead even if it's the life of a dog. Ah, but, Dinnlay, we are exactly poised now between two continents floating upon peaceful oblivion. Please tell me how you are."

DO YOU REALLY WANT TO KNOW

"Yes."

I FEEL CONTENTED
ENOUGH
JUST TO WANT TO DIE
FOR
I NEVER EXPECTED TAIL BETWEEN MY LEGS
TO BE RETURNING WITH *S.D.*
UNPUBLISHED

"Ah, Dinnlay. Patience, my friend. You must come out of your lovely gloom and put to rout all maudlin misgiving. Remember that now we come back to a land where one knows that there will soon be so many things to be sad about that it will be hard to make a choice. But as for Sebastian Dangerfield, it seems your opposition is censorship. The liberal world of France may be your answer. And from whence, once the words you have written have been made known in print they will burn holes through all opposition. Mike, everything is going to be all right. Provided you stay out of Wales. And the mother of all of us, whomever she is, will take care of us."

"Me fine. Me very fine. Me only sorry me miss wigwam. Ah, but my sight, Dinnlay, with these glasses is now passably good. My thinking, my understanding, my memory, concentration, mood and mobility are, to say the very pessimistically least, absolutely magnificent. Confidence restored. Depression and frustration put to rout. Gonads, as a result, possibly overactive. And except for our not being able in tourist class to have our breakfasts served in bed, one makes no complaint aboard this ship. I do believe we are being given a sample of what we have held as being our true way in life."

IT SEEMS AT THE MOMENT
THAT YOU ARE A MAN OF
INVISIBLE MEANS

"Which, Dinnlay, sadly are certainly not private by any stretch of the wallet or imagination. But as a man who expected to be of at least semiprivate means, I have found that one of the hardest things to do in life is to patiently and complacently wait for one's inheritance. For one has to assume that when it comes in the expectedly not too distant future, things are going to be different and that one's present state is not worthy of the effort to particularly change it."

AND APROPOS
OF NOTHING AT ALL
PLEASE LET ME STATE
THAT LIFE IS BUILT
ON RESISTANCE
NOT SATISFACTION

"Mike, you know, had we been to April's party, everything could have changed for us in America. But perhaps not. As we return to Europe, I think now we should both know better. We should always live by each other's advice and never trust our own. And, Dinnlay, everyone in that land that we have now left some distance behind us, is in a repressed rage. Everyone wanting to strangle and kill each other for all slights and indifferences that have been ethnically and economically heaped upon them and accumulated from the moment they were born or left the nest of their parents, if indeed they did have a nest and if indeed they did have parents. But let us now raise these glasses of good grog and be of good cheer. Here's to your good health and your quick return to colloquial discourse."

I'LL MOST GLADLY

DRINK

TO THAT

The approaching culmination had come now to the magical pleasure of shipboard routine. As if the whole world approached an end. And it had. We were west now of Ireland, with only a day's sailing ahead. The swells of the sea under the *Franconia,* moderate. Gainor, instead of being an international ambassador at large, reverting again to being the lonely highway man. No longer having to be on his shipboard toes for every contest from Ping-Pong to guessing the number of eggs used that day in the kitchen. He instead bowed, smiled and clicked heels to everyone and also let drop the rumor that upon landing at Cobh, he was about to have secret talks with the Irish government on behalf of the bearded silent gentleman in the fur-collared greatcoat who would continue to travel incognito on to Liverpool. At Halifax I had written and posted my last letter to Valerie stamped PAQUEBOT POSTED AT SEA. I showed the ten-cent stamp to Gainor which was a picture of an Indian stretching his fur skins outside his wigwam. This produced, as I knew it would, a paroxysm of immense delight, and I was summoned below to Gainor's stateroom for a drink as well as to collect back clothes prior to his embarkation at Cobh.

"Ah, my dear Dinnlay, the trip is well nigh over. We have weathered every storm and the destination we sought is won. Our injuries healed, our modest if not meek self-esteem restored, we now gird our loins for the challenges ahead. Let there be no looking back. Let there be no regrets. And let there be much mercy. And upon those words you have written. Which tell of the wild ginger man. Let the eyes of the world be ready to look. For they shall. And I fervently know that one day somewhere I will sit delightedly turning those printed pages. And your day and the day of Dangerfield will come."

THANKS

FOR THE HOPE

THANKS

FOR THE FLATTERY

Gainor poured out yet another swig or two left in his apparently inexhaustible gallon bottle of Chianti wine stowed in his Pan American Airways bag. And it seemed to be one of the few things he had brought back with him from America. I watched him pack his *Ocean Times* newspapers and thrust a magazine into his brown paper bag he still had. And in his single suitcase, there seemed nothing but a motley array of soiled and tatty underclothes. But then from beneath these, he lifted up a neatly tissue-wrapped parcel and carefully opened it. And from out of his own bedraggled clothes came these two pristine children's cowboy outfits. One for each of his daughters that he had promised to bring back to them from America. I watched as he lovingly held up these small reddish suits one at a time to the light, each pinned with a star-shaped sheriff's badge. It seemed as if he had lost all his personal possessions and only had left now these two precious things, shiny and smelling new. Which carefully he refolded and laid back reverently in his suitcase. And I was suddenly stunned with the utter sadness of this sight. Of something of which he never spoke. Was the deep devotion and obvious love he had for these two of his little beautiful daughters. Each with her own small beautiful name.

Mariana
The eldest and the youngest
Called
Jane

31

GAINOR'S LAST NIGHT aboard the *Franconia* was indeed gala. Sporting every article of clothing I had left suitable to lend him, he danced with lady after lady on the dance floor. And never a dull moment as he would return to the table where I sat to play "Raggle Taggle Gypsy" on his devised instrument of comb and paper. The first-class passengers trespassing out of control among us. Anxious to pay their respects to me, the pretended prince of the principality, and my equally deceiving chief of protocol. As I sat slightly apostate, my friend Joyce demanding but only once getting me to hopelessly waltz.

"Come on, J.P., get your curmudgeonly old bones up out of that chair and shake a leg."

The serenely attractive Joyce at last overcoming her charming reserve and strangely sounding like my dear April, whose voice, sadly, I did not hear again over the sea waves. And as I watched Gainor dance wearing my smoking jacket and dancing pumps, and looking every inch the ambassadorial representative of a decently important principality, I thought again of the first time we ever met, in the Pearl Bar in Dublin. A drinking place of journalists and poets in a shadowy street just a short stroll from the north side gates of Trinity. Here the portly figure of Bertie Smylie, the editor of the *Irish Times,* held court in the upstairs lounge with reporters and those who would be such. I was standing at the ground-floor bar having a rare drink with the elusively shy James H. Leathers, with whom I shared rooms. And who, by the account of anyone who had ever met him, was beheld as the most charming man ever to set foot in Ireland.

"Hello, Mike."

I turned from the bar to be confronted by two gents, one of whom, a Randall Hillis, a few days previously had asked me if I could lend him a silk shirt with French cuffs, a pair of gray flannel trousers and a yellow sweater because his brother-in-law was applying to perform a job as a male model. And these three articles of clothing of mine, a bow tie added, I now saw upon the man to whom I was introduced. None other than the present man Gainor Stephen Crist out on the dance floor doing a boogie-woogie. And I recalled again that back that day in Dublin there was not even the slightest trace of self-consciousness, condescension nor embarrassment that Gainor was walking around in my wardrobe but he merely gave me a look of benign curiosity as we were introduced and shook hands. Even with the incident of the broken watch which allowed me to keep time an hour at a time. Gainor instantly proving that I was hoaxing myself. Which indeed I was, but in Dublin such things were encouraged. However, this interjection of correction in matters of accuracy in the face of my abstracted musefulness undoubtedly formed the basis of our relationship ever since.

Aboard the *Franconia*, excitement now with every hour passing. Ahead on the horizon the towns and places we knew well. From Slea Head to Cape Clear. The bays, inlets, jutting peninsulas, and towns. Dingle, Killorglin, Cahirsiveen. And now it was nine-fifteen A.M. in the morning as we rounded the southern coast of Ireland and its low hills lay there softly green and silent. Gainor and I taking what would be our very last early morn, post-breakfast constitutional on the open deck in the chill breeze of the Atlantic Ocean. The taste of salt on one's lips. The roaring sound. The dark sea passing by. And as he was taking deep breaths of sea air, I was about to listen to the very last of Gainor's conversations.

"Ah, Dinnlay, the contours of Erseland are just there on the horizon. And strolling here as we do, I want you to know that I can recall all that has ever happened. And with the understandable exception of cunnilingus, buggery and blow jobs you need only come to me to learn of any details concerning past fights, insults, betrayals, calumny, backbiting, infidelity, cuckoldry, Judas kisses, stabs in the back or just general banjaxing."

HOW GOOD TO KNOW
THAT I SHALL BE ABLE
TO KNOW
ALL THERE IS
TO KNOW
WITH THE VERY UNDERSTANDABLE

EXCEPTION OF BUGGERY
BLOW JOBS AND
CUNNILINGUS

"Ah, and, Dinnlay, do you remember when you were not so silent on a memorable night in Dublin some years ago when I had in a pub run out of money, having most inconveniently not yet established credit with the barman. And you said you would get money from the very citizens of the city so that I could continue to drink. And I did not believe you."

ALWAYS
THE WISEST
POLICY

"Ah, but you led me out to the middle of the O'Connell Street Bridge, where you spoke and gathered a massive crowd. Who stood there in the cold gray night. As beneath us, the dark Liffey waters ebbed out to sea. You preached to them a new philosophy to which they avidly listened and which I must confess the substance of which slips my mind at this moment. But I acted as your front man, making sure you were not mobbed and had space. When you requested money in appreciation for what you told them, I was astonished that they threw you pennies, a few of which landed and rolled loose on the grimy pavement and were chased after by a band of barefoot urchins that one had to shoo away from the larger dimensions of coin. And I was even more astonished when you took the threepenny bits and threw these back into the crowd and asked for six pences and shillings. And when such were unbelievably forthcoming, I picked up the coins from the pavement and handed them to you. You then threw these too back into the crowd and asked for half crowns. Mike, I now have a confession to make. Concerning a matter which has made me feel quite guilty ever since. I must now, as we approach Cork, Ireland, at these steady eighteen or slightly more knots, own up to you. I pocketed a lot of that change. For as you threw a few of the half crowns back and asked for paper pounds, I knew that no matter how marvelous your words that we were about to get fuck all."

WE DID,
IF
I REMEMBER CORRECTLY

"Ah, quite right we did. But then too if you remember, the whole plan backfired. Although my pockets were heavily loaded with coin, you were simply too bloody convincing about everything you said and we found we could not disband the crowds nor stop the ardent who followed you from the bridge. We had in fact to flee to your Trinity rooms and be admitted by the porters into the front gates which had to be shut and locked behind us. And thus were we prevented from being able to get back into a pub to drink. Dinnlay, I often remember that night as an object lesson. That one must not be too good at what one attempts to do else everyone is after you to keep doing it. But here let me write something for you on your piece of paper."

DINNLAY
AS WE NOW ARRIVE IN CONDOM-
FREE IRELAND
I HAVE SOME CONTRACEPTIVES I AM GOING TO AUCTION
OFF
ON THE QUAY IN COBH

"Ah, too, Dinnlay, let me say in parting that we hope to see no more. No more of the weak cunning and treacherous scheming in conspiracy against the valiant, honest and brave. And that such shall be ceased, desisted and stopped. That it shall be proclaimed that the perpetrators of same shall not benefit. That they shall not be glad or be made greater. That they shall instead be banished from us to languish forevermore in their ignominy. And leaving us, the innocent, with our ears wagging, eager to listen, and our gonads still intact. And so say I now good-bye."

GOOD-BYE
AND JUST LET ME ALSO SAY
THAT NEVER HAVE I
EVER SEEN SUCH OUTRAGEOUS
GLUTTONY

"Dinnlay, I merely store up for the spiritually lean days that may be ahead, and the sustenance that may be in it. For in this respect, I don't trust God, for He has disappointed me once too often. But now may the blessed Oliver Plunket intercede for us both. *Adios, bueno amigo.*"

The previous hour we had steamed past the Old Head of Kinsale and on this misty, chill morning had entered Cork harbor. The small tender had come out on the gray-black choppy water and pulled alongside. The few passengers disembarking had already descended the ship's ladder. For some reason, as I saw Gainor standing there below on the tender's open deck, I felt I was looking at an apprehensive man. I do not know how those high up on the *Franconia* and peering down over the railings might have looked to him, but I was there with them and could see that tears were running down the cheeks of his lady friend, who had put him in possession of some funds. And the strikingly elegant widow of the ambassador seemed similarly bereft. Gainor now waving as he stood looking up from the tender's tilting deck. White dots of cottages and houses to be seen on the distant shore. And there he finally was, lonely deposited back in Ireland. The woes of the world having left him all the way across the Atlantic. And now leaving him lonelier still. Blue Aran Islander's cap on his head. He was going to hitchhike from Cork to Dublin. And I warned him he would more likely end up in Dingle. Or a muddy ditch. I asked him to give my regards to Behan and McInerney and to write me news of the old sod to the Isle of Man. And I wondered, as the tender, making its white wake as it pulled away, its bells ringing and diesel throbbing, if Gainor still had his coiled rope in his paper bag.

The *Franconia* weighed anchor. And we passed out again into the Irish Sea. Watching toward shore, one could see again along its eastern coastline this innocent-seeming but infernal land one had come to love. As Gainor did. Its silver and cold mountain streams. Its grassy soft, green mounds of hills. Its bleak bogs and bereft spaces which grew pretty little flowers. Its hedgerows, where you could find the moist, glistening holly with its red pearls of berries sparkling bright on its sharp-thorned leaves. Providing, like Ireland itself, beauty which could prick your flesh like a nettle sting. But where one could go where no other soul goes. By old lakes, muddy ditches and over stony fields, where the dried brown thistles stand lonely sentinels withering away the winter. On the land from which this ancient nation grew its people.

But it was to be many years hence before I would again walk this cold ground when spring was coming. After the frost had gone. And taking a lonely stroll, trying not to let the sorrow stored up in one's

life overflow. And one's sadness spill over into grief. And so it was
that Gainor Stephen Crist, the eternal tourist and almighty optimist,
was unsafely back upon the Emerald Isle. And the next time I was
to see him, several debacles in his life later, he would, just as he had
predicted,

Be sitting
And turning those
Printed pages
Of
The Ginger Man

32

ON THIS LAST DAY aboard the good ship *Franconia,* the reassuring, pleasant Joyce was my only companion. And in her cabin she was reading the last pages of *S.D.* The Irish newspapers got in Cork were now the first I'd seen in over a year. Making me familiar again with this small world which lived in its own perversely illogical concerns mostly with itself. With Gainor gone, and without our telepathic communication, it was lonely to have lunch. And at another table I could see his bereft lady friend, her head bowed. It was as if the ship had lost its vital force and heartbeat. Our waiter too was in drooping spirits at Crist's empty chair. And he actually set the place and brought all the dishes on the menu which he said was to placate and atone to the deities, so as to ensure that Mr. Crist would eat as well ashore.

God only knows and not even He would be sure what confidential arrangement Gainor made in the way of a gratuity with this droll and dedicated waiter. But now we were plying St. George's Channel and making toward Anglesey and were abeam of County Wicklow and passing where I had first sat down on this coast to write the beginning pages of *The Ginger Man.* And here I was, lugging all these dormant, silent and unsung words back with me. To heaven knows what, except a desperation and resolve to get them printed and see the light of day somewhere. And it had better be sometime soon. Before the despairs of disappointment finally, as they were bound to do, overtook me. But at least I had, with a carbon copy, the words themselves still there on the page to read and inspire one to go on and never, never to give up.

The afternoon light was growing dim on the waves as we rounded the point of Holyhead, where the Dublin mail boat landed its Irish bound for England. As the light faded, one had gone below to pack and then had dinner. Following which one had gone to walk out on deck with Joyce and her friend Lorie and suddenly in the darkness we found with surprise that we already lay midstream in the river Mersey. The ship now silent and stopped, having earlier passed all the sad sounds of tolling bells of the buoys in Liverpool Bay. Making it seem as if I had come back here to Europe by magic. And I had. Seeing now in the shadows the docks and the grimy blackness of this dark city of the sea. And silhouetted against the sky the great birds' wings outstretched on top of the Royal Liver Building. The hill of this massive port climbing up behind it with the red tint of its brick buildings darkened over the years by the smoke of coal fires. Behind their polished windows, the rich merchants, their fortunes built from the commerce of this seaport, had their offices through these gloomy streets. Tingling went down my legs and I was on my toes and beside myself with excitement. Looking again and again up at the familiar big looming birds on top of the white-faced clock, past which I would pass so many times over so many future years.

Now vanished from my mind, I felt that I had never been to America. That it was still the land I had yet to return to across the sea. While packing, I found a scribbled draft note of mine which I had given Gainor to deliver to Tony McInerney:

DEAR TONY,
AMERICA IS JUST A
MASS OF DISSIPATED PRIDES
AND
IT'S LIKE TAKING AN
ETERNAL
EXAMINATION THAT ONE
CAN NEVER
PASS
AND THESE TWO FAILED
CANDIDATES
HAVE JUST ARRIVED
BACK
ONE OF WHOM,
IN HIS USUAL WAY
AND WITH HIS USUAL CHARM
HAS LEFT ABOARD THIS SHIP MANY A MOIST FEMALE EYE.
SEE YOU SOON.

My imperceptible arrival in the darkness of the Mersey River made Europe now seem a mysterious place. And a mild soft wind was blowing as the *Franconia* maneuvered alongside its dock. With the steamer to the Isle of Man moored just behind, I was relieved to know that it was not far that I had to go with all my trunks. Although there was dancing and the band playing and one's heart quickened, the last night aboard was like a wake. I sat alone drinking Bass beer while watching the foxtrotting and waltzing. Gainor's little lady friend briefly coming to sit near and we exchanged a few words. Hers spoken and mine by note. She seemed so believing and honest. Always generously insisting on the trip in buying Gainor and I drinks. America had disappointed her too. And on my *Franconia* notepaper, I wrote,

IN THAT LAND BACK

ACROSS THE SEA

THEY HAD A MACHINE

WHICH SOLD HAPPINESS

UNTIL THIS CONTRAPTION

BROKE DOWN

WITH EVERYONE TOO UNHAPPY

TO FIX IT

I recalled how Gainor seemed nervous as I met him the evening before his departure in a ship's gangway with this pleasantly business-like and so proper a lady. And I wondered what his feelings could be and how it was that he managed to instantly receive such selfless, devoted loyalty from women. As well as an odd gouge down the cheeks and broom handle in the ribs. Which, as he said, was better to get there than up the arse. Then having seen this little person watch Gainor with his Pan American Airways bag on the tender as it went off toward the green fields and the many little colored dots on yellow and white squares which was the city of Cobh, and as the small vessel moved away, with Gainor slowly growing smaller and smaller as his blue Aran Islander's hat disappeared in a tiny dot, I knew now why I had asked in the words of *The Ginger Man,*

And how was love so round?

We disembarked next morning and I shook hands good-bye with the deep-sea diving submariner. I had already the previous day at Cobh waved encouragement to the departing kid who'd been banished to

365

another cabin. But although I disagreed with his top-bunk pissing, I knew at least he'd be a winner ashore on the Emerald Isle and would, as his family obviously thought he might, find a ready environment for all his waywardness. At British immigration, held in the ship's lounge, I wrote a matter-of-fact note that I was a writer, and for all time, now changing my identification from that of a painter. Always suspicious of the intruder, my passport was finally after ten minutes stamped and I was permitted to land at Liverpool on the morning of February 24, 1953, on condition that the holder of the permission did not remain in the United Kingdom longer than nine months.

I got a porter to handle my several heavy trunks and on this Tuesday of the week I boarded the familiar Isle of Man steamer called *Manx-man,* which was still moored, waiting just behind the *Franconia,* and set to sail at fifteen minutes before noon. But before leaving the *Franconia* pier, and as folk disembarked, one could see those who had been entangled in other limbs aboard the ship at sea, now rushing into the different waiting arms of their loved ones ashore. Setting not exactly the best example of loyalty and faithfulness. Then, as passengers were departing off into Liverpool, a taxi pulling away suddenly stopped and a girl got out and came running over to me. It was Gainor's lady friend on the trip. Who, as most women did, had done everything she could for Gainor. She seemed so small and funny when I first met her. And now she came up smiling, but with her eyes full of tears on her jauntily pretty face. Her little brown eyes, thin lips and upturned jaw. She said good-bye and wished me very good luck and all good hopes about my book. And I gave her a kiss on the cheek. And even knowing that I would more than likely never see this little person again, it did not come strange that there should be what already seemed to be a lifelong bond between us. And there was now no question that as I stood on this side of the Atlantic Ocean, I felt I had come home.

As we sailed for the Isle of Man out the Mersey and passed the docked *Franconia,* one felt so small. Seeing the parts of the ship where I had spent over eleven days. And in its unrushed world, life had taken on at least a vestige of vitality unknown to me over these past several weeks. When one could take tactile pleasure from the most simple and banal of things in life. In nearing England, the Tannoy on the ship was broadcasting familiar sounds and programs, such as "Housewife's Choice" and "Worker's Playtime." The former program by request often playing the "Sabre Dance," during which it was said housewives all over the United Kingdom dropped their brooms and scrubbing brushes and collectively threw themselves on their backs on their

366

Valerie and Philip (above)
and Philip and I (left) *on
the beach below the
Anchorage, Port-e-Vullin,
Isle of Man, where many
an hour was spent playing,
and where later, my daughter,
Karen, would swim for
hours unperturbed in the
ice cold waves.*

floors, tables and beds and kicked and shook their legs in the air. That is, if they hadn't already invited the gas man, milkman or breadman in.

Sensing friendliness in the world again, there had been at Liverpool a welcome letter waiting for me from Valerie. But still, left over in me from America was the vague feeling that people didn't want to have anything to do with me, nor, as it happened, I with them. And now I was finding it a continued surprise as folk approached me without hostility. Plus the lack of suspicion when I approached them. But with Crist gone, I felt a forlornness. I missed too, the nervous panic I could induce into him as I would rear up over the chessboard and mime the devastation I intended to mete out to his pieces. We did play twenty-seven games of which I won eighteen and he, nine. But most I missed our exchange of comments. But could at least play some of them over again in my mind.

"Ah, Dinnlay, I'm working for the resuppression of the working classes. And I am noteworthy at least as the first to introduce formal-ized hitchhiking to Ireland. And the first man ever to run up credit in pubs. In America I was the first man ever to knock another man into the subway tracks and to then, not that much later, walk off the platform myself, and on both occasions to have a train coming in the station that stopped only inches away from mangling us. And my last two nights in America, as I rode the subway through the night from last stop to last stop, I would awake thinking I could hear the Sunday bells of Dublin tolling out mournfully."

The Isle of Man, as it often did, seemed to have disappeared, until it suddenly rose out of the sea mists and we suddenly cut speed and maneuvered in to dock at Douglas. Empty now in winter without the holiday makers who swarmed here in the summertime. My mother-in-law was still away, as she frequently was, either visiting Zurich in pursuit of the teachings of Carl Gustav Jung or in India at an ashram. And so in this marvelous house on the sea, Valerie, Philip and I stayed on our own in the comparative luxury of the Anchorage. Two things now seemed to matter most. Rewriting and finishing *The Ginger Man* and getting somewhere to live. Which simply would mean a house and Valerie first obtaining from Mrs. Heron her modest inheritance. Meanwhile I set to work. Rewriting and amending passages through the novel. Taking sometimes breakfast and often tea on the terrace when the sun shone there and always spending hours staring out again on the waves of the Irish Sea. And even if it were wet chill and a gale blowing, one enjoyed heading out for bracing walks in heathers up on the promontory along the deserted road to Maughold Head.

Slowly now recovering from my discouragement in this endearingly familiar place, and regaining full use of my voice, I let Ernest Gebler know I was back and issued him an invitation to come for a visit. Remembering Ernie's sensible encouragement that had come from him just before leaving New York. And recalling that he himself in America had had the same feeling of helplessness and hopelessness. But he did assure me that my sanity would save me. Gebler's letters always having purposeful ways of lifting one's spirits. And I took sustenance from his mention of the daffodils which would soon be budding in his fields. And of the paradise of Lake Park, nestled as it was in its hill of pine copses. Its walled gardens planted for food. Its Ladies Garden landscaped for pleasure and scented with its medley of roses overlooking its exquisite lough. We'd walked and talked, tramping along the edges of this ancient oak forest which grew beside this glistening lough of black water. When even the most deeply solemn days had their lighthearted joys.

And there was also in the last letter Gebler wrote to me in America a note to bring back a full copy of my manuscript and that he had been thinking about French publishers and that there were a couple of firms in Paris. He said too that New York was a fearsome place for loneliness which my dismal letters reflected. And one knew now what was wrong with such as Gainor and I, nonconforming persons abroad in North America and surrounded by a sea of conformity. And it was true that many a bleak time in America I longingly cast my mind back to Ireland, with all its abounding eccentricities. Remembering days at Lake Park when Gebler was still asleep and I'd walk alone out on his darkening winter fields through the dull, rusted, wet leaves on the ground. And then how Ernie at midnight, after he'd milked his cow, would, as we sat before the turf fire, wax eloquent over Irish whiskey, telling stories and, as the gales blew over these lonely hills, predicting the transplanting of human organs and dissecting the atom sometimes till dawn. And Gebler would remind me of these times of this eternal place hidden in the shadows of its small mountains.

"Mike, if you go, don't stay in America. You've got to come back to the stark and vivid, gusty light that beats out of these temperamental skies, where all is alive with silent life. Never mind that up here in the Wicklows and over there in the west of Ireland they are maiming each other with kettles of boiling water flung at you for the smallest imaginary slight. The cold and ancient remoteness of Ireland, Mike, is what we come back to from the wrecked land of America, where you'll be wasting the living breath of life, day by day. But here in the old sod, spiders are flying their fine lines across the sparkling moisture on blades of grass. And there still is a hole above us through the cancerous cap of civilization through which our thoughts can escape out to the freedom of the cold void of the universe."

And now Ernest Gebler wrote to say he was soon on his way to the Isle of Man. And carrying plenty of news. First of Gainor, who, off the boat in Cork, disappeared for two weeks. Rumored to be in the company of the random met on highways and byways and in secretive little pubs. Talking and listening as he always did in these spellbound realms on the edge of our earthly universe. And finally to show up in

Dublin to be present the evening before Ernie caught the plane and was having dinner in the Bailey Restaurant. Where Behan, in his full vaudevillian manner and in his sometimes bullying way, was berating one of his usually timid admirers, who dared express an original opinion. Behan was plunging a pointing finger into the poor man's chest, which he had just done six repeated times this night. Whereupon a perfect stranger at a nearby table got up, walked over and remonstrated,

"Don't molest that little man."

Then, with a single blow of his fist, smashed Behan in the face. And then the man went and calmly sat down again while Behan, covered in blood, was thrown out on the pavement. To be ministered to by a just-arrived Gainor, who returned inside the restaurant and promptly demanded to know who had visited pain upon his pal Behan. And that he would challenge such person to a duel. But the man in question, thinking there was a better and quicker solution, got up to hit Gainor. And according to witnesses at the time, your man instead found himself flying at the end of a fist over John Ryan's bar.

As it was Gebler who witnessed this event in full, and hearing this story told by him, it was reassuring to know that whatever happened in the rest of the world to any of us, nothing had changed in Ireland. And Behan once confiding to me,

"Mike, in this fucking predictably unpredictable country, where Protestant devout declare that they know their redeemer liveth, I've taken many a push, shove and punch, not to mention bullets sent at me. But I'll tell you one thing that I wouldn't tell any of me so-called own. It's only the likes of you and Gainor that I'd trust with my life and, what's more important, trust with any of the secrets of my soul."

Ernest Gebler, who grew up with Behan in their North Dublin slums, always warmly recalled watching this cherubic small boy Behan, with his characteristic bravado, take his bare-arsed dangerous dives from high places into the flotsam and jetsam of the Royal Canal. Bumping into dead cats and dogs as he would surface like a walrus, from the muddy depths, shouting his witty curses on all sides. And now Gebler was on his way to see me, having read what he thought were my terribly depressing letters from the New World. Few were ever to know the humane warmth of this dear man whose dour expression and hard shell tempered by stubbornness and his unbelievable struggle to become a writer made his external demeanor such to frighten folk from his vicinity. But held within him was a reservoir of sympathy and feeling that in the bitter begrudging climate of Ireland,

and particularly Dublin, traditionally hostile to its writers, had to be kept well hidden from those who would do him harm. And who were at this very moment, as I waited for him on the Isle of Man, planning to do just that.

And so, as the weather warmed in the subtropical environs of the island, and my mother-in-law away, doors were opened to the terraces to let the breezes blow through these comfortable rooms where Valerie and I were to have our first visitor who could be thought of as a friend. And we awaited Ernie eagerly, who, deserted by his former beautiful glamorous American lady, one had now learned had a new chatelaine in his life at Lake Park. She was called by the simple name of Edna and had the distinguished surname of O'Brien. Numerously occurring in County Clare, some of these folk were descendants of Brian Ború, High King of Ireland, and warriors all. And let me tell you, we were about to confront in not that many hours hence, a contingent of them, that would make the battle of Clontarf seem like a picnic for a Protestant church choir.

We motored to the south of the island to meet Ernie and Edna at the small homespun airport of Ronaldsway. There were smiles and warm handshakes aplenty. But there was with this air of delight, one also sensed, immense relief evident in Ernie and Edna in their safe arrival. Which they soon explained was the result of drama which had recently unfolded in Ireland. Lake Park had been under siege by Edna's relatives, who, thinking Ernie had dishonorable intentions in sweeping this young attractive girl off her feet, had commandeered friends and allies to take the guilty culprit to task. A situation in Ireland, where, with the people so devout, relatives could be soon put behind every bush and shrub and could set the entire nation against you. But now here they safely were, taking a breather on this small, neutral volcanic outcropping in the middle of the Irish Sea. A subtropical oasis free for the most part of crime and where no particular stigma attached to carnal knowledge. And where wenching, gambling and illegitimacy were quietly tolerated if not accepted and even encouraged. And on this pleasantly balmy day, it was a glorious trip up over the mountain road back to the north of the island. After much laughter, dining and wining, and brandy and coffee on a terrace overlooking the sea and chatting till midnight, we all retired happily to bed. Next day Ernie asked for a copy of the manuscript and went to sit on the front lawn in a deck chair under a palm tree, where he read the novel upon which, up in a bedroom, I was still working my few hours of every day. And Ernie, after a pleasant morning and afternoon and again dining as the calm wind blew through the house, finally pronounced, "Mike, this manuscript of yours is that of a real writer and aside from a few fanciful gyrations of an overstimulated mind from which much wants to explode, and does, it's fantastic. And I'm impressed enough to tell you here and now that I'm prepared to financially support you completely until it's finished and the book finds a publisher, no matter how long that takes."

These were astonishing and unequivocal words to hear spoken by another writer and, after America, much appreciated ones. High hopes were suddenly beginning to again emerge in life. But much living drama was soon to intervene over that of the literary. Hours of the day were spent with Edna, whose sense of humor could be played upon until she could no longer sit or stand up with laughter. And she in turn embellished and painted amusing word pictures of the circumstances in which she and Ernie had found themselves and which were soon to be unamusingly added to. It was about to be discovered that Edna, beautiful, sweepingly charming and curvaceous as well, did not have relatives who could even remotely be described in such glowing terms. Her lilting, colorful use of the English language belied an original, for whom the Irish expression "charm the birds down off the trees" might have been invented. And of course she was the perfect foil for my elaborate exaggerations, as well as an eager listener to my counsel.

"Mike, you have laid the ghost to rest for me of all my nightmares at Lake Park, haunted as I've been by the previous inmates there. And your mental and moral advice is sticking to me like flypaper."

Edna, as well as having to tolerate the lurking auras of previous ladies at Lake Park, had also been more than a little intimidated by Ernest's much older friends, some of whom were bullying and envious of this flower of Irish maidenhood. And all of whom had already been hardened in the bitter and boiling bile of Dublin's literary and artistic circles. Which anyone would be forgiven for thinking were hardly much more than a gang of layabouts with sheets of blank paper in their typewriters and looking for handouts. Ernie, being nearly the single exception to these unachieved, was the target for their somewhat resentful jealousies. And they wasted no time to describe Edna as having just daintily stepped out from behind the respectability of the aspidistra in order to foster her ambitions with Gebler, a much older and an already internationally acknowledged successful author. But in Dublin, that was certain cause to get you branded as being less than mediocre. And gave instant license to both those who knew you and those who didn't know you, to insult, berate and malign the bejesus out of you until you were thoroughly reduced back down to where you started from and where everyone fervently believed you belonged and should stay. And, by God, let the lady in your close proximity go in tatters with you.

Ernie, I knew, had suffered a long bout of loneliness before this young Irish dream had stepped into his life. Normally abstemious, he solitarily and curmudgeonly had been for months drinking quantities of whiskey and wasting away each day. For he'd been much and deeply smitten by the loss of his previous lady. Which once was revealed in an unguarded moment when someone said something critical of her in his company. Not only did the remark bring tears to Ernie's eyes but caused a fist to be sent to the jaw of the speaker, who found himself suddenly sitting a few yards away on his arse. And I'm sure there were more than a few moments in Ernest's life which were equally agonizingly sad. And especially the saga of Sally Travers, the loveliest of all of Ireland's ladies. But he never let it be known to anyone how deeply he'd loved this young woman Lea from Hollywood who fled his sylvan domain back to America.

But now Ernie was more than content with this new, tall, willowy, attractive lady, full of drollness when not full of tears. And she had already broken away from the Irish way of life prescribed by her respectable Irish farming family from the west. And genteel from a convent education, she had recently emerged from behind a chemist shop counter, where she had worked in Dublin engagingly dispensing soaps, perfumes and emetics and was overnight coping with her new grander role as the companion of an acclaimed author with whom she was presently staying without the blessing of marriage as a long-term guest in his manor house. And there was more innocence than native cunning in her behavior as she now arrived with Gebler at the Anchorage, Port-e-Vullin. This splendid sprawling stone house of my mother-in-law's perched on a rock outcropping, and its gardens nearly sat on the waves. We took tea on the lawn under the subtropical palm trees. But the atmosphere of this idyllic visit slowly began to change when suddenly out of the blue a Manx detective arrived inquiring in general about the weather, which was agreeably bright, balmy and sunny. And then asking if my mother-in-law took in paying guests. I became suitably surprised if not aghast at this question, and the detective retreated and for the moment I thought no more about this strange intrusion.

Ah, but then not that long after, other folk had surreptitiously come in two more laden cars. Which parked above the house on the road and were out of sight but full to the brim with pure Irishmen. Plus a bishop from somewhere. To me, at first it looked like the unexpected arrival of friends and a version of an impromptu family reunion. And when Ernie got up to meet and talk with them and with the detective acting as equerry, I decided to leave my guests with their guests and repaired back up to my study, whose window faced out upon the sea and where I was writing my revisions of *The Ginger Man.* Ah, but the visitors had requested of Ernie that because of the private, confidential nature of their call, he accompany them outside the precincts of the Anchorage. I had not been long upstairs when suddenly I heard screams from Valerie.

"Mike, come quick, come quick, they're beating up Ernie."

Leaping from my desk, I tore myself away from the serenity of my sea views, papers flying as I went jumping down the stairs three at a time. I took off my jacket and a heavy sweater. Swinging around the bollard of the bannister at the bottom of these softly mint green–carpeted steps. Rolling up my sleeves as I ran through a hall. Depositing my watch on the Mouse Man–made dining room table as I sailed across that room. I was able to see one of the mice this furniture maker carved on each of his pieces. I now could hear the young lady Edna sobbing somewhere. And I increased speed out through the kitchen, already throwing shadowboxing blows to warm up my arms. Past the laundry room and scullery, I raced along a conservatory passageway full of peaceful plants and out a door which led across paving and up steps to the front gate which was a doorway in a tall stone wall. This entrance opened out onto a slipway which went down alongside the house, past which it sloped into the sea. I could already hear the Irish-accented, raised voices and shouts and the Gaelic reference to testicles: "That's it, lads, give him one in the goolies."

And now I could see as I emerged onto this bit of roadway, Ernie at the bottom, cornered and caught between the high garden wall at his back and a railing fencing him from the sea waves. He was clearly battling for his life as six or so folk rained blows and kicks upon him, with a seventh acting as a lookout up the slipway. And, by God, who saw me coming. I had no idea that the tongues had been wagging across Ireland and that avenging legions had been mustered over the association of Edna and Ernie. And there is nothing quite like the contretemps that can be created in the old sod from such situations. Or the alacrity with which those who abhorred such could be banded into an army of farmers and rugby players to end such relationships. Now, Ernie as a writer would have been an unknown quantity as a fighter, but I knew he was as strong as an ox and could snap his sinewy steel muscles like a whiplash. And I could already see that he was giving his seven antagonists one awful surprise. To which was added news that I was now coming roaring on the scene. I did at least know that if people back in Dublin had doubts as to whether I could write or paint, the one thing no one seemingly disputed was my being able to give a decent account of myself in an affray. And as I sallied forth, appearing on the slipway, a cry of warning was shouted by the lookout.

"It's him. It's Donleavy, he's coming."

"You bet your bloody Irish fucking arses I am, and this fighting amphibian is going to kick the living, bigoted shit out of every single fucking one of you."

In America one said little or nothing before a fight, but somehow dealing with these vigilante Irish bullies invited a vigorous announcement of one's unmitigatedly vicious intentions. Of course I must have said "bigoted" at the time. Especially as it at least would deflect some of the acrimonious attention being paid to the poor, woefully outnumbered Ernest Gebler. And I knew by the expression "It's him" that my violent reputation had preceded me. But even as I approached the battle, Ernest had already himself flattened two of the seven prone on the slipway and had just sent with an uppercut a third hurtling skyward, head arching first and feet last over the rusted railing and into the rough sea that was battering the slipway wall. And as I reached the brawl, I was able, in an authentically Irish manner, to level one more with a grossly unsportsmanlike blow just to the rear of his right ear while this victim's back was turned. Then as two of them set upon me at once, it was positively delicious to land hooks, bolos and uppercuts into this pack of persecutors. With one of the four remaining putting up his imploring hands to scream.

"Don't hit me, I'm an old man and haven't climbed Croagh Patrick yet, and I've a Friday left to make of the nine first Fridays."

There could be little or no dubitation here that we were dealing with a bunch of devout Catholics. And there were more yelps and squeals of discomfort as the religious-referring gent, who admittedly wasn't in the springtime of his prime, was, once let alone, then trying his damnedest to gouge Gebler's eyes out. It is entirely possible that this incensed person may have been Edna's father. But now I had no hesitation in hauling him away by the scruff of the neck, turning him around and bopping him a light one on the jaw and then turning him around again unleashing an almighty boot up his backside, to send him pitching forward on his face to be then followed by yet another kick as he got to his knees to scuttle away up the slipway, to escape while mumbling.

"Oh God, have mercy upon the hateful libertine infidel and the heinous pagan."

There was no doubt that Gebler and I were both the pagan and infidel being referred to. And this seemed the signal for the three gents who remained facing the two of us, and clearly the rugby players of the contingent, who could now be enjoined in what could reasonably be termed a fair fight, to promptly, speedily depart. One having to proceed hopping on one shoeless foot, for Gebler had a firm hold of the other leg. It was at this moment that I spied two more figures who were all this time lurking behind a wall in reserve but who now thought the better of leaping into the breach as their cohorts limped, hobbled and crawled as fast as they could back up the slipway to their cars. The rear now being taken up by the chap Gebler had socked flying into the drink, who, with water pouring out of his shoes and with copious amounts of seaweed hanging down around his ears, now resembled a female impersonator transvestite. And the poor sodden bastard, as he scrambled backward away, had now the incredible nerve to shake his fist at us.

"We'll get ye yet, you filthy fornicator."

Clearly, the intention of these unannounced visitors had been to beat Gebler to within an inch of, if not entirely extinguish, his life. And in the present rout of this gang of Irish retreating up the slipway, and me still outraged by such bullying behavior, I had no hesitation in landing further kicks here and there on the various backsides as they fled. While at the same time shouting dire warnings as to what would happen to them if any of their lot were to be found still on the island after sundown. On the road at the top of the slipway and in this unseasonably warm afternoon sunshine, the first peaceful buzz of the bees was to be heard in the honeysuckle. And the bishop from somewhere stood with a crucifix and rosary blessing himself and giving the last rites to Edna's father, who had collapsed to his knees with what was thought to be a heart attack. The bishop now declaring, I thought, most unfairly and inappropriately,

"It's the likes of the violent pair of you down there who have brought disgrace upon a decent family and an innocent young girl."

As the culprits of the attack crept back into their cars and disappeared in a cloud of exhaust up the road and over the headland and Gebler finished thanking me for saving his life, I counted six incisor and three bicuspid teeth on the slipway and quickly ran my tongue searchingly back and forth in my mouth. Happily, neither I nor Gebler was missing any, and indeed I seemed not to have suffered a scratch. Under our own power, we made our way back again through the garden door in the wall and locked the latch. And Ernie, who did receive cuts and bruises, was a genius with home remedies and bathed and bandaged his injuries while comforting his pretty Edna, who, sobbing before, was fortunately now, as I gave ringside descriptions of the infighting, able to see the amusing side of the imbroglio and was holding her stomach, falling off her chair laughing, which equally had the rest of us doing the same as she added her own embellishments with her lilting brogue, melodiously coining poignant phrases and making observations in her inimitable Irish way.

"Mike, I do hope your mother-in-law has a sense of humor and won't be outraged by the marauding tribes of Clare on their mission to protect young virgins and who in the process have desecrated her respectable doorway."

I now made a series of threatening phone calls to the local police that my gracious and considerably prominent and influential mother-in-law's lovely villa had been besmirched by a bunch of Irish ruffians. And that one of my guests, an internationally acclaimed author, had been viciously set upon and that unless the Manx constabulary had them off the island this day I would play my own form of besmirching pop with the entire police force. I was always amazed at how I could so convincingly bullshit in this manner. But of course, the young lady Edna was not only charming but also innocent of the culpability being alleged by the ostensibly well-meaning vigilantes out to save her good name and to prevent her from being led astray by a carnal-minded best-selling writer and to put her back on the previous good path laid down for all well-bred Irish country girls. In any event, Gebler was, for all his sometimes dour qualities, one of that rare breed, a consummate gentleman. And fully deserving of the battle fought to save him from the unjust punishment intended by Edna's would-be protectors. But these Irish in revenge never give up, or at least not until you marry the girl. Which Gebler finally did as his second wife. And alas, another talented Irish writer came into being and to ultimate world acclaim. Years later it did make me remember how, before the latter lady achieved her recognition, she had been made to suffer obtuse ridicule at the hands of some of Gebler's contemporaries, pretenders to artistic sophistication, who, ready to pounce, lurked resentfully in the bitter world of Irish letters. And to whom I once announced,

"You are making fun of a young lady who will one day be the literary queen of England."

Of course, the young lady could well take care of herself and certainly needed no help from me, but I was full of such bizarrely grandiose predictions and never wasted an opportunity when I felt they could be expressed, and perhaps only for a second thinking that any of them could ever come true. In any event, as Gebler was already a literary king, it was easy enough to throw titles about. Especially as I already had in my earlier Dublin days, pretentiously as possible, readily assumed them myself. But one never knew for absolute sure who all these volunteer vigilantes were who landed out of the blue on the Isle of Man, for as participants in the most famed Irish literary fisticuffs of all time, they weren't exactly ready to admit being routed by a pair of scribblers of the written word. But they did represent a faction and a mode of action frequently resorted to in Ireland to stamp out any carnal impurity that might be thought afoot and publicly affecting the morals of the female citizenry of that land. And one knew such contingent could be gathered in a thrice by merely a whisper in an ear in any pub, especially if the perpetrator of such alleged debauchery had a foreign-sounding name. And so had I come, in my little interim away from the old sod, into contact with Ireland and the Irish again. And would you believe it:

America
Was beginning to suddenly seem
Like the land of
The free
And home of the brave
Once more

33

COMING BACK from her Jungian sojourn to Zurich and a quick visit to an Indian ashram, my mother-in-law returned. Broad-mindedly good-natured as she was, she seemed not to be too much aggrieved at the imbroglio enacted in the confines of her idyllic villa. Except that one could sense a trace of alarm as she became aware of the resulting spread of the story like wildfire across the island which alleged concupiscence and mayhem had raged through the Anchorage. But in the course of the subsequent days, she was more concerned with Valerie's and my situation of having to find somewhere to live, and not too keen regarding money Valerie could receive under her father's will. Understandable enough considering her three other children and now numerous grandchildren in whom she took much interest and even delight, and did want to see the best done for each.

And wanting to see the best done for Valerie and young Philip, I was also my usual good-natured, broad-minded self. At least up to the point when required to act as administrant of canapés and drinks at her eagerly attended cocktail parties frequented by the elite of the island. Among whom were the returned colonists deserting Africa and India, who now, without their previous numerous servants, stood about over their gins and tonics generally trying to find chinks in my continued incredibly impenetrable armor of utter and unfailing politeness. But Mrs. Heron having let it be known she wasn't going to support my ego, I soon let it be known that I was not to be used as an excuse for depriving her daughter of a modest inheritance. These entirely civil back-and-forth sentiments were discussed over tea and once over after-dinner brandy when, as the embers of the drawing room fire were beginning to fade, it suddenly developed into honesty night. As I was reminded that I did not get my book published in

America and then I in turn rudely inquired of my mother-in-law as to how it felt with so many people waiting for her to die. This unforgivably matter-of-fact remark of mine did not go down well. But again, my mother-in-law could be equally matter-of-fact. "Mike, I do assure you I will not let the thought make the rest of my life any less pleasant. And surely it's not the worst thing in the world of your having to think of getting a job."

Of course it was the very worst thing. Heinous in fact. Indeed utterly unthinkable. And now with my impatience with nonbelievers in *The Ginger Man* heightened, I was quick to respond to even the vaguest suggestion that I might be an indolent, sponging parasite. And salt was surely going to get rubbed into the wounds of these exchanging remarks, which I was the first to administer, but which, of course, were said in my usual polite manner, and again one had to admit that she took them better than well, not only inviting me to have another pale old brandy but making a smiling response.

"Well, Mike, I assure you that I shall take as much pleasure in your success as you will and, in fact, will regard my archives, which include many remarks about and many pictures of you, with renewed interest."

It was characteristic of this very attractive and mostly bravely understanding lady that she was fully prepared to take her bombastic son-in-law in stride. Assured as she was that her own four children were as talented as they were handsome. Ah, but my angst was not lessening over my predicament of where to go and what to do. I made a brief trip to Ireland, a mere half an hour away by airplane, and saw Ernie and Edna at Lake Park. They seemed to have survived their ordeal but were still living under a threat of siege. Ernie revealing that while they were away under attack on the Isle of Man, they had been invaded at Lake Park as well. Both clergy and police keeping Ernie's staff closeted in rooms to be cross-examined for several hours. Edna, although holding out, was still on tenterhooks and concerned, as Ernie, with his face of gloom and guns loaded, would wonder what was going to happen next. But would at least be able as a crack shot to knock notches off any approaching unfriendly ears, with Edna advising him,

"They'll be for the time being, especially with Mike here, withdrawn into their burrows with only their little horns sticking out to gore us. Then, their nerve restored, they'll come crawling out to crouch behind every stray stone and shrub to ambush us. And, Mike, they have me every minute I hear the dog bark running upstairs to see if I can see out the window any of them coming like the cunning caterpillars they are, creeping this way."

Returning to Dublin, I saw Tony McInerney. He'd decamped from the Catacombs, where he was to be the very last to hold sway over those dungeons, albeit upgraded by him, which had for so long been the refuge of the damned and those supremely elegant of intellect and especially those eager of further and better carnal knowledge. However, these chambers were now being occupied in a dignified family way, the former "host," so referred to endearingly, and having made a disparaging remark about a visitor and having his throat promptly reduced that night to the diameter of a shoelace by the gent this otherwise extremely pleasantly entertaining man, as a result of this violent happening, thought it safer to abandon these famed premises for all time. But then shortly afterward, Tony, with his increased brood, moved to a suburban large house. And, ah, but who should soon call just back from America but that would-be eternal tourist, Gainor Stephen Crist, who, in taking up brief residence as a guest, did by his behavior get himself barred from this McInerney mansion and Tony's hospitality for all time.

Of course these disbarments had a way of being temporarily lifted in order that they could rigidly and permanently be reimposed again. And I could imagine the kind of behavior and the goings-on that Gainor might have been involved in upon his return from the New World. He seemed now to have formulated further and more distant destinations to seek his fortune in such as Nigeria and Tanganyika. However, meanwhile he was reawakening old acquaintanceships upon making a prolonged pub pilgrimage through the ancient settlement of Dublin. But as I now walked alone through the streets of this city, I realized that a poignantly memorable era was fully and finally over. That any celebratory life that one might now anticipate to be lived might never again be lived as it had been in the romantic past. That the struggle now was just to survive with uppermost in all minds not to make the fate of young children growing up too grim. And with Ernie and Edna's recent life reminding me of the bitter narrowmindedness and bigotry, and such free-minded oases as the Catacombs gone, somehow I did not relish the thought of setting up again in what seemed Ireland's intransigent intolerance.

Trinity College too was showing its first signs of change as native Irish influence became greater within its once exclusively Anglo-Irish walls, where once Catholics feared to tread. And now through these familiar streets, I walked in bereft loneliness, one's spirit crushed further as raindrops fell upon one's back and head. But there were still erupting out of pub doorways and coming around corners the odd face that one recognized. And even some mainstays, such as the tall former heavyweight boxing champion Jack Doyle, the gorgeous Gael, back from London. Who would with assured noteworthiness always nod to me as he passed and always appeared as if walking upon a stage. Taking afternoon tea in the better cinema cafes. And always with a young lady in tow. To whom he would bow in seating her and, with an accent to match, display his elaborate internationally acquired social graces. These were the Dublin actors at large and long known to their audiences. Ready to flaunt a bogus title or make an entrance, or having caused an expected embarrassment, make a dramatic exit. But first, if there were any sign of it, be poised to take a bow to any applause.

It was such eccentric constancy that threaded together this city's random life. And it needed only the briefest of encounters to make one feel that the old Dublin one knew was still there with its antique fixtures of its citizenry intact. And as I walked down Grafton Street to its intersection with Suffolk, there was still the Jewish gentleman of these environs happily in action. Who, as rush hour approached, was still stepping out into the thoroughfare to direct traffic and courteously allow pedestrians to cross. Of course he was damn good at stopping motorcars, bicycles, barrows or drays, and was always left to do so by the Garda Siochana. His assistance being highly appreciated as might not be the case in any other city in the world. And being from a highly regarded and prosperous family he was better dressed and frequently wore a cutaway coat and striped trousers and was never without his rose or carnation in his buttonhole. But just past this point of Grafton Street, some other ancient delights were still intact, such as Jammet's restaurant. Its back entrance hidden down a narrow alley. And into which upon so many an undergraduate evening one popped to take a draft stout or two and a dish of oysters. Tucked away in the tiled sanctum of the Gentlemen Only bar. And where once, as I drank there, a chap entered who, seeing me, declared as he paused on the raised entrance step, "That beard, sir, that you are wearing is bogus."

Such a remark of course in the Dublin of that day instantly called for a challenge to a duel and the death of one of us. But the chap, upon quickly hearing who I violently was, was escorted out of sight as I laughed at his quite charming Anglo-Irish bravery, even as temporary as it turned out to be. And here I was again back in this tiled, cozy sanctum, but at the same time, feeling somehow driven away. Simply by the Old World I had known there now grown silent. Of the adventure of the roaring voices and the clowns. The chat and the ghosts. That could endure through the night, and at times go on for

A photograph taken by Murray Sayle in my aviator-looking mode, which Sayle felt would add a sense of adventure to my image.

days. And these same ghosts still chatting to whom I now listened once more. But not even this familiar and pleasant place and the sound of its phantoms seemed able to convince me to return to settle back on this isle and continue to fight in defiance of obscurity and death.

Ah, but meanwhile, back at the Anchorage Nora Heron had relented and agreed to hand over Valerie's modest inheritance, which she had promised of her own volition before we went to America. She'd already been through a similar problem with her other son-in-law, married to the eldest of her beautiful daughters. And daughters, both of whom had been hopefully destined by their parents to marry the sons of the aristocracy of the great Yorkshire mill-owning families and who had been desperately pursued by these same young gentlemen. But it was to be otherwise than according to plan. Along came her first son-in-law, who, during the war was a traditionally dashing handsome British marine corps major, and was known by the simple one-barrelled name of John Ross. Christmas holiday winter evenings in the sumptuous lounge of the house in Ilkley, Yorkshire, aflow with potted meat, ales, cheeses, vintage port, we convened and played parlor games together with our beautiful spouses such as one on the Ouija board. Guided by our fingers to spell out mediumistic messages, which I think more than occasionally I may have dared force to read.

THIS GAME IS FULL OF SHIT

Such an antic somehow reminding me of my earliest inspiration, the Katzenjammer Kids, a color strip in the Sunday newspapers in New York, over which my brother and I would delight at their misdemeanors, for which they would, in the last frame, end up being soundly spanked and seen bawling their heads off for their misbehavior. Which I, now grown up, seemed to playfully exhibit on any seemingly serious spiritual occasion. And especially to amuse my fellow brother-in-law John Ross, who had been the son of small coal merchants in a not very large town in a not very prominent southern county. And indeed thought not to be the most socially suitable prospect for the eldest beautiful daughter of my mother- and father-in-law. But Ross not only looked like a field marshal, but comported himself as such. And as his own many children arrived, and as I did one day once inquire as to how he was faring, he announced prophetic words.

"Poverty has me by the ears, but my balls still swing free."

And so at last thinking that I had the modest wherewithal to pay for somewhere to live, Nora Heron asked me when I was going to do something about it. And I, in my battle-station-ready-for-action manner, instantly said that I would be aboard a Manx steamer sailing for the mainland the following morning. Ah, but there were to be suggested covenants in Nora's overtones. That I was not to stick her beautiful daughter and grandson in another Irish pigsty or slum like the West End of Boston. But I was to buy something socially acceptable. However, with such limited funds, this I knew was not going to be easy. But I made a start. Visiting old friends I knew in Kent, Randall and Teresa Hillis. And in my first outing to look, I found the most idyllic and stunning cottage with its small garden in the town of Tenterden. The owner, a pleasantly pukka ex–service type who one sometimes found surprisingly existing in England, of a modest and unpriggish behavior and to whom one did not have to ceremoniously establish one's social credentials. With a young growing family getting too large for their little house, he was anxious to sell, and, indeed, with an abode so attractive, had no shortage of buyers. Much disposed toward me, he instructed the estate agent that even if it were a matter of one or two hundred pounds, I was to get preference over any other potential purchaser.

Ah, but this was not to be. Nora suddenly without warning reduced the amount of money available. And back in London, Gainor Stephen Crist was standing outside the telephone kiosk where I heard this news, in what was a spot and area which was as a result to come to play a future intimate role in one's life. But a stone's throw from the converging borders of West Kensington, Kensington and Fulham, it was a location near the junction of Lillie and North End roads. The red kiosk nearly arising from its foundations as I raged with flailing fist and stormed out announcing my war cry. Gainor reporting the incident to Desmond MacNamara.

"Mac, let me assure you of one thing. In Mike's difficulties with his mother-in-law, the gloves are off."

And the gloves were. And to hell with all snobberies. With money suddenly halved, instantly, if not hysterically, I abandoned all thoughts of the bijou socially acceptable country residence such as my mother-in-law had been qualifying. There could no longer be any entertaining the idea of settling in the Kent countryside, where the cricket-playing folk, as I viewed houses, referred to me as Commander because of my beard. And where, with a long face one night, after a long day's house hunting and alone at a respectable hotel bar in the idyllic town of Tenterden, a nearby drinking dentist inquired of my crestfallen demeanor. Buying each other pints of ale till closing time, we then went loudly voicing mock jocular world-weary opinions together down the main street, parting as great lifelong friends, who, as it turned out, would never see each other again. But it was back to the big smoke, London. To find somewhere suitable to my straitened circumstances, if not my family's comfort and solace within this massive conurbation through which the river Thames wends its way. And where I would now begin the search for somewhere to live, bound to be socially unacceptable and which also had to be dirt cheap.

Edward Connell became my London guide. Born there and knowing the city well, but not well enough to escape in an IRA attempt to blow up Hammersmith Bridge over the Thames. Having got caught before his bomb exploded, spending ten years in a British prison, he acquired and so had a wide reading knowledge, which served him both as a literary critic and a general fixer, having many useful criminal contacts in London's underworld. Upon passing with him through an area called Walham Green, which one could describe only as possessing a somewhat unprepossessing village aspect, I said to Connell that it was exactly the type of anonymous area that one might choose to settle in. And directly across from the tube station Fulham Broadway, I suddenly saw a cheap freehold house for sale in an auctioneer's window. It was the strangely nondescript upper-working-class aspect of this part of London in which I felt I could continue a hand-to-mouth struggle. As well as to give my mother-in-law an absolute fit.

The borough of Fulham possessed within its boundaries 1706 acres and 122,195 residents in the year 1953. And it at least could boast of some proximity to more socially acceptable districts in respect of the British life-and-death concerns with such matters. Plus it had other colorful aspects, which Connell and I observed as we reconnoitered the area and walked past a vaudeville variety theater, called the Granville. Posted at its doors were weekly changed photographs of topless love-lies. And of attractions to come. Proof for certain that one was now many moral miles away from Ireland. There were pubs, cinemas, secondhand furniture shops, a church, a town hall, a large ironmonger, greengrocers, butchers and an entire street full of market stalls and barrows. And you could buy pork pies, fish and chips and jellied eels. With its own tube station and several bus routes threading through it, although an outlying area, it was comfortably accessible to central London. But let me tell you, you'd search long and hard to find a single sign of any pukka folk within its borders.

However, as I went to investigate the cheap freehold house, things were looking up in other amenity aspects. On a footpath, I made my way across an open grassy space called Eel Brook Common, over-looked by a terrace of small but pleasantly appealing houses. Then I thought all could not be that bad as I made my way farther beneath a straight avenue of cropped poplar trees lining Wandsworth Bridge Road. However, along with the name of the borough, Fulham, every name now of every street sounding socially taboo. But on a corner, I came to the most marvelous Victorian edifice of one of London's very first cinemas called the Star. Its front elevation like that of a Grecian temple. There was a tiny post office and, directly across the street, a library. I entered a narrow, slightly crooked alley, which emerged into what could distinctly be socially less than your upper-working-class precincts. Now revealed were sprawling acres of drab, small and woe-fully humble houses, beyond which lay a vast gasworks. Turning right and past a corner bakery and row of shops and a hundred or so yards down the street, I came to number 40 and 40A Broughton Road. Resolutely I entered 40A. Almost knowing already that here within this doorway and up the narrow flight of stairs lay my fate. In this grim little street, which was to play a long and significant role in the history of *The Ginger Man*.

With two self-contained flats, one on top of the other, both had side-by-side front-door entrances. The upstairs being vacant, the downstairs flat had already-installed, long-established tenants. Paying a pittance in rent, it was not long before this getting elderly couple told me the place was falling down. And as I got a tour of their rooms, it was not hard to see that they had been discouraging previous buyers with their descriptions of damp and dilapidations and the numerous repairs required. But from my pioneering days in Ireland, I at least had a vague idea as to what made houses stand up and as to what I could do to keep them up and from falling down. Plus Eddie Connell agreed with me that the general premises, with its postage stamp garden and indoor toilet facility of combined basin and bathtub, were sound. Driving as hard a hard bargain as I could, I bought this nonbijou residence for 800 pounds. And again, as I did previously in Boston, viewing the long haul into the future, I once more deposited myself and family firmly on the wrong side of the tracks and in the most blatantly wrong part of town. So wrong, in fact, that with a bare handful of exceptions no one to whom I revealed my address either bothered to write or visit me there. Thus doing my mother-in-law no favor, but she now could hardly complain. Her disapproval shown over the many years one was destined to be there, for while I was in residence I can't remember her ever making a single visit.

Ah, but in many ways that lady was right. For let me tell you, I soon had early second nightmarish thoughts as I spent my first night in Broughton Road. Through the ceiling from below came chronic lung-rupturing coughs. My tenants, otherwise as quiet as mice, seemed to put themselves to sleep with long conversations, which I could hear as uninterrupted muttering. Then at the approach of dawn, one was awakened by a pair of talkative ladies quickly approaching with their click click click of footsteps. Passing as they rapidly would below my window every day but Sunday, the drone of their loud words finally fading at the bottom of the road, where they worked in the laundry called Sunlight. An apt name, as looming massively on the horizon above the rooftop of this cleansing business were the four vast chimney stacks of Fulham Power Station, spewing an endless white cloud of smoke out into the sky above London. And the words one most often heard spoken in this borough of Fulham, which might have applied to the winter foggy air of this vast city.

"Ere, ere, now, it makes you think."

And what made one think was an occasion which came soon enough. Of a fog so thick, turned into smog and prolonged for days, that bus conductors had to walk step by cautious step with flaming torches in front of their vehicles. And one could literally not see one's hand held up a foot or two in front of one's face. The fog seeped into the house and formed a white opaqueness across the room. Prize cattle in the then being held agricultural show suffocated to death along with four thousand people. I now knew what my tenants' lungs had gone through. However, the local electricity power station's chimneys being so high, its smoke did not offend those so near. Worse was the gasworks to the east, and it was with some relief that I would now hear aircraft pass overhead on their way to the London airport, knowing it meant then that the wind was from the west and not from the gasworks. But now with each breath I took, I despaired for Valerie's and Philip's bronchial tubes and my own.

As a nonsmoker and after the comparatively clean air of the Isle of Man and Ireland, I was appalled over one's helplessness concerning the vital air one breathed. For the first time, I became politically sensitive to the victimization of a population unable, or worse, disinterested, to do anything about it. And it did provide the one single exception to my not ever looking for a job. Upon seeing an advertisement in one of the better journals for the post of secretary to what seemed to be the first-formed Smoke Abatement Society, I applied but alas received no response. I did, however, over the next few years as a resident of Fulham provide as best I could my own remedies and made every effort I could upon every occasion available to get us away into the pure air of rural climes.

Meanwhile, I kept submitting the manuscript of *The Ginger Man* to a small variety of English publishers, and always with rejection as the result. Either turning it down out of hand or someone holding on to the manuscript to wait for an opportune time to show it further up the corporate ladder. But then it always seemed that before that could be effected by such good-intentioned people, one would sense their qualms if not their squeamishness and upon my request the manuscript would be sheepishly returned. But I had now a minutely tiny handful of admirers. And some with literary connections, such as Desmond MacNamara and his wife, Skylla. Plus here and there a literary type or two who pronounced positively upon instead of denouncing the manuscript. Then, after many a barren month went by, things suddenly began to happen to me as a plain, ordinary writer. And finally a solemn day in May dawned in the year 1954. A famed and revered English newspaper, the *Manchester Guardian,* accepted a short sketch I sent them called "My Painful Jaw." Telling of a brief encounter of sportsmanship that in fact had taken place in the ring of the New York Athletic Club.

During this time, I did have, occasionally penetrating beyond the social pale, my few visitors to Fulham. Valentine Coughlin from Ireland came. The only man ever known to be able to pledge a few pounds of your best raw steak in a Dublin pawnshop. And who had now commenced a Robin Hood life of benign villainy in London. Also visiting were two socially stalwart former Trinity men, David Romney and Glin Bennett, who, having qualified in medicine, were now both practicing doctors in London. Desmond MacNamara too braved the social opprobrium and brought his own pillow to cushion his vegetarian-nourished bottom on the hard kitchen chairs. Ah, but few in their social dread dared to tread in this district. Indeed, some of them in becoming suddenly aware of crossing the border into Fulham actually stopped in their tracks and not only retreated but ran. One such doing so, when he thought he was out of my sight, was actually sprinting to get as deep and as far and fast as he could back into the socially safe geography of Kensington. I was so dumbfounded by this that I persisted to witness this incredible phenomenon from the bridge separating the boroughs and watched him till he reached the gates of Brompton Cemetery, where he tripped and, so help me God, fell on his face into a mud puddle.

But I began to more and more understand Nora, my mother-in-law, and what she had said she did not want to have befall her daughter and grandson which had now befallen them. The social status of boroughs and postal districts in London was clearly a matter of pathological concern. Leaving me more flabbergasted than appalled. And I was quickly finding that along with my own status and that of my elegantly beautiful wife and charming little son, that we were all, save for the few visiting stalwarts, truly to be left bereft, abandoned and alone. And I remembered back to the Isle of Man, where I briefly went to write in the lonely silence of a room over a garage, across from the Anchorage, and how, bringing the world of Dangerfield with me, I could find in this snug chamber in this small stone building that it could become in minutes my own world. As did these small ten-by-ten rooms in Broughton Road, where I now worked on an oak table from the secondhand furniture store. And where I was certainly not making any new friends, and was in fact losing even all the old ones, hand over fist. Ah, but then, by God, didn't there come visiting, two others. Himself, Brendan Behan, with his equerry in tow, Lead Pipe Daniel the Dangerous, also himself. I knew that these two latter had braved the social opprobrium of the borough of Fulham because an indisputable description was given of them as they appeared at the local library, where next day the terrorized porter came up to whisper confidentially to me.

"Mr. Donleavy, two gentlemen called here at the library yesterday looking for you, saying they knew you and asking for your address. Now by the look of them, I didn't think they would be friends of yours and I thought the better of giving them your address. They wouldn't give their names, but they said they'd be back."

And finally getting my address, back Brendan did come a few days later. Bringing about one of those signal evenings in the history of *The Ginger Man.* Himself rarely to be met but by chance, he came calling as he would out of the blue. Rarely too did he ever make an appointment, and if he did you could depend upon it that it would not be kept. Just as he mostly went on his merry way, singing through the anonymous streets of London but always traveling toward a destination where he might cadge money from someone he knew. And without a single passing Londoner knowing what to make of him. Except to usually find what were meant to be friendly remarks, insulting and assisted by a quickly commandeered group of sympathizers, attacking poor Behan on the spot. But if allowed in time to use it, he could, with his cockney accent, fool them into thinking he wasn't the Irishman they thought he was and was only imitating one. However, after Valerie giving him tea and cake, he seemed more discreet in my company as we went wandering throughout the afternoon together, crossing London and proceeding as if on some strange odyssey as we might have done in Ireland. Behan stopping to chat with and striking up a camaraderie with any workmen he saw at work. Either painting, bricklaying or digging a ditch or fiddling with telephone wires. When Behan's comments were usually at their best but sometimes not that much appreciated.

"Ah, now that wire there you've got in your hand, I'd know by its royal color of crimson that it would be going straight to the queen herself."

On the beginning of our journey, village to village through London and proceeding along King's Road, we stopped in the pub The World's End to have the first of many drinks. And farther on into Chelsea. We took a surprising cup of tea at Sloane Square. The occasion being notable as the first and only time I could remember ever being in Behan's company in a premises not serving alcoholic beverages. Behan making passing quips with the waitresses and chatting across the table to anyone minding his own business. From Sloane Square, along Eaton

Square we wandered into Pimlico, somehow in London certain streets attracting one to walk them again and again. Ebury Street being one, which took us past Buckingham Palace. Behan, whose belly had become considerably rotund, was shuffling along in his down-at-heels shoes and over his open-necked, crumpled shirt, he wore a gray sweater that could originally have been of another color. He was at the time staying at the indigent man's Rowton House. And just as he would sentimentally recall his Borstal days, as if it were a time he'd spent at Eton, Harrow, Winchester or Marlborough schools, he paid lip service to the queen. And it always took one aback as Behan, the anti-British revolutionary, did so in the same fashion as would any well-connected upper-class Englishman.

"Mike, there are many more times when I'd have to say that being at Borstal were some of the very happiest days of my life. I'd be as loud as any of them singing "God Save the King" and, bejesus, I'd be at the same time trying as well not to be as sincere. Of course, in me own Dublin accent, I'd be making it known to other paddies for the same decent royal family to go fuck themselves. But speaking for myself now, Mike, I often thought I'd like to be invited in there to the palace to have a cup of tea and maybe then knock back a few balls of malt with herself. And I would too, only that I'd be shot for it by the IRA unless I had with me a bomb hanging between my legs instead of a pair of balls. But Jesus, Mike, walking now through here, this St. James's Park they call it, with no Irish gobshite ripping up the tulips or drunkenly pissing on the petunias or trying to steal and eat the pigeons, you'd have to say this was a fucking civilized city and place."

Praising as we went, Behan even waxed lyrical as we wandered past Churchill's wartime bunker, where at last I was able to tell Behan something, concerning Gainor having this war leader's private number to ring during the hostilities. Then under Admiralty Arch and across Trafalgar Square and through the swarms of pigeons fluttering and shitting everywhere. Behan continuing like a tourist guide. Announcing that we were now at Charing Cross, which marked the center of London. And that the vast edifice of Bush House, in which part of the BBC was housed, was the largest office block in the world. Behan still stopping to make quips or to talk with any stationary workman at work we passed. At the same time seeming to carry with him in his head a word count of the manuscript of *The Ginger Man*. Its numbers of chapters and its characters. And able to recall its incidents, always referring again to his own cameo appearance in the novel.

"Mike, I'm proud to appear in your book, as fictionalized and as minor as I am. For bejesus, if you told any of the major facts of my life, I'd have to sue you. But, Mike, as a writer and achieving the quality you have, you've caught up to me in age and it would make me that bit concerned now that I'm the three years older. And you've already appeared in two well-thought-of journals, *Punch* and the *Manchester Guardian*."

In reaching Fleet Street, we visited the London office of the *Irish Times,* which seemed to be regarded as an Irish literary outpost in London, and a steppingstone to greater things. Behan being well known to, and knowing, the various reporters on the Irish newspapers as well as one or two investigative journalists on the Sunday tabloids. And with any of whom he would go to drink in the pubs. Fleet Street also seemed a place for Behan to rendezvous with other Irish who'd taken up to living in London, where somehow this famed thoroughfare gave them a sense of being where it mattered. And anxious as they were to raise themselves up by their bootstraps. Behan explaining his own attraction to this canyon inhabited by Britain's national newspapers.

"Mike, it would give you the feeling being here with the presses trembling the ground beneath your feet, that you'd be at the center of the universe with the news coming in from every corner of the globe and then sending it out again twice as bad-sounding as when it came in. And it would give you an awful urge to go in somewhere fast and have a drink. And to stay there and not to worry about the world going on outside. For if it fell down, blew up or if it went off on a tangent into the nether regions of the universe, or if the Irish discovered they were Jews, and had six-sided stars instead of three-leafed shamrocks coming out their arses, you'd be the first to hear of it and ask fast for another bottle of stout."

And ask for another bottle of stout we did. Desmond MacNamara turning up briefly but unlike the rest of us always meticulously pursuing and keeping intact his careful life-surviving routines. He was probably one of the world's best perfectionists regarding the poison-free quality of food, nothing but nature's pure best ever passing his lips. MacNamara on this day had been on his cycle to Billingsgate to buy the freshest of fresh fish for his cats. And before the night was out, he would also head to Covent Garden for vegetables just in from the countryside. But this slight build of a man who by all appearances wouldn't hurt a fly, was possessed of a formidable temper, and was Dublin's first Bohemian who had long provided the hub around which apprenticing Bohemians clustered. He was also marvelously adept at inciting people's wrath and getting their goat, which he seemed to do innocently enough by merely repeating the truth. He was, however, tolerant of all, especially Gainor, and was also one of the very few to whom Behan would ever defer and about whom Behan never had a harsh word to say. A friendship that always seemed to me astonishingly strange as it was enduring and continued to exist as this night roared on. The drink flowing till the money ran out. With Behan confiding to me as we drank our last round.

"Mike, I know who will publish your book for you in Paris, a nice bunch of Americans. Let me put it down in your notebook who to get in touch with. He's the correspondent for the *London Evening Standard*. You should write to Sean White about getting published with the Olympia Press."

This information seemed like an afterthought after our long day together, and we left the pub with MacNamara and a couple of the other folk and started to walk westward up the slight incline of Fleet Street. I said to Behan that I had a ten-dollar bill in my wallet and that if it could be cashed we could buy further rounds of drink. This news instead of being welcomely received produced a vehement reaction in Behan, along with the accusation that I was withholding money in the pub which could have been spent on drinks. The fact that you could exchange dollars only at a bank did not lessen the offense that I had breached the sacred principle held by all Irishmen that you drink down every penny you have in your pocket to the last drop. As to Behan's generosity, there was no doubt. But I was also someone who had over the years been one who could be counted on to dispense constant hospitality and had bought the likes of Behan many an unreciprocated drink. But it did not lessen Behan's anger to explain that dollars were not legal tender, nor had it occurred to me in the pub to make a declaration of my assets, but here I was, now doing so. Nor did this placate Behan, as he continued his abusive diatribe. "I'll fucking well kill you, hoarding money. Well, you fucking well know the pub's shut. You're a no-good, fucking, mean, miserly cunt."

On the pavement, as I stood slightly higher on the incline than Behan, he suddenly charged, his arms outstretched to grab my lapels and his head lowered to butt me in the face. Knowing that Behan was no respecter of the Marquess of Queensberry rules, I instantly assumed he was about to kick me in the balls. And so, while fending him off with my extended arms, I had raised up my knee over my privates. Behan shouting,

"Don't you try to kick me in the balls, you fucker."

"I'm not. My knee's up to block you if you're trying to kick me in the balls. But now let me tell you, you can forget your balls because I'm going to beat the absolute living shit out of you."

Behan, in an equally belligerent mood, accompanied me out into the middle of Fleet Street, where we squared off with room to punch. MacNamara, who preferred to preserve his habit of conducting his life in a civilized manner and who had fish to bring home to his cats, disassociated himself from the both of us. Especially as Behan, once in calling on him when he was briefly out, had promptly found the fish for the cats and had cooked and devoured the lot down to the very last fin. But now the fight that nearly happened years ago was about to unfold with me assuming the role of aggressor and loudly announcing,

"I am for once and for all and at long last going to knock the living fucking shit out of you, Behan."

"That you've said twice now and it remains to be seen, you mean, miserly fucker."

Behan, when required, could always reply in his best Shakespearean English, just as he could mimic half a dozen European languages and twice as many accents. And as we stood facing each other, midthoroughfare, the traffic now stopped and piling up behind both our backs, he let off a hail of linguistic curses, especially in French, German and Gaelic. An appalled MacNamara, although keeping his safe distance, did try to keep the fast accumulating denizens of Fleet Street from harm, announcing,

"Would you ever now for safety's and fuck's sake keep well out of the way of these two highly ridiculous and mistaken adversaries, for soon the bicuspids will be flying."

With news breaking right on their doorstep, the sidewalk was collecting with printers and reporters delaying their return from their favorite pubs to their respective buildings to complete their night's work and publish their papers in the morning. Horns were honking and faces appearing at the windows of these famed emporiums of the daily printed word. And clearly one shout must have come from one of the reporters on the *Scotsman,* a revered Scots newspaper.

"Hit him in the haggis."

I feinted a fist and feigned a lunge at Behan and then skipped backward without striking a blow. As Behan came forward, I found myself aiming at a red mark in the middle of his nose. I feinted again with a left, but this time followed with an overhand right directly toward my target. My fist landed smack on the crest of Behan's nasal bone. Even with the honking horns of piled-up traffic, there was a sound of contusing flesh. Behan went down falling on his back. As he slowly seemed to regain his senses, he got up, wiping the blood pouring out of his nose on the back of his fist. As deserving as I thought it might have been, I was horrified to have hit this friend. And one of the few who had unhesitatingly acknowledged me as writer merely upon the sight of my written word.

"Are you all right, Brendan."

"I am but for my nose needing a new bridge to it and the taste of blood in my belly. That was one hell of a swipe you gave me."

And the fight just over, the police had already arrived to arrest us. Behan and I were brought up a side alley alongside the Cheshire Cheese public house. After a warning from the arresting constable not to fight again, to one's surprise both Behan and I were suddenly released. And especially to Behan's relief, as, having been deported, he was barred from entering Britain by the Home Office. I heard it later said that in it being the city part of London, the constabulary were not keen to have to be up early in the morning and travel to give evidence in Bow Street magistrates court. Meanwhile, abject apologies were exchanged between Behan and I and, arms around each other in renewed friendship, we forgave each other our trespass. I went off home back to Fulham. With Behan's fatal instruction scribbled out by him in my notebook.

> Get in touch
> With Sean White in Paris
> About getting published
> With
> The Olympia Press

34

THE NEXT DAY in Fulham, I was out attempting to investigate what I could concerning the Olympia Press. Upon returning to 40A Broughton Road, Valerie said that Behan, with a big bump on his nose, had called, along with his equerry, Lead Pipe Daniel the Dangerous, in tow, but not it seemed to wreak revenge upon me for the previous night but to borrow my typewriter, as Behan claimed his own had broken down. And perhaps there might have been some truth in this, as I knew Behan was incapable of even changing his typewriter ribbon, having more than once carried his machine to a shop for this to be done. That is when he wasn't hocking this same machine tucked under his arm as he sang his refrain, "Come meet me at the pawnshop and kiss me under the balls."

Valerie gently but firmly refused Behan's request, and said that Behan sheepishly laughed when reminded that he would be dispossessing me of the tool of my trade. Our fight was to be next to the very last time I would ever see Behan again. However, despite being socked on his arse in Fleet Street or having broken his typewriter, the momentum of his literary career was to accelerate and he was soon to become what is commonly referred to as a celebrity. And indeed an international one at that. But if anything, Behan was already a celebrity in the immediate area of wherever he went. And having been one in close quarters and now in the media at a longer distance, it was a role Behan, believing in his publicity, took on with deadly seriousness. Appearing where necessary and obeying his responsibilities to his growing fame, he also made sure his old friends got as little as none. And especially if they were in his company when he was quick to dismiss and shunt them away back into their obscurity. "Sorry, you'll have to fuck off now because I'm busy with the BBC."

I was always surprised, however, by how I would retain a deep regard for this man. For Behan, as quick as he was to become a friend, was even quicker to become an enemy. And it might never be known if he might have played both roles in the future of *The Ginger Man.* However, I somehow think not, as he was never a sneaky man. But our day in London and night in Fleet Street was to be the last time I would ever talk with him on a friendly or intimate basis. And his relationships were conducted with a vicarious haphazardry, much as they were in the early Dublin days of his more carnal associations, as he had once described to me.

"Now as to my sexuality, Mike, about which you'd hear various circulating opinions, all of which I'd be the first to admit would contain a certain accuracy and grain of truth. Incarceration in a prison for long periods without too much distraction would cultivate the mind in that respect. But the simple matter of it is that I'd have a go at anything. Except maybe attracting too much attention might be a cardinal dressed in his full regalia and him up on an altar at St. Peter's in Rome and saying mass to the devout. But many is the time I'd be somewhere like down in the Catacombs and come that inglorious time of morning with the first faint light filtering down through the dungeon windows, and you'd be yourself slowly coming back into your senses and you'd still be on top of what you'd been shagging through the night and it would, with nothing better to do with your curiosity, put you to wondering whom or what it was beneath you. And bejesus if their backs were to you and you couldn't see the face, and if they weren't bald, you'd be as gently as you could taking them by a tuft of hair to turn their heads over to see who it was, male or female, doctor or nurse, priest or nun, members in good standing of the purgatorial society or someone from the very top in government or in the meat or rag trade and you'd wonder how did you start the conversation about Ireland needing a labor leader, or about fabrics or the poor price of livestock. And bejesus it would be sometimes a shock to find somebody to my utter surprise if not horror that I'd been fucking or buggering through the night and I'd be wanting to disconnect the private parts of us both as soon as etiquette permitted and introduce myself in order that we might sensibly discuss if there were any better way to do what we were doing and arrange for a more decent place and a time convenient to do it again. But in all these encounters, Mike, I'd always give of my best and dispense to all an equal and deep amount of prodding, showing favoritism to none."

But like Behan himself on this day in London, I was out attending as best I could to my profession as a writer. In any event, I might have been in the vicinity of Tottenham Court Road, as this was an area of London with which I had long been familiar. Having as an undergraduate during my Trinity College days and on my unpremeditated mystery tour excursions of England, always finding myself when ending up in London, holed up in a hotel somewhere not far from Euston Station and in the neighborhood of Holborn and St. Pancras. From here, I would then wander on the periphery of Bloomsbury, west by southwest toward Soho and through streets where there were, following the war, still many a vacant bomb site or a temporary makeshift replacement building. And one particular pub, which, put back together with temporary partitions, gave its character such a curious ugliness that I could never pass by without finding myself drawn in and ending up drinking a pint or two of mild and bitter.

As the drama of *The Ginger Man* would unfold, I was to get to know this area of London well. For it was not that far away from this war-wounded pub that I walked into Zwemmer's, one of the many bookshops that lined Tottenham Court Road, and here found my first evidence of the existence of the Olympia Press, Paris. The name appeared on the cover of a literary magazine called *Merlin*. Nearby I came across a copy of the novel *Watt* by Samuel Beckett, printed in paperback with a mauve cover and published August 1953 by the Olympia Press in what was designated "Collection Merlin." The mauve paper cover of Beckett's book was edged by white asterisks and had the black imprint of the silhouette of a bird. I assumed the word Merlin was to mean as interpreted in the dictionary, both a small European falcon and the name of the soothsayer of Arthurian legend. Beckett's work, as did Joyce's before him, had on its last written page notice of where and when the novel had been completed.

"Paris 1945."

There was a stirring of a certain romantic excitement in the whole idea of Paris, for generations long reputed as a friendly home away from home for artists and writers and a city where I had visited and a place where such as Henry Miller had roamed. Beckett too had previously been made known to me by an early girlfriend who mentioned *More Pricks Than Kicks* to me down in the Catacombs. I then quickly interpreted this title as meaning and being what many a lady got given her down in such infamous dungeons. Beckett himself, however, always seemed to safely stay away in Paris well out of the reach of

Dublin's resentment and begrudgers. And the occasional references to Beckett were always made with a feigned indifference, as if, having eliminated himself from Dublin's bitterness and its smoldering envy, he was no longer deserving of its attention. And like Joyce before him he seemed also to be setting an example of exile and cunning. And too, we had something in common, both our mothers had houses and had lived in Greystones, County Wicklow.

Conscious enough of having already found numerous interferences and delays in using intermediaries in dealing with the manuscript of *The Ginger Man,* and upon finding the address of the Olympia Press, I wrote directly off to 8 rue de Nesle. Which vaguely reminded me of the name of a chocolate bar one knew of growing up in America. But in the years to come, there was to be nothing sweet about this address. And my visits there would grow into a gargantuan nightmare to haunt me. Unlike Behan, who, now enjoying recognition and whose first radio play, "An Giall," written in Irish and later translated into English as "The Hostage," did not hesitate to sing the praises of this city of grandness called Paris.

"Being a writer in that city, Mike, it wouldn't strike you as strange to be walking into a cafe and have everyone jump to their feet to applaud you. They wouldn't, of course, liking their food and drink too much and for fear of upsetting the glasses, cups and saucers. But they'd regard you with a bit of awe. Whereas in fucking Dublin, they'd be on their feet all right, next to you, trying to figure out how to cadge another drink or get a loan of a fiver out of you first before they'd be blackguarding you behind your back, hammering verbal galvanized nails deep as they could get them into your reputation. And if not doing that, then they'd be sidling up in order to appear like an intimate acquaintance, only on their mind would be thinking how they could give your balls a kick."

Paris was to play a significant role in both our lives. And I had myself hearing of the splendors of the spaciousness of the boulevard of the Champs-Elysées and the ambience of the cafes, set off there in 1947 to experience my first bedbugs. Surviving these bloody little creatures, I went again in 1948 with Valerie to spend the weeks of one summer in the top-floor room of a hotel in rue St.-André-des-Arts. There was no doubt that one found it easy to feel at home on the banks of the Seine with a bottle of wine, a baguette and *saucisson.* And Behan's romantic visions of Paris were amazingly years hence to befall him and be exactly as he described. Applause greeting him not only in cafes but on the boulevards as he would, with his garrulousness and grand gestures and despite his atrocious Irish grammar, turn his fluent Irish into a form of French argot and mimic and repeat anything in this new personal language of his which struck his fancy. Behan anyway would have been the life of the party in any language and in any place, but the French especially seemed to take to his bonhomie. Although along with such adulation and with being many a time drunk and disorderly, he got the occasional attention of Paris's gendarmerie, who would courteously remove him into custody to preserve the peace.

"Jesus, Mike, if I wasn't a fucking writer and them knowing it, the fucking police could be a fucking vicious lot."

For myself years hence, when seen in a Paris cafe, it was more likely to be an American who would glance my way. But if it were the odd habitué of that city, he would stare at me as if he had seen a ghost and then as quickly be back minding his own business as if I were a ghost. And I nearly became one. Saved only by having got up on my own two feet and shaken my lone fist against the enemy I was discovering inhabited the literary and art world. For I had got some very early and memorable lessons taught me of the cunning, intrigue and fervently friendly arse kissing that governed such domain. John Ryan, one of my earliest friends in Dublin, and I had decided to exhibit our pictures. We had previously been going to have a joint exhibition of paintings together until he had been advised by an American pal I'd introduced him to not to have such an association with me, as it could ruin his reputation. This of course I might have done, as I was already being accused of being all nerve and no talent. But all was solved by splitting the two weeks for which we had rented the gallery. And fooling critic and public alike, and even myself, I was then adjudged as being not much worse than anybody else in Dublin as a painter.

But more intrigue and backbiting was to be forthcoming when Ryan decided to start a literary magazine, which he finally named *Envoy*. I got money from my mother to invest in this new excursion into this world of the written word. My enthusiasm being for the best work to see the light of day against Ireland's bitter intolerance and repression. I extolled the names of two deserving, the poet Patrick Kavanagh and Behan, who in good Dublin fashion grew to detest each other. But it was only Kavanagh who early managed to enter the pages, with Behan following later. But as I saw the magazine, and not unreasonably and well meaning in Ryan's case, take on what was to me the wrong bias and purpose, namely that of publishing writers and extolling painters already established and famed, I withdrew. As the magazine went on without me, Ryan brought about a communion of writers, artists, poets and composers which was to make for a literary period in Dublin. Meanwhile, I had, through my good-natured manner, introduced my own cultivatedly literate friends to Ryan, who helped foster artistic matters while I retreated alone to fight my own battles. And those who did not hinder me in this regard refused to resist against those who intended detriment and bane, isolating me yet further.

I had not then nor have I done since ever taken up a position of hindrance to another's work. But by God, I was soon finding out what sly experts they were who did, and who are to be found lurking in abundance among the literary fraternity and against whom one had to hone one's resolve. However, back in those early days, Ryan, as the entire finance of the magazine, persisted, and so for my first time in print, "A Party on Saturday Afternoon" was duly published in *Envoy,* volume 2, number 1, April 1950. But in the battle to stop it, the powers behind the scenes made sure my little story did not get even a first page all to itself, and it started midpage, at the end of another's work. But at least and at last, the words were out and printed there between the covers of this Dublin literary magazine for all those interested to read. However, I was about to embark upon a mountainous sea of nothing but obstruction, deception and betrayal and a protracted battle fighting for, not only my literary life, but my very life. And during the coming years that old refrain of my naval days would often come wafting back to mind and is now worthy again to repeat with an added stanza.

When you find a friend
Who is good and true
Fuck him
Before he fucks you

And even if he isn't a friend
Good and true
Don't worry
He will still try
To fuck you

35

IN THE MONTH OF AUGUST 1954, I started to write the novel *A Fairy Tale of New York*. A month later I wrote to the Olympia Press, Paris, as follows:

40A Broughton Road,
Fulham, London, SW6,
Sept. 7th 1954

Dear Sir,

I have a manuscript of a novel in English called *Sebastian Dangerfield* of approximately 125,000 words. While in America I submitted it to Charles Scribner's Sons in New York City. Although impressed by it they felt they could not publish it because of obscenity. The obscenity is very much a part of this novel and its removal would detract from it. Extracts of it have, however, been published in *Manchester Guardian*.

I would be very pleased if you could give me any information as regards your position in considering manuscripts, such as mine in English, for publication in English in France.

Yours sincerely,
J. P. Donleavy

Mail of the time must have been gossamer swift, for back came, on this gray notepaper I was to get to know better than well, an immediate reply.

THE OLYMPIA PRESS

8 rue de Nesle, Paris 6,
September 8th 1954

Dear Sir,

We thank you for your letter of the 7th September.

We should be glad to consider your manuscript for publication. Will you please take good care to send it registered.

Yours sincerely,
Maurice Girodias

I had these days been taking my son, Philip, daily on a Number 28 bus to Holland Park to play there. Meeting a young French au pair girl, whose charge had become a friend of Philip's, and having carried the letter with me, I showed it to her. The first thing she did was to run her thumbnail across the black imprint of the name Olympia Press and say with satisfaction that the lettering was engraved and that at least it indicated something of consequence in the matter of substantiality. But there was, she said, also to be regarded a slight flippancy in monsieur's signature. Further correspondence ensued.

40A Broughton Road,
Fulham, London, SW6,
October 18th 1954

Dear Sir,

I sent you a MS called *Sebastian Dangerfield* insured, September 11th.

It seems there is some difficulty checking on it from this end and I'm a little anxious to know if you received it safely.

I would be very pleased if you could let me know.

Yours sincerely,
J. P. Donleavy

8 rue de Nesle, Paris 6,
October 30th 1954

Dear Sir,

We have finally received your MS which has been detained some time by the French Customs who wanted to ascertain whether it had a negotiable value or not. This, of course, explains the delay.

We will write to you within two weeks in order to let you know what is our readers' report on the book.

Yours sincerely,
M. Girodias

With relief at the safe arrival of the manuscript, there was now the added bonus of this reply letter sounding like a publishing house. Although the words "our readers' report" did rather remind of these lurking opportunists lying in wait in such capacity, who would, if left unnoticed, dare to suppress and drive away the original. Which had already seemed to be the case with all the British publishers the work had been submitted to. But I had been further breaking out of the confines of my obscurity with my third piece, "Fraternal Fraud," accepted and soon to be published in the *Manchester Guardian.* A young editor on this famed paper, John Rosselli, who told me later upon meeting him that he knew exactly how I wanted my words to read and wrote "follow copy" in the margin of each of my pieces wherever he thought any printer's doubt might creep in to make a well-meant corrective change.

Instead of two weeks, there was now a gap of November and nearly all of December, and following Christmas, and rabbit for dinner on the thirty-first, I wrote to the Olympia Press requesting a decision. The significance of rabbit for dinner was survival. However, there were two people invited to celebrate this with us, one Valentine Coughlin, who masqueraded as Percy Clocklan in *The Ginger Man,* and the other Eddie Connell, who, after his stint with the IRA, was now, of all things, a lamplighter along the private roadway of Kensington Palace Gardens and the vicinity of the palace itself. Coughlin arrived on time, and, as we waited further for Connell, he asked if I'd told Connell what we were having for Christmas dinner and I said yes I had, I had warned him just as I had warned them both.

"Ah, well sit down then now and eat the dinner. There's no point in wasting time waiting for him another second, for hearing of rabbit he won't be here, he'd be elsewhere thinking he'd do better with an invitation to turkey. Sure how would the insensitive likes of him know a rabbit is a true gourmet's delight."

THE OLYMPIA PRESS

December 30th 1954

Dear Mr. Donleavy,

First of all, I must apologize for the delay in replying to your last letter; your book, considered from a publisher's point of view, raises a number of problems and we did not want to give you a full report on it without first comparing the opinions of several readers.

Let me say at once that all its readers have been able to find very striking qualities in your novel; but it has also been their feeling that it would not be to do you or *Sebastian Dangerfield* justice were the novel to be brought out in its present form. Apart from the manuscript's need of a considerable amount of editing (spelling, syntactical ambiguities, missing words) which could conceivably be done by ourselves, there are two more major problems. Firstly: the opening part seems to drag, to be hesitant, to be ineffective: it needs sharpening, it needs to be made more incisive. Secondly: elsewhere, indeed, almost everywhere, there is a need for condensation.

The reader does not become engaged in the book, nor feel its impact, until he reaches page 100 or thereabouts. It is hard to explain just why, especially hard when one rereads this opening hundred pages after having gone through the entire book, for then the vagueness disappears, and what seemed inaccessible at first reading is vivid upon second. Nevertheless, several readers have, independently, reached the same conclusion: action, they feel, should appear almost at once, the main characters should be distinguished more decisively . . .

We would suggest shortening these opening 100 pages; but almost all the book calls for the same revision. Above all in the long soliloquies, the interior monologues, proportion and control seem sometimes to falter, with the result that what would often benefit from terseness, prolongs into vagary and repetition. Were it reduced in length by one fifth, or one quarter, or even one third, the book would gain thereby. It is not a question of deleting episodes, but of weeding out what blurs them, of sharpening and lightening. This is the difficult job, this is the author's, and it is very possible you do not share our views. But we do feel that the matter deserves your thought.

The problem of the title is relatively minor. However, the deliberate modesty of simply *Sebastian Dangerfield* is a little stark and, in a sense, rather than giving the book a name, suggests that it lacks one.

I will be awaiting your response to these various points before I take a final decision regarding your book whose clear virtues have prompted us to mention faults—only because we would like to see them, if faults they are, eliminated. I earnestly hope that we will come to an agreement as to these matters of form.

Our custom is to pay a round sum for each printing of the books we publish, and we will make a definite offer as soon as your answer to this letter is received.

Can you at the same time let us know what extracts from the book have been printed by the *Manchester Guardian?* Can you provide any acknowledgments or reviews which we might use as publicity? We are keeping your MS with us until we hear from you.

Yours sincerely,
M. Girodias

P.S. Just before closing this letter I receive yours of December 31st. I will do as you wish regarding the MS, but I will not send it back before I hear from you.

M.G.

Although I was unaware of what Girodias was ultimately planning, I knew that the nature both in style and language of *The Ginger Man* was unlikely to have come across this publisher's bows before. It seemed, despite his fluency, as if a certain naive dichotomy existed with Mr. Girodias, especially as in rereading the manuscript he was finding it vivid and the vagueness disappearing. However, having gone through the book, I myself was aware of inconsistencies and misspellings. I also got the feeling that he simply wanted a shorter book. However, my first more serious uncertainty came concerning his letter's mention of page 100. For when referring to this part of the manuscript, there appeared at this point the first considerable account of a sexual nature. In considering the remaining matters raised in the letter, which, although sounding well-meaning, I thought erroneous and they were not suggestions I could follow. No such criticisms had been raised by Gainor Crist, Brendan Behan, John Hall Wheelock, A. K. Donoghue nor Julian Moynahan. The last to become a distinguished critic and novelist. However, above all other things, I had to take seriously the fact that here at long last was at least a publisher undeterred by obscenity, indeed making no mention of it at all, who seemed willing to publish. And one week later, I put my fingers to my typing keys and I accordingly replied. Following my precept that thou shalt not bluff in love, negotiation or litigation. But attempt to be diplomatic and polite to all.

January 6th 1955

Dear Mr. Girodias,

Thank you for your letter of December 30th, I am pleased you are interested in my MS.

I have read your letter carefully and note the points you make. As I'm sure you will understand, the amount of work to be undertaken to revise the MS as you suggest is considerable and would mean, for me, laying aside for some time, work I am now doing. I therefore feel that under the circumstances any decision I would make in the matter of revision would largely depend on your offer.

Could you let me know the size of a printing and the approximate price you charge for a book? If you have a catalogue you could send me I'd be very pleased to see it.

One extract I have switched to a revision which is not yet with copy you have. The other appears on page 244 and starts with 'I got off at the back gate out of the green upholstered tram and there was the university through my apprehensive eyes. . . .' and ends 'but I was smiling so pleasantly so willing to please.' These appear by way of sketches on the review page of *Manchester Guardian* and are not reviewed that I know of. . . . However, I have received a request from University of Dublin's graduate magazine for permission to reprint the extract which appears in your copy. It is an annual which is sent free to graduates. Other work of mine has also appeared in *Punch*.

I do hope you see my position regarding *Sebastian Dangerfield* and I would be very happy to discuss the points you suggest when I hear from you.

Yours sincerely,
J. P. Donleavy

P.S. I tried to get copies containing extracts from *Guardian* office here in London but they appeared May and June last year and this office only keeps back copies for 3 months. However, I got a more recent copy which has some of my work and I am sending it to you under separate cover.

Our letters now, if their dates were to be believed, were swift in passing back and forth. My own post office being located in a shop just around the corner within a couple of minutes' walk up the shortcut narrow confines of Bryan's Alley. Selling greeting cards, stationery, chocolate and even toys, it was the sort of shop you might expect to find in a rural English village. Behind her counter, rapidly dispensing service, was an always smiling, rosy-cheeked, raven-haired lady of ample proportions, who sold stamps, weighed parcels and administered pensions to retired folk. Also assisting the swiftness of communications were two deliveries by the postman every weekday. The letters to be seen from the top of the stairs, dropping through the letterbox and falling to a mat on the floor. And the trepidation and dread was to increase over the years as one would descend these wooden steps to discover what new threatening words were to be found within the envelopes lying there. But for the time being I was still pleased enough to get correspondence and the financial representations now proffered by Maurice Girodias.

THE OLYMPIA PRESS

January 7th 1955

Dear Mr. Donleavy,

Thank you for your letter of January 6th.

In reply to your questions concerning our terms, our customary practice is to offer a standard sum of 200,000 francs (paid half upon delivery of the final MS, half upon date of publication) for the first printing of roughly 5000 copies, and an additional 300,000 francs for each subsequent printing.

The retail selling price will be about 750 francs. In the case of your book, our idea would be to print over and above the regular paperbound edition, another 500 probably clothbound copies for the British and American markets. It is of course more than likely that *Sebastian Dangerfield* would be banned in both the U.K. and U.S. While the publicity created by banning often favours sales, banning does also often involve risks for the author as well as the publisher, and we would only proceed with our proposed 500-copy American and English edition if it were to receive your approval. Upon these 500 special copies we would pay a royalty of 10% of the retail price on all copies actually sold.

That in general is the offer we should like to make you as soon as we receive your agreement regarding the revision of the MS.

Your MS is being returned to you by registered post.

Yours sincerely,
M. Girodias

The businesslike look and sound of the Olympia Press letters were welcome enough, but as I was more familiar with a percentage royalty on each book sold I was not entirely happy about Girodias's standard and customary practice of payment of sums for each printing. But after nearly five years following beginning to write *The Ginger Man,* my concern for the actual publication of the work was now considerable. Especially as Valerie was expecting another child in three months. I could not avoid the slight tendency to letting myself assume the notion that publishers would, since their livelihood depended upon it, automatically look after and protect an author's interests. And although I was wary, there seemed to be an element of this in Monsieur Girodias's letters and of his giving warning of the risks involved in the novel being banned. I had also been brought up by parents who, in their astonishingly un-Irish way, exampled and taught to their children scrupulous honesty and a policy of fairness with others. And alas something which one perhaps overly expected to be reciprocated. However, because of this, one held an equally strong principle of revenging a wrong. But being cheated on a large or serious scale, or coming across someone daring to do this, was the least of one's expectations. And now in my most reasonable, businesslike manner I could muster, I replied.

January 11th 1955

Dear Mr. Girodias,
Thank you for your letter of January 7th and your list enclosed.
In view of your offer, which I don't consider unreasonable within its

terms, I would prefer, in the case of *Sebastian Dangerfield,* to deal on a royalty basis with one initial advance, half on delivery of MS and half on publication. The following arrangement is something I would be prepared to accept as it stands. For the publication rights of *Sebastian Dangerfield* in English in France, 150,000 francs as an advance on 10% royalty of the retail price on first 5000 copies, 12$\frac{1}{2}$% on next 5000 copies and 15% on copies sold over 10,000.

I would agree to undertake a revision which would reduce *Sebastian Dangerfield* by at least one fifth condensing, sharpening and cutting where necessary. It is conceivable that I could introduce action earlier in the book, but this is something, as I'm sure you will understand, I can't promise for such a promise might easily have the opposite effect and restrain me in dealing with this part. As you say, the problem of a title is relatively minor. However, *Sebastian Dangerfield,* although stark and perhaps modest, does offer scope in its use on a cover and in advertising, being eminently suitable as two very large letters on the cover, and as *Sebastian Dangerfield* is an inductive book this would seem appropriate. But this, of course, is something that can be worked out.

Should we be able to reach a final agreement and presuming that I revise *Sebastian Dangerfield* in say within two to three months, when would you propose publication?

In the matter of 500 probably clothbound copies for British and American markets, I would be prepared to accept your offer of 10%, but, as you point out, it involves risks for author and publisher, and I think it would be best for me to make a decision on this later.

I note you have returned my MS by registered post and thank you. I look forward to hearing from you.

Yours sincerely,
J. P. Donleavy

My assertions concerning my revisions in the manuscript did reserve my position, as my reply to John Hall Wheelock did, which I knew beforehand could not be fully carried out, but at least it let the publisher know that I was in some sympathy with his observations. However, as I had already been long accustomed to the fact that everyone's opinions would be as subjective as one's own, and vary accordingly, that one's own opinion in the end must take priority over all. The manuscript of *The Ginger Man* was certainly hefty enough. And although the style of one's writing was already concise and condensed, I knew there existed sentences and descriptions which might beneficially be either shortened or eliminated. But I was now aware too that I had perfected knowing when words had reached the point where they were saying exactly what I wanted them to say and also knew instinctively that they were in their final form, and each word relying on every other in a paragraph for its full meaning.

THE OLYMPIA PRESS

January 13th 1955

Dear Mr. Donleavy,

Thank you for your letter of January 11th.

I am afraid that I cannot accept your counter proposal. I am willing to raise amount payable for the first printing to Frs. 250,000, but I have good reasons not to go any further.

Our "Season" begins in April; if we could receive the final MS by the end of March, we could bring out the book in April or May.

Yours sincerely,
M. Girodias

As the grip of negotiation tightened, our letters immediately constricted in wordage, and there was added a couple of more days to these recent exchanges.

January 17th 1955

Dear Mr. Girodias,

Thank you for your letter of January 13th.

I will accept your offer.

Could you let me know what formalities, if any, are necessary to obtain Copyright protection in my name in France and on Continent?

As an alternative to *S.D.,* I offer *The Ginger Man* as a title.

Due to the possibility that my final MS might again be held for some time by customs and delay delivery to you, I wonder if you would be good enough to keep in mind and let me know of any person who may be making trip, London–Paris, end of March, with whom I could entrust MS.

Yours sincerely,
J. P. Donleavy

The significance of the title was that "Ginger" did to some degree describe Dangerfield not only in coloration but also in mettle and spirit. And this letter in its stamped envelope I gave to Philip to post in the local letterbox. We then took a Number 11 bus to Victoria to look for a chair to buy in the Army and Navy store. Meanwhile, in Fulham, I had continued to repair and improve the rooms we lived in and laid the best quality obtainable of squares of linoleum on the small sitting room floor. One evening the two gentlemen from whom I'd bought the squares and who had been laying the same at the new London Heathrow Airport called to see how I was getting on. Upon observing my floor and the expert job done, I was offered for the first and last time in my life a job which was to join them finishing their contract at the airport. I was of course greatly delighted but declined this pleasing suggestion, feeling that I was on my way as an author, and especially now as came the first signs from Girodias of publishing cheerfulness, optimism and hope.

THE OLYMPIA PRESS

January 19th 1955

Dear Mr. Donleavy,

Thank you for your letter of January 17. I take good note of your agreement.

I do hope that we will help to make a success of your book. I think that we might find a publisher for an eventual French version, if you are interested.

Your new title, *The Ginger Man,* seems much better than *Sebastian Dangerfield* to me. However, if you find something else, please let me know.

I am anxious to know when the final MS will be available.

Yours sincerely,
M. Girodias

My previous year's income from writing was thirty-six pounds, ten shillings. An amount that at the rate of my abstemious outgoings of five pounds a week did mean in Broughton Road that I had added seven weeks to my family's survival. A period not seeming a lot longer to stay alive but emotionally encouraging if one thought sunnier climes were ahead and one generously applied one's imagination. And now with the suggestion of a French version, there was even a modest hint of fulfilling Behan's predictions in Paris of a cafe's habitués getting to their feet to applaud one's appearance. Indeed for the first time, one felt a considerable measure of anticipation and accomplishment as I immediately applied myself every day to the manuscript. Plus my four previous publications in Britain had been meeting with an admiring word or two from odd readers. Although I wisely stayed true to my usual policy of allowing myself to remain wracked with humility.

January 27th 1955

Dear Mr. Girodias,

Thank you for your letter of January 19th and also for MS, which I have safely received.

At moment I can't predict exactly when MS will be ready. At present I'm finishing revision of last 50 pages. Then must rewrite first 100 but in middle part, I may be able to paste over revision and this should save time. However, in a fortnight or so, I should be able to give an approximate date.

Meanwhile, I'd be very grateful if you could send me a draft of your proposed contract to which your offer is subject.

I do appreciate your kind wish for the success of my book, and look forward to hearing from you.

Yours sincerely,
J. P. Donleavy

Ah, but here in my last two sentences of this January 27th letter are, as one sees now, some slightly timorous and innocent words suggesting more than just modesty and perhaps just that little hint of inviting to get hit soundly from behind with a crowbar. But also my letter contained the first mention of that all-pervading legal word, "contract." And if Girodias was already planning to publish *The Ginger Man* as a pornographic work and perhaps even scheming to cheat me, the word "contract" should have alerted him to some measure of caution. But at this stage, I could think only that at last the bitter battle to put the mealymouthed in their cowardly place along with the doubters and begrudgers had arrived. I was even for the second time taking the initiative in correspondence.

February 10th 1955

Dear Mr. Girodias,

I've finished a revision which includes last one hundred pages from which I've cut thirty-seven. And am now working on first hundred and middle.

As far as I can now judge, I should be able to finish MS by March 25th and, of course, will try to do so sooner, if possible. At that time I hope to find someone to deliver it to you.

I would be interested in an eventual French version. Could you let me know what page size you intend book to be.

Yours sincerely,
J. P. Donleavy

Throughout the previous month of January, I was not without worry pangs over *The Ginger Man* but felt the work itself would always withstand all that might be adverse visited against it. My life now including visits to Holland Park also consisted of daily walks and travels around London with Philip, visiting museums and galleries. And even calling at the Ritz Hotel to pee. Here observing people in elegant clothes and glittering with jewels, and a long, long way away from Fulham. And then arrived a letter which seemed like a forthright piece of information and warning.

THE OLYMPIA PRESS

February 11th 1955

Dear Mr. Donleavy,

Thank you for your letter of February 10th.

I am glad to hear that your revision is progressing in a satisfactory manner. I do hope that you will be able to complete the job quickly.

We should now start advertising the book for publication in May, and we therefore have to decide on the title *and* the author's name.

The Ginger Man does suit me as a title; but I would like to know whether you want the book to be published under your own name or under a pseudonym? Please think it over. Of course, my firm has a rather scandalous reputation, and it might harm you in some way to publicly admit any connection with us. . . . On the other hand, we have published the works of a few quite genuine writers; so I will leave you free to choose your own solution. . . . Please let me know what you decide in that respect.

Yours sincerely,
M. Girodias

This letter came somewhat as a surprise, for it now appeared written by someone who assumed there could be a question as to the author declaring himself the creator of a work the publisher referred to as having striking qualities. But for the first time it indicated that Girodias's opinion of the work, and referring to its striking qualities, might be in the sense of "pornography," a word I interpreted as meaning deliberately written obscenity which was obvious in titles listed in the catalogue I had now received. I had not yet come across the Olympia Press's pseudonymous and pornographic works which, if they were then in existence in England, were not openly circulated or openly available for sale. But since I had seen Samuel Beckett's book *Watt* and the literary magazine *Merlin,* and Girodias had mentioned that he published genuine authors, I assumed by his most recent letter and sending his catalogue that I was not to be left innocent of his other less literary works. In any event, if I had any qualms concerning his warning, I waited no longer than twenty-four hours to state my position.

That I had written a work now called *The Ginger Man* and wanted it published under my own name as the author.

*Self-portrait of the
honest-faced young man.*

THE OLYMPIA PRESS

February 17th

Dear Mr. Donleavy,

Thank you for your letter of February 14th.

We are prepared to send you review copies outside France and would like to know whether you have a list of reviewers, etc., to whom you would like the books to be sent.

As to advertising, we might also, if we obtained a few good reviews, advertise in certain English and eventually American papers.

Yours sincerely,
M. Girodias

Upon the arrival of Girodias's reply, it seemed now as if we were back on course, with the steps to be taken to assist *The Ginger Man*'s assault upon the world. And as momentum increased toward publication, I attempted to find names to have the book sent to, and wrote the following letter.

February 28th 1955

Dear Mr. Girodias,

Thank you for your letter of February 17th.

I don't have a list of reviewers offhand but one or two to whom I would like copies sent and will forward these on to you.

I offer another possible title: *Even on Judgment Day.*

Yours sincerely,
J. P. Donleavy

From Trinity College, Dublin, there had come into being a small group consisting of Paul Allen and Brian Parker, who, along with an Igor Chroustchoff, a Londoner, would occasionally invite me to assemble with them and take walks along the Thames towpath or meet in Fleet Street for a drink. All of these gentlemen had seen the manuscript of *The Ginger Man* and were interested to hear of its progress with the Olympia Press. They were, unlike Behan and Lead Pipe Daniel the Dangerous, quietly studious and eminently polite. But, like Behan and Lead Pipe, were scholarly and highly literate, and were the closest I was ever to get in England to associating with men of letters who soberly took the culture of the written word seriously. Brian Parker one evening in Fleet Street saying,

"Mike, you've got to read a wonderful book, *Catcher in the Rye,* by J. D. Salinger, a work that's gone hand to hand around the world."

And it was from such gentlemen not only that I was to get an idea of what books to read, but also a list of possible reviewers to send to the Olympia Press.

March 1st 1955

Dear Mr. Girodias,

The following is a list of the publications to which you might send review copies. Should I find more or reviewers who want to review book, I will send these on to you.

Irish Times
Irish Press
Spectator
Manchester Guardian
Truth
Punch
Paul Allen, c/o *Courier*
Time & Tide
Brian Parker, c/o *Belfast Newsletter*
Sunday Times
Encounter
The London Magazine

I realize my last suggested title may have been sent too late to you. However, could you let me know what you've decided, as it bears on one or two points in book.

I have cut about twenty pages out of first hundred. In middle I find most revision is a matter of cutting and I may be able to finish sooner. Could you advise me on any special way I might mail MS to prevent its being held by customs. Will you send me any copies for my own use.

Yours sincerely,
J. P. Donleavy

I was now rapidly working on the last manuscript pages, bringing them with me with Philip on the 28 bus to Holland Park. As Gainor had gone to Spain, the place he always planned to go to, this route reminded of him as it went along the long line of market stalls of the North End Road and passed near the pork pie factory and the purple house, where Gainor had lived in well-organized respectability with Pamela on Lillie Road. The bus route continued through West Kensington and past a drinking spot of Gainor's in North End Crescent which sported an open fireplace, carpets and mahogany staircase, and was his most frequently visited. Then further on came one of Gainor's favorite names for a pub, the Live and Let Live. And into this tavern, he had more than once tugged me by the arm to drink.

As the weather got warmer we made this trip to Holland Park nearly every day. I came to sit near the formal gardens and on a terrace where each day nannies and au pairs wheeled their charges and where I would frequently meet the same charming French au pair. But if I came early enough, I chose to go sit alone on a bench in a brick shelter built into the garden wall. There were occasional contretemps among these mostly well behaved children. However, more often there came a particular situation which seemed to arise in a thicket of shrubbery where various little boys would, having disappeared into these bushes, suddenly emerge running, screaming and leaving behind them another little boy whom they would accuse of hitting them. It was with this alleged perpetrator of such crime that Philip, but no one else, seemed to get on famously. And one day a man came to sit down next to me.

"You don't mind if I sit down here, do you. For moral support. My boy seems not to get on with anyone else's children except your son. My name's Robert Pitman."

It was true that Philip seemed to exert an extraordinary charm with other children. Even leading to an ambassador's son refusing to go away on holidays because he could not bear to miss playing with Philip

416

in the park. However, Philip occasionally chose to be less than his pleasant charming self, when, one day returning from Holland Park and waiting for the bus, he leaned over and sank his teeth deep into my thigh and my scream of agony opened up windows for miles around. However, in my more peaceful moments, I was now writing in my last corrections and emendations and making my final preparations to sending off the manuscript to the Olympia Press. Upon Pitman seeing the manuscript, he inquired concerning it and the work I was doing. He then said he wrote articles for a Labour Party newspaper and occasionally for the *Sunday Express,* which latter paper's staff he'd just been asked to join. He asked if a review copy of *The Ginger Man* might be sent him on publication. An eventuality that was to bring about the fame of *Lolita* and to affect the entire literary career of Vladimir Nabokov.

As the news spread of the impending publication in Paris, Chroustchoff, Parker and Allen knew of further names interested to get a review copy of the novel, and I duly added these to send to Girodias. And as Robert Pitman would come to play a role in the saga of *Lolita,* drawing his newspaper's attention to Graham Greene's recommendation of this work, so also would Derek Stanford, a name I was about to send to the Olympia Press, come to be instrumental in eventually finding a British publisher for *The Ginger Man.* And the title of this novel at last confirmed. Never having regarded my ability as being outstanding to name a work, and somehow having always felt my attempts to do so inadequate, I did have sense enough in this case to leave well enough alone.

March 11th 1955

Dear Mr. Girodias,

I have but to go through the MS once more quickly and I should then be able to send it on to you. I will leave the title *The Ginger Man.*

Following are two reviewers and a periodical to which I would like review copies sent:

Robert Graecen, c/o *Truth* (have sent address with original list)

Derek Stanford, 46 Lulworth Avenue, Lampton, Houndslow, Middlesex

The Listener, BBC, Broadcasting House, Portland Place, London W.1.

Unfortunately at this time I can't find a person going to Paris with whom I could entrust MS, so must post it. However, I will wait till I hear from you before doing so.

Yours sincerely,
J. P. Donleavy

March 15th 1955

Dear Mr. Donleavy,

Thank you for your letter of March 11th.

The best manner to send the MS is by registered mail, or through the British railways as you did on the first occasion (I have established connections with the customs people at this end, and we will not have any difficulty to clear the MS this time). In any case, do register, or insure the parcel, and write on the wrapping *"Manuscrit littéraire, sans valeur commerciale."*

I look forward to receiving your book in its final version.

Yours sincerely,
M. Girodias

I sent the manuscript to Girodias as advised, writing on the wrapping *"Manuscrit littéraire, sans valeur commerciale."* The first two of these words one might have thought true enough but the latter three over the years were to prove inaccurate indeed. And the manuscript finally sent off, I gave by letter my final advice to be followed.

March 22nd 1955

Dear Mr. Girodias,

Thank you for your letter of March 15th. I mailed MS yesterday, March 21st, following your instructions and hope you receive it soon and safely.

I've used American spelling. However, there may be one or two English I've overlooked. I've also tried to correct misspellings. Where I have crossed out, I mean for it to follow preceding sentences without a new paragraph except where I've put a paragraph mark. I think this occurs in one or two places only. At page 55 there is a jump in numbering to 71 due to cutting 16 pages in first 55.

Could you please let me know as soon as you receive MS?

Yours sincerely,
J. P. Donleavy

I had long been aware that the work was already written the way I wanted and that any attempt at rewriting was making me tense. And I found I could rewrite only minimal parts I thought could suffer to be shortened. MacNamara especially was against cutting or condensing what he felt should be regarded as the natural character of the novel. But too, as a wordsmith I found one could capitalize and embellish here and there and often to one's amusement. I had, however, despite my overlooking many a misspelling, meticulously gone through the manuscript, making doubly certain that each and every word could be understood and my corrections exactly followed.

Although the name Maurice Girodias was becoming familiar to me, it still somehow seemed enigmatic, if not hinting of mystery, including his signature which continued to consist of three strokes, four dots, a small scribble and a long loop at the bottom of the page. However, it seemed as if nothing could have warned me of a lifelong life-and-death nightmare to come. But in fact a few things should have caused me to be more than cautious, and one event actually did give a premonition of disaster looming.

A day came in Fulham in the mild spring of this fatal year of 1955. I was sitting at my desk in the middle of the afternoon in the front bedroom of 40A Broughton Road when suddenly, as my fist pounded down upon my desk in rage, I knew something gravely catastrophic and inimical to me had happened. Someone somewhere had betrayed me. The foundations of the little house in Fulham shook, and my voice and the word "goddamnit" trembling the windowpanes, could be heard reverberating far away up and down the street. I could only guess that the catastrophe, whatever it was, involved *The Ginger Man,* which, after the welfare of my wife and now soon-to-be two small children, was the most important thing in my life. I again swore that whomever it was or whatever it was and wherever it was, I would seek out the perpetrator and avenge such wrong or die doing it.

Shortly after this explosive abreaction, there came scribbled on a scrap of paper an eminently legible note from Behan, who said he'd just been in Paris, and that the Olympia Press was publishing *The Ginger Man.* This was an ordinary enough habit of Behan, who had, and not without justification, assumed all the prerogatives of royalty. His elegant, eminently legible penmanship would appear on scraps of paper and would by someone's hand be delivered to one. Behan taking upon himself the role of official chronicler, whose emissary in passing on such news meant that such was guaranteed to be a fact and being so, had his imprimatur. Which indeed, it had to be admitted, was always the case. But information far more ominous reached my ears just following Behan's communication and related to me by Desmond MacNamara:

"Mike, someone passing through London and just in from Paris, whose identity is unknown to me, was heard to say that *The Ginger Man* was a dirty, filthy book and deliberately written pornography."

My confidence in *The Ginger Man* allowed to ignore all kinds and types of criticism and although I could take no serious view of this opinion, treating it as misconstrued, it did at the time strike me as odd, if not suspicious. Even MacNamara, the most eminently tolerant of the world's foibles, thought this was altogether contrary news to be coming from Paris over a manuscript he had read and admired. And unable to pinpoint the cause, I must have known in my bones that something was badly amiss, for an anxiety was beginning to show three weeks later, following these sinister forebodings.

April 13th 1955

Dear Mr. Girodias,

I am most anxious about my MS. Do let me know if you have not received it.

If you still intend to do my book at this late date, please let me know the terms of your proposed contract, rights, translation, etc., as they are extremely important to me.

However, should MS arrived too late for you to go ahead or for any other reason, let me know and I will send coupons for its return.

Yours sincerely,
J. P. Donleavy

And a pity for us all, except those dedicated lawyers, that this latter had not happened and the manuscript repatriated. For, by God, in the quarter of a century ahead, there was going to be hell to pay.

Which happily
Was not all going to be
Paid by me

Indeed
A sovereign or two
Would tinkle
My way

36

MEANWHILE the correspondence with the Olympia Press was to continue, and Valerie, having a cup of tea in the kitchen, said she thought she was feeling contractions and would feel better if she went to go and lie down. Not that many minutes later in the front bedroom of 40A Broughton Road, with the district midwife summoned and still on her way, Karen was born. She was already lustily crying even before she'd half entered the world.

As these waiting days passed, one of my frequent walks now was westward down Clancarty Road, which, amid its lookalike Victorian terraces, provided a vicarage behind a few trees and an actual for-the-purpose-built artists' studio on the edge of South Park. Philip went to school here, and one could pass farther along Peterborough and Hurlingham roads to Bishop's Park along the river. Where under the great shadowy plane trees one could watch rowing crews training and practicing on the Thames. From here the annual Oxford and Cambridge boat race would begin, and one would witness these longtime adversaries going through their daily routines. It was from my many perambulations along this riverbank that my inspiration to write "Persons and Paddling at Putney" came, a piece which again was published in the *Manchester Guardian.*

These weeks there was no mail and little further news. In what could be thought, or what I imagined was the French literary manner of the eighteenth century, I'd taken an odd Sunday walk along the Thames again with Igor Chroustchoff, Paul Allen and Brian Parker, and we would then repair to take tea in Richmond. Valerie, always willing to do all, one tried to make her work burden less. Washing nappies, dishes, hanging clothes out to dry. One then sat in the warming sunshine on the back iron steps, reading as Philip dug in the tiny garden.

We dined off baked beans, ham and pears. My thoughts at this time were highly random. Words appearing in my notebook. How light can refreshment get. And if one goes around the world, does one meet someone in the middle and then say, "I know I am a stranger but feel I've known you all my life." And leaving my desk, one occasionally lurked at the front bedroom window to watch the passing pale white pudding faces of the poor. Their tales always the same. For any two ladies talking in this district were always recounting their happy days in the hospital, where, free of charge, they had on the National Health scheme been served meals in their beds for perhaps the only time in their lives. I was relieved of writing my meandering words when finally a letter arrived from Paris and I was temporarily reassured as I was plunged back into thinking of business, where, alas, the consequences of every word were to legally reverberate and upon which would hang a fortune.

THE OLYMPIA PRESS

April 15th 1955

Dear Mr. Donleavy,

Thank you for your letter of April 13th.

I have had some difficulties once again with the French customs about clearing your MS, which I received only two days ago. I have given it to one of our editors for a final revision before sending it to the printer. It should be printed within one month.

It is quite unnecessary to have a separate contract; an exchange of letters will, I think, be quite sufficient. These are the terms I suggest:

a) You grant us the right of printing and selling your book in all countries.

b) On the first printing, which will be of 5000 copies, we will pay you an outright royalty of Frs 250,000. On every subsequent reprint, we will pay an outright royalty of Frs 300,000.

c) We are liable to print a special edition, clothbound, for sale in England; on this edition, we would pay you a royalty of 10% on the selling price of copies sold.

d) Every transaction relative to the disposal of translation rights or reprints by other publishers, or any adaptation or use to which the book might be subjected, should be approved by both parties and the monies to proceed from such transactions should be divided equally between us.

Please let me know whether these terms meet your approval. I am anxious to settle this before sending the MS to the printer. As to the payments, I could arrange to have part of the money paid to you in England, and the rest in France. Would that suit you? It is possible to let you have all of the money in England, but that will involve some difficulties.

Yours sincerely,
M. Girodias

Although I had not yet the full grasp of copyright and that it vested in the full and absolute ownership of the author until such time as he would assign and do otherwise with it, as an amateur I had the fundamental idea.

April 19th 1955

Dear Mr. Girodias,

Thank you for your letter of April 15th.

Concerning the right to print in all countries: Does this mean, for example, that as publishers you might print and sell book in USA or elsewhere? This is not something I object to, but I should like to be in a position to give my approval and consider terms.

You have my approval for a clothbound edition for sale in England, and for equal division of monies secured from rights.

Will you send cloth or papercover books for review in England?

Concerning payment: If it is at all possible I should like to have all money in England.

I do wish you all luck and prosperity in dealing with my book and offer any help I can from this end.

Yours sincerely,
J. P. Donleavy

Girodias, as it became apparent in his next letter, was depending less on my wishes of good luck than he was on making sure of preserving his prospects of prosperity.

THE OLYMPIA PRESS

April 22nd 1955

Dear Mr. Donleavy,

Thank you for your letter of April 19th.

As regards American rights, I want to be free to sell as many copies as we can in the USA. If it proves possible to find a publisher willing to print an American edition (with a few cuts), we could sell him jointly the rights and share the returns, which would only be fair as our own market would thus be considerably limited. In any case, nothing will be done and no negotiation will be opened without your approval.

Your MS has been now nearly entirely revised, and a section has been sent to the printer. With a little luck, the book should be on the market within three weeks.

As to the money, we will arrange to have it paid to you in England, but we won't be able to settle the first half before the beginning of May and the balance in June.

> Yours sincerely,
> M. Girodias

And Girodias's response had put him nicely back in the generous position of a fifty-fifty share of rights, which my immediate reply agreed in the case of America.

April 25th 1955

Dear Mr. Girodias,

Thank you for your letter of April 22nd.

I am willing to sell jointly and share returns equally with you as regards American rights. I should like to have my share paid in dollars.

I am pleased book is progressing satisfactorily and look forward to seeing it.

Herewith a tragedy which appeared few days ago in *Manchester Guardian*.

> Yours sincerely,
> J. P. Donleavy

The money due was the equivalent of 250 pounds sterling. Considering that my budget was a steady 5 pounds per week, where owning a house with modest overheads and provided one had only an occasional bottle of wine or bottle of pale ale from the off license a short distance away, this was a considerable amount of money and represented nearly an entire year's survival at Broughton Road. And now for the first but not last time, some small adventure intervened in my dealings with the Olympia Press. A letter arrived from Girodias authorizing payment of the 250 pounds on presentation of the letter to a gentleman called Mr. Cliff in Old Compton Street, Soho. Despite the address, I half expected to enter some august office, flowers on desks, and to be received by a smiling receptionist who would, taking my letter, then hand me a check drawn on a reputable bank. I telephoned the number and seemed to get some evasive answers as to how to contact Mr. Cliff or how to determine his whereabouts and make the arrangements to collect the 250 pounds. Following what I thought to be prevarication, I clearly was alarmed and immediately scribbled a note off to Girodias suggesting another means and place of payment. An immediate reply came back.

THE OLYMPIA PRESS

May 9th 1955

Dear Mr. Donleavy,

I have just received a rather disturbing phone call from Mr. Cliff, who says that there seems to have been some misunderstanding when you phoned the number I gave you. Mr. Cliff appeared rather surprised by the manner in which you had requested payment of the agreed £250 from the person who answered your call.

I am sure that this incident was the result of some misapprehension. In any case, Mr. Cliff is a friend of mine, and is taking care of this transfer at my request on a friendly basis. I would not like to cause him any inconvenience over this that I can avoid. I'm sure you will understand my position and that, when you contact him again, this slight confusion will easily be cleared.

Yours sincerely,
M. Girodias

Next day I again directed my attentions to Soho and arrived by tube at Piccadilly and set off to the address in Old Compton Street. At a doorway I rang a bell, and as I stood on the street I was viewed from a window above. Then the door opening, two cautiously friendly gentlemen appeared and bid me to accompany them directly across the street into a fruit and vegetable shop. Inside, past the potatoes, cabbages, carrots, lettuces and leeks, we went down a narrow dark stairs into the basement. The dank cellar full of and smelling of stored vegetables, we proceeded forward to a table which was faintly illuminated beneath a skylight of glass blocks in the pavement of the street above. Businesslike, one of the gentlemen proceeded to count out 250 pounds from a stack of five-pound notes. I handed over my letter and bundled the cash into an envelope and squeezed it into an inside pocket of my jacket. Any second I thought I might feel a cosh on the back of my skull. But the two gentlemen, who seemed pleased at our exchange, were suggesting that we would be making such a transaction frequently in the future. The prospect of which, despite the less than elegant circumstances, I found not provoking in me any increased dismay.

However, as I climbed back up the dark cellar stairs and again past the carrots, brussels sprouts and cauliflowers and back out into the street, it was more than vaguely dawning on me that beyond these present gentlemen, who seemed totally innocent of such, that I could be coming close to rubbing elbows with a world commonly referred to as the dirty book trade. Nor could I help feeling that with so much cash upon my person, that in the close-knit community of Soho that anyone else knowing of the transaction might take it into their heads to dispossess me of my very first literary earnings from *The Ginger Man.* Which, instead of having been paid by official-looking check from a respectable publishing house, was rather a wad of much-used bank notes counted out to me down in the dank cellar of a Soho vegetable shop. And which had guaranteed, along with two recent pieces published in the *Manchester Guardian,* my yearly income of 5 pounds a week and in a stroke made me fully supporting as a writer.

Heading left out the vegetable shop door, I also turned left down Dean Street past the York Minster Pub, which, as the door happened to open, my eye caught sight of its smoky interior, full of its literary and artistic habitués. Looking back over my shoulder to see if I were being followed, and resisting running, I approached Shaftesbury Avenue. And here, with my best boxing footwork, I smartly nipped across through the two-way moving traffic. Glancing behind again, I could spot no particular pursuer, and it seemed so far, so good. But on my first steppingstone to fame and fortune, I was eager to avoid all jeopardy and I realized that if there were any foolproof way of telling that I was not being followed, I need now only slip through two narrow alleys I knew of off Macclesfield and Wardour streets, a hop, skip and a jump away.

I must have looked strange enough accelerating with a sudden burst of speed and turning abruptly into Dansey Place, a grim pedestrian alley through which one made greater haste, as it indeed seemed a place where one could be ideally murdered or mugged. However, I continued out into Wardour Street and a few yards down and into Rupert Court, a shorter, narrower and more civilized walkway, in which was located one of the best and cheapest-priced Chinese restaurants in London. And then before emerging from the other end, I waited at the corner of the Blue Posts pub to see if someone at speed also turned into this alley. And who would, by a guilty look in sudden confrontation, alert me to knowing I was being pursued. But in the next minute, during which I stood my ground, not a soul came rushing into the alley foaming at the mouth with a cosh or gun at the ready to rob me. I may have even been a little disappointed, but it did dawn on me that in starting my literary career as a novelist, I was being paid in this most bizarre manner of all time and was already seeming to be running for my life.

But if anything, payment was at least some proof of impending publication. And before I left the alley, I was tempted to step into the Blue Posts, located on the corner where the alley entered into Wardour Street, and have a glass of ale. And do as I so often did, listen to the voices around me of the inmate regulars having their usual and losing their anonymity in this great vast city of London. Where now so many years and miles away from County Wicklow, where I first sat down to write this novel for which after nearly five years, my first pay was bulging in my pocket. And a work about which I was recalling Behan's words which he had said as we walked in a soft misty rain on the muddy drive at Kilcoole past where I sat to first write the manuscript, now sent off to Paris.

"Mike, I'll make a prediction. This book of yours is going to go around the world and beat the bejesus out of the Bible."

And now following what was to be my strangest ever literary transaction, I duly wrote back to Girodias.

May 11th 1955

Dear Mr. Girodias,

Just a note to add to my hurried one yesterday.

As you mentioned in one of your letters that payment here would involve some difficulties and since I had no idea I was dealing with a friend of yours nor that this arrangement was anything more than temporary and perhaps quickly made, I naturally was apprehensive when I was unable to get in touch directly with Mr. Cliff. However, I now understand the position and it is satisfactory as far as I am concerned. I do hope I haven't caused any difficulty between you.

I note there are two names, "Collection Merlin" as well as "Olympia Press." Could you let me know to which I refer for mentions and reviews? A note appeared in an Irish newspaper last week and I wondered how or if you want me to make reference to your firm.

Yours sincerely,
J. P. Donleavy

If Girodias in Paris had any understanding of what initial fate he was planning for *The Ginger Man*'s first publication, my mention of "Collection Merlin" in my letter should have made him nervous indeed. However, it was more probable that he had already begun to regard me as he would any of his so-called dirty book writers, who were happy enough to be so for the money and who found it a ready means of survival in Paris. And it may have been indicative that just over a month would elapse before I would hear any more from Girodias. But too I was for the first time sensing caution in respect of the Olympia Press in my use of the word "if" in my asking concerning making any reference to Girodias's firm. But now June had come. And it would prove to be the month in which *The Ginger Man* was printed. However, no copy of the volume was in evidence.

July 12th 1955

Dear Mr. Girodias,

I've heard no news concerning book and am anxious to know if you've had some delay with printing.

I'd be very grateful if you could let me know if book is out or when it's likely to be available and also if you'd let me know where you might send copies for review.

Enclosed a sketch which appeared in the *Manchester Guardian* last week.

Yours sincerely,
J. P. Donleavy

The sketch in the *Guardian* I'd referred to was "The Mad Molecule." And as little known as one's name as an author or anything else was, it would, of all my sketches in the *Manchester Guardian,* be one of the best remembered by readers. For shortly after its publication and upon meeting and being introduced for the first time to Lindsay Anderson, the stage director, and later to become a distinguished film director, he had said to me upon our shaking hands,

"You wrote 'The Mad Molecule.' "

Such encouragement was always needed and considerably appreciated. But now July 15 of this fatal year of 1955 had dawned. The postman banged on the front door of 40A Broughton Road. And I descended the stairs to be handed a parcel from Paris. Standing there in the hall, I opened it immediately. The wrapper removed, I found two copies of *The Ginger Man.* The volume, in its green format, had its cover decorated by a thin white border inside a black border which enclosed the title and, in small black letters above it, the author's name. Listed below the title was the number 7 and below it the legend "The Traveller's Companion Series." Inside on the copyright page appeared "Printed in France, all rights reserved by the Olympia Press, Paris, France." Then there was the title page and again further mentioning the legend "The Traveller's Companion Series" published by the Olympia Press, 8 rue de Nesle, Paris, 6e. I turned over the page, and opposite the first page of text appeared

FOR CATALOGUES
OF BOOKS PUBLISHED
IN THE TRAVELLER'S
COMPANION SERIES
APPLY TO:
THE OLYMPIA PRESS,
8 RUE DE NESLE, PARIS, 6E
FRANCE

I read the first lines of the book. They were mine, as I had written them. Then flicking quickly through the 353 pages, I came to the last page of text in the volume, which was followed by another page giving the list of the Traveller's Companion Series.

Catastrophe already acknowledged, as I had begun to climb back up the narrow stairs, I stopped midway and my right fist descended with all my might upon the cover of the top book I held in my left hand. And within this cramped, dim lit hallway down this grim and grimy street in Fulham, my solemn declaration was made aloud. I would, if it were the last thing I ever did, redeem and avenge this work that I'd put my very life into writing. And that no matter how long it took and no matter what I had to do,

I would do
While I lived
With the life
I had left

37

Ah, but wait. One had to remind oneself not to jump immediately like a scalded cat to recrimination or to wreak instant vengeance and reprisal. For I had a good example to follow. My mother throughout her very long life always kept a poem within sight of her very bright blue eyes. And it seems now no question but that judging by her own reaction to disasters, she followed such precepts as were penned by this anonymous author. And I hope hereby not to infringe anybody's copyright in reproducing such wise words.

> Never cherish the worries
> That meet you each day,
> For the better you treat them
> The longer they stay.
> Just put them aside
> With a smile or a song
> And something much better
> Will hurry along.

Well, let me tell you, there was not one trace of an iota of a smile or a song or even the spending of the briefest fraction of a second waiting for something much better to come along as I hurried in one awful quick step right out my front door and up Bryan's Alley and over to my local library just across Wandsworth Bridge Road, and under that friendly roof went to delve into the nearest thing I could get to being a law book. And from which one could try to piece together words and phrases that might say anything about redressing disaster and aggrievement in the sphere of the subject of contract and copyright. Nor could there be any doubt whatever, that if this man Girodias,

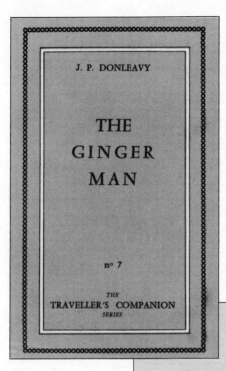

J. P. DONLEAVY

THE
GINGER
MAN

n° 7

THE
TRAVELLER'S COMPANION
SERIES

This now famed list of works, whose authors were pseudonymous and whose existence adorned the last page of the first edition of THE GINGER MAN, *and such becoming the basis for my swearing revenge on Maurice Girodias and the Olympia Press. Although the use of the words "special volume," according to Girodias, was meant to set it apart from the other titles, it could also be interpreted to mean in such context that* THE GINGER MAN *was a particularly raunchy variety of dirty book.*

THE
TRAVELLER'S COMPANION
SERIES

whoever he was, if he was, had he been within an immediate physical distance to be reached, he would have been smashed by me into a bloody pulp.

My most major concern was that the book, in its pornographic and pseudonymous series, could never be taken seriously for what it was and could never be reviewed by any reputable periodical. And with the exception of Paul Allen being able to write something mildly commendable in a journal he worked for, called *Courier,* the book was trapped and frozen, if not forgotten, in its tracks. Everything I was or hoped to be as an author simply no longer existed. I noted the use of the words "special volume" appended after *The Ginger Man*'s back page listing, which I could consider meaning in the context of the books it was published with, only that this particularly pseudonymous book was especially pornographic. Even number 10 on the list, Frank Harris, author of *My Life and Loves,* was a pseudonym for Alexander Trocchi, a genuine writer but also one of Girodias's most reliable and trusted pornographers. And thus it was, on what was to be the first of many dismal disaster days, I sat down this midsummer to write to what was to become nearly a lifelong bane in Paris.

July 15th 1955

Dear Mr. Girodias,

I have received two copies of book.

I had no idea you intended to include mine in your Traveller's Companion Series and under no circumstances will I approve of this book being sent to England with it included among list at back or this list being advertised with my work. You may sell more copies of book this way. However, in publishing my book you were publishing a book of genuine literary merit and it seems a pity to waste this merit by including it with books obviously written with ulterior motives.

I would like to point out that it cost me £2000 to write this book, keeping myself and family while doing it. The £250 that I've been paid as an advance means nothing in payment for my work or for the heart and soul I've put into it. I want this book removed immediately in subsequent printings from your Traveller's Companion Series.

I also note you are charging Frs 1500 per copy. In your letter of January 7th 1955 you state that the retail selling price will be about 750 francs. You are charging twice this price. This is a breach of our agreement. It was on this basis that I accepted your offer of £250 for a first printing of 5000 copies and agreed to an equal division of monies secured of rights and as an act of good will, American rights also, which may prove to be valuable ones and which rights are normally reserved by an author. I'm afraid that this matter will get somewhat involved unless I get some straightforward explanations. Obviously you underestimate the literary worth of my work. This I don't mind since the book will ultimately speak for itself. But I have no intention of letting my work be exploited in this way and will take every step necessary to prevent it.

Yours sincerely,
J. P. Donleavy

From my letter, it seems I knew more than I revealed in my first letters of negotiation with Girodias and certainly knew that what he had obviously, deliberately done would not forever ostracize *The Ginger Man* away from the attentions of the kindred to whom this work was directed, and upon whom I would always depend as an author.

THE OLYMPIA PRESS

July 21st 1955

Dear Mr. Donleavy,

I suppose that you are a rather difficult person, with a tendency to ignore other people's problems, and to indulge in bouts of violent self-pity. As, however, you do not seem to be a bad character, I will refrain from launching into a tedious and ridiculous argument with you, and will not answer the first two paragraphs of your letter dated July 15th.

Regarding the third paragraph, which raises the question of money and therefore deserves attention, my position is the following: your book proved *much* longer than I expected; I had asked you to cut out about $^1/_3$ of the original typescript, and my first idea was that the cuts were not as important as I had expected. This made it necessary for me to raise the selling price. It has never been my intention to deprive you of your rights, and I am ready to pay a supplementary £150 *when* this first edition is exhausted. I hope this will seem satisfactory and that you will understand that, if I had "underestimated the literary worth of your book," I would not have published it (which, incidentally, I have done *against* the advice of my readers).

Yours sincerely,
M. Girodias

If it ever would be hard to fathom the motives of one's now unquestionable adversary, in Girodias's masterly reply there was little doubt that he had parried my objections by merely ignoring them. Nor is there much doubt that in his eyes I was a victim and that as a victim I was intended to remain, at least for the considerable time being. But the one word he uttered which was in lieu of any explanation for what he'd done in publishing *The Ginger Man* as pornography was, if any word was, a woeful mistake, and was not to be forgotten by me. And

433

that word was "self-pity." I would, over the years to come, often be reminded of it as it more aptly applied to Girodias as our fortunes became reversed.

Without being able to afford a lawyer or legal advice, I had to totally rely on my wits, as in the matters of law, equity or copyright or contract, my knowledge was amateurish indeed. It would seem that the matter of mistake had interjected itself, for what proof could there be that what had happened and the risk that it would, could not have been clearly forseen by me. A view given me immediately upon my seeking advice from the Society of Authors, to which society it did not take me long to let my membership lapse. In any event, I had now to try best as I could to pick up the pieces. With no prospects now of making my name or a title of a book known, there was little hope of earning more as a writer in order that I might remain as one, my priority above all priorities. For this work once predicted by Behan that it would go round the world like the Bible, it had now gone only in a package from Paris to London and maybe under the counter of a few dirty bookshops in Soho, whose proprietors would immediately stop selling it when their customers stopped buying it as a very poor imitation of pornography indeed.

What I had now if I had anything was five thousand or however many copies were actually printed of *The Ginger Man*. And as I read through the now published book, there were a few major blunders and distantly misplaced paragraphs and an odd misprint here and there, but the work with these exceptions had meticulously followed the manuscript. And I still retained the draft and working pages plus a carbon copy of the original and unrevised manuscript. In any event, from my point of view of Girodias's commercial stupidity, as well as his clear ignorance as to *The Ginger Man*'s literary worth and future, I knew not to trust the contents of Girodias's letter of July 21 and replied mildly enough. But hidden beneath my words was a deathly ruthless intention. I knew I had to get the book published in England free of the Olympia Press's imprimatur of pornography as soon as possible and to redress my first publishing disaster.

July 28th 1955

Dear Mr. Girodias,

I am difficult, but I think you will find that it is not a matter of self-pity so much as that I am proud of my work and want to see the best done by it. I am pleased when someone likes and recognizes my work for being what it is, but I have no illusions about art world and have far more respect for opinions passed in wool trade. But as a writer, I do

434

know my business as I'm sure you know yours as a publisher, especially so since you obviously make money. But I was considering in my objection to your list the fact that it can deprive book of reviews here which book would have received and can also prejudice any case brought against book under Obscene Publications Act, which I would fight. However, what's happened has happened and nothing can now be done about it, but you may as well know that I feel my objections are sound. I realize work in running a firm can be complicated and heavy, but if some explanation were given me beforehand concerning your intentions with book, you would get my complete cooperation even if this were a matter of silence.

As regards your adjustment in price; £150 paid when this printing is exhausted is reasonable as far as I am concerned.

I've received four copies of book but would be grateful for two more to have some for loaning for possible reviews.

Yours sincerely,
J. P. Donleavy

Removing the offending pages advertising the Traveller's Companion Series from the volume, *The Ginger Man* was again sent to an odd English publishing house. And was even seen by such as the poet Cecil Day Lewis, an editor at Chatto and Windus. One knew of this gentleman, for his wife, Jill Balcon, who was possessed of one of the world's most beautiful speaking voices, had been an acquaintance of Valerie's and we had occasionally met to all walk together around the round pond in Kensington Gardens, little Philip kicking a football and the Day Lewises' young offspring, later to become Daniel Day Lewis, the actor, pushed in his pram. But Chatto and Windus returned the work without comment and indeed Day Lewis later seemed at once evasive upon seeing me walking down St. Martin's Lane. However, Paul Allen, editing the magazine *Courier,* had literary friends whom he'd already told about the book, and the words of my July 15 letter to Girodias, "the book will ultimately speak for itself," were in fact already beginning to happen. Allen recalling that he was standing in a group of people at the York Minster Pub when someone suddenly exhibited for the company to see a copy of *The Ginger Man* in its green format of the Traveller's Companion Series. Allen adding that at the sight of this work and mention of my name, an Irish poet from Dublin who was present, shrunk back out of sight. The power of *The Ginger Man* was working against its first ever known begrudger.

But much more positive matters were also surfacing. Paul Allen also had an uncle who ran a rather debutante type of drinking and dining club called the Renaissance in the very socially acceptable area of South Kensington. Where in an attractive upstairs, tall-ceilinged room, the uncle had a bar, dining booths and a dance floor. Allen had on a few occasions invited me and a few of his other friends here. And one evening such was the case as a few of us sat in one of the booths and I was introduced to a shyly attractive young lady and her gentleman companion. Both of these pleasantly sympathetic people were like Allen, considerably knowledgeable about the literary world. Derek Stanford, a poet, had read *The Ginger Man* and said he knew of an English publisher who might be interested in an English edition. The quietly studious lady concurred with Stanford on this idea and seemed unusually erudite for this debutante hangout. When I opinioned that I thought the work might be attacked, she confidently predicted *The Ginger Man* would be well received. Her acumen in the matter to be explained only many years later when her name turned out to be Muriel Spark.

During these months of August and September 1956, the work was now at least a little circulated and talked about. News soon arrived that a Neville Armstrong of the publisher Neville Spearman Ltd. indeed would be interested to look into considering to publish *The Ginger Man* in England. The book also came to the attention of a Keidrick Rhys, a Welsh literary person working on *The People* Sunday newspaper and who wrote a column for its Welsh edition. Rhys, who founded a literary magazine, was one of the first ever to publish a poem by another Welshman, Dylan Thomas. But now the momentum was fast increasing, with suddenly crucial now the fact that a piece of mine published in the *Manchester Guardian* had been chosen to be reprinted and read by children in a volume used as a text in modern secondary schools. And this matter in concert with *The Ginger Man* and its list of dirty books published in Paris interested *The People* newspaper, to whose offices I was invited.

Rhys assured me that his interest in writing about *The Ginger Man* was of an entirely literary nature. However, as one was to find, he was also a gourmet. And while nearly licking his chops and with yours truly, his Paris pornographer, in tow, Rhys showed his editor the list of dirty books in the back of *The Ginger Man* and asked if he might call Rules, the restaurant, to make a booking for lunch. The editor read the list, looked at me and agreed to the expense. And so at this old established eatery in Covent Garden, my first paid-for entertainment as an author was about to take place. Rhys tucking in his napkin over duck à l'orange and a vintage bottle of Burgundy. There were crepes suzette and equally splendid jolts of brandy accompanied by delicious coffee to drink us back to our senses. We sat eating merrily away till nearly four o'clock. And now returned to the newspaper office, Rhys, who had already written much of his interview, now concluded it and, with it typed, further presented it, along with his gigantic lunch bill, to the editor. It did not take long for this gentleman to look up from his desk with a grimacing and disapproving face. Following which Rhys vanished and did not reappear.

As I sat waiting out in this large outer room of desks and reporters, I was suddenly confronted by a tall, quite distinguished-looking Australian. Whose no-nonsense words were now shot out at me like lethal bullets from a gun. And who, as he pulled up a nearby chair, swung his legs and feet up to rest on the edge of a desktop.

"Hey, what's this business about this dirty book of yours you've published in Paris with the Olympia Press."

"It's not a dirty book."

"Well, you tell me what it is, then."

This tall gentleman was Murray Sayle. A journalist who I was to later learn was already famed in Australia. And like many from that country, who'd made their mark in their native territory, he had come farther afield to again achieve celebrity in what was then thought to be the mother country. One immediately got the impression that Sayle was trying to break through what his editor saw as a defense and disguise to my being engaged in the dirty book trade. A trade that *The People* newspaper regarded as fair game to expose and bring to the attention of the police and director of public prosecutions. And Sayle's words, although disarmingly mild and even friendly, were relentless in their probing into what he clearly felt continued to be my cover for this prosperous activity of purveying porn and known to be much alive and thriving under certain booksellers' counters in many a British city and which *The People* newspaper especially let it be known they would expose and stamp out. There was no doubt that despite the wonderful lunch, Rhys still wanted to keep his literary conscience clear and stand by his representations to me. However, the article he had written, one was told by Sayle, had been met by his editor's predictable reaction.

"Hey, you're praising this guy. Get to the bottom of this guy. We can't have innocent children reading the work of a dirty book writer in Paris."

Rhys, albeit well fed, was extremely apologetic that he had his favorable article put aside. And clearly Murray Sayle had replaced him on the job of what now was an investigative matter with Sayle's interest in my story continuing as six P.M. now approached and he invited me to go with him to a nearby pub. Sayle looking and probing for holes in my story but also seemed to be impressed by my continuing adamant affirmation that I was a genuine writer whose work was of literary merit. I was also finding Sayle's intelligent company equally strange and deceptive. No longer interrogating, he became a generous host as we drank a few beers and he was actually listening to what I said. Along with an Australian associate, he invited me back to Notting Hill Gate and his flat up three floors in Palace Gardens Terrace and looking out back on part of the Russian embassy. Populated with a stunningly beautiful girl, a mastiff dog and a couple of Australian friends, as the beer flowed and canapés were passed about, his gramophone was soon playing and thundering out for perhaps the first time in England the composer Carl Orff's music. This was an entirely new breed of mankind. Intelligent, tough, erudite, without English social snobberies and pleasantly letting you know it as they called each other digger, a favorite Australian cognomen to denote comradeship. And Sayle, after our evening at Palace Gardens Terrace, had pronounced,

"Based on my judgment of men, so far, I believe your story. But based on the ways of the world, I'd feel happier if I could know a few more facts."

Back in Fulham, I'd told Eddie Connell about my brush with *The People* newspaper and how now my concern existed over what might turn out to be an exposé of me as a dirty book writer for the Olympia Press. But that I had met both a literary man and an intelligent Australian journalist to whom I was attempting to let know the truth of the matter and that the story, if one there was, I felt would be fair and factual. But Connell immediately cautioned me: "Mike, from my knowledge, *The People,* once they get on to a story, they never let go and they pursue it to its ruthless end. And believe me when I say they are not in the business of painting a flattering picture of an author whose work is published along with the likes of *The Sexual Life of Robinson Crusoe.*"

Again Connell reminded me of the plight of Oscar Wilde, who, when released from prison, had finally to flee to the continent for good to escape British persecution and opprobrium. And now as if by design, I seemed to be provided by Girodias with all the ingredients to enable me to be described as a pornographer and a dirty book writer and to be about to suffer exposure and endure the first pitfalls and to risk prosecution for having written *The Ginger Man.* The fact that I'd been published in *Punch* and the *Manchester Guardian* could mean now only that here was a pornographer posing as a literary type and who assumed such disguise as a protection, which the headline due to appear in *The People* would soon widely disavow. For as a Sunday newspaper whose circulation was in the millions and whose readers were in the many millions, and which was required reading by the underworld as well as all law enforcement agencies, I was sure to undergo more than just a little of ridicule and contempt.

> "MOTHERS AND FATHERS, DO YOU WANT YOUR
> CHILDREN TO READ THE WORK OF A
> DIRTY BOOK WRITER?"

And as I dreaded, indeed, the worst was about to happen. According to Rhys, who regretted the development, *The People* newspaper was planning to use exactly such a headline. And a further reaffirming urgent message reached me at Broughton Road from Eddie Connell, who, in inquiring of his underworld contacts, now informed him that I was indeed to beware of *The People* newspaper, as they were well and truly after me. And, as befitted the sensational nature of the story, had put their ace reporter on the job. Anguish on all sides. Trust no one. And of course it did not help to have recently read a biography of Oscar Wilde. Fame now at long last imminent. But to be accompanied by arrest, prosecution and imprisonment and immersion in a bath of shameful ignominy. In mildly befriending me, Sayle, for this public crucifixion, was also presumably reading the book and finding out more about the Olympia Press. And I of course was imagining even grimmer headlines.

> "PORNOGRAPHIC PEN—WIELDING
> DIRTY BOOK
> WRITER CAUGHT
> FILTHY HANDED
> ESCAPING AT
> DOVER"

A day or two passed, during which I walked the miles away much depressed but not totally in a state of fatal despair, but, living through what I thought were to be my last moments in Fulham before I made my escape across the channel to France. And worst above all now, a gloom and doom descending with the awareness that no British publisher, once *The People* newspaper had written its exposé, would dare publish *The Ginger Man* in Britain. As was my wont in such dilapidated spirits, I had wandered the dismal, empty isolation of the streets around the Fulham Gas Works. Staring into the grime and grit of the streets over which I walked along Sand's End Lane and Imperial Road. Then emerging through Harcourt Terrace and down Bagley's Lane, I could come to the more cheerful open space and grass of Eel Brook Common. Here, in from the traffic of New King's Road, I chose a bench with my back facing Musgrave Crescent, where I had always thought it would have been pleasant to live in such houses facing a few trees, and in front of which I had often sat in reverie and pleasant daydreaming, which on this solemn evening only seemed to conjure up dread and another headline.

"ESCAPING PORNOGRAPHER
IN DISGUISE
CAUGHT COWERING
IN CROSS CHANNEL
SHED"

It was Thursday at just past six P.M. By Friday sometime Murray Sayle would have scratched his head for the last time and the story would be written. And by Saturday the printing presses of *The People* newspaper would begin to whine and then begin to roar and finally thunder as the bound bundles of print slammed down on the loading piers and were shoved into lorries and heaved on trains. And through the night would be all over England, Wales and Scotland to be ready on Sunday morning to be brought into households all over Britain. If they hadn't already got me in handcuffs in bed that night, by Monday the latest, Broughton Road would be full of the vice squad, and, with curtains twitching and fingers of the neighbors wagging, I would be hauled across the pavement into a squad car to face oblivion. And worse, leave a young family of two children minus a father who left them to be ridiculed in headline disgrace.

"PARIS
PORN PURVEYOR
CORRUPTING YOUNG
ARRESTED"

Having before me the soon approaching Sunday, I was already wondering what to pack, thinking it best to gather sparse luggage to accompany me with an apple, orange and banana on the train ride to Dover. Once on the ferry I'd be at least half safe and could have the orange. Then halfway across the channel have the apple. And finally reaching what could be temporary respite and shelter in France, I could eat the banana. And there in that country, with the work not yet translated into French, I would for sometime at least be free of prison bars, affording me a chance to continue to fight the battle of *The Ginger Man.* But then according to Behan and now according to Connell, even if the worst did happen, the standard of accommodation and the library facilities of Her Majesty's prisons were not half bad and in befriending your better class of criminal, introductions to whom they would readily provide, much influence could be wielded and much additional physical and intellectual comfort was available.

Meanwhile, as I sat in the gathering darkness of Eel Brook Common suffering my growing sense of intimidation and keeping an eye open around the park for the gathering forces of *The People* newspaper henchmen, who were noted for their fearlessness in tracking down the guilty, and just as Connell predicted to happen, I was already feeling that I should now, prudently, before it was too late, be making for Victoria Station on the number 11 bus that passed nearby. And not be physically present while I and the Olympia Press were at last being brought to book before the righteous population of Britain, who were to be richly entertained with this exposé of dirty books. Being able to imagine getting into *The Enormous Bed,* or joining the *School for Sin,* or feeling the lash of *The Whip Angels,* or squeezing their thoughts between *White Thighs,* or last but not least, fantasizing on *The Sexual Life of Robinson Crusoe.* And let me tell you, the gossipy residents of Broughton Road would especially be gloating.

As darkness had nearly descended over Eel Brook Common, I could hear the hammering of the final nail in the coffin of *The Ginger Man* and the lid sealed over what now promised to be the remnants and tatters of my life. I was on the verge of making up my mind to escape, as Connell had already suggested I should, and that he would get me a phony passport and could send word down the criminal grapevine to have someone hide me out overnight in Newhaven or Dover before I caught the boat. And at that moment, as I considered this prospect, and was already deciding that I would instead stay and fight, a shadowy figure had entered the otherwise empty park and was directly approaching me across the grass. From the menace of this large shadow and the purposeful walk, it looked at least like a detective inspector of some special criminal venereal vice squad. Size in an adversary had never particularly perturbed me and in fact I took a suicidal interest in such contest and was already contemplating sending this approaching brute's trilby hat flying and laying him out with one punch. But then surely I'd have to run for it back to Broughton Road, collect luggage and a few sandwiches Valerie could hurriedly make me and head for Victoria Station. But now the converging figure was nearly upon me. And was, in fact, Murray Sayle.

"Your wife, J.P., said if I looked around, I would no doubt find you sitting here in the park."

Sayle was well known, according to Connell, to be a man not to be intimidated nor deterred from tracking down quarry as a reporter. Nor indeed was he any slouch in a fight. Nevertheless, I felt my muscles relax and glacial calm settle over me as I awaited provocation to spring to the attack. But Sayle's voice was friendly enough. He was clearly stunned to find me in the twilight sitting alone in the empty park and asked if he could sit down. He seemed to think that I must be waiting for someone and asked how long I had sat there. When I said I was waiting for no one and would perhaps sit for an hour or two, he voiced surprise at my reclusiveness.

"Your wife, Valerie, told me that this is where I would probably find you. I'd like to accompany you back to Broughton Road and have a talk. But first I want to give you my opinion about this book of yours. I've read it twice. It's a work of literary distinction. In fact, when I first read it, I thought it one of the best novels I'd ever read. On second reading, I figured it was the best novel I'd ever read. And in my opinion, in no sense is it a dirty book and had no business to be published among the work listed at the back. You're a genuine writer. As far as I'm concerned, the story is dropped."

"I've been told by a friend that *The People* newspaper never drops a story."

"They're dropping this one. They're going to be told there is no story. You have my word on it."

After these sentiments were exchanged, I walked with Sayle back to Broughton Road, where, at the nearby off-license shop, he bought a half bottle of Bell's whiskey, for us an unusual luxury. As Philip played noisily till his bedtime and Karen already lay asleep, Sayle sat in our kitchen room, revealing a large and sensitive awareness about literary matters. He talked of the formation of sentences and the abbreviation of language and of the distinctive style in which he thought *The Ginger Man* was written. He enthusiastically quoted lines and laughed recalling incidents from the book. The transformation from what I had imagined was a tough investigative journalist and ogre pursuing me, into a man of learning and culture who confidently expressed his opinions over the worth of *The Ginger Man,* brightened the bleak darkness of my recent days. But upon telling Connell of the evening with Sayle, he immediately cautioned me that it was a trap. Which would close upon me the coming Sunday morning when *The People* newspaper hit the newsstands and I would more than deeply regret that I wasn't already halfway across the English Channel to France.

However, I stood firm and took and trusted Sayle's assurance. And Sunday came. When *The People* newspaper was opened, there was no mention of me, *The Ginger Man* nor the Traveller's Companion Series. For like many of the ancient Manx from whom he descended, Sayle was true to his word.

And now
I lived to fight
Another day
While not knowing
There would be
More than
Nine thousand
Of them

38

Aυτυμν of the year 1955. And five months since *The Ginger Man* was published in Paris. It was becoming time to confront one's nemesis in his lair. I was armed with only the vague possibility that *The Ginger Man* would find a publisher in England. But there seemed some hope in the air. The world silence over the novel's publication was at least breached here and there with sounds made by its few readers who recommended it should be read.

And now, instead of fleeing in the previous manner I thought would befall me, I sedately departed by train, boat and train to reach this long-famed city and the Gare St.-Lazare. By the familiar garlic scent of the Métro, I traveled to the Latin Quarter to a room up two flights at the small Hôtel Square in rue St.-Julien-le-Pauvre and overlooking its little park. This district, from Trinity days still familiar to me as I crossed boulevard St.-Jacques and traversed the narrow alley of rue de la Huchette. As one maneuvered a crowded place St.-Michel, it was now as it always seemed, full of students. I proceeded along rue St.-André-des-Arts, where Valerie and I stayed for our summers in Paris and which street entered the notorious junction converging in carrefour de Buci. Here on my first ever visit I was told by Jim Walsh, a Trinity scholar, that I would be awakened that very next morning by an enormous collision of cars. And indeed, just as daylight dawned, five cars crashed into each other, making for a chaotic shambles and hysterical shouting match between the gesticulating drivers.

I was fervently conscious of the importance of my mission, as I now walked this sunny morning from the carrefour de Buci toward the Seine, down rue Dauphine and at the second turning on the left, found the rue de Nesle. And there it was, number 8, hidden away in this quiet side street on the Left Bank. A stone archway within which seemed to be the source of all my troubles, and where now one might hopefully find a solution. With my meager French, I inquired of a passing lady in the courtyard for the Olympia Press and was pointed to an open entrance and up some steps. In the shadowy gloom of the stairwell, one was feeling more and more wondering what to expect to find upon this, my unannounced, visit. On the first floor, I knocked and entered through a great gray door and into a large room. The premises, with elegant carpets and glass doors, seemed attractively businesslike enough. At the immediate desk inside, there appeared sitting a very serious and academic-looking gentleman, whom I expected might be Girodias but whose identity I was later to learn was that of Jean-Jacques Pauvert, who, among other distinguished books, had published the works of the Marquis de Sade. I was referred to a further inner room. And in I stepped. As I declared my identity, there was no question but that there was considerable nervous surprise at my sudden unexpected morning presence. Girodias was slowly up out of his seat and from behind his desk proffering an apologetically limp hand, with what I am also sure was a fleeting trace of fear.

"Ah, you are in Paris."

"Yes."

"Ah. I trust your trip was comfortable."

"Yes."

"Ah, please, sit down."

"Thank you."

At last one finally had a look at this man who was behind the flamboyant signature and seemed to be, at this time, doing a lot of coughing and moving of chairs and whose handshake was far less than vigorous. With a slight French accent, he spoke English fluently. In his sober gray double-breasted suit, white shirt and gray tie, one could use the words "casually debonair" to describe his appearance. Conversation, slow to get started, was improved on by Girodias's inquiry as to where I was staying and until when. Displaying a politely cautious affability, along with his clear relief that he was not about to be punched or shot, he shortly suggested repairing for coffee at a cafe, the Old Navy on the boulevard St.-Germain, which he said served the best coffee in Paris. I was fast realizing that till now I actually thought there was some doubt as to the existence of a Maurice Girodias at all, and I took some slight comfort from what seemed a modestly busy office and from the first indication of his being a bon vivant.

Outside in front of 8 rue de Nesle, there sat, like a squat big black bug, a gleamingly new Citroën. Girodias pulling on his driving gloves, we made for the Old Navy, parking on the boulevard near one of the splendid metal-paneled pissoirs, where the urinator's lower legs were on view and which absolutely convenient convenience alone made Paris, Paris. As Girodias became more at ease, his bilingual ability seemed to involve more facile use of British and American slang. I was relieved but nevertheless wary at his steadily growing friendliness, and I early let it be gently known that the thrust of my visit was to organize a future for *The Ginger Man*. Although he pretended to appear to be listening with interest, I noted his basic reaction was somewhat evasive. It was quickly made evident that to him the publishing of *The Ginger Man* was a matter past and water under the bridge. And although it may have been secretly otherwise, he continued to give the impression that he was utterly indifferent to the book's future, and indeed to the fact that it could even have one.

Following a bland enough conversation at the Old Navy, which was clearly an exercise of disposing of my inquiries and any problem his publication of *The Ginger Man* might have presented, Girodias with great apology excused himself to return to his office. In parting, he asked if I would like to join him for lunch, to which I agreed. Although I sensed that he regarded I clearly served no further use to him in an author-publisher relationship, he seemed anxious not to behave inhospitably. I then went walking in and about my old haunts around the rue de Buci, past the markets where little had changed. And, indeed, where much new matters could unfold with the likes of Murray Sayle, who had departed working for *The People* newspaper and was now also in Paris and had in fact booked my ultracheap room at the Hôtel Square.

Girodias was already at the table as we met again at a restaurant in the carrefour de l'Odéon. And he was exhibiting a distinct degree of affluence. An elaborate enough menu consisted of pheasant, which was ordered and was now accompanied by wines appearing at the table and shown Girodias, which were kept for him reserved in the restaurant's cellars. And this became my first sample of signally stylish largess in the world of book publishing. Reminding of my own golden days at Trinity College and on the Isle of Man prior to my return to America. As the splendid wines flowed, Girodias now spoke more openly about including *The Ginger Man* in his pornographic Traveller's Companion Series.

"That was a mistake. But I had to do it to make money. And of course, like anybody, I like being rich. The book does a brisk trade in the Arab quarter of Jerusalem. My biggest customer is a provincial bookseller near an American army establishment in Germany who specializes in religious books and sells this English line on the side and is not, evidently, aware of what they are. The American sailors aboard ship in the Mediterranean are also good customers. Of course, my biggest ambition is to flood Ireland and Russia with pornography. And then I should like to manufacture dutch caps in France to sell in these territories, as that would be the natural sequence to commercially follow for a publisher of dirty books. Ireland especially, I would like to visit one day. The Miss Frost scene in your book made me weep."

We had now been joined at lunch by an attractive young American lady, Muffie Wainhouse, who seemed to be involved with the Olympia Press but who had to prompt Girodias to tell me so. Girodias, although sniffing, sampling and tasting and drinking the wines, disclosed that the next day he was to commence self-denial and would no longer be drinking, having been instructed by his doctor to abstain for two weeks. I continued to enjoy the wine with Mrs. Wainhouse, married to a gentleman called Austryn. And Paris suddenly seemed to behold pleasures. Girodias, over his pheasant, was deliberating on the mystery of conception, which, from my zoological studies, I was able to explain came about through an *anima humana,* which could be thought divine or chemical but which provided sperm with a homing instinct for the ovum. I went on to reasonably explain that all was not yet fully understood by science but such phenomenon was as close as any living thing could get to thinking it was God. It was the only time in Paris that Girodias seemed to be taken slightly aback by my company and he turned to Mrs. Wainhouse.

"This man knows a lot."

I was still uncertain as to when to raise the subject of an English edition, but as I left lunch at now past four P.M. in the carrefour de l'Odéon I recalled how in the years following the war that this city of Paris seemed to have had a way of constellating people. Who gravitated there from all parts of the world, and in staying, however briefly, seemed to meet most unexpectedly others they knew doing exactly the same. For only a few steps away, I was on the corner of this boulevard and rue de l'Ancienne-Comédie, where I sat one summer with Valerie in a cafe, when I spotted a familiar face from the Bronx across the street and shouted out the name Walter Silbernagel. The man I saw was a childhood acquaintance who lived in a house diagonally behind ours in Woodlawn. He stumbled forward as if shot with shock to hear his name called out aloud in this foreign place and of course did not recognize me because of my beard. Frowningly pointing to himself as he faced me across the boulevard and calling out, "Who, me."

Yes, I meant him. Because he lived down the street from John Duffy with whom I'd often discussed the two dogs his family always kept. One a St. Bernard, called Putsie, who was so massive it could hardly walk, and another, a tiny dachshund, or frankfurter dog, named Esmé, who was so small its belly scraped the slate pavement as it maneuvered forward on its four short legs. Silbernagel's family business of making optical lenses took him on trips to the various cities of Europe. And Walter was then staying in a large respectably bourgeois flat in Paris. To which we were invited that very night to dine with him. And thereafter, I never met again anyone from Woodlawn in Europe but found that whenever there appeared dogs in my novels, they were always named either Esmé or Putsie.

And in terms of constellation, on this October visit to Paris, Murray Sayle, who'd now become a friend, and taking a sabbatical from London since leaving *The People* newspaper, had become director of publicity for the Fédération Mondiale des Anciens Combattants and was for the time being living in this fabled city. He had also become an expert on the cafe pinball machine and vastly knew of the ins and outs of Paris life. I was finding pleasant enough the room he had booked for me in the Hôtel Square, from whence one could see across the river to the cathedral of Notre-Dame. I was taking morning constitutionals in the small park just outside and enjoying walks with Sayle, who knew the Paris streets well. And it seemed as if it were a constant round of celebration as he held court and constellated an astonishing assortment of people. There were pleasantly aimless afternoons in the cafes and less aimless evenings of delight in friends' apartments or in Russian and Greek restaurants. In the company of Betty Dalgarno, a generously sympathetic Australian lady, and Bob Marx, an American of singular sensibilities with whom Sayle waged devastatingly traumatic chess contests and equally furious pinball games, there would then be the spiritual examination of existence, always summed up by Sayle, who, with the music throbbing and at the magic height of such evenings, would announce, "The party's over, men. The decline of our lives has begun."

We traveled in the direction of Montparnasse to dine with Sylvia Sayers, a painter and whose husband, Michael Sayers, a writer, wrote short stories and for television and who was away in London. They lived behind a strange high wall in which there was a door on the street which, when entered, then led across a garden under fruit trees to a house in which a sumptuous meal was taken and which house would, on another return to Paris, play a curious role. For on a crucial day in the beginning of the battle of *The Ginger Man,* I would visit this city on a last-ditch desperate mission to hope to avoid an impending injunction to stop *The Ginger Man*'s publication in England. And in dire straits, I sought the company of someone who might temporarily distract me out of my anxiety.

But the present excitement in Paris at this time was continuing wine, women and song and a marauding, massive American who fought all other Americans and expatriates from any land who thought they were in any way intellectually impressive, and who was terrorizing nightclubs and cafes, where people sat in trepidation at his appearance, which included the police but excepted Sayle. Meanwhile in the intervening week, a party was arranged by Girodias to which Muffie Wainhouse said she would escort me and that I should meet her in the La Boucherie alongside the quai de Montebello for a drink. That afternoon at the Hôtel Square a telegram arrived. Sent from Newhaven harbor and by its cryptic and sparsely blunt instruction could be from the one and only Gainor Stephen Crist:

DONLEAVY OR SAYLE

SQUARE HOTEL

ARRIVING ST.-LAZARE, 6 P.M., TUESDAY

GAINOR

Gainor, who was on a mission from Spain to England, had been stopped at the port of Newhaven by the Home Office, his arrival there being alerted to immigration by a lady who did not wish to have him loose in England. Refused entry to the United Kingdom, Gainor was temporarily kept under mild arrest aboard ship until he could be sent back across the channel the next day. Ah, but true to his charm, it was not long before he had befriended a member or two of the immigration authority, who, in joining him that evening in his cabin, had a little party and polished off a bottle or two of duty-free spirits. Then these kindly, understanding gentlemen stamped his passport and saw to it he was served a sumptuous breakfast prior to releasing him to land. Whatever embroilments then ensued on terra firma, it was only a day or two later that Crist decided to flee to Paris.

Although I was finding it not unusual for Gainor to show up out of the blue at a critical time in one's life, for he was rarely not enduring one similar in his own, I did not relish all the chaotic complications that I foresaw coming with him. But as always, it was usually another's dilemma that took priority over his own. And such was the case when I duly arrived at Gare St.-Lazare at the appropriate time. I waited at six P.M. at the end of the platform for the Calais train to come in and for the passengers to get off. But ten minutes later, with the platform emptying, there seemed no sign of Crist. Then with the train doors being banged shut again, and at what seemed the very last moment at which I was deciding to go, there he was. Approaching down the platform with his Pan American Airways bag and a dog in his arms. Alongside him walked another gentleman with whom it seemed, by nods of the head, he was talking in sign language. Without preamble or explanation an introduction was about to be attempted.

"Mike, I'd like to introduce this gentleman I've met on the train who needs to get to Gare d'Austerlitz and who we shall for the time being designate as Mr. XYZ. Mr. XYZ, this is Mr. Mike Donleavy. And this is Mr. XYZ's bow-wow, who is called Kuninganna."

The man gave a slight bow, and I thought, in the still noisy station, I detected a click of heels. But I had never before in all my life seen such an expression of resignation on any human face as was on this strange gentleman's carrying a frayed green canvas valise in either hand. Although it appeared that Gainor seemed able to converse with this man in nods of the head and grunts and signs, neither was doing so in anything resembling a language I had ever heard before. It reminded me of a previous incident of Gainor's in Paris when, on top of the Eiffel Tower, he had appeared with another stranger in tow, a blind man to whom he was describing the sights of the city far below.

"Mike, come with us while we find on the station someone to assist this man and his blind dog, who sadly has cataracts in both eyes and whom I must carry because she is blind. But she is an entirely friendly little mutt. Mike, come, bear with us."

All three of us and the blind dog, licking Gainor's face, shuffling down the platform. It was thought best by Gainor to escort his extremely foreign friend and dog to the information booth in the station where there might be found persons who could translate. Inside at the counter of this tourist helping office, the first pair of translators said they could not interpret or even tell what language the man was speaking but that they had a gentleman whom they could get who was regarded as a world authority and who had a working knowledge of eleven languages. Gainor, of course, as he had done for Pan American Airways, very conspicuously orchestrated VIP treatment for his friend.

450

With a steadily larger and larger crowd collecting to hopelessly assist. Meanwhile it took twenty minutes to find this additional linguist, who, upon his carefully listening to Gainor's friend, finally shrugged his shoulders and professed total ignorance of your man's tongue or any tongue remotely resembling. But now the crowd, some of whom were exchanging views on semantics with Crist, had grown so large that the stationmaster, who had been summoned, insisted we all move onto the open space of the station. Gainor meanwhile calling for water for the dog, whom he was now petting and comforting with words in Spanish.

"Mike, you must bear with me. We must see that this man gets proper directions to get him to Gare d'Austerlitz."

"But, Gainor, this is causing an actual brouhaha. We're disrupting the station."

"Mike, everything is going to be all right."

The stationmaster, suspicious that Gainor and I were conducting an elaborate hoax, was now, along with two members of the Paris gendarmerie, sizing us up. The stationmaster now somewhat heatedly saying he had never heard such a language or words ever spoken before. But Gainor, with the blind dog happily lapping up its water at his feet, seemed to have collected an even larger group behind him, who were regarding him with much sympathy, especially as Gainor brought attention to the dog's cataracts. Indeed, if the stationmaster didn't soon shut his mouth, he could be in danger of being attacked by the crowd of dog lovers. While Gainor still remained the only one who could make any sense with the dog's owner, I was already well past showing more than some signs of impatience and was harboring an increased distinct fear of being arrested.

"Gainor, for God's sake, this is going to turn into a debacle if it isn't one already. I've booked you a room at the Hôtel Normandie, rue de l'Ancienne-Comédie in the sixth district. Just make sure you don't mention the name Behan, who's stayed there and still owes the bill."

"Mike, we've got to get this man and his dog to Gare d'Austerlitz. He needs to get there."

"Gainor, that's miles all the way across Paris. Plus they probably don't let mutts on the Métro."

"That's the very reason, Mike, that we must help him get there. If not for his sake, then for the dog's. We could take him with us. It must be on the way."

Clearly there was nothing for it. Any second further of delay now would get us arrested. I knew no obstacle could deter Crist in seeing to it that this unintelligible man, intelligible only to Gainor, got to Gare d'Austerlitz. And although I never inquired, I knew this must be a gentleman whom Gainor had never met before and would consider it his solemn duty to interpret his language, which all the linguists in the station had never heard before. I was sorely tempted to bring to Gainor's attention the fact that he had not hesitated an instant in sending numerous hapless air passengers who were innocently on their way to San Juan, Puerto Rico, off to Helsinki, Peking and Spitzbergen. And here he was now, hardly arrived in Paris and already totally dedicated to seeing that this absolute stranger catch a train at some other station miles away. Gainor could be all things to mankind just as all mankind were all things to him. Except that I knew that this was now a life-and-death commitment to get this man and his blind dog to Gare d'Austerlitz. As I had planned to meet Sayle shortly at a cafe near the Opera and near his office in rue de la Michodière and which one reached on the Métro in the direction of Porte des Lilas, I now dragged Gainor to the Métro map to try to talk sense into him, Gainor standing with the mutt back in his arms as I pointed out the route to Austerlitz.

"Gainor, why can't you just stick this poor unfortunate in the bloody Métro with his mutt on the right train, destination Mairie d'Issy."

"We can't do that. He's got to change at Sèvres Babylone. And being that he is completely unable to interpret signs and he could instead of heading for Austerlitz head for Porte d'Auteuil and end up way out by the Bois de Boulogne."

"Well, he could at least take the dog for a walk and a crap there."

"Mike, please don't try to be funny. He may have someone to whom he's a father waiting for him at his destination. That's if he ever now gets there in time to catch his train at Gare d'Austerlitz."

"Gainor, it's only one change and about a dozen stops. He's bound to see Austerlitz written up all over the place. It couldn't be simpler."

"Mike, what happens if his dog, Kuninganna, goes off loose as he is trying to put his bags on the Métro train. The poor man is absolutely banjaxed then in trying to fetch him back with the Métro train leaving with his luggage."

"Gainor, what if he hadn't met you. How the hell was he then going to get to Gare d'Austerlitz."

"Mike, that's a damn silly and an entirely hypothetical question and completely beside the point. Don't you understand the man has to get to Gare d'Austerlitz and doesn't speak French or any other known language."

"Well, how the hell are you talking to him."

"Your man seems to savvy a little Serbo-Croat and, combined with a bit of Esperanto and a tiny bit of Catalan, I have, if I may say so, become communicative with him. However, with a bit of sign language and my grunts in that language used by earliest humanity, the primordial utterings, we now understand each other perfectly. That indeed was the mother tongue, which has since regrettably become the global babble in which no one understands each other."

"Well, Gainor, I do hope you'll understand when I tell you that I've got to be at a cafe near the Opera in just a few minutes."

"Mike, don't worry. There's no need for two of us to go to Austerlitz. Just lend me a few francs and I'll meet you somewhere. Or back at the Hôtel Square in an hour or so."

"Done. Meet me at the Square. Here's some francs. Good-bye."

Even though Gainor was the world's most devout humanitarian, I did think in this case he was going far beyond the call of duty. But I bid him, along with his good friend and his blind dog, bon voyage. I also girded my financial loins, for in borrowing money I correctly assumed Gainor was broke, and more than likely was without the means to travel back to Spain. Despite the strange sainthood of this man Crist, at no time did I really think that he would actually do what he was doing on the station of Gare St.-Lazare and escort this incomprehensible gentleman whom he had never met before to Gare d'Austerlitz. If I had, I might have accompanied him. But instead, in total disbelief I stood there mute and more than a minute dumbfounded as off he walked, the handle straps of his small Pan American Airways bag pushed over one wrist and carrying the man's dog for him. I watched them disappear down the steps into the Métro, and as they did I had a sudden vision of catastrophe and rushed off after them only to lose them in the rush-hour crowd.

Having missed my appointment with Sayle, but at least having avoided ignominious defeat in a pinball game, at which Sayle was a master in popping the ball in the skill hole, I returned to the Hôtel Square, where Gainor did miraculously appear an hour later. Knocking on my door, his face was wreathed with concern. He had already been to his room in the Hôtel Normandie overlooking the carrefour de Buci, but he was now nervously twiddling his thumbs, which was always a true sign of his being agitated.

"Mike, I can't tell you, the most bloody wretchedly unbelievable happened. At Gare St.-Lazare, we mistakenly in the Métro got into a first-class carriage with second-class tickets. And some bastard sporting the Légion d'Honneur on his lapel spotted me hiding the dog under my coat. When we got to Sèvres Babylone and were about to make the successful change, we were no sooner on the platform to Austerlitz when this bastard now following us precipitated exactly what I described to you could happen, which did happen. The train's doors opened. My friend put his luggage on, and turned to me to hand him the dog. Then the bastard with the Légion d'Honneur shouted just as the train doors were closing that the dog was rabid and illegally on the Métro. You could hear the shout 'Prenez garde hydrophobie,' all over the station. Then, as I tried to hold the train doors open, the dog jumped down and got loose. In all the noise and commotion, the poor mutt, who was, I must admit, foaming a little at the mouth, just ran through a fast-panicking crowd. The bloody train then pulled out of the station with your man's two green canvas valises aboard. Meanwhile, the poor terrified dog ran right the bloody hell back out past the ticket collector from whence we came, which led to this ancient bitch who called the police to try to stop me. I ended up having to run for it. I lost sight of the dog, who couldn't see where it was going anyway. Then I couldn't find the man. Anyway, he'd already lost all his luggage. I mean after what happened, one had to wonder, was his life worth going on living anyway. I can now conclude only that the fate of the blind dog was to fall into the tracks, and the mutt's owner, poor fucker, is somewhere banjaxed for all time in the neighborhood of Sèvres Babylone."

As Gainor was about to relate further and better particulars of his most unhappy mishap, I handed him a copy of The Ginger Man, for which, by letters over previous months, he had badgered me. This seemed to cheer him up and relieve him of his disconsolate state and we went out of the Hôtel Square and appropriately enough I left him in a cafe in rue de la Harpe, stopping to look back at him through the window where he sat quietly with his calvados and a cup of coffee, and, with The Ginger Man already open, he was absorbed with a grin on his face. However, the sight of him there in the nearly empty cafe, left me feeling an overwhelming sense of loneliness. For there he sat, so anonymous, this strange traveler who yet could utter in a universal primordial tongue. Of which I had to admit I couldn't understand a bloody word.

I now went to meet Muffie Wainhouse just around the corner in the La Boucherie, sitting with her over a drink as she told me of her involvement with The Ginger Man and preparing the manuscript for the printer. She related how she meticulously had made sure that every word could be followed without mistake, conscious as she was of the book's unconventional style, grammar and punctuation. She had thought that the work would be published as had Beckett's and Genet's in a special edition of its own and was surprised to find it included in the Traveller's Companion Series. She seemed to have a likable opinion of Girodias, that he was not all good nor was he all bad, but that his intentions could be unpredictable. And whether he would do something or not often depended upon the humor he was in. Then this attractive girl with attractive legs led me up the stairs to Girodias's abode above the restaurant below. And here within sight of Notre-Dame Cathedral across the Seine, drink flowed and food in abundance was everywhere.

I had no idea the party was being given in my honor. Girodias's brother Eric, who seemed far less flamboyant than Maurice and rather more serious and erudite, came up to talk to me. In the early course of the evening, I spoke to Girodias and brought up the matter of a cut English edition of *The Ginger Man* and asked that if such were pro-ceeded with, would he agree to my having the English rights and that as a result of the English publication and reviews, that it might bring about an American edition and that we would continue to share these rights equally. Girodias thought this a good idea, that it would help advertise and sell his edition and was agreed to the arrangement should I find a British publisher. Years hence the story of this evening of October 25 was to be repeated many times and when told by Girodias would allude to my inebriation. Which, if there were any truth in this, and whatever drinking did take place, it never reached the point where my impressions or exact memory of the evening, or the words said, were in any way impaired or blurred. In fact, quite the contrary, every word spoken was writ large and indelible on my mind, for it was the very reason I had come to Paris.

But it was true, as Girodias described, that he did accompany me around the corner to the Hôtel Square. However, it was with much amusement and laughter resulting from my cheerfulness in now being able to envision a future for *The Ginger Man*. And so ended my first ever literary party. But not my enjoyment of more bizarrely pleasant nights in Paris. Gainor settling down to his usual daily routine of urgent errands interrupted by taking a calvados in the various cafes. Then by evening, assembled with Crist, Sayle, and Marx, we all went visiting Sayle's favorite bars in and around the streets near the Church of St.-Sulpice. Gainor immediately making himself a cherished cus-tomer in one of these smaller bistros, where a Spanish patron made him welcome, and one could leave him past midnight contentedly administering his charm and wisdom. However, there was one night which ended up with toreador Crist in the middle of boulevard St.-Germain performing a mock bullfight, with Bob Marx the charging bull. With his jacket off and used as a cape, Crist fought a battle up and down the boulevard. Both gentlemen being brilliant as they jousted with one another and then turned their attention to the on-coming traffic, which Crist, following a few quites, then standing his ground on this famed Paris thoroughfare, received *recibiento*. Pedestrians, collected in their plenty on the pavement, were incited to shout *olé* above the blare of automobile horns. But then came speeding down the boulevard at Crist a vehicle with a head out its window shouting, "Make way for the best drunken driver in Paris."

I couldn't determine who spoke these words, but they were followed by the man being declared so qualified, having, by the method of sideswiping, knocked off the door handles of one hundred yards of parked cars. A pass was exquisitely executed by Crist as the car's fenders swept harmlessly by. Mercifully bringing this particular night safely to a close. But the days seemed to increasingly weigh heavily on Gainor as he now asked for a loan of money to buy his ticket. And to some degree, I was responsible for his obvious glumness as I stubbornly withheld funds for his return to Spain, but always trying to remind him that I did so simply to ensure that he did not drink the money and fail to get back to Barcelona. I had already known from Pamela's letters of her supreme frustration over his failure to do what he said he would and how when he was expected to travel somewhere, would change plans at the very last minute and fail to arrive. Then, often as not, having already spent the money, she would get a summons to send yet more money to buy tickets.

Gainor now commenced an odyssey all over Paris to borrow what he could, visiting the few friends he knew and even diplomatic institutions. Gainor's impatience with me was now far more adamant, as I would reiterate that he would in fact get money for his ticket but that it would only be at the point of his saying good-bye and getting on the train. Even in our last days in America, I had not refused him at least the offer of some money. But Gainor this time seemed to be strangely agitated in a way I had never known him to be before. There is no doubt that he somehow now regarded my financial position as having been made more affluent with the publication of *The Ginger Man*. And that although I was providing for everything he needed in Paris, that my refusing to give him an amount of money was meanness. And that my offer to give him his fare, but not until he was actually leaving, seemed to irritate if not actually anger him.

"Mike, please don't prevaricate, equivocate and evade. I need the money now, at this moment."

His voice was raised and insistent. Previously he would philosophically have shrugged such a matter off and gone about his business. And my being in any way obtuse to a request would have merely led to the subject being changed, while always knowing I could at least be relied upon to buy the next round. Even my attempt to compromise and actually buy him the ticket was stubbornly refused. He had now already made his last attempt to get money and succeeded in obtaining a thousand francs from some strange source deep inside the American embassy which I suspected was female. And we were now back in his room, overlooking the traffic-noisy carrefour de Buci. There was a strange seriousness in his behavior. And he spoke in a way that I had never heard him speak before.

"Mike, I don't feel right, there's something wrong with me."

I had just contributed a small further amount of money for him to go out and buy some food at the market just around the corner, and he excused himself while I remained in the room. He was gone for ten or so minutes and returned and was standing in the middle of the room when, in placing his baguette on the dresser, he suddenly began reaching about himself and patting his pockets. He then said that he'd left behind in the market his piece of Camembert cheese he'd bought. At that moment, his recent story of the blind dog and its incomprehensible owner to whom he spoke in primordial mutterings, and the luggage lost in the Métro, flashed through my mind and I began to laugh. Knowing too that if his cheese was past praying for that I would replace it for him. But for the first time in all the time I had known him, there was anger in his voice directed at me.

"You think that's funny."

As Crist went out again to fetch his cheese, I was totally taken aback and realized suddenly that something was really wrong. One had always presumed upon his iron strength and his stoical ability to shrug off and even be amused by all the world's ills heaped upon him. And these words he said over the loss of his piece of Camembert cheese were, because of their vehemence, among the most wounding words I'd ever heard him speak. And a solemnity overcame me, that such a brief and trivial event might make one feel so. As I left, I thought I would leave it to him to show up at the Hôtel Square before he left for

457

Spain. Girodias meanwhile had organized yet another lunch at yet another eating house to which Muffie Wainhouse's presence was invited.

I was now feeling the pace. But, according to his doctors, so was Girodias, who kept a reference list of Paris restaurants and was sampling this one recently opened which seemed to have made an effort to resemble an Elizabethan country manor, its interior paneled in oak and, along with reputed great cuisine, somberly furnished. Although an acknowledged bon vivant, upon asking Girodias about what he would regard as his favorite meal, he announced it was roast beef and Yorkshire pudding. This was a meal I knew a great deal about, having had myself many times enjoyed it expertly prepared by both Valerie and her mother. Girodias seemed a mite different on this occasion and somewhat more guarded, and I recalled that earlier, when I had mentioned British newspaper interest, he said he was interested in publicity but wished one to be discreet, which was hardly advice to be followed when seeking mention by the press.

However, I vaguely suspected now that Girodias had second thoughts and was reviewing the commercial prospects of *The Ginger Man*. But I had no idea that he had a scheme already in preparation, according to Terry Southern, who, having written *Candy* with Mason Hoffenberg, published by the Olympia Press, disclosed such information years later. Girodias was intending during my visit to Paris to wholesale cheat me of my rights in *The Ginger Man*. And indeed later was even attempting to claim that the novel had been actually written by one of his editors. And, dear me, had I known it at the time, I could have warned him that such as he was plotting had no chance of going according to plan. But there were already other reasons to be cautious. Upon mentioning to Muffie Wainhouse that Girodias and I had agreed concerning an English edition, she immediately asked if I had it in writing. When I said no, she intimated that it would be better that I should, and that Girodias was not a man upon whose word alone one could depend. My reaction was swift and certain. I said that I would depend upon Girodias's word and that he would have to depend on mine as well.

Lunch ended early. And in the remainder of the afternoon, I went off alone wandering the Paris streets and to make my way to finally visit the church of Sacré-Coeur, which shone so radiantly on its mount overlooking Paris. Upon arriving I found a venerative ceremony in progress, and the church full of women in black. I took a pew. Candles on the altar blazing alight. Jesus above all. And his arms outstretched across the dome vaulting over the altar. The white host on display in its golden, gleamingly jeweled monstrance. The smoke of incense hovering between the massive towers of stone as the sacring bell rang and bells in the tower boomingly tolled. The recitation and litany as the organ thundered, piercing the great gloom. And voices of the choir soared. In crimson vestments, a cleric carried a crucifix and followed by priests and altar boys slow-marched, parading aloft the monstrance with its sacred host, up and down the aisles. The sorcery of these strange benedictions and vespers cast a spell on this darkening day. And the carefully moving feet of these figures in procession, with their liturgical raiment, their staring eyes and judicial faces, haunted the air of this seraphic chamber. The organ thundering out Charles-Marie Widor's Toccata Symphony no. 5 in F Minor. And in such solemn devoutness, although a total pagan atheist, I was stunned to putting paper francs into the passing collection plate.

Leaving the church, I stopped on the stone white steps to look out over the skyline of Paris in the fading gray light of its rooftops. From the Eiffel Tower to those of Notre-Dame. And beyond to the dome of the Pantheon. And farther to Gare d'Austerlitz. Below me, past Montmartre, were Paris's rich, fashionable streets. The glowing gleam of luxury along rue St.-Honoré and rue de Rivoli. And the grandeur of the Palais-Royal. And across the Seine, this city stretching to its southern horizon was now forever the place in which I so ignominiously had begun my literary career. Leaving me now to go in a trance of gloomy concern. Slowly proceeding down the long series of steps of rue Chappe toward Pigalle. Remembering the cafe where Jim Walsh, the Trinity scholar, had sold a pair of shoes to an Oxford scholar and, both speaking such impeccable French, neither knew the other spoke perfect English. Until one of them saw the other's old school tie reveal itself from beneath a covering sweater. But such memory leaving me walking now along rue de Steinkerque, an ever growing deeper disquiet overcoming me.

I had now reached the busy boulevard de Rochechouart at the foot of this rising hill crowned by the Sacré-Coeur. And walking along past rue des Martyrs, as I waited for the signal light holding back the traffic to change, rain began to fall. Then as I looked at the first line of cars, there waiting was a black Citroën. And through the downpour, I could see Girodias himself crouching behind the windscreen. Seeming as if to want to avoid me, if indeed he saw me. I stood solitary and still and watched as his car passed and speeded away. I felt that the strange coincidence of seeing him was an ill omen. And then with a sense of haunting horror, I absolutely knew that doom was looming and that against one, one had an enemy. And who knows now that this man Girodias hadn't in fact unbelievably been shadowing me. Which could be believable considering the events to follow. And especially from the description given many years later by Terry Southern of a scheme that was to be attempted to distract me, drunk, into an exotic whorehouse. For purposes ill-intentioned indeed. And if it were true that Girodias was keeping me under surveillance, he must have got a delightful confirmatory surprise thinking I was a meek and humble churchgoing worshipper of God. Over whom he might walk with impunity. And who wouldn't hurt a fly.

Or
Kick the living
Shit
Out of
A publisher

39

Bᴜᴛ ʙᴇғᴏʀᴇ ɪ ʟᴇғᴛ ᴘᴀʀɪs there continued to be other positive and pleasant distraction back again in the company of Murray Sayle and Bob Marx. Spending one's last evenings over aperitifs and the pinball machine or watching them play their soul-destroying games of chess. Although during their carefree playtime outside their office hours, there were times when both Marx and Sayle could be withdrawn and introspective, and paid heed to mapping out the future of their own lives. And as it happened, Marx to become rich and retire to his estate in Spain and Sayle himself back in Britain to become a distinguished, famed journalist and writer and to go reside in his oriental dwelling in Japan. But Gainor, on this fatal trip of mine to Paris, was not to be seen nor did he come to the Hôtel Square nor did I go to see him at the Hôtel Normandie to say good-bye. As far as I knew, he was still in Paris when I left to return to London. And I relied on his passwords he had always given me.

"Mike, everything is going to be all right."

But sadly, I never saw nor communicated with this strangely aristocratic midwesterner from Dayton, Ohio, U.S.A., again. And I always had my doubts about his passwords. Especially in the tough business of writing whereby every word the integrity of your life is at stake. However, over the passing years, a good bit was related back to me about Gainor. But little in reference to times past and commonly known as the good old days. He, instead, upon his return to Barcelona, had bitter words to say about me. And these would have been justified had I known of his state of health. For he was shortly thereafter diagnosed as having tuberculosis. Entering a sanatorium high on the side of a hill from which it was said he could see a jail, a lunatic asylum and a graveyard out his window. All three of which by a hairsbreadth he had so far in the past variously escaped. I heard also in the passing years that he was quoted as saying, "I taught Donleavy everything he knows."

And hearing these words pleased me, although I am certain they were not meant to. For they at least indicated that we had some purposeful bond and more than a little in common. But we did not fight the world in the same way. Unlike Crist, and with little of his philosophical patience, or his ability to run the passenger traffic of airports, I had no sense of the absurd to sustain me through my own struggles. Nor could I walk in his well-tailored way the Bohemian tightrope of caprice and chance, as he did. I may have been Bohemian in where I had to choose to live, but I never was one. In contests of knowing knowledge, I was frequently and carelessly wrong when Crist was frequently and exactingly right. My words always being fictionally grandiose, and his always factually down to earth. But there was certainly a thing or two I may have known as a New Yorker more than he did as a midwesterner, about staying alive. And needed now to know more than ever in the 8995 days ahead that I would be walking the tightrope of caprice and chance, trying not to fall, as Gainor did, into the subway tracks of fate.

But one would envy his death. For he, Crist, would die just as bizarrely as he had lived. Again by amazing coincidence. Running into and recognizing a face he knew on a Madrid street from seventeen years previously in the latter days of the Second World War. An army major with whom he'd gone on a wild drinking spree in London, and Gainor being a yeoman, able to commandeer naval travel, their adventures took them wandering. Days later they ended up waking and coming back to their senses in the back of a large lorry full of broomsticks and stuck in the mud on the banks of the river Rhine in Germany with artillery shells flying overhead in the last months of the war. And it was this same man, the army major that Gainor now saw passing in this Madrid street. They repaired immediately to a bar to reminisce and Gainor to be invited to accompany this former military person on a ready-to-leave ship, sailing with its handful of teetotal tourists on its way to South America. And as Crist always did and was always ready to do, he packed his toothbrush. And always an intending teetotaler, he made doubly sure he did not go without calvados.

With the other guests, Gainor and this gentleman continued their celebrations aboard the vessel as it left to cross the Atlantic. Gainor was on his last spree. For good luck he always carried with him in a match box Desmond MacNamara's small replica of blessed Oliver's head. But this former naval person was not now to be given safe conduct in his travels by this patron, who had by Gainor's publicity, and aided and abetted by me, been elevated from being blessed to becoming canonized as a saint. Aboard ship, Gainor suddenly became deathly ill and was put ashore on the island of Tenerife. Here he died three days later, adored by all in the hospital who ministered to him. And Pamela, now his wife, to learn of his death in England by telegram when the bill arrived from the funeral director.

And all so typical of Gainor's life. Pamela had been in London visiting their old friend David O'Leary, one of the cultural stalwarts at Trinity College and legendary as one of its most handsome and socially elite of the university's undergraduates, who at the time of Pamela's visit was reminding her of an occasion when Gainor, in Limerick, holed up in the city's best hotel in amorous pursuit of Pamela and in order to call on her at her home and not to appear disrespectably to the servants, had borrowed an appropriate pair of O'Leary's gray flannel trousers. But upon making his appearance in Pamela's boudoir, heard her parents returning, who disapproved of his attentions toward their elegant and well-brought-up daughter. Gainor promptly jumping out the window and plummeting twenty or so feet, landed bottom first into a just freshly manured rose bed. When returning to Cruise's Hotel to O'Leary with his trousers deeply, brownly stained, Gainor announced,

"My dear chap David, I do most humbly apologize. But, in confronting an unpremeditated spot of bother, I am most frightfully sorry to have rather countrified your trousers for you."

And so it was with this Amish man from Ohio, who would extoll the taste of methylated spirits diluted with lemon or orange juice and drink it as he would the finest champagne. Who would cackle and further damn the deservedly accursed. And would happily in satire accept the most miserable of mankind's unreasonable dogmas and beliefs. Who would always take his sustenance as if it were the last supper before the crucifixion. And proceeded through life as a pilgrim might to a shrine. A compassionate man to whom, if I had known I was, I could never be cruel.

At Trinity College, Crist had once described me as the most silent man he had ever met. And if I did finally start to talk too much, Gainor was always a foe to my own humbug. And a foe to how one struggled to give a better impression of oneself until always deciding to give none. The man from Ohio was always a staunch companion in grief and despair, who, as I showed impatience to the unintelligible man at Gare St.-Lazare, had simply said,

"Mike, help this weary pilgrim stranger on his way."

And both George Roy Hill and I, as we once were together out in the midlands of Ireland reminiscing about Crist and recalling some of Gainor's communications, we, for nearly three days round the clock, were holding our stomachs in laughter. Till finally we concluded that the only thing Gainor could have been was a saint. To whom one might to the now Saint Oliver Plunket, pray to be saved from the unpredictable. And we both knew that Gainor, even as a devout agnostic, was directly heading for a Roman Catholic heaven and that he had earned in life his remission from purgatory.

For left down here on earth, one is in envy of how finally and unpredictably and exotically Gainor came to be laid to rest in a grave on an island where banana trees grow. His tombstone bathed by balmy, moist Atlantic winds from an ocean we'd both crossed together on the good ship *Franconia*. To be back again where we first were. In Ireland. And where as an eternal tourist still he remains as a ghost never gone. See him in Blackrock, where he used to get off at the station. Scurrying in terror, having left his fly open on the train. Watch him hurry along the Monkstown Road. Or go as he did for his one and only picnic high on the hill above Dalkey. Where the larks are. Who rise now above him.

Ascending
Singing

40

DESPITE MY GLOOMY PREMONITIONS of my last days in Paris, I reasonably contentedly returned to London. To the whiffs of the gasworks coming in the window and the early clank of milk bottles and noisy garbagemen passing in the street. Working mornings writing *A Fairy Tale of New York* and taking my daily afternoon wanderings with Philip, pushing Karen in a pram to the park or across London. My first communication back to the Olympia Press contained with my letter a long list of names and addresses to whom review copies of *The Ginger Man* might be sent.

Daughter Karen in the front garden of the Anchorage, Isle of Man, with her cat. When we moved to our cottage at Maughold and when darkness fell she loved to chase with her pet between the tombstones of the nearby graveyard.

465

Dear Mr. Girodias,

Your wines have ruined me and I find it hard to face the drab ones I can afford here. Paris is a relaxing city and I enjoyed the stay and meeting you. Give my regards to your brother, who for some reason I remember vividly. And must thank you again for a most pleasant meal with Mrs. Wainhouse.

With best regards.

Yours sincerely,
J. P. Donleavy

The immediate response which came from Girodias's secretary was the first time that Girodias had delegated someone else to reply to me in correspondence. However, the secretary's signature was illegible.

THE OLYMPIA PRESS

November 7th 1955
Dear Mr. Donleavy,

Please find enclosed a copy of the letter we received today from Messrs Hodges Figgis & Co, 6 Dawson Street, Dublin.

We thank you for your list of reviewers which will be attended to immediately.

Yours sincerely,
[signature of a secretary]

Enclosure letter from
Hodges & Figgis Ltd.

The Hodges Figgis and Company letter referred to was from this old established Dublin bookseller, to whom *The Ginger Man* had been sent, and who wrote that they had read it "with the greatest enjoyment and are filled with admiration for it." However, they said that as booksellers they thought it "rash in the extreme" to import it into Ireland with its puritanical censorship laws. This letter became one of the first ever from Ireland to contain a positive reaction to at least the literary aspect of *The Ginger Man,* before this work endured a ban, which was to last for over twenty years. But the book, in true Irish fashion, would end up to be read by every cultured man, woman and literate child in the country.

Being sent out along with *The Ginger Man* at this time, by the Olympia Press, were three other titles, which included Beckett's *Molloy,* Jean Genet's *The Thief's Journal* in their collection of Merlin editions, and Nabokov's *Lolita.* However, this last work, when it arrived, came in Volume One and Volume Two and had been printed in France, August 1955. *Lolita* sported the same green format as that of the Traveller's Companion Series, but with one significant difference. Unlike *The Ginger Man*, *Lolita* was not included in and contained no mention of this series. But it did strike me that Mr. Nabokov, whoever he was, would kick up a stink over having his novel chopped in half in two volumes, which one might have considered was further ample evidence that if this publisher knew what he was doing, his real expertise lay in publishing pornographic books.

As I looked for evidence of the existence of this possibly pseudonymous writer Nabokov in the library, I was pleasantly surprised to find a previous book of his. In the margin of this work, a reader had noted in pencil, "Nabokov is drawing attention to a novelist he highly regards in Russia. The writer to whom the author alludes is Nabokov himself." Back in those days, this was astonishing erudition on the part of a reader in Fulham. But at least one discovered that Vladimir Nabokov was a real name and real author who felt frustration at his own unsung merit but which through happenstance, and my association with Robert Pitman in Holland Park, was to bring about world recognition. And even Samuel Beckett at this time, with his play *Waiting for Godot*, was fast rising from his obscurity. A month now elapsed and I wrote to the Olympia Press.

December 8th 1955

Dear Mr. Girodias,

Many thanks for letter from Hodges & Figgis. No doubt the result is the same in England. *Molloy* will, however, make your position here much easier since *Godot* success. What a fearful terrified bunch the British are. The Irish have excuses and I always feel it a privilege to be banned by them. Even Frank Harris met his match in West of Ireland — think it was only time he failed to seduce.

And thanks for copies of *Ginger Man* and *Lolita*. I read something else here of Nabokov's but not nearly so good as *Lolita*. A really dramatic moment when Humbert's mixing a drink and Mrs. Haze is killed.

Could you look up MS of *Ginger Man* and send it on. And I'd be grateful if you could send me six *Ginger Man* which I'm sending on to people here who do my work in hope that something can be done about reviewing. I hope your doctor's orders are to drink fine wines again — I must admit that I arrived back in London suffering a painful liver.

Would you check to see if books have gone to Arland Ussher? I sent his address c/o *Irish Press* because he moved — or rather *Irish Times* — and they will forward it on.

And you might send copies to Nancy Spain, *Daily Express,* Fleet Street, London EC4, unless copies have already been sent.

With best regards.

Yours sincerely,
J. P. Donleavy

This letter of mine was not to be responded to. And a gap of communication of nearly nine months was to intervene until August 16, 1956. By the month of December 1955, I had published another two more sketches in the *Manchester Guardian,* which included "Dear Sylvia" and "You Murdered My Cat." But I was also taking my first steps as a dramatist in response to the BBC's call for excellence in radio drama and had dramatized the opening chapters of *A Fairy Tale of New York,* as a radio play called *Helen.* It was submitted and short-listed and finally chosen to be broadcast. And soon I was to find myself amid actors and listening carefully as my words ethereally floated out over loudspeakers to an English public still listening to the radio.

But there was to be another blow and perhaps one of the most disappointing yet for a young writer. A sketch of mine, which had appeared in the *Manchester Guardian,* had been selected to be re-printed in the *Bedside Guardian,* an annual book published, containing pieces published in the newspaper during the previous year. In November 1956, I was paid one guinea but was soon devastated to find that the piece was then withdrawn. Although told it was due to lack of space, I couldn't help believing those who suggested that it could also have to do with *The Ginger Man*'s growing circulation in the Traveller's Companion Series and the fact that the *Bedside Guardian* was being published by a highly respectable firm, who also published a version of the Bible.

Derek Stanford had now related to me that Spearman was indeed interested to see *The Ginger Man.* On January 7, 1956, I posted an Olympia Press copy of the book, with the offending pages referring to the Traveller's Companion Series removed, to Neville Spearman Ltd. along with the following letter.

40A Broughton Road,
Fulham, London SW6
January 7th 1956

Neville Spearman Ltd.,
10 Fitzroy Street, London, W1.

Dear Sir,

Herewith a copy of my novel, *The Ginger Man.*

Mr. Derek Stanford said you might be interested in it as regards publication of a somewhat revised edition in England and said he would mention it to you. In case he hasn't, I might explain that *The Ginger Man* was published last June in France. This because parts were objected to here by publishers. However, an extract has appeared in the *Manchester Guardian* and been reprinted in *Trinity,* an annual record published by Trinity College, Dublin.

Although this book presents a problem as regards a rather outspoken realism, there are many here who feel its publication in England would be defensible and warranted by the merits of the book. I am aware, however, that this is a great problem here but do hope you can give *The Ginger Man* serious consideration.

Yours sincerely,
J. P. Donleavy

Clearly I had improved my choice of words with those of "outspoken realism" to refer to *The Ginger Man's* difficulty for a publisher, and Neville Armstrong responded January 10, 1956, with a cautionary letter concerning the obsession authority currently had with obscenity and therefore he did not want to raise false hopes, but he knew he would enjoy reading the book. On January 20, he briefly wrote to say he thought *The Ginger Man* a fine book and would enjoy to meet me.

And so it was that on January 23, I was making my way to 10 Fitzroy Street and finding myself right back again in these familiar climes of Soho. Only this time a little farther north in the vicinity west of Bloomsbury and not far from the famed pub the Fitzroy Tavern, long a haunt of the poetic and painting Bohemians of this area and one or two times visited by myself and Michael Heron when on our undergraduate traveling jaunts from Trinity College. Nor indeed was it that far from the pub where took place the famed kangaroo battle that was described in the pages of *The Ginger Man.*

I entered up steps of a less than pristinely preserved Georgian building now commercialized in which on the ground floor was the office of the publisher Neville Spearman, Ltd. A small sign directed one to the first doorway on the left. I knocked and, after being told to come in, I found rising from behind his desk inside this long narrow room a disarmingly good-looking and nattily bow-tied, smiling gentleman, dressed as befitted someone who lived at an address Rose Cottage in the rural splendor of Sussex.

"Ah, I'm Neville Armstrong and I presume you are Mr. Donleavy."

"Yes. How do you do."

All was extremely polite. I was now, having met a few, at least able to compare publishers. And Neville Armstrong had a lively, breezy and brisk enthusiasm about him, and bid me take a seat in his unpretentious office.

"Well, Mr. Donleavy, I'll come straight to the point. I liked *The Ginger Man* very much and would like to publish it. I'm sure it will be prominently reviewed and well received by the perspicacious and more than probably attacked by the more conservative of the establishment. But I would expect it to make a stir upon its publication in England and to receive lead reviews in the better journals. However, I think one must warn that as the book stands, it could also land the author and publisher in legal difficulties if not prison and involve the printer in the same plight. It's being an offense, as I am sure you know, to publish indecent books and to deprave and corrupt those into whose hands such publications may fall. If I am allowed to make some judicious cuts in the Paris edition and perhaps have an introduction written drawing attention to the work's literary merit, this will help allay a printer's misgivings and avoid the book's being prosecuted as an obscene publication. If you agree to this, I will assume fully all risks of publication and would defend publishing *The Ginger Man.* But not only would I like to publish *The Ginger Man* but would like to have an option on your next novel."

Despite his caveats, Armstrong seemed to be optimistic, not to say cheerful, about bucking the status quo and said he would draw up a contract. But this was certainly something new in publishers' reactions, in encountering someone who thought I had a future as a writer and whose next book might be worth publishing. I then said I had already been to Paris and seen the Olympia Press who were agreed to a cut English publication and that it would advertise and sell more of their unexpurgated edition. Armstrong throughout our talk clearly knew considerable of the Olympia Press's existence and its business but gave no hint of any previous troubles he had had with Girodias. Nevertheless he did seem to gently suggest that the less the Olympia Press came into matters the better.

In the ensuing year of 1956, from January to December, the logistics of *The Ginger Man*'s English edition preparation and publication took place. Signed contracts with Neville Spearman Ltd. were exchanged by March 19. Arland Ussher, the aristocratically Anglo-Irish philosopher and a friend of Gainor's, had agreed to write an introduction. I published "You Murdered My Cat" in the *Manchester Guardian,* and the blurb and my biography were ready to go to Spearman Ltd. And Armstrong, it transpired, was also a man of the theater and having seen

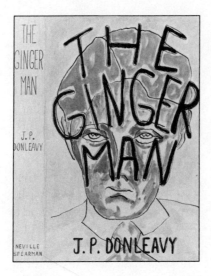

In order to make use of my artistic accomplishments, Neville Armstrong suggested I do a cover for THE GINGER MAN. *Alas he felt it not to his liking.*

John Osborne's *Look Back in Anger* on the London stage, and known that *Helen* was to be broadcast on the BBC, thought that I should dramatize *The Ginger Man*.

On July 4, I commenced to undertake to write the first draft of the play based on the novel *The Ginger Man*. Neville Armstrong, who exhibited an ease of informal communication, was sending further encouraging words and even apologizing once in a letter, that to pardon his typewriter as the machine was jumping. We were now referring to each other as Neville and Mike. But as galley proofs were now coming and a copy of a proposed cover, it immediately provoked my response that I might be heading down the same road as paved by Girodias and the Olympia Press. And I invoked the name of Robert Pitman, who, as a journalist in the world of newspapers, was now becoming considerably conspicuous and more right wing than left in his leanings.

40A Broughton Road,
Fulham, London SW6
July 20th 1956

Dear Neville,

Re: Dust jacket. I don't think that one the way it stands. Any suggestion of sex on cover is fatal. It clashes with introduction since cover draws attention to what intro is trying to avoid. I'm sure you must feel this yourself. Didn't want to say anything yesterday till I got some opinions and slept on matter. Pitman for one thinks it's absolute suicide and I feel it instinctively. And it's robbed me of all hope for book.

I think take out woman entirely and substitute a sinking red sun on horizon with black outline of road. This will center red and balance picture as enclosed. Do let me know as soon as possible.

Sincerely,
Mike

To my utter relief Armstrong took my advice concerning the cover and by August 14, his representatives were subscribing the book and making efforts, as do authors, to tie in matters where an association might be of benefit. In this regard Ilkley, Yorkshire, and the bookshop Broadbent's was mentioned by Armstrong to his rep as a possible place to subscribe book "as the author and his wife have big connections there." And his London rep had stayed up till four A.M. and, reading the book in one sitting, reported next morning that it was "terrific." To which Armstrong replied that it must be a "man's book." This was all heady stuff and was like being like an author is supposed to be, with the world, in response to his scribbling, making sounds back to him. Ah, but small but significant enough further flies were getting in the ointment. Following the salacious jacket being scrapped as a result of my objection, Neville in the nicest possible way suggested I should pay for half of this cost. My response was swift and sure. Not on your nelly, I said.

By September 21 and in response to a set of galley proofs being sent, the very first genuine interest was being shown by Barney Rosset of Grove Press to publish *The Ginger Man* in America and he was actually offering a contract to do so. Which agreement as it turned out was the very first and last which was not designed to screw the author down unconscionably, and was in fact an agreement drawn up by an agent or league in favor of authors. Providing one to believe there at least existed an example of a publisher prepared at the outset to be fair to a writer.

But faint war drums were beating. Matters in July were about to hot up. Neville Armstrong may have had second thoughts about my representations concerning the Olympia Press or in the fact that he now could be responsible for obtaining an American edition of *The Ginger Man* and knew that I was sharing this fifty-fifty with the Olympia Press, and he had sent without my knowledge a gentleman P. A. Dinnage to Paris to see Maurice Girodias. I had not met Dinnage, whose name was only later to appear listed as a director of Neville

Spearman Ltd. But I now had myself made plans to visit Paris to deal with the matter that might arise over an American edition. Not having heard from Girodias in over nine months, I wrote to Muffie Wainhouse. A reply was not long in coming, which was undated from Girodias and was received by me on August 20.

THE OLYMPIA PRESS

Dear Mr. Donleavy,

Muffie Wainhouse passes on your letter — of course I'll be in Paris on the 28th, and I'd be delighted to see you then.

I expect you must be very disappointed in me, and feel that I should apologise for my protracted silence. Things have been a bit tough of late, and I've really had very little time. I saw some vague bastard sent by Spearman, some time ago, who came to enquire about the English rights to *The Ginger Man*. I told him I controlled them as long as my edition of the book would be in print. Anyhow, if you contemplate doing anything with Spearman, be very careful, they are very dishonest people according to my experience with them.

Well, toodle oo.

Yours,
Girodias

The first shot across one's bows had now whistled by and not yet having to duck, it was difficult to sense whether and how soon larger guns were going to come into play. So far one had found Spearman Ltd. quite straightforward, but there was no doubt about Neville Armstrong's attitude, which was in a nutshell simply expressed as, "To hell with Girodias."

I too began to sense that this might have to be the case and a very measured response was made to this gentleman signing off with "toodle oo," which would elicit lawyer amusement if not laughter many years into the future. However, the expression would indeed grow fainter and fainter very soon on this singular gentleman's lips and pen and entirely disappear as a lighthearted form of eloquence.

August 23rd 1956

Dear Mr. Girodias,

Thank you for your letter and catalogue received August 20th.

I wrote sometime ago about a matter serious to me, you did not answer and that's that. On October 25th 1955 you gave me the English rights. I hold you to this.

I wanted to come to Paris to discuss future of book. Your letter makes me wonder if there is much point.

Yours sincerely,
J. P. Donleavy

And now a more serious-minded Girodias began to rear his extremely astute head. With very carefully couched words all designed to elicit from the author, who was thought prone to suffer from outbursts of self-pity, as many admissions as possible which might be prejudicial to his rights. But the second paragraph of such letter made extreme sense and seemed written with words heartfelt and true but one could only surmise they were so stated to establish this gentleman's publishing bonafides should push come to shove and legal guns start to blaze.

THE OLYMPIA PRESS

August 24th 1956

Dear Donleavy,

What is it all about? I fail to understand your mysterious letter, and its subterranean implications. You say that you wrote some time ago about a matter serious to you, but I don't even know what you are talking about! You say that on October 25th 1955 I gave you the English rights. What do you mean by that? Don't you think you should be more clear — unless the whole thing is another private joke.

In any case, as your letter leaves me rather perplexed as to your projects, I wish to remind you, 1) That I have published your book not because of some sordid motive, but only because I liked it, and was the only publisher so far to like it enough to publish it; and 2) That, having published it, I consider that I own the English rights at least as long as my edition is in print, and will protect my rights quite definitely.

I will be looking forward to a word of explanation from you. Don't hesitate to tell me all that's on your mind, it is the only way to deal with problems caused by moodiness and London fogs.

Yours, as always truly,
M. Girodias

In referring to "a matter serious to me," although I did not fully realize it then, I was in fact raising a question which would many the years hence provide the legal bedrock upon which the entirety of Girodias's action in the London law courts would come to grief and founder. As I sat down now to make my reply to Girodias, I already realized that the barbed legal arrows I was attempting to fashion would have to sink deep and permanently into the enemy. And which now in my bow were aimed to be lofted leisurely but would from their high arc descend lethally to finally hit their bull's-eye, Girodias. For here clearly was a man who from his thought to be in a superior position, regarded another man a naive fool. And I realized as I wrote such a letter that whatever words it said would have to say them as writ in stone. I was not without remembering of what the Society of Authors had advised me. That I had no redress over the work being published by the Olympia Press with their warning to me, which in my failure to question was tantamount to my entering into their business as purveyors of pornography. However, I had now looked more deeply into the laws of contract and copyright and also the terms exact of our agreement. It was now, at least for the appreciable time being, firmly "toodle oo."

September 3rd 1956

Dear Mr. Girodias,

Your letter August 24th. A matter I consider serious, recovery of MS copy of *The Ginger Man*. This is valuable to me.

I went to Paris last October 1955 to see you since I considered our agreement, constituted by our exchange of letters, in abeyance, for reasons I will give below. On October 25th 1955 I told you a publisher here was interested in *The Ginger Man* and the publication of a cut edition in England. I asked you if you were agreed to my having entire rights to the publication of a cut edition in England and you said yes, that it would help sell your edition and advertise book. I accepted this as an agreement and on this basis I was in turn agreed that you should share with me in an equal division of monies secured of American rights resulting from such publication.

You mention your motive for publishing book. The fact is that you published it as pornography in a pseudonymous and pornographic series, it is distributed and sold as such. You will understand that I do not have to remain party to an agreement where the subject matter has been used for an unlawful purpose and which has resulted to my prejudice. Had I known your intentions I would have withdrawn my book. My rights are protected by common law where there has been a breach of trust or confidence. I accepted your letter of February 11th 1955 as a genuine concern for my work which was offered to you in good faith and accepted our correspondence as evidence of yours.

According to our agreement you were to pay me outright royalties in advance. This in fact has not been the case, it was upon this basis of payment of an outright royalty in advance that I accepted your agreement and the sharing of rights in English speaking countries. As it now stands my royalty is approximately 3%, a supplementary payment of

£150 brings it to approximately 5%. My acceptance of your agreement stood on the basis of an outright royalty payment in advance of approximately 6½%.

Yours sincerely,
J. P. Donleavy

Down my narrow Fulham working-class street, and popped into my letter slot came the Girodias response, adamant and uncompromising, as one might have expected it to be. But unlike being confronted by the surprise of Girodias's publication of *The Ginger Man,* this time I was on guard and ready. And saw instantly that the arrows had struck home, with my letter having mapped out a defense in a future legal action, but not knowing then that the law proceeds in unpredictable and strange ways.

THE OLYMPIA PRESS

September 8th 1956

My dear Donleavy,

I consider your letter of September 3rd as a piece of schizophrenic nonsense. Do not think for a minute that I find your infantile attempt at blackmail impressive, or even interesting.

As to the moral aspect of the quarrel, please refer to your own first letter, dated September 7th 1954, in which you offered us your MS., and explained the circumstances with none of your present blue-eyed righteousness.

As to the legal aspect: I have with you a contract which is perfectly good and sound in any court, be it British or French. It consists in an exchange of letters ours of January 7th and 13th, April 15th and 22nd 1955 and yours of January 11th and 17th and April 19th 1955. I will add that I have never agreed to letting you sell the rights for a cut edition in England; you have dreamt that.

Sincerely yours,
M. Girodias

I was to know early that anyone making a distinction between what was moral and legal was likely to be a dangerously unpleasant customer indeed. And that one should hasten to make these words mean the same as soon as possible, and squeeze the less than palatable result down their unwilling throats. But meanwhile, this Girodias reply had to mean that a serious situation could be accruing, for all was geared now toward *The Ginger Man* being published in England. A publication date set and the book subscribed to booksellers. October 15,

Grove Press and Barney Rosset had agreed terms for an American edition. The first press news announcing the publication was beginning to appear. After a struggle of six years, what one had first thought possible for *The Ginger Man* might at last be realized. Ah, but fatefully just as it would always be in the history of this work, there came an ominous warning from what one had to surmise was to be a first salvo from a heavy Girodias gun. No "toodle oos" now. And loading was in progress for further and heavier warning salvos.

THE OLYMPIA PRESS

October 26th 1956

Dear Donleavy,

From a clipping of the *Publishers' Circular,* October 13th 1956 I see that you have decided to go ahead with an English edition of *The Ginger Man.*

If this project is not abandoned immediately, I shall have to take legal action to prevent publication and to obtain adequate damages.

Sincerely yours,
M. Girodias

Registered

A similar and longer letter from Girodias was also to arrive at Neville Spearman's. And I was to find in the years to come that often as not two publishers in conflict would, if they could, fast make the author the scapegoat in between. But this possibility did not now seem to present itself between Girodias and Armstrong.

THE OLYMPIA PRESS

October 26th 1956

Neville Spearman, Publishers,
10 Fitzroy Street,
London W.1.

Dear Sirs,

From the October 13th issue of the *Publishers' Circular* we learn that you intend to publish a cut version of J. P. Donleavy's *The Ginger Man.*

We must remind you of the visit of one of your directors to this office some months ago to enquire about our intentions concerning this book. At that time we stated clearly that as the original publishers and owners of the English-language world rights, we were not prepared to consider sharing those rights with any other publisher as long as our own edition was not exhausted.

In any exchange of correspondence with Mr. Donleavy we have again expounded our position on this, to us, extremely important subject. We are shocked, therefore, to learn that you and Mr. Donleavy have persisted with this project — no doubt founding your decision on the belief that our peculiar position would prevent us from taking legal steps against you.

We must state once more and emphatically that we do not intend to be imposed upon by piratical methods, but will defend our own good right in a most energetic manner.

Of course we are at your disposal to give you in case you pretend not to be acquainted with Mr. Donleavy's contract with us, all the necessary information concerning our legal rights.

> Yours sincerely,
> M. Girodias

MG/mw
Registered

It seemed that the time was now fast approaching when we might have to consult with lawyers. But I simply did not have the wherewithal to do so. But meanwhile, first on November 3, Neville Armstrong took up the cudgel and sent off his own salvo toward Paris.

NEVILLE SPEARMAN LTD.

3rd November 1956

M. Girodias,
Olympia Press,
6 rue de Nesle,
Paris 6e, France.

Dear M. Girodias,

I have your registered letter and I am at a loss to understand its meaning or why it has been written. You know very well that you do not hold the rights in Donleavy's *The Ginger Man* that you claim and I am amazed that you have the audacity to make such a frivolous claim and use the threatening words that you have written. What is the motive behind this?

Earlier in the year, as you say, my fellow-director came to see you while in Paris. He *never* approached you with the request that we might be allowed to publish an English edition in England of this title. Why the hell should he? We had already signed the contract with the author and previously took legal advice that it would be in order to do so.

Let's get this quite straight. Your edition has already been on the French market 18 months: further, the book in its French edition would not, I imagine, be admissible into this country in view of certain passages (which we have deleted) and therefore you have no claim on this point of implied competition.

Kindly be good enough to drop, therefore, these spurious claims, particularly in view of the fact that I am informed that you already owe the author a considerable sum of money on the French edition. I cannot believe that you wish to be involved in litigation to substantiate your claims.

All further correspondence on this matter will be passed to my legal advisers who are already informed on this matter and who will take the appropriate action necessary.

Yours truly,
Neville Armstrong

CC. J. P. Donleavy

There could be little doubt that Armstrong took comfort from the nature of Girodias's overall business and his removed position in France. But this gentleman with the bow tie was to be just as adamantly persevering as his letter more than amply pretended. However, Girodias could certainly be portrayed in a British court as the depraved devil incarnate to the British establishment of magistrates, police commissioners, customs officers and the queen. Not to mention the British public at large, and to such as *The People* newspaper, who could now have, at last, a heyday, were they still interested. And to extol that Girodias was the happy source of tomes concerning bottoms being thrashed by bishops and perhaps could be thought of as a beneficial influence in the spread of such cautionary tales. But I did not take such comfort, nor did I underestimate my adversary, knowing for a start that Girodias was perhaps laying claim to a work he might have now found he wanted to boast about having published and discovered had serious commercial prospects.

THE OLYMPIA PRESS

November 6th 1956

Mr. Neville Armstrong,
Neville Spearman Ltd.,
10 Fitzroy Street,
London, W1.

Dear Mr. Armstrong,

I think it is unnecessary to answer in detail your letter of November 3rd concerning J. P. Donleavy's *The Ginger Man* since you yourself propose it is preferable that all further discussion of this extremely disagreeable affair be carried out through the offices of our lawyers.

Will you please, therefore, make known the name and address of your legal counsel so that he can be contacted by mine?

Meanwhile I wish to make quite clear the following: 1) When your fellow-director visited me in Paris he *did* ask whether we would let you produce an edition of *The Ginger Man* and I very definitely replied that we could not grant such an authorization; 2) We *own* the world English rights to *The Ginger Man*. How can you presume we do not with no knowledge of what is in our files?; 3) Concerning any disagreements between Mr. Donleavy and myself, I would be very pleased to dispense with your comments and intervention, as, once again, you can only know one side of the picture; 4) veiled threats contained in your letter, as well as rather unseemly insolence, will not influence me toward changing my absolute determination to straighten out this business quite completely.

In conclusion, I would advise you most earnestly to take the advice of your legal counsel before going any further, either with your threats or with the production of the book.

Sincerely yours,
M. Girodias

MG/mw
Registered
A registered copy of this letter is being sent to Mr. Donleavy.
(MG)

There was now in Girodias's letters for the first time a nuance showing of serious regard in even referring to me as Mr. Donleavy. But even in invoking the use of lawyers and such words as "unseemly insolence," Girodias's reply again seemed to possess a curious underlying reasonableness. Which was not about to last for long. For on November 13, we heard from his lawyers, Rubinstein, Nash and Company, with an address in Gray's Inn who "as a matter of courtesy" were informing that if after a perusal of papers and considering the matter, and should the circumstances justify, they would advise their clients to issue proceedings.

The legal chess game had begun. And except for the countdown to publication now twenty-nine days away, I was not to know that there was to be oodles and oodles of time to stretch strategies to the limit. And in many lands also keep numerous lawyers far from the poorhouse. But paramount now, above all things, and an absolute matter of life and death and especially my life, was that the book, no matter what, get out into publication, and be itself the answer to Girodias. I had no money for lawyers. And with nothing else to back me up except my wits and my ability to quick-spot wile in others, I awaited the worst. Noting that Girodias did not in his August 24 letter flatly deny any agreement over the British rights but waited until his letter of September 8 to do so.

But what was to amaze me now most was my satisfaction at having at last made Girodias the enemy I meant and knew him to be. And also that the work *The Ginger Man* could be, like my own name, real, and both could become known for what they were. I could also dimly regard I'd achieved a sense of redress in that this publisher in Paris had had to come to the realization and recognize that *The Ginger Man,* as a so-called literary work, had commercial worth. But which, to my mind, he had absolutely no right to, whatsoever. He had instead incited a wrath in his budding author adversary that would be carefully and forever concealed.

And which
Even in total victory
Would never be
Undone

41

As the chillier days of middle November 1956 came to London and the ladies' footsteps on their way to the laundry at the end of Broughton Road sounded dimmer through a closed window, the front door letterbox flapped more frequently and sounded louder as I now came to unpleasantly anticipate the legal correspondence arriving.

Armstrong had sent the Olympia Press matters for advice to his solicitors, with whom he'd now spoken and who had counseled that having seen the relative papers and copies of letters, that we indeed had a very poor case and that the contract consisting of an exchange of letters was enforceable by injunction and the only thing to do was to negotiate as best as one could and get Girodias to agree to a compromise and share of royalties and by so doing stop them issuing an injunction against publication scheduled for December 7, 1956.

A four P.M., November 16, meeting was now made with Norman Shine of Samuels and Shine. I met Armstrong beforehand at his office and we both strolled toward Goodge Street but were early for our meeting. Neville proposing we repair meanwhile to have a cup of tea. It was to be my first social entertainment in England by a British publisher. And so inside a little tea kiosk full of cigarette smoke and serving fish and chips and populated by the local road sweepers, lorry drivers and shop assistants, we stood at the counter. This was a dramatic change from Paris's best restaurants. And despite my being a lowly resident of Fulham, I indeed might never have actually been in such a place before. Armstrong asking me would I also like a cup of tea and I said yes, I would like one weak without sugar and a tiny bit of milk, and Armstrong, taking command, ordered tea for us both. The brew served up in plain white cups and saucers and placed on the wooden counter by the aproned cook at four pence per cup. Making a total of eight pence. Neville dug into his pocket and drew out a half crown coin, which then was one eighth of a pound sterling and which he looked at as it lay heads up in the middle of his outheld palm.

"Mike, you don't happen, do you, to have any small change on you. I don't want to break into a half crown."

Although completely stunned, I reached into my own pocket and fetched out a six pence and few pennies and, totaling them to eight pence, placed the sum down on the counter. I somehow imagined that Neville must have been an army commissary sergeant major in the war and was carefully conscious of comestibles. But in fact I had no idea as to what role he had played in the Second World conflict. But one thing was imminently clear, this was no flamboyantly spendthrift publisher who put on airs and was out to impress authors. And which in the case of British publishers even in further years was not to greatly change.

At Gerald Samuels and Shine's office, Norman Shine appeared to be quite enthusiastic with dealing with our case. With this rugged, young and surprisingly handsome gentleman looking more like a rugby player than a lawyer. Although it seemed it might not be the usual type of literary litigation in which he got engaged, I nevertheless got an impression of confidence as he reviewed the papers, examining all scrupulously, even down to the loops of Girodias's signature. And then even taking up one of Girodias's letters and holding it up to the light to examine it for its watermark and quality of paper and both passing muster. He laughed as he advised how it was often a grave mistake to ever answer letters from anybody, and especially those sent by a lawyer. Then Shine observed the serious mien upon my face, which in fact, disguised vengeance and the disbelief that I was actually, for the first time in my life, going to be sued and knowing that deep down in my soul, come what may, I would fight to the death.

"You mustn't be so glum, Mr. Donleavy. I've painted the worst possible picture of yours and Neville's position. I've read this *Ginger Man* of yours, and I must confess I enjoyed it and thought it a very good book. Your adversary in Paris has a certain grandiloquence with which, it already appears, he has slandered Mr. Armstrong. And he has retained a prominent law firm, but you mustn't be intimidated. I'm just a poor Jewish boy from the East End of London who's come up the hard way, but more times than you'd imagine, we end up kicking the hell out of these bigger West End law firms and these public school boys who operate them."

Throughout the conference with Norman Shine, Neville Armstrong mostly remained quiet and businesslike and very much putting himself in the hands of his solicitor. However, these comments of Shine's were among the first unsolicited reactions to *The Ginger Man* and at least provided me with one of the very few times since the difficulties had begun that I could take comfort from someone's words, and the other unbelievable thing that was happening, that at long last I now actually had people reading and enjoying the book, and knowing who the author was, albeit all members of the law profession. And Norman Shine, Neville Armstrong's and now also my solicitor, did, in spite of all the dire prospects indicating that Girodias could hang us, duly dispatch a letter, and in the good way of protecting his clients.

GERALD SAMUELS & SHINE

19th November 1956

Rubinstein, Nash & Co.,
Gray's Inn,
WC1.

Dear Sirs,
The Ginger Man

We confirm our several telephone conversations in respect of the book entitled *The Ginger Man*. We have viewed the long correspondence between the Parties, and are by no means certain that there is a contract between the Parties in which your clients receive the English printing and publishing rights. We have not had the opportunity of obtaining full instructions from the Author, and are dealing, at the moment, merely with the correspondence. However, our clients Neville Spearman Limited have no desire to litigate on this matter, and if some sort of amicable arrangement can be come to between the Parties, we would consider this possibility in the interests of all.

We await to hear from you at the earliest possible moment, as our clients wish to proceed with the proposed publication.

Yours faithfully
Samuels & Shine

Bleak now indeed were prospects and gloom blackening ever blacker by the hour. Rubinstein and Nash asked for a copy of the galley proofs. However, along with such advice, adverse as it was from Norman Shine, Armstrong, and clearly seeming able to sustain optimism in spite of the overwhelming pessimism of our present case, was, perky as ever, in the midst of all, still gung ho toward publication, and even imploring me to go ahead and sign the Barney Rosset agreement with the "please be an angel." He also told me not to be too worried, although he feared that financially I looked like being the loser to Girodias, but that half a loaf was better than none.

Indeed the drums toward publication were beating furiously now. The dust jacket orange and blue. And Dangerfield portrayed on a couch with a bottle. Then of all amazing things, a photograph taken by Murray Sayle was there for all to see on the jacket flap. Advance copies were in hand with Arland Ussher's quite marvelously erudite introduction, which Armstrong believed should, by its scholarship, stay the hand of the public prosecutor. With bulk supplies on their way and the book being subscribed in London, the review copies were being sent out. I also got the author's six free copies, in two of which the pages were blank here and there throughout the volume. And now as we were continuing to get closer day by day and hour by hour to publication, we were inadvertently helped by Girodias's solicitor, who, having other business there, was going to Paris and would also be seeing Girodias. However, in giving us more time, it still did not remove the threat of an injunction hanging over us, which not only could stop all distribution of the book but have all the copies already shipped, recalled.

The month of November was coming to a close. And to achieve, as Shine had suggested in his letter, some sort of amicable arrangement, a meeting was arranged with Girodias's solicitors. The fact of settlement being suggested in the letter of November 19 had, it seemed, introduced a degree of leisure to the proceedings. But with the clear unpleasant prospect of Girodias imposing terms for settlement, which one had no encouragement to believe would be reasonable. But we did at least now have again the luck of a further postponement of this meeting. I was beginning to learn something most important in the matter of law, that provided one was the defendant, a delay could be something to be looked forward to. And in this case, ever so infinitesimally increasing the chance that publication day, now less than a week away, might still be achieved. It also increased the dubious comfort of thinking that literary editors and their various reviewers had got the book and were belting out paeans of praise on their typewriters. There was also a strange vague comfort taken from the fact that Girodias had chosen to be represented by a highly reputable firm of solicitors, distinguished for their probity, and to whom turpitude was an anathema. And who, in possession of seven telephone lines to Spearman's one and my none, had also to be unhappily presumed, extremely expensive, a major consideration for me, as I might end up having to pay them.

485

But now this end of November a new appointment was made with Rubinstein and Nash. The fatal meeting to be on a Friday at eleven A.M. at their offices in Gray's Inn. I met Armstrong at his Fitzroy Street office to be driven with Norman Shine in Armstrong's fairly up-market car around to these offices located in a sedate terrace of old buildings standing in their somber wintry park under leafless elms. Rubinstein and Nash, with their prominent clients, especially in the world of arts and publishing, were reputed by their mere prominence and influence to be able by their intervention as lawyers often automatically to effect settlements. Their weight added to that of their clients, now to be imposed upon Neville Spearman Ltd. and myself. And here they were quite appropriately located in the Inns of Court, surrounded by trees and lawns, and these gray buildings were just as the place was named.

Up we went upon these ancient, musty and stern steps, where many a litigant one felt must have preceded us. And as one would learn, our adversary Maurice Girodias had also climbed. After a brief wait in an outer space, we were ushered by a legal ostiary into an austere office, humanized discreetly by a few photographs of the family sort that one was to become familiar with over the coming years. And seen in other lawyers' offices, would be the only consoling sight there was, and only to be found in the visages of those near and dear to such legal counselors. But here, now in the offices of Rubinstein and Nash, as a few tentatively friendly words were passed with Norman Shine, there seemed to be a degree of graciousness exhibited by this gentleman behind his desk as he was about to follow his client's instructions in Paris. First to come were the terms for settlement in regard to the publisher Neville Spearman. Armstrong listening intently but unamused and becoming increasingly so, as he heard the ruthlessly tough terms laid down by Girodias and now dictated, which were not only to severely cut into the prospect of his profit but even to just about leave him without one, plus undermine his due credit as publisher. My terms and sentence of my punishment was to be last, to which a question was raised by Norman Shine and which in the course of answering Mr. Rubinstein used the following words.

"Of course the terms of Mr. Donleavy's agreement with Mr. Girodias will be spelled out."

These words, when I heard them spoken, seemed entirely reasonable enough. I had always thought and understood that I would remain in a position to be consulted and have my approval required and to consider terms in any matter of negotiation by the Olympia Press concerning the rights affecting *The Ginger Man*. And one took the words "spelled out" as being a process to effect an exact written agreement which would avoid any misinterpretation. But there was felt in Girodias's terms a bullying quality which I sensed severely provoked Armstrong's anger, and he had already spoken of suing Girodias for slander. And indeed I myself felt a growing reluctance to agree and settle. Although lurking still within me was the sense of the reasonable man, but it was progressively getting less and less so. But there seemed now no question that unless a settlement was reached, an injunction would be brought to stop publication and distribution and against booksellers selling the book. Reminding one now that there had been in one of Armstrong's recent letters a comment with three words underlined.

"Rubinstein wants to see our edition but *under no circumstances* can we send him an advance copy which will give him a clue as to our publication date."

Norman Shine had the details of settlement written down in notes and remained friendly and confident, suitably disguising the apprehension felt by the author and the anger of Neville Armstrong. We now together got up from our chairs and left these offices dedicated to the practice of law. As the door closed behind us and we were in the hall and had begun to descend the stairs, Shine spoke.

"Neville, as a matter of interest, how much money is at stake in this and do you think you might make a profit out of this book and if so how much."

As we had now reached the front stone steps and there was an appreciable pause and awkwardness and hesitation in Armstrong answering the question, Shine waited patiently. I sensed that Armstrong did not think it appropriate to discuss matters as sensitive as his profit in front of the author, and certainly would want to be discreet in mentioning figures to his solicitor, who would one day soon be billing him. But on the pavement fronting 5/6 Raymond Buildings, Gray's Inn, his breath steaming out on the cold air, Armstrong, after pausing to calculate a final time, answered Shine.

"I suppose I might make about two hundred and fifty pounds."

"Well, Neville, in that case I think it's worth spending ten pounds to get counsel's opinion."

At this, a further incurring of expense, Armstrong clearly was in some resistance and asked Norman Shine why he thought it was worth throwing more good money after bad.

"Because, Neville, there were some words used back there in that meeting we've just had and which were used in the discussion concerning Mr. Donleavy's settlement which bear further looking into. The words are simply, 'spell out.' They may mean nothing at all but certainly indicate that Girodias's rights are not clear-cut as they presently might seem to be in his exchange of letters with Mr. Donleavy. Therefore, I would advise you to get counsel's opinion."

"Norman, this is Friday, publication day is now next week and only a matter of days off. If settlement isn't reached, Girodias could move to get an injunction and stop the book."

"That's true and it's a chance you're taking. But I'll have the papers brought to counsel this afternoon and ask for an opinion by Monday at the latest."

This was a crunch time. But even now, the mood, if not the absolute intention, remained, that both Armstrong and I could refuse settlement. But anyone's opinion which could change anything to our advantage would be more than welcome. However, I put no hope whatever in any further legal advice. Thinking only that meanwhile, if one could now delay just these further few days, the novel would be published, reviews appearing. Then, if an injunction did come, at least the book would be out, and whatever legal mishmash ensued, at least some of the British public would know that as a writer and author of *The Ginger Man,* I existed. I now proffered my own two cents and said I would immediately go to Paris and do so without prejudice, and see Girodias and see if a better settlement could be reached. But to me my trip was more so, and more importantly, to borrow more time that I knew we desperately needed. Still, however, if it were possible, I was also concerned to attempt to settle the matter with Girodias. He had agreed with me to the English publication. And I even found myself vaguely thinking that he would one day regret denying it.

On December 3, 1956, and four days left to publication, I embarked at Dover and landed in France at Calais after one of the roughest crossings in the history of the Channel. Passengers even screaming in anguish as they upchucked again and again over the rails into the mountainously thrashing gray sea. I saw one Oriental gentleman so distressed that he seemed to be pleading for someone to come end his misery by shooting him, even demonstrating how it should be done, by putting his pointing finger up to the side of his head. Unlike my voyage on the *Franconia,* I astonishingly in my gloom took not a whit's notice of the pitching and rolling ship, strolling through the agonized passengers, and even chewing down an apple. Making port two hours late, I went onward by train to Gare St.-Lazare, arriving there and almost thinking I might encounter on the station Gainor's friend and blind dog still wandering around trying to find their way to Gare d'Auster-litz. Which station Gainor had reminded was named after Napoleon's greatest battle.

Lugging my single black leather bag, I took the Métro second-class and got off at rue du Bac. I found what was an inexpensive hotel and stayed in a first-floor front room near the corner of rue Jacob and rue Bonaparte. I chose badly for the night ahead. If the cars did not roar by, then they crashed. Arguments ensued and came more crashes. I stayed awake till nearly dawn, in what I was to adjudge was the noisiest if not the most dangerous spot in all of Paris. Which made the carrefour de Buci seem like an oasis of silence inside the tomb of a pharaoh's pyramid.

Next morning, bleary-eyed and weary, I duly took my *petit déjeuner,* splashed cold water on my face, stepped out on the street and headed eastward along rue Jacob to cross to rue de Buci and navigate its carrefour, and then heavy-footed down rue Dauphine to turn left into rue de Nesle. There was little to prepare or shield one for the further utter grimness one would encounter at this address of number 8. Could it ever be thought in such pain, that one ever wrote for glory, or for money or for fame. And upon this day of December 4 in the year 1956, I would sink into an abysmal, desperate state of depression.

Out of which I
Deeply sincerely
Thought I might
Never
Get

42

I MADE MY WAY under the stone arch of number 8 and into its courtyard and up the steps to the big gray doors at the top. My mind battered by traffic noise through the previous night was growing crystal clear by the second. Inside there was an air of bustle and business and Girodias seemed to have expanded further into the interior of this floor of offices, inhabiting yet another and more distant room with a large window overlooking this *cour de maison.* I had not too long to wait to be shown in. And to find an unfriendly grimness upon Girodias's face, as one might have expected.

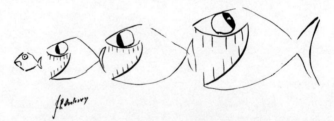

My longtime favorite fish cartoon, which I frequently sent to friends and submitted to THE NEW YORKER *the year during my stay in America in 1951 but which was rejected with the note that the magazine had something similar in the works.*

Perfunctory greeting made, and following informing him that his terms were unacceptable and that I had come to see if an agreement could be reached in settlement, it did not take additional time to discover that Girodias considered my visit a distinct and verifying sign of weakness. Growing heated, he said that he was not compromising in any way and that I should prevail upon Spearman Ltd. and Armstrong to accept the terms he had laid down or face the consequences. As to my own position, he referred me back to his solicitors in London and to their terms that had been dictated, and then added,

"I think we should be realistic."

"Very well, in that case I will see you in court."

I was astonished at my reaction, delaying not a second to rise from my sitting position. From behind his desk, Girodias, ashen-faced in anger, got slightly up out of his seat as if to stand, but more as if he were reaching for the telephone. But the telephone was already easily in reach, and Girodias leaning forward put his two hands on his desk and sat back down. I was already at the door, and now on my way out. Almost disbelieving my own words sentencing myself to death. But in so doing I was absolutely willing so to do. And one thing was for sure, if ever I needed to know. Was that I would stand there in battle fighting as I died.

I walked down those steps of 8 rue de Nesle and out of that courtyard back onto these narrow Paris streets. I knew exactly at that moment that Girodias was telephoning London to instruct to issue an injunction. All one could see was dismal disaster. My own fate no longer on my mind. But the overwhelming thought of what would be the possible and greater nightmare fate of my wife and two innocent young children. Whose futures would now be destroyed by the destruction and demise of their father. Who was to be put in a different kind of battle. Not of physical courage but one not less courageous. Fought with money that could buy words. That would be writ by legal hands and would accumulate in documents stacked mountainously high. And played as cards to win a pot of gold. That was, as no one could have known then, to grow and grow increasingly large.

As I proceeded up rue Dauphine, such was the terrible grimness of my thoughts that I realized that I had to find some distraction to keep me out of my rapidly deepening abyss and get me through the desperate hours remaining until I again boarded the train the next day at Gare St.-Lazare to return to London. Sayle and Marx had long left Paris. There was now no one whom I knew I might see and with whom I might talk. It was still only the morning. And a long, long way to go through the day. Then I suddenly thought of the only other single person I knew who might still be in Paris. Sylvia Sayers. I hadn't her phone number but remembered the appearance of the street in Montparnasse where behind a door in a long brick wall she lived with her husband in part of a large house which sat in an idyllic garden. I knew the number was 8, the same as that of the Olympia Press and that the street was near a hospital and an observatory that could be seen at the end of a long vista from the Luxembourg Gardens. I also knew that I could somehow find my way there by dead reckoning and recognizing the passing atmospheres of the boulevards and simply heading in the direction southwest, as one might do to Porte d'Orléans on the Métro. But such was my urgency that I took a taxi.

I gave at best garbled instructions street by street as we passed identifying landmarks. Then, as we turned off the boulevard and proceeded a little way down this side street and almost by a miracle on this otherwise nearly deserted thoroughfare, there was the strange door. Upon which I would now thump the knocker and ring the bell. And I waited. And waited. Fully five minutes and no answer. Reluctant now even to let myself walk away in this unfamiliar territory and have my despair and grim foreboding turn me into dust and the meekest breeze blow me away out of existence. But having now nearly waited ten minutes and knowing the sound at least of my knocks must have been heard across the walled garden inside, I knew no one must be home and I turned away into my fate.

I walked now up the street and back toward the boulevard to retrace my way back to the Latin Quarter. But thirty or forty yards away, something made me stop and look back. A man's head was peeking out the door and was surveying up and down the roadway. I turned round and retraced my steps. But this gentleman, whoever he was, had already closed and locked the door. I banged and knocked. The seconds went by. Then the sound of a latch being undone and the door opening. A man stood there in a robe over his nightwear. In French, I inquired after the Sayerses, and this gentleman replied in perfect English. I then vaguely remembered Sylvia referring to this person as being of the legal profession.

"Ah, Monsieur and Madame Sayers have moved. They are gone some many weeks now."

"Do you have their address to where they have moved."

"Ah, I am absolutely sure I have. But you must come in a moment while I attend to finding it."

The garden door closing behind us, we crossed on a path under the fruit trees which led up to a pair of French doors. As my friend opened one of these to enter a room, its windows shuttered, he switched on the light. And my heart sank at the sight. The walls covered with bookcases and books from floor to ceiling. Upon every shelf were stacked volumes of every size in every tiny conceivable space. His large desk was a sea of papers. Documents, files, notebooks and albums. Piles of paper with their edges curled over the edge of the desk. Every single nook and cranny seemed occupied by beribboned files, half-open books, newspapers, magazines, drawings and maps.

"Ah, monsieur, please, do step in. It will of course take me a moment. I know the address is somewhere here."

There was hardly any room to step into, but one did find a space directly ahead inside the door. The ceiling light was weakly beaming down. He switched on a desk lamp and more light helpfully was radiated out from under a green glass shade. And I watched this kindly gentleman still in his pajamas under his bathrobe and shuffling in his bedroom slippers, tentatively flick up a few pages on a few stacks here and there. But there was one thing that was becoming quickly and absolutely certain. I knew that in the several years it would take and that I did not now have at my disposal, that there was not the remotest ghost of a chance of this obviously scholarly and most accommodating gentleman ever finding Sylvia and her husband Michael's address without the assistance of every archivist at the Sorbonne. How would he, for a start, ever know which stack to look in. There being at least a hundred or more in nooks and crannies from floor to ceiling, never mind the uncharted surface of his desk.

But courtesy must be reciprocated by even greater courtesy. I stood my ground, my appreciative smile locked on my face. The minutes went by. I watched as a frown would appear on monsieur's face as he would abandon one stack of papers and repair to another stack. And then dig systematically downward through the parchments, dockets, forms, and documents. As he would begin at another pile, I began to silently count, as deeper down he went, one two three, and all the way to forty-six. Suddenly stopping, he would frown again and now move to yet another piece of furnishing, this time a lectern holding its towering weight of paper stacks. Monsieur continuing the careful lifting up of scratch pads, albums and diaries. I caught brief sight of a partly buried desk calendar useful to count the passing days.

"Forgive me, monsieur, I shall only be these few more moments. Please do step a little more inside out of the chill. I just know, I am absolutely certain that I have this address somewhere."

I was now feeling like the terrible imposition I was on this kindly gentleman's life. But I moved forward over the doorjamb and stood in some minimal further floor space, where I was just able to position myself between two stacks of literary and legal journals. And there was one thing I was sure of, that the Sayerses' address would simply have to wait to abide until another time that I might be in Paris. But that in facing this incredible sight of this gentleman's study, down this strangely lonely street of this city, and entering this world hidden away in the scholarly existence of this man's life, it was essential now to show one's appreciation and gracefully withdraw. And the one thing I knew I could do with some brilliance was to be damn polite to those deserving it.

"Monsieur, please don't bother further. If the address is for the moment not easily readily available, it is of no serious consequence whatever. I have already inconvenienced you enough. I shall be able to telephone a friend who may have it."

"Oh, it is no trouble, I assure you. In any event I shall require it myself soon, and it may as well be unearthed now as well as later."

I was anyway for these many moments at least enjoying being utterly transported celestial distances out of my own cares and woes. With only the worry now that this desperate pilgrimage to find the Sayerses, in being in vain, was also slightly unbalancing me mentally, and perhaps an omen that Paris should as quickly as possible become a forgotten chapter in my life. But I was thinking too that the French for some strange reason never seemed to be rude to me. However, I had never encountered nor expected such marvelous courtesy and manners as this good gentleman displayed in intrepidly facing the impossible. And in itself, a triumph of patience. Indulged only by those whose compassion could embrace an outsider trespassing among their fellow man. One could also see by the elegant vellum of diplomas, citations and testimonials that monsieur was most distinguished by considerable achievements, which alas, by my intrusion, only made one to feel even further acute embarrassment.

"Ah, monsieur, now I know. I well and truly know. Yes. Yes. It was Tuesday two months ago exactly that I was in here and that I had come to place the address and to put it exactly where I knew it could be found. Ah. Yes. Now if I could only remember exactly. But I am convinced. Absolutely convinced that I have put it somewhere on this desk. And that it has somehow become obscured."

Had I been obtuse enough I would have now ventured to suggest to this courteously kindly man that one might have added or substituted the word "buried" to that of his use of the word "obscured." But never mind, for more than a few moments I had totally forgotten the

Olympia Press and the name Girodias. And that by bowing deeply enough, I could show my appreciation for something that would be done for a desperate stranger by few other Frenchmen in all the wide breadth of France. But had, however, been done by Gainor for the man of the unknown language and his blind dog at Gare St.-Lazare. Through my desperate mind now went thoughts of Gainor Stephen Crist and blessed Oliver Plunket, to both of whom I did not feel I could rightly pray, being an atheist idolater, and not even in my extreme crisis did I think it fair that an exception could be made. In spite of this gentleman, still with his back bent and poring over yet more stacks and documents and now with a magnifying glass raised.

"Ah, *voilà. Presto. Passez muscade.* Here it is."

I did not believe my ears. Nor my eyes. As a tiny torn little scrap and slip of paper was unearthed and pulled from beneath a mountain-high stack of documents and newspapers at the corner edge of his desk. This gentleman's face wreathed with a satisfied smile as he made his way around to me, sidestepping the piles of books and other papers on the floor. His arm raised, to triumphantly show fluttering from his fingertips, a scrawl on a small slip of notepaper.

"Ah, but of course I will write the address out for you. It is in fact a hotel, quite a good one, the Montalembert, near the rue du Bac."

I could not believe how delighted I was. The Sayerses now had most definitely become a serious quest and mission. And they had already provided, even if only for these minutes, a wonderful relief from contemplating my life's ruin. To have within my actual fingers now this address and somewhere to go, somewhere to be. And to have this erudite and scholarly gentleman in his robe, pajamas and slippers delighted too to see my pleasure and to now give me a little bow and smile as I thanked him from the bottom of my heart and from all the bottoms of all the hearts I could think of. And indeed if anything was true. It was that Gainor Stephen Crist in Spain and his cohort in heaven, the blessed Oliver Plunket, had between them wrought a miracle. Because idolater that I was, I did nevertheless secretly madly pray to both of them.

As I now left this strange cloister in the company of this man and crossed his garden under the leafless apple trees, he gave me another little bow as I departed back out his door onto the streets of Paris. He seemed indeed as we said our good-byes to have thoroughly enjoyed himself. And my whole vision of the future seemed to have changed with this address that I now carried with me. Later I was to learn that I had spent the last half hour in the company of the descendant of another man who wrote much to change the thinking of the world. And whose great-grandson had now just given me hope once more.

And the name
Of whose
Great-grandfather
Was
Karl Marx

43

Bᴜᴛ ᴛʜᴇ ǫᴜᴇsᴛ for the Sayerses, I was to find had only just begun.
I went dutifully back first-class on the Métro to the Latin Quarter to
find the Hôtel Montalembert concierge helpfully informing me that
the Sayerses indeed had been staying there but had now moved at least
three or more weeks ago. And to yet another hotel. I looked up the
address in my atlas of Paris and figured the shortest route across the
interwoven confusion of all these streets. Walking instead of using
the Métro, for then at least I would know step by step where I was
going.

I set out across the boulevard St.-Germain and along rue du Bac,
crossing rue de Grenelle and rue de Varenne. Feeling now the first
sense of tiredness accosting one's legs and feet, and disgruntlement
when taking a wrong turning and having to find my way again. But at
last to go correctly down a quiet little street. The Sayerses must suddenly have decided they wanted peace and tranquility. An iron gate.
And a path beneath an arbor to the entrance door of a quiet, well-
starred and sedate little hotel which one might find tucked away in the
English countryside. To make my inquiry yet again for the elusive
Madame and Monsieur Sayers, who, clearly, one was learning, liked a
frequent change of scene.

"Ah, yes. We have their address. They have left a week ago."

Another address. Another hotel. Another perusement of my little
red Paris atlas. More rues, avenues and boulevards. Another mile.
Another wrong turning. Another half mile. And then this four-star
hotel. The afternoon fading. Now feeling desperate. It could not possibly be that I hadn't now at long last tracked them down. Having moved
only a week ago. Again into the lobby. Less English spoken. But surely
they would have found exactly what they were looking for and settled

497

in nicely in this most comfortable-looking and fairly luxurious establishment.

"Ah, yes, Monsieur and Madame Sayers. They have left. Just the day before yesterday."

"Oh, I was just wondering if you might have their new address."

"One moment and I shall look, monsieur. But I do not believe we have."

My elbows came down to rest on the hotel counter. As I now waited, it seemed as good a time as any to choose to give up. Before my legs folded up underneath me. There was no question but that with such erratic moves and such romantically elegant people, that they were next planning to travel to London or New York, or Hollywood. And that all finally packed would have been heading toward Le Havre and were this very morning boarding ship and taking up comfortable residence in their stateroom. It also seemed the more recently someone had left a hotel, the longer it took to find a forwarding address. But having embarked so purposefully on my mission and pursued it without pause, it was as if this hotel had become a suitably appropriate place to end it. A nice little bar with palm shrubs and a few comfortable leather chairs. Even the Paris *Herald Tribune.* Knock back a quick cognac, or better still, two cognacs. And just a short distance away along rue de Vaugirard, I could go, in my abject despair, sit in the Luxembourg Gardens.

"*Merci bien,* mademoiselle."

"Ah, wait, monsieur I have found it, a forwarding address. 172 rue de l'Université."

I went anyway to rest my weary legs in the Luxembourg Gardens, where the lonely didn't seem to mind remaining alone. And sharp-beaked seagulls became white specks on the green lawns. Strolling past the pale gray stone statues which peer over all from the past. Students chewing sandwiches. Old men playing chess and cards in the chill. At least Paris hadn't stopped being what it was since I was last there. And one goes to take a long pee in the pissoir. And an even longer sit on a bench. Where I looked again at the new street address scribbled and added to all the other previous addresses in my notebook. Except for the first time, this wasn't a hotel. And maybe, who knows, the elusive Sayerses could finally be found somewhere. I gathered my wearying legs once more beneath me. And just as did the boatswain mate in the navy at six A.M. in the morning, say, "Let's go, up and at them."

I proceeded down rue Bonaparte past a large police station taking prisoners in handcuffs out the door. Opposite and across the square, the church of St.-Sulpice. As I passed by this somber edifice of worship, one remembered the strange afternoon of Sacré-Coeur. And Girodias in his Citroën. That black vision all now a reality. With an indication of a man, who, assuming one was weak and vulnerable, was stimulated to the attack. Inspiring one to fight. And to now plow on to find a friend. Even though there seemed no doubt that the Sayerses were gone from Paris and probably France. No one moving so much could have been contemplating anything else. But go I must still in search to this last address.

In the familiar rue des Canettes, it was near the bar where Gainor visited his favorite little bistro, presided over by his Spanish *patrón*. My legs most severely now tiring. But only a short distance to walk down rue des Sts.-Pères and turn left to reach rue de l'Université. And having duly done exactly that, I commenced what was for me to become the longest walk of my life. Anticipating first that number 172 would only be one block over, then in the next street, then over the next avenue or boulevard. And I walked and walked. Westward across Paris. On what seemed now this endless street. Passing the Ministère de la Guerre. The Chambre des Députés, the Ministère des Affaires Étrangères. And still onward across the esplanade of the Hôtel des Invalides.

I stopped briefly to find I was still not disabled and still on my own two feet. Taking a *citron pressé*. Then up again and ever onward. In the distance now I could see the actual very end of rue de l'Université crossing avenue Bosquet and just a little further on to avenue Rapp. I knew this was going to happen and that the last building would be numbered 171 and there would be no 172! But suddenly there it was. A grand old venerable structure. Which looked to be housing anciently elegant apartments. I entered the *porte cochère*. Looked about, all seemed empty. A locked door admitted to a further vestibule and to what must be the staircase to the building's residences. Then, as I was contemplating to leave, a door of an office opened to reveal a diligent lady concierge. In my limited French, I inquired after Monsieur and Madame Sayers. She looked at me and shook her head. She had never heard of them. She even looked at a list of names and again shook her head. At least this was it. My day of walking and tracing was over. I could head back out through the gloom and shadows to the daylight of my nightmare again. Go back to my hotel, lie down and try to cure the tiredness of my legs, knowing I had tried my best. But a voice now was calling. The concierge had come out of her little office after me.

"Monsieur, monsieur. *Deuxième étage*. Monsieur and Madame Sayers. They move in only yesterday."

I went up the two flights of stairs. Stood in the gloom of this large hall and knocked on the door. It opened quickly. And it was Sylvia. Who could not believe her eyes, as they had not yet made known to their friends where they were and had just taken up residence in these commodious and grand apartments. Invited in, we chatted. Michael, her husband, whom I had not yet met, was working in his study, writing. She was on her way out to shop and said, can you come and have dinner here with us tonight. Yes. I could. About seven. My ordeal was over. The dismalness and much of the despair gone. I fairly skipped and danced and trotted all the way back to my hotel on this the nearly longest street in Paris.

A long soak of my legs in a minuscule hot bath and promptly at seven I was back. Magnificent smells pervading these vast chambers. Champagne poured in the grand salon. Normandy butter on whole-wheat bread. Lemon juice squeezed to anoint the slivers of smoked salmon. Michael Sayers and I sitting to talk about Dublin. From where he had gone to Monte Carlo as a young man to live in the Hôtel de Paris in order to attend nightly at the casino tables and to enjoy a fortune he'd inherited. He chuckled as he told this story of youthful imprudence. We talked about London. And about Paris. He had read *The Ginger Man.* As many had, he said, in Paris. The book was talked about. I mentioned the trouble with Girodias. He said in reply that with a book like *The Ginger Man,* I had no real worries. It would defeat those who would exploit or attempt to damage it. So have another glass of champagne.

In the large dining room in the candlelight we had oxtail stew and vegetable delectables with Clos de Vougeot 1947 and Romanée-Conti 1949. These stunning velvety wines descending the throat as one had second and third helpings from a magnificent steaming tureen set center of the table. Brie and salad. And an ice cream of stunning ingredients. But all now was explained as to the Sayerses' impatient and nervous wait to move to the splendor of these apartments. Where, heels clicking on the parquet, we repaired back from the dining room to the grand salon. Furnished with such as Louis the Sixteenth secretaries, the kingwood, tulipwood and marquetry all gleaming under an eight-light Louis the Fourteenth chandelier. On the gilded chairs we sat to listen to records and drink an elixir of apricot brandy. The songs we heard were sung by workers in the Pennsylvania coal mines. Michael Sayers able to trace and compare the origins of the words and melodies. And listening to the truth of all this sadness, they sounded indeed as if they had come out of the grief and sorrow of Ireland. And they had.

For the first time in this battle of *The Ginger Man* and in this grand salon of Paris, here was another writer telling me I had written a fine novel, which had already been circulating hand to hand across the various arrondissements. And that it would inevitably, as any good work did, produce some battles. And that the book, having readers talking about what they had read, I had the war already won.

And no day
And no night was
Ever to be as memorable
As this one
In my life

44

THE BOW plunging through the still rough gray waves, I sat solitary below decks, meditating upon the defeat I now faced in London as the cross-channel steamer made its way from Calais back toward the white cliffs of Dover. The ship finally no longer pitching and tossing in the great gray swells as it glided at last into the peaceful water of the harbor. The disappointing trip somehow at least had softened the aspect of the future, now knowing that the book had already found sympathetic readers in Paris, such as Michael Sayers.

The next day in Fulham, and on the last day left till publication, I waited till early afternoon to relate the most gloomy news of my visit to Paris to Armstrong, already realizing that he would no doubt be in his office staring at a notice of an injunction stopping publication and recalling the book from booksellers. My destination, as it was on many of these afternoons, was Bishop's Park along the river Thames where Philip could run while Karen, in her pushchair, and I could stroll under the tall, hauntingly somber plane trees. And where also on the way, in the comparative privacy of a country lane, I could stop to telephone Neville Armstrong at his office.

The route one walked took one past a housing estate and an adjoining athletic field, where once there had been a polo field. But still this area strangely seemed to retain its rural atmosphere from long ago. And at one end of a slightly crooked alley joining Peterborough and Hurlingham roads, there stood a red telephone kiosk posted like a sentry. At least it was just past lunch and, avoiding the likelihood of ruining someone's appetite, and Neville Armstrong following my pennies clanking was immediately on the line. And who, having listened to my voice convey my dismal news, sounded surprisingly cheerful and asked me did I otherwise enjoy Paris. When I said it hadn't been too bad, I found it difficult to believe his chirpiness or the words he was saying or the words that he now went on to say.

"We've had counsel's opinion. Norman Shine was right, there was indeed something not spelled out in the agreement you have with Girodias based on the exchange of letters with him, as no document exists signed by you in which you state that you convey the right to the Olympia Press to print and sell in all countries. Such a right can only be conveyed under the written signature of the proprietor and copyright owner, which you are as the author, and therefore Girodias without this right conveyed to him can't obtain an injunction and stop the book. Frankly I wouldn't want to be in his shoes. Publication will take place as planned."

Although I wasn't as sanguine as Neville Armstrong, knowing Girodias could still sue for damages and in my judgment would remain an enemy who still existed across the channel and who showed little or no regard for an author's work but whom I knew would show much regard for any money or profit such an author's work might bring, it was nevertheless bliss at last to hear for the first time that an author somehow had rights hidden buried in the technicalities of the law that could, even though by accident, result to his benefit. Walking along now, my step was lighter. And even though such information was hard to comprehend, it was, after all the months not to mention years, most welcome that now, when least expected, straight out of the blue, good and positive news had struck without warning.

And as Armstrong predicted, this last day did quietly tick by without a writ and without an injunction. And the day December 7 struck. Publication. *The Ginger Man* at last free and out on its own. But had not this victory come and the book achieved its freedom from its undeserved yoke of pseudonymous pornography imposed upon it by the Traveller's Companion Series, there is no question but that I would have been arise with a rage so great, Girodias's life would have been at stake. And as indeed it turned out *The Ginger Man* would anyway inextricably wind around and haunt the every future day of his existence.

Reviews came. Mixed, as they say. But the best of the praising ones overwhelming the dissenters. It seemed I had crawled up out of a bleak, black abyss of encroaching jurisprudence to the brighter sands of moral hope on the beach. And on a day shortly following publication, I called on Neville Armstrong, busy as a bee in Fitzroy Street, from which he was already planning to move to a larger premises.

Behind his desk, he was pretending a little that all was proceeding as routine and as was to be expected of a highly successful publisher. Nevertheless, he was beaming. He had the reviews laid out and had quotes selected for back of the jacket of the second printing, and which he now handed across to me to read.

THE SUNDAY TIMES
FICTION OF THE WEEK
BY JOHN METCALF

"*The Ginger man,* whose Sebastian Dangerfield is as central a version of the new Byronic hero as anyone could ask for."
"A fine and genuine verbal talent."
"He has fire enough for a dozen books, dexterity and liveliness to spare."

EVENING STANDARD
FICTION SHELF
BY PHILIP OAKES

"Plotless, picaresque story. Originally published in Paris, and lightly censored for the English edition, it displays a raging, randy talent."
"Brilliantly comic writing, but decidedly too gamy for gentle tastes."

MANCHESTER GUARDIAN
BY ANNE DUCHENE

"The total impact of the book seems incontestably one of outrageous and fantastic comedy."
"It is the comedy of enjoyment, with nothing destructive about it."
"Full of love and preposterous energy and laughter."
"People who don't think randiness and riotous good company are subjects for comedy will not be amused, of course: but they would not have been asked to the party anyway. And that is all one needs to know, morally, about this book."
"An ultimate comic triumph."

Here seated in this small office in London's Fitzroy Street, this was my mini victory, lightening my weight of concern, that might have happened three years previously in its major way in America. And as I sat reading these paeans of praise, Armstrong's phone kept ringing as book orders were pouring in. Harrods's large department had already reordered twice. Neville's grin each time he put down the phone was

504

on the verge of laughter and his bow tie seemed to be spinning like an airplane propeller. It was truly, for the time being at least, To hell with Girodias. As Brendan Behan had predicted,

The Ginger Man
Was at last
On its way
Chasing the Bible

As a repressed botanist, one always felt reassured
by an ecclesiastic-looking gentleman
pausing in his religious fervor to admire
an instance of beauty in nature.

45

Aₙ MORE REVIEWS FOLLOWED. At the end of January in the
periodical *Truth,* Peter Shaffer wrote.

> *The Ginger Man* does not sell out. He lives defiantly without compromise
> — and without proceeding virtue either. Mr. Donleavy in his invigorat-
> ing book displays the vices of indelicacy, formlessness and no sense of
> selectivity whatever. His Sebastian Dangerfield, young, American, mar-
> ried with a brat, comes to Dublin to read law at Trinity: but his feeling
> for law is not that of the Scarsdale (and Sunningdale) bourgeois. In its
> context, Mr. Donleavy's world is a blasphemy, and his Dangerfield is
> anti saint. Life, says he, is for living: not necessarily for solving. And live
> he does. *The Ginger Man* is the saga of his lunatic unplanned existence
> on the fringe of starvation, most often drunk, most often quarrelling,
> never working though dreaming continually of his future wealth as a
> lawyer, moving moodily through the pub and alley world of an amiable
> nightmare (the contradiction is not impossible at all in Dublin) sustained
> by an ever richening private mythology. It gets better as it goes on; his
> wife, quite properly, leaves him, and he himself embarks for England —
> though not before holed up in a house to dodge his villainous landlord
> Egbert Skully. He has an affair with his tenant, the spinsterish but
> complaisant Miss Frost, which is surely one of the funniest incidents in
> modern fiction. Thereafter the atmosphere (because it is portable)
> haunts London too, to produce the magnificent MacDoon for the my-
> thology, and provide a suitable background for the final appearance of
> dewy, innocent insatiable Mary, a worthy love for the anti saint whose
> hagiography Mr. Donleavy tells so well.

From Ireland there came a different message and my first ever fan
mail concerning *The Ginger Man.*

Dear Mr. Donleavy,

Your book *The Ginger Man* was given to me by accident. I write myself and know how tiring it is to write and cross out the words to put in their place the correct words.

I wonder did you think of what effect your book would undoubtedly have on your readers? Human passions are very strong and at times it's an effort to subdue them. Why then try to make life harder for men? You would be sad if your children were poisoned by some heartless wretch? Or your wife led away from you? Or their names dragged in the gutter by people who knew you? You seem to be doing these things to others. Married life is difficult oftentimes, why make it worse? Passions are strong, why make men worse than brutes? The Holy Name of Jesus belongs to a Person who will judge you soon. Why drag your Saviour's name in the mud? I hope your next book will lift people up a little. Oscar Wilde had a beautiful style and was clever. Try to do something constructive.

There's no use giving you my name.

AE

With John Osborne's *Look Back in Anger,* the so-called "angry young man" had come on the scene in London. But there now descended an ominous silence from Paris, where apparently the French government had imposed a ban on the Traveller's Companion Series, which was being appealed by the Olympia Press. As the prospect of litigation continued to haunt me, my resolve to continue writing *A Fairy Tale of New York* was weakening. I was languishing. All was not well. Although there was the victory of publication, still stifling my spirit was the stigma of litigation clinging to *The Ginger Man.* Any moment, any day, I was expecting a writ to arrive. I now had to finally abandon the writing of *A Fairy Tale of New York.* As I forced myself to run back and forth along the Putney embankment of the Thames just beyond the boathouses, I could sense that my reserves had, during these past racking weeks, been diminished. With no such bacterium ever having taken up residence within me before, I discovered now I had an abscess.

Dr. Rosemont, the pleasant Jewish doctor, with his small neat surgery across from Eel Brook Common on King's Road, referred me to St. Stephen's Hospital. I was shot with penicillin. And advised to return in a day or two when the abscess had localized and could be drained. Hovered over by doctors and nurses, they said the pain would be alleviated by taking gas. However, as they insisted, I declined. Physical pain could be nothing to me but immense relief. But I was told the agony I would be subjected to would make it difficult to operate and I did finally relent. To have a dark mask come over my face. And the bother and peeve of the world to be briefly taken away. I was to find out what it was like to die. In the wind and growing darkness of an autumnal afternoon beseated on that evening bench on Eel Brook Common, you arise. Death was coming. With the life of others leaving. As you began to flee, running. Chasing along under the clumps of branches of the plane trees of Wandsworth Bridge Road. And all those nearest and dearest that you loved were blown away by the wind. You shouted out. Calling after their names. Come back. Stay. Be with you. With you.

I was at my lowest ebb. But as *The Ginger Man* was to do so many times in the future, it did now for the first time come to my aid. The morning following my attendance at hospital as I lay convalescing on the daybed of this tiny Fulham sitting room, Philip brought up to me from the front hall an envelope forwarded to me by Neville Spearman Ltd. And upon such letter's heading were the much familiar words "Ealing Films" in red.

EALING FILMS

EALING FILMS LTD., M.G.M. BRITISH STUDIOS

BOREHAM WOOD

HERTS

3rd January 1957

J. P. Donleavy Esq.,
c/o Neville Spearman Ltd.,
10 Fitzroy Street,
London, W1.

Dear Mr. Donleavy,

That's a marvellous book. Do you really hate films as much as the Mary-Dangerfield stuff at the end suggests? If not, do you think we could meet some day and see if you have any ideas that might be put on celluloid? Dialogue like yours would be something of a godsend to British films.

Ring me any afternoon at Elstree 2000 or any morning at GRO 4934.

Yours sincerely,
Kenneth Tynan
Script Editor

Kenneth Tynan was an Oxonian and already legendary as a theatrical critic and enfant terrible of the show business world. As I gathered my more positive wits about me, I arose from my bed and found a telephone kiosk and gave Tynan a tinkle, delighted as I was to be so casually invited to put one's words on the silver screen. I was immediately bid come to 120 Mount Street in Mayfair, with its calm red brick elevations. Ascending in a small lift, I was greeted and shown in by a butler, with a pretty little smiling girl called Tracy charmingly introducing herself. I was put waiting briefly in one of this flat's two grand reception rooms as suddenly entered this tall, slender, satin-adorned gentleman who offered me a drink and said,

"Mr. Donleavy, assuming that your characters will be human beings and not locusts or something and you have the beginning of an idea and if you can tell me verbally or in a letter or on a match book cover, we can give you a contract and pay you money to write your conceptualization into a screenplay at your leisure and convenience. How does that sound to you."

"Awfully nice."

"And I'd like you to meet with Seth Holt. Who's been involved in the making of a few such little films as *The Lavender Hill Mob* and other films too fabled and numerous to mention. And should you not both detest each other, it's possible he'll direct the film you will write. By the way, let me fill up your drink."

Kenneth Tynan, if occasionally stammering, turned out to be every bit as good as his glibly spoken word. I wrote an idea on a sheet of paper and I signed a contract. We met Seth Holt at Ealing. We had a conference. Interspersed with some laughter. The name of my film would be *The Rich Goat*. About an American who comes to track down money left in a will out in the west of Ireland. Seth Holt was as quiet and introspective as Tynan was hyper and pleasantly talkative. With the latter I rode in a taxi back into London, as he was remembering words from a song and humming a piece of music. His fingers clicking and the palms of his hands alternately beating his knees. He seemed to lightly pirouette and dance his way across the cultural froth of London, upon which I had just become a rising bubble.

It was my first sense of largess since moving to my outpost in London SW6 near the gasworks and north of the power station. From oblivion, overnight I had been transported from the social untouchability and unrecommended wilds of Fulham into the sumptuously enveloping pastures of Mayfair. As only a matter of a week or two later, Peter

Brook, the distinguished theatrical director, came on the scene. To take me to lunch at an elegant restaurant in Dover Street. He proposed that I should write yet another film and this he would direct. Beforehand, we took drinks with Tynan in his palatial flat in Mount Street, where all was deft with diplomacy. With the pinging and zinging of the ricochets of intellectual delight, there was not a murmur nor sign of a begrudger anywhere. The tiny first trickle of gold had begun. And with my disposable income now exceeding 420 pounds a year, I was turned down for legal aid, for which Norman Shine had applied on my behalf. But I was to beware of the flashy moments of blithesomeness.

> For most
> Of life's blows
> Fall then

46

I HAD NOW THEATRICALLY DRAMATIZED *The Ginger Man.* And a gentleman, John Gibson, a BBC producer, was interested to stage it. Gibson was a romantic enthusiast, wanting to see alive these new and brave words that might be spoken and performed on stage as had been John Osborne's. And I now heard more of a real and living Samuel Beckett, who was visiting London. The man with the world's most kindly eye and of whose existence I first became aware down in the Dublin Catacombs. Gibson and Beckett had become great friends, and Gibson spoke in glowing terms of this Irish person from Paris as a man who was honest and true. And Gibson, enamored of matters Irish, led to our occasionally celebrating together in the various pubs located around Broadcasting House. One afternoon of which was to lead to an evening both of us would regret.

It was upon a night following closing time in a pub, the George, near the BBC, and we were on our way home down Great Portland Street. Singing my latest lyrics as we went. Gibson, passing a doorway, accidentally tripped over some milk bottles and in so kicking one, it was sent breaking into the roadway. There were a group of good British citizens on the opposite pavement who remonstrated with the pair of us, and Gibson, who in effect was innocent of any vandalism, took exception with words quickly becoming heated and the group crossed the street. More angry words ensued. We of course, equally inspired as good citizens, suddenly found we were having to fend off these gentlemen also inspired to doing their duty as responsible Londoners, who had, following our exchange of rude words, rightly accosted us to press their objections.

When a fight began, a car-starting handle from some other pedestrian landed across the back of Gibson's head, who indeed was not to be trifled with in this way. As the fists flew, my own were extremely busy as I found myself confronting two and three faces at a time. Our opponents indeed were formidable enough. One gentleman with whom I was exchanging blows seemed to be made of steel. Then I saw Gibson's fist pass over my shoulder, which ended the affray and the group were dispersed. But the police, summoned, had already arrived. As Gibson and I appeared unscathed, we were arrested and charged with actual bodily harm. Taken to Savile Row police station, up at the less exalted end of that famous tailoring street, one was sat at a desk, and particulars were taken, including the fact that John Gibson was a BBC producer.

There was indeed a note of strange grimness felt as a cell door clanked after me and I found I was back again in prison for the first time since naval days. The hospitable police brought one a cup of tea. Then checking on the address I had given, I was released with the undertaking to appear that very next morning at Bow Street magistrates court. I had a guest staying in Fulham. None other than the indomitable Arthur Kenneth Donoghue, who had nearly fainted in his tracks in Boston the three years previously when I said I was going to abandon *The Ginger Man*. And here he was now close at hand, suffering new and different panics in his own life and viewing my suspicious behavior with suspicion as I gulped back coffee and disappeared out my door and up Broughton Road that early morn.

I could sense John Gibson, as we met in Bow Street, was an extremely worried man. Married to an elegant and beautiful French wife of a prominent family and not a reviled banned author like myself, he was put in the most invidious position. I said that I would do and plead anything that he wished in order to soften this matter in any way I could, since publicity of this nature I knew would damage him in bringing ridicule and contempt down upon the good name of the BBC. For he had rushed to my rescue when I might have needed it. He was too, like his good friend Samuel Beckett, full of a strange love and glorious devotion to the theater. Advised to plead guilty by detectives, as this would lead to a small fine and an undertaking to keep the peace, we appeared before a Judge Robey, whose father had been famed in English theater as a distinguished music hall artist. It was in fact duly the case. We were let off as lightly as possible. Gibson and I had each to forfeit ten pounds. But of course news of our affray was promptly plastered over the newspapers and we were sued for damages by our adversaries.

And now, along with the unpleasant wagging finger of the more smug English raised against us, I was to find in this enormous city of London, that it was a small world indeed. Gibson's wife, a lady of considerable influence, had to find a lawyer to represent him in his defense in the matter of being sued for damages. And as momentous coincidence would have it, who do you think would be recommended and chosen. None other than the highly regarded and good solicitors of Rubinstein and Nash. And so came the fateful month of June in this year of 1957, and the specter loomed again of that arch-enemy, Monsieur Maurice Girodias. A letter clanking in through the letter slot at Broughton Road.

GERALD SAMUELS & SHINE
40 GOODGE STREET
LONDON WI

18th June 1957

J. P. Donleavy Esq.,
40A Broughton Road,
London, SW6.

Dear Sir,
Re: The Ginger Man
     The solicitors for Girodias have issued a Writ in connection with the above and wish to know whether we have instructions to accept service thereon.
     Kindly let us hear from you within the next day or so.
                                        Yours faithfully,
                                        Gerald Samuels and Shine

It was to be from this day forward that one would quietly shrink back from all bonhomie but the most heartfelt and needworthy. To be ever ready and cautious. To write no word that might upon being sent out from one's pen, come back to bite one. And Neville Armstrong now voiced an opinion of Girodias: "Mike, he's tough."

And I was now finding that such as Neville Armstrong as a fighter was even tougher. We would need our resilience. As Girodias was to discover more than any of us that he was going to need his. However, in my foreboding, now I found my resistance hardening. Monies for the first time were forthcoming for litigation. It was too, now that the fame of *The Ginger Man* had spread to other climes and countries. Publishers in America were presently making louder and bigger offers for *The Ginger Man*. But sad tidings too were arriving. My father's life in the Bronx was coming to a close. I was so informed by my mother by telephone, where I received the prearranged call at Murray Sayle's

His was sexual pain

The News of Death

Creaky mouths of Green.

His hands refuse to labor

The Red Sun ~~He was dead in the morning~~ *the over*

tram?

He thought that

NI-MAY-SHILTEAK BITEAK

Several things mattered being alive in the agricultural,
pauperel, ~~sodden~~ *myth* drugged greenery that is Ireland.
These things are not love, faith or happiness. These
things are money, land and servants. It is a land ~~which~~
which best demonstrates the ingredients upon which the world
fosters itself and the world fosters itself on manure. It
is not a country where the stranger is killed, but where
fathers, mothers, sisters, brothers and neighbors live from
day to wet day in fear of poison, the gun or the hook.
Friendship ~~is on the~~ *for foreigners* lips but not in the heart. Death is a
visitant greeted with shrewd glee, for another greedy mouth
is dead.

On the day that these three of graduate age and demeanor
were talking in a public house on Tara Street, one of them
had taken his first bath in three months. This to him was
one of the most desirable of those things which are considered
to be luxuries. He had carefully selected, washed and dried
his best underwear for the occasion and had a towel specially
laundered; this man lived his poverty with caution and design,
being forever careful not to encourage the company of those
people with less money than himself, or to pass his time idly
with the drug of collective, celtic wit. His interests cen-
tered and ranged around the Dialogues of Plato, prefaces of
Shaw, the early novels of Henry Miller and the source books.
He had one consummate preoccupation which was with sex. He
was a graduate of Harvard University. His name was Kenneth
O'Keefe.

The tallest of these three, most respectable, was
spare and red. He wore a pair of borrowed grey fla
ill fitting woman's raincoat, bowler hat and had
for two months. This man had attended at Dartmo
He was drinking a bottle of guinne having just
electric fire. He was interested in the plays
compositions of Bach, the ~~milieu of~~ *writings* of Rousseau.
Swift and was disarmingly erudite. He had one co.

The first formal draft page of THE GINGER MAN *with my earliest
struggles to also find a title. Having written the first one hundred and
forty pages, this and the earlier pages were returned to and over the
months were systematically cut down to the starker words which were
finally chosen to begin* THE GINGER MAN.

flat at 44 Palace Gardens Terrace. Following which, on this warm, beamingly sunny day, I walked in some despair to Holland Park, where Philip, Karen and Valerie were parked on the grass. And I realized that at least I had a little surviving family left.

My father died the end of September. But not without holding and reading a copy of the English edition of *The Ginger Man* in his hands. Then, as it had done during those grim days in America, my heart cried out for the landscape of Ireland. To free oneself to its soft, moist cleanliness and not always balmy breezes. I spotted an ad in a Sunday paper for a house to rent in the west. And the four of us packed up the end of October and crossing by boat, landed in Dublin to take the train through Mullingar to Galway. Met by our kindly landlord, who seemed inordinately solicitous, we were entertained to a meal at the Great Southern Hotel before heading in darkness farther west in his car over the bleak landscape through a gale and driving rain. Past the miles of black shiny lakes and heathery deserted hills. It seemed like we were going to the very end of the earth. And we were. To a large isolated Georgian mansion sitting on its lonely hillside. A storm blowing in from the Atlantic, shutters rattling and rain splattering the windowpanes. Philip and Karen put to bed in the great dark, cold rooms. As one lay attempting to sleep, I had to wonder had I now done the worst thing in all my life. Stranded from everywhere in the all-pervading damp chill I had first known at Trinity College. But morning came. Along with some sun streaming in the windows. Philip and Karen jumping from bed to bed in their room, with their noise and laughter of life rescuing me with hope, which flooded back into one's soul.

It was out in this vast isolation that George Smith of *A Singular Man* was born. In being able to see the postman on a distant hillside and still two hours away, I was also able to gather my reserves of resistance to the unpleasant if such was to be found in an envelope. And I was already among friends. Mr. and Mrs. Kelly, the kindly landlords, turned out to have both read *The Ginger Man*. At the foot of these windswept, heathery hills, the Atlantic Ocean separated by an isthmus, came with high tide to nearly join in the distance in front of the house and make where it stood, an island. One could walk on the stony meandering paths to the lonely beaches, where shell fragments had turned them gold. And near where a hermit lived, reading last year's newspapers. For there was no other news of the outside world. But such as Murray Sayle, long now become a trusted partisan back in London, was variously watching out for my interests and keeping me informed. From the distanced lawyers, as affidavits were sworn, I would learn of the term, further and better particulars. And leave to apply for this or for that. And learning too that judges are always looking for excuses to be fair. But I was finding too, in the words of George Smith, my own reply. Dear sir, only for the moment am I saying nothing.

And one day dawned cold and misty. I was sitting at my makeshift desk over my typewriter and surveying the distant windswept landscape from the sunroom over the front door. Suddenly a man came jumping over the hedge and running across the lawn, wildly gesticulating with his arms. He was shouting and pointing up into the sky.

"There's a dog up there."

I called to Valerie down in the kitchen to get the children in from what might be a dangerous local, already gone or rapidly going insane. But after sixteen billion years out in this primitive landscape, the Space Age had begun. Even while on the rising moors of heather, sheep grazed like tiny white maggots on the far mountainside. And across the dark hills, the rains still fell washing brighter the brightness of the dirt lanes. On which the postman would come. To reach one's door. Taking two hours with bad news and usually three for better tidings.

I was not to know that this was merely the very beginning of this battle over *The Ginger Man*. And that before I reached the end of such saga, it would endure for nearly half my life. Nor could I have ever imagined then that I was to end up as the actual owner of this now most fabled publishing company of all time. Which even as it languishes seems to grow ever greater in fame. My second wife, Mary Wilson Price, and my secretary at the time, Phyllis MacArdle, both stunningly beautiful women, flying to Paris with enormous drafts drawn on the Chase Manhattan Bank of New York. And as they charmed and cajoled the civil authorities over two days as foreigners to be allowed against all the reigning rules, to bid, presented themselves in this commercial tribunal's surprisingly jammed chamber. Where, with the auctioneer's customary three candles guttering out between bids, and in the presence of Maurice Girodias himself, trench coat debonairly draped over his shoulders, was secretly bidding through a nominee. At first laughing and enjoying himself as he planned to surreptitiously buy back his bankrupt firm for a minuscule sum, he slowly and painfully grew hysterical as Mary Price's own attorney methodically again and again upped every Girodias bid by one hundred francs, and finally after nearly half an hour of a cliff-hanging suspense, the Olympia Press was purchased in what was reputed to have been the most dramatic auction in Paris commercial history.

Girodias in this battle having lost the war, barged his way, knocking over chairs and with trench coat flying from his shoulders, swept in a rage from the auction room. And totally unaware there was news even worse to come. That instead of a beautiful pair of exotic ladies, he was to discover weeks later that his most terrible and most dreaded nemesis of all had ignominiously taken his beloved Olympia Press from under his nose. And so, with my enemy finally becoming mine, I ended up in the Paris courts actually in litigation with myself. Which I soon and wisely decided to settle. This bizarre event and turning of the tables on Girodias, perhaps redressing a little and atoning for some of my own long-suffered life-and-death struggle in litigation and at last avenging a young author's dream for his work, into which he had put his heart and soul seventeen years ago. But at least I had over all that intervening time, amid the hoot and holler, and the coming and going baying of the wolves, accomplished one thing. My fist had steadily grown strong to raise against sneaks and bullies. Shaking my knuckles in the mealy-mouthed faces brought silence to the slurs and sneers. I had surest control of and had saved my book, which would not ever again leave my care. And as the good ship *Franconia* had, when all but Gainor Stephen Crist were prostrate below, I faced my prow to cut apart the oncoming buffeting waves. Resolved to keep battle pennants flying, and my sail raised to catch the breeze and cruise safely to port.

But come here till I tell you. Of a further word I have to say. Out here in the windy, wet remoteness of the west. Where the dead are left to be under their anonymous stones. So quiet in their unmarked graves. The grass growing long above their tombs in the salty Atlantic air. They who were once animated on this speck, whirling through the universe. And who would no longer have to wonder about the stars. Or who would know or care. That I had set out one June near the sea in County Wicklow, Ireland. To write a splendid book no one would ever forget. I knew then that the years would come and go and the book would live. But it has taken more years than I ever could have imagined and more battles than I ever felt I'd have to fight. But the fist I shook and the rage I spent has at last blossomed. And before it should fade, I'd like to say that I am glad. That there is. And has been.

> God's mercy
> On the wild
> Ginger Man

Publisher's Note

Forty years after publication in Paris by the Olympia Press in its pornographic Traveller's Companion Series *The Ginger Man* has achieved the status of a world classic. Royalties flow in from various sources: theatrical rights, motion picture rights, foreign language editions (published in fifteen countries), and from its continued success as a bestseller with more than five million copies sold throughout the world. A celebrated restaurant in New York City was called The Ginger Man. In 1965 *The Complete and Unexpurgated Edition of The Ginger Man* launched the distinguished literary imprint of Seymour Lawrence. *The Ginger Man* has never been out of print.

DONLEAVY